Representation and Misrepresentation

Edwaert Collier, *Trompe l'œil* still life, c.1700 [Reproduced by courtesy of the Hunterian Art Gallery, University of Glasgow.] This depiction of a letter-board was painted around 1700 by a Dutch artist, Edwaert Collier, who worked in England after the Revolution of 1689. The *trompe l'œil* deceives about space and depth. But the illusion extends further, to the printed words. We are asked to 'read' the picture. We do so by looking at 'public prints'—yet this is a private scene, apparently celebrating the man depicted in the miniature portrait (whose birth may perhaps be dated from one of the tracts as 1676). The individual is reflected through *political* prints—a king's speech and a newspaper, the whiggish *Flying Post*, reporting on affairs in Europe. It is as though political print helps to constitute the character of the individual depicted here, though we are left worrying whether he is really the subject at all. Moreover, the tracts and newspapers which hang in the rack, themselves representative of the mass of print that rolled off the presses in the wake of the permanent lapse of pre-publication censorship in 1695, seem to be real. Yet at least one of them is not what it seems. The printed speech by the king does not match anything known to have been published—the dates do not tally. Why? Is the speech a mere invention, another trick? This painting, ostensibly a straightforward still life, bristles with illusions and allusions to the political culture of the day. As such it raises key issues explored in this book about representation and the fictions on which it relies.

Representation and Misrepresentation in Later Stuart Britain

Partisanship and Political Culture

MARK KNIGHTS

OXFORD
UNIVERSITY PRESS

OXFORD
UNIVERSITY PRESS

Great Clarendon Street, Oxford OX2 6DP

Oxford University Press is a department of the University of Oxford.
It furthers the University's objective of excellence in research, scholarship,
and education by publishing worldwide in

Oxford   New York

Auckland Cape Town Dar es Salaam Hong Kong Karachi
Kuala Lumpur Madrid Melbourne Mexico City Nairobi
New Delhi Shanghai Taipei Toronto

With offices in

Argentina Austria Brazil Chile Czech Republic France Greece
Guatemala Hungary Italy Japan Poland Portugal Singapore
South Korea Switzerland Thailand Turkey Ukraine Vietnam

Published in the United States
by Oxford University Press Inc., New York

© Mark Knights 2005

The moral rights of the authors have been asserted
Database right Oxford University Press (maker)

First published 2005

British Library Cataloguing in Publication Data

Data available

Library of Congress Cataloging-in Publication Data

Knights, Mark.
Representation and misrepresentation in later Stuart Britain :
partisanship and political culture / Mark Knights.
p.   cm
Includes bibliographical references and index.

1. Great Britain—Politics and government—1660–1714.   2. Public opinion—Great Britain—
History—17th century.   3. Political parties—Great Britain—History—17th century.   4. Political
culture—Great Britain—History—17th century.   5. Politics and literature—Great Britain—History—
17th century.   6. Representative government and representation—Great Britain—History—17th
century. I. Title.
DA435.K69 2005 941.06—dc22   2004030382

0–19–925833–3

ISBN 978–0–19–925833–8

1 3 5 7 9 10 8 6 4 2

Typeset by SNP Best-set Typesetter Ltd., Hong Kong
Printed in Great Britain
on acid-free paper by
Biddles Ltd.
King's Lynn, Norfolk

Acknowledgements

Whilst researching and writing a book on public discourse it has been a pleasure to have had so many enjoyable conversations with a number of colleagues. I particularly wish to thank Simon Middleton, John Arnold, Steve Pincus, Andy Wood, Colin Davis, Linda Waterman-Holly, and Gaby Mahlberg for characteristically perceptive comments and advice. David Hayton, Joad Raymond, Clyve Jones, Andy Hopper, Jan Pitman, Jason McElligott, Philip Hines, Stuart Handley, Justin Champion, Carolyn Nelson, and Anne Kugler have all been kind enough to share ideas and material with me. Audiences at a variety of research seminars and conferences have also helped to clarify my thinking; it would be impossible to thank them individually but I would like to do so collectively. I am also grateful to Edward Acton and Blair Worden for their encouragement and support. Blair, Nigel Smith, and Steve Pincus all made helpful suggestions when the book was accepted by Oxford University Press.

A number of librarians and archivists have also been particularly helpful in locating and providing primary sources. Whereas some of the material published before 1700 was available to me first on microfilm and then through Early English Books Online, I had much more trouble tracking down later publications. I therefore wish to thank Cambridge University Library, the British Library, the University of Liverpool Library, the Deputy Keeper of the Devonshire Collection, The Library of Illinois, Birmingham Central Library, the National Library of Scotland, the Kress Library (Harvard), Trinity College (Cambridge), the Beinecke Library (New Haven), The Harry Ransome Humanities Research Center at The University of Texas at Austin, and the Newberry Library (Chicago) for providing me with copies of rare items.

Images are reproduced by kind permission of the British Museum, the Houghton Library, Cambridge University Library, Huntington Library, Hunterian Art Gallery, Bodleian Library, Magdalen College Cambridge, Public Record Office, and Norfolk Record Office.

The University of East Anglia and the Arts and Humanities Research Board have provided me with periods of funded study leave, for which I am very grateful.

Finally, Emma has often forced me to think about why the subject matters, and family and friends have been an important source of support and sometimes inspiration. There are some pictures in this 'chapter book', which will please Sam and Caitlin, but not, I fear, as many as they would like.

Contents

List of Illustrations

Abbreviations

Add. MSS	Additional Manuscripts
BIHR	*Bulletin of the Institute of Historical Research*
BL	British Library, London
BM	British Museum
Bodl.	Bodleian Library, Oxford
CHJ	*Cambridge Historical Journal*
CJ	*Journals of the House of Commons*
CLRO	Corporation of London Record Office
CSPD	*Calendar of the State Papers, Domestic*
CUL	Cambridge University Library
DNB	*Dictionary of National Biography*
EcHR	*Economic History Review*
EHR	*English Historical Review*
ESTC	English Short Title Catalogue
HJ	*Historical Journal*
Harl. Misc.	*The Harleian Miscellany: A Collection of Scarce, Curious, and Entertaining Pamphlets and Tracts, as well in Manuscript as in Print, Found in the Late Earl of Oxford's Library*, 12 vols. (London, 1808–11)
HR	*Historical Research*
HMC	Historical Manuscripts Commission
HOP I	B. D. Henning (ed.), *The History of Parliament. The House of Commons 1660–1690*, 3 vols. (London, 1983)
HOP II	E. Cruickshanks, S. Handley, and D. W. Hayton (eds.), *The History of Parliament. The House of Commons 1690–1715*, 5 vols. (Cambridge, 2002)
JBS	*Journal of British Studies*
JMH	*Journal of Modern History*
LG	*London Gazette*
LJ	*Journals of the House of Lords*
Luttrell	*A Brief Historical Relation of State Affairs, from September 1678 to April 1714*, 6 vols. (Farnborough, 1969)
MSS	Manuscripts
n.d.	No date
NS	New series
OED	*Oxford English Dictionary*

Parl. Hist.	*Cobbett's Parliamentary History of England from the Earliest Period to the Year 1803*, 36 vols. (1806–20)
PMLA	*Transactions and Proceedings of the Modern Language Association of America*
P&P	*Past and Present*
PRO	Public Records Office, London
RO	Record Office
State Trials	*Cobbett's Complete Collection of State Trials and Proceedings for High Treason and Other Crimes and Misdemeanors from the Earliest Period to the Present Time* (London and Dublin, 1809–28)
Somers Tracts	*A Collection of Scarce and Valuable Tracts . . . selected from . . . private libraries; particularly that of the late Lord Sommers* (first collection 1748; second 1750; third 1751; fourth, 1752)
TRHS	*Transactions of the Royal Historical Society*
Works of Halifax	*The Complete Works of George Savile, First Marquess of Halifax* ed. W. Raleigh (Oxford, 1912)

Author's Note on Conventions

Dates have been given in old style but with the year taken to have started on 1 January.

Spelling of quotations has not been modernized, and original punctuation retained, but capitalization has been modernized where it was possible to do so without altering the meaning or significance of the quotation.

Place of publication is London unless otherwise stated.

Chronology of National Events

1660   Restoration of Charles II; elections to a 'Convention' parliament.

1661   New elections deciding the composition of the 'Cavalier Parliament' that was to sit until January 1679.

1660–5   Legislation passed to: restore episcopacy and the church of England; re-establish religious uniformity, at least for the clergy and to penalize dissenting ministers; to repeal the Triennial Act that required the automatic assembly of parliament after three years; to prevent 'tumultuous petitions'; to re-impose pre-publication licensing of print; regain royal control of the militia; remove the army as a political force through disbandment; and secure greater control over corporations by attempting to proscribe dissenters from holding office.

1665–7   War against the Dutch.

1670   Conventicle bill designed to extend uniformity to the laity; secret Anglo-French treaty by which Charles bought French support in a future war against the Dutch by promising to convert to catholicism.

1672   Declaration of war against the Dutch (ends 1674), prompting the issue of a declaration of indulgence to dissenters; the 'Stop of the Exchequer' signals royal default on debt.

1673   Charles II forced to retract the declaration of indulgence; passage of the Test Act disqualifying from office-holding any catholics and dissenters who could not take the sacrament according to the rites of the church of England.

1675 and 1677   Disputes over the longevity of the parliament without an election and anglican-royalist court policy.

1678   Revelation by Titus Oates of a 'popish plot'.

1679–81   Three general elections; parliamentary attempt to prevent the catholic James, duke of York, from succeeding to the throne; lapse of licensing law; campaigns of mass petitioning; parliamentary attempts both to grant toleration and widen the base of the church to embrace moderate dissenters; first use early in 1681 of the terms Whig and Tory to describe politico-religious groupings.

1681–5   'Tory reaction' regaining royal control over the press, prosecutions against leading Whigs and remodelling of borough charters to remove Whigs and dissenters; king fails to summon parliament in 1684, ignoring the injunctions of even the revised Triennial Act of 1684 that he should do so; persecution of dissenters.

1683 Widespread arrests of Whigs after the Rye House Plot, allegedly proof that radicals were prepared to assassinate the king.

1685 Death of Charles II and accession of James II; renewal of licensing act; west country rebellion led by Charles II's illegitimate son, the duke of Monmouth, and rising in Scotland, both suppressed; general election returns largely Tory parliament but also one suspicious of the king's catholic agenda, and it was short-lived.

1686–8 James insists on royal prerogative to intrude catholics into the army and other offices; king rules without parliament; king alienates the high churchmen and seeks an alliance with dissenters, issuing a declaration of indulgence in 1687 and 1688 and working towards securing a parliament that would repeal the penal laws against catholics and dissenters.

1688 Tension between James II and the churchmen comes to a head with the trial of Seven Bishops who had issued a statement why they were unable to read the 1688 declaration of indulgence to their flocks; churchmen and dissenters appear to unite against a common threat; invasion by William of Orange, defection of key elements of James's army, and the king's flight to France.

1689 Election to another 'Convention' parliament; William and Mary become joint monarchs; declaration of rights attempts to define abuses of royal power; declaration of war against France; James II heads armed force in Ireland; Jacobite forces in Scotland suppressed; William increasingly frustrated with Whigs.

1690 Elections return a parliament with a small Tory majority; battle of the Boyne signals Williamite supremacy in Ireland. Scottish legislation to establish a presbyterian form of church government.

1694 Establishment of the Bank of England; William turns back to the Whigs, who are now led by a 'Junto' of those anxious to yoke court to their party. Passage of Triennial Act requiring elections to be held at least every three years.

1695 Elections: small Whig majority; permanent lapse of pre-publication licensing.

1696 Attempt to assassinate William III fails but provokes a nationwide 'Association' of loyalty to him; re-coinage creates considerable shortage of money.

1697 Peace of Ryswick concludes first stage of war against France; calls for disbandment of the army divide the Whigs.

1698   Elections: anti-army issue complicates party slates.

1699–1701   Parliamentary attacks on Whig leaders and perceived court corruption.

1701   Two elections; debate over the threat still posed by France, particularly after Louis XIV's recognition of catholic James Edward Stuart and passage of Act of Settlement confirming protestant succession.

1702   Death of William III and accession of Anne; elections result in decisive Tory victory. Declaration of war against France (ends 1713).

1702–5   Attempt to enact Occasional Conformity Bill to proscribe from office those dissenters who took the sacrament according to the rites of the church of England in order to comply with the Test and Corporation Acts. Tory ministry wrecked by the divisions this produced.

1705   Election: Whig gains.

1706   Compromise ministry, but 'country' MPs attempt to exclude office-holders from sitting in parliament.

1707   Union with Scotland ratified.

1708   Election: Whig majority.

1709–10   Dr Henry Sacheverell preaches inflammatory sermons against dissenters and 'revolution principles', is impeached by parliament, and triggers bitter ideological conflict.

1710   Election: Tory landslide.

1710–14   Tory supremacy in parliament and at court, leading to enactment of Occasional Conformity Bill (1711); a measure requiring MPs to be substantial landowners (1711); and a Schism Bill aimed at dissenting academies (1714). Controversy over peace negotiations with France.

1713   Election: Tory victory.

1714   Illness and then death of Queen Anne results in mainly Whig regency government and proclamation of George I.

1715   Election: Whig victory.

1715–16   Jacobite unrest in England and rebellion in Scotland.

1716   The Septennial Act repeals the provision for elections every three years, stipulating elections only once every seven years.

1716–21   The Whigs, although dominating the government, temporarily split into factions; repeal of Occasional Conformity and Schism Acts (1718–19); 1720 South Sea Bubble creates huge financial uncertainty but Walpole re-establishes financial and Whig credibility.

1722   Election increases Whig majority. Whig oligarchical rule established.

Part I

Representation and the Public

The word 'representation' is one of the most difficult of all the words used by the historian because its meaning may reflect deep-seated historical changes.[1]

we ought . . . to be prepared to ask ourselves quite aggressively what is supposed to be the practical use, here and now, of our historical studies.[2]

The best lectures in politicks are deduced from occurrences of moment, that have happened either within the compass of our own memories or those of our predecessors. These we are furnished with from history . . .[3]

---

[1] D. Ogg, *England in the Reigns of James II and William III* (Oxford, 1984 edn.), 128.
[2] Q. Skinner, *Liberty before Liberalism* (Cambridge, 1998), 107.
[3] *What Has Been, May Be; or, A View of a Popish and Arbitrary Government* (1713), introduction, iii.

CHAPTER ONE

Introduction

THE ARGUMENT

This is a book about later Stuart political culture. The central theme is an examination of the concept and nature of representation at a key period in its history. I argue that in the later Stuart period England witnessed a significant shift towards a representative society. This was the result of the conjunction of several factors. General elections were held, on average, every two and a half years in the period between 1679 and 1716. A huge and expanding electorate voted more regularly than ever before. Prepublication licensing lapsed, temporarily in 1679 and then permanently in 1695. Political parties—Whigs and Tories—were born and flourished in bitter conflict with one another. Men and women engaged in an ideological struggle about the nature of the church, the state, authority, and obedience. And there was a financial revolution that created a publicly funded national debt for the first time. These factors combined to produce a partisan political culture that was truly national and in which the public became a routine, participating, part of the political process. Yet the involvement of the public, and its expanded role as a source of authority, raised questions about the capacity of the people to make informed, rational, political judgements. The partisan press, clubs, coffee-houses, electioneering, addresses, and petitions were a means of informing and involving a reified public, but also potentially a means of subverting its rational judgement through mendacity, impartiality, passion, and even rage. The period thus witnessed an experiment in representation but also, in the eyes of many contemporaries, one in misrepresentation through slander, political lying, and partisan fictions.

To be sure, many aspects of the later Stuart political culture can be seen earlier, particularly in the 1640s, and it is easy to exaggerate the 'Glorious Revolution' as the key turning-point. There was a coup in 1688–9, but a revolution process spanning at least from 1640 to 1720. We can therefore find instances of the anxieties that have just been outlined well before the 1670s. Indeed, one can find continuity across the early modern period (and before and after it) between periods of great political and religious tension. Polemic, an appeal to popularity, a fear of the effects of print, anxiety over truth-claims can all be found in the sixteenth and earlier seventeenth centuries, as well as in the eighteenth. Contemporaries were particularly aware of the role that the mid-century revolution played in changing the political culture. From the 1670s onwards, when the failures of the restoration settlement of the 1660s became apparent, explicit reference was made to 1641 and to a lesser extent 1648, in order to warn against repeating earlier mistakes. Yet, as this focus on the 1640s suggests, alongside the perceived continuities there were also recognized shifts over the seventeenth century. The mid-century revolution was certainly one such period of change. But this book focuses on the second half of the 1640–1720 revolution, partly because it has been much less well studied than the first, but also to emphasize the importance of innovations in the later phase that have sometimes been overlooked.

The shifts over the seventeenth century were quantitative. Whereas the 1584 bond of association was a relatively circumscribed affair, subscribed for the most part by men of substance and amounting to about two dozen sets of parchments, the parallel 1696 oath of association was signed by men of all social levels and about 430 were collected.[4] Similarly, whereas the irreverent satire of the 'Martin Marprelate' controversy ran to about fifteen or sixteen tracts in the late 1580s, there were about 128 polemical titles a century later, debating the revolution of 1689–90.[5] One important difference between the late sixteenth and the late seventeenth century had therefore to do with scale. There was a wider, more consistently invoked, public.

This shift in scale was accompanied by a qualitative shift. Although the later Stuart period was in many ways the culmination of trends over a 'long seventeenth century', spanning from the 1580s to the late 1710s, the nature of the later appeal to the public and of public politics was different. This was the result of changes brought about during the mid-century revolu-

---

[4] P. Collinson, 'The Monarchical Republic of Queen Elizabeth I', *Bulletin of the John Rylands University Library of Manchester*, 69: 2 (1987), 394–424; D. Cressy, 'Binding the Nation: The Bonds of Association, 1584 and 1696', in D. J. Guth and J. W. McKenna (eds.), *Tudor Rule and Revolution* (Cambridge, 1982); E. Vallance, 'Loyal or Rebellious? Protestant Associations in England, 1584–1696', *The Seventeenth Century*, 17 (2002), 1–23; D. M. Jones, *Conscience and Allegiance in Seventeenth Century England: The Political Significance of Oaths and Engagements* (Rochester, 1999). See also Ch. 3.

[5] P. Collinson, 'Ecclesiastical Vitriol: Religious Satire in the 1590s and the Invention of Puritanism', in J. Guy (ed.), *The Reign of Elizabeth I: Court and Culture in the Last Decade* (Washington, 1995); M. Goldie, 'The Revolution of 1689 and the Structure of Political Argument: An Essay and an Annotated Bibliography of Pamphlets on the Allegiance Controversy', *Bulletin of Research in the Humanities*, 83 (1980), 477.

tion but also by the later seventeenth one. As a result, whereas scholars of the early seventeenth century have seemed reluctant to embrace the notion of a 'public sphere' based on early capitalism, new communicative practices, and public rational discourse, such a model seems far more suited to the late seventeenth and early eighteenth centuries. This book therefore examines the two key components of this qualitative shift. First, it seeks to demonstrate the centrality of the public to politics: as voters, as readers, as a legitimating authority, as umpires and judges of state and church. Second, it explores attitudes to the public and identifies public judgement as one of the key issues causing concern. Part one focuses on the first of these, and part two on the second, although both themes will recur throughout the following chapters.

The public acquired new prominence and importance as a collective fiction with an enlarged role as a legitimizing power and as an umpire. The vacuum of authority resulting from the undermining of traditional authorities such as the crown and church during the mid-century crisis was thus partly filled by the public. This becomes clear when we examine frequent electioneering, the proliferation of cheap political print, and the expansion in the number of public petitions and addresses. In each case the scale of such appeals to popularity was either unprecedented or matched only (and then temporarily) during the 1640s. Such appeals worked to create a national political culture, with labels and structures recognized in every borough and in which every borough was expected routinely to participate. The public was asked repeatedly, and consistently, to judge. It had to decide how to vote, whether it believed what it read, and whether or not to sign petitions and addresses.

Much of this debate was carried out in public, and in print. The expansion of the political press had a transformative impact on the 1640s but also on the later Stuart political culture. Thus although the genre of printed electoral advice literature had emerged in the 1640s, it is a reflection of the later development of mid-century innovations that such literature flourished only when electioneering became frequent and routine after the 1670s. Moreover, by then the short cooling-off time between elections ensured that print had become a decisive player in the new political culture. Print was not only a means to communicate but also a political tool. Printed interventions became an intrinsic part of the political contest. Finally, and in part facilitated by print, debates about political economy and printed news about stocks and trade, the public acquired new importance because of the revolution in public finance. After the 1690s it was the public that supported the national debt and conferred the 'public credit' necessary to fight a large-scale, and semi-global, war with France. Public opinion gave value to stocks and even to money itself. The fiscal revolution after 1689 was a public, representational, one.

Greater stress on the public and the role of public judgement neverthe-less led to anxieties about 'popularity' and public reason. Again, these were not new; but they were writ large in new ways. We can find anxieties about the seditious nature of print, the irrationality or credulity of the multi-tude, and the subversion of truth well before the age of party. Yet parties, a new development characteristic of the late Restoration period, intensified these anxieties and gave them a new context. Party was symptomatic of, and fostered, state zeal, political heat, or 'rage'. Such vehement partisanship was thought to transport men and obscure their ability to discern what was true. Truth became relative to partisan conviction and party institu-tionalized a system of rival truth-claims. Anxieties about the abuse of lan-guage and the public's inability to discern right reason and truth thus became embedded into the structure of politics. Partisans championed, or admitted, the public as an umpire, and yet feared that many might not have the capacity for rational judgement and to discern the truth. Know-ledge and truth were thus political issues. In that sense, the period is important in stressing the early stages of a political enlightenment that coincided with the religious and scientific ones. Moreover, such debates were routinely fought out at a local level, and spilt far beyond the religious sphere—into matters of political economy, electioneering and personal credit, and into the nature of language itself.

Contemporaries across the political spectrum had, by the accession of the Hanoverians, come to fear a paradox at the heart of publicly competi-tive politics: an appeal to the public was an integral part of such politics, but it was through such an appeal that truth could become subverted. Po-litical knowledge was both conveyed by public discourse but also poten-tially undermined by it. This was no abstract problem. A failure on the part of the public to judge properly threatened defeat by the most powerful military force in Europe, the destruction of civil and religious liberties, and the destabilization of an emerging capitalistic economy. Once again, the means by which partisanship corrupted public discourse were not par-ticularly new, but they were certainly intensified. Contemporaries across the political spectrum feared deliberate and systematic campaigns of propaganda designed to mislead. They worried that slogans, words, and phrases were routinely being given different meanings by each interest-group so that a shared language was dissolving, replaced by cant and jar-gon. Contemporaries thought their age had perfected the art of political lying, with each side seeing the other as based on a series of lies. Partisanship thus ensured that everything political could be seen in two ways—the same words, phrases, people, and events were routinely represented differently according to party allegiance. As a result men and women of all stripes saw themselves surrounded by a world of ambiguities, misrepresentations, and fictions. Such a culture could be highly creative, with imaginative fictions embedded in partisan polemic, so that the political and the literary were fused. Later Stuart political culture intensified, and made routine representational phenomena and anxieties associated with earlier crises.

The consequences were profound. In order to try to control and order such phenomena contemporaries developed a series of informal and formal controls. The languages of politeness and reason were prized because they appeared to offer an antidote to the incivility and passionate irrationality of partisan discourse. As ideals they were increasingly articulated in response to partisanship. The language of moderate, rational politeness was thus the inverse of how contemporaries characterized partisan polemic and discourse. But as well as a stress on an idealized way of talking, there were also shifts in attitudes to the press. Printed vindication or rejoinder, rather than censorship, was recognized as the best means of countering an opposing viewpoint—an implicit recognition that the mind could not be forced in politics any more than in religion. The press was thus regarded not just as a corrosive influence but also as an antidote to partisan poison. For this to happen readers had to read rightly. And they were encouraged to learn how to become critics capable of deconstructing a political text in order to learn its true meaning. Literary style duly became part of the political contest. More formally, the Triennial Act of 1694, that had guaranteed frequent parliaments, was repealed in 1716 in favour of a provision for elections only once every seven years. This was defended in terms that drew on anxieties about a decayed public discourse and public judgement that had been mounting over the previous forty years. In other words, the later Stuart period not only offers us a culmination and in part a resolution of the preoccupations of the seventeenth century but also an explanation of the concerns of the eighteenth century. The later Stuart period helped to place on the agenda matters to do with partisanship, politeness, sociability, public opinion, political economy, truth, fiction, and reason, together with the means available for the construction of individual, group and national identities.

The book thus studies how diversity of opinion—seemingly made dangerous by its public nature in an age of extensive print, new communicative practices, frequent elections, civic conflict, a financial revolution, and religious division—could be accommodated peacefully within the state. It argues that partisanship shaped the political culture in innovating ways but also that such a culture explored means of containing the resulting passion and party rage. The book pursues the relationship between the style, language, and content of public discussion between the 1670s and 1720, with a particular stress on the reign of Anne, during which division was both intensely bitter and widespread. It aims to connect a number of different strands—political, intellectual, literary, economic, social, and religious—by focusing on how public discourse operated to legitimize or undermine authority and allegiance. My analysis situates the political culture of the later Stuart period as one of transition: towards new ways of talking and acting; towards new anxieties about how the abuse of words imperilled political choice. It is thus part of a larger narrative about the development of a representative society. By that I mean a society (not democratic) in which public representation, defined both as a political concept and as a mode of communication, was key to the justification and exercise of power. This involved a curious re-blending of monarchy, aristocracy, and democracy, the combination of which produced something rather extraordinary, centred on a representational form of politics. As Montesquieu recognized when trying to classify it, the British system that emerged in this period, particularly after 1689, was a fascinating, delicately balanced hybrid, reliant for the preservation of its liberty on a potentially tyrannous public that nevertheless checked itself through the party system.[6]

By studying both the inventiveness of, and anxieties heightened and created by, the publicly partisan political culture the book also seeks to engage with problems inherent in all representative societies: how are voters best informed? How, if at all, does the language of politics aid or enlighten public choice? How can political judgement best be inculcated? Is partisanship a positive or negative force? Later Stuart political culture thus posed and sought to answer timeless questions about the nature of representation.[7] It explored the relationship between the represented and their representatives, the claims of minorities to represent the whole, the means by which opinion could be determined, and how misrepresentation might be avoided.

---

[6] Charles-Louis, Baron de Montesquieu, *De L'Esprit des lois* (1748), bk. 19, ch. 27.

[7] For their continuing relevance see, for example, H. Redner, in L. Diamond and R. Gunther (eds.), *New Science of Representation; Political Parties and Democracy* (Baltimore, 2001).

Rethinking periodization

The study of later Stuart political culture gives us an important piece of a historiographical jigsaw that so often has the late seventeenth- and early eighteenth-century pieces missing. The period saw the culmination of trends that had been evolving over the long seventeenth century (1580–1720) but also offers a starting-point for our study of the long eighteenth century (1689–1832). And the period is crucial not just for our understanding of Britain but also of Europe. In that context this book also seeks to contribute to the ongoing debate about the nature of the enlightenment.[8] Although the European enlightenment is often characterized (or caricatured) as confident in rational truth, unity, 'progress', and objective knowledge—virtually everything that postmodernism sets itself against—the early, English enlightenment displayed considerable scepticism about the nature of truth, about the possibility of unity, and about the nature of progress. And it did so not (or not only) through grand philosophical texts but through the cut and thrust of everyday politicking that affected nearly every borough in the country. Questions about knowledge and human understanding were routinely explored in partisan political literature that offered rival versions of the truth to the public. As a result, it was an age of uncertainty about how to discern truth, an era obsessed with the nature of language, anxious about the degradation of politics and about the absence of universal frameworks that gave common meaning. In other words, the study should make us question not only how we periodize the past but also where we look for 'enlightenment' debates.[9]

The later seventeenth and early eighteenth centuries are usually conceived as constituting the end of the 'early modern' period and a starting place for the 'modern'. Yet the era often tends to fall out of both historiographies.[10] The partly justifiable attack on a Whig interpretation of

[8] For an English or British Enlightenment embracing this period, see R. Porter, *Enlightenment: Britain and the Creation of the Modern World* (London, 2000); J. Champion, *Republican Learning: John Toland and the Crisis of Christian Culture, 1696–1722* (Manchester, 2003); M. Jacob, *The Radical Enlightenment: Pantheists, Freemasons and Republicans* (London, 1981).

[9] French historians have, of course, been much more alive to the importance of the press and public debate for the enlightenment. See the works of Robert Darnton, François Furet, Mona Ozouf, Roger Chartier, and Keith Baker.

[10] For discussions of periodization, see J. Scott, *England's Troubles: Seventeenth-century English Political Instability in European Context* (Cambridge, 2000); J. C. D. Clark, *English Society*, 2nd edn.; and A. Houston and S. Pincus, *A Nation Transformed: England after the Restoration* (Cambridge, 2001), introduction. Scott (46, 492–3) does not see 1660 as a watershed but thinks change may have occurred 1688–1714. Clark praises Scott but nevertheless sees 1660 as a key watershed, with continuity over 1660–c.1820s. Whilst both accounts are flawed they do at least engage with the question of 'early modernity'. For accounts spanning

history (one that stressed progress towards secular values of civil liberty achieved through the efforts of one party) has had two unfortunate consequences. First, it has resulted in a neglect of the study of partisan political culture that gave birth to that Whig interpretation; and second, it has tended to give centre stage to the mid-seventeenth-century crisis and divorce it from its aftermath.[11] Without restoring a whiggish teleology, we should aim to recover a study of partisanship and explore the shifts as well as continuities apparent after 1640. At a time when issues to do with identity, the negotiation of authority, state formation, the nature of truth, and the historicizing of texts are at the heart of current research agendas, a sidelining of the era of party rage and political literature seems not only odd but also indefensible. So to some extent this book represents another attempt to persuade early modernists to look beyond 1640 and modernists to consider the period before 1720. If we look to the consequences of processes of reformation and revolution, as much as to their origins, we open up exciting lines of enquiry.

As these remarks suggest, it is worth restating at the outset that change and continuity are not mutually exclusive. In many ways the period 1670–1720 displays important continuities with the sixteenth and earlier seventeenth century, and these should be fully recognized. The later Stuart period witnessed the culmination, expansion, evolution, and development of a number of trends apparent far earlier, especially those concerning polemical appeals to the public.[12] Nevertheless, it is equally important to discern how changing contexts led to an evolving political culture. This study thus seeks not only to connect the later and early Stuart worlds but also to link the Stuart and the Georgian political cultures. To do so begs the charge of a whiggish concern with linear progress culminating in the birth

---

the period, see J. H. Plumb, *The Growth of Political Stability in England, 1675–1725* (London, 1967); G. Holmes, *The Making of a Great Power. Late Stuart and Early Georgian Britain 1660–1722* (Harlow, 1993); P. Halliday, *Dismembering the Body Politic: Partisan Politics in England's Towns, 1650–1730* (Cambridge, 1998).

[11] For a reconsideration of 1689 as a turning-point, see H. Dickinson, 'How Revolutionary was the "Glorious Revolution" of 1688?', *British Journal for Eighteenth-Century Studies*, 11 (1988), 125–42.

[12] N. Smith, *Literature and Revolution in England, 1640–1660* (New Haven, 1994); J. Peacey, *Politicians and Pamphleteers* (Aldershot, 2004); S. Achinstein, *Milton and the Revolutionary Reader* (Princeton, 1994); Achinstein, 'The Uses of Deception: From Cromwell to Milton', in K. Z. Keller and G. J. Schiffhorst (eds.), *The Witness of Time. Manifestations of Ideology in Seventeenth Century England* (Pittsburgh, 1993); Achinstein, 'The Politics of Babel in the English Revolution', in J. Holstun (ed.), *Pamphlet Wars: Prose in the English Revolution* (1992), 14–44; E. Skerpan, *The Rhetoric of Politics in the English Revolution, 1642–1660*, (1992); J. Raymond, *The Pamphlets and Pamphleteering in Early Modern Britain* (Cambridge, 2002).

of modernity. Such a critique is not just. Change does not need to be equated with progress; and representation can be the preserve of authoritarians as well as liberal democrats, a means to exclude as well as include the 'people'.

FIVE FACTORS FOR CHANGE

An outline of factors at work and the changes they effected will provide the reader with some sort of a map by which to chart later—hopefully more nuanced—discussions.[13] It is possible to discern five main factors promoting (and reflecting) change.

Frequent elections and parliament's coming of age

The first factor was a new role for parliament, involving frequent elections, frequent sessions, and an expanded electorate. Frequent elections had been a feature of the 1620s (1621, 1624, 1625, 1626, and 1628) and then again in the late 1650s and 1660s (1654, 1656, 1659, 1660, 1661); and during both these periods the frequency had marked effects on the political culture.[14] But they had not been sustained. Frequent elections after 1679, by contrast, occurred over a period of almost forty years. Between 1679 and the repeal of the Triennial Act in 1716 there were sixteen general elections: on average, about one every two and a half years.[15] This intensity was profoundly influential. It sharpened a trend already apparent by the 1680s, but largely brought about due to the mid-century conflict, for *contested* elections. But the consequences of the shift Mark Kishlansky identifies, from selection to election, are clearest after his end-point of 1685. In the period 1690–1714 only one English county, Dorset, and a dozen English boroughs failed to experience a contested election.[16] Electors were presented with choices

---

[13] What follows should be regarded as overly schematized, ignoring the subtlety of the way in which continuity and change work dialectically.

[14] D. Hirst, *The Representative of the People? Voters and Voting in England under the Early Stuarts* (Cambridge, 1975); M. Kishlansky, *Parliamentary Selection: Social and Political Choice in Early Modern England* (Cambridge, 1986).

[15] There were general elections in 1679 (twice), 1681, 1685, 1689, 1690, 1695, 1698, 1701 (twice), 1702, 1705, 1708, 1710, 1713, 1715. For their context, see the 'Chronology of National Events' at the start of the book.

[16] The lowest number of contests was 85 (in 1695), the highest 131 (in 1710), representing 32% and 49% of seats, respectively (for more detailed analysis of contests, see D. W. Hayton, 'Introduction', in *The History of Parliament. The House of Commons 1690–1715* (Cambridge, 2002), Vol. 1). Compare these figures with only a dozen or so contests at the beginning of the

between candidates in well over a third of all elections in that period; and many more were disputed before polling day. In other words, protracted electoral conflicts occurred in nearly every borough and county in the land. This novel situation served to tie civic and national politics ever more closely. Such a trend was also encouraged by the marked shift in the longevity and productivity of parliamentary sessions. After 1689 there were sessions every year without fail, and each session lasted longer, averaging 112 days, almost double the Restoration figure. This greater regularity and longevity had a great impact on legislative initiatives. From 1660 to 1688 parliament passed on average about 26 statutes per session; between 1689 and 1714 this rose dramatically to 64 per session. Legislation became, constituencies realized, a reliable means of getting things done. As Julian Hoppit puts it, 'Parliament as a legislature had come of age'. It was responsive to both central and local initiatives in a new way; but its role needed working out at both a practical and theoretical level.[17]

The relationship between parliament and the public was also shifting. More people were eligible to vote than ever before. A growth in the size of the electorate was not in itself new—the expansion occurred over the seventeenth century.[18] But the increase for the later Stuart period was remarkable.[19] Determining the size of electorates is not a precise science and we should probably talk of those who actually voted (a 'voterate') rather than those eligible to vote.[20] Nevertheless the number voting in 1715 amounted to at least 250,000, almost 20 per cent of the adult male population—a higher percentage than *after* the 1832 Reform Act.[21] Expansion of

century, a peak of 40 in the 1620s in 1624, and a sharp rise in 1640 to 80 in the second election of that year; 79 constituencies were uncontested in the early Stuart period (Hirst, *The Representative of the People?*, 111).

[17]   J. Hoppit, *A Land of Liberty? England 1689–1727* (Oxford, 2000), 26. For local lobbying, see S. Handley, 'Provincial Influence on General Legislation: The Case of Lancashire, 1689–1731', *Parliamentary History*, 16 (1997), 171–84; Ibid., 'Local Legislative Initiatives for Economic and Social Development in Lancashire, 1689–1731', *Parliamentary History*, 9 (1990), 14–37.

[18]   J. Plumb, 'The Growth of the Electorate in England from 1600 to 1715', *P&P*, 45 (1969), 90–116; Hirst, *The Representative of the People?*, 2.

[19]   G. Holmes, *The Electorate and the National Will in the First Age of Party* (Lancaster, 1976).

[20]   The numbers voting were only a proportion—perhaps 75%—of the electorate as a whole. For a discussion, see *HOP II*, i. 40–2.

[21]   F. O'Gorman, *Voters, Patrons and Parties: The Unreformed Electoral System of Hanoverian England 1734–1832* (Oxford, 1989), tables 4.2 and 4.3. In Bristol almost all adult male householders were freemen qualified to vote in parliamentary elections (J. Barry, 'Popular Culture in seventeenth-century Bristol', in B. Reay, (ed.), *Popular Culture in seventeenth-century England* (Sydney, 1985), 60). Geoffrey Holmes has argued persuasively that the total English and Welsh electorate was 330,000–340,000 by 1722 (Holmes, *Electorate*). Although

the electorate was all the more remarkable given the slow-down in the rate of population growth in the later Stuart period. For Holmes, all this was proof that the representative system did express the opinion of the electorate. Bill Speck similarly concluded from his work on poll books that not only was the 'electoral system more representative in Anne's reign than it had ever been before' but also that voters enjoyed considerable autonomy.[22] Although the degree of voter independence and political awareness has been questioned by some studies, the size of the increase and the increasing pressure this placed on the need to manage and influence voters has not.[23]

The development of a fiscal-military state and commercial expansion

The second factor promoting change was the development of a fiscal-military state and commercial expansion. The development of a fiscal-military state began in the 1640s, when innovative methods of raising revenue and improved collection dramatically increased the state's resources.[24] We should not under-estimate how far the nerves of state were strengthened before 1689, particularly during the civil war but also under the pressure of naval wars against the Dutch in the 1650s, 1660s, and 1670s. Even so, sustained warfare against France between 1689 and 1713 (with only a short break between 1697 and 1702) fostered a financial as well as a military revolution.[25] Not only was the size of the armed forces

---

the English counties had a uniform 40*s* freehold qualification, the franchises of the English, Welsh, and (after 1707) Scottish boroughs varied significantly—the variety is mapped out in the introductory volume of *HOP II*.

[22] Holmes, *Electorate*, 30–3; W. A. Speck, *Tory & Whig: The Struggle in the Constituencies, 1701–1715* (London, 1970), 17, 26.

[23] For views of the electorate as relatively uninformed and deferential, see J. C. D. Clark, *English Society, 1688–1832: Ideology, Social Structure and Political Practice During the Ancien Regime* (Cambridge, 1985), 17–19. Clark drew support from Norma Landau, 'Independence, Deference and Voter Participation: The Behaviour of the Electorate in early C18th Kent', *HJ*, 22 (1979), 561–83; and L. Colley, *In Defiance of Oligarchy: The Tory Party 1714–60* (Cambridge, 1982). A study of Cheshire evidence also suggests a strong correlation between landlord and tenant in voting patterns, and therefore questions the 'participatory model' (S. Baskerville, P. Adman, and K. Beedham, 'The Dynamics of Landlord Influence in English County Elections 1701–1734: The Evidence from Cheshire', *Parliamentary History*, 12 (1993), 126–42).

[24] M. Braddick, *The Nerves of State. Taxation and the financing of the English State 1558–1714* (Manchester, 1996).

[25] J. Brewer, *The Sinews of Power: War, Money, and the English State, 1688–1783* (New York, 1989); P. G. M. Dickson, *The Financial Revolution in England: A Study in the Development of Public Credit, 1688–1756* (London, 1967); M. Duffy, *The Military Revolution and the State 1500–1800* (Exeter, 1980); D. W. Jones, *War and Economy in the Age of William III and Marlborough* (Oxford, 1988); P. K. O'Brien and P. Hunt, 'The Rise of a Fiscal State in England

unprecedented—there were, for example 48,000 seamen in 1710 compared to 20,000 in 1660 and not even 10,000 in the 1630s—but unheard of amounts of money were needed to finance the war effort.[26] Average tax revenue during the war years of the 1690s was £3.64 million, about double the state's tax income before 1689. In 1720 the state took 10.8 per cent of income in tax, compared to just 3.4 per cent in 1670.[27] The state's capacity to tax outstripped the growth of the economy. Even so, this increase was insufficient to pay for the armed forces, necessitating the new phenomenon of public credit. Public indebtedness, which was unknown before 1689, stood at £16.7 million by 1697, £36 million in 1713, and over £50 million by 1720.[28] Fiscal innovation and reform brought about not only major recoinage in the 1690s but also the introduction of long-lasting expedients, such as the creation of the Bank of England in 1694, paper money, and the development of the stock market.[29] At the same time, commerce expanded, boosted in particular by the re-export trade from the colonies, and a mercantile culture was strengthened.[30] Each of these developments was overseen or shaped by parliament. Moreover, parliamentary taxation not only underwrote the debt, but had itself increased in relative importance. Again the 1640s had been instrumental in shifting state revenue from royal demesne to parliamentary grant; but by 1714 only 3 per cent of national revenue was of a non-parliamentary nature, compared to about 75 per cent in the early Stuart period.[31] Thus two features of the 'political economy' need stressing. The first is the role of parliament as the institu-

1485–1815', *Historical Research*, 66 (1993), 129–76; B. Carruthers, *City of Capital: Politics and Markets in the English Financial Revolution* (Princeton, 1996); C. Brooks, 'Public Finance and Political Stability: The Administration of the Land Tax 1688–1720', *HJ* 17 (1974), 281–300.

[26] Braddick, *Nerves of State*, 31.

[27] P. K. O'Brien, 'The Political Economy of British Taxation, 1660–1815', *Economic History Review*, 2nd ser., 41 (1988), 1–32.

[28] A distinction should be made between a royal and a national debt.

[29] Besides the works cited above see also, Ming-Hsun Li, *The Great Recoinage of 1696–9* (London, 1963); P. Laslett, 'John Locke, the Great Recoinage, and the Origins of the Board of Trade, 1695–1698', *William and Mary Quarterly*, 3rd ser., 14 (1957), 370–402; J. E. T. Rogers, *The First Nine Years of the Bank of England* (Oxford, 1887); W. Scott, *The Constitution and Finance of English, Scottish and Irish Joint-Stock Companies to 1720*, 3 vols. (Cambridge, 1951); J. K. Horsfield, *British Monetary Experiments, 1650–1710* (London, 1960).

[30] P. Gauci, *The Politics of Trade. The Overseas Merchant in State and Society, 1660–1720* (Oxford, 2001); R. Grassby, *The Business Community of Seventeenth-century England* (Cambridge, 1995); W. E. Minchington (ed.), *The Growth of English Overseas Trade in the Seventeenth and Eighteenth Centuries* (London, 1969); R. Davis, *A Commercial Revolution* (London, 1967); J. G. A. Pocock, *The Machiavellian Moment: Florentine Political Thought and the Atlantic Republican Tradition* (Princeton, 1975).

[31] Braddick, *Nerves of State*, 13.

tion where innovation was ratified and debated. The second is the new phenomenon of public credit. It was not only linked to representative politics—credit fluctuated with political power—but it was itself a representative system, based in part on paper money, exchequer bills, and stocks that had representative rather than intrinsic value. The fiscal-military revolution was also a representational one.

Print, coffee-houses, and clubs

Developments in communicative practices are a third factor explaining change. Again, we should not exaggerate the innovations of the later Stuart period. A number of scholars have suggested that information about, and discussion of, public affairs was common and vigorous in the early Stuart period. Others argue that the real watershed occurred in the 1640s, when the abolition of Star Chamber not only unlocked the floodgates but also destabilized control over print's content.[32] Similarly, it has been suggested, it was the 1640s that breached the norms of secrecy that had hitherto prevailed and made an appeal to public opinion both routine and justifiable.[33] In terms of the quantity of print, the control over print, and the conventions that applied to public discourse, the mid-century crisis undoubtedly marked a step-change. Yet there were marked developments in all three of these areas during the later Stuart period. The quantity of print is often difficult to assess, but a count of titles is one, albeit unsophisticated, guide to availability and influence. Using the database of printed titles compiled by the English Short Title Catalogue (ESTC), the output of the press can be measured over time, using cumulative counts per decade.[34]

As the graph shows, the 1640s were indeed a turning-point; but output achieved that decade was not sustained. Rather, it contracted in the 1650s, only regaining its previous height during the crisis of 1679–81.[35] But from

---

[32] See below, n. 54.

[33] D. Zaret, *Origins of Democratic Culture: Printing, Petitions, and the Public Sphere in Early-Modern England* (Princeton, 2000); D. Freist, *Governed by Opinion: Politics, Religion and the Dynamics of Communication in Stuart London, 1637–1645* (London, 1997); J. Raymond, *The Invention of the Newspaper: English Newsbooks, 1641–1649* (Oxford, 1996); S. Achinstein, *Milton and the Revolutionary Reader* (Princeton, 1994).

[34] The graph is taken from ESTC web-site. It does not take into account the frequency of editions. For important caveats about such statistics, see D. McKenzie, 'Printing and publishing 1557–1700: Constraints on the London Book Trades', in J. Barnard and D. McKenzie (eds.), *The Cambridge History of the Book. Volume IV 1557–1695* (Cambridge, 2002).

[35] The remarkable quantity of print was noticed at the time (M. Knights, *Politics and Opinion in Crisis, 1670–1681* (Cambridge, 1994) part 2) and subsequently (*Remarks Upon the*

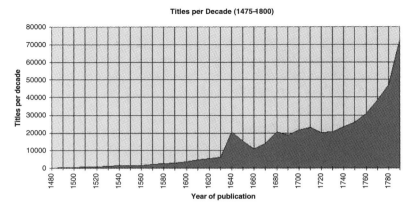

Titles per Decade (1475-1800)

Output of printed titles per decade 1480–1800 [Reproduced by courtesy of Alan Veylit, Center for Bibliographical Studies and Research, University of California at Riverside.]

1695 the quantity remains reasonably consistent for the next half-century, before sharp rises in the second half of the eighteenth century. If we examine the number of titles by year, the output of 1641 and 1642 was unprecedented, but the level was almost matched at key moments during the restoration and then surpassed regularly (and importantly far more *consistently*, year on year), from 1703 onwards, reaching a first quartile peak in 1714. In part the pattern correlates with pre-publication censorship, which lapsed in 1641, again in 1679, but only permanently in 1695.[36] Again, we might be wary of reading too much into this, since bills continued to be introduced to regulate the press, and taxation in the form of the Stamp Act was introduced in 1712, curbing production.[37] But in the 1710s the average yearly output of titles was 2,416, 25 per cent higher than that of the 1640s; and by the 1720s there were twice as many printers as there had been in the late 1640s.[38] We can conclude that the mid-century crisis broke the mould

Most Eminent of our Anti-Monarchical Authors (1699), 'introductory remarks', alleging that treasonable print had turned 'every corporation into a pest house').

[36] F. S. Siebert, *Freedom of the Press in England 1646–1776* (Urbana, 1952); T. Crist, 'Government Control of the Press after the Expiration of the Licensing Act in 1679', *Publishing History*, 5 (1979), 49–97; R. Astbury, 'The Renewal of the Licensing Act in 1693 and its Lapse in 1695', *The Library*, 5th ser., 33 (1978), 296–322.
[37] See Ch. 5.
[38] M. Treadwell, 'Lists of Master Printers: The Size of the London Printing Trade 1637–1723', in R. Myers and M. Harris (eds.), *Aspects of Printing from 1600* (Oxford, 1987), 141–70.

but that paper warfare was waged and *sustained* at similarly high or higher levels after 1695.

We should also note that literacy levels continued to rise over the second half of the seventeenth century and early eighteenth century.[39] To be sure, much of the improvement in literacy occurred before the rage of party got underway; oral and manuscript culture continued to flourish; and there was tremendous variation in literacy according to region, urbanization, gender, trade, and class. Nevertheless male headline illiteracy had been reduced from 70 per cent in 1640 to about 55 per cent by 1715, with corresponding decreases for women from 90 per cent to 75 per cent.[40] In urban areas, illiteracy was far lower. Thus for male artisans and tradesmen in London and Middlesex it fell from 25 per cent in 1640 to 13 per cent by 1696, and a mere 8 per cent by the 1720s.[41] It is more difficult to establish that the greater quantity of print was reaching new readers. Yet it is in distribution that the later Stuart period was most innovative. Improvements in the postal system, especially after the introduction of London's penny post in 1680, facilitated dissemination. Coffee-houses were locales specifically designed to cater for the highly literate, news-hungry public who flocked there to read and debate as well as drink. Coffee-houses spread rapidly in the capital after their introduction in the 1650s, so that by 1700 there were about 500, but they were also established in most provincial towns.[42] They were, moreover, a forum for the numerous clubs and societies that began during this period.[43] Of course, taverns, inns, and alehouses had earlier provided venues for discussion, debate, and association; but, as we shall see, the new spaces seemed to pose new challenges. Moreover, the lapse of the Licensing Act had the dramatic consequence (perhaps more important than that of removing censorship) of opening up provincial

[39] D. Cressy, *Literacy and the Social Order: Reading and Writing in Tudor and Stuart England* (Cambridge, 1980); K. Thomas, 'The Meaning of Literacy in Early Modern England', in G. Baumann (ed.), *The Written Word: Literacy in Transition* (Oxford, 1986); R. S. Schofield, 'The Measurement of Literacy in Pre-Industrial England', in J. Goody (ed.), *Literacy in Traditional Societies* (Cambridge, 1968); W. Ford, 'The Problem of Literacy in Early Modern England', *History*, 78 (1993), 22–37; A. Fox, *Oral and Literate Culture in England 1500–1700* (Oxford, 2000).

[40] Cressy, *Literacy and the Social Order*, 176.

[41] Ibid., 154 and table 7.3.

[42] S. Pincus, ' "Coffee Politicians Does Create": Coffee-houses and Restoration Political Culture', *Journal of Modern History*, 67 (1995), 807–34; L. Klein, 'Coffeehouse Civility, 1660–1714: An Aspect of Post-Courtly Culture in England', *Huntington Library Quarterly*, 59 (1997), 30–51; P. Borsay, *The English Urban Renaissance: Culture and Society in the Provincial Town 1660–1770* (Oxford, 1989), 145–6.

[43] P. Clark, *British Clubs and Societies, 1580–1800: The Origins of an Associational World* (Oxford, 2000).

publishing, which had been forbidden by statute. Thus the first provincial newspaper was printed in Norwich in 1701. By 1710, 13 provincial newspapers had been started and the capital had 18 newspapers, including a daily.[44]

Ideological conflict and politicized religion

A fourth motor for change was ideological conflict. Again, this was hardly a new force. The early and mid-seventeenth century had been wracked by contested notions of religious and political authority. But continuity in the importance of ideological division does not negate its enduring influence as a factor for change; nor was the nature of the conflict quite the same.[45] Disputes over the succession (occurring 1659–60, 1679–83, 1685, 1689, and then periodically renewed by fears about the strength of jacobite plotting, especially in 1692, 1696, 1701–2, 1708, and in the aftermath of the accession of George I in 1714) focused debates about the extent and legiti-

[44]   E. S. De Beer, 'The English Newspapers from 1695 to 1702', in R. Hatton and J. S. Bromley (eds.), *William III and Louis XIV. Essays 1680–1720* (Liverpool, 1968). J. R. Sutherland, 'The Circulation of Newspapers and Periodicals 1700–1730', *The Library*, 4th ser., 15 (1934), 110–24; J. M. Price, 'A Note on the Circulation of the London Press 1704–14', *BIHR*, 31 (1958), 215–24; J. Feather, *The Provincial Book Trade in Eighteenth-century England* (Cambridge, 1985).

[45]   For discussions of later Stuart ideology, see J. Kenyon, *Revolution Principles: The Politics of Party, 1689–1720* (Cambridge, 1977); H. Dickinson, *Liberty and Property: Political Ideology in Eighteenth-century Britain* (London, 1979); R. Ashcraft, *Revolutionary Politics & Locke's Two Treatises of Government* (Princeton, 1986); J. H. Burns with M. Goldie (eds.), *The Cambridge History of Political Thought 1400–1800* (Cambridge, 1991); M. Goldie, 'The Roots of True Whiggism, 1688–1694', *History of Political Thought*, 1 (1980), 195–236; Goldie, 'The Political Thought of the Anglican Revolution' in R. Beddard (ed.), *The Revolutions of 1688* (Oxford, 1989); Goldie, 'The Revolution of 1689 and the Structure of Political Argument', *Bulletin of Research in the Humanities*, 83 (1980), 473–564; T. Harris, *London Crowds in the Reign of Charles II: Propaganda and Politics from the Restoration until the Exclusion Crisis* (Cambridge, 1987); Harris, *Politics under the Later Stuarts: Party Conflict in a Divided Society 1660–1715* (London, 1993); J. G. A. Pocock, *Politics, Language and Time: Essays on Political Thought and History*, 2nd edn. (Chicago, 1989); J. G. A. Pocock, 'The Varieties of Whiggism from Exclusion to Reform: A History of Ideology and Discourse', in his *Virtue, Commerce and History* (Cambridge, 1985); G. Schochet, *Patriarchalism in Political Thought* (New York, 1975); B. Behrens, 'The Whig Theory of the Constitution in the Reign of Charles II', *Cambridge Historical Journal*, 7 (1941), 42–71; O. W. Furley, 'The Whig Exclusionists: Pamphlet Literature in the Exclusion Campaign, 1679–81', *Cambridge Historical Journal*, 13 (1957), 19–36; G. Straka, *The Revolution of 1688 and The Birth of the English Political Nation* (Lexington, 1973); D. Bahlman, *The Moral Revolution of 1688* (New Haven, 1957); J. Daly, *Sir Robert Filmer and English Political Thought* (Toronto, 1979); T. Claydon, *William III and the Godly Revolution* (Cambridge, 1996); Champion, *Republican Learning*; J. Rudolph, *Revolution by Degrees. James Tyrrell and Whig Political Thought in the Late Seventeenth Century* (2002); M. Zook, *Radical Whigs and Conspiratorial Politics in late Stuart England* (Pennsylvania, 1999); A. Houston, *Algernon Sidney and the Republican Heritage in England and America* (Princeton, 1991); J. Scott, *Algernon Sidney and the Restoration Crisis, 1677–1683* (Cambridge, 1991).

The Coffee House Mob (1710) shows how integral print was to the coffee-house culture but also how it engendered bitter dispute—here a dish of coffee is thrown in anger. The dating of 1710 is significant, since the nation was divided then over the impeachment of a high-church cleric, Dr Henry Sacheverell. [Reproduced by courtesy of the Trustees of the British Museum.]

macy of royal or popular sovereignty and power. There were real or imagined plots first to create the Restoration monarchy in 1660 and subsequently to overthrow or reform it, and then to bring about the Revolution
of 1688 and to try to restore the Stuarts.[46] These plots forced the public to
decide to what or to whom they owed loyalty and allegiance. Ideology in
these circumstances was not a luxury but a fact of life. At the heart of these
disagreements lay polarized views about contract, consent, the right to
resist, freedom of conscience, and hence also the power and rights of the
people. The Restoration settlement, especially its religious dimension, was
hotly contested. Foreign policy split contemporary opinion about what
constituted the national interest. The impact of war and fiscal change
created fierce passions. And contemporaries constantly revisited the
ideological origins of the civil war in a search for explanations that could
guide them away from similar rocks. This last point is important because
it suggests another way in which the later Stuart period was different from
the early or mid-seventeenth century.

But the nature of ideological conflict had also slightly changed. To put
it most provocatively, we sense a shift in the way religion was defined
and debated; and a heightened sense of a public (as opposed to the 'godly')
that was engaged in, and even judge of, those debates. Such an assertion
immediately raises the spectre of 'secularization'. But, as Blair Worden
has persuasively argued, even if this term is problematic there are important differences between early and later Stuart approaches to 'religion'.[47]
Religious dispute did not cease to be important; but was treated in
different ways (for which the decline of Calvinism may have played a key
part), judged by a lay public as much as an informed clerisy, and explicitly
tied to debates about civil governance.[48] 'High church', a term in use by

---

[46] R. L. Greaves, *Secrets of the Kingdom: British Radicals from the Popish Plot to the Revolu-
tion of 1688–1689* (Stanford, 1992); R. L. Greaves, *Enemies under his Feet: Radicals and
Nonconformists in Britain, 1664–1677* (Stanford, 1990); R. L. Greaves, *Deliver us from Evil: The
Radical Underground in Britain, 1660–1663* (New York, 1986); P. Hopkins, 'Aspects of Jacobite
Conspiracy in England in the Reign of William III', Ph.D., Cambridge (1981); E. Cruickshanks
(ed.), *Ideology and Conspiracy: Aspects of Jacobitism, 1689–1759* (Edinburgh, 1982); J. Garrett,
The Triumphs of Providence. The Assassination Plot of 1696 (Cambridge, 1980).

[47] B. Worden, 'The Question of Secularisation', in Houston and Pincus, *The Nation Transformed*. See also my ' "Meer" religion and the "church-state" of Restoration England: the
impact and ideology of James II's declarations of indulgence' in the same volume; and
C. J. Sommerville, *The Secularization of Early Modern England* (Oxford, 1992).

[48] Justin Champion sees continuity with the seventeenth-century's periodic convulsions
that centred on the relationship between priest and civil society (*The Pillars of Priestcraft
Shaken: The Church of England and its Enemies, 1660–1730* (Cambridge, 1992), 17–18). He challenges notions of secularization, arguing that the radical programme sought not to destroy
religion but to deprive a corrupt priesthood of political power (24). In his most recent work,

1677,[49] was as much a political label as a religious one. The toleration enacted in 1689 broke the intrinsic overlap between church and state, and by
the early eighteenth century conscience had lost much of its power as a
guide to political judgement, so that state oaths became more routine, political, affairs.[50] For these reasons I think it viable to talk about the highly
politicized debate about church–state relations as 'politics', a term that also
embraces other forms of power struggle, and to consider it as part of 'political culture'. Claims to freedom of conscience were treated as political
claims as much as theological ones, on the grounds that there was an intrinsic link between dissent and political sedition. In turn the established
church was accused of exercising, or wanting to exercise, a form of political power, 'priestcraft', over the laity. Controversy over religion was seldom
solely about private belief, but also or mainly about public practice and the
ideal relationship between civil and religious power. We can therefore call
most of the arguments about religion consciously political in some form
or other.

This viewpoint challenges a current later-Stuart historiographical trend
that stresses the *predominance* of religious concerns and hence emphasizes
continuity with the first half of the seventeenth century and/or between
the seventeenth and eighteenth centuries on religious grounds.[51] At its

---

Champion suggests that Toland pursued political concerns through religious discourse (*Republican Learning*, 13). Yet the language of priestcraft itself seems to suggest a contemporary
recognition of the politicized nature of clerical authority and a sense of religion as a political
veil. The importance of religious language in introducing the concept of political pluralism
is also ably explored in P. Ihalainen, *The Discourse on Political Pluralism in Early-Eighteenth
Century England. A Conceptual Study with Special Reference to Terminology of Religious Origin* (Helsinki, 1999). Ihalainen admits (244–5), however, that there was a gradual 'shift from a
religion-dominated political discourse towards an increasingly secular political discourse'
and quotes Peter Paxton, *Civil Polity* (1703), 588, that 'the very nature of the dispute between
the two parties is gradually changed: For now it is not, as formerly, so much upon the score of
religion (though that is continued, or rather revised) as it is upon points of government'. For
the civil implications of the rejection of puritanism see D. Zaret, 'Religion and the Rise of
Liberal-Democratic Ideology in 17-Century England', *American Sociological Review*, 54
(1989), 163–79. For primary sources, see J. A. W. Gunn, *Factions No More: Attitudes to Party in
Government and Opposition in Eighteenth Century England, Extracts from Contemporary
Sources* (London, 1972).

[49] M. Goldie, 'Danby, the Bishops and the Whigs' in Harris, Seaward, and Goldie, *The
Politics of Religion* (1990), 81 n. 22.

[50] E. Vallance, 'The Decline of Conscience as a Political Guide: William Higden's *View of
the English Constitution* (1709), in H. Braun and E. Vallance (eds.), *Contexts of Conscience in
Early Modern Europe 1500–1700* (Basingstoke, 2004).

[51] See n. 1. For more detailed and nuanced views of continuity, see C. Rose, *England in the
1690s: Revolution, Religion, and War* (Oxford, 1999); Claydon, *William III*; Goldie, 'Political
Thought'; Bahlman, *Moral Revolution*.

most extreme, such an interpretation calls for historians to turn 'away
from so-called political and constitutional history' and to recognize that
'the rise of the middle class, religious toleration, free speech, contractual
government and parliamentary supremacy have all been imposed on 1688
retrospectively'.[52] 'Religion' was what mattered, it is alleged, and it continued to do so before and after 1688. Such views are important in so far as
they correct a liberal, secular, tradition that sidelined the power and importance of religious belief and practice. To be sure, political views were
shaped by religious ones and only by recovering their religious context can
we fully understand them; we should see political and religious concerns
as entwined. But to neglect the politics of religion, or deny change, would
be to miss what was obvious to most contemporaries, that religion, as
opposed to private faith, was a tool in a partisan, political contest. It was
said, for example, that Sir Edward Seymour, one of the Tory leaders who
lamented the 'danger' the Whigs and low churchmen posed to the church,
had not been inside one for seven years.[53]

Partisanship and parties

The fifth factor for (and facet of) change was the public partisanship that
emerged during the mid-century crisis and became formalized in the later
Stuart period as party politics.[54] Many of the features of the impact of
party, of course, can be seen earlier, whenever sides engaged in adversarial
conflict sought to appeal to the people.[55] Indeed, it is to be hoped that this

---

[52] Scott, *England's Troubles*, 35; Clark, *English Society*, 2nd edn., 82. For attacks on the idea
that contract and Lockean theory was prevalent after 1689, see Dickinson, *Liberty and Property*; Pocock, 'The Myth of John Locke and the Obsession with Liberalism', in J. G. A. Pocock
and R. Ashcraft (eds.), *John Locke* (Los Angeles, 1980); Kenyon, *Revolution Principles*; H.
Nenner, *The Right to be King. The Succession to the Crown of England 1603–1714* (Chapel Hill,
1995), ch. 8; M. Thompson, 'The Reception of Locke's Two Treatises of Government
1690–1705', *Political Studies*, 24 (1976), 184–91 and the debate in vols. 26 (1978) and 28 (1980).
[53] J. Oldmixon, *The Life . . . of Arthur Maynwaring* (1715), 245.
[54] Halliday, *Dismembering the Body Politic*, 5–18.
[55] This is not to deny that politics (or religion) could be contested publicly before the civil
war; rather that an appeal to 'popularity' was not routine. For some illuminating discussions
of early Stuart political culture, see T. Cogswell, R. Cust, and P. Lake, *Politics, Religion and
Popularity. Essays in Honour of Conrad Russell* (Cambridge, 2002); P. Lake and M. Questier,
'Puritans, Papists and the "Public Sphere": The Edmund Campion Affair in Context', *JMH*, 72
(2000), 587–627; P. Lake with M. Questier, *The Antichrist's Lewd Hat. Protestants, Papists and
Players in Post-reformation England* (New Haven, 2002); A. Bellany, *The Politics of Court Scandal in Early Modern England: News Culture and the Overbury Affair 1603–1660* (Cambridge,
2002); Bellany, 'Libels in Action: Ritual, Subversion, and the English Literary Underground
1603–42', in T. Harris (ed.), *The Politics of the Excluded* (Basingstoke, 2001); A. Bellany,
'Rayling Rhymes and Vaunting Verse: Libellous Politics in Early Stuart England 1602–28', in

study has relevance for anyone interested in partisanship and polemic across time and space. Yet in the later Stuart period the formalization, popularization, and politicization of partisanship were developed to new heights. Party was thus both a reflection of change and a motor for further change. Party has nevertheless become controversial in recent years.[56] The coherence and novelty of parties as organized bodies, rather than ideological groupings, has been questioned and the demise of more traditional court–country sensibilities and religiously determined divisions debated.

K. Sharpe and P. Lake (eds.), *Culture and Politics in Early Stuart England* (Basingstoke, 1994); T. Cogswell, 'Underground Verse and Early Stuart Culture', in S. Amussen and M. Kishlansky, *Political Culture and Cultural Politics in Early Modern England: Essays Presented to David Underdown* (Manchester, 1995); T. Cogswell, 'The Politics of Propaganda: Charles I and the People in the 1620s', *JBS*, 29 (1990), 187–215; T. Cogswell, *Home Divisions: Aristocracy, the State and Provincial Conflict* (Manchester, 1998); P. Croft, 'The Reputation of Robert Cecil: Libels, Political Opinions and Popular Awareness in the early Seventeenth Century', *TRHS*, 6th ser., 1 (1991), 43–69; P. Croft, 'Libels, Popular literacy and Public Opinion in Early Modern England', *HR*, 68 (1995), 266–85; A. Fox, 'Ballads, Libels and Popular Ridicule in Jacobean England', *P&P*, 145 (1994), 47–83; A. Fox, 'Rumour, News and Popular Political Opinion in Elizabethan and Early Stuart England', *HJ*, 40 (1997), 597–620; A. Fox, 'Popular Verses and their Readership in the Early Seventeenth Century', in J. Raven, H. Small and N. Tadmor, *The Practice and Representation of Reading* (Cambridge, 1996); J. Raymond (ed.), *News, Newspapers and Society in Early Modern Britain* (London, 1999); F. Levy, 'How Information Spread Among the Gentry 1550–1640', *JBS*, 21 (1982), 11–34; R. Cust, 'News and Politics in Early Seventeenth-century England', *P&P*, 112 (1986), 60–90; E. Shagan, *Popular Politics and the English Reformation* (Cambridge, 2002); I. Archer, 'Popular Politics in the Sixteenth and Early Seventeenth Centuries', in P. Griffiths and M. Jenner (eds.), *Londinopolis* (Manchester, 2000); E. Shagan, 'Constructing Discord: Ideology, Propaganda, and English Responses to the Irish rebellion of 1641', *JBS*, 36 (1997), 4–34; A. McRae, 'The Literary Culture of Early Stuart Libeling', *Modern Philology*, 97 (2000), 364–92.

[56] Much of the literature is summarized in Harris, *Politics under the Later Stuarts*. The existence of party was challenged first by the Namierite school and more recently by Jonathan Scott's revisionism. For the Namierite view and the refutation of it, see R. Walcott, *English Politics in the Early Eighteenth Century* (Oxford, 1956); R. Walcott, 'English Party Politics, 1688–1714', in *Essays in Modern English History in Honour of W. C. Abbott* (Cambridge, Mass., 1941); D. Rubini, *Court and Country 1688–1702* (London, 1967); G. Holmes, *British Politics in the Age of Anne* (London, 1967; rev. 2nd edn. 1987); G. Holmes (ed.), *Britain after the Glorious Revolution 1689–1714* (London, 1969); H. Horwitz, *Parliament, Policy and Politics in the Reign of William III* (Manchester, 1977); Speck, *Tory & Whig*; C. Jones (ed.), *Britain in the First Age of Party, 1680–1750: Essays Presented to Geoffrey Holmes* (London, 1987); C. Jones (ed.), *Party and Management in Parliament, 1660–1784* (Leicester, 1984); B. W. Hill, *The Growth of Parliamentary Parties, 1689–1742* (London, 1976); G. De Krey, *A Fractured Society: The Politics of London in the First Age of Party, 1688–1715* (Oxford, 1985). A host of local studies reinforces these works, the most important of which are listed at *HOP II*, i. 32, though the constituency articles in *HOP II* add considerably to them. For the debate generated by Scott, for the Restoration period, see the special issue, 'Order and Authority: Creating Party in Restoration England', *Albion*, 25 (1993); discussions in my *Politics and Opinion in Crisis, 1678–1681*, 5–15; and J. Montaño, *Courting the Moderates. Ideology, Propaganda and the Emergence of Party, 1660–1678* (Newark, NJ, 2002), 27–52.

Even so, the use of new labels, Whig and Tory, after 1681 is significant.[57] As Terence Ball argues, party was not a term that simply replaced other ways of describing division; it reflected conceptual change and a shift in the nature of division.[58] It denoted a move away from expectations of uniformity, that had been current in the early Stuart period and that the Restoration regime attempted to resurrect, towards a situation in which diversity of opinion was seldom embraced but had come to be expected and even accepted. The rise of the idea of the polity as an artificial body, into which individuals contracted, challenged traditional rationales for the construction of authority and created a debate about how to represent the collective people or public. Whereas faction represented the interest of an individual or sectional group, party claimed to represent the public and the public good. The achievement of scholars such as Holmes, Speck, Horwitz, and others has been to show that later Stuart politics was not Namierite in character, but that party allegiance was ideologically driven, increasingly well organized along bipartisan lines and went beyond local loyalties, personal connections, and social deference. This was a new version of the political game. Certainly by Anne's reign, but often from the 1670s onwards, contemporaries were well aware of what they themselves called the 'rage' of party. A caveat is necessary, however. Although Whig and Tory provided the basic structure of politics, contemporaries also displayed a court–country mentality that could at times (most notably 1697–9, in the wake of the pause in warfare) temporarily disturb party lines.[59] Moreover, as we shall see, high church and low church were also employed as labels (often, however, overlapping with Tory and Whig), and there were also those who rejected, or professed to reject, all parties. However, whether Whig–Tory, court–country, or anti-party predominated, contemporaries still saw the world in polarized terms and commented on

[57] R. Willman, 'The Origins of "Whig" and "Tory" in the English Political Language', *HJ*, 17 (1974), 247–64.
[58] T. Ball, 'Party', in T. Ball, J. Farr, and R. L. Hanson (eds.), *Political Innovation and Conceptual Change* (Cambridge, 1989). For a very stimulating discussion of the nature and language of party, see Ihalainen, *Discourse on Political Pluralism*, 159–228. Ihalainen argues that political pluralism owed much to a developing notion of religious pluralism. See also, J. A. W. Gunn, *Beyond Liberty and Property: The Process of Self-Recognition in Eighteenth-Century Political Thought* (Kingston, 1983), 50; Tone Sundt Urstad, *Sir Robert Walpole's Poets. The Use of Literature as Pro-Government Propaganda 1721–42* (Newark, NJ, 1999), 174.
[59] D. Hayton, 'The "Country" Interest and the Party System, c.1689–1720', in C. Jones (ed.), *Party and Party Management in Parliament 1660–1784* (Leicester, 1984); D. Hayton, 'Moral Reform and Country Politics in the Late Seventeenth-century House of Commons', *P&P*, 128 (1990), 48–91; L. Schwoerer, *No Standing Armies! The Anti-Army Ideology in the Seventeenth Century* (Baltimore, 1974).

the impact that organized ideological communities had on political culture. The focus of this book's discussion is therefore not on the chronology or definition of parties, nor their precise identity at any one point (interesting though these may be), but on the nature and impact of partisanship.

These five key factors, all in some sense concerned with an appeal to the 'public', were often intertwined; and it is the combination rather than the factors individually that might be said to have been most innovating. The elections of 1710, 1713, and 1715, for example, were partisan contests fought over the problems created by divergent ideologies and competing notions of war and commerce, producing paper warfare and public debate on a huge scale. It is also important to recognize that none of the factors just outlined relied on central direction for their impetus but were fuelled by local and personal contexts. The dispersed governance of the early modern state ensured that the nature of electioneering and the voterate, the collection of revenue and the economic response to war, the role of print, and the nature of party were all locally conditioned and arose out of local circumstances.[60]

Generalizing without regard to differences between urban and rural communities, between English and British communities, or between regions or towns is a foolhardy undertaking. For this reason it must be acknowledged that what follows relates primarily to the experience of English civic communities, and that the book's conclusions may be less applicable to rural areas or even to all English towns at all times.[61] This is

---

[60] Three years working on constituency articles at the History of Parliament drove this message home. *HOP I* and *HOP II* chart numerous varieties of localized political culture and offer a wealth of references to local studies. For important studies of provincial political cultures, see P. Gauci, *Politics and Society in Great Yarmouth, 1660–1722* (Oxford, 1996); Halliday, *Dismembering the Body Politic*; D. Beaver, *Parish Communities and Religious Conflict in the Vale of Gloucester, 1590–1690* (Cambridge, Mass., 1998); D. Rollison, *Local Origins of Modern Society: Gloucestershire, 1500–1800* (London, 1992); J. M. Triffitt, 'Politics and the Urban Community. Parliamentary Boroughs in the South West of England 1710–1730', Ph.D., Oxford (1985); Speck, *Tory & Whig*; Barry, 'Popular Culture'; and works cited in Knights, *Politics and Opinion*, 14. For the early eighteenth century, see also K. Wilson, *The Sense of the People. Politics, Culture and Imperialism in England, 1715–1785* (Oxford, 1995); N. Rogers, *Whigs and Cities: Popular Politics in the Age of Walpole and Pitt* (Oxford, 1989). For explorations of Scottish and Irish political cultures, see *HOP II*, i. 141–77; in J. G. Simms, D. W. Hayton and G. O' Brien (eds.), *War and Politics in Ireland 1649–1730* (1986); D. G. Boyce, R. Eccleshall, and V. Geoghegan (eds.), *Political Discourse in Seventeenth- and Eighteenth-century Ireland* (Basingstoke, 2001); and forthcoming studies by Tim Harris and Clare Jackson.

[61] Research on the town is synthesized in R. Sweet, *The English Town, 1680–1840: Government, Society and Culture* (1999). See also P. Withington, 'Two Renaissances: Urban Political Culture in Post-Reformation England Reconsidered', *HJ*, 44 (2001), 239–68; Withington, 'Views from the Bridge: Revolution and Restoration in Seventeenth-century York', *P&P*, 170

primarily a study of urban representational politics. Since four-fifths of
MPs were elected by borough constituencies, this position is defensible. Indeed, an analysis of London's political culture alone would be worth while,
given the capital's importance and size, able to draw one in six adults to live
there at some point in their lives. But much of the argument put forward in
the following pages applies to, and is based on studies of, other urban societies, particularly those with large freemen or inhabitant franchises.[62] As
the work of Peter Borsay and others indicates, after 1660 English civic life
was taking on not only a new material appearance but also a new self-
conscious urbanity.[63] Indeed, 'cit' and his rural counterpart, 'bumpkin',
were stock representations that were increasingly used in polemic.[64]

   One important dimension of this caricaturing was the difference in the
potential to acquire knowledge. John Locke argued that knowledge was
deeper in urban societies where reason could be polished by conversation
and debate, so that, he said, a city cobbler's understanding surpassed that
of a mechanic in the country and this in turn surpassed that of a day-
labourer in a country village. Indeed, he claimed, 'an ordinary coffee-
house gleaner of the city' was 'an arrant statesman' compared to the
country gentleman.[65] This knowledge gap in rural areas may help to explain why some studies of county electorates have seen popular deference

(2001), 121–51; Withington, 'Citizens, Community and Political Culture in Restoration
England', in A. Shepherd and P. Withington (eds.), *Communities in Early Modern England*
(Manchester, 2000), 134–55; P. Borsay and L. Proudfoot, *Provincial Towns in Early Modern
England and Ireland: Change, Convergence and Divergence* (Oxford, 2002).

   [62] E. A. Wrigley, 'A Simple Model of London's Importance in Changing English Society
and Economy, 1650–1750', *P&P*, 37 (1967), 44–70; De Krey, *Fractured Society*; A. L. Beier and R.
Finlay (eds.), *London 1500–1700: The Making of the Metropolis* (London, 1986); *HOP II*, ii.
374–96; P. Griffiths and M. Jenner (eds.), *Londinopolis. Essays in the Cultural and Social
History of Early Modern London* (Manchester, 2000); N. Rogers, 'Popular Protest in Early
Hanoverian London', *P&P*, 79 (1978), 70–100. For an analysis of the wider franchises, see
HOP II, i. 78–96, 105–24. Besides the counties, about a quarter of borough constituencies
had over 1,000 voters each, but of course electoral contests could be fierce even in restricted
franchises.

   [63] Borsay, *English Urban Renaissance*; P. Clark, *The Transformation of English Provincial
Towns, 1600–1800* (London, 1984); Klein, 'Coffee-house civility'.

   [64] R. L'Estrange, *Citt and Bumpkin* (1680), which went into five editions in the space of a
year and prompted a sequel that also ran to four editions. See also *The Humours and Conversation of the Town* [*c*.1681] for an extended satire of town life in comparison with country living; *Spectator*, 119, 17 July 1711. For a discussion of stereotypical rural dialects, see Fox, *Oral and
Literate Culture*, 104–11. A distinction between court and country had drawn on a similar di-
chotomy, but the city appears to have been replacing the court. For the resistance of rural
communities to urban influence, see C. Estabrook, *Urbane and Rustic England: Cultural Ties
and Social Spheres in the Provinces, 1660–1780* (Manchester, 1998).

   [65] J. Locke, *Works* (1823), iii. 211–12.

rather than ideological commitment.[66] This study will be concerned with exploring how such political knowledge could be gained but also how political truths could be *discerned*. Voters and readers were faced with hard choices. Consequently the problem of political judgement will loom large.[67]

Some of the features analysed in this book, particularly those to do with the press and the nature of polemic, can be found in other European countries, but a comparative framework also highlights the precocity of public debate in England and the unique combination of factors that contributed to its partisan political culture.[68] Of the Europeans the Dutch were the most similar. The United Provinces saw a high degree of participation in representative politics and restrictions on the press had never been strong.[69] The Dutch also had a developed financial system and religious toleration. Yet because of its highly devolved and oligarchical representative system, the country had nothing like national parties or general elections to maintain partisan feuding or develop a national 'public'. France, too, lacked the institutional framework for such a participatory politics, and had much lower literacy levels. Although its press could still reflect vigorous debate at moments of crisis, its public sphere was stunted throughout the seventeenth century.[70] Outside Europe, colonial America closely followed English political life, adopting metropolitan political labels and slogans, and emulating English provinces by participating in the addressing campaigns explored in Chapter 3. But neither its press nor financial system was as developed as in England and its much smaller urban

---

[66] Baskerville *et al.*, 'Dynamics of Landlord influence'; *HOP II*, i. 36–72, which nevertheless notes many examples of deep politicization. For the role of estate stewards as electoral agents, see D. R. Hainsworth, *Stewards, Lords and People* (Cambridge, 1992), ch. 7. My aim is not to deny the power of landed influence, which was huge in the counties and some boroughs; but to examine the vigorous public debate about politics.

[67] P. Steinberger, *The Concept of Political Judgment* (Chicago, 1993) is a useful, but ahistorical, treatment.

[68] J. Van Horn Melton, *The Rise of the Public in Enlightenment Europe* (Cambridge, 2001); T. W. Blanning, *The Culture of Power and the Power of Culture. Old Regime Europe 1660–1789* (Oxford, 2002); B. Harris, *Politics and the Rise of the Press: Britain and France 1620–1800* (London, 1996).

[69] C. Harline, *Pamphlets, Printing and Political Culture in the Early Dutch Republic* (Dordrecht, 1987); J. L. Price, *Dutch Society 1588–1713* (Harlow, 2000).

[70] J. Sawyer, *Printed Poison. Pamphlet Propaganda, Faction Politics and the Public Sphere in Early Seventeenth Century France* (Berkeley, 1990); C. Jouhard, *Mazarinades: la fronde des mots* (1985); J. Klaits, *Printed Propaganda under Louis XIV* (Princeton, 1976); P. Burke, *The Fabrication of Louis XIV* (New Haven, 1992); A. Farge, *Subversive Words: Public Opinion in Eighteenth-century France* (Cambridge, 1994); J. A. W. Gunn, *Queen of the World: Opinion in the Public Life of France from the Renaissance to the Revolution* (Oxford, 1995).

populations made for a rather different context.[71] Yet if England was first to experience the rise of public and nationally contested, partisan, representative politics, few countries during the eighteenth century escaped the increasing pressures of public opinion and passionate polemic. And in that sense, this study should offer useful points of comparison across time as well as space.

AN EVOLVING POLITICAL CULTURE

To summarize the changes that will be outlined more fully in the following pages:

1   England (and then, after 1707, Britain) moved from a nation in which elections and parliamentary sessions had been held irregularly to one in which both were regular and frequent. Alongside this, the electorate expanded so that a higher percentage of adult males could vote than at any time before the Second Reform Act of 1867.

2   The later Stuart period witnessed the development of a national political culture in which allegiance to national political identities (Whig, Tory, high church, low church) was routine. Thus one of the key features of this nationally applicable and nationally understood political structure and language was the emergence of political parties.

3   The parties were groupings of allegiances that were based on shared ideologies but also increasingly on techniques developed over the course of the seventeenth century and refined in the later Stuart period, such as signing petitions and addresses; electioneering; political oath-taking; partisan polemic; and linking reward to party loyalty. Under such conditions, the notion of unity through uniformity became problematic and unsustainable.

4   The press, freed at moments in the seventeenth century from pre-publication censorship, was permanently unshackled in 1695. Regulated by the market rather than the state (except in cases of libel or

[71] M. Warner, *The Letters of the Republic: Publication and the Public Sphere in Eighteenth-century America* (Cambridge, Mass., 1990); P. Thompson, *Rum Punch and Revolution: Taverngoing and Public Life in Eighteenth-century Philadelphia* (Philadelphia, Pa., 1999); M. L. Lustig, *Robert Hunter 1666–1734: New York's Augustan Statesman* (Syracuse, 1983). I am very grateful to Simon Middleton for discussing these, and showing me his forthcoming *Privileges and Profits: Tradesmen in Colonial New York City.*

sedition), print was regarded as its own best censor. Moreover, 1695 also allowed for the emergence of a provincial periodical press and hence further to integrate a national political culture at the local level.

5   All these developments invigorated a role for the public. The appeal to popularity was not new; but the public as a collective fiction that was both frequently appealed to as an umpire of politics and as a legitimating force was a phenomenon that grew to new proportions. Moreover, the culture of plots and elections that dominated the later Stuart period repeatedly invited the public to participate by exercising its judgement.

6   That public found new importance structurally within the state because of the factors outlined above and because for the first time a national debt was funded by the public and based on public credit.

7   The public was also restricted and at times excluded by new political languages or shifts in existing ones. There was a reassertion of the language of consent, a new stress on popular sovereignty and an attack on 'priestcraft'. Perhaps the most striking shift was the increasingly frequent appeal to a language of politeness and reason.

8   Such a language was in part a response to growing fears about the uses to which language was being put. To be sure, anxiety about words permeated much of the early modern period, but this was sharpened in the later Stuart period because partisans (a) necessarily offered rival, opposing interpretations; (b) sought to use all means possible to persuade the public that they had a monopoly of truth and reason; (c) had new means and opportunities (for reasons enumerated above) to effect their perceived designs; and (d) the consequences of being misled by words were now so much the greater, because Britain was at war with France and because public credit necessary to fight that war rested on notions of credibility.

9   Because of such fears and anxieties, the conspiratorial mindset and hostility to particular interests that characterized the early modern period was carried over into the eighteenth century, albeit shaped less by traditional 'anti-popery' or anti-factionalism and more by suspicions of 'interest', whether of self, party, crown, money, or even state. Party was a vehicle that could carry anxieties previously manifest predominantly in the religious sphere into the political.

10 Party was nevertheless also a creative force that impacted on literary culture and wherever truth-claims were made, fostering a sense of ambiguity, relativity, dissimulation, and fiction.

The key aims of this book are thus to relate public discourse to the practice of politics, and to explore the concept of representation at a crucial time in its development. Two recurrent questions are: why and in what ways did Britain become a more representational society in the later Stuart period? And what were the characteristics of a national political culture based on publicly contested, partisan politics?

THE PROBLEM OF REPRESENTATION

Conceptually, the study of representation and party politics might appear 'old hat', part of an agenda irrelevant to modern historiographical questions. It might be dismissed as a branch of 'political history' or 'high politics' of the type defended (albeit needlessly aggressively and in limiting ways) by Geoffrey Elton.[72] Yet this book is conceived as a study of later Stuart political culture, by which I mean the intersection between politics, society, ideas, and modes of communication.[73] Broadening our definition of the political in this way opens new lines of inquiry that blur the boundaries between cognate studies in political science, political thought, social history, and literary studies;[74] and doing so provides new reasons for returning to the passions aroused by party politics. An expanded sense of the political requires us to draw on different approaches, for, as Kevin Sharpe puts it, 'history as the study of representations collapses the boundaries traditionally placed between rhetoric and truth, play and politics: it makes all accounts of the past a cultural history'.[75] As applied to the later Stuart period, this creates a very large agenda, but one that helps link it across time and across disciplines and sub-disciplines.

The book focuses on several overlapping types of representation. The

[72] G. R. Elton, *Political History* (1970).

[73] For a discussion of the meaning of political culture, see K. Wilson, *The Sense of the People. Politics, Culture and Imperialism in England, 1715–1785* (Cambridge, 1995), 1–2; P. Griffiths, A. Fox, and S. Hindle (eds.), *The Experience of Authority in Early Modern England* (Basingstoke, 1996), 1; Withington, 'Urban Political Culture', ch. 1; K. Sharpe and P. Lake (eds.), *Culture and Politics in Early Stuart England*, introduction; S. Amussen and M. Kishlansky, *Political Culture and Cultural Politics*, introduction; J. Vernon, *Politics and the People: A Study in English Political Culture c.1815–1867* (Cambridge, 1993), introduction.

[74] S. Hall (ed.), *Representation: Cultural Representations and Signifying Practices*, (London, 1997), 2. The limits to what is 'political' are perhaps best defined by considering the central concern of politics: power. Power is always exercised unequally and whenever power is exercised over others it is political, but it is not necessarily *politicized*.

[75] K. Sharpe, *Reading Revolutions: The Politics of Reading in Early Modern England* (New Haven, 2000), 12.

two most important are the formal representation of elections contested by partisans, and the informal representation of words produced by partisans to persuade the public of their viewpoint. The underbelly of both was misrepresentation: a corrupt parliament or MPs who did not genuinely reflect the will of the people; and words that misled or lied.[76] Words had political import. A vote was even called a 'voice'. An election, the site of much public discourse, was the voice of the nation.

The links between a formal and informal sense of representation can be seen in a printed tract advising the electorate about the choices before them in 1702. Objecting to the dissemination to electors of printed lists of MPs' voting behaviour, writer and physician James Drake complained that Tories were liable to be 'branded' with unjust labels, 'scandalous stories, libels and pernicious lying accusations'. Publicly contested politics thus, he claimed, stimulated discourse that was designed to mislead rather than inform. Such arts, Drake feared, were all too easily successful and 'prevail'd upon the simplicity of the well-meaning people'. Drake thus wrote 'to undeceive' them. In this world of political dissimulation, he alleged, 'lying and defamation' had become standard tools for his enemies, the Whigs: 'by virtue of this single quality has their faction been propagated . . . By these arts have great numbers of our bravest gentlemen and the nation's best friends been aspers'd, and render'd unpopular in most parts of England, and many thousands of simple credulous people banter'd almost out of their faith and principles. When therefore any of the electors hear these men lay about them with the tremendous noise of Popery and French gold, those Bug-bear words, which fright the poor silly vulgar out of their senses: they may prepare themselves to hear some egregious lie.' Party politics thus relied on the manipulation of key terms and phrases, 'bug-bear words', to 'seduce numbers of people' to vote the way the partisans and polemicists desired.[77] Political representation was thus about the way in which choices and candidates could be represented, or represent themselves, to the public. And political parties themselves offered a new form of representational activity. The public and the press assumed a new importance but in doing so created uncertainties about public discourse.

[76] A tract of 1702 referred to as the 'Year of . . . Misrepresentation' (*The Tryal, Sentence, and Condemnation of Fidelity* (1702), dedication).
[77] [J. Drake], *Some Necessary Considerations Relating to All Future Elections* (1702), 3, 5, 15, 17. Apparently reworked as *Necessary Considerations touching the election of members to serve in parliament* (1702).

MERCURIUS POLITICUS:

O R, A N

Antidote to Popular Mif-reprefentations:

CONTAINING

Reflections on the prefent State

O F

AFFAIRS.

Malicious Mif-reprefentation of the Church of England *an Ag-*
gravation of Schifm. Yet daily practic'd and by whom.
Reafons and Confequences of fome Men's Clamour for Mode-
ration. The Moderation of the Church examin'd and prov'd.
Penal Laws made for the fecurity of the Civil Government.
But repealed by the Church.

In a tract of 1702 the high-church Tory Dr James Drake drew an explicit link between representation at the polls and misrepresentation of candidates. Immediately after the 1705 general
election he also began a periodical, *Mercurius Politicus*, designed as an 'antidote to popular
misrepresentations'. He was prosecuted in November 1706 on the grounds that the paper was
a 'scandalous and seditious libel'. [Reproduced by courtesy of the British Library.]

Given this context it is no surprise that the period examined the theory
of representation as well as its practice. Hannah Pitkin's survey of the ety-
mology of the term 'representation' suggests that 'in the second quarter of
the seventeenth century, no doubt spurred by the pamphleteering and political debate that preceded, accompanied and followed the civil war, the
"represent" family [of words] became political terms', and there was 'a
transition from the earlier [meaning of] standing for others by way of sub-
stitution, to something like acting for others'. This shift reflected the need
for a new examination of 'the relations of an individual member of the

Commons to his particular constituency'.[78] Pitkin thought the first use of the word 'representative' (to refer to a member of parliament) occurred in 1651 and noted that this was the year in which Thomas Hobbes's *Leviathan* was published. In it Hobbes made, she says, the first systematic examination of the idea of representation, for he argued that 'a commonwealth is said to be instituted, when a multitude of men do agree and covenant, every one with every one, that to whatsoever man, or assembly of men, shall be given by the major part, the right to present the persons of them all, that is to say, to be their representative; every one . . . shall authorise all the actions and judgments of that man or assembly of men, in the same manner as if they were his own'.[79]

As *Leviathan* stated:

a multitude of men, are made *one* person, when they are by one man, or one person, represented . . . every man giving their common representer authority from himselfe in particular; and owning all the actions the representer doth, in case they give him authority without stint: otherwise, when they limit him in what and how farre he shall represent them, none of them owneth more than they gave him commission to act.[80]

Hobbes thus applied a concept of individual authorization, via contract, to the representative, and he explicitly linked political representation and the representation of language. He thus began his account of political power, *Leviathan*, with an account of speech and the proper signification of words. Hobbes recognized that control of language conferred power. But he also argued that an artificial person or actor was a personator or representative of others. Such representatives had 'their words and actions *owned* by those whom they represent', and it was this authorization that was the basis of authority. Thus political actors and representatives were authorized *fictions*.[81] Every man was the author of everything that their representative said or did; and the voice of the majority 'must be considered the voyce of them all'.[82]

[78] H. Pitkin, 'Representation' in Ball *et al.* (eds.), *Conceptual Innovation and Change*, quotations at 139–40. For a more extended treatment, see Pitkin, *The Concept of Representation* (London, 1967). A. H. Birch, *Representation* (London, 1971) is also a useful conceptual analysis.
[79] T. Hobbes, *Leviathan* ed. R. Tuck (Cambridge, 1996), 121.
[80] Hobbes, *Leviathan*, 114.
[81] 'There are few things that are uncapable of being represented by fiction' (*Leviathan*, 113). John Locke also refers to 'the image, phantom or representative of the commonwealth' (*Two Treatises of Government* (1690), second treatise, ch. 13, para. 151).
[82] Hobbes, *Leviathan*, 84–5.

The relationship between represented and representatives was repeatedly confronted in the later Stuart period. In particular, contemporaries were forced to consider how far representatives were actors who remained responsible to those who authorized them. Hobbes conceived of a transfer of power from the represented to the person representing. But not all agreed. As one critic put it in 1716:

> I cannot therefore agree with Mr Hobbes, that when a person chooses a representative, he resigns the power of resumption, unless it be expressly mention'd in the compact; for a representative acts not by virtue of his own power, but another man's power, who may exercise his own powers, if he pleases, himself. Hence also a representative must be accountable to the person he represents.[83]

The relationship between the represented and representative, including the power that each had, was under constant scrutiny. But there were also other dimensions of Hobbes's formula that were contested and debated. Some denied the contractural basis of representation altogether; others queried who were the people who could legitimately authorize a representative, an issue raised every time a franchise was contested or an appeal to the 'people' was made; others worried about what was being represented—interests, land, or people? These ideological debates arose out of routine political practice.

The debate about representation, of course, went back much further.[84] But in the seventeenth century its development ran alongside assertions of popular sovereignty that were formulated soon after the outbreak of civil war.[85] Representative legitimacy was frequently questioned during the mid-century revolution. Pride's Purge, removing moderates from the Commons, heightened the representational dilemma, for the Rump's claim to be representative was challenged by many. The Presbyterian

---

[83] M. Earbery, *Elements of Policy Civil and Ecclesiastical in a Mathematical Method* (1716), 8.

[84] G. Elton, 'The Body of the Whole Realm: Parliament and Representation in Medieval and Tudor England', in G. Elton, *Studies in Tudor and Stuart Politics II* (London, 1974); H. M. Cam, 'The Theory and Practice of Representation in Medieval England', in E. Fryde and E. Miller (eds.), *Historical Studies of the English Parliament*, Vol. 1 (Cambridge, 1970), 262–78.

[85] D. Wootton, *Divine Right and Democracy: An Anthology of Political Writing in Stuart England* (London, 1986), 52. Edmund Morgan's *Inventing the People: The Rise of Popular Sovereignty in England and America* (New York, 1988) is particularly useful in exploring some of these issues. Samuel Rutherford's *Lex Rex* (1644) talked about the people as 'constituents' of power who entrusted not only to the king but also their knights and burgesses ('representators') revocable 'commissions' in parliament (151–2, 170, 178). Rutherford asserted that the king 'doth unproperly represent the people'. His work was burned by Oxford University in 1683.

William Prynne, for example, drafted a declaration on behalf of a dozen counties, eight cities, and fifty-two boroughs repudiating the Rumpers who, it was claimed, had erected a 'new representative . . . which neither we nor our ancestors ever heard of nor desired'.[86] Yet the declaration of a commonwealth on 4 January 1649, asserted that the Rump, 'being chosen by, and representing the people, have the supreme power in this nation'.[87] In March the act abolishing kingship claimed to 'return' the nation to 'its just and ancient right of being governed by its own representatives'. A year later the Rump required subscription to the 'engagement' in order to procure (or manufacture) representative consent. And the Rump continued to deliberate its own representativeness.[88] So when Hobbes was applying the language of representation to the Leviathan he was doing so against heightened claims about representing the people and novel arguments that representatives had the authorizing consent of individuals.[89] The later Stuart period thus explored and worked through problems and a language that had arisen in the 1640s.

In 1660 the Convention Parliament's first address to Charles II assured him it was 'the true representative of the whole nation'.[90] But during the 1670s Charles's failure to dissolve the parliament that had been elected in 1661, a second 'long parliament', placed the issue of representation back at the top of the agenda.[91] In 1677, for example, a number of tracts argued that parliament's longevity broke the link between the people and representation. One of these, 'The Young Men's plea . . . for dissolving this present parliament', was (like the works of the 1640s) grounded on the necessity of individual authorization of representatives.[92] It argued that all those aged between 21 and 37, '(which is a 3d part and more of the men of England) are not represented in this parliam[en]t', having been too young to vote in

---

[86] [Prynne], *A Remonstrance and Declaration of Severall Counties, Cities and Burroughs* (1648), 6.

[87] *CJ*, vi. 111.

[88] B. Worden, 'The Bill for a New Representative: The Dissolution of the Long Parliament, April 1653', *EHR*, 86 (1971), 473–96. For the mid-century debate more generally, see V. F. Snow, 'Parliamentary Reapportionment Proposals in the Puritan Revolution', *EHR*, 74 (1959), 409–42.

[89] Wootton, *Divine Right*, 57; Q. Skinner, 'Conquest and Consent: Thomas Hobbes and the Engagement Controversy', in G. Aylmer (ed.), *The Interregnum: The Quest for Settlement, 1646–60* (1972), 79–98.

[90] Morgan, *Inventing the People*, 94.

[91] For arguments in 1675 about the unrepresentativeness of parliament, see PRO, SP 30/4 *Two Seasonable Discourses Concerning this Present Parliament* (Oxford, 1675).

[92] PRO, SP29/391/67, endorsed 'Ag[ains]t the parliam[en]t Febr. 1676/7'. There is another copy at BL, MS Stowe 354, f. 133.

1661. Thus while the 'law books say that parliaments are the people of England collectively taken', the young men had either to disown their MPs 'or ourselves for being a part of the people of England'. Freeborn Englishmen who were denied their representative rights were, it was asserted, neither obliged to obey the laws nor pay taxation.[93]

Even when the 1661 parliament was finally dissolved in 1679, concepts of representation remained controversial. The issue was kept prominent by three general elections in as many years, by the king's refusal to allow the second parliament elected in the late summer of 1679 to sit until October 1680, by a mass of 'instructions' to MPs and campaigns of mass petitioning, and by the temporary expiry of the licensing laws, all of which allowed public access to a revitalized debate about popular sovereignty.[94] During the later 1680s James II fuelled the controversy by embarking on a systematic campaign to pack parliament. And between 1688 and 1714 popular sovereignty and the nature of representation were debated vigorously. But, by then, new threats to a 'true representation' of the people had emerged, it was thought, in the form of a fiscal-military state that could corrupt elections;[95] an increasingly powerful concept of the sovereignty of *parliament* as the people;[96] a press free from pre-publication licensing but capable of misleading as much as informing; and, most ironically of all, the very process of frequent elections. The study of representational practices must

[93] Lord Holles, *A Letter to Monsieur Van. B—de M—at Amsterdam, Written Anno. 1676* [1676], 5–6, argued that the cavalier 'Parliament represented the sickly times in which they were chosen, when the people of England were in a kind of delirium or dotage, so a new Parliament would represent a People restored to their wits, cured of the evil, and steadily pursuing the great Interest of the Commonwealth.' Another tract suggested that the cavalier Parliament, by the 1670s, could not be said to have been representative, 'many of those who chose them being dead, and others were either grown up or had purchased estates, whose opinion both of the persons and things might be much changed from what the sense of the nation was when that parliament was first called' (*An Enquiry; or, A discourse between a yeoman of Kent and a Knight of the Shire* (1693), 11). *A Collection of State Tracts* (1706), Vol. II, 'contents', ascribes this to 'Major Wildman, Mr Hampden etc'.

[94] Treated in my *Politics and Opinion*; 'London's "Monster" Petition of 1680', *HJ*, 36 (1993), 39–67; 'London Petitions and Parliamentary Politics in 1679', *Parliamentary History*, 12 (1993), 29–46; 'Petitioning and the Political Theorists: John Locke, Algernon Sidney and London's "Monster" Petition of 1680', *P&P*, 138 (1993), 94–111.

[95] Brewer, *Sinews of Power*, 155–61; G. Aylmer, 'Place Bills and the Separation of Powers: Some 17th Century Origins of the "Nonpolitical" Civil Service', *TRHS*, 5th ser., 15 (1965), 45–69; G. Holmes, 'The Attack on the "Influence of the Crown", 1702–16', *BIHR*, 39 (1966), 47–68; C. Brooks, 'The Country Persuasion and Political Responsibility in England in the 1690s', *Parliament, Estates and Representation*, 4 (1984), 135–46; *HOP II*, i. 189–96, 491–3; D. Hayton, 'The Reorientation of Place Legislation in England in the 1690s', *Parliament, Estates and Representation*, 5 (1985), 103–8.

[96] H. T. Dickinson, 'The Eighteenth Century Debate on the Sovereignty of Parliament', *TRHS*, 5th ser., 26 (1976), 189–210.

therefore be seen in this changed context. The later Stuart period faced some old problems, but it did so in new circumstances and, this book suggests, accordingly stands between the seventeenth and eighteenth centuries conceptually as well as chronologically.

If a study of representation may appear whiggish, it also seems at odds with current historiographical trends that stress self-governance in the early modern state through office-holding, the experience of authority at the parish level, and institutions of negotiation, such as the law.[97] Participation rather than representation, it is urged, is more important for understanding the nature of early modern authority. Such an interpretation explicitly downplays the importance of parliament, elections, and representative institutions in order to investigate the interlinked variety of institutions through which authority could be exercised.[98] I have no quarrel with the focus on participation. To be sure, participatory mechanisms remained important, long after 1720.[99] But even advocates of a highly participatory model of early modern society discern a shift in the later Stuart period when 'a more regularised routine of local government gave a more "institutional" appearance to the activities of local officeholders', especially as a result of more frequent parliamentary sessions.[100] So, it seems to me, we should do well to chart the growth of a representative culture and discern ways in which it interacted with a participatory one. In doing so we should not see participation and representation as necessarily rival

[97] M. Braddick, *State Formation in Early Modern England* c.*1550–1700* (Cambridge, 2000); M. Braddick and J. Walter (eds.), *Negotiating Power in Early Modern Society: Order, Hierarchy and Subordination in Britain and Ireland* (Cambridge, 2001); S. Hindle, *The State and Social Change*; P. Griffiths, A. Fox, and S. Hindle (eds.), *The Experience of Authority in Early Modern England*; A. Shepard and P. Withington (eds.), *Comunities in Early Modern England: Networks, Place and Rhetoric* (Manchester, 2000); M. Goldie, 'The Unacknowledged Republic: Office-holding in Early Modern England', in T. Harris (ed.), *The Politics of the Excluded* c.*1500–1850* (Basingstoke, 2001); J. Kent, 'The Centre and the Localities: State Formation and Parish Government in England c.*1640–1740*', *HJ*, 38 (1995), 363–404; P. Rock, 'Law, Order and Power in late seventeenth-century and early eighteenth-century England', in S. Cohen and A. Scull (eds.), *Social Control and the State* (Oxford, 1983). For a pre-1660 focus, see also C. Herrup, 'The Counties and the Country: Some Thoughts on C17th Historiography', *Social History*, 8 (1983), 169–81; and K. Wrightson, 'The Politics of the Parish in Early Modern England', in P. Griffiths, A. Fox, and S. Hindle (eds.), *The Experience of Authority* (1996). For an older, but still very useful, outline of local governance, see S. Webb and B. Webb, *The Development of English Local Government, 1689–1835* (London, 1963).
[98] Goldie calls for a shift of attention 'away from voting and towards governance' and criticizes the 'psephological' approach to participation ('Unacknowledged Republic', 153, 156–9).
[99] D. Eastwood, *Government and Community in the English Provinces 1700–1870* (Basingstoke, 1997); J. Vernon, *Politics and the People: A Study in English Political Culture, c.1815–1867* (Cambridge, 1993).
[100] Braddick, *State Formation*, 170.

concepts, for they were often intertwined.[101] And, rather than paint out parliament, we should seek to explore how its role changed. A key dimension of this book lies, therefore, in stressing participation *through* representation and its processes. This is not just because in the later Stuart period elections provided a major opportunity for participation,[102] or because parliament found a new importance, but also because representation involved much more than Westminster or voting. Representation required many other forms of participation, through reading and debating, through allegiance to party, through ideology, and through varying forms of signalling consent. Representation was thus a cultural phenomenon. As Roger Chartier puts it, representation 'is . . . one of the foremost concepts manipulated by writers of the ancient regime when they set out to comprehend the functioning of their society or to define the intellectual operations that enabled them to apprehend the physical or social world. This is a first and an excellent reason to make it the cornerstone of a cultural approach to history'.[103] My own study suggests that participation needs to be explored by including, rather than excluding, means of representation. Indeed, the parish state only functioned through sophisticated concepts of representation, with households being represented by their heads and parishes by their office-holders.

The nature of public dialogue is particularly important if we understand the state not so much as a set of institutions as authority constructed by and through negotiation and processes of legitimation. Because those processes involved dialogue between interested parties, the language in which negotiation occurred was therefore important. Legitimization of authority in part depended on the right choice of language for the right audience; but partisan language could make the internal dialogue of state negotiation more difficult, or change the way in which that dialogue occurred, and hence reorient state formation. Reward for partisan allegiance and national networks of patronage, for example, changed the way in which office-holding worked. A state capable of paying salaries was a different beast. And the language of negotiation changed, in part because of the new player, public opinion, and in part because the languages of inter-

---

[101] I hope to write more extensively about the interaction between participation and representation elsewhere.

[102] Goldie ('Unacknowledged Republic', 161) estimates about 50,000 parish officeholders *c.*1700; yet even if contests only regularly affected a third of constituencies, some 250,000 voted in general elections, and many more in annual local elections for borough officials.

[103] R. Chartier, *Cultural History: Between Practices and Representations*, trans. L. G. Cochrane (Cambridge, 1988), 9.

est and politeness were becoming increasingly powerful. The balance within the state also shifted, as parliament assumed a less occasional role. If political partisanship placed new strains on dialogue and public discourse, as I argue that they did, then this necessarily affected the nature of state formation.

A study of representation also appears at odds with a philosophical and political emphasis on participatory or 'republican' forms of citizenship.[104] Discussions about representation have been much less vociferous, despite the paradox that there is some sense of crisis of democracy in the West occurring at the same time as an attempt to export representative principles and practice to other countries.[105] Recent commentators have also had relatively little to say about the problems facing public political dialogue, even though popular hostility to what is perceived as political lying and a corrupt or unheard political discourse seems to be connected to a dangerous alienation from the representative process.[106] Neither has there been a great effort to place these issues in a historical or conceptual context. Hannah Pitkin's classic study of representation, written in 1967, remains one of the most useful treatments of the theme; yet her conclusion would suggest the imperative of historical analysis. She argued that representation was 'not vague and shifting but a single, highly complex concept that has not changed much in its basic meaning since the seventeenth century'.[107] As she was happy to admit, hers was primarily a history of an idea, 'tracing the treatment of representation by major political theorists', and her study lacks any sustained contextualization. Nor was she particularly interested in how language shapes political representation. This book therefore aims to suggest some features intrinsic to partisan politics and representative practices as much as being a study located in a certain time and place.

Pitkin's argument that representation has not changed in its basic meaning since the seventeenth century has been given a new twist by Bernard Manin. He suggests that 'what today we call representative

---

[104] For a stress on the virtue of republican ideas about participation, see P. Pettit, *Republicanism: A Theory of Freedom and Government* (Oxford, 1997).

[105] But see P. Hirst, *Representative Democracy and its Limits* (Oxford, 1990); D. Judge, *Representation: Theory and Practice in Britain* (London, 1999); A. Przeworski, S. Stokes, and B. Manin (eds.), *Democracy, Accountability, and Representation* (Cambridge, 1999). Much of the literature on parties is overly preoccupied with organization, but for the relationship between parties and representation, see B. D. Graham, *Representation and Party Politics: A Comparative Perspective* (Oxford, 1993).

[106] The translation and discussion of Habermas (see next chapter) is nevertheless testament to a desire to explore these problems. There is, of course, a substantial literature on politics and the media.

[107] Pitkin, *Concept of Representation*, 8, 240.

democracy has its origins in a system of institutions . . . that was in no way
initially perceived as a form of democracy or of government by the
people'.[108] He argues that there was a fundamental shift from a participatory ideal of personal representation to one based on delegated imper-
sonal power. Manin outlines four key criteria of a representative form of
government:

1   Those who govern are appointed by election at regular intervals.
2   The decision-making of those who govern retains a degree of independence
    from the wishes of the electorate.
3   Those who are governed may give expression to their opinions and political
    wishes without these being subject to the control of those who govern.
4   Public decisions undergo the trial of debate.[109]

Each of these criteria can be related to the period 1660–1720 (an era that
helped to determine them in the first place) and in doing so, we begin to
examine some of the birthpangs of representational politics. As John
Pocock has suggested, from about 1700, 'we date the centrality of the notion that the defining characteristic of the citizen is his or her capacity to
be represented'. From then on the question was 'how much of myself I had
retained in making myself over to these characters'. [110] In the context of
globalization, the collapse of communism, and voter alienation, this seems
a particularly pertinent question to ask.

   I have sketched large problems and big questions. But at the outset the
limits of the current project's concern with representation should be recognized. A comprehensive study of representation should include, far
more than I attempt here, a study of visual representation. The images in
this book are only suggestive of the importance of integrating the visual
and other forms of culture. One could also say much more about the way
in which representations worked socially. Important themes, such as the
representation of women and children by adult male heads of households,
and the political uses of the representation of love and of sex, are touched
on but the connections between the political and social need to be drawn
more consistently than is attempted here.[111] The book does seek to show

---

[108]   *The Principles of Representative Government* (Cambridge, 1997), 1.
[109]   Ibid., 6.
[110]   J. G. A. Pocock, 'The Ideal of Citizenship since Classical time', *Queens Quarterly*, 99
(1992), 33–55, quotations at 52–3.
[111]   The best account is R. Weil, *Political Passions. Gender, the Family and Political Argument
in England 1680–1714* (Manchester, 1999). See also, A. Kugler, *Errant Plagiary. The Life and
Writings of Lady Sarah Cowper 1644–1720* (Stanford, 2002); P. McDowell, *The Women of Grub
Street. Press, Politics and Gender in the London Literary Marketplace 1678–1730* (Oxford, 1998);
K. Shevelow, *Women and Print Culture: The Construction of Femininity in the Early Periodical*

ways—through the study of petitions, addresses, print, discourse, and electioneering—in which social, cultural, and political history should overlap; but the points of contact do need more attention.[112] Representation outside England also receives skimpy attention. I hope to treat some of these important themes elsewhere. But, primarily for reasons of space and focus, the book will centre on a study of representation and misrepresentation in politics and language. It seeks to complement existing studies of the organization and personnel of party politics, available in the array of secondary material already outlined.[113] It does so by aiming to reconnect parliamentary history with public politics, political discourse, and state formation, and by pointing to connections between cognate bodies of secondary literature—in political and social history, but also in the history of ideas, of science, and literary criticism. Discussions are based on primary evidence drawn from research into electioneering and into the vast, and still under-used, archive of contemporary pamphlets and printed ephemera which runs into millions of words. The sources for this study are therefore numerous and wide-ranging. Petitions, addresses, associations, speeches, pamphlets, periodicals, borough records, state archives, court cases, newsletters, personal correspondence, memoirs, and diaries have all been used in order to investigate public discourse and representation. But how should those themes be approached and interpreted?

CONTEXT AND METHODOLOGY

The linguistic turn

Geoffrey Holmes opened his classic study of politics in the reign of Queen Anne with the plea that we should 'study the vocabulary which

---

(1989); H. Smith, 'English "feminist" Writings and Judith Drake's *An Essay in Defence of the Female Sex* (1696)', *HJ*, 44 (2001), 727–47; R. Perry, *The Celebrated Mary Astell: An Early English Feminist* (Chicago, 1986); H. Berry, ' "Nice and curious questions": Coffee Houses and the Representation of Women in John Dunton's Athenian Mercury', *Seventeenth Century*, 12 (1997), 257–76; H. Berry, *Gender, Society and Print Culture in Late Stuart England: The Cultural World of the Athenian Mercury* (London, 2003); *Women Writers and the Early Modern British Political Tradition*, ed. H. L. Smith (Cambridge, 1998); B. Cowan, 'Reasonable Ecstasies: Shaftesbury and the Languages of Libertinism', *JBS*, 37 (1998), 111–38.

[112] The work of John Walter, Andy Wood, Steve Hindle, and Mike Braddick offers excellent examples of the fruitful integration that is possible. I intend to write more about this elsewhere.

[113] Thus, although I will mainly be discussing perceptions of political practice, as articulated in print, many parallels can be found in *HOP I* and *HOP II*. Indeed, my interpretation of the public discourse is informed by three years working on the mechanics of constituency and parliamentary politics for *HOP II*.

contemporaries used to describe the political attitudes and questions of their own age' on the grounds that 'in the language of early-eighteenth century politics are to be found some of the most valuable clues to its character'.[114] Holmes was identifying, even if he did not fully exploit, the importance of 'the linguistic turn'. What, then, does the term mean and why is it important?

The 'linguistic turn' involves the recognition that language 'acts'. This happens directly, as when we are told to do something, but also indirectly, when the words used can *implicitly* rather than *explicitly* tell us something. Certain words and phrases thus have a power of their own, because the way in which they are understood can shape and order behaviour and experience. As Quentin Skinner recognizes, contemporaries were familiar with much of this theory simply as the art of rhetoric.[115] The focus on language, then, is not an abstract bit of modern theorizing, but something taught routinely in schools, universities, and inns of court. The way in which men and issues were represented in words—the text of an address, printed advice at election time, the words of a speech, and so on—mattered intensely. So a concern with language is not driven by a modern, or even postmodern, critical agenda, but stems from the preoccupations of the combatants in partisan conflict. The abuse of language, and the uncertainty of meanings were, as we shall see, prominent later Stuart concerns.

The approach mapped out by Skinner, John Pocock, and others, suggests that change can be understood through the study of language; or, rather, the study of how language was used at any point in time can tell us a great deal about the society in which it was used. Contextualizing political language has thus been particularly important for historians of political thought, a discipline which 'is now more accurately described as the history of political discourse'.[116] Contextualization has also been important for a movement within literary scholarship known as 'new historicism'. Louis Montrose summarizes the approach as being 'characterized, on the one hand, by its acknowledgement of the historicity of texts . . . and on the other hand, by its acknowledgment of the textuality of history'.[117] Significantly the journal most associated with this movement is

---

[114] Holmes, *British Politics*, 13.

[115] Q. Skinner, *Reason and Rhetoric in the Philosophy of Hobbes* (Cambridge, 1996).

[116] J. G. A. Pocock, 'The Concept of Language and the Metier d'historien: Some Considerations on Practice', in A. Pagden (ed.), *The Languages of Political Theory in Early-Modern Europe* (Cambridge, 1987), 19.

[117] L. Montrose, 'Renaissance Literary Studies and the Subject of History', *English Literary Renaissance*, 16 (1986), 8. That issue of the journal is devoted to 'studies in renaissance historicism'. See also J. Goldberg, 'The Politics of Renaissance Literature: A Review Essay', *A*

called *Representations*, founded in 1983. Since much of this book is concerned with how representation worked verbally as well as structurally, and how the two influenced one another, this contextualist line of enquiry is worth pursuing further.

If we accept that an author is doing something when speaking or writing, Skinner argues, then the words and phrases chosen will help to recover something of what the author intended.[118] A full understanding of texts 'presupposes the grasp both of what they were intended to mean and how this meaning was intended to be taken'.[119] Thus an author might describe a man who opposed the wishes of the court as disloyal, seditious, factious, a fanatic, and self-interested (all negatively charged terms), or more positively as patriotic, independent, moderate, rational, and virtuous. There was a variety of different 'languages' from which to choose. These included, for the later Stuart period, the languages of scripture, common law, classical republicanism, patriarchalism, natural rights, reason, and 'politeness'. Such languages had their own vocabulary, rules, tone, and style; and they also had their own preconditions and political implications. The dominance of any one language and the interplay between languages thus tells us a good deal about a political culture at any given time.

To give an example: in the 1690s some Whigs became highly suspicious of the way in which the power of the court and the emerging fiscal-military state could distort men's principles. They began to be labelled, and talk of themselves, as 'true' or 'old' Whigs, as opposed to the 'new' or 'modern' Whigs who complied with the court and sought to profit from state

Journal of English Literary History, 49 (1982), 514–42; S. Greenblatt, *Renaissance Self-fashioning* (Chicago, 1980); K. Sharpe and S. Zwicker (eds.), *The Politics of Discourse: The Literature and History of Seventeenth-century England* (Berkeley, 1987); D. Norbrook, *Poetry and Politics in the English Renaissance* (1984; rev. edn., 2002); D. Norbrook, *Writing the English Republic: Poetry, Rhetoric and Politics, 1627–1660* (Cambridge, 1999); Raymond, *Pamphlets and Pamphleteering*; N. Smith, *Literature and Revolution in England, 1640–1660* (New Haven, 1994); T. Corns, *Uncloistered Virtue: English Political Literature, 1640–1660* (Oxford, 1992). D. Womersley, 'Literature and the History of Political Thought', *HJ*, 39 (1996), 511–20, notes that Pocock and Skinner were nevertheless very guarded about how much engagement with 'literature' to allow their method. Womersley also warns that historians are frequently insufficiently alert to literary techniques and arguments.

[118] Perhaps the clearest treatment comes in his 'Bolingbroke vs Walpole', in N. McKendrick (ed.), *Historical Perspectives: Studies in English Thought and Society in Honour of J. H. Plumb* (London, 1974), now extensively revised as 'Augustan Party Politics and Renaissance Constitutional Thought', in Q. Skinner, *Visions of Politics Volume II: Renaissance Virtues* (Cambridge, 2002).

[119] Q. Skinner, 'Meaning and Understanding in the History of Ideas', *History and Theory*, 8 (1969), 48–9, now revised as ch. 4 of Skinner, *Visions of Politics Volume I: Regarding Method*.

expansion. They adopted a language, derived in part from Machiavelli via James Harrington, that stressed virtue, independence, and participation in the state—particularly through the militia.[120] Their choice of such language was deliberate, for they might have couched their complaints in different ways. A biblical language, say, might see the court as sinful; one based on natural rights might see the court as subverting an abstract contract between government and individual. By analysing shifts of language—how words and concepts change their meaning and use—we can track change over time.[121] Politics and language have to be related to each other and the political struggle often occurred over and through a linguistic one.[122]

A problem arises, however, in terms of *how far* words have agency.[123] If words are powerful, how and what we think or speak (and hence also behave) may therefore partly be determined by the discourse around us.[124] A second form of the linguistic turn embraces this position. A group of historians working mainly on late eighteenth- and nineteenth-century problems of class have argued that political language constructs, sets boundaries to, and even *determines* social identities.[125] By restoring politics to its proper place, it is argued, we can find that changes in political discourse explain larger changes. Language is thus not simply a medium in which experience finds expression, but shapes or even creates that experience. One of the principal exponents of such a view, Gareth Stedman Jones, intended 'to dispel the illusion of the independence or even primacy of social history, to restore the central position of political history and to recast the pre-occupations of the social historian as a set of concerns encompassed within it'.[126]

---

[120]   Pocock, *The Machiavellian Moment.*

[121]   C. Condren's *The Language of Politics in Seventeenth-century England* (Basingstoke, 1994) is an ambitious attempt and he notes that 'it is a pity that so much of what people might have been doing with words is skipped in the hurry to get to the concepts' (136).

[122]   M. Knights, 'Politics after the Glorious Revolution', in B. Coward (ed.), *A Companion to Stuart Britain* (Oxford, 2003).

[123]   'Words absolutely force the understanding' (Bacon, *Novum Organum* (English translation, 1676), section II, aphorism vi).

[124]   'The modes of speech available to [an author] give him the intentions he can have' (Pocock, *Virtue, Commerce, and History*, 5). Thus, although Pocock shares many of Skinner's views, for him it is not always clear that languages are *deliberately chosen*. For a similar criticism, see A. Cromartie, 'Harringtonian Virtue: Harrington, Machiavelli, and the Method of the *Moment*', *HJ*, 41 (1998), 987–1009.

[125]   G. S. Jones, *Languages of Class: Studies in English Working Class History* (Cambridge, 1983); P. Joyce, *Democratic Subjects: The Self and the Social in Nineteenth-century England* (Cambridge, 1994).

[126]   G. Stedman Jones, 'Neo-Marxism and the Discursive Approach to History' in A. Ludtke (ed.), *Was Bleibt van Marxistischen Perspectiven inder Geschichtsforschung?* (Gottingen, 1997),

It is not difficult to see how an approach that seeks an explanation for social and political identity in language might be useful, for party, like class, involves an identity, or set of identities, which need to be constructed. Might party identity and allegiance, therefore, be constructed by and through language? And might the language of party have had real social importance, ironically serving to reinforce unity by stressing horizontal ideological ties at a time when there were growing social and economic polarities that might have erupted in significant conflict? And did the reaction against the rage of abusive and mendacious party discourse foster the invocation of an ideal of rational, polite discourse that necessarily affected how the 'people', represented as irrational or lacking in judgement, were regarded? There is, as following chapters show, some mileage in these thoughts. Nevertheless the postmodernist approach alone cannot explain shifts in political culture. It is too bent on claiming language as the sole construct of 'experience', too linguistically determinist.[127] As Wahrman points out, such an approach ironically underestimates the importance of politics, for politics makes the choices between different conceptualizations of society matter, and this version of the linguistic turn removes agency and contingency.[128]

But the Skinnerian use of the linguistic turn is also in some ways problematic. Its stress on contextualizing language and examining the rhetoric of political discourse is enormously important. Nevertheless, what precisely is the 'context' that has to be explored to recover the contemporary meaning of a text or discourse? All too often the history of political discourse is written with reference either to canonical writers or to a few articulate, well-known, pamphleteers. This is partly because the Skinnerian school is not interested in the minor works *per se*, but in what they can tell us about the 'major works'.[129] As James Tully puts it: 'minor texts of a period are carefully dusted off and surveyed to identify the constitutive and regulative conventions of the reigning ideologies and their inter-relations

183. I am grateful to Simon Middleton for drawing this piece to my attention. See also D. Wahrman's review essay 'The New Political History', *Social History*, 21 (1996), 343–54.

[127] For critiques, see D. Mayfield and S. Thorne, 'Social History and its Discontents: Gareth Stedman Jones and the Politics of Language', *Social History*, 17 (1992), 165–88; J. E. Cronin, 'Language, Politics and the Critique of Social History', *Journal of Social History*, 20 (1986), 177–83.

[128] D. Wahrman, *Imagining the Middle Class: The Political Representation of Class in Britain, c.1780–1840* (Cambridge, 1995), 9.

[129] Although his earliest work on Hobbes was rooted in an analysis of the pamphlet literature of the engagement controversy, Skinner's later work is far less based on such material, perhaps as a response to the accusation that his approach encourages antiquarianism (*Liberty before Liberalism*, 107–8).

before they are employed as benchmarks to judge the conventional and unconventional aspects, and so the ideological moves, of the major texts'.[130] Yet, as Tully's account explicitly recognizes, the minor works are only minor if one is interested in exploring canonical writers or assumes that it is the latter that are the main motors of linguistic and conceptual change.[131] As Richard Ashcraft showed in his contextualization of the thought of John Locke, apparently minor, ephemeral and even anonymous works could be, and were, innovative and influential.[132] The ebb and flow of political, religious, and economic disputes could change the meaning of words and concepts. As I hope to show, meanings were vigorously contested in this minor canon that was itself the product of disputed political practice. In other words, the 'benchmarks' used to chart change were themselves contested constituents of change *and* the means by which change could be effected. This is particularly important because in the later Stuart period (as in others) contemporaries were acutely aware of the instability of meanings, of the ways in which words could be abused or misused. John Locke, for example, observed that it was 'hard to find a discourse written of any subject, especially of controversy, wherein one shall not observe, if he read with attention, the same words (and those commonly the most material in the discourse, and upon which the argument turns), used sometimes for one collection of simple ideas, and sometimes for another, which is a perfect abuse of language'.[133] In order to recover these dimensions this study is rooted in what might be called ephemeral political literature that was itself rooted in everyday political practice.

Such material raises a further problem, about the degree to which any political language was 'pure'. When we talk of the variety of political languages, and the choices made by authors, the implication is that a single idiom is chosen. But the pressure of party polemic, the need to convince or cajole as many as possible, frequently necessitated employing more than one 'language' within any pamphlet. The anonymity of print audiences was problematic for a single idiom. To sell and be read in a market, controversial polemic necessitated different voices, and different types of appeal through different types of language, either within the same text or in

---

[130] J. Tully (ed.), *Meaning and Context: Quentin Skinner and his Critics* (Cambridge, 1988), 12.

[131] There is also a question here of how the canon is invented by the Whig and Tory traditions.

[132] Ashcraft, *Revolutionary Politics*, 7, makes a plea to expand the remit of political theory to 'newspapers, pamphlets, sermons, broadsides and various literary forms', see *Revolutionary Politics*, 7. See also R. Tuck, *Philosophy and Government 1572–1651* (Cambridge, 1993).

[133] Locke, *Essay Concerning Human Understanding*, iii. vi. 26; x. 5.

a series of different speech acts aimed at different audiences. And it may also have been the case that authors themselves thought in more than one 'language'. As we shall see in the next chapter, Henry Booth, who might otherwise be categorized as an 'old Whig', talked about natural law, natural rights, the ancient constitution, scripture, and interest, even though each has often been labelled a discrete 'language'. Such points of overlap, and the interplay between languages, merit more discussion. So too does the way in which the variety of readers interpreted polemic and hence gave it different meanings.[134] In other words, we might move away from charting the variety of political languages towards mapping the contested words and concepts, the political framework or the moments of crisis that drove the contest, and the variety of rhetorical strategies employed to contest them.[135] And to do this will necessitate examining genres of texts—such as petitions and addresses, election advice, letters, and dialogues—as well as the meanings they contain and the meanings, so far as we can recover them, conferred by readers or listeners as well as authors. Although an author may intend a language to perform in a particular way, the reader or listener is also part of that process, and may impose different interpretations, both from that intended by the author and from each other. By studying elections—how the sum of individuals reacted to the public discourse that surrounded them—we may in part be able to examine a response to the word games being played.

[134] For the literature on readers, see M. Spufford, *Small Books and Pleasant Histories: Popular Fiction and its Readership in C17th England* (London, 1981); T. Watt, *Cheap Print and Popular Piety 1550–1640* (Cambridge, 1991); S. Zwicker, 'Reading the Margins', in K. Sharpe and S. Zwicker, (eds.), *Refiguring Revolutions: Aesthetics and Politics from the English Revolution to the Romantic Revolution* (Berkeley, 1998); K. Sharpe and S. Zwicker, *Reading, Society and Politics in Early Modern England* (Cambridge, 2003); Sharpe, *Reading Revolutions*; I. Rivers (ed.), *Books and their Readers in Eighteenth-century England* (Leicester, 1982); J. Raven, H. Small, and N. Tadmor, *The Practice and Representation of Reading in England* (Cambridge, 1996); A. Patterson, *Censorship and Interpretation: The Conditions of Writing and Reading in Early Modern England* (1984); R. Chartier, *The Order of Books: Readers, Authors, and Libraries in Europe between the Fourteenth and Eighteenth Centuries* (Cambridge, 1994).
[135] R. Ashcraft, 'The Language of Political Conflict in Restoration Literature', in *Politics as Reflected in Literature, Papers presented at a Clark Library Seminar 1987* (1989). Ashcraft identified about fifty key words, all linked as 'a constellation of meaning', out of which he makes five related groups, by which one might chart linguistic and conceptual change. One group, followed in this book, included *lying, betraying, hypocrisy, deceived, disguise.* Such words, he argued, 'should be viewed as the site of a political struggle between partisans on both sides to gain control of their meaning' (15). Definitions of meaning were thus made not just by great thinkers but by everyday polemicists. Ashcraft wondered whether, during the 1680s, political conflict did not increase 'the sensitivity of individuals to the ways in which words were used' (19). For a similar sensitivity to sets of words, see M. Richter, *The History of Political and Social Concepts* (New York, 1995).

There are, then, methodological issues that this book aims to raise. It stresses the importance of the practice of politics in shaping language, seeking to widen the 'context' that students of political discourse must examine. But it also argues that the historian of party must also be alive to issues of language, as a means by which allegiance and identity was constructed and as a tool in political conflict. The book recognizes the shaping power of 'ways of talking' without withdrawing the potential for individual or group agency. On occasion participants were conscious of making a choice about certain vocabularies, not least because the meanings of words and phrases were contested; but languages, such as those of conspiracy or politeness, shaped political processes. Moreover, as the conflict became more protracted, the public became more aware and suspicious of human agency in political affairs but also of the misuse to which language could be put.

Habermas and the public sphere

If approaches to 'language' can be helpful when thinking about public discourse, so too can ideas about the nature of the public itself. Politics was fought out in a dialogue of different claims to represent the public. How, then, should we conceptualize what the public was? One of the most influential models has been provided by German sociologist Jürgen Habermas's idea of a public sphere.[136] Habermas identified a linguistically constructed interface between the public state and its private citizens, the 'public sphere'. This was created, he suggested (drawing on Kant), whenever citizens met to use their private reason to discuss matters of general interest. Thus the expansion of opportunities and greater freedom for such discussions gave rise to 'the public sphere': a unified, collective, but also idealized, voice and site of rational debate.

Habermas argued that this expansion took place in Britain in the later Stuart period and offered a number of reasons for this timing. One was the growth of a mercantile, capital economy that gave information a new cachet and made it economically important. Merchants and tradesmen needed to know about state affairs in order to be able to conduct their business, but they also needed to be able to convey their own opinions about trade back to the government.

---

[136] J. Habermas, *The Structural Transformation of the Public Sphere: An Inquiry into a Category of Bourgeois Society*, trans. by T. Burger and F. Lawrence (Cambridge, 1989). The book was first written in German in 1962.

We are speaking of the elements of the new commercial relationships: the traffic in commodities and news created by early capitalist long-distance trade . . . almost simultaneously with the origin of stock markets, postal services and the press institutionalised regular contacts and regular communication . . . [and] there existed a press in the strict sense only once the regular supply of news became public, that is, accessible to the general public. But this occurred only at the end of the seventeenth century.[137]

This press was first a vehicle for criticism of literary works but rapidly became a vehicle for political discussion. Such talk took place in the coffeehouses that proliferated in the late seventeenth and early eighteenth centuries, enabling men to meet more frequently, and in a new public space, to talk about matters of public interest. The expansion of the state also enlarged the public sphere. The growth of a fiscal-military state and the regular frequency of parliaments meant opportunities to lobby, seek patronage, assess the impact of state policies, or to discuss who was in and who was out. Public discussion was thus linked to the activities of the state and in part acted as a controlling mechanism on it, important because it was not intrinsic to the state itself. The later Stuart period, Habermas argued, thus witnessed the emergence of a bourgeois public sphere, appropriated by an educated élite who came to think of themselves as constituting the public and who formed public opinion.

Habermas argued that the public sphere was founded on the principle of access to all those who engaged in rational debate.

The bourgeois public sphere may be conceived above all as the sphere of private people come together as a public [in order to] engage public authorities in a debate about the general rules governing relations in the . . . sphere of commodity exchange and social labour. The medium of this political confrontation was peculiar and without historical precedent: people's public use of their reason.[138]

The public sphere was thus the product of rational debate. But Habermas argued that this rational debate decayed over time, producing a process of structural transformation. As new forms of communication evolved they changed the way in which the public sphere operated. The function of the public sphere as an interface between the public and the state, he argued, has broken down in the modern world.

The process of the politically relevant exercise and equilibration of power now takes place directly between the private bureaucracies, special-interest associations, parties and public administration. The public as such is included only

[137] Ibid., 15–16.   [138] Ibid., 27.

sporadically in this circuit of power, and even then it is brought in only to contribute its acclamation.[139]

Instead of a rationally constructed public sphere, therefore, we occupy a
consumer culture, in which individuals are passive. 'Rational critical debate had a tendency to be replaced by consumption'.[140] The new public is
not participatory but consumptive and 'the world fashioned by the mass
media is a public sphere in appearance only'.[141] It is clear from this analysis
that Habermas's early rational public sphere is an ideal, from which he
constructs a story of decay and corruption.

Habermas's ideas have been examined by many historians and literary
scholars.[142] Criticisms are various. Some think that Habermas may be
right in discerning the creation of a public sphere but wrong about its timing, which, it is argued, can be found much earlier (though there is no
agreement about precisely when) and brought about by factors which he
had failed to consider (such as religion). Others suggest that the public
sphere was not a single entity. Work by a number of scholars has suggested
that a number of different public spheres could operate, not quite independently of one another but at different capacities at different times.
Thus, it is said, it makes more sense to talk in terms of public *spheres*, which
could open and close in vitality at different times and often, before the later
Stuart period, at the government's bidding. Other scholars remark that the
concept of the 'public sphere' is a vague one, with ill-defined notions of
what was private and how the 'space' (physical or virtual) operated. The
emphasis placed on the novelty of print and coffee-houses also jars with
those who stress that manuscript, speech, and ale-houses had performed
similar functions a hundred years beforehand.[143] There is some truth to all

---

[139] Habermas, *Structural Transformation*, 176.   [140] Ibid., 161.   [141] Ibid., 171.

[142] There have been curiously few attempts to relate his ideas to the later Stuart period.
But see T. Claydon, 'The Sermon, the "Public Sphere" and the Political Culture of Late
Seventeenth-Century England', in L. A. Ferrell and P. McCullough (eds.), *The English
Sermon Revised: Religion, Literature and History 1600–1750* (Manchester, 2001); Berry, *Gender,
Society and Print Culture*; McDowell, *Women of Grub Street*. For an excellent overview of
how Habermasian ideas have been treated more generally, see H. Mah, 'Phantasies of the
Public Sphere: Rethinking the Habermas of Historians', *JMH*, 72 (2000), 153–82.

[143] Besides works listed in Ch. 1, see also B. Robbins (ed.), *The Phantom Public Sphere*
(Minneapolis, 1993); A. Halasz, *The Marketplace of Print. Pamphlets and the Public Sphere in
Early Modern England* (Cambridge, 1997); D. Norbrook, 'Areopagitica, Censorship and the
Early Modern Public Sphere', in R. Burt (ed.), *The Administration of Aesthetics: Censorship,
Political Criticism and the Public Sphere* (Minneapolis, 1994); P. Lake and M. Questier, 'Puri-
tans, Papists, and the "Public Sphere" in Early Modern England: The Edmund Campion Af-
fair in Context', *JMH*, 72 (2000), 587–627; G. Schochet, 'Vices, Benefits and Civil Society:

these objections and in the chapters that follow other criticisms will be outlined. First, the stress on the rationality of the early public sphere will be questioned,[144] and hence the degree to which there was a linear degradation or decay. Second, the priority of a literary public sphere before a political one will be questioned, not least because a distinction between politics and literature is often hard to define.

And yet there is clearly something of value in the notion of a new force of public opinion emerging in the early modern period and acquiring a new status under the later Stuarts.[145] As historians of the French revolution remind us, the idea of a fusion of individual participants into a representative, collective unity (the public) is extremely important.[146] It forces us to examine how such a fiction could be justified and encouraged; how the representation of the public as a single unity was compatible with, and actually fostered by, the development of conflicting groups of partisans; and the way in which such a collective unity could be used in political struggles. The concept of the public sphere relies on a notion of the public as something different and separated from, but also in dialogue with, the state. Again, this is a useful way of understanding the state itself. Early modern social historians have stressed a model of a participatory state, in which office-holding was widespread and in which power was negotiated; state and public were thus overlapping entities. Yet by the later Stuart period (and evident at moments of crisis earlier too) there is also clearly a public that lies outside the ranks of office-holders; and the state is regarded as an 'other', with its own set of interests and against which a public opinion ought to act. If this is right, Habermas was correct to talk about his public sphere emerging in the late seventeenth and eighteenth centuries, for before then the state was not regarded as an entity with its own interests. Scholars of sixteenth- and early seventeenth-century political culture have, perhaps for that reason, generally been more sceptical of the value

Mandeville, Habermas and the Distinction between Public and Private', in P. Backscheider and T. Dystal (eds.), *The Intersections of the Public and Private Spheres in Early Modern England* (1996).

[144] See also, Klein, 'Coffee-house civility', n. 5 and 35–9, 44.

[145] J. Miller, 'Public Opinion in Charles II's England', *History*, 80 (1995), 359–81; B. Sharp, 'Popular Political Opinion in England 1660–1685', *History of European Ideas*, 10 (1989), 13–29; I. Atherton, 'The Press and Popular Political Opinion', in B. Coward (ed.), *A Companion to Stuart Britain* (Oxford, 2003); S. Pincus, *Protestantism and Patriotism: Ideologies and the Making of English Foreign Policy, 1650–1668* (Cambridge, 1996); Pincus, 'Coffee Politicians'; Harris, *London Crowds*; Montano, *Courting the Moderates.*

[146] K. Baker, 'Public Opinion as Political Invention', in his *Inventing the French Revolution* (Cambridge, 1990); M. Ozouf, ' "Public Opinion" at the End of the Old Regime', *JMH*, 60 (1988); F. Furet, *Interpreting the French Revolution* (Cambridge, 1981).

of the Habermasian model. Peter Lake and Michael Questier have thus talked about a 'de-Habermased notion of the public sphere'.[147] But their hesitancy may well be a sign that the political culture *did* change and that hence a model inappropriate to one era might be more applicable in another. Habermas was right to highlight the transforming conjunction in the later Stuart period of new factors such as the rise of parties, frequent parliaments, a free press, the coffee-house, the appearance of a stock market and the expansion of a capitalist economy, the funding of a national debt, the legal recognition of religious dissent, the permanent lapse of pre-publication licensing and the expansion of the press, the rise of literary criticism, and the unprecedented amount of tax extracted by the state which could then afford to maintain armed forces on a new scale.

Habermas can also productively help us with a problem identified in the discussion of the linguistic turn, namely the response of readers rather than authors to the power of words. One way of thinking about the public as a unified collective is to think of it as a reading public. Partisan politics involved reading events, either metaphorically or more literally, with voters and actors as authors and consumers of texts. Sharon Achinstein has suggested that the mid-seventeenth century witnessed 'a revolution in reading', since more readers were exposed to a greater diversity of reading material than ever before, leading to shifts in rhetoric and reading practices.[148] She suggests that readers became responsible judges of what they read, though, for her, their judgement was informed not so much by reason as by conscience. The readers therefore constitute the public sphere, in part because they were encouraged to think of themselves as a conscientious jury and because ' "the public" was . . . an ideological construct of an audience'.[149] This produced 'nothing short of a new mode of political consciousness . . . turning English people into political activists', accompanied by 'a qualitative change in the ways people wrote and thought about political ideas'.[150] The public appeal to a revolutionary tribunal of readers,

---

[147] They reject the Habermasian model as inappropriate to the conditions of early Stuart England and suggest that cultural change occurs through 'processes of appropriation and reappropriation, of interpretation and reinterpretation, whereby the "popular" or "the traditional" were taken over by a variety of ideological factions and fractions only to be resold to (and appropriated for the often very different purposes of) the people'. This process results in a 'bricolage' of 'ideological materials, core assumptions and resonant figures' (Lake with Questier, *The Antichrist's Lewd Hat*, 324, 360–1, 483; 'Puritans, Papists and the "Public Sphere" ', 590). For reservations about the applicability of Habermas to the early Stuart period see A. Bellany, *The Politics of Scandal in Early Modern England* (Cambridge, 2002), 17–18.

[148] Achinstein, *Milton and the Revolutionary Reader*, 3.

[149] Ibid., 9–10, 32.   [150] Ibid., 18, 31.

she suggests, led to a confusion of conflicting voices, with the result that printed exchanges 'were clashes *in* language, verbal disputes, but they were also clashes *about* language—about the proper use of words'.[151] Exploring the public thus involves something of a paradox: because it is an ideal construct of a collective unity, it can only be examined through the disparate and conflicting voices that helped create it. Achinstein raises the question of how partisan polemic was read and received. This is always difficult to answer. Nevertheless, voters were a set of readers, bombarded with electoral advice; and though their behaviour was not solely the result of such material, the way they polled was in part influenced by what they read. This is an issue that will be tackled in Chapters 4 and 5.

Public discourse circumscribed: politeness and reason

One further salvageable element of the Habermasian concept of the public sphere is the stress on rational public discourse governed by new conventions. Although the transition away from a medieval concept of 'courtesy' to one of 'civility' took place gradually over the course of the sixteenth and seventeenth centuries, Lawrence Klein has written about a more marked development that coincides with Habermas's notion of a late seventeenth- and early eighteenth-century innovation: the rise of 'politeness'.[152] Politeness was defined in 1702 as 'a dexterous management

[151] Ibid., 86.
[152] A. Bryson, *From Courtesy to Civility. Changing Codes of Conduct in Early Modern England* (Oxford, 1998), 50, 276–7, 283; P. Burke, 'A Civil Tongue: Language and Politeness in Early Modern Europe'; and J. Barry, 'Civility and Civic Culture in Early Modern England: The Meanings of Urban Freedom', both in P. Burke, B. Harrison, and P. Slack (eds.), *Civil Histories. Essays Presented to Sir Keith Thomas* (Oxford, 2000); J. G. A. Pocock, 'Post-Puritan England and the Problem of the Enlightenment', in P. Zagorin (ed.), *Culture and Politics from Puritanism to the Enlightenment* (California, 1980); N. Phillipson, 'Politics and Politeness in the Reigns of Anne and the Early Hanoverians', in J. G. A. Pocock (ed.), *The Varieties of British Political Thought 1500–1800* (Cambridge, 1993); L. Klein, 'The Political Significance of "Politeness" in Early Eighteenth Century Britain', in G. Schochet (ed.), *Politics, Politeness and Patriotism*, Folger Institute Center for the History of British Political Thought Proceedings Vol. 5 (Washington, 1993); Klein, 'Coffee House Civility'; L. Klein, 'Liberty, Manners and Politeness in Early Eighteenth Century England', *HJ*, 32 (1989), 583–604; L. Klein, *Shaftesbury and the Culture of Politeness* (Cambridge, 1994); 'The Third Earl of Shaftesbury and the Progress of Politeness', *Eighteenth Century Studies*, 18 (1984–5), 186–214; L. Klein, 'Politeness and the Interpretation of the British Eighteenth Century', *HJ*, 45 (2002), 869–98. But B. Cowan, 'Reasonable Ecstasies: Shaftesbury and the Languages of Libertinism', *JBS*, 37 (1998), 111–38, argues that Shaftesbury's 'vision of who should be included in the public sphere was far more restrictive than that of many of his fellow Whig ideologists' (137). Civility was, as Barry points out, necessary for a wide number of people in their urban relationships; politeness was more exclusive but ironically more necessary when expectations of civil unity had broken down.

of our words and actions, whereby we make other people have better opinion of us and themselves'.[153] It was concerned with representation through words and manners, and 'came into extraordinary prominence in the later seventeenth century, especially after 1688, and endured for a good deal of the eighteenth century'.[154] Crystallized in the writings of Addison, Steele, and the third earl of Shaftesbury, and disseminated in the coffee-houses where the ideal of 'polite conversation' was pursued, politeness was, Klein suggests, 'hammered . . . into place roughly in the years between 1700 and 1715'.[155] It offered 'the opportunity to create a new public and gentlemanly culture of criticism' or 'public, secular gentility'.[156] It 'invented a new ideal of elite culture', widening the gap between patrician and plebeian.[157] Klein rightly links the rise of politeness to the 'urban renaissance' described by Peter Borsay, seeing a 'unified elite cultural standard' that was 'quite tangibly a way of articulating and mastering actual changes in elite cultural life' in urban centres.[158] Klein thus accounts for politeness in cultural and social terms. He argues that 'stability could co-exist with partisanship in the eighteenth century because of elite social and cultural cohesiveness, summed up in the language of "politeness"'.[159] Similarly, Borsay suggests that during the eighteenth century 'civility and sociability replaced the divisive aspects of politics and religion'.[160]

The concept of politeness is very useful when discussing rules governing discourse or anxieties about sincerity, hypocrisy, lies, and dissimulation raised by partisan behaviour. In other words, it can help us to understand reactions to partisan political culture. But Klein does not, perhaps, sufficiently stress how far politeness was linked to the political process (the word was, after all, derived from 'polis' and hence shared a root with 'political'[161]), and how far it consciously distanced itself from political conflict. Two of the chief proponents of politeness, the Whig journalists and politicians Joseph Addison and Richard Steele, condemned party mentalities

For urban civility see also P. Withington, *The Politics of the Commonwealth: Citizens and Freemen in Early Modern England* (Cambridge, 2004). I am grateful to Phil for showing the chapters of this before publication. He argues that civility had a much longer gestation than a focus on the later seventeenth century would imply, and that it owed much to the conventions of city commonwealths.

[153] A. Boyer, *The English Threophrastus* (1702), 106, quoted by Klein, 'The Third Earl of Shaftesbury and the Progress of Politeness', 190.
[154] Klein, 'Political Significance', 75.
[155] Ibid., 76; Phillipson, 'Political Politeness', 243.
[156] Klein, *Shaftesbury*, 8–9, 21.   [157] Ibid., 3.
[158] Klein, 'Political Significance', 75, 88, 90.   [159] Ibid., 75.
[160] Borsay, *English Urban Renaissance*, 282.
[161] Burke, 'A Civil Tongue', 38.

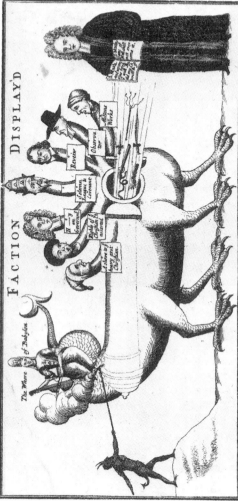

The hydra is depicted with heads of writers, suggesting that the church was under devilish fire from Daniel Defoe, John Milton, Benjamin Hoadly, John Tutchin, and the pope. The image represents the destructive power of polemical words. The first-known use of the term 'journalist' was in 1693. [Reproduced by courtesy of the Trustees of the British Museum.]

for obstructing sociable behaviour.[162] Addison noted that a furious party
spirit filled the nation with spleen and rancour, extinguished good sense
and humanity; and he regretted that 'a dull scheme of party notions' or
abuse should pass for 'fine writing'.[163] He thus suggested that 'we should
not any longer regard our fellow subjects as Whigs or Tories, but should
make the man of merit our friend and the villain our enemy'.[164] He said he
endeavoured 'to extinguish that pernicious spirit of passion and prejudice
which rages with the same violence in all parties'.[165] Yet in the following
chapters it will become clear that the invocation of an ideal of aloofness
from, or disdain for, the impolite rage of party could be a partisan move
made by Whigs and Tories as much as those who disliked any party. It is
worth recalling that Addison and Steele were both Whigs, writing in some
sense to draw the sting of passionate high-church Toryism. The language
of politeness, at least in the later Stuart period, was not a politically neutral
one but itself part of the political game. Controlling the rules of public discourse was an important move.

    Associated with politeness is the rise of rational discourse. The degree to
which concern for rational judgement affected political behaviour will be
an important concern of the second half of this book. The discussion will
be informed by the work of two (overlapping) schools of historians: those
charting changes in religious attitudes over the sixteenth and seventeenth
centuries; and those mapping the rise of 'scientific' attitudes. The first of
these tend to see a new emphasis on a rational religion espoused by the
Great Tew circle before the civil war, but gaining momentum with the
Cambridge Platonists in the mid-seventeenth century. The Platonists
argued that reason was itself divine.[166] In the late seventeenth century,
their intellectual heirs, John Toland and others, urged a rational religion
accessible to all. Frederick Beiser sees Toland's 'criticism in public, for the
public and with the intention that it eventually be also done by the public'
as 'the beginning of enlightenment in early modern England'.[167] Toland's
most recent biographer concurs, but stresses that the attack on priestcraft

---

[162] Borsay, *Urban Renaissance*, 280, also suggests that while polite urban culture could on
occasion be exploited for political ends, even before 1720 'fashionable town culture developed
an apolitical, even anti-political complexion, that may have helped to stem the tide of party
prejudice and warfare'.
    [163] *Spectator*, 125.   [164] Ibid., cf. nos. 57, 81.   [165] Ibid., 126.
    [166] F. Beiser, *The Sovereignty of Reason: The Defense of Rationality in the Early English
Enlightenment* (Princeton, 1996), 149.
    [167] Ibid., 223–4. For Toland, see also R. Sullivan, *John Toland and the Deist Controversy*
(Harvard, 1982); S. Daniel, *John Toland: His Methods, Manners and Mind* (Montreal, 1982);
Champion, *Republican Learning*.

and tyranny still took place through religious discourse.[168] Freedom of religion could thus underpin political controversies and the critique of the enthusiastic puritan or overly formal conformist was transmuted into the criticism of zealous and passionate Whigs and Tories. But again it is important to recognize that reason, like politeness, could be a political tool, a way of denying legitimacy to a rival point of view.

Public discourse and truth-claims

The critique of enthusiasm and the championing of reason, together with a concern about the effects of rhetoric, overlapped with developments in natural philosophy.[169] Since the latter embraced religion, the natural world, language, and the nature of truth, it is not surprising that work by historians of science helps with the central themes of this book. Both scientists and politicians (and there is often a fascinating fusion of the two[170]) worried over the rules governing public discourse and the meaning of words. As is well known, the Royal Society urged the reform of language by promoting a plain style in an effort to bring words and things closer together.[171] Similarly the language of mathematics and science could be appropriated by those engaged in political debate.[172] The precise influence of science on rhetorical practices has been the cause of much debate, for many literary scholars reject a simple correlation between the new science and plain language or even that there was a transformation of prose

[168] Champion, *Republican Learning*, 13; I. Rivers, *Reason, Grace, and Sentiment: A Study of the Language of Religion and Ethics in England, 1660–1780*, 2 vols. (Cambridge, 1991 and 2000).

[169] Beiser, *Sovereignty of Reason*, 184–5; M. Heyd, 'The Reaction to Enthusiasm in the Seventeenth Century: Towards an Integrative Approach', *JMH*, 53 (1981), 258–80; Heyd, *'Be Sober and Reasonable': The Critique of Enthusiasm in the Seventeenth and Early Eighteenth Centuries* (1995); B. Shapiro, *Probability and Certainty in Seventeenth-century England: A Study of the Relationships between Natural Science, Religion, History, Law, and Literature* (Princeton, 1983); B. Shapiro, *A Culture of Fact: England, 1550–1720* (London, 2000).

[170] Among the medics and scientists who became involved with politics and polemics were John Locke, Bernard de Mandeville, James Drake, Samuel Garth, Hugh Chamberlen, John Arbuthnot, Isaac Newton, Richard Lower, William Wagstaffe, and James Welwood.

[171] R. F. Jones *et al.*, *The Seventeenth Century: Studies in the History of English Thought and Literature* (Stanford, 1951); R. Adolph, *The Rise of Modern Prose Style* (Cambridge, Mass., 1968); George Williamson, 'The Restoration Revolt against Enthusiasm', *Studies in Philology*, 30 (1933), 571–603. S. Clauss, 'John Wilkins' Essay Towards a Real Character: Its Place in the C17th Episteme', *Journal of History of Ideas*, 43 (1982), 531–54; M. Slaughter, *Universal Language Schemes and Scientific Taxonomy in the Seventeenth Century* (Cambridge, 1982).

[172] M. Poovey, *The History of the Modern Fact: Problems of Knowledge in the Sciences of Wealth and Society* (Chicago, 1998).

This 1709 Tory satire suggests that there was a hidden republican and anti-clerical agenda behind the work of the Whig, low church polemicist Benjamin Hoadly (the Whig canon of authors, of which Locke is the last, stand in the bookshelf). Hoadly himself invited readers to guess at his meaning, since on at least one occasion he wrote impersonating a Tory. But the image also asks us to confer meaning: is the axe raised to execute Hoadly? The 'truth' and 'meaning' were thus both disguised and created by the partisan reader. [Reproduced by courtesy of the Trustees of the British Museum.]

style.[173] The controversy nevertheless reminds us that language was a quite overtly contested subject in the later Stuart period on a number of fronts and that a study of politics might help to explain why.

Moreover, 'science' has been reinterpreted as a public activity. Public science and public politics relied on rather similar bases. 'Popular lectures and cheap pamphlets smashed the boundaries of public education. And Whig coffee-houses formed the matrix of Newtonian persuasion.'[174] Science adopted the rhetoric of public interest and hence 'it was the public that would increasingly be the arbiter of the value of natural philosophy in the first half of the eighteenth century'.[175] There is also an intriguing, though by no means straightforward, correlation between Newtonians and whiggery.[176] But the most important way in which the study of the history of science overlaps with that of publicly contested politics has to do with the nature of truth, of fact, of credit, credibility, and judgement. These are social and scientific constructs. But, as might already be apparent from the discussion so far, such concepts are political as well. Political contest turned on the credibility of key participants, on how the public could be informed of political 'truths' and how the public might judge what was politically true. At a national level public credit and party identity rested on partisan truth-claims and credibility. Given this overlap it is important to review some of the recent literature about science, for it contains valuable concepts that are applicable to any study of public politics and political discourse.

A ground-breaking book by Steven Shapin and Simon Schaffer focused on the controversy between Thomas Hobbes and Robert Boyle over how knowledge should be constructed.[177] Shapin and Schaffer contrasted the experimental methods of Boyle and the Royal Society with those of Hobbes. Boyle sought to privilege a restricted public space within which free debate and private judgement about uncertain things could flourish.

---

[173] R. Markley, *Fallen Languages. Crises of Representation in Newtonian England 1660–1740* (New York, 1993), 22. R. Kroll, *The Material World. Literate Culture in the Restoration and Early Eighteenth Century* (1991), sees the restoration as marking a major shift in discursive practices, largely through a revival of interest in Epicureanism.

[174] L. Stewart's *The Rise of Public Science: Rhetoric, Technology and Natural Philosophy in Newtonian Britain 1660–1750* (Cambridge, 1992), 108, 118, and ch. 5, quotation at 146. For coffee-houses, print, and science, see also A. Johns, *The Nature of the Book: Print and Knowledge in the Making* (Chicago, 1998), ch. 8.

[175] Stewart, *Rise of Public Science*, p. xv.

[176] Ibid., 153–4, 156, 163–4, 206–11, 317–18. For a less subtle attempt to link Newtonianism and Whiggery, see M. Jacob's *The Newtonians and the English Revolution* (1976).

[177] S. Shapin and S. Schaffer, *Leviathan and the Air-pump: Hobbes, Boyle, and the Experimental Life* (Princeton, 1985).

Such a debate could take place without animosity so long as members agreed on certain rhetorical and methodological rules. Yet Hobbesian philosophy sought right reasoning that could enforce assent on a public that included all men. In outlining the differences between Boyle and Hobbes, Shapin and Schaffer recognized that 'solutions to the problem of knowledge are solutions to the problem of social order' and that hence the disagreement over experimentation was a contribution 'to political history as well as to the history of science and philosophy'. Thus, they concluded, 'the solution to the problem of knowledge is political'. Indeed, their book ends with a suggestive section on 'the relationships between knowledge and political organisation'. They (rightly) argue that the history of science occupies the same terrain as the history of politics because scientific practitioners helped to create and shape the polity in which they worked and 'the knowledge they produced and authenticated became an element in political action in a wider polity'.[178]

Shapin took this insight a stage further, or perhaps in a slightly different direction, in his book *The Social History of Truth*, which argues that truth is as much a social construct as an intellectual one. Thus what is 'true' rests on validation by men of credit, and credit is conferred socially, through wealth and status and ways of talking. Shapin argues that there was a 'special relationship between the idea of a gentleman and the idea of truth-telling. To acquire the reputation of a liar was to endanger membership in gentlemanly society'.[179] He suggests that conceptions of free action and virtue were regarded as reliable indicators of truth-telling and contemporaries perceived these to be the qualities of gentlemen. Truth was a matter of collective judgement, decided by the majority, and relied on shared notions of trust. Research by social historians on the use of the courts made by men and women quite low down the social scale to defend their reputation suggests that Shapin's stress on gentility is overstated. But there is also a political history of truth that is largely ignored. Though partisans may have drawn on social status to reinforce truth claims, partisan allegiance could also confer credibility on what might otherwise seem highly implausible or even erroneous; and parties had a credit and credibility that had to be defended through the vindications of individual adherents. Political parties routinely made truth-claims, even though they contradicted one another. As we shall see in future chapters, truth could be something dependent on, even determined by, the authority of party. In some ways,

---

[178]   Shapin and Schaffer, *Leviathan and the Air-pump*, 332, 342.
[179]   S. Shapin, *A Social History of Truth: Civility and Science in Seventeenth-century England* (Chicago, 1994), p. xxi.

then, we might agree with Barbara Shapiro, who has charted the emergence of a probabilistic society in the later seventeenth century, one that accepted degrees of certainty about what was true. On the other hand, her more recent suggestion that this was a culture of fact seems far more questionable.[180]

Collectively these works offer us means of approaching issues that were common to later Stuart politics and its wider religious, political, scientific, and cultural context. These were issues of enthusiasm and rationality, certainty and credibility, and public judgement.[181] Put crudely, the concern to establish the criteria for establishing truth which had preoccupied religious thinking in the aftermath of the Reformation and which also concerned those working in scientific fields, also preoccupied those engaged in publicly partisan politics, who found themselves in a contest to establish credibility with the public. Truth was a political issue. 'Enlightenment', if by that term we mean a movement concerned with the rational inquiry and the discernment of 'truth', was thus not just the product of science and political thinkers but also the result of everyday political culture.[182] And science provided a new language in which politics could be discussed. For example, the later Stuart period witnessed the flowering of 'political

[180]   Shapiro, *Probability and Certainty*; *Culture of Fact*; H. G. van Leeuwen, *The Problem of Uncertainty in English Thought 1630–1690* (The Hague, 1963). I. Hacking, *The Emergence of Probability* (Cambridge, 1975), argues that a modern concept of probability emerged around 1660 [9, 23, 82]. D. Patey, *Probability and Literary Form: Philosophic Theory and Literary Practice in the Augustan Age* (Cambridge, 1984), offers a critique of the Hacking thesis but admits that probability 'is on every pen' after 1650 (272).

[181]   The best application of these to the later Stuart political culture are C. Condren, *Satire, Lies and Politics: The Case of Dr. Arbuthnot* (Basingstoke, 1997); R. Weil, ' "If I did say so, I lyed": Elizabeth Cellier and the Construction of Credibility in the Popish Plot Crisis', in S. Amussen and M. Kishlansky (eds.), *Political Culture*; S. Schaffer, 'Defoe's Natural Philosophy and the Worlds of Credit', in J. Christie and S. Shuttleworth (eds.), *Nature Transfigured. Science and Literature, 1700–1900* (Manchester, 1989). For important application to the rest of the seventeenth century, see also Achinstein, 'The Uses of Deception'; B. Dooley, 'News and Doubt in Early Modern Culture', in G. Dooley and S. Baron (eds.), *The Politics of Information in Early Modern Europe* (London, 2001); P. Hinds, 'Roger L'Estrange, the Rye House Plot, and the Regulation of Political Discourse in Late-Seventeenth Century London', The *Library*, 7th ser., 3 (2002), 1–31. Since writing his book Kate Loveman has finished an important dissertation exploring the relationship of shams plots and deception to the development of the novel (K. Loveman, 'Shamming Readers: Deception in English Literary and Political Culture *c*.1640–1740', Ph. D. diss., Cambridge (2003). She shows well how uncertainties and deceptions could be enjoyable and entertaining as well as cause for concern. Nevertheless she also relates deception primarily to catholicism and freethinking rather than to partisanship *per se*.

[182]   Roy Porter, who did so much to foster the study of the eighteenth century, nevertheless confessed he did 'not give much space to political debate' in his account of the British enlightenment (*Enlightenment*, p. xix).

arithmetic', the attempt to use the language of certain mathematics to describe the uncertainties of political calculations.[183]

Fiction and disguise in public discourse

Ideas of credit and credibility have also fascinated economic historians and literary scholars who therefore also have something interesting to tell the student of partisan politics. Craig Muldrew has investigated the early modern economy and concluded that it was one dominated by credit. He argues that such financial credit was dependent on an array of social and religious factors that conferred credibility.[184] Muldrew's work suggests a wider economy reliant on notions of credit. Though he does not make the link, Muldrew's notion of a credit economy has applicability in the political sphere. Parties maintained public credit or their stock would fall. And this credit was created and sustained by public discourse.

A connection between the new mercantile economy, the production of fact, and partisanship has, however, been asserted by Margaret Poovey. Although stressing the way in which science borrowed from mercantile habits before the later seventeenth century, Poovey recognizes that the financial and scientific revolutions were linked by concerns with objectivity, credibility, credit, and impartiality. But, she recognizes, these also relate to the partisan struggle between parties which was fuelling debate over the financial revolution. Both experimental observation and political parties made claim to be impartial, disinterested, and true. There is thus a nexus of concepts to do with credit, credibility, and credible information that intersect with science, economics, politics, and culture. And hence 'inevitably, although in some unpredictable ways, the rise of modern political parties affected the relation between facts and interests'.[185]

Credit was something constructed, representational, dependent on opinion, and therefore in some sense fictional. For this reason, credit has interested literary scholars. Stocks and shares, lotteries, and the new forms of finance that constituted the financial revolution of the later Stuart period were both dependent on fictions and helped to foster a fictional

---

[183] S. Schaffer, 'A Social History of Plausibility: Country, City and Calculation in Augustan Britain', in A. Wilson (ed.), *Rethinking Social History* (1993). Hobbes, of course, attempted something similar in *Leviathan*.
[184] C. Muldrew, *The Economy of Obligation: The Culture of Credit and Social Relations in Early Modern England* (Basingstoke, 1998).
[185] Poovey, *History of the Modern Fact*, 145.

mentality. Important links have been uncovered between the historical context of the later Stuart period and the development of new forms of fiction, most notably the novel. The literature on this subject is huge and varied.[186] But it is possible to discern a number of fictional impulses stemming from the transformation of political culture.

The first is the fictional potential of news. News was contested. A 'fact' had to be created; and contemporaries frequently accused each other of inventing the news.[187] The second is the epistemological uncertainty created by this but also by a wider contest over meaning. Literary scholars have tended to examine this in relation to contests over religion, economy, and credit. But the analysis can very usefully be extended to embrace partisan political culture. Indeed, this book seeks to demonstrate that the contest over meaning necessarily produced by public political strife was a key element of later Stuart political culture and hence an important element in preparing and stimulating a public appetite for prose fiction. Party polemic is, for this reason, full of interest. A third element to emerge from literary studies is the fictions deployed in historical writing. As we have already seen, partisan politics was embroiled in rival interpretations of the recent and not-so-recent past, which could be condemned by the rival parties as fictitious. We should, then, return to the 'Whig interpretation of history' with new eyes, seeing it less as a tired formula insistent on progress and more as a creative, contested, and utterly political view of the past. A fourth, rather undeveloped, strand in literary analyses has been to stress the relationship between the conspiratorial, plotting mindset of the later Stuart period and the plot offered by politics to writers.[188] Politics offered a narrative peopled with characters and rogues. To this catalogue of fic-

---

[186] Besides works already mentioned, see I. Watt, *The Rise of the Novel: Studies in Defoe, Richardson, and Fielding* (Berkeley, 1957); M. McKeon, *The Origins of the English Novel 1600–1740* (Baltimore, 1987); L. Davis, *Factual Fictions: The Origins of the English Novel* (New York, 1983); J. P. Hunter, *Before Novels: The Contexts of Eighteenth-century Fiction* (New York, 1990); R. Ballaster, *Seductive Forms: Women's Amatory Fiction from 1684 to 1740* (Oxford, 1992); J. Spencer, *The Rise of the Woman Novelist: From Aphra Behn to Jane Austen* (Oxford, 1986); S. Sherman, *Finance and Fictionality in the Early Eighteenth Century: Accounting for Defoe* (Cambridge, 1996); M. Schonhorn, *Defoe's Politics: Parliament, Power, Kingship, and Robinson Crusoe* (Cambridge, 1991); C. Nicholson, *Writing and the Rise of Finance: Capital Satires of the Early Eighteenth Century* (Cambridge, 1994); J. Thompson, *Models of Value: Eighteenth-century Political Economy and the Novel* (Durham, NC, 1996); D. Eilon, *Faction's Fictions: Ideological Closure in Swift's Satire* (Newark, NJ, 1991).
[187] J. Raymond, *Invention of the Newspaper*.
[188] Some of this is explored in R. Braverman, *Plots and Counterplots: Sexual Politics and the Body Politic in English Literature, 1660–1730* (Cambridge, 1993).

tions we might also add the fiction of party, of a national will, and of the public—all were in some sense abstractions that nevertheless, because they could appear real, exerted real political force.[189]

Indeed, political fictions were of great concern to contemporaries (and still to us in the twenty-first century). The later Stuart period was one fascinated by disguise and dissimulation.[190] Steven Zwicker's studies of the Restoration recreate a world 'where the enterprise of literature is understood as political'.[191] As such 'the self-conscious manipulation of language for political interest characterises the dominant mode of political discourse in the later seventeenth century and suggests that an important change had taken place, not only in politics, but also in the perception of language'. At the heart of this manipulation lay a passion for disguise. Zwicker finds deception and deceit to have permeated all genres: in comedy, in epic, in satire, in the rise of fables, and in the refinement of historical parallels so that they became political commentaries. The Advice-to-a-painter genre is a particularly good example. Such a preoccupation with disguise suggests to Zwicker that 'words had come loose from things, and this condition had an effect not only on the way in which political discourse was practised but on discourse in general, on the language of politics and on the language of high culture'. He also speculates that such ambiguity may have been 'a necessary means of political accommodation' and that 'by using the rift between words and things, men brought about change and explained its legitimacy to one another as stasis'. Divorcing words from things thus accommodated conflict.[192] Zwicker's analysis, and the detailed study of Dryden on which it is based, is wonderfully suggestive. Above all, it demands two responses: does the historian find supportive evidence and, if so, might we not extend such analysis? John Spurr, for example, has recently found considerable evidence in the politics of the 1670s to reinforce Zwicker's conclusion. This book will seek to show that

---

[189] For this last point see Mah, 'Phantasies', 168.

[190] Such an interpretation had also preceded new historicism (see, especially, M. Novak (ed.), *English Literature in the Age of Disguise* (Berkeley, 1977), albeit in a form less explicitly related to politics. See also, L. Trilling, *Sincerity and Authority* (1974) for a wider context.

[191] S. Zwicker, *Lines of Authority: Politics and English Literary Culture, 1649–89* (New York, 1993), 5.

[192] S. Zwicker, 'Politics and Literary Practice in the Restoration', in B. K. Lewalski (ed.), *Renaissance Genres: Essays on Theory, History and Interpretation* (Harvard, 1986), 269–98; S. Zwicker, 'Language as Disguise: Politics and Poetry in the Later Seventeenth Century', *Annals of Scholarship*, 1 (1980), 47–67; 'Lines of Authority: Political and Literary Culture in the Restoration', in K. Sharpe and S. Zwicker, *The Politics of Discourse* (Los Angeles, 1987). For Dryden and the problems of words and meanings, see also Kroll, *Material World*, 308–11.

disguise, dissimulation, and deceit were high on the political and literary agenda throughout the later Stuart era.[193]

CONCLUSION

Later Stuart political culture, building on a representational revolution that had been gathering head at least since the 1640s, was one of competing public voices, each claiming to represent the majority will or the public good or both. This competition was facilitated by the dispersed and overlapping nature of the early modern state, though the contest to capture public speech also helped to change the relationship between state and public. Ultimately, though not completely in this period, a public of office-holders gave way to a representative public. Electioneering, petitioning, publishing, and public debates helped to contribute to that shift, within a framework of an expanding state. In order to understand this process, we need to highlight contemporary anxieties: about the nature of the representative process; the abuse of language; the corruption of the state and the individual; the danger of self-interest and misrepresentation. And these are best explored by adopting and adapting techniques and models developed outside the study of partisan politics: sensitivity to linguistic usage and context; a notion of a public opinion and a public sphere; the languages of politeness, reason, and truth; debates about truth; and the mask of literary representations.

If a study of cognate disciplines can assist our understanding of the later Stuart period, an appreciation of partisan political culture may also extend the insights developed in these other areas. By foregrounding the importance of political practice and public discourse, it is possible to restate the importance of political history to a holistic understanding of the past. This is not a plea to prioritize political history over any other branch; but to stress its usefulness in ways that may not always have been apparent as a result of the sub-discipline's eclipse.

The structure of the book

The next chapter offers two case studies to apply some of the approaches already outlined and to highlight some of the interconnecting themes of the book. Probing the political culture of Hertford and Chester also serves

---

[193] J. Spurr, *England in the 1670s: 'This Masquerading Age'* (Oxford, 2000).

to set out the aim of the first half of the book: to show how the public was repeatedly invoked and asked to judge public affairs. The third chapter pursues this theme further by taking one genre—the petition and address—in order to show the interplay between politics and language. It also seeks to answer a series of questions: given the dispersed and overlapping nature of authority in the early modern period, what happened when legitimately authorized voices conflicted? And how were partisan rivalries and allegiances formed, maintained, and articulated within such a structure of authority? The fourth chapter examines the emergence of advice literature that was printed in large quantities to influence the frequent elections of the period. Again, the genre is taken in order to explore questions about the nature of representation in the period: what was the imagined character of the represented and their representatives, and how did such fictions influence the practice of politics? The election literature also raises the question of judgement: if voters were idealized as a rational and impartial public umpire, how could they preserve a sense of judgement amid partisan polemic that sought to manipulate them?

The first section of the book thus attempts to show the centrality of the public and a contest to represent it. The second section of the book then explores in more detail the nature of public discourse, or at least how contemporaries viewed the appeal to the people. Chapter 5 examines its dialogic and rhetorical nature, and its boundaries, particularly after the lapse of the pre-publication licensing laws in 1695. Chapter 6 studies the problem of how, in a partisan world, voters and readers could know what was true or right, and of how contemporaries feared that partisan polemic was abusive, slanderous, uncivil, lying, and fictitious. The final chapter suggests that the reaction against the rage, irrationality, and abusive nature of the partisan political culture fostered notions of an ideal, rational, and polite discourse. It argues that this trend sought to restrict the turbulent public sphere and exclude the people. The year 1716 thus witnessed the repeal of the 1694 Triennial Act that had guaranteed frequent elections. By then the Whigs feared that Tory and jacobite misrepresentations were in danger of winning the day. But it was also the case that, despite the repeal, the political culture had been changed for good. The tensions observed by Montesquieu remained embedded in the hybrid British political system.

CHAPTER TWO

Public Politics

This chapter seeks to provide the reader with some idea of the forms which partisan politics took and how the 'public' took on a new significance and importance. The central theme is public politics and the aim is to explore the nature of partisan conflict as it was played out in front of, and with, the public. It is important to sketch some of the ways in which the representation of the public was conceived in theory and worked out in practice. This is best done by examining particular local contexts, since these not only make conceptual problems concerning representation both concrete and personal, but also highlight many of the questions facing contemporaries. A key one was how might, or should, a (or the) public voice be represented? As will become apparent, voting was only one form of representative practice. We need to obtain a sense of the varieties of political representation and also how the representation of politics was itself a centrally important concern. Offering brief studies of two particularly interesting examples of partisan conflicts, Hertford and Cheshire, it argues that representative politics centred on public discourse: the public articulation of opinion expressed through elections, petitions, addresses, print, and speech. The two case studies stress that later Stuart political culture needs to be seen as a form of public dialogue. In such a dialogue representation was not limited to electioneering but encompassed a wide range of interlinked representative practices, each of which involved the public. These practices require us to study the politics of language and the nature of public discourse.

The second half of the chapter examines the notion of the public as a collective entity and explores the ambiguous definitions of the 'people'. It argues that ideas about the public as a generality, with a will and an interest, matured, so that the 'public' became central to political discussions and a concept invoked in partisan disputes. Alongside this expanded role for the public there was a competition over the representation of the voice of the people. Frequent elections strengthened parliament's and partisans' claim to this, while new notions of public credit further strengthened the notion of a collective, fictional entity. An appeal to the public also lent weight to the language of public interest, and raised anxieties that private, particular, or self-interest was facilitated by partisanship. This leads to an examination of discussions about who constituted the public and hence who might be represented. There were different ideological positions about the role of the people. Ideas about contract and popular sovereignty created radically different notions of the power of the people from those inherent in patriarchal thought; but it was also the case that the identity of the people, and hence of the public, was something contested, and in part politically contingent, throughout the later Stuart period.

POLITICS AS PUBLIC DIALOGUE: REPRESENTATIVE
PRACTICES IN HERTFORD

The links between the representation of politics and political representation can be seen in the partisan political culture of the borough of Hertford.[1] The representational struggle there worked at a number of different levels. First, there was a struggle over the franchise. Hertford had 'above three hundred inhabitants',[2] who were in conflict with the corporation, which alleged that the inhabitants had been 'introduced' to the franchise in 1640. Their right was only finally recognized in 1705. But there was also a dispute over the right of the corporation to create honorary freemen, who also had voting powers. Both controversies ensured that over the later Stuart period the number of voters rose from 520 in 1690 to 670 in 1701 and to 750 by 1710.[3] Many of these new voters were honorary freemen, created by the corporation's high church faction. Over 400 were enrolled in the last twenty years of the seventeenth century. A power struggle partly occurred over the franchise; but the representation of dissent was also at stake.[4] Perhaps as many as a third of the inhabitants were dissenters and

---

[1] L. M. Munby, 'Politics and Religion in Hertfordshire 1660–1740', in Munby (ed.), *East Anglian Studies* (Cambridge, 1968); V. Rowe, *The First Hertford Quakers* (Hertford, 1970); V. Rowe, 'Hertford's Borough charters of 1680 and 1688', in D. Jones-Baker (ed.), *Hertford in History*, (Cambridge, 1991), 174–83; D. Hirst and S. Bowler, 'Voting in Hertford 1679–1721', *History and Computing*, 1 (1989), 14–18; W. Urwick, *Nonconformity in Herts.* (1884); A. Kugler, *Errant Plagiary: The Life and Writing of Lady Sarah Cowper* (Stanford, 2002); *HOP II*, ii. 282–93; B. Adams, 'The Body in the Water: Religious Conflict in Hertford, 1660–1702', London Ph.D., (2000).

[2] Hertfordshire RO., borough records, 23/446, Case of Clarke and Boteler, 1715. For the population, see ibid., bor. recs. 33/52.

[3] These figures are deduced from polls in the borough records, vols. 23 and 25/53–9, list of freemen 26 Aug. 1710.

[4] Herts. RO, bor. recs., 23/320 for the Whig claim that 'none of the ch[arte]rs give any rules or take notice how or by whome members of parliam[en]t shall be chosen; soe it remaines in

one estimate for 1720 put the number of dissenters eligible to vote at 150, with a further 124 votes 'influenced' by them. The corporation, however, tended to be dominated by high churchmen. Joseph Hoppey probably summed up the feelings of many inhabitants when in October 1684 he said the corporation was 'governed by ten fools, sixteen asses and two knaves'.[5]

Key to these representational struggles were the fortunes of the Cowper family, who owned Hertford castle. The high church faction used a new charter to make new freemen on an unprecedented scale in the early 1680s, in an effort to ensure the electoral defeat of Sir William Cowper, who was a staunch Whig, a follower of the first earl of Shaftesbury, and a strong ally of the dissenters.[6] Cowper was certainly a polarizing influence. In 1682 two of his men, Henry Radford and George Draper, asked inhabitants to drink a health to the duke of Monmouth, and allegedly struck or threatened anyone who refused to join them.[7] And in the summer of 1683 Sir William was himself indicted for 'making nag mouthes and distortid faces' at the vicar, Ralph Battell, when the latter prayed for the king and duke of York, and for claiming that the entire episcopal bench was popishly affected.[8] The Revolution of 1688–9 allowed a revival of flagging Cowper fortunes. In 1690 Sir William regained his seat and in 1695 was joined by his son, also called William. That election 'produced scuffles' and the Whig victory pushed the Tory faction into new extremes.[9] In December 1696 one of the Tory aldermen was bound over 'for speaking many desperate and profane oaths and uttering many threatening, malicious and scandalous speeches against' the Cowpers.[10] A year later the leader of the Tory aldermanic faction, John Dimsdale, became mayor and remained so, 'contrary to the charter and usage of the town' for four years, during which time more

---

inhabitants, as it did before any ch[arte]r'. For estimates of the number of dissenting voters in each constituency, see appendixes to E. D. Bebb, *Nonconformity and Social and Economic Life 1660–1800* (Philadelphia, 1980).

[5] Herts. RO., bor. recs., 9/307, indictment 24 Oct. 1684. In 1691 a Benjamin Hoppy was alleged to have said that all the justices of the peace were 'rogues and that they were all bribed' (ibid., 9/347, information 24 July 1691) but also that the people 'would be no better until the king came home again' (ibid., 9/397). John Stout, a Quaker, was alleged to have said 'in the publique market place' that the mayor and aldermen 'were a pack of as great rogues as any that robbd on the highway' (ibid., 9/373, information, 9 Sept. 1695; ibid., 21/2, court book 4 Dec. 1695).

[6] Herts. RO, bor. recs., 1/76, extracts from corporation book. For prosecutions for nonconformity, see ibid., 9/270, 278, 297, 328. Sir William Cowper did have a clerical friend, John Patrick, prebend of Charterhouse, who was his 'inseperable companion' in 1685, but Samuel Parker described Patrick as 'the sowrest Whigg in the nation' (Bodl., MS Tanner 31, ff. 166–75).

[7] Herts. RO, bor. recs. 9/285, information of Nelson Stratton, 17 Aug. 1682.

[8] Adams, 'Body in the Water', 208–9.

[9] Herts. RO, Panshanger MSS, D/EP F81, f. 78, Sir William to Sarah Cowper, 16 Oct. 1695.

[10] Herts. RO, bor. recs. 9/386, Mr Squire to Sir Humphrey Gore, 8 Jan. 1696/7.

sympathetic honorary freemen were created to bolster the Tories' electoral position.[11]

This abuse of the formal process of representation provoked another type of representational activity in the form of petitions from the inhabitants. The first petition, signed in January 1698 by 138 residents (including most of the town's prominent Quakers) was launched against the mayor and aldermen. The actions of the Tory clique were said to 'impoverish the trade of this town; and greater detriment may follow for that thereby our poor are greatly increased, our rights and priviledges greatly obstructed, our commons eaten up and destroyed by them who have no right'.[12] When redress was not forthcoming, Sir William Cowper and seventeen others petitioned the king, and another petition appears to have been drafted for parliament, complaining that the creation of honorary freemen aimed 'to overbalance such as were the rightful electors'. The Tory faction was alleged to desire 'the power of imposing what representatives they please upon your petitioners without any title or colour of right'.[13]

These representative struggles, in which petitions offered a legitimate public voice against the corporation, spilt over into rancorous public discourse. About this time Sir William called the mayor 'a blockhead' and the aldermen 'a pack of rogues'.[14] The election of 1698 only exacerbated the feuding. At a meeting on 3 August the Tories made 83 more potential voters and 72 of the town's Tories signed a petition complaining that Cowper and his cronies were disaffected to the church and had abused the 'magistrates in the said borough with opprobrious language and print and publish scandalous libels against them and do all they can to create disturbances in the said borough'.[15] Petition had thus provoked counter-petition and public discourse had descended into libel. The Whigs retaliated by taking court action, in January 1699, to secure a ruling against the creation of non-inhabitant freemen.

But disaster struck the Cowpers before the court could rule. On 20 July 1699 Spencer Cowper, Sir William's younger son, was tried for the murder of a Quaker, Sarah Stout, the daughter of one of his father's former election agents. Spencer Cowper alleged that he had been accused of murder

[11]   Herts. RO, 23/149, petition of inhabitants, 7 Mar. 1701.
[12]   Ibid., 25/27, names of those who signed the petition; 25/37 and 25/39, petition from the inhabitants.
[13]   Ibid., 23/446–7, petition of inhabitants 1698.
[14]   Ibid., 33/52, Sir Thomas Trevor's legal opinion.
[15]   33/52, Sir John Trevor noted that the mayor produced a scandalous printed paper but he could not prove who printed or published it.

by witnesses who were prejudiced against him 'upon feuds that have risen at the elections of my father and brother in this town'.[16] At stake in the trial was the reputation of the family and of Whiggery more generally. Here, then, the private represented the public, fused as a result of the public way in which politics and personal rivalry was contested. Although a not-guilty verdict was returned, the trial damaged the family's reputation and split the Quakers. The Cowpers' hold on the borough was temporarily broken.

These disputes showed a clear tie between the process of representation and representational practices. Not only was the franchise disputed but other representations of the people were made, notably through a series of petitions and counter-petitions.[17] Participation was about much more than office-holding and such petitions were an important form of public discourse to which we shall return. Such voices could also be heard because of the variety of public institutions of the dispersed early modern state. Shortly after the 1708 election, for example, the Whigs sent a commission of charitable uses to Spencer Cowper and other Whigs, authorizing an investigation of the corporation's finances designed to make it repay £2,495 of allegedly misappropriated money belonging to the town's poor.[18] A dialogue between the various branches of institutional power was, of course, nothing new; but the institutionalized partisanship of the later Stuart period posed intriguing new problems for a state founded on assumptions of harmony not cacophony.

Another form of public discourse was print that aimed to inform, advise, comment, and cajole. Thus in 1689 Sir William Cowper issued his own election tract, *The Case of the Ancient Burrough of Hertford in Relation to their Electing Burgesses*, which alleged that all inhabitants, whether free or not, had always been eligible to vote and that the corporation had a design, 'which is very near treason', to transfer power into its own hands.[19] The magistrates were thus represented as 'arbitrary' for having 'exasperated the inhabitants'. Print, then, was not only important as a platform; it can also help us to understand the languages used to fight political contests. Cowper was here invoking the languages of law and conspiracy, as

---

[16] *State Trials*, xiii. 1149.
[17] Herts. RO, bor. recs. 23/181, copy of the petition presented 7 Jan. 1701/2; ibid., 23/282 and 23/289, petition of 1705; ibid., 33/56–8, petition for the removal of the recorder, c.1725. 212 of the 'principal inhabitants' counter-petitioned.
[18] Ibid., 5/35–50, decree of the charitable commission 1709; ibid., Vol. 75 for many papers relating to the commission.
[19] Herts. RO, bor. recs. 23/331, endorsed 'Sr Wm Cooper's reflec[ti]ons conc[erning] the charter & corpora[ti]on of Hertford'.

well as the language of public good.[20] It was not just Cowper, of course, who used print and public discourse against his enemies. The town's Tory, and jacobite, parson, Thomas Hodgkin, was said to have 'made it his business to libel the [Cowper] family in prose and rhimes'.[21] Public discourse in a variety of forms thus shaped the political contest.

Print and reading does seem to have changed minds, or at least justified shifts of opinion and emboldened individuals' resolution. There is an example of how political theory and practical politics meshed in the figure of a Mr Cranfield, who in 1701 deserted the Whigs. When asked why, 'his answer was that he had read Machiavel, and learnt from him; he was to own no cause or party longer than they could protect him, and the Whigs were so plainly none down here they could not'.[22] Such ideological literacy was common-place. As the borough addresses of July 1710 show, ideological polarity was intrinsic to the publicly partisan contest. The Whigs, for their part, were able to present an address that year from the 'principal inhabitants and freemen' that represented the high church Tories as the real national enemy. The address informed the queen that 'the persons truly dangerous to your Majesty and the protestant succession are those who traduce the honour and justice of the Revolution; those who seditiously suggest the church to be in danger'. But a rival address from the Tory mayor and corporation attacked the 'factious, anti-monarchical and rebellious' notions afoot.[23]

Hertford politics generated print. The trial of Spencer Cowper for the murder of Sarah Stout, for example, attracted a wealth of printed commentary and reportage.[24] The case was still in the public eye as late as 1728 when, on Spencer Cowper's death, *Sarah, the Quaker, to Lothario, lately deceased, on meeting him in the Shades* ran to at least three editions. Private

---

[20] See also Herts. RO, bor. recs. 1/64, petition to the king against Marmaduke Alington, appointed in 1714 as recorder, for his denial of freedoms to traders and his deliberate infliction of higher costs on them; and ibid., 23/448, information relating to the 1714/15 election.

[21] Herts. RO, D/EP F 31, p. 159. Sarah Cowper possessed 'two inveterate libels' that Hodgkin had written (ibid., F32, p. 95).

[22] Herts. RO, D/EP F 81, f. 97, Cowper to Lady Cowper, 18 Sept. 1701. Sir William Cowper was scandalized 'that a rogue of his low condition should be undone by Machiavel, or go to square his private life to rules which, if good, are laid down only for princes and men in public characters who have the good of the people to answer for'.

[23] For the addresses, see J. Oldmixon, *The History of Addresses* (part 1, 1709; part 2, 1710), ii. 350–1.

[24] *The Tryal of Spencer Cowper* (1699); *An Account of the Full Tryal and Examination of Spencer Cooper* (1699); *The Case of Spencer Cowper Esq.* (1701); *The Hertford Letter* (1699), *A Reply to the Hertford Letter* (1699); *Some Observations on the Tryal of Spencer Cowper* (1701); *A Dialogue between a Quaker and his Neighbour in Hertford, about the Murder of Mrs. Sarah Stout* (1699); *The Case of Mrs. Mary Stout* (1699).

scandal thus had public, political consequences. This continued to be true for several members of the Cowper family. William Cowper rose to become lord chancellor but his bigamous marriage (he had two illegitimate children) left him vulnerable to Tory pens. Delariviere Manley, who, like Swift, wrote for the influential periodical the *Examiner*, made the most of the scandal in her fictionalized account of political intrigues, *The Secret Memoirs and Manners of Several Persons of Quality* (1709).[25] In it, Manley represented the Cowpers as the epitome of hypocritical dissemblers, whose outward show hid private designs. William Cowper thus had 'religion in pretence, none in reality' and was 'violent' in the pursuit of pleasure and riches, 'quitting his interest for nothing but pleasure and his pleasure for nothing but interest'.[26] Both the fictional dimension of political representations—also apparent in the manuscript annotation on a printed Tory election case of 1705 which was dismissed as 'all fiction'[27]— and the apparent mismatch between representation and reality in a world of deceit are striking.

Sarah Cowper, the mother of two scandal-ridden sons, found such print deeply offensive but also misrepresentative.[28] 'A paper battle is on foot between parties who pelt at each other all the dirt they can rake up', she observed. Her son William, she believed, was the victim of misrepresentation. A wise and good man, she said, could be made to 'look like a madman: and yet if his life were fairly represented, and his vertues set over against his failings he wou'd appear an admirable and excellent person'.[29] But, for all its ability to mislead, the creative potential of print was central to Sarah Cowper's world. It would be no exaggeration to suggest that she constructed her own identity out of her reading.[30] Seeking refuge from a very difficult husband, she found reading books, pamphlets, libels, or ballads and writing her diary to be her principal joys. Indeed, she frequently copied extracts from printed works into her diary entries and recorded ballads at the end of volumes. She found the more ephemeral political print 'diverting enough'.[31] Constructing her own identity in part through

[25] Cowper himself published partisan pieces (*HOP II*, iii. 763, 770).
[26] Manley, *The New Atalantis*, ed. R. Ballaster (London, 1991), 115.
[27] Herts RO, bor. recs. 23/329, annotation on *The Case of the Borough of Hertford* [1705].
[28] For the public display of lampoons, see Herts. RO, D/EP F 30, p. 10 (23 Jan. 1702/3). For the sense of offence, and concern that the people were being 'impos'd upon' by 'rascally scribblers' see ibid., F 34, p. 238 (22 Apr. 1713).
[29] Ibid., F 33, p. 214 (7 Sept. 1710 (punctuation altered)). The reference is to Elizabeth Cullen, Cowper's 'first' wife.
[30] Kugler, *Errant Plagiary*, ch. 5.
[31] Herts. RO, D/EP F 34, p. 64.

print, she expressed her own plight in the language of Whig discourse, articulating and conceiving the private through the public. Thus she referred to her domineering and wilful husband as an 'absolute tyrant' and herself as a 'slave'.[32] Similarly, she viewed the public through a private lens. For example, when in 1701 Robert Harley was chosen speaker of the House of Commons 'contrary to the mind of the king', Sarah sympathized because 'to have a right and title to power and governm[en]t without the exercise is a hardship an[d] greivance equal to slavery. I speak it from experience in the low and little sphere I move in as a wife and mistress.'[33]

The public and private also mixed in print and discourse. Sir William Cowper loved free discussion and his table was often the scene of mixed religious disputants knocking corners off each other. On one occasion Sarah recorded that four different opinions were represented at the dinner table: a 'Latitudinarian, another for the Church, a papist, and a preaching Anabaptist'.[34] Such cacophony of conversation had already been satirized in a public print, *The Best Choice for Religion and Government* (1697), which recorded (or imagined) a conference between controversialists meeting in 'an obsolete and neglected castle'. The reader of the copy in the British Library was convinced that this was Hertford Castle, noting that the key participant in the dialogue represented 'Sr WC', who is depicted in the tract as an advocate of the family of love, a freethinker who scoffed in the coffee houses at his son's immorality, and as a man who had done nothing for his borough.[35] Clearly this was an electioneering 'libel', representing Cowper and his son in the worst possible light and hence preparing the public for the polls in 1698.[36] But the printed dialogue also highlights what Sarah Cowper herself felt was the erosion by partisan zeal of polite behaviour and conversation.[37].

Before leaving Hertford, we must briefly return to the allegations of murder made against Spencer Cowper, for they also highlight the way in which truth-claims were contested and in some sense warped by partisan

---

[32] Herts. RO, F 29 p. 162.   [33] Ibid., F 29 p. 172.   [34] Ibid., F 30, p. 150.

[35] *The Best Choice*, 9, 20–6. For the annotation see BL, T.2032(20).

[36] A rejoinder was issued that also made the electioneering nature of the print controversy clear, aiming to help voters distinguish between 'truth and falsehood' (*The Trial and Determination of Truth in Answer to the Best Choice for Religion and Government* (1697), preface). The tract exploits a fictional, dialogic, framework, with Hertford renamed as Scydromedia and representatives of the religious communities there placed on trial in order to discover the 'truth'.

[37] For her persistent complaints about the state of conversation, see Herts. RO, Panshanger (Cowper) MSS D/EP F 29, 16, 49, 72; F 30, 49; F 31, 65; F 32, 22; F 33, 239, 323, 328; F 34, 145.

THE

Trial and Determination

OF

TRUTH:

In ANSWER to

The Best Choice for Religion and Government.

Believe not every Spirit ; but try the Spirits, whether they are of God ; for many false Prophets are gone out into the World, 1 John 4. 1.

That thou may'st know how thou oughtest to behave thy self in the House of God, which is the Church of the Living God, the Ground and Pillar of the Truth, 1 Tim. 3. 15.

LONDON:

Printed in the Year 1697.

This tract satirized Hertford politics by fictionalizing the borough and its citizens. As the title makes plain, the issue of truth loomed large in both political and religious debate. It aimed to show 'all freemen and freeholders' how to judge between 'truth and falshood'. [Reproduced by permission of the Syndics of Cambridge University Library.]

allegiance. We have already seen how the accusations against Spencer were in some sense political: the Hertford Tories sought to destroy the dominant Whig family's interest among voters. Yet most of the evidence against Spencer Cowper at his trial for murder was medical, and politics was conducted under the cover of science. Disputes centred on determining whether or not Sarah Stout had been dead when she entered the water. The prosecution alleged that Sarah had not drowned but had been murdered and then thrown in the water. Key to the prosecution case was the testimony of John Dimsdale junior, a local surgeon, who testified that he had found swelling and bruising around the neck. Dimsdale had changed his evidence, for at the time of the death he had reported to the coroner that the marks were no more than was usual in dead bodies.[38] Four more physicians, including John Dimsdale senior, who had attended the postmortem, also gave evidence against Cowper. The doctors had, they reported, held 'a consultation to consider whether she was drowned or not drowned; and we were all of opinion that she was not drowned' because they found no water in the lungs. An affidavit was drawn up to that effect, which was also signed by Robert Dimsdale, another member of the local physician family. But the Dimsdales were not impartial medics; the veracity of their claims was questionable because of their political animus against the Cowpers. Indeed, Dimsdale senior was the controversial mayor with whom the Cowpers crossed swords.

Spencer Cowper conducted his own defence, alleging that only a very small quantity of water in the lungs could cause drowning. This, he said, was 'a certain and established truth'.[39] In order to reinforce his case Cowper called 'some physicians of note and eminency' from London, numbering seven in total and including Sir Hans Sloane and Samuel Garth, two of London's most sought-after doctors. Sloane and the others testified that a small amount of water, even 'some spoonfuls', in the lung would indeed cause suffocation.[40] Such water, Sloane maintained, would then have been absorbed into the lungs during the six weeks that the body had lain underground. Garth—a committed Whig who also wrote in the party cause—concurred, adding 'we have not only philosophy but experiments for this'.[41] In the trial contested medical evidence thus took a party line, with experts lining up on each side to confer credibility on their version of the truth. To be sure, the case was unusual. Issues of credibility and veracity were not often so explicitly resolved through experiment and the language

---

[38] *State Trials*, xiii. 1123.   [39] Ibid., 1145.
[40] Ibid., 1155–6.   [41] Ibid., 1157.

of reason and science; but the larger point here has to do with a contest over what was true and over the credibility of those who made truth-claims. Just as a scientist had to convince a public of the veracity of his experiment, so a politician had to persuade voters that his version of the truth was worth backing.

Hertford politics thus emphasize that representation meant much more than voting and that there were several interconnected (but also some-times competing) representational spheres. The formal representation at the polls was thus supplemented and challenged by the representative realm of petitions and addresses. In such a contest it was not always appar-ent where the public voice actually lay. Moreover, the frenzy of interest in the Cowpers reflected a larger interaction of politics and print. The representations of print were intended as contributions to a political struggle; and through the reaction of readers, whether the voter who read Machiavelli or Sarah Cowper and her political ephemera, we can glimpse a private as well as a public contest for allegiance. Hertford's political cul-ture therefore reveals a number of intersecting representational realms: elections, electioneering, and publicly competitive politics; print culture and public discourse interacting with private dialogue; petitions and ad-dresses as rival articulations of a public voice; and rival truth-claims. These will provide the main threads of the chapters that follow. They are also all apparent in a second case study, that of Chester and Cheshire, which serves to underline the various and interrelated ways in which representative practices worked. What again emerges is a contest to speak for, and to, the public.

REPRESENTATIVE POLITICS IN CHESHIRE

In Michaelmas term 1683 a Cheshire grand jury made a presentment against Sir Willoughby Aston, who kept notes of the incident in his diary.[42] He and twenty seven others were alleged to have: promoted a 'seditious' address to the candidates at the 1681 county election; abetted the 'riotous'

---

[42] Liverpool RO, 920/MD/172, diary entries for 17 June 1683, 17 Sept. 1683, 7 Apr. 1684. Cheshire politics at this time are particularly well documented, with diaries kept by Aston, Roger Whitley, Sir John Mainwaring, and Henry Booth. The Cheshire material has been ex-amined by P. J. Challinor, 'Restoration and Exclusion in the County of Cheshire', *Bulletin of the John Rylands University Library of Manchester*, 64 (1982), 360–85; Challinor, 'The Structure of Politics in Cheshire, 1660–1715', Ph. D., Wolverhampton (1984); Baskerville *et al.*, 'The Dy-namics of Landlord Influence'; *HOP I*, i. 151–4; *HOP II*, ii. 58–67; G. W. Keeton, *Lord Chancel-lor Jeffreys and the Stuart Cause* (London, 1965), 161–85.

entertainment of would-be heir the duke of Monmouth when he visited
Chester in 1682; and frequented conventicles or harboured dissenting
ministers. Aston and his colleagues responded by issuing a writ for *scan-
dalum magnatum* against the grand jury, suing them for malicious conspiracy in making the presentment. When the case came to court, shortly
after royal commissioners took over Chester's government, Aston and his
associates were all bound over on recognizances of £500. The case together
with its origins and consequences reveals a number of different representative practices.

The address at the centre of the dispute was, the indictment claimed, the
product of a 'dissatisfied party' that had urged the alteration of the succession 'with other dangerous and seditious purports'. The address was one of
the so-called 'instructions' that had been presented immediately after the
election of MPs, in Cheshire on 7 March 1681. It claimed to represent the
'sentiments and desires of the gentry and freeholders' and thanked Hon.
Henry Booth and Sir Robert Cotton, the county's representatives, for their
'sincerity and proceedings' in parliament. The address, which was itself
published, desired that the House of Commons continue to print its votes,
so that the people 'may be truly acquainted with your proceedings', thereby
invoking, as well as utilizing, the representative forum of print. And the
address urged the MPs 'to adhere to what the late Parliament designed
relating to the duke of York', the defence of the king, and the pursuit of
popish or 'sham' plotters. It thus sought to strengthen the hand of the
knights of the shire with the force of public opinion.

The address had been printed in a 'true collection' of similar texts called
Vox Patriae, the title itself appropriating the representative voice of the
country. The tract carried an assertive preface that defined the people and
how their voice worked. It is worth quoting at length:

It has for many ages been received a maxim, vox populi, vox dei, the voice of the
people, is the voice of God, and though some flashy wits pride themselves in speaking contemptibly of the populace, calling them the rabble, the mobile &c they must
either mean the meer vulgar, the dreggs of mankind, persons without estates, reason and judgment, bankrupts of common sense, as well as beggars in fortune, or
else they put the greatest affront imaginable on the body of the nation, especially in
England, where under the title of Commoners, are included all degrees of gentry,
under peerage . . . able merchants, discreet citizens, understanding burgesses, and
such substantial yeomen and freeholders, as no kingdom besides can boast of. Now
since interest will not lye, how is it morally possible, that the major part of a nation
so qualified should act so contrary to the true and proper interests of their countrey? For tho particular men may be imposed upon by artifice, or deluded with pre-

tences, or biassed by private advantages, yet tis not imaginable, that the whole body should either be so infatuated as not to see or so stupidly tame, as not to oppose, as far as lawfully they may, what tends their universal ruin . . . Whatever distempers may have seiz'd some parts, yet blessed be Heaven, the head and heart of England is sound, as is manifest by the following numerous addresses, so general and so unanimous, that they may justly be styled the voice of the realm.[43]

The people, then, were far more than the nobility and gentry; and they spoke through addresses *and* elections. The tract went on to claim that 'he was certainly no fool, that first said, parliaments were the pulse of the people . . . nor will it be less plain, what is the common sense of the body of the people in this juncture of eminent danger, if the unanimous addresses from so many considerable parts of England be regarded'.[44] The text defines who is being represented; makes claims about their unanimous voice and 'common sense'; explains how that will was to be discerned and represented, particularly through parliament; talks the language of interest, rationality, and majorities; raises the possibility that the public could be misrepresented and misled by 'artifices'; and makes all these claims in print as an appeal to the public 'reader'.

A similar address, in Essex, had been read out to allow an opportunity to show that 'it was the sense of each individual person in that numerous assembly', and a same process of authorization occurred in Cheshire.[45] This was necessary because the address was not quite as unanimous as *Vox Patriae* suggested. A manuscript account, written by Booth, explains how, having finished his speech to the voters, a rival text had been presented:

an address was tendered to me & Sr Robt Cotton by 3 of ye psons concern'd agt us, & twas subscrib'd by about 30 psons, twas delivered to me, but I told them I could not consent to have anything of yt nature read being subscribed; unless ye number & quality of ye p[er]sons were such as might induce me to believe yt ye consent of ye county went along with it, but this was subscribed by so few & most of them of so mean quality, yt I must look upon it as ye act of those particular p[er]sons, so it came to nothing.[46]

---

[43] *Vox Patriae; or, The Resentments & Indignation of the Free-born Subjects of England* (1681), 17.

[44] *The Speech of the Honourable Henry Booth Esq.* (1681), printed in Chester but also sold in London. The wording of the address in this version, though not its sense, was slightly different from that published in *Vox Patriae*. Booth was refuting misrepresentations of his views made by Dr Ardenne, rector of Nantwich.

[45] *Vox Patriae* (1681), 12.

[46] BL, Hargrave MS 149, ff. 73ᵛ. For a discussion of this manuscript, see below.

U6540 6.1

VOX PATRIÆ:

OR, THE
RESENTMENTS & INDIGNATION
OF THE
Free-born Subjects of ENGLAND,
AGAINST
Popery, Arbitrary Government, the Duke of *YORK,*
OR ANY
POPISH SUCCESOR;
BEING A TRUE
COLLECTION
OF THE
PETITIONS and ADDRESSES lately made from divers *Counties, Cities,* and *Boroughs* of this Realm, to their respective *Representatives,* chosen to Serve in the *PARLIAMENT* Held at *OXFORD* March 21, 1680.

Et si non profunt Singula, Juncta juvant.

With a *Perfect List* of *Both Houses* of that *Parliament.*

LONDON, Printed for *Francis Peters,* 1681.

A collection of petitions and addresses in 1681 claimed to be the representative 'voice of the country'. Print facilitated such claims to speak for the nation. [Reproduced by permission of the Syndics of Cambridge University Library.]

But although Booth had refused to make the rival address public at the time of the poll, it was published in a London newspaper, illustrating how difficult print made it to control representative politics.[47] Critics of the addresses more generally also pointed out that they could not be representative of the nation since only 12 out of 52 counties, and 11 out of 250 boroughs, had presented them. The chief court apologist, Sir Roger L'Estrange, concluded that the addresses acted 'in the name of the people, without the people's commission'. Indeed, secretary of state Sir Leoline Jenkins claimed that they were 'the contrivance of a very few . . . & meerly imposed upon the people by artifice and surprize'.[48] Were the addresses, then, the true voice of the people? Booth thought so, for he invoked the Cheshire address during a parliamentary speech in favour of the bill to exclude James, duke of York from the succession, telling the Commons that it was not just his opinion but that of his county which they had 'comanded' him to support.[49] Yet the prosecution of the address in 1683 suggested that it was no more than the voice of a seditious faction.

We might at this point pause and ask in what way was any of this different from earlier political practice? Hadn't petitions been presented before? Hadn't MPs been looking back to their constituents for representative legitimacy in the early Stuart period? Certainly all was not novel. On 27 February 1641 Sir Willoughby's father, Sir Thomas Aston, had presented to the House of Lords a Cheshire petition with over 6,000 names in defence of episcopal government, and had repeated the trick a year later with 8,000 signatures. These petitions were in dialogue with anti-episcopal petitions; and linked to electoral rivalries within the county. The counter-petitioners accused each other of fathering fictional texts that had never been circulated and hence were unrepresentative and libellous.[50] And they broke with the tradition of manuscript, private, petitions to invoke the public through print. The conflicts of 1641–2 thus displayed many of the features of later partisan conflict. It is important to link moments of crisis across time for what they had in common, rather than look for linear continuity or discontinuity. To acknowledge this does not, however, mean that nothing had changed. The earlier petitions were preoccupied with the

---

[47] *True Protestant Mercury*, No. 21, 5–9 Mar. 1681. It desired that the MPs 'embrace with thankfulness his Majesty's most gracious intimation of his royal assent to secure us ag[ain]st the danger of a popish successor'.

[48] Knights, *Politics and Opinion*, 300–1.

[49] BL, Hargrave MS 149, f. 74.

[50] P. Lake, 'Puritans, Popularity and Petitions: Local Politics in National Context, Cheshire 1641' in T. Cogswell, R. Cust, and P. Lake (eds.), *Politics, Religion and Popularity: Early Stuart Essays in Honour of Conrad Russell* (Cambridge, 2002).

issue of church government; the later petitions (both at Hertford and Cheshire) with issues of national and local politics, albeit ones with a religious undercurrent. What had been an extension of godly politics became an expression of political opinion. The earlier petitions, as Peter Lake suggests, helped 'religion' to transmute into 'politics'; but this was a process that needed time to mature. Moreover, although the scale of the earlier campaigns was impressive it cannot, as we shall see in Chapter 3, compare with the repeated waves of petitions and addresses presented over the later Stuart period. Whereas earlier petitions were mostly county petitions, later ones came even from the smallest boroughs in the land. And in the later period they were intrinsic to electioneering in a way that they had not been previously.

The misrepresentations of political and religious difference

Key to the representative contest was claim and counter-claim about misrepresentation. Sir Willoughby Aston and others had claimed to be representative of county opinion; but were presented in a public court for acting as a conspiratorial minority. Aston was outraged and thought he had been misrepresented as well as mispresented.[51] As the son of a sequestered anglican royalist who had attended prayer-book services before 1660 and who was devoted to the established church, there was more than a grain of truth in his protestations of loyalty. Aston argued that the charges against him and his friends were 'stains upon our honour, which is dearer to us than our lives, and these stains will spread themselves upon our posterities'. Correcting a misrepresentation *in public* was thus essential for his good character. He was 'resolved to bring it into all the Courts of England' in order to make his 'vindication as publick as the aspersion was infamous and false'. Behind the concern for personal misrepresentation there lay larger political motives too. By late 1683, after the Rye House Plot, all criticism of the court was represented as seditious and factious. Part of this campaign meant depicting all critics as dissenters or blackening their characters. Misrepresentation thus fed into the formal system of representation, for it influenced the chances of re-election. The presentment, Aston said, had been made 'only to cast an aspersion upon such men as [the court] thought likely to stand for election themselves or had a considerable interest and number of voters to serve their friends'.[52]

---

[51] Cf. Edward Blundell of Liverpool, who, in 1712, moved 'to quash a presentment (or rather a mis-representation)' against a clergyman which had been 'scandalous, malicious and illegal' (*Post Boy*, No. 2683, 19–22 July 1712).
[52] Liverpool RO, 920/MD/172, diary entry for 7 Apr. 1684.

The prosecution was a contest about which voice truly represented the will of the people. Booth and Cotton's election, together with the address that was presented to them, had represented the county as critical of the court and supportive of the ardent prosecution of catholics. Yet rival addresses and grand jury presentments subsequently sought to represent the county as loyal, resolutely opposed to sedition and to protestant dissent. Indeed, counsel for the grand jury was later to claim that its members were 'the representatives of the whole county', though Aston collected evidence that the grand jury had been threatened into making the presentment.[53] Many petitions and addresses emanated from grand juries, which were both participatory and representational institutions.[54] Grand juries had long been accepted as an authoritative voice, legitimized by the substantial but middling status of their jurors and by their legal function.[55] Whig lawyer John Somers called them, in terms of their role in securing liberty, 'of most concern, next to the legislative'.[56] The grand jury could therefore claim, as Kent's in 1701 did, to be 'the representative body' of the county.[57] Legitimate platforms within the overlapping institutions of the dispersed state thus offered rival opportunities to claim to be representative of the public.

Such a struggle over representation led to greater participation in politics as each side sought to appeal to a wider public for support. Cheshire had almost 5,000 voters, ranking it among the largest electorates in the country. The struggle over representation thus involved and invoked a wide public, both as participants and as an umpire between competing claims. Politics in Cheshire was thus often popular politics at its most violent and festive. The reception in September 1682 of the duke of Mon-

---

[53] HMC 13th Report, Appendix Part v, *House of Lords MSS 1690–1*, 29; Liverpool RO, 920/MD/172, diary entry for 1 Jan. 1684; [E. Stephens], *Authority Abused by the Vindication of the Last Years Transaction and the Abuses Detected* (1690), 35. For the convention that grand juries were 'the authoritative voice of county opinion', see J. Morrill, *The Cheshire Grand Jury 1625–1659* (Leicester, 1976), 6.

[54] N. Landau, *The Justices of the Peace 1679–1760* (Berkeley, 1984), 46, argues that charges made to juries and addresses had a representative function. The grand jury itself helped to ensure a participatory, consensual, system (C. Herrup, *The Common Peace: Participation and the Criminal Law in Seventeenth-Century England* (Cambridge, 1987)); S. Roberts, 'Juries and the Middling Sort: Recruitment and Performance at Devon Quarter Sessions 1649–1670', in J. S. Cockburn and T. A. Green (eds.), *Twelve Good Men and True* (Princeton, 1988), 182, 184; P. Withington, 'Urban Political Culture in Later-Seventeenth-century England: York 1649–1688', Ph.D., Cambridge (1998), 44, 102, 112; J. Beattie, 'London Juries in the 1690s', in *Twelve Good Men and True*, 227, 234, 238, 241, 242.

[55] 16 & 17 Car. II cap. III required quarter session and assize jurors to be worth £20 p.a.

[56] J. Somers, *The Security of English-men's Lives* (1681), 19. Cf. Sir John Hawles, *The Englishman's Right* (1680).

[57] *True English Advice to the Kentish Freeholders* [1702], 2.

mouth, Charles II's illegitimate son and therefore rival to the catholic duke of York, had prompted exuberant street politics in Chester. A panicky eye-witness

saw the city as it had been in a flame. The occasion was that the duke of Monmouth had won the plate at Wallasey [in a horse race]. The bonfires got the rabble together. They broke the windows of St Peter's church to get to the bells, broke down two doors belonging to the steeple to get to the ropes and then rang the bells and among them the firebell. Then the rout got into the streets, crying a Monmouth a Monmouth and at several loyal persons' doors sang a ballad Long Live the Duke of Monmouth &c 500 of them, as I am credibly informed; while the ballad was a-singing at my door, at the end of every verse [they] threw stones and shot guns at my windows . . . God help the poor cavaliers that must live here'.[58]

A local clergyman duly 'preached against tumultuous gatherings of the people and . . . said that it looked like the beginning of the last rebellion'.[59] Both the cleric and the eye-witness account deliberately sought to represent the events as highly dangerous and like those of the 1640s—so the 'poor cavalier' and the 'last rebellion' were invoked. But was the depiction of a state on the verge of civil war justified? Booth claimed not. Certainly, he admitted, some 'piss pots were thrown out of a window' at some boys who were making a bonfire to celebrate his horse-racing victory '& thereupon ye boys threw stones & broke ye windows to ye damage of 2 shillings', but he doubted if this amounted to a riot and even 'a speciall commission of oyre & terminer . . . could make nothing of it'.[60] Booth told a grand jury about this time that he heard 'it positively affirm'd that 80 & 81 is become 40 & 41', but said he could find no grounds for the parallel.[61] Representations of the past were thus powerfully political and partisan. A 'Whig' interpretation of history, which sought to counter the Tory version of rebellion, was born.

Municipal politics: Chester

Electoral politics did not just mean Westminster politics, though it was certainly the case that local and national were intertwined. Representational struggles were fought at the municipal level, particularly after the purges of the 1680s and the manipulation of the size of the electorate that occurred as a result of partisan contests. Indeed, since elections to local

---

[58] *CSPD 1682*, 393.   [59] Ibid., 398.
[60] BL, Hargrave MSS 149, f. 75.
[61] *The Works of the Right Honourable Henry Late L[ord] Delamer* (1694), 627.

office were held annually they could often maintain party feuding. This was the case in Chester. Its history again highlights how partisanship took advantage of the representative platforms of the state; how petitioning facilitated representation at local as well as national level; and how misrepresentation was a key concern in the localities.

Shortly before the 1690 general election Chester's Tories created over 120 freemen in two months in order to bolster the number of their freeman supporters.[62] The tactic was successful and, despite an allegation that during electioneering Sir Thomas Grosvenor had spoken words against William and Mary, he and fellow Tory Richard Levinge were elected. This victory infuriated the Whigs, who sought revenge at the local level. The city had a system of mayoral election that involved rounds of voting to select two candidates; in the penultimate round the city's freemen (just short of 1,000 of whom had voted at the general election) chose two nominees, from which the aldermen then chose one. In 1691 the Whig Roger Whitley paired with Henry Booth (now Lord Delamere), and the latter was elected mayor. Booth delivered a speech, later printed, in which he lamented how the corporation's liberties had been 'ravish'd' from them by a party of men who complied with the 'wicked' demands of the court. He thus attacked the 'fullsome addresses' made when the charters had been surrendered. Their 'nauseous stuff' was 'much fitter to be offer'd to some eastern monarch or the French king than to a King of England governing by the laws of the realm'. He mentioned this not to 'keep up divisions', for he wished 'we were all of a mind', but he was sure no man could be 'hearty for this government who does not abhor such proceedings as these were'.[63] The rabid partisan thus appealed for unity by redefining his opponents as the seditious ones. In 1692 it was Whitley's turn to become mayor, an office that he held tenaciously for the following four years. Chester was thus represented at Westminster by Tories but, on the same freeman franchise, by Whigs in the mayoralty. Again, different representative elements of the state competed with each other for dominance and legitimacy. Party thus intensified the dialogue between the institutions of self-government.

This political dialogue was a contest for supremacy in which both sides sought to destroy the other, whilst at the same time disowning partisanship. Capitalizing on his new local power, Whitley thus sought support for a proposal to make annual elections of the entire common council, aimed

---

[62] *HOP II*, ii. 64; Halliday, *Dismembering the Body Politic*, 280–6.
[63] *A Collection of Speeches of the Right Honourable Henry late Earl of Warrington* (1694), 2–3.

at purging the councillors inserted under Tory dominion in 1685. With the
backing of an address signed by over 400 citizens, who claimed they
wanted the restoration of ancient rights, Whitley was able to oust over half
of the councilmen, prompting a boycott of council proceedings by Tory
aldermen which lasted throughout Whitley's mayoralty.[64] A legal challenge against Whitley's actions failed in 1694. Even so, the Whig bid for
dominance ultimately failed. Whitley shared the parliamentary representation in 1695 with Grosvenor, in what was another violent contest that
took eight lives.[65] The following autumn Whig fortunes collapsed. Whitley
did not stand—perhaps due to ill health—and his rivals secured a
favourable mayor. Mayor Peter Bennett promptly attempted to undo
Whitley's mode of annual elections. Whitley had simply presented a slate
of councillors for freemen to approve; Bennett now proposed choosing a
new, permanent, council but called the names individually. The result was
a Tory council that in July 1697 finally revoked the provision for annual
council elections. The Tories represented Chester at local and national
level for the remainder of our period.

Conflict in Cheshire in the 1680s and 1690s thus centred on a struggle
between different and legitimate representative elements of the state: parliamentary representatives, the 'people', the grand juries, the city council,
the clergy, and the press. This interaction created a dialogue that eroded
distinctions between national and local politics. And one of the key means
by which such dialogue took place was the petition or address. Addresses
allowed rival voices to be heard. And just as petitions could come from different branches of the state, so they could also be directed at different
elements of the state. The legality of Whitley's manœuvres had been questioned by petition, first to privy council and then to King's Bench, though
both were unsuccessful.[66] And the public nature of the petitions had also
involved the people as an umpire, irrespective of the stated recipient. Petitioning thus offered a highly flexible representative tool that could both

---

[64] Whitley explained to secretary of state Trenchard the severity of threats to 'ye well
affected loyall party of us' and that annual common council elections were the only remedy
to remove 'ye roote cheife cause of o[u]r oppression', which was the common council chosen
by Jeffreys in the 1680s (John Rylands Library, Manchester, Mainwaring of Peover MSS, Bundle V, No. 74, Whitley to Trenchard, 14 June 1693). He asked Trenchard to 'represent it
favourably to their Ma[jestie]s' (ibid.). John Trenchard promised he would 'represent' the
dispute in Chester in 1693 to the queen 'in such manner as may be most for your service'
(ibid., No. 73, Trenchard to Whitley, 22 June 1693).
[65] Chester RO, Earwacker MSS, CR63/2/691, Crewe to Cotton, 20 Sept 1695; CR63/2/181,
Aston to Crewe, 22 Nov. 1695; Chester RO, Assembly Books, A/B/3, ff. 54ᵛ–57ᵛ.
[66] Chester RO, Assembly Books, A/B/3, ff. 54ᵛ–57ᵛ, petition to Lords Justices, 11 Aug. 1697.

challenge and support authority. And it was a process that inevitably invoked the 'public' as a force.

How was that 'public' informed? One way was through electoral 'advice'. In 1679 Booth offered a grand jury 'some rules for the choice of members to serve in parliament'.[67] He suggested that it was necessary to be 'very cautious who we choose to represent us'.[68] He advised voters to avoid ambitious men, and prefer instead 'a man that has a good estate in the country; for though he may possibly forget us, yet he will remember himself and avoid all unnecessary charge upon the country'. Self- and public-interest were thus combined. The ideal candidate, he suggested, was also 'a moderate man, one that is not strict or rigid, neither one way nor the other, either in church or state'. Yet, ironically given the fine line between 'advice' and direction, he urged 'let your own judgment and not another man's interest or inclination, direct you in this case'. Booth was thus invoking the ideal of a rational, impartial voter and a publicly minded candidate even though he was a partisan, urging his own election.

His appeal was successful. But we know from a speech that he made to electors on 6 October 1679 that he had found it necessary to battle against misinformation that had been given to the electorate. Booth was concerned to dispel 'ye reports & stories yt some have industriously spread abroad concerning me . . . tho they are most false & malitious'.[69] He listed the fictions that had been pedalled against him. He had been reported to have said he would 'vote agt ye Court, right or wrong' but also that he was too free to grant supply, allegations which contradicted each other; that he was 'a Presbyterian & no friend to ye church', even though he was a scrupulous conformist; and when that failed to sway voters, he had been accused of being a 'most furious p[er]secutor of them who do not come to church'.[70] Clearly what he saw as misrepresentations of his views had been circulated deliberately in order to prevent his election. This was a permanent feature of electioneering, on both sides of the political divide. Fearing an election in 1704, Sir Henry Bunbury thought that Sir George

---

[67] Booth, *Works*, 646–68. The dating is inferred by references to the popish plot and a current opportunity to elect MPs (652, 657).

[68] Booth, *Works*, 651. He went on to condemn those who 'thirsted after a commonwealth'.

[69] BL, Hargrave MSS 149, ff. 62–4.

[70] For Booth's habit of commonplacing Scripture, see R. Wroe, *A Sermon at the Funeral of the . . . Earl of Warrington* (1694), 23. Whitley was also alleged to have 'forsaken the church not coming within those holy walls this 6 mo[nths]' (John Rylands Library, Mainwaring of Peover MSS, Bundle v, No. 101, undated account of events in Chester).

Warburton would be set 'aside by the influence of false reports and malitious wrongfull representations'. Bunbury saw these as gaining hold because of the public's weak capacity for judgement. He was anxious about
those who 'have not had the good fortune either by naturall abilities or
education to make a true judgment of what may conduce to their own advantage'.[71] His fears proved justified, for one man was condemned by the
Commons in March 1705 for 'misrepresenting' Bunbury's voting record to
the freeholders.[72] Misrepresentation thus raised the problem of how voters could discern the truth and see through private designs.

Discourse in Cheshire

As we have seen, petitions and addresses or electoral advice literature
yoked public discourse with political events; indeed, such discourse
was the stuff of politics. Private opinion is, of course, more difficult to
recover. But for Cheshire a unique set of overlapping diaries, prints, and
papers allows some attempt to be made. It is important to do so in order to
emphasize other key themes of later Stuart political culture: disguise, dissimulation, deception, and the apparent disparity between the private and
the public, all of which appear heightened by partisanship and the nature
of later Stuart contests. Through the diary of Roger Whitley one can
glimpse the interaction of public and private, not just in its repeated
entries about his public movements—with whom he dined or talked—
but also the ambiguous function of the diary itself. One motive for beginning it in 1684 (the year after the Rye House Plot had led to the execution
of Algernon Sydney, Lord Russell, and other Whigs) may have been to ensure that false information could not be used against him: Whitley could
prove where he was and who he met.[73] The diary may thus have been security against misrepresentation. One can see why he needed it, for Whitley
mixed with London radicals who had been arrested in 1683.[74] Early on he
recorded a conversation with Robert Yard, one of the under-secretaries of
state, in which he protested his loyalty to Charles II and requested the king

[71] John Rylands Library, Legh of Lyme MSS, Bunbury to Peter Legh, 15 Aug. 1704.
[72] *HOP II*, ii. 61–2.
[73] G. Aylmer, *The Crown's Servants: Government and Civil Service under Charles II,
1660–1685* (Oxford, 2002), 235.
[74] He mixed with John Wildman, Aaron Smith, John Hampden, Robert Molesworth,
Aaron Smith, Sir Walter Yonge, Michael Godfrey, and Sir William Cowper (Bodl. MS Eng.
hist. c.711, ff. 8, 9ᵛ, 19ᵛ, 23, 25–6, 28, 33, 75, 78).

'not to believe ill of me w[i]thout evident proof'.[75] Whitley carefully noted that he regarded Monmouth's rebellion as being 'as foolish & mad as wicked'.[76] The ostensibly 'private' diary thus may also have had a public purpose, in case he needed vindication.

The parallel concern with a public reputation for 'loyalty', evidenced by his friend Aston, also emerges in the diary when Whitley was taken to court about the embezzlement of post office moneys. The attorney-general, Sir Robert Sawyer, told him that he had been 'loyall but [was] now degenerated'.[77] Yet Whitley continued to profess his loyalty, a word that it was important to appropriate in order to claim legitimacy (even if there were competing loyalties). In 1685 he swore he would 'lay my life & fortune at his Ma[jesti]es feet' and that he had 'always bin loyall, would live & dye soe; it were not only wicked but madness to doe otherwise'.[78] Even when he heard of the massacre of protestants at Piedmont, Whitley remarked that 'preachers taught us better, yt subjects must use no weapons but prayers & tears'.[79] Yet the 'true' Whitley was hard to discern. In May 1688 he condemned any potential 'designe from Holland' as 'mad' and declared that the country was 'well pleased w[i]th ye governm[en]t, yt all partyes were at ease, enjoyed their libertyes, payd no taxes had no grievances'.[80] Yet in December that year, when Lord Derby appeared with a declaration for adhering to the prince of Orange, the protestant religion, and the laws, Whitley was a signatory.[81] Whitley's representation of his actions and beliefs is thus carefully fashioned even in his private writings, perhaps because he feared they might become public.

Of course, James's reign forced many to dissimulate or leave the king's agents none the wiser about their true intentions and views.[82] But Whitley is enigmatic in other ways. On one reading of his actions, in espousing freemen rights, he might be described as a populist. Yet entries in his

[75] Ibid., f. 4. For conversations that he may have feared were attempts to entrap him, see ibid., ff. 31, 51, 55, 69.
[76] Ibid., ff. 36, 51.
[77] Ibid., f. 9ᵛ. He had fought for the king, lost two brothers in action, and was involved in royalist conspiracies, including Booth's rising in 1659. He was rewarded after the Restoration with minor court offices and made deputy postmaster general. As an MP in the Cavalier parliament he supported the court, whilst vowing in 1673 to pursue 'a moderate middle way to keep things well betwixt King and people'. The first earl of Shaftesbury marked him 'doubly vile' but by the end of the 1670s his loyalty to the court was being strained (*HOP I*, iii. 710; Aylmer, *Crown's Servants*, 230–6).
[78] Ibid., f. 41.   [79] f. 55.   [80] Ibid., f. 91.   [81] Ibid., f. 100.
[82] In May 1688 Whitly left Sir John Crewe 'as wise as when he came' (ibid., f. 91), despite (or perhaps because of) the latter's attempts to persuade him to accept office.

commonplace book, apparently made in the 1660s, reflect a fascination with the instability of popular politics and the necessity for strong monarchical government.[83] He made copious notes out of Machiavelli, Thomasso Campanella (nicknamed the 'second Machiavel' in one translation of 1659)[84] and accounts of the French wars of religion. Whilst Whitley included the observation that 'authority should not be used to oppresse ye meaner sort of people', he also recorded that the liberty of the people 'doth not consist in a licentiousness to interrupt ye governement of their superiors & change ye governement according to their fancyes'.[85] Indeed, he noted that 'the judgments of ye people are judgements of folly; and theire affections are always indiscreete; they reject ye good for ye bad; what they say is false; wt they commend is infamous; wt they undertake, fury'.[86] He also recorded that 'the abused maxime, salus populi suprema lex (ye safety of ye people is ye supreme law) hath bin ye mother of rebellions in all ages' and, echoing comments in the diary, he noted that 'none (except madmen) will ever offer to conspire ag[ain]st a prince', even if he 'betray his trust'.[87] Whitley may have changed his mind during the 1670s; but it seems likely that while he welcomed the Revolution of 1688, he retained a paternalistic suspicion of the populace. He noted in his diary that in November 1688 there was 'great disturbance' in Chester when 'many of ye citizens fell to theire armes to preserve ye peace, ye streets full of ye rabble & very great disorder'. Whitley was one of those who helped to 'keep things quiet'.[88] His concept of popular representation seems thus a relatively narrow, patrician one.

Whitley had noted that 'in ye beginning of civill discords ye pens are (usually) more busy then ye swords'.[89] His friend Henry Booth was busy with both in 1688. Booth had been MP for Cheshire since March 1678,[90] and, having retired from court 'to cultivate the popularity he had so ancient and so good a title to', he was one of the leading English peers to take up arms in 1688.[91] At that time he had written to his tenants, inviting

[83] Bod. MS Eng. Hist. c.712.
[84] *Thomas Campanella an Italian Friar and Second Machiavel His advice* (1659).
[85] Bod. MS Eng. Hist. c.712, ff. 42, 455.
[86] Ibid., f. 641.   [87] Ibid., ff. 176, 574, 641.   [88] Ibid., f. 99.
[89] Ibid., f. 154.
[90] For his biography, see *HOP I*, i. 679–81.
[91] *A True Account of the Lord Delamere his Reception and Wellcome in Cheshire* (1689), 3. He made a schedule of bequests, dated 16 Oct. 1688, presumably in case of death in action (PRO, Prob. 11/446/178). He also appears to have written 'advice to his children' about this time, fearing that he would be 'swept away in the common calamity' that was impending (Booth, *Works*, 1).

them to join him; he also appears to have made a speech to them at which they 'huzzared and threw up their hats and promised to follow him wherever he went'.[92] That public plea was challenged in print by *The Lord Delamere's Letter to his Tenants at Warrington, in Lancashire, Answered; by One of his Lordship's Tenants*, which accused him of preparing the 'common people . . . [to] be ready for riots and insurrections, and that upon any flying story and however false report'.[93] Rather than being a leader and defender of the people, then, Booth was depicted as a dangerous demagogue. In order to counter such slurs, Booth's cultivation of the public, before and after the revolution, included making numerous speeches to grand juries. These appeared in print, either at the time, in his collected 'works' published in the year of his death in 1694, as a collection of speeches published by the veteran Whig publisher Richard Baldwin in the same year, and in the collection of *State Tracts* published during the reign of Queen Anne.[94] Booth's public discourse was thus both oral and literate, and consciously canonized. But, like Whitley's diary, the speeches are deeply manipulative and deceptive.

The collection of speeches and essays that make up Booth's *Works* were a masterpiece of self-representation. In the opening essay, for example, in which he offers advice to his children immediately prior to the Williamite invasion of 1688 (which he either foresaw or knew of in advance), Booth emerges as a man independent of faction, devoted to the public, hostile to the sycophancies necessary for advancement at court, tolerant of protestant dissent, but also a devout churchman and a champion of revolution principles. The success of this self-representation is clear when we compare it to a hostile verse portrait in which he is depicted as a rabble-rouser, 'stiff for religion, which he ne're professt . . . lewdly profane and wicked like the rest', a man who had 'learn'd to varnish wickedness with zeal'.[95] Publicly partisan politics thus created two versions of the same man and rendered the real or true character difficult to discern. Perhaps because he was adept at representing himself and his ideas in a certain language,

[92] BL, Add. MSS 41,805, ff. 232–3; *Lord Del-r's Speech* (1688).
[93] *The Lord Delamere's Letter . . . Answered*, unpaginated.
[94] *The Speech of the Right Honourable, Henry Earl of Warrington, upon his being Sworn Mayor of Chester, in Novenber* [sic] *1691* (1691); *The Speech of the Right Honourable Henry Earl of Warrington, Lord Delamere, to the Grand Jury at Chester. April 13. 1692* (1692); Booth, '*Works*; *A Collection of Speeches of the Right Honourable late Earl of Warrington* (1694); *State Tracts* (1706), ii. 195–200, 201–8, 342–8. For his charity, see R. Wroe, *A Sermon at the Funeral of the Right Honourable Henry Earl of Warrington* (1694), 24–6.
[95] A. Maynwaring, *The King of Hearts* [1690], broadside. He was called this by his sister 'because he had that interest in the peoples affections' (ESTC, MS annotation).

Booth was sensitive to the ways in which an alternative depiction, which could be called a misrepresentation by its opponents, had political importance. He thought, for example, that Machiavelli had been misrepresented as a friend to tyrants and hence disregarded; and that popery was misrepresented as a religion when it was really nothing 'but an interest, which endeavours our destruction'.[96] And he noted how ambitious high churchmen who sought to restore James could not 'for shame talk any more of their unshaken loyalty' and had therefore 'wholly laid aside that word, and now their mouths are filled with nothing but the Church'. The slogan of the church was thus, he thought, a piece of sophistry hiding self-interest: 'the name of the Church is made use of as a stalking horse to serve the designs of a self-seeking party'.[97] Indeed, he thought the words hid hypocrisy, for 'those who bawl most of the danger the church is in, have the least of religion in their lives'.[98] Booth was a pious advocate of the prosecution of vice and immorality, but saw religion as dependent on civil liberty.[99] Overall, then, he was thus engaged in a complex task of redefining key words and attempting to replace one discourse (that of a biblically inspired politics) with another (derived from the law of God, nature, reason, and the ancient constitution) that invoked the language of the public good and public interest. At a personal, political, and discursive level, then, misrepresentation was a key concern.

The controversies in Cheshire and the discourses produced by Booth and other protagonists highlight a number of key themes. First, the disputes stress the key roles played in fostering a new political culture by frequent elections and the interaction between print and electioneering. The public was thus invoked as a reading and voting umpire. Second, the rival addresses and petitions—which not only competed with each other but also with the results of elections—raise the problem of how rival opinions were represented, the legitimacy of different public voices, and how institutions and language could be used to misrepresent the will of the people. Third, the disputes focus our attention on the ways in which the public was addressed and advised, how it acquired political knowledge, and how (and if) it discerned what was true and in its own 'public' interest. Fourth, it is clear how partisan politics generated anxieties about representation at local as well as national level, and how party politics was both local and

---

[96] Booth, *Works*, 658.   [97] Ibid., 391, 398, 493–6.
[98] Ibid., 496. Cf. *An Impartial Account of the Behaviour of the Tories* (1716), 24; *HOP II*, v. 410.
[99] Booth, *Works*, 486–7.

national in its everyday implications. Fifth, Booth's works in particular show a contest between competing definitions and political languages, and an anxiety about the discrepancy between outward representation and inner design, producing nervousness about private interest and dissimulation. Sixth, the indictment of Aston and all the other forms of public representation point to the way in which words could be misapplied in order to mislead, and how politics could be conceived as a process of contested meanings and hence one in which truth was uncertain and even fictional. The problem of language and definitions, of labels and the abuse of slogans such as 'the church', will also be tackled in later chapters.

Public discourse was not only dangerous for contemporaries; it also poses problems for historians. Booth's parliamentary speeches illustrate this well. A number were published in the edition of his *Works* of 1694. Although no dates were given defining when they were delivered, the speeches in the volume clearly refer to the period 1677–81.[100] Yet the speeches published in the *Works* were only a selection of speeches recorded by Booth himself in a—previously unattributed—manuscript journal of his own contributions in the House of Commons between 1675 and 1681.[101] Or rather the speeches in the published works are *not* to be found in the manuscript diary even though they were clearly delivered on the same occasion. The *Works*, for example, includes a speech in favour of the Exclusion Bill.[102] It reads as though it refers to the first Exclusion Bill, introduced in May 1679. The manuscript journal does indeed record a speech given by Booth on 11 May in favour of exclusion; but it is nothing like the printed version.[103] The manuscript records that Booth spoke on the matter again on 6 November 1680, 4 January, and 26 March 1681, but all three texts bear little resemblance to the published speeches.[104] Either the manuscript journal omits a speech (which would be odd, given that the rationale for the volume appears to be its careful record of Booth's parliamentary rhetoric) or the printed speech was never given in the form it appears.[105]

---

[100] Ibid., 94–9, 100–6, 107–14, 115–20, 121–8, 129–32, 133–7, 138–44.

[101] BL, Hargrave MSS, 149. Booth's authorship is clear from the entries on f. 61ᵛ and f. 70 relating to his election in 1679 and 1681. The diary entries relate to the period 1675–81, but also contain some notes relating to 1682.

[102] Booth, *Works*, 94–9.

[103] BL, Hargrave MSS 149, ff. 54–54ᵛ.

[104] Ibid., ff. 64ᵛ, 67ᵛ–70.

[105] The manuscript is also evidently an attempt to place Booth at the centre of parliamentary opposition to the court. The volume begins with the speech delivered by the earl of Shaftesbury on 20 Nov. 1675, calling for the dissolution of parliament, and there are speeches by numerous MPs on the debate over the adjournment on 9 Feb. 1678; but thereafter the focus

The print might thus represent what Booth might have liked to have said, or even what he intended to have said, but did not.

Similarly, the published speeches include a seven-page diatribe on 'the corruption of the judges', presumably delivered in November 1680 when the infamous Jeffreys was under attack—an attack for which Jeffreys's part in the prosecutions in Cheshire in 1683 might be seen as sweet revenge. The manuscript journal records a speech delivered by Booth on 13 November but this and the published version overlap for just one paragraph, in which Booth complained that Jeffreys had 'a very arbitrary power'.[106] Which version is the true representation of Booth's speech? Was the public, printed, representation of Booth as a patriot concerned for large principles of justice not in tension with the manuscript, private, version's focused attack on a local political rival? Is the historian able to reconstruct Booth any more clearly than a bemused contemporary? These documents are a reminder that just as words and print misled contemporaries, we are also potential victims.

THE PUBLIC AND THE PEOPLE

> 'The people is a word that is thought to be under-
> stood; but upon better thought, it will be found im-
> possible to define it'.[107]

As these case studies suggest, during the later Stuart period the 'public' came of age. For this reason we need, as the following sections will do, to map out some of the ways in which the public was conceived. In particular, the relationship between the 'public' and the 'people' needs to be explored, not least because the concept of representation that is being examined in this book requires us to understand what or who was being represented—even if, as is the case, our conclusion is that this was ambiguous and fluid. A focus on the 'public' is also useful because it highlights how it acquired a new significance, enlarged by the five factors identified in the previous chapter. That is to say, the public acquired a larger role through frequent appeals to the public as voters and readers capable of exercising a public judgement; the development of public credit; partisan-

---

narrows almost exclusively to Booth's contributions. The journal is thus not a parliamentary diary of proceedings in the House but rather an account of Booth's part in them.

[106] BL, Hargrave MSS 149, f. 65; Booth, *Works*, 143; Grey, *Debates*, vii. 461–2.
[107] M. Brown (ed.), *Works of George Savile Marquis of Halifax* (Oxford, 1989), iii. 212.

ship that sought to speak for the public good and represent the public interest; new contexts for public discussion; and ideological struggle over the legitimate power of the public. This last point is considered in most detail here in order to tease out the range of contemporary attitudes to representing the people; but the other points will be considered at large in the following chapters. The word 'public' was not a new one, but part of an established nexus of related terms, such as 'people' and 'nation';[108] the latin tag '*vox populi*', which carried some of the connotation of a single voice of the people, had a long history.[109] Nevertheless, later Stuart linguistic creativity prompted a proliferation of new meanings around the stem 'public', such as 'public interest', 'public minded', 'public happiness', or 'public credit'. Moreover, there was an important mid-seventeenth century shift in the use of the word, from an adjective describing a condition to a noun that described an imagined generality. The word 'public', in this second sense, finally appeared in the 1696 edition of Edward Phillips's *The New World of Words*.[110] Once the concept of the public as a generality had been developed, the idea of a 'public opinion' could emerge.[111] Although the term was not commonly used until the 1730s, even in 1677 an MP could declare that 'discourse of people abroad is a great thing and not to be slighted'.[112] By Anne's reign the pressure of public opinion was intense. The public demanded explanations of state affairs. As one tract put it, 'if the populace, upon the first appearance of any state-measures, cannot penetrate into the depths of them, the prime minister must either . . . decypher his meaning, or else be threatened with some impending fate'.[113]

The linguistic and conceptual shift reflected ideological change. As ideas about popular sovereignty gained sway, so the public assumed a greater role and importance. In 1689 William Denton, for example, argued that 'publick consent' was superior to royal power, 'or to express it in

---

[108] J. Wilkins, *Essay Towards a Real Character and a Philosophical Language* (1668), 264.

[109] The full tag was 'vox populi, vox dei' (the voice of the people is the voice of God). For an uncontextualized history, see G. Boas, *Vox Populi: Essays in the History of an Idea* (Baltimore, 1969). For a discussion of earlier usage, see Phebe Jense, 'Vox Populi, or News from the Stage', *Literature and History*, 7 (1998), 1–20.

[110] G. Baldwin, 'The "Public" as a Rhetorical Community in Early Modern England', in Shepard and Withington, *Communities in Early Modern England*, ch. 11.

[111] J. A. W. Gunn, 'Public Spirit to Public Opinion', in Gunn, *Beyond Liberty and Property*; J. A. W. Gunn, 'Public Opinion', in Ball, Fair, and Hanson (eds.), *Political Innovation*, 250.

[112] A. Grey (ed.), *Debates of the House of Commons, from the Year 1667 to the Year 1694*, 10 vols. (1763), iv. 70. Interestingly this remark was made during a debate on the extent to which MPs should let public 'libels' and 'rumours' about the representativeness of the parliament influence their proceedings.

[113] *Arguments Relating to a Restraint upon the Press* (1712), 31.

another dialect, the publick power and authority of all societies is above
every individual contained in the same societies, of what quality soever,
kings or not kings'.[114] But more importantly the public had become a unified and personified abstraction with a will that could be displayed and
publicly discerned. The notion that the public had a 'will' necessitated a
means by which that will could be discerned, voiced, and represented.
Once the 'people' were identified as sovereign, and once the consent of
individuals was required to sanction what was done in the name of the
public good, the power of public judgement was sanctioned and made
important. The sovereignty of the people was, of course, contested, and
ideologically whiggish, but even Tories accepted a *de facto* need to court
and shape public choice; and both high churchmen and jacobites invoked
popular power.

   This set of notions was creative. It made elections, petitions, addresses,
and the press important means by which the public will could be discerned
as well as the means by which the public was forced to make choices and
judgements. It created a contest to claim to represent the public will and
made this contest an essential part of partisan politics. But the public was
also something that could be imposed on and deceived. As Sarah Cowper,
an acute observer of party and polemics, put it in February 1708, 'the publick is made to be cheated in many things, and some take advantage of its
disposition'.[115] The legitimacy offered by the public was thus sought and
abused by parties. And this necessitated an emphasis on the language of interest and majority. Indeed, the language of interest emerged at roughly
the same time as the new idea of a public community.[116] This is significant,
since contemporaries described electoral influence as an 'interest'. In other
words, the language of interest was linked to the language of representation and the public.

   There is a substantial literature for the sixteenth and early seventeenth
centuries pointing to something like public opinion operating as a pressure well before the Restoration.[117] Certainly by the 1640s, it is argued, the
public—in part created by publication—was a vibrant entity. This is undeniable, and following chapters will draw on this material to stress continuities over the period. Nevertheless, the later Stuart period developed the

   [114] W. Denton, *Jus Regiminis* (1689), 29. The tract employed thoroughly Lockean arguments and, like Locke's *Two Treatises*, had also 'been written several years and kept close, because the government would not bear such prints' ('Advertisement to the reader').
   [115] Herts. RO, Panshanger MSS D/EP F 32, p. 165.
   [116] See Ch. 8.   [117] Ch. 1, no. 54.

public in important ways linked to the five factors for change identified in the introduction.

First, frequent elections and an expanded electorate enlarged an already familiar idea that parliament was the voice of the public. One tract graphically described parliament as 'the throat of the publick; it is the neck that joyns the head and body'.[118] The more frequent the elections, the more strongly parliament could claim a monopoly of representation. Elections were thus said to be 'the pulse of the people and discover the sense and temper of their minds'.[119] An election was an appeal to the judgement of the public and the resulting voice reflected national choice. So frequent elections magnified the importance of public judgement. A tract of 1689 eulogized the 'divine institution of a publick judgment' and John Trenchard argued that 'it is certain that the whole people, who are the publick, are the best judges when things go ill or well with the publick'.[120] This was no inconsiderable matter when England was at war after 1689 and when the parties offered different visions of society. Never before had the character of the voting public mattered so much. Moreover, frequent elections worked to delegitimize rival public voices. The overlapping and dispersed nature of the state in early modern England had offered many such voices—grand juries, petitions and addresses, the press, the pulpit, vestries, and corporations. The later Stuart period thus witnessed an intensification of the struggle to represent the voice of the public.

Second, the development of the fiscal-military state also affected the nature of the public. Private wealth put at the disposal of the public now became not just a matter of taxation but also a matter of credit. There was now public credit, public debt, and public stock. The government was no longer merely reliant on money-lenders but on an army of private investors who thereby gained a vested interest in the public. And the buoyancy of public credit was inextricably linked to the actions of politicians and how investors reacted to them. Public credit was dependent, Defoe noted, 'upon the honour of the public administration in general and the justice of parliaments in particular'.[121] The public was thus rendered capitalistic.

---

[118] *The Popish Damnable Plot against our Religion and Liberties fairly laid Open* (1680), 30.
[119] *An Enquiry into the Inconveniences of Public and the Advantages of Private Elections. With the Method of a Ballott* (1701), 15.
[120] *A Discourse Concerning the Nature, Power and Proper Effects of the Present Conventions in Both Kingdoms called by the Prince of Orange* [1688/9], in *Collection of State Tracts* (1705), i. 219; *London Journal*, 21 Jan. 1721.
[121] *The Review*, 7 (166), 463.

Third, party raised fundamental questions about the divisibility of the public. For all its diversity, each party clung to the idea of a united public and a public good subverted by faction. The idea that the public was a single entity thus caused huge problems, for whilst invoking it contemporaries were all too aware that there were competing and different publics and interests. Whether these divergent publics were legitimate and whether the public interest prevailed, were questions with creative tensions in the later Stuart period. Many were convinced that there were conspiracies against the single public good, and the public interest was nearly always juxtaposed to a claim about a private interest. That this was usually done to denigrate private interest explains the reaction against Bernard de Mandeville's assertion in 1704 and then 1714, that private interest was beneficial to the public interest.[122] One anxiety that emerges very strongly is that the political culture was conducive to the pursuit of the private not the public. Indeed, how far this sense of a self-interest (a term first used, according to the *OED*, in 1649) can be linked to an emerging idea of the 'self' will be worth considering.[123] Party raised questions about the self—about allegiance, about personal representation, about the disparity between outward and inner appearance, about private interest against public good, about private ambition, private judgement.

Fourth, communicative developments also shaped the concept of the public. Public space was developed in the squares and assembly rooms that were becoming fashionable; but also in the new institution of the coffee-house. But development of the press ('public-ation') also changed perceptions of the public. The public as an imagined set of readers—readers connected by what they read but who might not necessarily physically meet—could develop alongside, and as part of, other similarly imagined communities of voters and party. Moreover, the nature of polemical print and the public's apparent lack of capacity to read rightly questioned the rationality of the public. Many contemporaries, even those with strong party allegiances, feared that by its nature party (or at least the rival party) led to an irrational, undiscerning, public.

Fifth, ideological conflict ensured vigorous debate about the role of the people. Ideas about popular sovereignty, a contract between king and peo-

---

[122] M. M. Goldsmith, *Private Vices, Public Benefits: Bernard Mandeville's Social and Political Thought* (Cambridge, 1985); S. G. Burtt, *Virtue Transformed: Political Argument in England, 1688–1740* (Cambridge, 1992).

[123] *OED* notes that many words with the prefix 'self-' appeared around mid-seventeenth century. The first given occurrence of 'self-interest' is 1649, 'selfhood' in 1649, 'selfishness' in 1643.

ple, the necessity of public consent, and a right of resistance (whether exercised by the public as a collective or by individuals collectively) had, of course, been raised during the 1640s and 1650s. But the Restoration had been unable to put the genie back in the bottle, and all of these issues came to the fore during the succession crisis of 1679–1681 and again after 1688, when they were called 'revolution principles'. At the core of the debate about revolution principles thus lay the problem of the public and its legitimate role. Whigs asserted that the public was sovereign and that it had both a right to judge when tyranny was perpetrated and to resist it. The Tories denied such sovereignty and often asserted a duty of passive obedience, but they implicitly asserted the right of the people to judge—indeed frequent electioneering necessitated as much.[124]

The public thus acquired a new meaning as a collective fiction and an expanded role, made more important by its involvement in frequent elections, public finance, public discourse, and revolution principles.

The people and concepts of their representation

The growing importance of the 'public' raised important, but longstanding, questions about the identity of the 'people'. 'I would fain understand what is meant by the People?' wrote one pamphleteer, 'for now every man calls himself the People; and when one man calls for one thing, and another for something directly opposite, both cry out, that if this or that be done, the People is betray'd'.[125] When Jonathan Swift attacked the ideas of the Whig newswriter John Tutchin, he observed 'this word People is so delicious in him, that I cannot tell what is included in the idea of the people. Doth he mean the rabble or the legislature?'[126] The answer was to some extent in the eye of the beholder. The 'people' were, in Edmund Morgan's phrase, fictional and mystical, and their identity had to be invented.[127]

---

[124] The Tory denunciation of the concept of the sovereignty of the people and resistance was epitomized in the decree of Oxford University, passed and printed in 1683. For a discussion see Zook, *Radical Whigs*, ch. 2. A popularized version of the Oxford Decree sought to disseminate its proscription as late as 1705, and it was reprinted in 1710 as *University Loyalty*. The House of Lords condemned it in 1710 and ordered it to be burned by the common hangman.

[125] [Earl of Roscommon], *A Letter from Scotland* (1681), 1.

[126] H. Davis (ed.), *The Prose Works of Jonathan Swift* 13 vols. (Oxford, 1939–68), ii. 99.

[127] E. Morgan, *Inventing the People. The Rise of Popular Sovereignty in England and America* (New York and London, 1988), 49, 58. For other useful discussions, see D. Underdown, *A Freeborn People: Politics and the Nation in Seventeenth-Century England* (Oxford, 1996); C. Hill, 'Liberty and Equality: Who Are the People?', in C. Hill, *Liberty against the Law* (London, 1996); and 'The Poor and the People', in his *People and Ideas in Seventeenth Century*

How, then, were they (or 'it') to be defined and represented? This was, of course, a question posed far earlier in the seventeenth century and we need to acknowledge this debt and legacy; but the later Stuart period was also influential in offering an answer.

Popular sovereignty and government based on consent and contract were ideologies that encouraged debate about representation. The form of such representation could nevertheless vary. One strand was outlined by Thomas Hobbes. For him, the people (by whom he meant all naturally equal and free men) conveyed all their authority to a representative, reserving only their natural right to self-defence. This united the multitude into one 'person', 'the great Leviathan'. This argument required Hobbes to talk about the representative 'person': when a man is 'considered as representing the words and actions of an other, then is he a feigned or artificiall person'.[128] Thus 'to personate is to Act, or represent himselfe, or an other; and he that acteth another . . . is called in diverse occasions, diversely; as a Representer, or Representative, a Lieutenant, a Vicar, an Attorney, a Procurator, an Actor and the like'. For Hobbes, the people created an authorized representative person. Indeed, 'the sovereign, in every commonwealth, is the absolute representative of all the subjects; and therefore no other can be representative of all the subjects'.[129] This sovereign representer was the arbiter of all, even to the extent of controlling opinion, 'for the actions of all men proceed from their opinions, and in the well-governing of opinions, consisteth the well governing of men's actions, in order to their peace and concord'.[130] The 'people' became subsumed within and by their representative sovereign.[131]

Yet a different version of contract theory, based on the same principle of natural equality and freedom, gave far greater power to the 'people'. Philip Hunton argued, like Hobbes, that the people 'divested themselves of all superiority' once they had contracted with a king, but the people were nev-

England (Brighton, 1986), 247–73; D. Wootton (ed.), *Divine Right and Democracy: An Anthology of Political Writing in Stuart England* (Harmondsworth, 1986); H. T. Dickinson, *The Politics of the People in Eighteenth-century Britain* (Basingstoke, 1995); C. Robbins, *The Eighteenth-century Commonwealthman* (Harvard, 1961).

[128] Hobbes, *Leviathan*, 111.   [129] Ibid., 112, 155–6.   [130] Ibid., 124.
[131] In *De Cive* Hobbes argued that a distinction should be made between 'a *people* and a *multitude*. The *people* is somewhat that is *one*, having *one will*, and to whom one action may be attributed, none of these can properly be said of a multitude. The *people* rule in all governments, for even in monarchies the *people* commands; for the *people* wills by the will of *one man* . . . in a monarchy, the subjects are the *multitude* and (however it seeme a paradox) the king is the *people*. The common sort of men, and others who little consider these truthes, do alwayes speak of a great number of men as of the people' (*De Cive: The English Version*, ed. H. Warrender (Oxford, 1983), 145, 151).

ertheless to decide when the monarch acted outside the law, since then the government was dissolved and 'the superior law of reason and conscience must be judge'.[132] This concept was more famously outlined by John Locke, in print in 1690, though his ideas were echoed and in some cases prefigured by pamphleteers.[133] The key difference between Hobbes and Locke lay in the nature of the contract. Instead of Hobbes's analogy of the representative as an actor who is put on stage to impersonate others, Locke talked the language of the attorney, whose 'trust' to act on behalf of someone is strictly limited. Whereas Hobbes thought the sovereign representative could not be restrained by covenants, since they were 'but words . . . [and] have no force to oblige', Locke thought the terms of the covenant *were* enforceable.[134] Hobbes and Locke thus held different views of the relationship between the people and the representative, and on the nature of the representative. For Locke, 'where the legislative is not always in being, and the executive is vested in a single person who has also a share in the legislative' the monarch was only 'the public person vested with the power of the law, and so is to be considered as the image, phantom or representative of the commonwealth, acted by the will of the society declared in its laws . . . But when he quits this representation, this public will, and acts by his own private will, he degrades himself, and is but a single private person.'[135] For Locke, then, the electoral system had to offer a 'fair and equal representative'.[136] When the executive attempted to corrupt the choice of representatives, 'and endeavour to set up the declared abettors of his own will for the true representatives of the people', the 'people' could decide when their 'trust' had been violated and provide 'for their safety a-new by [establishing] a new legislative'.[137] The corruption of the representative legislative exposed 'the people anew to the state of war' and the people, individually or collectively, could judge when their trust had been breached.[138] Thus in civil society individuals came together, not as Hobbes argued, as subjects to a single will, but as 'one people', or a 'community', or 'commonwealth'.[139]

---

[132] For Hunton's views, see C. McIlwain, 'A Forgotten Worthy: Philip Hunton and the Sovereignty of the King in Parliament', in his *Constitutionalism and the Changing World* (London, 1969). For the claims to popular sovereignty made in the 1640s, see J. Sanderson, *'But the People's Creatures': The Philosophical Basis of the English Civil War* (Manchester, 1989).
[133] Ashcraft, *Revolutionary Politics*; Morgan, *Inventing the People*, 109–10.
[134] Hobbes, *Leviathan*, ed. Tuck, 123 cf. 94, 99, 117, 151.
[135] Locke, 'Second Treatise', para. 151.   [136] Ibid., para. 158.
[137] Paras. 222, 225–6. Cf. G. Burnet, *An Enquiry into the Measures of Submission to the Supream Authority* (1688).
[138] Locke, 'Second Treatise', paras. 227, 230, 240–1.   [139] Ibid., 89, 96, 133, 243.

Locke was in part refuting the ideas of Robert Filmer, who had challenged the idea of popular sovereignty and with it the new concept of the
power of the people. Writing in 1648, Filmer had sought to show how impossible it was for the consent of all the people ever to be gained to agree to
an original contract between all the people of a society: 'it cannot truly be
said that ever the whole part, or the major part, or indeed any considerable
part of the whole people of any nation ever assembled to any such purpose'.[140] The concept of power being passed from the people by means of a
contract was therefore ridiculous. But it was also hypocritical, he suggested, for while our 'modern politicians . . . talk big of the people, yet they
take up and are content with a few represeners (as they call them) of the
whole people'. Rather than the representation of all, Filmer sneered, the
contract men insisted a majority 'be reckoned for the whole people'.[141]
Milton, Filmer noted, only allowed the 'sounder and better part only'; yet,
he asked, 'if the "sounder, the better, and the uprighter" part have the
power of the people, how shall we know, or who shall judge who they
be?'[142] The alternative to a concept of power rooted in the people, Filmer
argued, was power authorized by God and his natural order. Thus Filmer's
Patriarcha, not published until 1680, had as its subtitle 'The naturall power
of kings defended against the unnatural liberty of the people'. In it, Filmer
argued that scripture and reason suggested that authority was vested by
God, and nature, in fathers, and that the king was the father of his kingdom. Such an explanation of authority excluded any role for the people in
choosing their governors, sharing in government, or judging their king.
This denial of mixed forms of government, and of any popular authority,
was, he argued, the means to avoid tyranny rather than embrace it, for the
multitude was a greater tyrant than any prince. Filmer's analysis was
shared by Restoration courtiers and high church Tories.[143] In Anne's reign
high churchmen were still repeating such ideas. Joseph Trapp, for example, castigated the Whigs for making the people 'the sovereign, the representative', so that anyone who wielded power was made only 'a sort of
agents or attornies for the people'. In this model, Trapp complained, 'the
govern'd are the governours, and the governours are the governed; or
(more properly) there is no such thing as any government at all'.[144]

---

[140] Sir R. Filmer, *Patriarcha and other Writings*, ed. J. P. Sommerville (Cambridge, 1991),
140–1.
[141] Ibid., 199.   [142] Ibid., 198–9.
[143] For Tory arguments pointing out the exclusion of groups of people from representation, see Knights, *Politics and Opinion*, 244–50; Grey, *Debates*, ix. 21–3; Bodl. MS Tanner 459,
f. 6, notes by Sancroft; BL, Add. MSS 32518, f. 31, notes by North; Add. MSS 32520, f. 226ᵛ, notes
by North; Add. MSS 32518, f. 261, notes by North.
[144] [J. Trapp], *The Character and Principles of the Present Set of Whigs* (1711), 5, 7.

The ambiguity, however, of the high-church Tory position can be seen in the work of Charles Leslie, who launched an all-out assault on the ideology of popular sovereignty and representation of the people. He defied any to 'shew from scripture or any authentick record, or from any history, your MOBB original of government in the PEOPLE'. This was the prelude to Leslie's assault on representative government as outlined by Locke. Leslie argued that the doctrine that a majority could bind the minority, inherent in Locke's (and Hobbes's) theory, allowed any band of thieves to assume the name of the people of England. 'The truth of the matter is that every party calls themselves the people', he remarked. Indeed, he believed that the voice of the people was 'commonly that of the devil'. He thought 'Vox Populi Vox Dei' a safe notion only if it meant the voice of all (confident that they would never agree on anything) and attacked the Whigs' 'foolish notion of the consent of every individual'. Such attacks, Leslie crowed, forced the Whigs to modify their arguments. In August 1706 he triumphantly remarked, 'they have now quit their Milton and Lock and Sidney'.[145] He and others had certainly exposed tensions within Whig ranks between those who defined the people as they were represented in their assembly and those who held to a wider definition.[146] One Tory tract of 1707 delighted in taunting the Whigs that the logical extension of their ideas about popular sovereignty was universal suffrage, which the Whigs disowned.[147] But there was also ambiguity in Leslie's position, for not only was his print an appeal to the people but the popular support the high churchmen received, especially after 1710, softened some of their rhetoric about the people as a mob. As Hoadly pointed out during the popular but high church violence against meeting houses the followed the trial of Dr Sacheverell, Charles Leslie now discerned 'a People distinct from the Mob. And is very angry at any ones calling his good people the Mob; though he can upon other occasions always call the whole nation so'.[148] As Leslie's argument suggests, the phrase vox populi vox dei, the voice of the people is the voice of God, was highly controversial.[149]

[145] C. Leslie, *The Rehearsal*, 6–13 Jan., 13–20 Jan., 7–14 Apr., 14–21 Apr., 28 July–4 Aug., 11–18 Aug., 8–15 Sept., 15–22 Sept., 11–13 Oct., 13–20 Oct. 1705; 3 Aug. 1706; 9 Apr. 1707; 19 Apr. 1707.

[146] Dickinson, 'The Eighteenth-century Debate', 194, 204.

[147] *The True Picture of a Modern Whig Reviv'd. Set forth in a Third Dialogue between Whiglove and Double at Tom's Coffee-House in Covent Garden* (1707), 20–1.

[148] [Hoadly], *The Jacobite Hopes Reviv'd by our late Tumults and Addresses* (1710), 12.

[149] Locke's ideas were quoted and paraphrased in *Vox Populi, Vox Dei* (1709), which was almost immediately reprinted under the title *The Judgment of Whole Kingdoms*, collectively running to 12 editions by 1714. Their publisher, and perhaps editor, Thomas Harrison, was bound over for publishing *Vox Populi* (BL, Add. MSS 70421, f. 122, newsletter, 25 May 1710). The work is explored in R. Ashcraft and M. Goldsmith, 'Locke, Revolution Principles, and the

A narrow view of the people was also promoted by ancient constitutionalism. Robert Brady used historical research to prove that 'community' meant only 'a select number' and a community of citizens to be a select band of *governors*.[150] He argued that by misunderstanding such important words, parliament had placed power in the wrong hands.[151] Similarly, William Prynne used the ancient constitution to prove that the word 'citizen' used in parliamentary writs applied 'only to some select Citizens and Burgesses who are of age, discretion and ability; or to the magistrates of the City or Borough'. Citizenship did not include 'the vulgar sort or popularity, as all accord and constant usage and our laws resolve'.[152] James Harrington took yet another tack, arguing that the ancient constitution had been based on a distribution of land that no longer prevailed. The balance of wealth, formerly weighted in favour of the monarchy, nobility, and the church, had shifted in favour of the people. Harrington therefore sought to remodel the political architecture to reflect this shift towards a landowning people.[153] His sense of an economically powerful people led him to suggest the need for widespread direct participation. The representative process he envisaged reflected this, in its elaborate scheme for elections from the parish upwards, as did provisions for the rotation of office and a citizen militia. Harrington's was, quite literally, a freeholding people who were freeholding voters. Yet their participation was representative only so far as it involved the right to choose, for Harrington limited their share in the formulation of policy.[154] Harrington distinguished between,

Formation of Whig Ideology', *HJ*, 26 (1983), 773–800. For replies, see *An Appeal to thy Conscience* (first published 1643, but repr. 1710 to refute *Vox Populi*) and *The Art of Lying and Rebelling* (1713). For attacks on the notion of *vox populi* as *vox dei*, see J. Collier, *Vindiciae Juris Regii* (1689); *Some Modest Remarks* (1691); and *An Examination of Dr Sherlock's Book* (1691).

[150] Brady, *An Historical Treatise of Cities and Burghs* (1690), 21, 75–6. Cf. Sir Henry Chauncy's *The Historical Antiquities of Hertfordshire* (1700), 241–2. The interpretation of the word 'commonalty' was also disputed at Tamworth, where, in 1669, Lord Clifford argued that it must imply a narrower franchise than the inhabitants or 'the consequences thereof would somewhat resemble anarchy' (Longleat, Thynne papers, Vol. 68, ff. 39–40).

[151] Brady, *Historical Treatise*, 78–9. For James Tyrrell's critique of Brady's views, see Rudolph, *Revolution by Degrees*, 65–6, 73–9, 88–9.

[152] Prynne, *Brevia Parliamentaria Rediviva* (1662), 320, 322. Prynne also argued that 'the words Burgenses, Inhabitantes and Communitas too . . . shall in cases of election extend only to the mayor, aldermen and common council or capital burgesses and chief inhabitants or burgesses who have freeholds; not to all the burgesses, inhabitants and commonalty of them; when and where prescription and ancient custom have restrained their general and larger construction' (321).

[153] C. Hill, 'James Harrington and the People', in *Puritanism and Revolution* (1968). The idea was repeated in Henry Neville's *Plato Redivivus* (1681).

[154] Skerpan, *Rhetoric of Politics*, 227–33.

and separated, the power to offer choices and the power of making them, 'debating and resolving'. Wisdom, he thought, lay in the gentry and aristocracy but 'interest' was to be found in the body of the commonwealth, which must be represented in a council 'so constituted as can never contract any other interest than that of the whole people'.[155] Harrington's concept of representation was thus a formalized one that left 'the people' relatively little room for debate though plenty of room for participation.[156] He conceived of there being a single interest of the people, discernible through an extensive electoral process that produced an assembly in which the public interest must necessarily be apparent. 'The people, taken apart, are but so many private interests, but if you take them together they are the public interest.'[157]

To these notions we should add a concept of the people developed in relation to the state—as office-holders, freemen of corporations, or tax payers. *The Claims of the People Essayed* (1701), a country Whig tract, depicted the people not as something separate from authority but the practical constituents of it. In England, the author argued, 'almost all the executive power of the law is lodg'd in their hands. Tis hard to find a man who has not sometime been call'd to bear office in his parish or borough, or who has not served on the coroner's inquest or on some jury or homage in court-baron or court-leet if not at the Quarter Sessions or Assizes: whereby the common people of England gain a greater experience in justice than the practice of law in foreign countries will allow to that sort of people.'[158] The participatory nature of the state has recently been emphasized; but equally it was a representative one. In London, for example, the taxpayers in the wards voted for aldermen and common councilmen; and all the liverymen who voted in parliamentary elections were also freemen.[159] The idea of the people as tax-payers was closely related to that of the people as freeholders. 'Old Whig' Thomas Gordon defended the

---

[155] *The Political Works of James Harrington*, ed. J. G. A. Pocock (Cambridge, 1977), 173–4.
[156] For the influence of this concept of representation on the American colonies, see Morgan, *Inventing the People*, 128–57. For a critique of Pocock's analysis of Harrington on this point, see A. Cromartie, 'Harringtonian Virtue: Harrington, Machiavelli and the Method of the *Moment*', *HJ*, 41 (1998), 987–1009.
[157] *Works of Harrington*, 280.
[158] *Collection of State Tracts*, iii. 3–4.
[159] London's political culture is explored in H. Horwitz, 'Party in a Civic Context: London from the Exclusion Crisis to the Fall of Walpole', in Jones (ed.), *Britain in the First Age of Party*; De Krey, *A Fractured Society*; I. Doolittle, 'Walpole's City Elections Act (1725)', *EHR*, 97 (1982), 504–29. For the claim that common hall was replacing common council as the representative body, see Francis North's notes at BL Add. MSS 32520, ff. 170–6.

people's rights but added that by the people he meant 'not the idle and
indigent rabble under which name the people are often understood and
traduced, but all who have property without the privileges of nobility'.[160]
   In a religious sense, a 'godly people' excluded the ungodly.[161] This again
implied a different notion of representation, based on piety. Such a view
created two peoples, one a 'people in virtue, spirit and power . . . [the
other] the people, in grosse, being a monster, an unwieldy, rude bulk of no
use'.[162] The former could only be represented by men who were similarly
virtuous; and the latter needed no representation.[163] The people as an excluding term nevertheless went far wider. Colonists,[164] women, children,
servants, and those in receipt of alms were all included only by virtue of
their relationship with other 'people'. Women, children, and servants were
deemed to be, according to James Tyrrell, 'represented by their husband,
fathers and masters'.[165] In practice, however, women could exercise considerable influence on representative practices. For example, Margaret
Burges of Chippenham 'said Mrs Webb gave her a good waistcoat for her
husband and a dressing for herself, and promised her a bushell of wheat
and a pair of breeches for her husband to vote for Sir Basil Firebrace'. Her
husband, John, confirmed this and said that he had switched his voting intentions.[166] Here then a woman influenced a woman to change the vote of
a man.[167] But it was such inversion of the normal relationship that allowed
a genre of 'parliaments of ladies' to flourish in popular literature.[168] Other

[160]   Robbins, *Eighteenth-century Commonwealthman*, 122.
[161]   Although a 'protestant people' could also mean a select nation.
[162]   Morgan, *Inventing the People*, 75–6, citing William Sedgwick.
[163]   Richard Baxter's *The Saints' Everlasting Rest* (1649, repr. 12 times including 1688) described heaven in the form of a parliament.
[164]   For North America, see J. Oldmixon, *The British Empire in America* (1708), introduction. For Ireland, see W. King, *The State of the Protestants of Ireland* (1691), 152–3; Sir W. Petty,
The Political Anatomy of Ireland (1691), 34–46; W. Molyneux, *The Case of Ireland's Being
Bound by Act of Parliament in England* (1698); J. Cary, *A Vindication of the Parliament of
England* (1698), 104.
[165]   Tyrrell, *Patriarcha Non Monarcha* (1681), 74, 77.
[166]   *CJ*, x. 637. *Suffragium; or, The Humours of the Electors* (1702), 9, suggested that female
electoral power was very strong and that candidates 'tongue-bob'd guineas into Mary's
mouth'.
[167]   There was an allegation that at the 1693 by-election for Clitheroe one of the Whig voters, Henry Mercer, was so drunk that he could hardly stand and when the vote came two
women standing next to him managed to raise his head, and that counted as his vote (Lancs.
RO, DDFr 7/7; I am very grateful to Dr Henry French for this reference).
[168]   Besides the series written by Henry Neville in the 1640s, see also *Now or Never, or, A New
Parliament of Women Assembled* (1656); *Votes of the House of Ladies or the Parliament of
Women* (1708). The genre took advantage of the *double entendre* of 'member'.

women achieved self-representation through the press, petitions, riots, and stocks.[169] The poor could be included as voters if they were freemen who had fallen on hard times or lived in broad franchises, such as pot-walloper franchises where theoretically one only needed to have enough to light a fire under a pot the night before an election.[170] But those in receipt of poor relief were mostly excluded from franchises. This forced reliance on the fiction that parliament represented all men.[171] Andrew Marvell suggested that 'the very meanest commoner of England is represented in Parliament'.[172] Or, as Sir Humphrey Mackworth put it, the 'whole people of England are vertually present' in the Commons and it was their right to be 'truly represented'.[173]

The people could be regarded in a number of diverse ways: as the sovereign and/or as the mob, as a collective and/or as individuals, as a civil community and/or as a select few, as citizens and/or subjects, as landowners and/or as taxpayers, as a unified public and/or the many-headed rabble, as the commons and/or the Commons. Defining the people was thus part and parcel of the political contest. This brief survey has highlighted how attitudes towards the people were dependent on ideology as well as social assumptions. Patriarchalists and their critics held very different views about the role of the people and how representation worked to those who championed popular sovereignty. But partisan concepts of the people were themselves fluid and in part shaped by political expediency and context. All this made for an ambiguous situation in which the nature of the public had constantly to be worked out and was therefore contingent on the partisan struggle. The people were thus participants in a political dispute that in part turned on their own definition and powers.

This chapter has drawn attention to the important but ambivalent role played by the public, to the problems of how the voice of the public might

---

[169] Smith (ed.), *Women Writers*; Weil, *Political Passions*; McDowell, *Women of Grub Street.* For female petitioning, see A. M. McEntee, ' "The [Un]civill-sisterhood of Oranges and Lemons": Female Petitioners and Demonstrators, 1642–1653', in Holstun (ed.), *Pamphlet Wars*; P. Higgins, 'The Reactions of Women, with Special Reference to Women Petitioners', in B. Manning (ed.), *Politics, Religion and the English Civil War* (London, 1973).

[170] *HOP II*, i. 105–7.

[171] Parliament 'representeth and hath the power of the whole realm, both the head and the body; for every Englishman is intended to be there present either in person or by procuration' (G. Petyt, *Lex Parliamentaria* (1690), 19–20).

[172] *The Complete Works in Verse and Prose of Andrew Marvell*, ed. A. B. Grosart, 4 vols. (London, 1872–5), iv. 249.

[173] Mackworth, *Free Parliaments* (1704), 22, 27.

be discerned, to the dangers of misrepresentation and to the ideological debate about the powers of the people. The next two chapters explore these issues more fully, asking when and how the public was invoked, what power it had, how the structure of the state offered it more than one voice and how the public might be informed.

CHAPTER THREE

Petitions and Addresses

it is the right of the People, under apprehensions of danger, to address to your majesty.[1]

the people themselves have taken up so many new ways to express themselves, that we are obliged to take new ways also, to understand them by . . . there is a thing call'd the Sence of the nation; by which all things of this kind are determin'd and under-stood . . . and is now become the only true rule to judge by.[2]

it does now appear that those petitions and addresses published in the names of several counties and corporations were mis-representatives, and not Vox Populi; for we now abound with addresses, letters and congratulations of a different nature.[3]

THE PUBLIC DIALOGUE WITHIN THE STATE

The case studies in the previous chapter highlighted the role of petitions and addresses in articulating diverse opinions, and this chapter examines the subscriptional genres more closely. Petitions and addresses are important because they shed light on the multi-faceted nature of the public: as a unity capable of articulating its will; as judge of state affairs; but also as potentially factious, contradictory, and irrational. Often it was the latter category that appeared most obvious. This was in part because of a contest over what institution(s) might legitimately claim to represent the will of the nation, for the early modern state consisted of legitimate but overlapping and sometimes competing representative bodies: grand juries, the commission of the peace, the militia, boroughs and corporations (including livery companies and trading bodies), convocation, dioceses,

---

[1] LG, 3757 [Brackley].
[2] The Character of a Modern Addresser (1710), 1, 3.
[3] The Loyal Protestant and True Domestick Intelligence, 19. Cf. Observator in Dialogue, 1.

and parish vestries. Each of these institutions could, and did, formulate petitions or addresses. The public could thus appear multi-vocal as well as a collective entity. The series of different voices and overlapping bodies, subject to varying degrees of control by different authorities, were part of a structure that historians of the state have seen as a participatory system. Petitioning and addressing were thus important ways in which the various parts of the dispersed state—whose key institutions were local as well as national—negotiated with one another. There was thus a dialogue, sometimes a sharp debate, between these local representative institutions. A process of statement, response, counter-response, and reply formed a dialogue that could extend over many months. Petitions and addresses erode the distinction between 'local' and 'national', for the local struggles over them became national ones and the national struggles were localized. Petitions and addresses were thus key points of interface. They are important to any understanding of how power, and in particular partisan power, functioned.

The dialogue and debate generated by the campaigns helped to constitute public discourse. Paradoxically, however, the cacophony of different and differing voices, exacerbated by overt partisan rivalries, masked claims to a unity of voice. For, although each petition or address spoke for a sectional interest, each usually made claims to speak on behalf of, and hence to represent, a larger whole. To make that claim often meant recourse to the language of majorities rather than consensus. Later Stuart petitioning and addressing movements thus involved contests to claim representativeness, attempts to 'capture' public speech from minorities masquerading as majorities. Petitions were instrumental in creating a notion of a representative public opinion (with the minority castigated as factional and self-interested). Petitions and addresses thus helped to constitute the public sphere. Moreover, they helped to shape a *national political culture*. As we shall see, virtually every part of the kingdom was affected by such campaigns. Certainly the towns with the parliamentary franchise were participants, down to the smallest of the west-country pocket-boroughs, but the campaigns also extended well beyond them, to minor towns that sought to be part of the national voice. Collectively a flood of such texts might claim to represent both the local and the national will. Lancashire's address of 1713, for example, insisted that it represented 'the general, the almost unanimous voice of your people, in great contempt of a clamorous but inconsiderable faction'.[4] This claim to a national voice—significantly one that

---

[4] *LG*, 5145.

stretched to Scotland, Ireland, and the colonies—was all the more important because the texts were usually made public through print—indeed that was in part how the national voice was created. Petitions and addresses thus articulated different voices within the state, but were also key to the developing notion of a unified, national, public opinion that was then instrumental within the state.

The resulting fiction of a public voice was used for political ends because the campaigns to gather signatures of support were very often linked to electoral contests, either at local or national level. To give just one example, an aldermanic election in Norwich in 1705 was contested by Whig petitioners who claimed that the majority claimed by the Tories at the polls was a false one manufactured by artifice. The 82 signatures that were gathered gave a collective voice to a group that claimed to speak for the majority in defiance of the Tory mayor's insistence that they were a minority. And this aldermanic contest bolstered the Whig position immediately prior to their victory at the parliamentary contest that occurred later in the same year.[5] After the early 1680s (and even arguably then) virtually every significant movement of petitioning and addressing was linked in some way to the formal representative contest at the polls. Petitions and addresses thus had multiple, secondary audiences that included the participating local electorates.

The culture of petitioning and addressing formed a staple part of 'news' and opinion and the texts were recorded, collected, and debated.[6] Analysis of such material can help us to explore the nature of representation and the shift towards a representative society. First, petitions and addresses raised questions about the relationships between the represented and their representatives. As such, they raised ideological questions about the rights, and identity, of the people, and allow us to pursue these questions through the practice of politics rather than an abstract discussion of political theory. It will be argued that attempts to restrict the freedom of elected representatives by means of 'instructions' and other addresses were resisted and that, although this tug of war was by no means over by 1720, such attempted restraints on representatives were viewed with suspicion.

Second, petitions and addresses helped to *construct* identities—whether political, religious, local, or national. The genre thus helped to shape the allegiances and communities that were vital to partisan politics. Petitions and addresses forced subscribers, or even those that read them, to

---

[5] *London Post*, 14 May 1705; PRO, S.P. 34/6/8.
[6] William Holgate made copies of addresses from Saffron Walden and elsewhere in Essex during Anne's reign (Essex RO, T/A 98, common-place book, ff. 149, 151, 152, 179, 259–60).

commit themselves to a 'side' or position. Daniel Defoe described the process:

> In the procuring [of addresses] we find terrible ragings, heats, divisions, and animosities among the people: one side opposing the other with all possible fury and artifice . . . It raises and maintains factions in every town and county, keeps up the heats and propagates the party-divisions, that are already come to too great a head among us.[7]

Rival addressers created 'a civil war among neighbourhoods and societies' through 'paper-combat'.[8] The rage of party was thus, in large part, the collision of rival sets of represented allegiances and communities generated by subscriptional acts.

Third, as texts, the petitions and addresses were rhetorically crafted. The words and language chosen, and the variation in wording between texts, could all reflect, as well as construct, genres of political discourse. Some—those promoted in 1710, for example—were bold statements of ideology. Yet the petition was conventionally couched in supplicating language, humbly requesting rather than demanding the redress of grievances.[9] Violation or acceptance of such rhetorical rules might spell success or failure, but also shift or confirm prevailing paradigms.[10] It will be argued that we can discern a shift from petition to address, a genre that relied more on panegyric than supplication. This marks a shift from popular agency to acclamation. To be sure, petitions continued to be promoted to parliament, ironically in increasing numbers after 1689 as sessions became more regular and longer, in order to lobby about specific pieces of legislation.[11] But the campaigns that attracted national public attention were primarily

---

[7] [Defoe], *A New Test of the Sence* [sic] *of the Nation Being a Modest Comparison Between the Addresses to the Late King James and those to her Present Majesty* (1710), 82–3. But, in the longer run, petitions may have defused as well as created partisan tensions, by providing a means by which legitimate but sectional interests could be expressed.

[8] Ibid., 85, 88.   [9] Skerpan, *Rhetoric of Politics*, 73–4.

[10] For some of the literary importance of petitioning, see A. Patterson, *Reading Between the Lines* (1993), ch. 3, 'A Petitioning Society'.

[11] P. Gauci, *Politics of Trade*, chs. 5–6; J. Brewer, *Sinews of Power*, 231–49; R. Sweet, 'Local Identities and a National Parliament, *c.*1688–1835', in J. Hoppit (ed.), *Parliaments, Nations and Identities in Britain and Ireland 1660–1850* (Manchester, 2003); D. Coleman, 'Politics and Economics in the Age of Anne: The Case of the Anglo-French Trade Treaty of 1713', in D. Coleman and A. H. John (eds.), *Trade, Government and Economy in Pre-Industrial England* (1976); D. A. Harkness, 'The Opposition to the Eighth and Ninth Articles of the Commercial Treaty of Utrecht', *Scottish Historical Review*, 21 (1924), 219–26; G. Holmes and C. Jones, 'Trade, the Scots and the Parliamentary Crisis of 1713', *Parliamentary History*, 1 (1982), 47–77. I plan to write elsewhere about the extent of petitions to parliament.

those addressed to the crown, to give thanks for military victory, peace or war, a royal accession, or against those labelled rebels by the crown. The shift in emphasis from public petitioning for redress of grievances to frequent addresses of thanks entailed an attempt both by Whigs and Tories to appropriate the language of panegyric to their cause.[12] Indeed, one attack on the addresses thanking James II for his declaration of indulgence thought that 'all those strains of flattery among ye Romans yt Tactius setts forth with so much just scorne are modest things compared to wt this nation has produced within these 7 years'.[13] These developments promoted a 'polite' discourse. Petitioning and addressing in the later Stuart period therefore contributed to, as well as being ruled by, the polite behaviour expected in the eighteenth century. But the careful language used by petitioners and addressers also needed to be deconstructed by subscribers and readers if they were not to be deceived. By the end of the Stuart period, commentators were alarmed about the way in which addresses used language to dissimulate the real intentions of their promoters. Thus although the process of petitioning often legitimized an enlarged public sphere, the vacillations over time that petitioning and addressing appeared to show contributed to the view that the 'people' were gullible and perhaps hypocritical pawns in a power game they only partially understood.

Finally, petitions, addresses, and other forms of subscriptional activity reconciled and fused the participatory with the representational and are thus particularly interesting given the apparent rivalry of the two models of the state. Petitions and addresses were clearly participatory—their subscribers, supporters, and readers became actively engaged in the processes of governance and authority. The numbers involved, as we shall see, could be huge and penetrate down the social scale. But petitions, addresses, and

---

[12] Shippen worried that the nation seemed only 'prepared to receive panegyrick' (*Moderation Display'd* (1704), preface). Panegyric has been treated almost solely as verse rather than prose, but see O. Hardison, *The Enduring Monument: A Study of the Idea of Praise in Renaissance Theory and Practice* (1962); J. Garrison, *Dryden and the Tradition of Panegyric* (1975); A. Williams, 'Panegyric Decorum in the Reigns of William III and Anne', *JBS*, 21 (1981), 56–67; D. DeLuna, '"Modern Panegrick" and Defoe's "Dunciad"', *Studies in English Literature*, 35 (1995), 419–35; C. A. Moore, 'Whig Panegyrick Verse 1700–1760', *PMLA*, 41 (1926), 362–401; R. Horn, *Marlborough: A Survey. Panegryics, Satires and Biographical Writings 1688–1788* (1961); Smith, *Literature and Revolution*, 277–86; A. Williams, *Poetry and the Creation of a Whig Literary Culture 1680–1715* (Oxford, 2004).

[13] BL, Stowe MS 305, ff. 46ᵛ–47, 'A Letter containing some reflections on his Majestyes Declaration'. Robert Ferguson agreed: 'if anything did ever cast a dishonour upon the English nation, it hath been that loathsome flattery and slavish sycophancy, where with the addressers, both now and for some years past, have stufft their applications to the two royal brothers' (*A Representation of the Threatning Dangers* (1688), 43–8).

associations were representative as well as participatory. They represented communities and institutions—by speaking on their behalf—and did so by 'representing' the state of affairs. So, for example, in 1701 Lancaster craved leave 'to represent' the town's hatred of French support for the Pretender.[14] They could also 'represent' the past. In 1701 Dublin remembered the rebellion of 1641 and declared that it 'represents to us afresh the very many and great blessings which we enjoy'; and Durham looked back to times when 'religion, laws and liberties are represented in the extreamest danger' and hence noted the happy change under William.[15] Petitions and addresses were also concerned to act as a means for correcting *misrepresentations*. In 1713 an address from Dumfries attacked the Whigs for daring 'to misrepresent' the queen's administration and hence 'to give your People a wrong impression of the best parliament that ever represented the British nation'.[16] Shropshire's, in the same year, hoped that 'the misrepresentations of those men of factious principles and ill designs [i.e. the Whigs] will no longer find credit, even amongst their own partizans'.[17] The genre thus made representative claims in a number of different senses whilst drawing legitimacy in part from their participatory nature.

Historiographical framework: petitioning and the public sphere

Historians of the later Stuart period have not yet systematically explored this rich terrain, even though the importance of petitioning and other forms of subscriptional activity has been stressed by historians of earlier and later periods.[18] The boldest model is offered by David Zaret, who

---

[14] *LG*, 3753.   [15] *LG*, 3756.
[16] *LG*, 5116.   [17] *LG*, 5122.
[18] For the earlier petitioning movements, see A. Fletcher, *The Outbreak of the English Civil War* (1981), ch. 6; R. Ashton, *Counter-Revolution: The Second Civil War and its Origins 1646–8* (New Haven, 1994), ch. 4; K. Lindley, *Popular Politics and Religion in Civil War London* (Aldershot, 1997); J. Maltby, *Prayer Book and People in Elizabethan and Early Stuart England* (Cambridge, 1998); J. Walter, 'Confessional Politics in Pre-civil War Essex: Prayer Books, Profanations and Petitions', *HJ*, 44 (2001), 677–701; D. Zaret, 'Petitions and the "Invention" of Public Opinion in the English Revolution', *American Journal of Sociology*, 101 (1996), 1497–555; P. Lake, 'Puritans, Popularity and Petitions'; A. M. McEntee, ' "The [Un]Civill-Sisterhood of Oranges and Lemons": Female Petitioners and Demonstrators, 1642–1653', in Holstun (ed.), *Pamphlet Wars*; Higggins, 'The Reactions of Women with Special Reference to Women Petitioners' in B. Manning (ed.), *Politics, Religion and the English Civil War* (1973); R.W. Hoyle, 'Petitioning as Popular Politics in Early Sixteenth-century England', *HR*, 75 (2002), 365–89. For the later movements, see P. Fraser, 'Public Petitioning and Parliament before 1832', *History*, 46 (1961), 195–211; J. Bradley, *Popular Politics and the American Revolution in England: Petitions, the Crown and Public Opinion* (Macon, 1986); C. Tilly, *Popular Contention in Britain*

argues that the 1640s witnessed the invention of public opinion in part because of the innovative use of petitions.[19] Before 1640, he suggests, petitioning was regulated by (a) conventions which required a language of deference; (b) the invocation of local and specific grievances experienced by the petitioners; (c) avoidance of criticism of the laws or of public authority in general; (d) manuscript production; (e) a sense of immediacy rather than pre-concerted action; and (f) the legitimacy provided by corporate bodies. These conventions were, Zaret argues, broken in the 1640s. Printed petitions and counter-petitioning, created textual communities engaged in a public dialogue and thus helped to establish a communicative space with the public as umpire. Public petitioning thus 'became a device that constituted and invoked the authority of public opinion'.[20] It produced a public sphere. Innovative petitioning, Zaret suggests, also generated ideas attaching importance to representation and consent. These, in turn, stimulated a demand for constitutional change to enforce the authority of public opinion. But, Zaret also argues, contemporaries were highly reluctant to admit the innovatory nature of the uses to which they were putting petitioning; and therefore (with what he calls the 'paradox of innovation') did not invoke claims about the will of the people or coin the phrase 'public opinion'.[21]

This chapter pursues some of these themes but also suggests a changed context after the Restoration. Zaret's analysis does not extend much beyond the 1650s. But he makes a number of claims to suggest that once born the democratic public sphere continued to expand. He sees in the later seventeenth century scientific impulse and the push for a rational religion a 'growing confidence in public reason' and, by implication, progress

---

(Cambridge, Mass., 1995); L. Colley, *Britons: Forging the Nation 1707–1837* (New Haven, 1992); P. Pickering, ' "And-your-petitioners-etc": Chartists Petitioning in Popular Politics 1838–48', *EHR*, 116 (2001), 368–88. For a collection of essays ranging from the early modern to modern, see *Petitions in Social History*, ed. Lex Heerma van Voss, Special Issue 9 of the *International Review of Social History* (2001). For discussions of associations and oath-taking, see E. Vallance, 'Loyal or Rebellious? Protestant Associations in England 1584–1696', *The Seventeenth Century*, 17 (2002), 1–23; D. M. Jones, *Conscience and Allegiance in Seventeenth-century England: The Political Significance of Oaths and Engagements* (Rochester, 1999); D. Cressy, 'Binding the Nation: The Bonds of Association 1584 and 1696', in D. J. Guth and J. W. McKenna (eds.), *Tudor Rule and Revolution* (Cambridge, 1982); P. Collinson, 'The Monarchical Republic of Queen Elizabeth I', *Bulletin of the John Rylands University Library of Manchester*, 69: 2 (1987), 394–424; J. Morrill, P. Slack, and D. Woolf (eds.), *Public Duty and Private Conscience in 17th-century England: Essays Presented to G. E. Aylmer* (Oxford, 1993).

[19] D. Zaret, 'Petitions and the "Invention" of Public Opinion in the English Revolution', *American Journal of Sociology*, 101 (1996), 1497–555; Zaret, *The Origins of Democratic Culture*.
[20] Zaret, 'Petitions', 1499.   [21] Ibid., 1532–5.

towards modern rationality and democracy.[22] I see the process as less linear, and this chapter therefore maps the ebbs and flows of petitioning and addressing on national issues. It examines the fluctuations in the number of petitions and addresses produced over time to show an expanding and contracting public forum. These fluctuations will be related in part to formal restrictions (on the right to petition) but also to informal restraints (on the timing and character of petitions). But the chapter also seeks to show how, even if conventions of traditional petitioning were broken in the 1640s, the scale of these earlier campaigns was still small and relatively short-lived compared to the addressing campaigns of the later Stuart period. The latter were truly national and they did aspire to invoke claims about the will of the people. Moreover, whereas Zaret sees a growing confidence in public reason, the evidence of the later Stuart petitions and addresses—or rather the reaction to them—suggests that such confidence was shaken by the partisan view of any rival text as a misrepresentation designed to gull the people.

MAPPING THE PATTERN OF PETITIONS AND ADDRESSES
OVER TIME

The neglect of petitions and addresses in the later Stuart period is surprising given their remarkable number. As the figure below indicates, over 5,000 addresses were presented between 1679 and 1716 to the crown on public, non-legislative matters. A further 40 addresses were presented as instructions to MPs, detailing constituent views; and 500 associations, mostly in the wake of the February 1696 assassination attempt on William's life,[23] might be added to the tally of national subscriptional activity. This excludes petitions presented to parliament about specific pieces of legislation, disputed elections, and private issues, not because these are unimportant but because they deserve consideration in their own right elsewhere.[24] Indeed, they strengthen the case made here that the later Stuart period had a truly national political culture. Thus between 1697 and 1699, the leather trades presented over 150 petitions from over 100 different localities in a successful campaign to have leather duties reduced after the cessation of hostilities with France. John Brewer discerns a grow-

---

[22] Zaret, *Origins of Democratic Culture*, ch. 9, citation at 272.
[23] J. Garrett, *The Triumphs of Providence: The Assassination Plot of 1696* (Cambridge, 1980).
[24] Some mercantile petitions are considered by Gauci, *Politics of Trade*, chs. 5 and 6.

Date	Occasion	Number
Petitions		
Dec. 1679–Jan. 1680	Petitions for Parliament to sit	7
Addresses		
Spring 1680	Addresses of abhorrence of the petitions calling for parliament	8
Summer 1681	Addresses of thanks for the king's Declaration	210
Jan.–Sept. 1682	Addresses against Shaftesbury's Association	199
Aug.–Nov. 1683	Addresses of abhorrence of the Rye House Plot	323
Feb.–June 1685	Addresses of congratulations on accession of James	361
1687	Addresses of thanks for the declaration of indulgence	197
Dec. 1694–Apr. 1695	Addresses of condolences on death of Queen Mary	201
Nov. 1697–Feb. 1698	Addresses of congratulations on peace	260
Oct. 1701–Jan. 1702	Addresses against France's recognition of the pretender	344
Mar.–May 1702	Addresses of congratulation on accession of Queen Anne	400
Feb.–Aug. 1704	Addresses of clerical thanks for Queen's bounty to church	25
Aug.–Dec. 1704	Addresses of congratulation on military victories	265
May–Oct. 1706	Addresses of congratulation on military victories	303
Mar.–Oct. 1707	Addresses of congratulation on Union with Scotland	213
Mar.–July 1708	Addresses against the jacobite invasion attempt	338
July–Oct. 1708	Addresses of congratulation on military victories	98
Dec. 1708	Addresses of condolences on death of Prince Consort	10
Sept.–Dec. 1709	Addresses of congratulation on military victories	40
1710	Tory addresses about dangers to state and pressing for election	92
1710	Whig counter-addresses	15
June–Nov. 1712	Addresses of congratulation on imminent peace	291
Apr.–Sept. 1713	Addresses of congratulation on conclusion of peace	231
Sept. 1714–May 1715	Addresses of congratulations on accession of King George	443
July 1715–Aug. 1716	Addresses against rebellion and thanks for its suppression	320
		Subtotal 5,187
Associations		
Dec. 1688	Revolution	8
Mar.–Sept. 1696	After assassination attempt	430
Dec. 1714–May 1715	Against the pretender	62
		Subtotal 500
		Total 5,687

Subscriptional texts presented to the crown, 1679–1716.

ing capacity for public pressure on such matters, culminating in the 1733 anti-excise campaign.[25]

Subscriptional texts are considered here as related genres. This may seem surprising. Certainly, petitions, addresses, and associations had different forms. Petitions requested action—redress of grievance, redrafting or rejection of legislation—while addresses could appear more passive— acclaiming, congratulating, thanking, assuring the addressee of allegiance and loyalty, or abhorring something done by others. Yet, by Anne's reign, Daniel Defoe remarked: 'the address is call'd a petition and the petition an address'.[26] This interchangeability perhaps reflected the growing popularity of the address to the crown, evident from the figures given, but crucially both forms were, according to Defoe, different from 'remonstrances', which were more peremptory claims of right. Anything else became a demand, 'a force or threatning of force' and hence 'absolutely destructive of the very being and substance of government'.[27] The essential characteristic both of petitions and addresses was that both were couched (however thinly) in the language of humility and loyalty, and they bound adherents into a community.

Petitions and addresses were thus akin to another subscriptional type linked to notions of loyalty: the association. The oath inherent in most associations, and their sometimes compulsory nature, did mark them as distinct; but associations were also closely tied to addresses in other ways, not least because an association could prompt an address. The draft Bill of Association found among the papers of the first earl of Shaftesbury thus prompted a national round of addresses in 1682, and the associations of 1696 and 1714–15 were often accompanied by addresses when they were presented to William III and George I. Like petitions and addresses, the texts of associations could be formulaic but variations could also reveal a good deal about local political cultures. The purist might want to exclude them from the figures, but they will be considered in this chapter alongside petitions and addresses because they combined politics, language, and allegiance in remarkably similar ways, and all turned on a nexus of ideas about loyalty, the public, and negotiation with authority.

The sheer scale of the later Stuart campaigns, compared to those of the mid-seventeenth and later eighteenth centuries, is impressive. The petitions promoted between December 1641 and August 1642 came from 38 of

---

[25] Brewer, *Sinews of Power*, 233, 236, fig. 8.1.

[26] *Two Great Questions Considered. I. What is the Obligation of Parliaments to the Addresses or Petitions of the People* (1707), 3.

[27] Ibid., 6.

the 40 counties but only a handful of towns.[28] Zaret has estimated there were about 500 public petitions printed between 1640 and 1660.[29] In the later eighteenth century the Wilkite Middlesex election affair provoked petitions from just 18 counties and 20 boroughs in 1768; the drive for economic reform in 1780 was supported by petitions from 26 counties and 11 boroughs; and the 1775–8 campaign against the war rallied 11 counties and 47 boroughs in England. Later Stuart campaigns, by contrast, not only regularly involved the majority of constituencies but, in terms of numbers of signatories, also matched or outdid their Hanoverian counterparts. The later eighteenth-century movements attracted between a fifth and a quarter of the total electorate, with between 50,000 and 60,000 signatures. Calculating the number of signatories to the later Stuart movements is more difficult, since the evidence is patchy, but single petitions and addresses could attract huge numbers. Petitioning in the winter of 1679–80, for example, found support from at least 16,000 Londoners and a further 50,000 signatures from the provinces. The overall total for the 1681 addresses, from the sketchy evidence we have, must have amounted to well over 40,000 signatures.[30] In 1696 the numbers who signed the association rolls have so far been too numerous to count but certainly run into hundreds of thousands. It may be true that as the frequency of addressing increased over the period fewer names were gathered; but on any reckoning the campaigns were national in scope and mobilized large numbers. Yet, because they have been uncharted, it is first necessary to map and explain the pattern of petitioning and addressing after 1660. This highlights their political importance.

THE NATURE OF THE CAMPAIGNS

The Restoration was in part ushered in with the help of a petitioning campaign.[31] On 5 October 1659 the army presented a petition and parliament's response provoked a coup, for six days later parliament voted that while

[28] Fletcher, *Outbreak*, 192.
[29] Zaret, 'Petitions', 1507. The number of petitions produced in this period is the subject of ongoing research, and may well represent a considerable under-estimate. Even so, the figure for the later Stuart period is likely to remain considerably higher because of the fashion of addressing the crown and the increase in economic legislation promoted in parliament.
[30] M. Knights, 'London's "Monster" Petition of 1680', *HJ*, 36 (1993), 39–67; Knights, *Politics and Opinion*, ch. 8.
[31] Between Dec. 1659 and June 1660, 29 petitions and addresses were presented for a free parliament and a restoration of the monarchy.

soldiers 'as freemen' had a right to petition, they had to do so in a 'peaceable' manner and 'submit their desires to the parliament and acquiesce in the judgment thereof'. The following day parliament voted to cashier the officers involved. The army response was immediate. On 13 October MPs were expelled. But agitation against the army motivated apprentices in London to call for a return to 'the condition and state of affairs where we begun'. In November signatures were duly gathered to a petition to the City's common council which demanded either new elections or the restoration of those members of the Long Parliament who had been purged. Despite a prohibition by the Committee of Safety, the petition was presented amidst chaotic and bloody street scenes in which soldiers were attacked. The apprentices therefore presented another petition to common council complaining of the murderous soldiers who had tried to prevent them from peaceably petitioning. By 12 December some 23,500 hands were said to have been subscribed to an engagement of citizens who bound themselves to defend, with force if necessary, the rights and liberties of the City.[32] This unrest prompted the Rump to resume power on 26 December. Petitions in favour of the Rump came from the London watermen and from 'thousands of . . . lovers of the good old cause'.[33]

But rival petitions were soon promoted to press for a free parliament.[34] Stationed at Morpeth at the beginning of January, Monck received a 'declaration' of the City of London demanding to have representation in parliament.[35] As he marched south, Monck received eight county declarations for a free parliament, five of which were presented to him as petitions.[36] Most of these combined the issue of representation and taxation. The Oxfordshire address, for example, argued that it was the privilege of a freeborn people to be represented in parliament, that the Rump violated this principle, and that therefore 'no taxes may be put upon us without our free consent in Parliament'.[37] This and the Leicestershire address argued that 'whereas every free-born person of England is supposed to be present in parliament, by the knights and burgesses of the place where he liveth, and thereby is presumed to give his consent in all things that passe in Parlia-

---

[32] *The Engagement and Remonstrance of the City of London, Subscribed by 23500 Hands* (1659).

[33] *CJ*, vii. 836.   [34] Harris, *London Crowds*, 42–9.

[35] T. Gumble, *The Life of General Monck* (1671), 200.

[36] R. Hutton, *The Restoration: A Political and Religious History of England and Wales, 1658–1667* (Oxford, 1985), 90. Gumble, *Life*, 223–4; *CSPD 1659–60*, 332, 335, 340, 341, 344, 347, 356, 361; BL 669. f. 23. (Nos. 68, 55, 51, 48, 42, 35, 31).

[37] *The Diurnal of Thomas Rugg 1659–1661* ed. W. L. Sachse, Camden Society, 3rd ser., 91, (1961), 40–1.

ment', many counties lacked any representation whatsoever.[38] *A Caveat for my Countreymen in General* (1660) accused the Rump of acting more like 'absolute lords than representatives and trustees of the people'.[39] Petitions and addresses alone are unlikely to have caused Monck to declare for the readmission of the secluded MPs; but they must have played a considerable part in exerting the pressure of public opinion on him. Certainly in his speech to parliament on 6 February 1660, the general mentioned the addresses 'with numerous subscriptions' that he had received on his way south.[40]

One address, ironically, also summed up the sense that during the civil wars and interregnum, petitions and addresses had been highly misleading about the state of opinion. In May the 'loyal-hearted' of Kent and Canterbury issued a vindication of themselves, which they felt to be necessary because

many several petitions, remonstrances, declarations and other like addresses, framed or rather forged by a few disloyal, factious and seditious time-servers (persons for the most part as inconsiderable for their estates as numbers) have with much impudence in the authors and injury to us, without our privity, and to our great and just regret, been fathered, foisted, and obtruded upon us and presented and exposed to the open view and all the world in print, under our name and stamp, as carrying the title of this counties, others of this cities addresses.

Yet such addresses, it was now claimed, and in particular one calling for justice against Charles I, had been

so far from being the acts or from speaking the sense and desires of our more loyal county and city that as they were hatch'd and bred in corners, and in sly and clandestine way carried on, without either counties or cities privity . . . scarce one hundred, we may truly say of a thousand, of the numerous inhabitants of either putting his hand or giving his consent to them.[41]

Petitions, then, were a means of correcting misrepresentations offered by earlier petitions.

Perhaps because the genre was discredited, or because of the memory of the 1640s and 1650s, or (as we shall see) because of legislative restrictions, the years after 1660 witnessed a sharp decline in public petitioning. In 1667 and again in 1676 there were rumours and hopes that the City of London

---

[38]   *The Humble Desires of the Knights, Gentlemen, Ministers, Freeholders and Inhabitants of the County and Burrough of Leicester* (1659).

[39]   *A Caveat*, broadside.   [40]   *Parl. Hist.*, iii. 1575.

[41]   *A Declaration and Vindication of the Loyal-hearted Nobility, Gentry and others of the County of Kent and City of Canterbury that they had no Hand in the Murder of our King* (1660), broadside.

might petition to request a parliamentary session, but these came to nothing.[42] It was not until 1679 that petitioning re-emerged as a major factor in the political process.[43] A campaign of mass petitions in the winter of 1679–80 pressed the king to allow parliament to sit on 26 January 1680, the date to which it had been prorogued. One massive petition from London and six provincial petitions were presented; but these provoked, in the spring of 1680, a set of 'addresses of abhorrence', castigating the petitions, and these were printed in the officially sponsored periodical, the *London Gazette*. Although few in number the 'abhorrences' in turn provoked reaction, first from a London grand jury, which in July 1680 attempted to couple its petition for parliament to sit with an indictment against the duke of York for popery, and then more successfully at a London shrieval election. But in 1681 the initiative again passed back to those loyal to the court. Although 16 peers petitioned the king to hold parliament at Westminster rather than at Oxford and the 1681 elections saw 23 addresses presented to MPs at their elections recommending how they should act in parliament, the loyalist backlash was evident in counter-addresses. At least 9 of these were presented at the time of the elections; but it was in the summer of 1681 that the counter-flow became most obvious. In response to a royal declaration, justifying the king's policy of dissolving the last two parliaments, a total of 210 addresses of thanks were presented to the king. These attracted mass subscriptions and the addresses were collected and printed in a two-part tract, *Vox Angliae*, as well as being published in the *London Gazette*. The following year there was another series of almost 200 addresses abhorring the Bill of Association which had been found among Shaftesbury's papers, and in 1683 a further round of 323 loyal addresses followed the discovery of the Rye House Plot. The death of Charles II in February 1685 and subsequent accession of James II offered another pretext for 361 laudatory loyal addresses.[44] The so-called Tory reaction thus used addressing as one of its principal tools to reflect and manipulate public opinion.

Having apparently benefited from the loyalist addresses, it was natural that James should have looked to addresses to thank him for issuing a declaration of indulgence for catholics and nonconformists in April 1687.

[42]   P. Seaward, *The Cavalier Parliament and the Reconstruction of the Old Regime, 1661–1667* (Cambridge, 1989), 307; K. H. D. Haley, *The First Earl of Shaftesbury* (Oxford, 1968), 409.
[43]   M. Knights, 'London Petitions and Parliamentary Politics in 1679', *Parliamentary History*, 12 (1993), 29–46.
[44]   D. N. Marshall, 'Protestant Dissent in England in the Reign of James II', Ph. D., Hull (1976), 110, citing *LG*, 2007–27; Luttrell, i. 329, 331, 332–9, 340, 342–4.

Such addresses were again printed in the *Gazette* for the best part of a year, 197 in all, encouraged by the progresses throughout the country made by the king and William Penn. But the limits of the address as a political tool were also exposed. Very few came unsolicited or without remodelling of corporations or livery companies, making them questionable representations of public opinion. This point was driven home when a single petition from seven bishops in 1688, against reading the declaration of indulgence, aroused more public fervour than all the pro-indulgence addresses put together. Indeed the bishops' petition brought the king's administration to its knees after James decided to prosecute for seditious libel.

The 1690s saw relatively few national petitions or addresses. Only in late 1694 did the death of the queen reawaken a nationwide desire to address the court, with some 200 condolences offered to the king, and even then the texts were highly formulaic. For much of the early 1690s, therefore, petitions and addresses were not popular. The later 1690s, however, witnessed some changes to this pattern, though addressing remained only an occasional feature of the political landscape. The attempted assassination of William in February 1696 provided the ideal context for the reanimation of a national subscriptional community. Throughout the country signatories to associations swore allegiance to William as 'rightful and lawful' king and promised revenge. Clearly modelled on the Elizabethan Association Bond of 1584, the associations invoked a much larger political nation than had been evident in the late sixteenth century, with hundreds of thousands flocking to sign their names or make their marks.[45] Northamptonshire's was signed by 14,000 freeholders, Hertfordshire's by 9,000, Yorkshire's by 25,000, Leicestershire's by 8,500, Lancashire's by 40,000, Buckinghamshire's by over 20,000, and Suffolk's by a massive 70,000 subscribers. Warwick's claimed to come from all the borough's male inhabitants over the age of 16 'except two papists and two quakers'.[46] The figures given by 30 of them suggested that 366,800 men had signed. Since there were 430 associations in all, and London was not one of the 30 that tallied its numbers, the actual total must have been really gargantuan. Each association was duly sent up, accompanied by an address of loyalty to the king. Yet the vast effort involved in gathering names did not immediately lead to a revival of petitioning and addressing. Although 260 addresses were promoted in the wake of the successful conclusion of the Peace of Ryswick in 1697, the movement was a relatively lacklustre one.

---

[45] Cressy, 'Binding the Nation'.
[46] Oldmixon, *History of Addresses*, ii. 199.

It was only in the last two years of William's reign and especially during Anne's reign that nationwide petitioning and addressing returned as part of the habitual mode of politics. The re-animating factor again appears to have been the threat from France. In the spring of 1701 freeholders in Kent urged a grand jury to 'consider of making some application to the Parliament, to acquaint them of the apprehensions of the people' about the French. The Tory-dominated Commons rejected the petition, provoking what became known as the 'Legion Memorial', a petition claiming to represent the grievances of 200,000 'good People of England'.[47]

Legion outlined the nation's grievances. These focused on the imprisonment of the five Kent petitioners and included a sharp reminder to MPs that 'the freeholders of England are your superiors'; but the memorial also reinforced the petitioners' request for war against France. Legion's demands were 'deliver'd by the very person who wrote it [allegedly Daniel Defoe], guarded with about sixteen gentlemen of quality, who if any notice had been taken of him were ready to have carried him off by force'.[48] The Kent petition and the Legion memorial were probably designed, as one tract claimed, as 'landmarks for the rest of the counties to steer by, or rather as beacons set on fire on purpose to alarum and set the whole kingdom in a flame, and to that end they were both printed in a public news paper'.[49] Certainly petitioning campaigns were launched in London, Warwickshire, Yorkshire, and Worcestershire 'after the example of Kent, that is to say they are getting subscriptions of hands to them and ye punishment of the Kentish gentlemen does not at all frighten them'.[50] It would appear that Yorkshire did actually send a petition, together with Buckinghamshire, Bedfordshire, and Hampshire 'but they all met with ill success'.[51] Petitioning had been reborn but its pulse was not strong.

Addresses, on the other hand, flourished. Louis XIV's recognition of the Stuart James III on the death of his father in September 1701 provoked 344 addresses. At the same time 17 instructions were presented from constituents to MPs and were collected in *The Electors' Right Asserted* (1701). The death of King William on 8 March 1702, and the queen's subsequent speech to parliament in which she said she was 'very glad to find in your addresses so unanimous a concurrence' in the resolution to reduce

---

[47] *Mr. S-r. The enclosed memorial you are charg'd with, in the behalf of many thousands of the good people of England* (1701), henceforth the Legion Memorial.

[48] Defoe, *The History of the Kentish Petition* (1701), 14.

[49] *A Letter to a Modern Dissenting Whig* (1701), 22.

[50] PRO Ireland, Wyche MSS 1/222, Francis Annersley to Sir Cyril Wyche, 15 May 1701.

[51] *The Several Proceedings and Resolutions of the House of Commons* (1701), postscript.

the exorbitant power of France, inevitably sparked a new shower of addresses;[52] 400 addresses were presented between March and July 1702 and again printed in a specially expanded *Gazette*. The addresses congratulated the queen on her accession and offered condolences on the death of her brother-in-law, but rapidly evolved into a more explicit attack on the claims of the Pretender and France's threat to the balance of Europe. They also echoed phrases in the queen's accession speech to parliament in which she had declared her 'heart to be entirely English' and that she would work for 'the happiness and prosperity of England'.[53]

As this campaign suggests, it was the war and the threat from France to English liberties, succession, and religion, and the partisan feelings these issues aroused, that provided the context for the rash of addressing in Anne's reign. Following the victory at Blenheim in 1704, 265 addresses flowed in.[54] A proclamation on 21 May 1706 for a day of thanksgiving for the duke of Marlborough's victory at Ramillies signalled another round of congratulatory addressing. From then until just into the new year, 303 addresses were presented. Success of a more political kind, though still linked to the security of the protestant succession, came with the conclusion of the Union with Scotland in March 1707; 213 addresses congratulating the queen on surmounting difficulties which had defeated all her predecessors were presented. They filled the pages of the *Gazette* throughout the summer up to the sitting of parliament in October. The Scottish reaction had nevertheless been markedly different. In late 1706 anti-Union addresses had been presented to the still independent parliament in Edinburgh. These had come from Tories but also from presbyterians who disliked unification with a parliament that still contained bishops; 15 of the 33 shires and 21 of the 67 royal burghs in Scotland petitioned against the Union; not a single petition was received in its favour.[55] Yet both Scottish and English addresses flowed shortly after, for on 6 March 1708 the queen announced that France intended to invade in order to support the pretensions of the Pretender. This prompted another round of 338 addresses assuring the queen of the justness of her own title and promising the subscribers' lives and fortunes in her defence. The capture of Tournay and the subsequent victory over the French at Mons provided another pretext for addressing

[52] *LG*, 3791.   [53] Ibid.
[54] These overshadowed a movement to thank the queen for her generosity in making over the revenue from first fruit and tenths to the support of impoverished clerics. At least 25 such clerical addresses were made.
[55] J. Young, 'The Scottish Parliament and National Identity from the Union of the Crowns to the Union of Parliaments 1603–1707', in D. Brown, R. Finlay, and M. Lynch (eds.), *Image and Identity: The Making and Re-making of Scotland through the Ages* (Edinburgh, 1998), 127.

in the autumn of 1709. But the campaign flagged, reflecting the bad economic conditions and war weariness and a paltry 40 addresses were
squeezed out of the boroughs, often by members of the administration.

Indeed, a change of public mood was shaped by the trial in early 1710 of
the high-church Dr Sacheverell for an anti-revolution sermon. In the later
spring and summer a Tory addressing campaign was waged in order to refute the Whig ideology of resistance, to brand the Whigs as atheists and republicans, and hence to prepare the public for the general election; 92
addresses therefore promised to elect MPs who would be loyal to the
church and monarchical principles. These provoked 15 Whig counter-
addresses but also a great deal of polemical controversy. Perhaps having
witnessed the success of the 1710 campaign, the Tories continued to use addressing as a political weapon. The summer of 1712 saw a further flood of
291 addresses in the wake of the queen's announcement to parliament that
peace negotiations were at an advanced stage. The tenor of the addresses
was overwhelmingly loyal and caught the tide of euphoria at the prospect
of an end to what they called a 'long and tedious' war. So when peace was
finally announced in April 1713 another 231 addresses offered thanks and
took the occasion to suggest that anyone who opposed the peace negotiations (as the Whigs had done) was unpatriotic, self-interested, blood-
thirsty, and conspiratorial. When Anne died, however, on 1 August 1714, the
addresses reflected a turning, Whig tide. Over the next ten months 443 addresses congratulated King George on his succession and rejected the Pretender; and jacobite rioting and rebellion in the summer of 1715 prompted
another 320 addresses. These may in part have been due to a proclamation
in July that condemned the 'open rebellion'. But as the crisis deepened towards the end of 1715, worried Whigs returned to the old idea of associating, and 62 of these were presented to the king in the spring of 1715. The
Georgian succession crisis was, therefore, fought out through addresses
and associations as well as militarily.

This account of the pattern of petitions and addresses in the period reveals that the communicative public sphere (at least in so far as it was generated by petitioning and addressing) was subject to contraction as well as
expansion in the years after the outbreak of the civil war. In other words, if
the 1640s provide an 'origin' for democratic politics, as Zaret claims, the
public space created was an uncertain one that could be eroded, reshaped,
and manipulated. It is clear that for much of the Restoration period the
public sphere created by petitioning and addresses had shrunk; that it expanded after the succession crisis but diminished again in the 1690s, before
being revitalized in the last years of William's reign; and that for much of

Anne's reign it remained vibrant. Yet this survey of the pattern of petitioning tells us only about the broad contours of the campaigns. It reveals very little about *why* the public sphere created by petitioning and addressing contracted and expanded. We need, therefore, to turn to the pressures for and against, together with the limits of, such activity.

ESTABLISHING THE RIGHT TO PETITION AND ADDRESS

This section seeks to show how the right to petition the monarch was established by the Bill of Rights and how the right to petition parliament or the monarch was, by the early eighteenth century, tacitly recognized. As a result of this legitimacy and availability, petitions and addresses were exploited for partisan purposes and became a representative tool in party struggles. But they also challenged parliament's claim to representation and after 1701 a vigorous debate occurred over the extent to which petitioning communities had power over MPs. Between 1701 and 1702 it was the Tories who rejected the representative claims of petitioners and addressers; but in 1706 (over Union with Scotland) and again in 1710 (against Tory addresses aiming at the dissolution of a Whig parliament) it was the Whigs' turn. Thus by the end of Anne's reign both parties had argued hard in favour of the supremacy of parliamentary representation. One might see this as the temporary conclusion to an argument begun by the critique offered by the Levellers (another petitioning community) in the 1640s.

The small and sporadic petitioning movements of most of Charles II's reign in part reflected a desire to break with the type of politics that had characterized 1640–60, and any attempt to orchestrate mass petitions thereafter were always seen as seditious. One of the first pieces of legislation enacted by the new regime was the Act against Tumultuous Disorders Upon Pretence of Preparing or Presenting Public Petitions or other Addresses to his Majesty or the Parliament.[56] The preamble suggested that 'tumultuous and other disorderly soliciting and procuring of hands by private persons to petitions, complaints, remonstrances and declarations and other addresses to the king' or parliament had been made use of for factious ends and had 'been a great meanes of the late unhappy wars confusions and calamities in this nation'. The act forbade the collection of more than twenty hands to any petition unless its content had first been approved by three or more JPs or by 'the major part' of a grand jury. A

---

[56] 13 Car. II c.5.

maximum of ten could present a petition. The re-imposition of press licensing also curtailed the publication of petitions. Legislation thus effectively forestalled any new mass petitioning campaign, though it did not entirely eradicate the possibility that corporate bodies might press petitions on the monarch on matters of national policy.

The succession crisis of 1679–81 witnessed a heated debate about the right to petition after a proclamation was issued on 12 December 1679 against tumultuous petitioning. The proclamation attacked the attempt to gather mass subscriptions as tending 'to raise sedition and rebellion' and warned subjects 'not to agitate or promote any such subscriptions, nor in any wise join in any petition of that manner to be preferred to his Majesty, upon peril of the utmost rigour of the law'. Invoking royal prerogative powers as they had been asserted in the reign of James I, the proclamation claimed that gathering 'the hands or subscriptions of multitudes' was 'contrary to the common and known laws of this land, for that it tends to promote discontents amongst the people and to raise seditions and rebellion'.[57] But when parliament resumed sitting the following autumn, the Commons reasserted the subjects' right to petition. On 27 October 1680 the House voted that to represent petitioning as seditious was to betray the liberties of the subject, subvert the constitution, and introduce arbitrary government. Impeachment proceedings were prepared against lord chief justice North for having prepared the 1679 proclamation and against others for their opposition to petitioning. Hoping to shelter under the protection of the Commons, the City of London provocatively resolved on 13 January 1681 on a petition that attacked the king's recent prorogation of parliament. Yet again this act of defiance brought down governmental anger, for the petition provided one of the grounds on which successful legal proceedings were launched in 1682 against the London charter. The crown alleged that the petition constituted a malicious libel. Since the judges included two men who had been victims of the Commons' campaign against 'abhorrers', Withens and Jones, an outcome against the City was never seriously in doubt.

The right to petition for the redress of grievances was again asserted in 1688, from an unlikely quarter. Seven bishops outlined in a petition to the king the reasons why they refused to read the declaration of indulgence in church, as the order of April 1688 had required. The petition was printed without the permission of the king and it was this act of publication, as much as the rebuke the bishops gave the king, that prompted the charge of

---

[57] *A Proclamation against Tumultuous Petitions*, 12 Dec. 1679.

seditious libel. Yet curiously the crown prosecution was not coherent on whether the petition constituted such a crime. Solicitor-general Williams alleged that the bishops had no right to petition outside parliament though the lord chief justice remarked that they might have such a right but should not have petitioned in a 'reflective way'. Judge Alibone concluded 'that every man may petition the government or the king in a matter that relates to his own private interest, but [not] to meddle with a matter that relates to the government . . . if every man shall come and interpose his advice, I think there can never be an end of advising the government.'[58] The acquittal of the bishops did little to clarify matters, so it was left to the Declaration (and subsequent Bill) of Rights to include provision safeguarding the right to petition the king.[59]

Although the Bill of Rights had settled the right to petition the king, it did not explicitly safeguard the right to petition parliament. This right became contested in 1701 in the wake of a petition from Kent urging MPs 'to have regard to the voice of the people; that our religion and safety may be effectually provided for; that the loyal addresses of this House may be turned into bills of supply; and that his Majesty may be enabled powerfully to assist his allies before it is too late'.[60] The petition was taken to the House by Sir Thomas Hales, who nevertheless betrayed its promoters by tipping off the hostile Tory leaders. Knowledge of the petition produced lengthy condemnatory speeches and Sir Edward Seymour was so incensed that he recommended that Kent be double-taxed and that the estates of those who had presented it should be confiscated and put towards the war effort. Undeterred, the petitioners allegedly sent a message that 'it is our right to petition' and that they had said 'nothing offensive'. After a five-hour debate the Commons voted that the petition was 'scandalous, insolent and seditious, tending to destroy the constitution of parliament, and to subvert the established government of this realm' and ordered the petitioners into custody.[61] This sparked a heated controversy over the right to petition parliament, a debate that rapidly evolved into an argument about popular sovereignty and the proper relationship between the people and their representatives.

---

[58] J. P. Kenyon (ed.), *The Stuart Constitution 1603–88* (Cambridge, 1969), 442–6.
[59] L. G. Schwoerer, *The Declaration of Rights* (Baltimore, 1981), 283.
[60] *CJ*, xiii. 518.
[61] *History of the Kentish Petition*, 5; *The Parliamentary Diary of Sir Richard Cocks*, ed. D. W. Hayton (Oxford, 1996), 114; *CJ*, xiii. 518; [J. Somers], *Jura Populi Anglicani; or, The Subjects Right of Petitioning* (1701) in *Collection of State Tracts*, iii. 257–89.

The 'Legion Memorial', written to support the Kentish petitioners, boldly claimed to come to MPs 'from [their] masters (for such are the People who chose [them])' and warned that

tho there are no stated proceedings to bring you to your duty, yet the great law of reason says, and all nations allow, that whatever power is above the law is burthensome and tyrannical; and may be reduced by extrajudicial methods: you are not above the people's resentments; they that made you members may reduce you to the same rank from whence they chose you; and may give you a taste of their abused kindness in terms you may not be pleas'd with.[62]

Thus

it is the undoubted right of the people of England, in case their representatives in parliament do not proceed according to their duty, and the people's interest, to inform them of their dislike, disown their actions and to direct them to such things as they think fit, either by petition, address, proposal, memorial or any other peaceable way.[63]

Moreover if parliament did betray the trust imposed on them, the tract claimed, it was 'the undoubted right of the people of England to call them to account for the same, and by convention, assembly or force may proceed against them as traitors and betrayers of the country'.[64]

Legion's assertion of the right to petition provoked an important pamphlet exchange about the supremacy of the people over their representatives. *The History of the Kentish Petition* agreed that even if the petition had come only from 'the meanest and most inconsiderable person in England and that singly by himself, provided he were a freeholder of England, he had a legal right to speak his mind'.[65] But the most important of the tracts, *Jura Populi Anglicani*, probably written by Whig grandee John Somers, defended the right to petition in ideological terms.[66] Like the *Legion Memorial*, the tract suggested the danger of a tyrannical Commons but then went on to justify the people's right of petitioning by sketching an account of the rise of government. Men, it argued in Lockean terms, gave up their right to secure themselves 'for the preservation of their property, which is the end of government'.[67] The people therefore had a natural right to petition, which was preserved in civil society. The tract justified petitioning by a long rehearsal of the campaigns of 1679–81 and invoked Algernon Sidney's

[62] *Legion Memorial*, 1.   [63] Ibid., 3.   [64] Ibid., 4.
[65] *History of the Kentish Petition*, 20–1.
[66] *The Old and Modern Whig Truly Represented* (1702), 55 nevertheless implies the author was Toland.
[67] Somers, *Jura Populi*, 30.

We are Many.

The Effigies of the Legion (1701) shows a hydra trampling on the church and monarchy. A Tory tract, *England's Enemies Expos'd* (1701), glossed the Legion of Luke 8: 30 as a devil who tried to 'misrepresent actions and be a false accuser'. [Reproduced courtesy of the Houghton Library, Harvard University.]

Discourses to argue that, although MPs represented the nation rather than the constituency that elected them, the people did not delegate power to their representatives 'for them to do whatever they please'. Rather MPs were sent with a trust 'which if they should manifestly betray, the People, in whom the power is more perfectly and fully than in their delegates, must have a right to help and preserve themselves'.[68] In this sense the right to petition was a natural right which was inalienable from a sovereign people.

The Tories sought to rubbish these claims, dismissing the Kent petition as merely a party thing, pre-concerted in London by the Whig lords, who

[68] Ibid., 51.

sought their own interest.[69] But in order to attack the Whigs, and their doctrine of popular sovereignty, the Tories also found themselves upholding the concept of the supremacy of parliamentary representation. They suggested that the Whig petitioners' claim

to the Voice of the People is nonsense; for every little faction lays claim to that appellation and have wore it so thread-bare that tis scandalous to make use of it, as appropriating it to a party; for none can be truly called the people of England in a divided capacity; and they are only whole and entire in their representatives in Parliament.[70]

The people were not the masters of parliament and 'if the inhabitants of the said places think themselves aggriev'd, they ought to address themselves only to those knights, citizens or burgesses they have had the immediate choice of' and not petition the whole House.[71] In other words, local representatives were the proper channel for public opinion. The people were not superior to their MPs but 'by the choice of their representatives resign up all their authority to 'em'.[72]

What is perhaps most interesting in this debate is that as it widened into a party and constitutional struggle about the role of the 'people' *vis à vis* their representatives, the right to petition was admitted by the Tories. 'Tis the right of the people to petition,' acknowledged the author of *England's Enemies Expos'd*, 'provided always that it be done in decent words and submitting their opinions to the wisdom of the house'.[73] The bone of contention was not whether petitioning was legitimate but whether the petition was representative of the people and whether the petition had been couched in the appropriate language, for 'not to distinguish between a modest petition and a scandalous, insolent and seditious one was to turn the world upside down'.[74] The acknowledgement of the right to petition was thus made only with the proviso that old rules about the etiquette of humility continue to be observed. 'It's the subjects undoubted right to

[69] *The History of the Kentish Petition, Answer'd Paragraph by Paragraph* (1701), 11–12; *The Several Proceedings*, preface; [Defoe?], *A Letter to a New Member of the Ensuing Parliament* (23 Dec. 1701 as printed date) (1702), 3. For the attack on the *Legion Memorial* as the contrivance of a few (including the veteran 'commonwealth' printer John Darby, see *England's Enemies Exposed* (1701), 28; J. Tutchin, *The Mouse Grown a Rat* (1702), 19–20.
[70] *The History of the Kentish Petition Answer'd*, 15; *Jura Populi Anglicani . . . Answer'd, Paragraph by Paragraph* (1701), 79.
[71] *Jura Populi . . . Answer'd*, 73–5, 79.
[72] *The Ballad; or, Some Scurrilous Reflections in Verse . . . Answered* (1701), 27. Cf. *England's Enemies Expos'd*, 31.
[73] *England's Enemies Expos'd*, 42.
[74] *The History of the Kentish Petition Answer'd*, 39. Cf. *The Old and Modern Whig*, 46.

petition, but not to make use of words that shew him superior to the power he makes address to . . . if their representatives were not wiser than themselves, why did they chuse them?' asked a Tory pamphleteer. MPs were therefore 'above being directed'.[75] The partial interests of petitioners could not compete with the ability of parliament to discern the true public interest. 'The interest of England is a compound concern' and a true judgement of it was best made by the House of Commons that contained 'representatives from every corner'. It was thus 'saucy as well as senseless' for 'a few men of one county to pretend to dictate . . . and to petition for the whole nation'.[76] The Kent petition had focused attention on the clash of rival representative institutions and the Tories upheld parliamentary rather than popular sovereignty. If there was a right to petition, the petition was necessarily subordinate in representative terms to an MP.

This was not quite the end of the story, however, for when parliament met again in February 1702 it considered, evidently with relation to *Jura Populi*, a Tory motion against 'libells and reflections upon the parliament'. The Commons voted that to assert that the House was not the representative of the body of the nation tended to subvert the rights and fundamentals of the constitution. The Tory majority went further by securing a resolution that to print or publish anything 'reflecting on the proceedings of the House of Commons or any member thereof, for, or relating to his service therein' was a 'high violation' of the rights of the House. William Bromley then moved 'to censure the grand juryes that addressed for a dissolution', urging 'that the promoting and presenting addresses to His Majesty containing reflections upon the House of Commons and desiring H[is] M[ajesty] to dissolve ye parliam[en]t tended to sedition and to the dissolution of the rights of the House of Commons'.[77] This threatened to undo the recognition of a right to petition. This attempt 'against the more public voice of the people' was duly resisted by the Whigs.[78] 'Many warm words' were exchanged during a long debate—indeed, the Whig Sir William Strickland died in the House of a heart attack after vigorously

[75] *Jura Populi . . . Answer'd*, 70.
[76] *A Letter to a New Member*, 7. One anti-Whig tract asked 'Shall two or three gentlemen over a bottle agree to arraign the proceedings of the House of Commons then carry it to the Quarter sessions and by their authority prevail with the grand-jury to sign it; and must this instrument be called the act of the whole country? by what law are the grand-jury the representatives of the whole country?' (*England's Enemies Expos'd*, 50). Cf. *The Old and Modern Whig*, 47.
[77] *Cocks Diary*, 217–18.
[78] PRO, 30/24/22/2, Shaftesbury to Furley, 27 Feb. 1701/2; BL, Add. MSS 7078, Stepney papers, newsletter by John Ellis, f. 73, 17 Feb. 1701/2.

defending the Yorkshire address—but the House could not be brought to condemn the grand juries and the matter fell.[79] The affair had ended with vigorous assertions of the right to petition balanced by the larger representative right of the House of Commons.

The legitimacy of petitioning and addressing was again questioned in 1706, in Scotland, when the legislative Union between the two countries was being promoted. The anti-Union addresses presented to the Scottish parliament once more questioned the propriety of petitioning. They were defended in *The Scottish Echo* (1707), which quoted from the 1701 Whig tract *Jura Populi* in order to embarrass the court Whigs (who were pro-Union). They were thus reminded that they had espoused a right to let MPs know 'what is the voice of the people and what they think the necessities of the publick'.[80] The tract also cited *Jus Populi Vindicatum*, 'a book printed in defence of the people of Scotland's right to defend themselves in 1669'. The latter asserted that all power came from the people and that the power of the people 'is greater than the power of any delegated or constituted by them'. Parliament thus 'doth represent the people but the people do not represent the parliament; therefore the power of the people must be greater'. Parliaments exercised power in trust for the people and when they transgressed their limits 'by commanding what god hath forbidden . . . or when they seek not the publick good of the land but their own private advantage, they are not but cease to be the ministers of God and of the people and become private persons, who ought not in these particular, where in they go beyond their bounds, to be obeyed'. Parliament, it was argued, could not transfer inalienable rights of the people. Thus 'parliament cannot tyrannize by any law or right over the people' and when they 'turn tyrants, wolves, tygers and enemies to the commonwealth themselves, or conspire, join or enter into a confederacy with a tyrant, and so seek the destruction of the community, the community is allowed to see to the preservation of their own rights and privileges the best way they can'. The tract argued that there was no hope that parliament would follow the ancient course and therefore 'the people of Scotland are as if they had no Parliament, nor inferiour judges, for that end; and cannot be supposed or imagined to be in a worse condition than if they never had any such to protect them . . . and therefore must be allowed to use the privilege and liberty which nature hath granted unto them to defend themselves from unjust

[79] *Cocks Diary*, 218.
[80] *The Scottish Echo to the English Legion* (1707), in *Somers Tracts*, third collection, iv. 198–9.

tyranny and oppression of parliaments and inferiour judicatures'.[81] This set of arguments showed the radical edge to the arguments invoked by the Whigs to justify petitioning in 1701.

With some irony, then, the petitions against the Union, were disowned by the Whigs. *Two Great Questions Considered* thus remarked how the anti-Union petitioners mistook the nature of the rights of the subject. MPs could not 'make laws against nature or reason but in everything else they have the full legislative and judicature committed to them and it can not be rational to subject them to the tumultuous authority of their constituents'.[82] The further irony of this tract was that it was written by Daniel Defoe, the man thought to be partly responsible for drafting the Legion Memorial which had claimed in 1701 that the people *were* superior to parliament. The legitimacy of petitioning and addressing had therefore moved out of the realm of governmental restriction into the contingent realm of party politics. This was most clearly apparent in 1710 when the Whigs vigorously contested the claims made by Tory addresses against the administration, Whig ideology, and whiggish parliament. Many of these addresses came from grand juries and were discounted by Whig journalist John Oldmixon as unrepresentative: 'the grand-jury is chosen by the sheriff and the knights [of the shire] by the freeholders; so that if I was to know the true sense of a county, I would take the word of the freeholders and not the grand-juries'.[83] He duly slighted the clique of 'two or three deputy lieutenants, a gentleman or two, half a dozen parsons and a couple of haberdashers' who might claim to be behind an address.[84] It was now the Whigs who were championing the sovereignty of parliament over the (Tory) addressers.

This section has argued that there was an ongoing debate about the legitimacy of appealing to the public through petitions and addresses. It has shown that by 1689 a right to petition or address the crown had been established, but that the relationship between parliament and the public was more problematic. Both claimed representative, collective, authority. Yet the pressures and contingencies of partisan politics ensured that both parties articulated arguments favouring parliament as the representative voice of the people. Even so, this did not impede vigorous partisan use of petitions and addresses, and the continued invocation of the public in such a process.

---

[81] Ibid., 205.   [82] *Two Great Questions Considered*, 11.

[83] Oldmixon, *History of Addresses*, ii. 9.

[84] Ibid., ii. 89. For a Tory statement along similar lines, see *England's Enemies Exposed*, 30: 'by what law are the grand jury the representatives of the whole country?'

WIDENING   THE   POLITICAL   NATION   AND   INVOKING
POPULAR   OPINION

Before moving to consider the politics of representation in more detail, we
need to examine the process involved in manufacturing petitions and addresses in order to show how it widened the political nation and invoked
popular opinion as the sense of the nation.

Petitions and addresses were either spontaneously produced or procured; often the outcome was a mixture of the two. Who generated a petition or address is important, for whether it came from an individual[85] or
from a community determines the extent to which we can regard it as representative of public opinion. The petition or address could be initiated
from above, the result of an initiative by the lord lieutenant, MP, cleric, or
national office-holder but also locally, from within a borough or club or
other assembly. But it was also clear that the number of later Stuart petitions and addresses owed a good deal to the establishment of a national
political culture in which boroughs as well as counties were *expected to
participate*. The emergence of such a culture can be seen in the reaction of
St Albans to a plea from its MP, Sir Harbottle Grimston, to draw up an address in the wake of the Rye House Plot in 1683. The town did so but felt the
need to apologize for not having done it before: 'howsoever we may be liable to misrepresentation in not bearing our part in the many addresses
heretofore made to your Majesty, yet since we never petitioned in relation
to the succession, nor meddled with other state affairs, we hoped that it
would be thought needless for us to make any address or abhorrence
against the practices of those that took upon them unmannerly to press
into your secret counsels and to prescribe a method for the future disposal
of the government. . . .'[86] The address itself recognized that it was no
longer possible to evade participation in national campaigns and that political loyalty would henceforth be measurable. The pressure to emulate
other boroughs in addressing was powerful.[87]

Once drawn up a text needed signatures, endorsement by a grand jury,

---

[85]   Roger L'Estrange, by his own admission, published a number of petitions which purported to represent the sense of the city for a free parliament (*L'Estrange his Apology* (1660),
43–54). He was also accused in 1682 of being the man 'principally employed in framing the
draughts which are remitted into the countrey, where lieutenants, justices and curates are
commissioned to procure subscriptions to them' (*The Addresses Importing an Abhorrence*
(1682), 3).

[86]   Herts. RO, Verulam MSS IX.A 268A, Grimston to mayor, 7 July 1683; ibid., Tho Bush to
Grimston, 13 July 1683; *LG*, 1842.

[87]   BL, Add. MSS 28895, f. 336, Charles Hedges to John Ellis, 31 Aug. 1704.

or a corporation seal. A dilemma faced the promoters. Should they seek large numbers, to show the weight of public feeling, or should they narrow support to the perceived leaders of a community? The Kent petition of 1701, for example, was signed by 21 of the grand jury and 23 JPs, and 'the freeholders of the county crowded in so fast that the parchment was filled up in less than five hours time; and many thousands of hands might have been had to it if the justices had not declin'd it, refusing to add any more rolls of parchment, as insisting more upon the merits of the petition than the number of subscribers'.[88] The decision about whether or not to canvass for mass subscriptions therefore had an ideological dimension, for it raised issues about the legitimacy of popular involvement in national politics. Although the quantity–quality argument was an ongoing one, partisan politics tended to ensure an active competition for popularity and, even more importantly, for publicity.

The mass subscriptions of 1679–80 and 1696 were thus reflections of the Whigs' desire to mobilize popular opinion and use it for political purposes, but also suggested an ideological readiness to embrace such popular involvement. The Tories did resort to similar tactics in order to outdo the Whigs at their own game, as in 1681 and in 1710, but only with some reluctance, for to do so involved them in a numbers game that caused them discomfort.[89] The number of signatures appended to petitions and addresses could be extremely impressive. In 1683, for example, the address from Guernsey claimed to be 'signed by all the inhabitants of the said island'.[90] 'About ten thousand tinners of the several stannaries in Cornwall' signed another, as did a further 9,175 in Derbyshire.[91] In 1708 Westminster's address against the jacobite invasion was 'subscrib'd by several thousand hands'.[92] The evidence suggests, though, that the number of subscribers did decline in proportion to the frequency of addressing. Surviving addresses promoted, mainly by Whigs, in 1710 generally carry only about a hundred signatures, and some considerably fewer.[93] Thus a Middlesex

[88] The proceedings are recounted in *The History of the Kentish Petition*. Cocks reckoned there were 200 signatures (*Cocks Diary*, 114).
[89] The Whigs thus taunted Tories about their reluctance to woo popular support and one tract of 1682 argued that the Tories had exposed the king as 'the head meerly of one part and that a very inconsiderable one if compared with the bulk of the nation' (*The Addresses Importing an Abhorrence of an Association*, 3–4; cf. *A Letter from a Person of Quality to his Friend, about Abhorrers and Addressers* (1682); *A Reply to the Second Return* (1682)).
[90] *LG*, 1852, 1859.   [91] *LG*, 1872, 1886.   [92] *LG*, 4418.
[93] There is collection of texts with signatures at BL, Add. Charter MSS 76108–23. An exception is Norwich with 533 subscriptions, perhaps a testament to the deep divisions there (M. Knights, 'Bloody Noses and Broken Heads: The Political Culture of Norwich 1660–1835', in C. Rawcliffe and R. Wilson (eds.), *The History of Norwich* (2004)).

address condemning the Sacheverell rioters for trying to 'move and incite your subjects (under a pretence of passive obedience and non resistance) to Rebellion and Sedition' and promising to stand by the queen's title 'founded upon the late happy revolution', was signed by only 62.[94] Similarly, a loyal address from Taunton against the 1715 jacobite rebellion was signed by only 107.[95] Both addresses were whiggish ones, fighting against a swell of hostile popular fervour; and we know relatively little about the numbers of Tories who signed on the back of the Sacheverellite disturbances in 1710. But the indications are that mass subscriptions had become less popular by the early Hanoverian period.[96] The important exception to this was the mass oath-taking of 1723, which will be discussed later.

Numbers alone, and especially the numbers claimed in print, were, however, not always what they appeared to be. For example, on 28 January 1660 an address from Norfolk was presented to the Rump Parliament.[97] Ostensibly coming from 'the gentry', the printed broadsheet carried just 45 names but alluded at the end to 'many hundreds more of the knights, gentry, citizens and freeholders'. The manuscript from which the print was made survives and more than bears out this latter claim, for although 5 of the names on the printed version do not appear on the original and were probably added in London, a total of 827 signed, the vast majority being citizens of Norwich.

The desire to attract as much support as possible did not, in any case, rely on numbers alone. A key feature of several of the addressing movements is the extent to which the usual or official mouthpieces of a community were by-passed or became part of a larger, more expansive, expression of the public. This occurred in a number of ways. First, although the petitions and addresses tended to come from parliamentary constituencies, this was by no means always the case. In 1712 Parshore, Worcestershire, acknowledged that although 'not distinguish'd as a body politick' the locale wanted to address because its inhabitants had 'read with

---

[94] BL, Add. Charter MSS 76111.

[95] PRO, SP 35/1/64.

[96] A loyal address from Rye in July 1715 carried 158 signatures (PRO, SP35/3/77b) and another from Shaftesbury in 1716 only 75 (SP, 35/5/49).

[97] It bewailed the 'miseries of an unnaturall Civil war, the too frequent interruptions of Government, the impositions of severall heavey taxes and the loud out-cryes of multitudes of undone and almost famished people'. It urged the readmission of the secluded members, especially since 'we of this county of Norfolk being by such seclusion deprived of any person to represent us in Parliament' (*CSPD 1659–60*, 332; *An Address from the Gentry of Norfolk and Norwich to General Monck in 1660*, ed. H. Le Strange and W. Rye (Norwich, 1913)).

pleasure the hearty addresses' made by parliament.[98] In 1713 a number of Devon boroughs, such as Bradninch, Great Torrington, and South Molton, sent addresses, and there were also contributions from other non-parliamentary boroughs, corporations, institutions, and trading bodies.[99] The borough of Lydd in Kent was a particularly frequent addresser, as was Leeds. In other words, petitions and addresses helped to enfranchise non-parliamentary boroughs in a representative form. Second, partisanship in a borough or county could lead to rival addresses, each seeking public support, or to a single address that cast about for backing outside the confines of the corporation. Thus in 1712 Shaftesbury's came from its mayor, recorder, 'and loyal part of the capital burgesses, gents and other inhabitants'.[100] In 1710 Gloucestershire produced two addresses. One, rabidly Tory, from (the Whigs claimed) an unrepresentative grand jury, promised to elect men 'religiously zealous for our holy church'; and another was promoted by the knights of the shire, 'of a quite contrary sense', with subscriptions allegedly procured by a dissenting minister among the 'spinners and weavers and other mean people under their teaching'.[101]

Partisan conflict could thus justify and even necessitate a widening of the political nation. Those not eligible to vote could become signatories. The 'public' who signed or gave approval was usually limited and identified in two ways: loyalty and status. Thus in 1713 Nottingham's address of thanks for the conclusion of the peace came from the mayor 'and dutiful part of the aldermen and corporation in conjunction with the clergy, gentry and other loyal freeholders, tradesmen and inhabitants of the said town'. This group used the address to appropriate loyalty, asserting that 'tho the whole body of this corporation are not sufficiently grateful for the same, yet we, who are the loyal part of that body in the communion of the church of England, and are true to its interest, do, in conjunction with other loyal inhabitants return thanks'.[102] Protests of 'loyalty' could therefore legitimize a public that might otherwise not have been conjured. More usually, however, the 'public', if it did not consist of qualified citizens or freemen, was described as consisting of the 'chief' or 'principal'

---

[98] *LG*, 5038.

[99] *LG*, 5123, 5129, 5130, 5132, 5139, 5144.

[100] Its divisive nature was evident in its reference to the queen's care of the church 'by excluding all vipers from her bosom' and a readiness to offer lives and the 'remainder of our fortunes' against any who 'through love for a Dutch commonwealth, beyond a British monarchy, shall oppose your prerogatives and the true interest of our country' (*LG*, 5054).

[101] Oldmixon, *History of Addresses*, ii. 16–19; Harris, *Politics*, 182.

[102] *LG*, 5128.

inhabitants.[103] Petitions and addresses seem thus to have enforced a trend
in borough life, also apparent at parish level, for a socially and economically dominant minority to assert themselves over their fellow townsmen,
even if such élites varied considerably in status when compared across the
board.[104] Indeed the petition or address gave the 'chief inhabitants' a national as well as a local stage on which to flaunt their status. Signing alongside fellows conferred a group rank, identity, and *esprit de corps*.[105]

Thus although petitions and addresses could reinforce status, the culture of petitioning could also give a voice to the marginally represented,
including them in a widely conceived—indeed almost self-selecting—
political nation. A petition arguing for a wider franchise at Bewdley, for
example, allegedly included 'the names of above thousands of married
women, apprentices and children not above four or five years old'.[106] Each
of those groups, often excluded from the political sphere, also found their
own voice in other petitions. The 'Children's Petition', against flogging in
schools, was presented to parliament by 'a lively boy' in 1669.[107] Apprentices organized their own petitions and addresses on national issues—
some 30,000 petitioned in 1681.[108] Women petitioners were active in the
mid-century crisis as petitioners, but the 1723 association appears to have
been the first time that a mass subscription routinely involved both men
and women across the land.[109] By then women, it would seem, had become
citizens whose loyalty was worth being sure of.

Even so, their right to participate remained ambiguous, as Addison's remarks in the *Freeholder* made clear when he considered their involvement
in associations and addresses in 1716. Addison said he considered women
'as the most important part of our community' and 'as members of the
body politick' able to 'judge for themselves; look into the state of the nation

[103] Taking the 1714–15 campaign as an example, see addresses from Coventry, Penryn,
Helston, Hertford, Minehead, Truro, Folkestone, Deal, Great Torrington, Dartmouth, Brid-
port, Portsmouth, Barnstaple, Bideford, Kings Lynn (*LG*, 5262, 5263, 5264, 5267, 5268, 5270,
5272, 5287).
[104] H. R. French, 'Social Status, Localism and the "Middle Sort of People" in England
1620–1750', *P&P*, 166 (2000), 66–99.
[105] This did not always hold true, however, and a number of sheets of the London 1679
address show gentlemen signing promiscuously with unknowns.
[106] BL, Harl. MSS 6274, f. 192 Bewdley Case.
[107] C. B. Freeman, 'The Children's Petition of 1669', *British Journal of Education Studies*, 14
(1966), 216–23.
[108] J. Dunton, *The Life and Errors of John Dunton*, 2 vols. (London, 1818), i. 49.
[109] NRO, NCR13d/4, oaths of allegiance to George I, 1723. For a Quaker petition against
tithes, see *These Several Papers were Sent to the Parliament* (1659), preface, signed by Mary
Forster. 'Above seven thousand' names were arranged by county. Even so, the level of female
participation in 1723, as I hope to show elsewhere, was unprecedented.

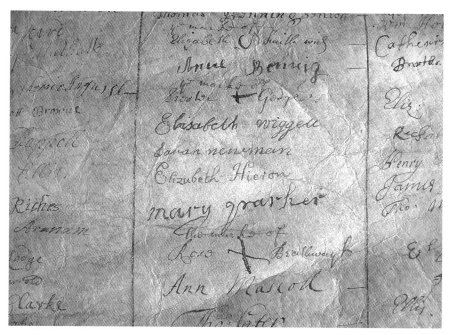

The 1723 Norfolk Association encouraged many women to demonstrate their loyalty to the Hanoverians but also thereby their citizenship. [1723 Association roll (NCR 13d/4) reproduced by courtesy of the Norfolk Record office.]

with their own eyes; and be no longer led blindfold by a male legislature'.[110] So, on the one hand, women were recognized as having assumed a new importance in the political sphere. But at the same time as addressing the 'ladies', Addison also sought to circumscribe their activity as petitioners and addressers because he feared that many had 'eloped from their allegiance' to the government, preferring a romanticized jacobitism.[111] Indeed, in order to mock female political zeal and petitioning, he duly related the story of Papirius, the son of a Roman senator who

was usually teized by his mother to inform her of what had passed. In order to deliver himself from that importunity he told her one day, upon his return from the senate house, that there had been a motion made for a decree to allow every man two wives. The good lady said nothing but managed matters so well among the

---

[110] 110 *Freeholder*, 32.   [111] Ibid., 11.

roman matrons that the next day they met together in a body before the senate-house and presented a petition to the fathers against so unreasonable a law. This groundless credulity raised so much raillery upon the petitioners that we do not find the ladies offer'd to direct the law-givers of their country ever after.

Telling the story was a deliberate excluding tactic. Subscriptional activity by the marginal offered a form of representation; but it was a limited one and at times the process of defining who could be included served only to exclude.

PETITIONING AND ADDRESSING AS PARTISAN TOOLS

Petitioning and addressing both reflected and fostered party conflict. It did so by creating communities of subscribers who defined themselves against a rival 'other', becoming locked into a dialogue of petition, counter-petition, and re-statement. This very public process hardened and shaped political allegiances but also helped to bind the provinces and boroughs into a national party system and forge a national identity. Since addresses were promoted in the provinces, even if instigated from else-where, they became focal points around which local rivalries and feuds turned.[112] They then appeared in a national press that deepened partisan-ship and made local contests available as part of a national political cul-ture. They were also partisan tools because many were deliberately promoted as part of electioneering campaigns. Their representation of public opinion was thus intended to influence the more formal representa-tive process at the polls.

Struggles in Canterbury in 1710 illustrate these points. Canterbury's first address in 1710 was a Tory one attacking 'all promoters of atheistical, im-moral and republican tenets'. This prompted the Whig *Flying Post* of 13 May 1710 to print 'the protestation of the several aldermen of the city of Canterbury against the pretended address'. The paper's report was consid-ered by Canterbury's burghmote, which found that it contained 'false and scandalous matter, unjustly reflecting on the mayor, aldermen and com-mon council of this City'. Central to the dispute was the claim that the Tory address 'was only a pretended address and not voted by the burghmote'.[113]

---

[112] See, for example, the disputes at Newcastle under Lyme detailed in *Post Boy*, 2695, 2716.
[113] The corporation's own records show that the Tory address had been approved in 'a pri-vate burghmote' attended by only some of the corporation (Canterbury Corp. Archives, CC/A/C 8, burghmote minute book 1695–1744, 397, 429).

A subsequent meeting on 30 May 1710 resolved to have a copy of the newspaper burned 'by the common cryer in front of the Guildhall' and notice of the burning was to be 'published in print'.[114] Even that was not the end of the affair, for one alderman, John Lee, broke his oath to keep burghmote matters secret. 'Designing and maliciously intending to slander and disgrace' the assembly, Lee wrote a 'false, scandalous and malicious libel', called 'The Protestation', which he published 'at divers public houses and places' in the city. This attacked the Tories' 'pretended address' as lacking in sincerity and castigated it for not making 'any mention . . . of the many and repeated mercies to these kingdoms either for the happy revolution, the memory of our glorious deliverer, or of any duty or gratitude to our present gracious sovereign for her great and good work in completing the Union, for the glorious successes of her arms, for her late gracious speech from the throne, nor for her constant care and zeal for the Church'. Lee also attacked the Tory declaration that the city would only send MPs who were known to be 'against all republican spirits and such as were the cause of her grandfather's murder'. He said this was subversive, since it intimated 'a dislike to our present representatives which we take to be men of honour and integrity, dutiful and loyal to our present gracious sovereign, zealous for the church, lovers of their country and its happy constitution, of penetrating judgements, who lately discovered the intended rebellion of the Cheveralites, so cunningly concealed in the doctrine of passive obedience'. The 'pretended address', it was suggested, was the work of the mayor and three aldermen, who had surprised eight other aldermen and not given them time to consider the address. The Tory response to this onslaught was vigorous. Lee was expelled from office; and another alderman, who had told one antagonist that he was 'endeavouring to impose on us a French government', had his gown 'immediately pulled over his ears' and was sent to prison.[115] Lee, in turn, sought a writ of mandamus to be restored to office, and was duly reinserted in March 1711, only to be expelled again five months later for refusing to withdraw from the burghmote when it discussed his misdemeanour in publishing the 'Protestation'. Lee was only finally restored in February 1712.[116]

The Canterbury case shows how addressing could split a corporation into rival parties (or harden existing schisms) but also highlights how the struggle in the constituency was related to the struggle over the electoral process, at both local and national level. The impact which petitions and addresses could have on the electorate was noted in February–March 1681,

---

[114] Ibid., 430.   [115] Ibid., 434–6.   [116] Ibid., 454, 459, 461, 469.

when rival sets of instructions were presented to MPs and again in the summer of that year when addresses loyal to the court sought to show that the elections earlier in the year had in some ways misrepresented the voice of the nation. Thereafter, addresses and petitions were inherently election- eering texts. Thus in 1682 and 1683 many addresses promised to return 'loyal' MPs, even though there was no imminent election.[117] Charles II never realized the potential of loyalty unleashed by such methods, for he chose not to summon another parliament in his reign, but the accession of James II in February 1685 forced new elections. It was no coincidence that the court encouraged a flood of addresses congratulating the king on his succession. Even though they were not perhaps as straightforwardly loyal as they might at first appear, many addresses promised to return MPs sym- pathetic to the court. For example, the freeholders of Haslemere declared that they would 'not elect, nor give any of our voices for the electing of any person or persons whatsoever to be a burgess or burgesses for this borough in the next ensuing Parliament who were members of Parliament' in 1680 or 1681. Nor would they support anyone who could not prove 'that he did openly and avowedly oppose and give his vote against' the bill to exclude James from the succession.[118] Such addresses were, of course, not the only reason for the overwhelmingly Tory parliament elected in 1685, but they surely played their part. James must have thought so, for when he sought to use addresses for electioneering purposes after 1687 19 addresses promised to elect MPs who would follow the court line and repeal the test and penal laws. Caught in the circularity of his own policy, James was probably misled by these into a false sense of security. As Sir John Reresby noted in his diary, the king was 'much deceived as to the opinion of his sub- jects concerning the indulgence, three or four men in divers places pre- tending to represent the thoughts of a whole corporation or county'.[119] The addresses had played a part in James's attempts to pack a parliament with compliant men; but just as they had helped to prevent the represen- tative assembly, it was claimed, so too did they misrepresent public opinion.

Using addresses for electioneering purposes was a technique revived

[117] For 1682, see Newark, Worcester, Oxon., New Woodstock, Bath, Portsmouth, Pontefract, Cumberland, Carlisle, East Looe, Lyme Regis, Great Bedwyn, Westbury (*LG*, 1696, 1704, 1706, 1707, 1710, 1720, 1722, 1723, 1727, 1731, 1736, 1746). For 1683, see Guildford, Oke- hampton, Richmond, Lincs., Pontefract, Sussex, Stafford, Plymouth, Cockermouth, Grantham, Kent, Ludgershall, Lyme Regis, Great Marlow, Weymouth and Melcombe Regis, Stockbridge, Poole, and Amersham (*LG*, 1844, 1849, 1851, 1853, 1856–60, 1862, 1865, 1867–8).
[118] *LG*, 2613.
[119] *Memoirs of Sir John Reresby*, ed. A. Browning (Glasgow, 1936), 495.

after the Revolution of 1688, though chiefly from 1701 onwards. In the spring of 1701 the Kent petitioners had sought to put pressure on parliament to listen to the voice of the people, but their intention to procure the dissolution of parliament to make way for a more whiggish one was certainly clear to contemporaries.[120] Thereafter addresses coincided with election campaigns quite regularly. The proclamation dissolving parliament in November 1701 even began with the observation that 'our loving subjects have universally, by their loyal addresses, expressed their resentment of the injustice and indignity offered to us and our People by the late proceedings of the French king'.[121] The death of King William on 8 March 1702, and the queen's maiden speech in which she played on Tory sensibilities by referring to her English heart, released another round of addresses, up to the election of 1702.[122] Effectively, then, addresses and petitions were promoted continuously through one election in the autumn of 1701 and up to the election called in the summer of 1702. Frequent elections and frequent addressing went hand in hand.

Just as the fear of France and the Pretender had been used in 1701 to promote the Whigs, so again in 1708 an attempted jacobite invasion, supported by France, provided the perfect occasion for Whig gains. The campaign to congratulate the queen on its defeat coincided exactly with the general election, which was called on 22 April. Electioneering was clearly evident in Westmorland's address which promised that they would choose men 'well affected to the glorious revolution'.[123] But the most visible link between addressing and electioneering came in 1710 in the wake of the trial of Dr Sacheverell. The parliamentary session ended in March 1710, shortly after London and elsewhere had witnessed riotous mobs destroying dissenting meeting houses. Between then and August, when parliament was eventually dissolved, there were persistent rumours that an election would be called and the preparations included addresses and counter-addresses. The Tory addresses were clearly designed to show the Whig parliament was unrepresentative of the nation and to reassure the queen that if she chose a Tory ministry she would find public support. The addresses thus aimed, said one whig critic, to be 'esteem'd . . . as the

---

[120] *The Diary of Abraham de la Pryme*, ed. C. Jackson, Surtees Society, 54 (Durham, 1870), 244; *The Several Proceedings and Resolutions*, postscript; *Cocks Diary*, 203–4.
[121] *LG*, 3757.
[122] *LG*, 3791. For addresses specifically mentioning voting intentions, see Malmesbury, Westbury, Fowey, Steyning, Newport, Isle of Wight, Higham Ferrers (*LG*, 3794, 3798, 3796, 3798, 3805).
[123] *LG*, 4435.

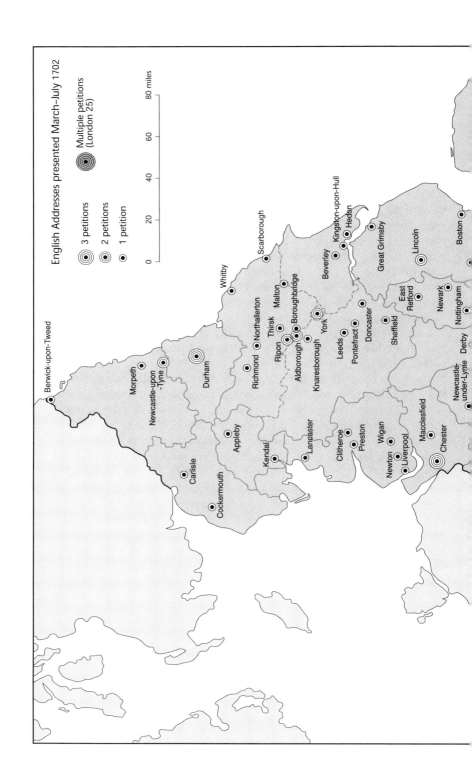

English Addresses presented March–July 1702

- ◎ 3 petitions
- ◉ 2 petitions
- ● 1 petition

⊚ Multiple petitions (London 25)

0   20   40   60   80 miles

Berwick-upon-Tweed

Morpeth
Newcastle-upon-Tyne
Durham
Carlisle
Cockermouth
Appleby
Kendal
Lancaster
Richmond
Northallerton
Whitby
Thirsk
Malton
Scarborough
Ripon
Aldborough
Boroughbridge
Knaresborough
York
Beverley
Kingston-upon-Hull
Hedon
Leeds
Pontefract
Doncaster
Sheffield
Great Grimsby
Clitheroe
Preston
Wigan
Newton
Liverpool
Macclesfield
Newcastle-under-Lyme
Chester
Derby
Nottingham
Newark
East Retford
Lincoln
Boston

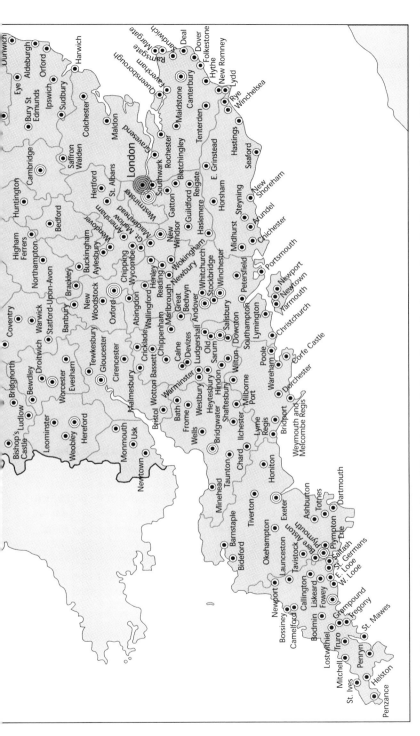

A nation-wide addressing campaign in 1702, mapped here, followed hard on the heels of one only a few months earlier. Between October 1701 and May 1702 at least 744 addresses were presented to the crown. Such activity helped to spread a truly national political culture.

voice of the people (and that is as the voice of God)'.[124] Before the election was called in August 1713, addresses were again promoted throughout the country, from April onwards. Again these were explicitly electioneering documents in which the Tories evidently hoped to proscribe whiggery as republican, schismatical, self-interested, promoters of blasphemy and irreligion.[125] But in 1715 the tide again turned and it was the Whigs' turn to use addresses for electioneering purposes.[126]

Such examples of the way in which petitioning and addressing coincided with electioneering should not, perhaps, be surprising. Petitions and addresses were alternative forms of representing the voice of the people and could buttress or challenge the more formal representative process. Nevertheless the struggle over representation through addresses and petitions raises a number of important questions about the political process that must now be explored. These relate to the role of such campaigns as propaganda rather than reflections of opinion; to the nature of the language used in the texts and how far this contributed both to a rational debate and to growing sensibilities about manners; to the function of the campaigns as assertions of loyalty; to the role of the campaigns in fostering national identity; and to the economic motivation behind petitioning and addressing in the later Stuart period.

PETITIONS AND ADDRESSES IN PRINT: REASON, NATIONALISM, AND POLITENESS

We saw earlier that petitioning and addressing expanded the public, but a further way in which that process occurred was through print. The texts litter the periodicals and pamphlets of the day. The petitions and addresses thus had dual audiences: the ostensible recipient (crown or parliament) but also the public who could read them in print. Readers were potential subscribers or counter-petitioners and hence interested parties. Many of the addresses promoted in the period were published in the officially controlled *London Gazette*. Displacing the foreign reports that usually headed the news, they reflected public opinion in the provinces but also shaped and even created it. The forum of print could thus collect local political cultures into a national one.

---

[124] [W. Stephens], *Dick and Tom: A Dialogue about Addresses* (1710), 13. For explicit references to elections, see Oldmixon, *History of Addresses*, ii. 129, 186, 204, 206, 244.

[125] See, for example, Gloucester, London, Dunwich, Fowey (*LG*, 5112, 5116, 5121, 5128–30).

[126] *LG*, 5293.

Yet the ramifications of the systematic printing of petitions and addresses go further. Zaret argues that the printing of petitions stimulated and indeed helped to create a rational public sphere. To a certain extent he is right. But there were also factors inherent in the very foundation of the rational public sphere that contributed to its decay. Habermas argued that the decay in rationality was essentially a modern, post-nineteenth-century, phenomenon, in part the result of a mass media that was obsessed by spin and by governments that sought to control their populations. In this modern phase, Habermas argued, the bourgeois public sphere has been replaced by the feeble criticism of consumers. In such circumstances, he suggested, the public is thus 'included only sporadically in th[e] circuit of power, and even then it is brought in only to contribute its acclamation'.[127] Yet it is possible to observe a similar degradation of the quality of discourse occurring at the very birth of the public sphere. The public sphere, it can be argued, is thus something in tension with itself: the very causes of its creation can also act to undermine it. Habermas, of course, saw this but argued that decay was a process that occurred over time. The later Stuart evidence, however, suggests that we should see the process as far more dialectical right from the start. Let us probe this acclamatory dimension more fully.

The proliferation of addresses in the later Stuart period has already been noted. Whig historian John Oldmixon blamed Oliver Cromwell for the development of the acclamatory address; such texts had also poured in for his son Richard in 1659.[128] But after the Restoration, and particularly from the 1680s onwards, the printed congratulatory address made a come-back. Governments deliberately encouraged such movements. William and Anne made speeches to parliament that stimulated addresses; they issued proclamations for fast days and days of thanksgiving to encourage the nation to think and thank; and publication in the *Gazette* offered its own incentive. Repeated victory in the war against France was also especially important in encouraging the panegyric trend. To some extent then, particularly in the 1680s and the 1700s and 1710s, the public was invoked in order to contribute its acclamation. The addresses to Queen Anne show this very well, since the victories in the war were often attributed to the

---

[127] *Structural Transformation*, 176.
[128] 94 were printed in a pamphlet in Sept. 1659, a year after they had first started to be presented, in order to show the 'late apostacy' of their promoters. The texts were thus described as 'blasphemous, lying, flattering addresses' (*A True Catalogue; or, An Account of the Several Places . . . where . . . Richard Cromwell was proclaimed Lord Protector* (1659), quotation from sub-title).

personal virtues of the queen herself, praise that led to an apotheosis of monarchy. The flattery inherent in addresses of thanks might be said to have reduced, rather than increased, the rationality of the process. This is not to suggest that the dominance of addressing with thanks was a *necessarily* irrational or destructive process. On the contrary, it can be shown that the charge of irrationality was often dependent on party loyalty and that the acclamatory address contributed towards growing sentiments about nationality and politeness.

The point about the alleged irrationality of addresses will be pursued later in the chapter so let us take the second of these points first. Pride in British achievements and the power of the nation was fostered by the nationwide nature of the addressing movements, which drew on support from nearly every borough in the country and bound them into a national campaign. Moreover, addresses increasingly came from Scotland, Ireland, and the colonies, marking the process of addressing as an important contributory factor in the forging of a British identity. A brief glance at the addresses of 1704 (to congratulate the queen on the victory at Blenheim), 1707 (on the Union with Scotland), or 1714–15 (on the Hanoverian succession) can illustrate these points. During the latter, out of 443 addresses, 93 came from Ireland, 53 from Scotland, 19 from the overseas colonies, and 3 from trading companies. This was coverage on a truly British scale.

Many of the addresses of 1704 represented England's defeat of France as liberating the Western world from tyranny and explicitly made a parallel with the defeat of the Spanish by the last female monarch, Elizabeth. As Norwich's address put it, the queen had extended her goodness 'to recover the languishing liberty of Europe'.[129] Warwick's enlarged on the theme: 'the whole world does, more or less, partake in the influences of that glorious victory' and the queen 'conquers for peace and the rights of mankind, and not the extent of dominion or power . . . you have sav'd [the Holy Roman] empire, loos'd the chains of kings, and given a fatal blow to the second attempt of universal monarchy'.[130] The language was thus nationalistic but counter-imperial: England freed rather than conquered. Europe had received its liberties 'a second time from an English queen' and Salisbury's address suggested the queen might be called 'defender of the oppressed as well as of the faith'.[131] Pride in liberating Europe infused a sense of national destiny and pride. Hereford's address thus exclaimed 'O happy England! where there is such a peace; where the church established by law religiously

---

[129] *LG*, 4052.   [130] Ibid., 4056.
[131] *LG*, 4058, 4059; cf. Westminster and Brackley, both in *LG*, 4061.

professeth and learnedly defends the true and apostolick doctrines; where there is neither tyrant nor slave; where the sovereign upholds the liberty of the subject and the people with their hands, hearts and purses endeavour to maintain the sovereignty as their own security'.[132] Morpeth's address was even more extravagant: 'If we look back into former ages, and consider the happiest state and condition that any of our ancestors ever saw, how imperfect does it appear and how short does it fall of what we now enjoy under your majesty both in church and state?'[133] There was also national pride in the courage shown on the battlefield. Launceston's address, for example, noted that Marlborough's victory showed 'the world what Englishmen can do under an English government'.[134] 'The ancient English prowess must no longer be said to be in its declention', claimed Staffordshire's address.[135] It is clear that the war therefore had the effect of boosting a national identity based on the security of liberty for the oppressed, the triumph of English arms abroad, and the perfection of the English constitution based on the monarchy. Each address strove to outdo the other in its praise; this had the effect of reinforcing national identity as well as a concept of national happiness as the end of government. The addresses of 1707 spoke a very similar language.[136] Gloucestershire's, for example, told the queen that her 'heroic firmness to your allies, the prudent management of our revenues, the free and impartial administration and dispatch in doing justice and growing regulation of the laws set ours upon the level with the politest and happiest of ages'.[137]

This reference to 'politeness' draws attention to the importance of the language and rhetoric of addressing, for the predominance of addressing for thanks rather than petitioning for redress of grievance both reflected, but also spread into every borough, the growing culture of politeness that historians of the eighteenth century have seen as such a feature of the political landscape. Indeed, it is possible to suggest that, for all their importance in fostering division, addresses also played a significant part in undermining the credibility or legitimacy of party feuding. At one level addresses sought to promote a unified response; and they also encouraged a dislike of passionate party rage, a term frequently employed by the addresses of 1712 and 1713.[138] The Whigs in 1712, for example, were depicted as

---

[132] *LG*, 4060.   [133] Ibid., 4070.
[134] Ibid., 4064.   [135] Ibid., 4067.
[136] East Retford, Canterbury, Leominster, Thirsk, Stafford, Winchester, Carlisle (*LG*, 4324, 4332, 4326–7, 4330, 4334).
[137] *LG*, 4332.
[138] See addresses from Stamford, Cambridge, Dublin (*LG*, 5123), Bradninch, Chichester, Blechingley (*LG*, 5119, 5121, 5123, 5127, 5133).

a 'restless faction' that pursued its own interest rather than the nation's and gloried in war. Such sentiments had been encouraged by the queen herself, who had made a speech castigating the 'ill minded persons who may attempt to sow sedition amongst my subjects and under specious pretences carry on designs they dare not own'.[139] The inhabitants of Honiton thus abhorred 'the many obstructions and crafty insinuations of some self-interested and discontented people who vainly would have it that nothings is for the Public Good which crosses the measure of their private interest and party'.[140] Indeed the Whigs were represented as little more than political vampires who had sucked the nation dry. Ilchester's address thus referred to the 'close designs of those who so long triumph'd in the misery of their fellow subjects, sacrificing their blood and treasure to insatiable avarice and ambition' and Radnor's referred to disloyal men who 'to gratifie their own resentments, ambition and sordid avarice, labour to obstruct your royal intentions'.[141] London's address therefore denounced the 'party-Rage of a Faction'.[142] The passion of party was impolite, even if it was condemned by a Tory party passionately hostile to the Whigs. The 'civilizing process' has often been seen in terms of the cultural diffusion of courtly values and urbane civility; the addresses were an important, though neglected, part of this process. The boroughs spoke and absorbed the language of civility.

The language of petitions and addresses was also important because specific words and phrases were laden with meaning. Addressing thus took on a form of code, which was in part fostered by hyperbole. Phrases had to be carefully weighed by drafters and readers; addresses were often not as anodyne as they appeared once they were read in context. John Oldmixon recognized that the addresses had to be linguistically deconstructed: the difference between them lay 'chiefly in the Lexicography of the adjectives and substantives us'd by both sides and the rendr'ring some particular words'.[143] Words, he suggested, were used creatively in addresses for 'the poetica licentia is as warrantable as in a poem, and all the beauties of fancy and fiction not only allowable but commendable'.[144] But this posed difficulties for the undiscerning, who needed to be supplied with definitions. Thus by 'anti-monarchical principles', Oldmixon argued, the Tories

---

[139] *LG*, 5021.
[140] *LG*, 5024. Cf. Appleby, Lancaster, Grampound (*LG*, 5031, 5033, 5037).
[141] Ibid., 5043.   [142] Ibid., 5112.
[143] Oldmixon, *History of Addresses*, ii. 162.
[144] Ibid., 230.

'meant such principles as are against the absolute government of one person by mere will and pleasure and without laws'; 'hereditary right' was that
right by which the Stuarts could be restored; and 'republican principles'
was a phrase used to attack 'revolution principles under covert terminology'.[145] So elusive did meaning become that in 1710 rival Whig and Tory
tracts published 'explanations of some hard terms now in use for the information of all such as read or subscribe addresses'.[146] These contested the
interpretation of party slogans, such as 'revolution principles' or 'hereditary right'. The addresses therefore helped to contribute to the uncertainty
of language and partisan cant that will be examined more closely in the
second half of this book.

   The printing of so many addresses of thanks helped to create a paradox:
the process both enlarged a public sphere but also placed one large part of
it into the hands of the government and its partisan minions. The boroughs and counties found a voice but often it was a subordinate one, for
they had been seduced into a format reliant on rhetorical submission, acclamation of monarchy, and hyperbole. Criticism had to be disguised in
compliment. Occasionally the format could be totally subverted, as it was
in 1710 when the Tories promoted addresses which appeared very loyal but
which were clearly designed to alter the ministry and procure a new government. Significantly, however, they were denied any space in the *London
Gazette* and had to be printed in the Tory *Post Boy* and a separate publication, *A Collection of all the Addresses that have been presented to her Majesty*.
Criticism through compliment was not, of course, new; but historians of
early Stuart political culture have tended to see it as operating within the
court, rather than acting on the court through the public sphere.[147]

   This section has therefore highlighted the creative dimensions of addressing, in terms of fostering notions of a national political culture, national identity, and pride, and in cultivating a sense of a polite discourse
spoken by the meanest borough in the land. Addressing and associating
was also creative, as we shall now see, in terms of manufacturing consent
and loyalty.

---

[145] Ibid., 269.
[146] [J.Trapp], *The True Genuine Modern Whigg-Address* (1710); [B. Hoadly], *The True
Genuine Tory-Address* (1710). *The True Genuine Tory-Address and the True Genuine Whig-
Address, Set One against the Other* (1710) set out definitions in dictionary format.
[147] Sharpe, *Criticism and Compliment: The Politics of Literature in the England of Charles I*
(Cambridge, 1987).

ADDRESSING AND ASSOCIATING: PROFESSIONS
OF LOYALTY

The etiquette of both petitions and addresses required a profession of loyalty. The ways in which early modern society procured loyalty and allegiance have recently come under some scrutiny. Historians have become
increasingly interested in the bonds that held society together, not least because they appeared to be under great strain, and even to be changing, as a
result of the mid-century crisis. Moreover, political scientists argue over
the degree of consent procured from individuals to the activities of the
state. Were citizens obliged merely, as Locke seemed to suggest, by breath-
ing the air and walking the highways, to abide by the original constitution?
Was consent something granted at the time of the original constitution
but never actively procured thereafter from a state that required only
passive consent to its actions? These are fundamental questions about the
participatory and consensual nature of the state and the addresses and associations promoted during the later Stuart period can help us to explore
them. Signing an address or taking an oath was an important means by
which citizens were induced to declare their consent and allegiance to the
state as well as to a party or set of concepts.

   Addresses and associations repeatedly engaged subscribers in declarations of loyalty to the monarch as well as to more abstract principles such
as 'the protestant succession' or 'the church as by law established'. Indeed,
the profession of loyalty lay at the heart of many of the addresses and was
certainly the whole point of the associations. Thus in 1708 Brackley's
corporation promised to 'stand by, support and maintain the protestant
succession, the happiest government and the best of queens against all
pretenders whatsoever. Which declaration (as a record to posterity) is not
only attested in the usual forms of our corporation; but we are ready upon
the first occasion to seal it with our blood'.[148] The vehemence of this may
have been unusual but not its general sense which was repeated in many
other addresses.

   Seeing the addresses as forms by which subjects repeatedly signified
their active consent to the state opens up a more radical dimension. As we
have seen, many addresses spoke not just for the corporation but also for a
borough's inhabitants. The statements of active consent therefore penetrated beyond a narrowly defined office-holding élite. The association
oaths of 1696, and the addresses that accompanied them, offer a wonderful

[148] *LG*, 4427.

example of this process, though the oaths of loyalty in the mid-century remind us that this process was the culmination of a longer trend.[149] Whig MPs promoted the association to defend William, their 'rightful and lawful' king, against 'the late King James and all his adherents'. It was intended to confront one political party, the Tories, with a dilemma about their allegiance to the revolutionary regime. Such a dilemma had been obvious ever since 1688 but now the dominant Whig party had their enemies over a barrel: if the Tories accepted the wording of the association they risked splitting their party, but if they opposed the association they ran the risk of being branded jacobites. John Evelyn saw through the partisan design and reported that the association was 'censur'd as a very intangling contrivance of the Parliament: In expectation that many in high office would lay downe & other succeed'.[150] The act enforcing the association did carry some relief for the Tories, for its compulsory nature for anyone holding office meant that fewer refused than would have been the case had the oath been purely voluntary. But the rest of the act's provisions did not make cheerful reading. MPs had to sign or be unseated and anyone who refused the oath was to be disenfranchised.[151] And whilst the Tories had to struggle with their consciences, Quakers (who refused to take any oath) were relieved of the need to swear and were allowed to make a simple declaration of fidelity. Worse still, although the act was not compulsory for non office-holders, the assassination plot made many want to sign the association voluntarily. The text of the parliamentary association was thus rapidly copied throughout the kingdom onto parchments, and signatures both invited and encouraged by Whigs.[152] At Doncaster the association was signed with a 'great noise in the town, so that the streets were filled and the windows decked with fair ladies'.[153] The clerical diarist Abraham de la Pryme recorded that 'over the whole nation there are few or none that refuses the same, but every one signs it with the greatest alacrity imaginable'.[154] Accordingly, associations signed with many thousands of names flooded up

---

[149] First framed in 1534, there were state oaths enacted in 1536, 1559, 1606, 1640, 1641, 1643 (twice), 1645, 1649, 1654, 1661–5, and 1702 (Jones, *Conscience and Allegiance*, appendix).

[150] Cf. HMC Portland, iii. 575.

[151] For a high church Tory campaign against the association as 'an overt act of treason', see *The Present Disposition of England Considered* (1701), 15.

[152] Sir Richard Cocks delivered a charge to the grand jury ('not approved by Mr Lane and Mr Stratford and Mr Sheppard') urging everyone to sign the association (Bodl. MS Eng. Hist. b.209, f. 39 charge to the Easter sessions 1696). See also, Liverpool RO, MD/174, entry for 16 Mar. 1696, diary of Sir Willoughby Aston, for the promotion of the association in Cheshire. For Tory hostility, see HMC Portland, iii. 575–6.

[153] HMC Various Collections, viii. 81.

[154] *Diary of Abraham de la Pryme*, 95.

to London. These oaths of loyalty and their accompanying addresses must be regarded as attempts to procure active consent to revolution principles. Such bonds were particularly necessary at a time when economic distress caused by the recoinage was at a height.[155] And the campaign penetrated all social levels. A detailed study of Earls Colne, in Essex, suggests that about two-thirds of that parish's adult males signed, ranging from the very poor to the wealthy.[156]

The association movement, like petitions and addresses, taught ideological lessons about the nature of political legitimacy to a very wide spectrum of men. In Norwich, for example, Henry Meriton delivered a sermon in the cathedral on 11 April (the anniversary of the king's coronation and at the height of the association movement) that paraphrased Lockean arguments about the nature of civil society. Meriton asserted that 'the consent of the People is God's Voice' and that all political authority was constituted 'by Compact and Agreement'.[157] Man, he said, was a sociable animal and when in a state of nature 'right reason which is the voice of God [did] direct them to place a supream Authority upon some or other of themselves, to be an umpire of their Controversies, and keep them in peace, according to such measures and limitations, as were thought fittest for the attaining the ends of Government, the Preservation of the People'.[158] Government was thus a divine ordinance but a human creation and Meriton explicitly rejected all Tory ideology about the nature of obligation, castigating patriarchalism, providentialism, and conquest theory, all of which had been used to salve Tory consciences about the legitimacy of William's accession. Meeting, as Locke had done, the charge that such an ideology opened the floodgate to popular disorder, Meriton argued that the 'doctrine, that political authority is derived from God by the consent of people' was 'certainly the only means to preserve government, and keep it steddy without tottering or shaking'.[159] The new king, Meriton asserted, thus had 'an undoubted Right to the Crown he wears' even though 'so many boldly dispute against' it and had attempted to kill him.[160] 'The Nation' rejected such disloyalty and 'condemned it in their Associations'.[161] Indeed, he hoped that the city's inhabitants would 'yield our Obedience to His

---

[155] In July 1696 Roger Whitley received a delegation of 27 women and a boy 'complaining of ye coyne; yt they were ready to starve' (Bodl. MS Eng. Hist. c.711, f. 206). For further descriptions of the poverty caused by the recoinage, see Somerset RO, DD/SF 1088(7), R. Snowe to [E. Clarke], 18 Nov. 1696; *HMC 10th Report app. iv*, 332; *Diary of Abraham de la Pryme*, 95–7.

[156] A. Macfarlane, *Reconstructing Historical Communities* (Cambridge, 1977), 189–90.

[157] H. Meriton, *A Sermon Preacht at the Cathedral Church in Norwich* (1696), 7–8.

[158] Ibid., 9.   [159] Ibid., 19–20.

[160] Ibid, 21, 25–6.   [161] Ibid., 32.

Two versions of the 1696 association were promoted in Norwich, one (shown here) promising to stand by one another in 'revenging' any successful attempt on the king's life, and the other merely 'punishing' it. The rival texts split the city. [Reproduced by permission of the National Archives.]

present Majesty for Conscience sake, as to one that hath a Right to govern us'.[162]

Meriton's encomium on William and his legitimacy was perhaps the more necessary because of Norwich's strong non-juring faction and divided politics. Indeed, the city sent up two associations, with rival wordings.[163] In February 1696 a Tory alderman, Philip Stebbing, was forced publicly to deny that on reading a 'printed paper' about the assassination plot he had declared in the Half Moon Coffee-house that 'the plott is mine Arse all over'.[164] But the Tory-dominated corporation was certainly suspicious of Whig intentions. A London newspaper, the *Post Man*, carried a hostile account of the corporation's prevarications. Although Norwich's MPs had sent down a copy of the association, the corporation, it claimed, 'never would promote the same till the mouths of all the honest part of the Citizens were filled with exclamations against them for their not doing it' and so 'the Citizens resolved to do it themselves'. Under pressure, then, the corporation copied the association signed by MPs but at first 'left out the word *Rightful*, implying that William was merely the king by law. Moreover, they replaced the word 'revenging' with 'punishing' in a promise of action against the papists 'because they thought the former too severe and unchristian (to use their own expression)'. After some debate the corporation did agree to add the all-important word 'rightful' but refused to alter 'punishing'. The citizens therefore promoted a rival address with just the one word different, and it was reported in the newspaper that it was like to attract '4 to one to what the Court has'.[165] This report itself proved controversial. The court of aldermen hunted for the source of the 'scandalous' report and a Nathanial Harthnance was forced to disown it publicly.[166] On 3 May the court sanctioned the prosecution of the newspaper's publisher, Richard Baldwin. The controversy of public discourse, facilitated by print, was thus at the heart of city politics, and raged over disputed words.

The rival associations listed the city's inhabitants along partisan lines; 3,124 signatures, including those of the Tory mayor, Augustine Briggs, and veteran pamphleteer Sir Roger L'Estrange (who was shortly afterwards arrested in connection with the plot), were appended to the 'corporation' text. A number of its signatories, including L'Estrange, had already been

---

[162] *A Sermon Preacht*, Meriton, 34.
[163] PRO, C213/182 and C213/184.
[164] Norfolk RO, N[orwich] C[ity] R[ecords], Mayor's Court books, Vol. 26, f. 10.
[165] *Post Man*, 7–9 Apr. 1696.
[166] Norfolk RO, NCR 16a/26, Book of Proceedings in the Mayors Court 1695–1709, fol. 26ᵛ.

prosecuted or suspected of jacobitism.[167] In all, 3,918 names were attached to the rival, more vigorous, 'citizens' text and included a number of prominent dissenters, including John Fransham, who acted as Daniel Defoe's contact in the city for the distribution of Whig prints and Robert Cooke, 'the wealthiest man in the city' and the apparent organizer of the citizens' association through the city's Weavers' Company.[168] Of the total 7,042 names, fewer than 4 per cent were common to both texts, suggesting a remarkable degree of polarization and popular participation. Norwich's population was about 28,500 at this time, suggesting that almost the entire adult male population might have been involved in subscribing.[169] The division in Norwich was in some ways an oddity, for rival associations were rare. Nevertheless the huge impact of the dispute in England's second city showed the power of words to divide.

The Whigs returned to the idea of an association to safeguard the protestant succession during the jacobite riots of 1715–16 and, more successfully, in 1723 in the wake of the Atterbury Plot. On this latter occasion really vast numbers of subscriptions were collected at quarter sessions. In Devon, for example, some 27,000 signatures and marks were enrolled over a six-month period.[170] In many places the entire adult population of a village paraded before the justices. Yet Speaker Onslow thought the exercise futile. 'It was a strange and ridiculous sight', he said, 'to see people crouding to give a testimony of their allegiance to a government and cursing it at the same time for giving them the trouble of so doing, and for the fright they were put into by it; and I am satisfied more real disaffection to the king and his family arose from it than from any thing which happened in that

---

[167] NRO, NNAS Frere Collection DS 604, persons disaffected to the government, 1693. The subscribers included Robert Poyn[t]er, who in September 1689 had allegedly said that 'King William was the elective king but not the hereditary king' (NRO, NCR, Case 12 shelf b (1), examinations and information 1684–9, information of Joseph Smith, 7 Sept. 89 and William Symonds, 12 Sept. 89).

[168] *Letters of Humphrey Prideaux to John Ellis, 1674–1722*, ed. E. M. Thompson, Camden Society NS, 15 (1875), 167, 169–70; F. Norgate, 'Correspondence between De Foe and John Fransham, of Norwich', *Notes and Queries*, 5th ser., 3 (1875), 261–3, 282–4. Prideaux referred to the weavers 'as distinct corporation of themselfes' and it is clear that economic issues were also at stake in the controversy, for the weavers wanted a bill to prohibit Indian silks and were persuaded by the Whig MP Sir Henry Hobart that the more zeal they showed the more likely they were to obtain the legislation.

[169] The assembly ordered that common councillors, with the assistance of a churchwarden and an overseer of the poor, were 'to goe from house to house and tender the same to be subscribed by all men who are housekeepers and alsoe all men lodgerss of the age of sixteeen yeares and upwards' (NRO, NCR, Court Books, Vol. 26, ff. 200ᵛ–201ʳ). I am currently engaged in a more detailed study of the associations.

[170] P. Langford, *Public Life and the Propertied Englishman, 1689–1798* (Oxford, 1991), 104.

time.'[171] Even so, the subscriptions were testimony of an inclusive, consensual, society but one in which the representation of loyalty was as important as popular participation.

THE VAGARIES OF PETITIONS AND ADDRESSES: THE GIDDY PEOPLE

As Onslow's disparaging remarks suggest, the activities of subscriptional communities were often slighted. The struggle for power in the localities, reflected in the dialogic nature of petition and counter-petition, seemed only to show the voice of the people to be inconsistent at the very least, and downright giddy or untrustworthy at worst. In the wake of the rash of addresses in 1710 Daniel Defoe argued that the 'sense of the nation' could be made to mean anything and that the addresses threatened the meaning of words to the point of 'non-signification'. The addresses were the clearest example that the people 'had no meaning at all in what they said'. Ever since the days of James II, Defoe argued, addressers had never performed a single word of what they said. The 1710 addresses likewise 'would be understood to have NO MEANING'. And this was a clever ploy, Defoe said mockingly, to protect them against the charge of insincerity: 'For having only muster'd up a Rhapsody of Words, which they meant for nothing; and which they hoped no doubt that her Majesty wou'd take for nothing; the want of truth in them was a thing of no signification, for what can it signify whether words that have no meaning have any truth in them or no?' Indeed, his tract was devoted to a lengthy outline of how words generally had become devoid of sense. He noted how meaning had so disappeared from the 'common conversation of men' that it had become like 'froth upon your drink'. In order to understand people, it was thus necessary to understand words in a new way, so that the 'literal' meaning was not to prevail over the truth of how men acted. He duly warned against the election of 'Nothing-Meaning Gentlemen' and recommended the return to parliament of 'men of meaning'. This was an election tract, explicitly making the connection between language and representation.[172] Defoe was playing with the different meanings of 'sense'; that is to say, sense as 'meaning', as 'opinion', and as 'political savvy'.

---

[171] W. Coxe, *Memoirs of the Life . . . of Sir Robert Walpole*, 3 vols. (London, 1798), ii. 555.
[172] Defoe, *A New Test*, 3, 7, 13, 17, 55, 76–8. The BL copy at 101.c.44 has a manuscript date of 3 Aug. 1710.

John Oldmixon, who analysed the addresses promoted over the period, was also ambivalent about what he found. On the one hand, he doubted if addresses showed very much at all about the sense of the people. Those at the 'head of affairs' would always be able to find men to address away their lives and fortunes, he thought. But part of him (and it was the Whig part, since he was writing in the wake of the surge of popular support for Dr Sacheverell) was deeply depressed about the vacillations of opinion which addresses revealed. Oldmixon therefore attacked the 'levity and inconstancy of people in changing their stile and sentiments'. He thought that 'if we could ever find one borough keep its word, we should highly extol the superabundant loyalty and zeal of those who are at pains of having an address drawn up'. The transience of representations of public opinion struck him forcefully: 'what is the sense of a county today may not be so tomorrow; and tis the same with Addresses as in knights of a shire'. He took the example of Gloucestershire, which appeared to have addressed on every major occasion and swum with the tide on each. Oldmixon's whiggish faith in the people was shaken by his analysis of addresses and his observations are shot through with contempt for the untrustworthiness and inconsistency of the nation. Oldmixon's conclusions about addresses were highly cynical. 'Those you make them for are not fond of them; those you make them against laugh at them; those you make them to do not value them; those that sign them do not understand them; those that understand them do not like them; those that like them, do not believe them.'[173] Addresses, then, played their part in distancing the Whigs from popular politics; and the rash of high-Tory addresses between 1710 and 1714 was one element pushing the Whigs to enact a series of measures after the accession of George I that reduced the scope for popular political activity.

SUMMARY

Petitioning and addressing contributed towards the formation of party allegiances and partisan politics; but the latter in turn also shaped the way in which petitions and addresses operated. Each party, as well as the government, sought to capture public speech through petitions and addresses. These documents therefore illuminate the interaction of political practice, rhetoric, and public discourse. They helped to form a fictional unity—the national public voice. But that was also a contested one. And it was one that

---

[173] Oldmixon, *History of Addresses*, i. dedication; ii. 2, 12, 29.

operated according to slightly different rules even from the campaigns of
the 1640s. There was thus a shift from petition to address; an attempt to
link informal representative practices to the formal representative process;
and a rejection of explicit accountability by representatives. The scale
of the later Stuart campaigns was unprecedented, and helped to foster a
national political culture. Zaret charts a shift from traditional to innovative petitioning; and we might extend his analysis to chart a shift from
innovative petitioning to a form of national acclamation. And that raises
important questions about the public sphere at the very moment of its
creation, for according to Habermas a public acclamation of politics is a
sign of a decayed, modern, form of presentational politics.

The subscriptional activity of the later Stuart period could foster partisan, party conflict and opened an important dialogue between the representative parts of the state. In the process petitions and addresses enlarged
the public sphere both in terms of the debate engendered and the broadening of the 'public' invoked in the struggles. Yet there was also a paradox
at the heart of public addressing. Its acclamatory nature in terms of format
and content could both restrain the autonomy of the public sphere and reduce its critical faculty. While this had creative dimensions, in terms of
helping to forge a sense of national identity and pride, as well as manufacturing consent and loyalty, in the longer term the vacillations of the
dialogue may have confirmed a fear that the people were not rational
participants in the debate but credulous, easily swayed, perhaps even hypocritical victims, and hence tools, of partisan polemic. The expansion of
the public voice was not thought to have coincided with the development
of popular rationalism. It is to this problem of public judgement that we
must now turn.

CHAPTER FOUR

Informing Public Judgement at the Polls

Tis not half a century ago, since twas common for a worthy gentleman who was fam'd for his publick spirit, to be chose in his parlour, and beg'd to represent his county, city or borough, in the House of Commons. The case is so strangely alter'd that now a Gentleman shall exhaust his estate and spend vast sums to get to be elected for a pitiful borough.[1]

Tis a great advantage in England that whatever be the changes continually occurring in Church or State there be so many learned men who immediately publish their advice pro and con that each may see and quickly choose what is safest and best to do without much study. Such are now the various papers directed to the freeholders and electors for choosing of Parliament men . . .[2]

[Beware] those officious politicians, who will surely be selling Advice of all prices, from a half-penny to six pence, and I forewarn the Freeholders not to be cheated, for what they vend is like Mountebank's poison. I never knew a New Parliament to be chosen but out came Advice upon it.[3]

The last chapter suggested that, through a partisan contest to capture public discourse, petitions and addresses fostered notions of a public will and raised queries about the nature of that public and the rationality of its will.

---

[1] T. Baston, *Thoughts on Trade and a Publick Spirit* (1716), 65–6.
[2] 'London in 1689–90', diary of the Revd R. Kirk, transcribed by D. Maclean, *Transactions of the London and Middlesex Archaeological Society*, NS, 6 (1929–32), 494.
[3] *Remarks on a Scandalous Libel Entitl'd a Letter from a Member of Parliament* (1713), 20.

Petitions and addresses forced individuals to make choices about the political world around them, and it was possible to come to very different, partisan judgements about that world. And we saw how contemporaries believed the vacillation of opinion to be, in part, the result of failures of public judgement and the tricks and deceptions practised by political opponents, who twisted language to manipulate the public. Petitions and addresses thus raised key questions about public judgement. How were the people to decide about national affairs? On what criteria should they base their choices? These were the issues raised by any appeal to the people. As such, they were not particularly new. But they applied with even greater force to electioneering, the subject of this chapter. The frequency of electioneering in the later Stuart period, and the routine appeal to public opinion, made answers to such questions far more urgent than ever before. The result was the development of new ways of guiding the people's judgement. This chapter examines the emergence of a genre of print that sought to advise the public how to vote and to inform them about how their representatives voted. This recognized a shift in the object of counsel.[4] Whereas advice had previously been offered to the monarch, it was now the public that needed counsel. Such a shift posed intriguing challenges.

Electoral advice literature is an interesting development in its own right, indicating both the rising profile of parliament at the heart of a representative society and the ways in which cheap print helped to change political culture. But it also has significance as another means by which the 'public' was fostered. Like the subscriptional activity examined in the last chapter, the contest of conflicting opinion helped to constitute public discourse and the idea of a people with a national political culture. Authors of printed advice assumed that Whig and Tory had a national applicability and meaning, and although some pamphlets were targeted at particular constituents, many more addressed a national platform or expected the local to have national resonance. The electoral advice literature is also important because of the representation it put forward of voters and their representatives. The material was engaged in a systematic exercise in imagining: imagining readers as voters, and voters as idealized selfless and dispassionate citizens. Published advice helped to shape the ideal of a rational public that set self-interest and partisanship aside in favour of the public good. And as well as creating representations of the ideal voter, printed

---

[4] For earlier notions, see J. A. Guy, *Politics, Law and Counsel in Tudor and Early Stuart England* (Aldershot, 2000).

electoral advice also depicted the ideal politician as similarly impartial and public-spirited.

These ideals, which in part drew on older notions of urban civility and the good of the commonwealth, had interesting implications. First, they militated against the partisanship that inspired or provoked much of the electoral advice in the first place. The claim to, and advocacy of, impartiality and rationality sat uneasily with the partisanship and passion evident in the elections themselves. Authors also entered print specifically to reject the irrationalities induced by blind adherence to party. Second, the ideal of a representational society encouraged the articulation of ideas about how to make elections more participatory. There was thus no theoretical tension between representation and participation, for a truly participatory representative system would determine the true will of the people. An active voter ensured true representation. Third, as we also shall see more fully in subsequent chapters, the electioneering discourse was seen to fall short of the standards of rationality that the convention of the 'rational voter' itself encouraged. Far from informing the people's judgement rightly, printed advice of all sorts seemed intent merely on leading public judgement astray. The printed appeal to the electorate was thus highly ambiguous. On the one hand, it cultivated the idea of a rational, independent, and uncorrupted voter who pursued the public rather than private interest. On the other hand, the need to advise voters reflected anxiety that they were often acting irrationally, subject to a host of pressures, from party and court, that perverted free and informed choice. The people were imagined both as the rational arbiter of the public good but also as vulnerable to irrationality or manipulation. Moreover, advice to voters was itself often seen as misleading. Hence the public discourse that might keep the public alert to the danger of corruption might also be the means to corrupt it. The advice to or from voters might *itself* be partisan, promoting sectional or private interests over public ones. Frequent elections were intended to secure a true representation but in this way they also threatened it. If the voters could not judge the misrepresentations perpetrated by the nation's enemies, the self-interested, and/or the corrupt, then national disaster lay just round the corner.

In the second half of the chapter the problem of public and private interest is pursued through a discussion of the role of 'instructions' to MPs. Some of the debate surrounding these, in relation to the right of the people to petition or address their MPs, was examined earlier. Here, the discussion seeks to show that advice about political judgement was a two-way process, flowing from people to representatives as well as from parliament to the people. More importantly it seeks to highlight the significance of the debate about the rationality or irrationality of the people. Instructions were only worth while if the people had the capacity for judgement and many publicly doubted that they did.

Throughout the chapter runs a discussion of the language of interest (the word used to describe an electoral following as well as a personal or public motivating factor). I argue that the anxiety over party interest provides an essential context for a debate over the role of representatives, who denied they were mere delegates and subordinate to the people who elected them. Partisan MPs thus sought to legitimize their status by claiming to rise above sectional interests. Similarly, anxiety over the prevalence of self-interest, among voters and parliamentarians, explains attempts to restrict corruption and bribery as well as the number of office-holding MPs. The political culture appeared to facilitate the pursuit of private over public interest. The language of interest was thus part and parcel of the representative contest.

PRINTED ELECTORAL ADVICE: A NEW GENRE

Your choice will now be the best standard by which to judge the present disposition of the kingdom[5]

Judgment is discernment of difference.[6]

the partiality of judgment is a central and ineliminable feature of all politics everywhere.[7]

There has been little close analysis of the voluminous printed literature that articulated anxieties about misrepresentation and offered advice about how to avoid it. What follows is an attempt to map out the form and contours of that public debate and to reveal some of its richness.

The development of printed electoral advice in the later Stuart period was testimony to the growing interaction of politics and print.[8] It is true

[5] *The Best Choice of Parliament-Men Considered* (1701), 11.
[6] Locke, *Essay Concerning Human Understanding*, bk. 2, ch. xi, para. 2.
[7] J. Dunn, *The Cunning of Unreason: Making Sense of Politics* (2000), 165.
[8] There is no general history of election advice literature, though Plumb long ago drew attention to this gap ('The Growth of the Electorate', 92). But see J. Richards, *Party Propaganda Under Queen Anne: The General Elections of 1702–13* (Athens, Ga., 1972); Speck, *Tory & Whig*; Speck, 'Propaganda in Augustan England', *TRHS*, 5th ser., 22 (1972), 17–32; J. A. Downie, *Robert Harley and the Press: Propaganda and Public Opinion in the Age of Swift and Defoe*

that print of all types, not just that specifically targeted at the voter, had an elector as the implied, imagined reader and this is a point to which we must return in future chapters, for in an important sense a good deal of public discourse in an age of frequent elections was necessarily conceived as public advice. Nevertheless the genre of electoral advice stands out as novel in the 1640s, another product of the liberated press. Yet it only reached maturity in the Restoration and post-revolutionary period, when frequent elections, a free press, and an expanded electorate fostered its development. Such print addressed the voters directly, imagining readers to be electors (and hence in a sense virtually enfranchizing those without a vote but who nevertheless read the material). In this sense the expansion in the output of controversial material after 1640 had a qualitative impact as well as a quantitative one.

Printed advice—mainly in pamphlet form but also, increasingly, to be found in periodicals[9]—was written by men of every political persuasion and was a flexible genre. Tracts often set out the criteria by which candidates should be judged. The aim was usually to confirm or loosen allegiances, and sometimes to try to overturn them. This could be combined with a history of recent events or an overview of the state of the nation. And the advice could be tailored to a national audience or to particular electorates (either specific localities or groups within localities)[10] or to ideological groupings, such as dissenters.[11] Advice demanded a reader response, by asking the reader/voter to judge the value of the arguments. Recent work has tended to focus on reading as a personal reaction; but viewing voters as readers allows us to examine readers as groups and actors. Implied activity was perhaps most obvious when the advice

(Cambridge, 1979); M. E. Ransome, 'The Press and the General Election of 1710', *CHJ*, 6 (1939), 209–21.

[9] Defoe's *Review* was published three times a week during the elections in 1705 and one edition devoted all four pages to his political message for the parties to study peace, of which some 5,000 copies were produced (Downie, *Harley and the Press*, 69).

[10] The first example of a tract tailored for a particular town's audience (outside London) seems to have been in 1690 (*A Letter to a Gentleman about the Election of Members for the County of Cambridge* (1690)). *A Letter from a Citizen of Worcester* (1710) argued that a pamphlet called *The Worcester Triumph* (1710) had been 'industriously spread' in that city. *Cameronian Whigs No Patriots* (1713) was addressed to the electors of King's Lynn (and hence against Robert Walpole) early in 1713—months before the election of that year (*Post Boy*, 2775).

[11] For example [T. Comber], *Three Considerations proposed to Mr William Penn . . . which may be Worthy the Consideration of all the Quakers and of all my Dissenting Brethren also that have Voyces in the Choice of Parliament-men* [1688]. *The Best Means to Defeat the Expectations of the Enemies to the Government* (1690), was endorsed by Luttrell as 'a fanatick thing in behalf of yis governm[en]t' (Houghton broadsides, B80).

literature appeared in the form of 'queries', which asked the reader to supply the albeit-implied answer; but it was present in most printed advice.[12] In this sense, the flood of words was meant to generate an active citizenry. Division lists, considered in the second half of the chapter, were another form of print that demanded reader/voter response. Such lists appeared to offer impartial knowledge in order to inform judgement and hence facilitate a rational choice. All too often, however, they were viewed as partisan attempts at misinformation designed to subvert true judgement.

Printed electoral advice became widespread in the later Stuart period but the first example of the genre appears to have been written by the poet and critic George Wither. His pamphlet *Letters of Advice* was first published in November 1644 (in the expectation of recruiter elections) and reprinted in September 1645 to coincide with the issue of writs for the Surrey constituencies with which he was most concerned.[13] In many ways Wither established the format of the genre, though he was in turn drawing on an older 'advice' literature, a tradition of manuscript letters of recommendation and electoral sermons. But he explicitly addressed the public, 'those of inferiour rank and meanest capacities' who needed to be instructed about the 'publick interest', and urged that his advice be read 'to those illiterate persons, whose voices are usually given by an implicit faith'.[14] Wither's example was copied in the 1650s but found maturity only with the advent of frequent elections. Large quantities of printed advice for the voting public began appearing 1679-81, around the revolution, and again 1698-1701; but the volume increased dramatically in Anne's reign.[15] James Richards lists 114 pieces of election propaganda published between 1702 and 1713, a figure that excludes the advice offered in numerous

---

[12] *Sober and Seasonable Queries Humbly Offered to all Good Protestants . . . The Second Edition with Considerable Additions by Another Author* (1679); R. L'Estrange, *Some Queries Concerning the Election of Members for the Ensuing Parliament* (1690); J. Harrington, *Some Queries Concerning the Election . . . Together with a Reply* (1690); Harrington, *Roger L'Estrange's Queries Considered; and Some Queries Put* [1690].

[13] J. Gurney, 'George Wither and Surrey Politics, 1642–9', *Southern History*, 19 (1997), 74–98. I am very grateful to Jason Peacey for drawing this to my attention. I have also benefited from reading his unpublished 'Parties, Polls and Print: Election Propaganda in the Civil War and Interregnum'.

[14] *Letters of Advice*, 2.

[15] Knights, *Politics and Opinion*, 206–19, 306–16, bibliography; Horwitz, *Parliament, Policy and Politics*, 51–2, 237–9. BL, Add. MSS 70421, ff. 177–8, newsletter 29 July 1710: 'the Whigs send a greate many pamphlets abt ye kingdome to prepare the people ag[ains]t a new Election'. A Norwich bookseller was prosecuted for selling Tory electioneering print (ibid., ff. 191–2, 15 Aug.).

periodicals; and about a fifth of this material went through more than one edition.[16] Indeed some tracts became bestsellers. Halifax's *Some Cautions* (which emulated Wither) went through at least four editions, reprinted to coincide with a number of different elections.[17] The sheer scale of production of such material suggests a large public appetite. Even if it is difficult to show a direct correlation with voting behaviour, there was a clear assumption on behalf of authors and publishers that the electorate *could* be influenced in this way. In February 1690, for example, Edmund Bohun (soon to be appointed licenser of the press) was urged by a correspondent from Ipswich to send a parcel of tracts that would be 'very useful' during the election campaign there.[18] One of the titles, *A Letter to a Friend* was also sent to Sir Ralph Verney in Buckinghamshire; and it is reported to have been circulated in Cambridgeshire and elsewhere as well.[19] The tract provoked several replies.[20] As this case illustrates, printed advice often provoked printed counter-advice in a paper battle to win hearts and minds, and therefore became part of the larger polemical battle.

Arrangements for distributing such material became sophisticated. *A Word of Advice unto all those that have a Right to Choose Parliament Men* (1690) urged

all sober honest citizens to send packets of these papers of advice into the country to your chapmen, and desire them to spread them abroad in the country, that the people may be awakened to their duty. What if it cost you a few shillings; it may be the last time that you may have occasion to stir them up to their duty; it will not undo you nor impare your estates by it and it may cost you many pounds, to little or no purpose, if we should through the people's ignorance or negligence, have another bad parliament.[21]

One whiggish electoral tract of 1714 even began with an advertisement offering cut-price bulk buys:

---

[16] Richards, *Party Propaganda*, 9.

[17] *Some Cautions Offered to the Consideration of those who are to Chuse Members to Serve in the Ensuing Parliament* was published in 1695, 1701, 1713, and 1714, and was still being reprinted as late as 1796. It was also reworked and plagiarized as *The Subjects Case, or, Serious Advice to all Englishmen who have the Right of Electing Members to Serve their Country in the Next Parliament* (1701).

[18] Cambridge University Library, Sel.3.237 item 26, 'MW' to E. Bohun, 27 Feb. 1689/90, requesting *A Letter to a Friend, Upon the Dissolving of the Late Parliament* (1690); *Some Queries Concerning the Election of Members* (1690).

[19] BL, Verney MSS, reel 44, John Verney to Sir Ralph, 18 Feb. 1689/90; *A Letter to a Gentleman about the Election of Members for the County of Cambridge*, 1.

[20] *An Answer to a Paper Entituled A Letter to a Friend* (1690); *A Letter to a Gentleman*.

[21] *A Word*, 2.

Since it is certain, the enemies to the present constitution will be very zealous for obtaining a parliament after their old manner, it is earnestly desired of every true Briton, who has any value for religion, liberty or the encrease of trade, to give this book gratis at every house in some one part of a county, city or shire-town in Great Britain, before new Members of Parliament are chosen; to the end the nations may not again be in danger of falling into the hands of the Romans.[22]

The apparent success of such means was indicated by a printed reply, which complained that 'great drifts' of the pamphlet 'were daily dispersed through the country, to influence elections'.[23] But Tory advice literature was equally successful in reaching voters. Francis Atterbury's *English Advice to the Freeholders of England* (1715) was 'dispers'd over every corner of Great Britain and Ireland with unparallel'd industry . . . publisht a little before the election'.[24] Its national dissemination was impressive, so much so that it was regarded as a deliberate attempt 'to raise disturbances in the approaching elections', and prompted a proclamation forbidding riotous behaviour at the polls.[25] Printed electoral advice, then, was produced in large quantity, particularly in Anne's reign, and circulated well outside London.

In the period 1679–1715 over 200 tracts were published with the explicit intention of influencing the judgement of voters. The number of pamphlets is significant—marking a real contrast with early or even mid-seventeenth-century electioneering—but so too is the way in which the advice genre addressed its readership. The freeholders and burgesses were treated as a national body of men, despite the very significant variations that existed in franchise and local political contexts.[26] Moreover, the message of the tracts was a national one. They gave criteria for choice that applied across the country. When the advice literature described Whigs and Tories they expected readers everywhere to know what they meant and for

----

[22] [C. Povey], *An Inquiry into the Miscarriages of the Last Four Years Reign, . . . Presented to the Freeholders of Great Britain against the Next Election of a New Parliament* (1714), 3. It ran to nine editions within a year. Copies were also printed in Ireland 'against the next election of a parliament there' and a 'counterfeit' or pirate version of the tract was also in circulation. *A Tender and Hearty Address to all the Freeholders and other Electors* (1714) cost 3*d* but 'any gentlemen that are willing to take a number to give away, shall have a considerable allowance'.

[23] *The Management of the Four Last Years Vindicated . . . Recommended to all True Englishmen, against the Election of a New Parliament* (1714), 6.

[24] J. Toland, *The State-Anatomy of Great Britain* (1717), 90–1. P. B. Hyland, 'Liberty and Libel: Government and the Press during the Succession Crisis in Britain, 1712–1716', *EHR*, 101 (1986), 886–7.

[25] *LG*, 5294.

[26] Gunn, *Beyond Liberty and Property*, 73–88 discusses eighteenth-century views of the people as freeholders.

their comments to have local applicability. And, as we shall see shortly, the literature often invoked the notion of Englishness: the freeborn Englishman became the freeborn voter whose horizons were not circumbscribed by locality or self-interest but were truly national.

Printed advice as a rival to the pulpit

The flourishing of the genre of printed electoral advice reflected a partial secularization of public discourse. The rise of the genre was in part a testimony to the need to counteract the politicized sermons of the clergy and dissenting divines. This is not to say that the pulpit ceased to be a very powerful means of attempting to manipulate the public choice.[27] Indeed the political influence of the clergy grew during the Restoration due to the re-establishment of the church-state, the enfranchisement of the clergy in 1665 after their payment of lay taxation, and the sermonizing on politically charged anniversaries (such as 30 January or 5 November). Sometimes electioneering sermons were explicit in directing choice. Thus in 1660 Samuel Kem preached a sermon in Gloucester 'the Lords day before the election of burgesses for parliament' in which he advised members of his congregation about the type of man they should choose.[28] Politicized sermons were also encouraged by the many fast days called whilst England was at war with France, and by the attempts by jacobites to invade or, as in 1696, to assassinate the king. Such clerical electioneering could be taken as symptomatic of 'priestcraft', the clerical exercise of political power, or 'flattery'.[29] As one pamphleteer (hostile to such clerical meddling) put it, 'the clergy have the greatest advantage in this particular, that if they happen to be disgusted at any thing, they presently get up into their pulpits and in a state-sermon ring the bell backwards and then their party come in'.[30]

The extent of such influence was highlighted by the torrents of clerical vitriol produced in the election year of 1710 after the impeachment of Dr Sacheverell. Provoked by the politicized sermons of their colleagues, a group of low church clerics declared that such sermonizing meant that there was

---

[27] Claydon, 'The Sermon and the "Public Sphere"'.

[28] *King Solomon's Infallible Expedient* (1660), 9.

[29] *Political Aphorisms* (1690) observed that the people had 'an implicit faith to believe whatever our guides declare to be the doctrine of the Gospel', even if it was contrary to reason, and attacked the 'flattery' of those who persuaded princes that they had more authority than they did (preface and 3). In Kent 250 out of 318 parsons allegedly voted Tory in 1705 (*Review*, 29 May 1705).

[30] *A Letter from a Clergy-Man in the Country to a Minister in the City* (1689), 15.

scarce a parish, where such sermons have been preached, but has been immediately put into a flame by it; families have been divided; old friends quarrel'd; neighbours become shy; trade itself has not suffer'd a little; and instead of the great duties of love and peace, and doing good, are you for or against the Doctor? has been the word and hereditary, irresistible, anti-monarchical, republican &c has been all the language.[31]

'Pulpit-statesmen', some feared, were corrupting the sense of the nation.[32] In doing so, as John Locke put it, there was the risk of them 'propagating wrong notions concerning government'.[33] The dividing line between acceptable and unacceptable political comment from a cleric was never a clear one; but it gave rise to frequent controversy and comment.[34]

Printed advice could be used either to *reinforce* the clerical message outside the environment of the place of worship or to *counteract* the influence of 'priestcraft' or, indeed, the conventicle. As such, conscience was a powerful weapon to invoke. The casuistical tone of some electoral advice can be seen in a high-church Tory tract of 1705. It posed the dilemma of a voter who had 'a father, a patron, a landlord, a brother, a kinsman, or benefactor, who desires or perhaps commands me to vote for an ill man, quite contrary to my judgment; and tells me I shall lose his favour if I don't vote as he directs'. The reply of a fictional high churchman (asked for his 'guidance in this difficult case') is revealing:

Though every man is not capable to judge for himself without the assistance or direction of others; yet he ought to be very cautious of being impos'd on, by any man, lest he act contrary to reason and a good conscience . . . in general I lay this down for a rule, that the person voted for so far as you can learn, be a hearty friend to the established government in church and state and if your father, patron, landlord &c shall command or importune your voice for any gentleman not so qualified, you are to consider; tis your duty to prefer the publick good, before any private consideration whatsoever; that you shou'd do nothing (in this case) for any personal relation or favour; for the public welfare is of greater value and requires a stricter regard than your own private honour or gain.[35]

---

[31] J. Swynfen, *The Objections of the Non-Subscribing London Clergy against the Address* (1710), 25.

[32] *An Answer to a Letter from a Gentleman in the Country, Relating to the Present Ministry* (1699), 9.

[33] Locke, *Two Treatises*, preface.

[34] Burnet alleged that the clergy sat down in coffee-houses on Saturdays to read the high church Charles Leslie's *Rehearsal* (Leslie, *The Good Old Cause; or, Lying in Truth* (1710), 28). The *Examiner* was used by one parson in Scarborough to counteract the influence of the whiggish *Review* and *Observator*, gathering parishioners around him every Sunday evening (HMC Portland, iv. 641).

[35] *A Dialogue; or, New Friendly Debate* (1705), 19.

The Loyal Subjects Free Choice :
OR, Their General Satisfaction in the Calling of a New
PARLIAMENT,
By King *William*'s Gracious Appointment, *Whom God ever bless.*
To the Tune of Grim King of the Ghosts. Licensed according to Order.

Let all Royal Glory and State
invest our Great King on his Throne;
Whose Prudence and Wisdom so great
all Protestant Subjects will own:
To spring from a gracious Design
to give all his People content,
That none may have cause to repine,
He hath called a new Parliament.

Let Murmurers now lay aside
their many insensible Fears;
The Church shall in safety abide;
for the loyal Commons and Peers
Are Men of Integrity,
all Fiends in this Realm to prevent;
And prosperous Days we shall see,
being blest with a new Parliament.

The Wrongs of True Subjects they'll right,
likewise the proud Papists oppose;
Maintaining an Army to Fight
and cut down those insolent Foes.
The Honour and Peace of the Realm,
they'll strive to maintain by consent:
God bless those that sits at the Helm,
the King and His new Parliament.

Ne'er was there a legaller Choice
in any past Ages before;
Each Subject hath here a free Voice,
not only the Rich but the Poor:
All Persons might Vote that was free,
no Courtier to hinder was sent;
His Majesty gave Liberty
for choosing a free Parliament.

An election ballad of 1690 stresses the 'free choice' available to 'not only the rich but the poor
| All persons might vote that was free'. [Reproduced by courtesy of the Pepys Library,
Magdalene College, Cambridge.]

On one reading of this, public good becomes defined as loyalty to the established church and conscience is the means by which the individual can discern this. Yet the passage is also more complicated than that. The appeal is to 'reason' as well as a good conscience; and although the voter needs 'assistance', he can and should judge and act impartially and free from influence. Moreover, the appeal to conscience was being made through a print dialogue *that derived its authority from outside the pulpit.* Indeed, the genre deployed secular homily that tended to eschew the type of prayer that Wither used at the end of his 1644 tract. In other words, although not supplanting clerical influence, and at times used to supplement it, printed electoral advice was inherently a more secular alternative, drawing authority from the nature of print and public opinion, and drafted for the most part in language far distant from the eschatological discourse of the mid-century crisis. To understand this more fully we need to examine both the type of advice offered and the type of voter imagined by the printed electoral advice.

THE PARADOX OF THE RATIONAL VOTER

Voters, it was said, had both a duty and right to vote. One 1654 tract reminded electors 'that the choice of your law-makers is your first common right by which you distinguish yourselves from slaves' because each man could exercise his 'inherent and natural right'. Voting was thus 'the foundation and root of all' liberties.[36] Even if this 'natural right' to vote was not often discussed after the Restoration, the exhortation to vote was still strong. The whiggish *A Word of Advice* (1690) sought to dissuade men from 'sotting at an ale-house' at election time and excusing their non-participation by saying to themselves: ' "There is enough without me, I am but one, and I cannot go; or I must go to Plough on that day in such a place, and I cannot go; and I have my shop to look after, and my customers to tend, or such a customer to come to town that day and therefore I cannot attend it; and I am but a poor man, though I have a vote to give, yet I have nothing to lose, let it go which way it will, I can be no worse than I am.' The tract insisted on active, participatory citizenship: 'your estates, lives, liberties, your souls, religion and the glory of God are all concerned herein and all lye at stake'.[37] Instead of succumbing to self-interest, the voter was thus advised to prefer the public good by voting. Much of the printed electoral advice made similar pleas. Clearly this drew on a civic humanist tradition that fostered active citizenship. Yet the urge to act was not impartial; indeed, it was part of the partisan culture. The voter, in this case, was advised to vote against popery and jacobitism. Inherent in the advice literature was

---

[36] *A Memento for the People about their Elections of Members for the Approaching Parliament* (1654), broadside.
[37] *Word of Advice,* 1–2.

a tension between the desire to appeal to readers as active, rational, independent voters and the desire or need to inform the voter in ways that
could shape how that free choice was exercised. There was also ambiguity
about how far interests, particularly socially based ones, should be set
aside. And there was a tension between claims to impartiality and the
partisan bias of many tracts.

Such tensions are apparent in a tract of 1701 that reworked the marquis
of Halifax's electoral advice. At first it appeared to urge disdain for any private influence, insisting that electors must 'set aside all private respects and
interests; and discharge the trust of voting with 'justice, candor and integrity'. And in this construction of the independent voter there was a good
smattering of patriotism.[38] The electorate must discern 'the safety of the
English interest' by avoiding 'degenerate self-interested persons'. Thus

he is unworthy of the name of an *Englishman,* that for a small reward, a meals meat,
a debauch, or to procure the favour of some great man, will sell his vote . . . for next
to a man's salvation, the welfare of his country ought to supercede all other obliga-
tions, and be dearest in his esteem.[39]

Here, then, was advice for the voter to act on his own reason, for the public, national good, and to reject men 'inseparably link'd to a party or faction'. But the same tract also set out 'rules for directing' voters' choice, 'for
their serious considerations'. Thus although the voter was to act independently, outside the power of a landlord's influence, they would also do well,
it advised, to choose someone who had 'either in possession or reversion a
considerable estate', for 'certainly the interest of the kingdom is best plac'd
in the hands of such gentlemen as have the greatest shares in it'. When a
man had 'but a small estate, a numerous family', then 'his circumstances
have so prepar'd him for corruption; that he must in this degenerate age be
more than man . . . to withstand the temptation of rising himself at the
charge of the publick'.[40] The appeal to public virtue could thus both cut
against and uphold the superiority of rational independence over influence. The language of virtue insisted on individual responsibility but also
suggested that virtue and reason would rationally be found in the landed
élite. The ambiguity of appealing to the independence of a voter whilst also
wanting his deference or submission to a certain way of reasoning was also

---

[38] The language of patriotism became a 'fully-fledged part of English political discourse'
in the 1680s and 90s (M. Dietz, 'Patriotism', in Ball, Farr, and Hanson (eds.), *Political Innovation,* 183).
[39] *The Subjects Case,* 2, 5–6.
[40] Ibid., 1, 12–13, 18.

apparent in another tract of 1701. It urged men to let 'no threats or terrors of men, how great and powerful soever, fright you from your duty as well as your interest', and hence to act 'with the pure and noble principles of free-born Englishmen'. But the tract ended by recommending electors to choose 'gentlemen consisting of the chiefest quality, best parts, firmest loyalty, most plentiful estates'.[41] The free-born Englishman should freely consent to representation by his social superiors.

On the one hand, then, the genre helped to create an image of the people as free, sovereign, self-governing men capable of making up their own minds and possessed of a duty to act for the public good. In this sense, such material was part of an early enlightenment discourse that was widely available and part of the political culture. The freedom of the electorate to choose for itself was frequently asserted and encouraged. As one put it, 'he's a free and disinterested elector, that mov'd by no private principle, elects according to the best of his judgment'.[42] Voters should choose with 'all the care, caution, deliberation and circumspection imaginable'[43]. They should take care their votes were 'free, without present, gifts or future promises of reward'.[44] *The Best Choice of Parliament-Men* (1701) reminded electors 'you have the balance of power in your hands and may turn the scales to which side you please.'[45] Influence, of whatever sort, was to be resisted where reason and the public good rendered it necessary.[46]

But, on the other hand, the voter was represented as in need of advice about all sorts of dangers. *A Letter from a Freeholder to the Rest of the Free-holders of England* [1689] claimed electors must be 'as well advis'd as much in earnest when they chuse persons to serve in Parliament as they usually are when they make their last will and testament'.[47] Such printed 'influence' was necessary for a whole host of reasons. There were, protested one tract, many 'whose distance from the parliament, multiplicity of business or other circumstances in the world, render them less able to penetrate the designs that are now carrying on for the total subversion of our most excellent constitution'; without advice the electors could be imposed

---

[41] *The Best Choice*, 13, 21. In 1708 the marquis of Worcester bought up the entire first edition of a tract that urged his tenants to throw off their 'yoke of bondage', in order to prevent its circulation (M. McClain, 'The Wentwood Forest Riot: Property Rights and Political Culture in Restoration England', in Amussen and Kishlansky (eds.), *Political Culture*, 127).
[42] *Enquiry into the Inconveniences*, 9.
[43] *The Subjects Case*, 1.   [44] *The Best Choice*, 1.   [45] Ibid., 6.
[46] *Considerations Relating to our Choice and the Qualifications of Our Members of Parliament* (1711), 35; *A Word of Advice*, 2; BL, Eg. MSS 3,348, f. 70, King's Lynn corporation to Danby, 31 Mar. 1675.
[47] S. Johnson, *A Letter*, 1.

on.[48] Given the importance of the European situation, argued another, 'it is highly necessary to offer some marks, whereby persons of the meanest capacities may distinguish their friends from their enemies'.[49] The large number of rival electoral candidates, particularly for London's four seats, might also justify advice.[50] One tract targeting the City's voters claimed there were 'so many candidates' that the 'great variety . . . distracts the choice' and that voters needed 'some plain rational directions' to guide them.[51]

The voter was thought to be particularly in need of warning against the increasingly sophisticated attempts to seduce him away from his rational choice. As competition for parliamentary and local elections increased, more money was spent on softening or manipulating the electorate. The costs of electioneering spiralled as candidates were forced to lay out on drink, food, and entertainment for voters and, indeed, for a wider public who might influence those who had the vote.[52] All this imperilled true representation. As one tract put it, if the electors and elections were corrupted 'such a house of Commons cannot pass for a representative of the people, but a representative of a few dissolute, mercenary persons, possesst of voices in the boroughs of England' and Englishmen would have 'to seek other ways of being better represented'.[53] Partisan, as much as court, corruption thus necessitated printed electoral advice to bolster the rationality of the electorate. 'The corruption of officers is not to be fear'd half so much as the corrupting of the electors', remarked one tract.[54]

On the one hand, then, the voter was depicted as independent and rational, not only capable of making a choice but capable if left free to do so; on the other hand, the voter was portrayed as in need of advice to help him make a choice along the most rational lines and also of exhortation not to succumb to treats, bribes, and intimidation. This tension was exacerbated by partisanship. For one of the corrupting pressures on voters was printed electoral advice that was partial, misrepresentative, and emotive. Such

[48] Toland, *The Danger of Mercenary Parliaments* (1698), (*Harl. Misc.* ix, 399).

[49] *The Candidates Try'd or a Certain Way how to Avoid Mistakes in Choosing Members* (1701), 1.

[50] In London print was also used to give notice of City and parliamentary elections or pre-meetings of voters (BL, Harl. MS 5996(39), (48), (76)).

[51] *Some Advice Humbly Offered to the Consideration of the Several Electors of Parliament-Men for this Great City* [1689], broadside.

[52] Knights, *Politics and Opinion*, 217–18; *HOP II*, i. 68–9, 102–3, 188–9.

[53] *Considerations on the Nature of Parliaments and our Present Elections* [1698], 1–2, 8; *A Friendly Letter to Such as Have Voices in Election of Members to Serve in Parliament* (1695).

[54] *A Serious Address to the Commoners of England Concerning the Approaching Elections* (1705), 8.

London, April 19th, 1708.

S I R,

O*N* Wednefday *next*, *being tbe* 21 ft *Inflant*, *divers Eminent Citizens have determin'd to meet at the* Sun *Tavern behind the* Royal Exchange, *to think of Four Per-fons fitly qualify'd to be Nominated at the Common Hall, to ferve for this City in the enfuing Parliament ; where your Company is defired, at Four in the Afternoon ; and to bring fuch Perfons with you, as you fhall think fit.*

S I R, London, April 26. 1708.

IT having been unanimoufly agreed at a General Meeting of many hundreds of Eminent Citizens, on the 21ft Inftant, That

The Rt. Hon. Sir *William Withers*, Lord Mayor,
Sir *Francis Child*, } Aldermen,
Sir *Richard Hoare*, }
John Ward, Efq;

fhould be Nominated in the Common-Hall to be the Four Citizens to Reprefent this City in the next Parliament ; being Gentlemen of un-doubted Loyalty and Fidelity to Her Majefty's Perfon and Government, of fteady Zeal and hearty Affection to the Eftablifh'd Church and Pro-teftant Succeffion in the *Hannover Line*, and well acquainted in the Laws and Ufages of this City ;

Your Intereft, Vote and Poll, is therefore defired for the abovefaid Gentlemen.

In London print was exploited to encourage participation in elections and to inform the public. In 1708 handbills urged voters to gather in order to determine candidates and then announced the Tory slate that had been decided on by 'many hundreds of eminent citizens'. [Reproduced by courtesy of the British Library.]

print was thought to appeal to fear, prejudice, and passion as much as reason.[55] But the best antidote was thought to be corrective, but equally partisan, advice. Thus partisan literature was both one of the means to subvert free and rational choice, but also provoked more such literature, and hence generated a vicious circle. Guidance was necessary to show where truth lay amid the torrent of lies that accompanied each campaign; and this provoked a dialogue of advice and counter-advice. Partisans thus complained about the misleading advice offered by their rivals; and sought to correct it, claiming to be offering true advice that might properly inform the people's judgement.

The weapon in this battle was reason. Partisan electoral polemic appealed to readers' individual judgement and reliance on their own reason, but it also sought to circumscribe that freedom by suggesting that some choices were irrational or erroneous. The paradoxical appeal to, and manipulation of, voters' reason was sometimes apparent within a single tract. In 1675, for example, in order to influence a Norfolk by-election, a group of clerics 'published' a manuscript 'paper'. This professed not to 'dare to be so positive and disingenious as to determine the votes upon any individuall p[er]son nor doth this paper designe to ravish from you your reason & understandinge your supreme pr[e]rogative'. Yet, on the other hand, it consisted of a set of queries so vehemently hostile to Sir Robert Kemp, a candidate favoured by Lord Townshend, that it resulted in a libel case.[56]

Sometimes even a plea for voter independence and rational free choice was itself an attempt at partisan manipulation. A Tory tract of 1714 attacked Whig printed advice, telling voters that they ought to resent being 'taught to give your vote', and rely on their 'interest' and 'religion' to dictate to them. In an ideal world, 'under a true state of liberty', it would 'be enough to warn every honest, unprejudic'd man'. But in reality there were 'mists raised' and voters had to be shown a way through them. The tract thus went on to advise the electorate from a Tory perspective: it defended the Tory ministry of 1710–14 and urged voters to let loyalty 'ever conspicuous in the true members of the establish'd church, be the compass you steer by'.[57] The tract sought to lead voters by the nose just as much as the

---

[55] For emotive appeals, see [A. Maynwaring], *Advice to the Electors of Great Britain; Occasioned by the Intended Invasion from France* (1708); *British Advice to the Freeholders of Great Britain* (1715); J. S. Barrington, *A Dissuasive from Jacobitism: Shewing in General what the Nation is to Expect from a Popish King and in Particular from the Pretender* (1713); *What has been, May be*; [Defoe], *A Word Against a New Election* (1710).

[56] NRO, MC 1601/73 and 60, Horatio Townshend to Lord Chief Justice North, 28 Apr. 1676.

[57] *The Management of the Four Last Years Vindicated*, 6–7, 26.

pamphlet it criticized; but did so on the grounds that its rival was an impartial attempt to subvert the rational, independent, voter.

Indeed, the invocation of the rational, impartial, voter was often part of a partisan ploy. For example, *The Election Dialogue between a Gentleman and his Neighbour in the Country* (1710) begins with a gentleman affecting a pose of impartiality. He would vote, he claimed, for anyone who loved his country, the protestant succession, and an honourable peace and 'if these characters belong to the Tories, they shall have me at their command; if to the Whigs, then I am on their side'. Yet, as the dialogue unfolds, it is clear that the rhetorically dominant 'gentleman' is strongly whiggish. He asserts that the right of resistance was 'the foundation of all our government' and that Tories denied the legitimacy of the Revolution.[58] It is clear which way the voter was being advised. Many other examples could be offered to show clearly partisan tracts assuming a veneer of impartiality and ironically advising voters to lay aside their own partisan and private interests.[59] Much 'impartial' advice thus veiled a party bias. This was recognized at the time and exposing the hypocrisy of such claims to impartiality was often the task of counter-advice. Thus John Oldmixon published a refutation of Atterbury's high-church *English Advice to the Freeholders of England* (1715), claiming 'there are almost as many false things as words said . . . [it was] the most abominable medley of lies and impudence that ever came from the press'.[60] The independent, rational, voter had to be addressed as though advice was appealing to his independent reason; the trick was to use impartiality to bolster a conclusion that only one choice made sense but also to try to claim that an opponent's claim to impartiality was mere hypocrisy.

A number of aspects of published electoral advice are thus evident. It made appeal to an ideal of rational, public-minded, voters who disdained influence and self-interest. The voters were imagined as Englishmen—a word frequently employed—capable of discerning the national interest. The voter was thus imagined as being able to judge national politics on a national stage, so long as he had the 'right' advice. That advice, however, often employed its own polemical cunning, making use of the very notion of a rational, independent, voter to bolster the credibility of partisan

---

[58]   Hoadly, *Election Dialogue*, 4, 8.
[59]   *The Best Choice*, 17, 21; *A Word in Season* [1690], broadside; R. Walpole, *A Short History of the Parliament* (1713); [A. Collins], *Priestcraft in Perfection* (1710); *A Serious Address*; [W. Wagstaffe], *The State and Condition of our Taxes Considered . . . with Some Directions to the Freeholders of Great Britain, Concerning the Choice of the Next Parliament* (1714), 44.
[60]   J. Oldmixon, *Remarks on a Late Libel Privately Dispers'd by the Tories* (1715), 2, 10.

claims. What was designed to assist judgement, therefore, risked leading it more astray. The culture of party both placed a high premium on reasoned impartiality and yet sought to use such claims to further partisan ends. Voters were to avoid representing their own interests but instead choose the public good, even though party represented its own interest as that of the nation.

It is worth pursuing the language of interest further, because it has important implications for the concept of partisan representation. For a condemnation of the pursuit of self- or particular-interests fostered an attack on party zeal, even when it came from the pens of partisans. Naked partisanship could thus provoke denunciation and hence contribute to the formulation of an ideal of non-party, public-spirited, discourse.

Loyalty to party was, by its very nature, loyalty to a sectional interest, unless that interest coincided with, or could be portrayed as coinciding with, the national one. The pursuit of self-interest, by definition, rendered a representative useless. Unmasking self-interest through print was thus a public duty. The language of the public good could be used to delegitimize rival partisan interests; and the deployment of such language by both parties tended to empower an important critique of partisanship. As one pamphlet put it, ''tis not Whig or Tory but the honest English Man that must be employ'd'.[61] Partisanship thus employed a rhetoric that undermined itself. Here then was a paradox: the passion of party provoked *partisan* condemnations of party zeal. If a party could identify its opponents as pursuing self-interest, then partisans could legitimately advise the electorate to avoid the self-interested. This was the achievement of the Whigs early in Anne's reign (successfully accusing supporters of the occasional conformity legislation of pursuing a party and self-interest) and of the Tories in the later half of Anne's reign (successfully accusing the Whigs of spinning out the war for party and self-interest).

An example of this can be found in a 1710 Tory tract that sought to expose the degree of financial corruption at the heart of the Whig administration, but did so in terms of the Whig subversion of the common good:

The Business therefore of a House of Commons is to represent the whole commonalty of England; that is, they are to do all such things and exercise all such

[61] *An Englishman's Thoughts of the Present State of Affairs* (1701), broadside.

powers for the welfare and safety of the publick, which the whole common people would be supposed to do and exercise could they meet together, to counsel and debate orderly and quietly and deliberate maturely, for their own common good and safety.

MPs were thus to ensure financial propriety and to protect the rights of the people 'whom they represent as a third estate of the Kingdom'.[62]

Such arguments coincided with attacks on partisanship from those who claimed not to belong to any party at all. There was a shared discourse suspicious of sectional interest. As a result, electoral advice produced in the age of party tended to urge against the choice of a party man. The latter was not a

free agent and for that reason is very unfit to be trusted with the peoples liberty, after he has given up his own; for in reality they are greater slaves, than any body else would care to make them . . . the only freemen in the House of Commons are such gentlemen as know no side but our laws, nor espouse any interest but that of their country.

Party men were 'tether'd to the stake of a particular interest' and their 'heat weakens their judgments, heat raigneth in the fancy, and reason which is a colder faculty of the brain, takes more time to be heard, than the other will allow'. Parties were thus 'like your Algerine Pyrates, they hang out false colours; their pretences are the publick good, their real business is to advance their private interests, and to possess themselves of the best places in the government . . . tis very sure that while these opposite setts of angry men are tossing the ball, they will break all the windows, and do more hurt than their pretended zeal for the nation will ever make amends for.'[63]

The critique of sectional interest combined with a longstanding hostility to court interest, for it was claimed that the struggle between Whig and Tory was a contest to see which side could monopolize office. Unlike the early or mid-seventeenth-century struggles, which could be depicted as religiously motivated, a key objective of the later Stuart game was thus perceived to be state power and the rewards it could offer. As one tract of 1703 put it:

all the disputes, heats and fewds that are or have been in the nation since the Revolution (for from that time we chiefly date our misery) have not at all been upon the

---

[62] *A Letter to a New Member of the Honourable House of Commons; touching the Rise of all the Imbezzlements and Mismanagements of the Kingdom's Treasure from the Beginning of the Revolution until this Present Time* (Amsterdam [London?], 1710), 23–4.
[63] *The Subjects Case* (1701), 18–19.

account of religion (tho indeed that has all along been made use of to amuse and deceive the people) but have been made, created and begotten by those who endeavoured to be Members of Parliament

who hoped to make themselves and their families great through office. The Commons had thus become 'the seat of faction, that is, the place where all factions centred, under denomination or appellation of the Church party and the Dissenting party (to which Tory and Whig were nicknames)'.[64] On this reading, the pursuit of place had a damaging effect on representative government because it turned the representative into a partisan arena for spoils. Such a pursuit for self-interest, via sectional interests, obscured the pursuit of the public interest. As Sir Richard Cocks declared, 'if places were not to be the rewards of our actions here men of small or no estates would never try to get in and the chief aim of everyone would more probably be the true interest of their country since they could propose to make no other advantage to themselves'.[65] The selfish thus represented themselves and were ready to sell the liberties of the people. They thus failed to act for the public good. An office-holding MP no longer represented the people but his employer, the state.[66] Bar them from such places, and true representation could be restored. Pursuit of the public interest would follow. 'Were this a true representative and free from external force or private bribery, nothing could pass but what is thought to be for the publick good.'[67] Country rhetoric—that which criticized the corrupting influence of the court—thus combined with the mutual hostility of Whig and Tory to condemn the corruption of the public interest by monarch and the party system.

This combined condemnation was reinforced by the sense that an MP's pursuit of personal reward not only distorted parliament as a representative of the people but also had a corrosive influence on the electors. Candidates eager to chase lucrative posts through their activities at Westminster would in turn bribe voters and hence turn them away from their true interest. The effect of bribery was thus that it turned frequent elections, a force for good, into something subversive of representation. John Toland's *The Danger of Mercenary Parliaments* (1698) warned that as a

---

[64] *A Vindication of the Constitution of the English Monarchy* (1703), 15.

[65] *Cocks Diary*, 5–6.

[66] A. Pope (ed.), *The Works of John Sheffield . . . Duke of Buckingham* (1723), ii. 295 [rect. 111, mispagination].

[67] Speech by Sir Arthur Kaye, 31 Oct. 1710 in *Camden Miscellany*, 31 4th ser., 44 (1992), 343. He plagiarized this from J. Trenchard, *A Short History of Standing Armies in England* (1698), preface, iii.

result of 'frequent meetings of parliament' the 'managers' of parliament
had learned 'so much dexterity and address in their applications to the
members of that assembly, that they are now become consumate masters
in that most detestable art of corrupting our representatives, by hopes and
fears of attaining and losing offices and preferments'. Such corrupted MPs
'represented not their country, but themselves, and always kept together in
a close and undivided phalanx, impenetrable either by shame or honour,
voting always the same way, and saying always the same things, as if they
were no longer voluntary agents, but so many engines, merely turned
about by a mechanick motion, like an organ'.[68] The people's judgement to
reject such men thus became vital to preserve liberty. Alarmingly, however,
it was very difficult to discern the mercenary from the patriot from their
words alone. Candidates said anything at election time: 'they shall be of
any religion, any party, and for any administation the electors shall propose, during the time their elections are solliciting; but what are they
afterwards? are they of any religion, for any party, or any ruling power, but
what is opposite to the interest of those they represent?'[69]

One safeguard was therefore to enact legislation either to ban all or
some office-holders from sitting in parliament, or require them to undergo a new election so that voters could decide whether they were still
able to represent them.[70] But a good deal of printed advice sought to warn
voters against electing place-hunters in the first place. Toland thus advised
the electors to 'spew them out as detestable members of the commonwealth; not only as unfit to be trusted with their liberties, but as unworthy
to breath in the air of a free government'.[71] One effect of this fear of self-
interested representatives was to strengthen the hand of those who advised
the choice of men of estates, for men without financial need would be
thought less likely to pursue places or pensions. Virtue and wealth were
thus linked. *The State and Condition of our Taxes* (1715) argued that 'a gentleman of an estate is undoubtedly the only proper representative of his
country, for a man of a small fortune is liable to the temptation of a bribe,
or a pension, and he who has no estate in land, to establish the funds upon

---

[68]   *Harl. Misc.* ix, 389, 393–5.
[69]   *The Art of Parliamenteering* (1722), 19–20.
[70]   For an outline of legislative attempts to enact place legislation, see G. Holmes, 'The
Attack on "The influence of the Crown", 1702–16', *BIHR*, 39 (1966), 47–68; E. Porritt, *The
Unreformed House of Commons: Parliamentary Representation before 1832*, 2 vols. (New York,
1963), 204–15.
[71]   Toland, *Danger*, 7. For a reply defending those who held court office, see *The True
Englishman's Choice of Parliament-Men* (1698).

its ruin'.[72] Moreover, the landed man was also likely to be an educated man, and therefore able to understand arguments in debate, and one who had the leisure and means necessary to attend parliament.[73] Choosing a man who had no local estate, Halifax thought, was 'more like chusing valentines than MPs' because they were unknown quantities.[74]

This section has shown that the partial, group-interest, of parties produced a counter-discourse that prized impartiality and the pursuit of the public good. Both Whigs and Tories espoused such a language in order to undermine the legitimacy of the other. They were joined by those who disliked both parties and who saw the expanding resources of the state as a danger when put at the disposal either of the court interest or a party administration. The attack on self-interest thus increased the power of the landed interest, since it could more easily veil the pursuits of its own interests under the cloak of impartiality and the public interest. Once again, then, the public had become an important term; but the public interest could actually serve to narrow the social criteria for selection as a representative.

REPRESENTATION AND PARTICIPATION

This is not quite the whole story, however. This patrician tendency was not incompatible with the advocacy of broader and more active participation in the electoral system, especially if that broader public was property-owning and had only circumscribed powers. This view recognized that long-term religious and economic changes had enlarged the landed public. For a small but vociferous group of pamphleteers, true representation was to be preserved by reform, much of it aimed at reconciling participation with representation. This often meant turning back to the mid-century insights of James Harrington. An examination of the later Stuart advice literature shows how neo-Harringtonianism, conceived by John Pocock as primarily concerned with participation, was as concerned with representation: the two were seen by contemporaries as intertwined and

---

[72] Wagstaffe, *The State and Condition*, 35; *Caution to the Good People*,1; *A Seasonable Memento to all the Electors* (1689), broadside; Cornwall RO, Carew papers, BO/23/63, 'A Caution to the Severall Cittyes Towns and Burroughs in their Eleccon', paper of 1698 sent from London; *Advice to the Gentlemen, Freeholders, Citizens and Burgesses* (1710), 11.

[73] The last wage paid to an MP appears to have been in 1678.

[74] *Works of . . . Halifax*, 155.

mutually supporting.[75] Attempts were made to channel the shift towards a
representative society back into the structures of the dispersed, participatory, form of governance of the pre-1640 period. One way of doing so was
to focus on the idea of a parish state, the very concept that has recently
found much favour with social historians who tend to prioritize participation over representation.

A parish-based system of representation was explored, for example, in
the utopian *Free State of Noland*, which made provision to give suffrage to
the 'meaner sort' through a system based on local representation.[76] Similarly Thomas Sheridan's *Discourse of the Rise and Power of Parliaments*
(1677), suggested that in 'every parish, freeholders and others, if they
please, should meet and choose two honest knowing men, on whom their
power of electing members should be devolved'. The two elected from each
parish then collectively chose two from every hundred; and the representatives of the hundreds were then to elect the MPs.[77] Written perhaps about
the same time, though not published until 1689, *Some Observations Concerning the Regulating of Elections* echoed this. It argued that although each
individual had 'a natural right to vote' it was 'impracticable' for all to exercise this and therefore representatives were necessary. The process by
which this transfer of power took place was both social and political, for
'whereas every pater-familias, or house-keeper is a natural prince, and is
invested with an absolute power over his family, and has by necessary consequence, the votes of all his family, man, woman and child included in his',
the parish house-keepers should meet to choose 'an elector for the county'
from a list prepared by the church-wardens. The 'electors' chosen by the
parishes were then to choose from a list of the gentry ('each worth in lands
and moveables at least £10,000 all debts paid and not under forty years of
age'). 'By this method the parliament will be a perfect representative of the
whole body of the people, and also of every numerical person in the kingdom. Here can be no partial (and consequently prejudicial) acts made by

[75] 'We can think of a period beginning in the late seventeenth century as one of debate between the liberal and participatory ideals; but in that debate Harrington and his successors
will be found invariably ranged on the side of participation' (Pocock (ed.), *Works of James
Harrington*, 146).

[76] This was the conclusion of the hostile *The Source of our Present Fears Discover'd* (1703),
11–17, which also discerned the influence of Harrington's *Oceana* and Sidney's *Discourses*. The
Free State was first printed in 1696 but then revised in 1701.

[77] *Discourse*, 29–30. The rest of Sheridan's tract is a visionary document that clearly
has state-*building* in mind, offering a blueprint of how to increase power and wealth, a reminder that a parish-based perspective was not incompatible with an aggressive commercial
mentality.

separate interests and factions; none will sit in this great council but men of gravity, wisdom, integrity and substance; no pensionary members; no unfair elections' and no 'unruly rabbles' or 'heats and animosities among the gentry'.[78] Paternalism, it was claimed, could be both participatory and truly representative.

The neo-Harringtonian flavour of these proposals was repeated in *The Claims of the People Essayed* (1701), which argued that in order to revive 'the true publick spirit of old England' all state public officers should be elected, as churchwardens, overseers of the poor and others were 'and hereby it is that parish-government carries nothing in it uneasy or unpleasing to the people. For naturally every one is best pleased with his own choice and hereby both honours and burdens are equally born.' Consent, then, was needed for state officers, such as sheriffs and lord lieutenants 'as was the ancient custom'.[79] The author desired a form of government in which the representative nature of the parish was writ large. He duly extolled London's form of government as most nearly resembling this model and saw in the drafting of the 1701 Act of Settlement an opportunity to liberate the people. The raft of measures thus sprung from a 'commonwealth principle'.[80] This tract was itself a form of election advice, published in July 1701, a few months before the second election of that year. The author urged the electorate to reject court pensioners, arguing 'that this court-style is only an art of hocus pocus to convey the idea of English government out of our minds and to slide the idea of French government in the room of it'. The freeholders, it claimed, owned England and therefore had 'a natural right to erect what government they pleased' and if there were no courtiers in the Commons parliament would 'represent not the court but people of England'.[81] This argument was important because it rejected the idea that the state, growing in power, could subordinate the representative and hence claim to speak for the people. First apparent, perhaps, in the Leveller discourse of the late 1640s, this idea was to be a powerful strain of oppositional discourse throughout the eighteenth century. In the later Stuart period it was testament to the growth of the representative state apparently becoming more divorced from the people it represented, but also to the growth of a party system in which the people were no longer truly represented. It was a voice seeking to turn back the tide, to recreate what

---

[78] *Some Observations*, 15–16, 18. The tract is sometimes attributed to Anthony Ashley-Cooper, first earl of Shaftesbury.
[79] *Claims*, 23–6. For the proposal to elect officers of state, see also *Some Remarks upon Government* (1689).
[80] *Claims*, 32–3, 111–15.   [81] Ibid., 94, 106, 110.

was admittedly its own rather fictional version of a glorious past in which
participation and representation had gone hand in hand.

Before leaving the neo-Harringtonians, it is worth lingering a moment
to notice another intriguing development, the advocacy of the ballot-box,
since this was another example of the 'rational' discourse governing much
of the election literature. Voting in the later Stuart period was a public affair—voting preferences were declared verbally to clerks at polling booths
devoid of privacy. A secret ballot, it was thought by some (always a small
minority[82]) might ensure a truer representation, since it would allow men
to vote according to their reason and the common good. It was 'a sure way
to prevent bribery and to make every man give his vote according to the
best of his judgment, because he can get nothing by doing otherwise, no
man can sell his vote, when it cannot be known he gives it'.[83] The ballot's secrecy also meant it was a remedy against partisan feuds. In the current
state, however, 'no man can live quietly . . . because his votes displease
some of his neighbours' and inevitably 'a publick way of voting breeds parties'.[84] Party voting, alleged one advocate of a ballot, weakened the ability of
citizens to reason independently and perverted the expression of the general public interest, since it encouraged a man to vote 'according to his private interest . . . so that 'tis the greatest odds whether in six thousand votes
you have six hundred *fair ones*' or 'so many guided by an unprejudiced
judgment'.[85] Once again, then, hostility to partisan electioneering produced election literature that condemned party and instead idealized rational and impartial judgement. As the same author put it, 'a party pursues
as distinct an interest from the society as an ill prince can do' and forced
free men into a dependency on others. In theory 'Elections are, as it were,
the pulse of the people and discover the sense and temper of their minds.
But undue elections are a cheat and like an intermitting pulse, lead the
government into a mistake of the dispositions of men'.[86] An election tract
of 1705 similarly queried whether the people had been 'duly represented'
and therefore recommended the ballot-box, even illustrating it for curious
readers.[87]

The radical nature of the proposal was clear when the author argued
that the ballot could widen participation in representation. Thus 'all

---

[82] In 1696 an Elections Bill committee was empowered to receive a clause 'that all elections
of Members of parliament to serve in Parliament be by a Ballotting' (*CJ*, xi. 427), though
nothing came of it.
[83] *A Ready Way to Prevent Bribery* [1689], broadside. Cf. *A Serious Address*, 9.
[84] *Enquiry into the Inconveniences*, 4–6.
[85] Ibid., 7, 11–12.   [86] Ibid., 13, 15.
[87] *The Patriot's Proposal of the People of England Concerning the Ballot, the Best Way of
Choosing New Representatives in Parliament* (1705), 3–4.

This image, in a 1705 election tract, appears to be the first English depiction of a ballot-box. The green and white box was to be used to select who should propose candidates. The scheme owed much to the ideas of James Harrington, though the author of this tract (unlike Harrington) refers to a 'natural right' to vote. [Reproduced by courtesy of the Newberry Library, Chicago.]

freemen' (defined as 'those that are not servants but can live of themselves and pay taxes') were said to have 'a natural right to vote and this right is deny'd many of them for no other reason but a supposed impossibility of so many giving their votes'. This could be overcome, since 'they might all vote by their representatives chosen before hand in every parish or division'. This pyramid system of choosing representatives by representatives could thus widen the franchise to include almost anyone who was public-spirited enough to vote.[88] Here the restrictive nature of much neo-Harringtonianism was abandoned and a radical voice, to be heard throughout the eighteenth and nineteenth centuries, articulated.

THE PRINTED LIST OF MPS AND THE PARTISAN FRAMING OF INFORMATION

Earlier in the chapter we saw how material claiming to offer impartial advice to electors could be partisan. In fact a whole new sub-genre of political information emerged, apparently designed to offer accurate, even impartial, knowledge to the public in a way that seemed to aid their independent, rational, electoral choices. This sub-genre was the printed list of MPs. It was further testimony to the way in which print could change the political culture, not just furthering a national political culture in which the activities of individual MPs were judged according to national debates but also providing means by which voters could apparently make informed choices. Yet such apparently impartial and neutral print was, in fact, highly partisan and could be read in a number of different, even

[88] Ibid., 9.

contradictory, ways. This section explores the paradoxes inherent in these printed lists, which can be taken as a case study of a political debate about the truth of practical 'facts'.

Precedents for such lists lay, like the printed electoral advice discussed earlier, in the mid-century crisis. *A List of the Names of the Members of the House of Commons* [1648] showed those who were army officers 'contrary to the self-denying ordinance'. In 1654 an annotated list of MPs who had sat in the Barebones Assembly was printed.[89] In 1660 a list of Rumpers and regicides was printed so that the people 'may be the better guided in their future elections'.[90] But it was only with the first age of party that such lists became common, published principally to influence electoral opinion. In the fifty years after the publication of *A List of One Unanimous Club of Voters* in 1679[91]—'very fit to be thought on at the next new choice'—over twenty such lists were published, despite a resolution of the House of Commons in October 1696 that it was a breach of privilege to print the names of members and to reflect on them for their proceedings in the House.[92]

The 1696 order had been provoked by a tract that claimed the people needed to be able to distinguish between the actions of MPs. *An Account of the Proceedings in the House of Commons* (1696) printed a list of members who had been in favour of Whig policy on the controversial recoinage, designed to eradicate clipped (debased and devalued) money. The tract's author, Thomas Wagstaffe, believed that without his list the public had

no opportunities to know the particular proceedings in Parliament, nor means to distinguish between their faithful representatives and others; for [although] the votes are printed, the yeas and noes, the names of the persons concurring and dissenting are not, and the nation hath no way of knowing that but by particular information.[93]

Moreover, Wagstaffe alleged, those who had been forward in promoting the recoinage were now back in their constituencies 'washing their hands and wiping their mouths, and craftily insinuating into the credulous mul-

[89] *A Catalogue of the Names of the Members* (1654)—I owe this reference to Jason Peacey.
[90] *The Grand Memorandum* (1660). *England's Directions for Members Elections* (1660) was a poem which listed many Rumpers and radicals whom the electorate needed to avoid.
[91] In 1677 *A Seasonable Argument to Perswade all the Grand Juries to Petition for a New Parliament*, which also listed MPs, had been published in order to use public opinion to secure new elections.
[92] *CJ*, xi. 572. The titles are to be found in *British Parliamentary Lists 1600–1800*, ed. G. Ditchfield, D. Hayton, and C. Jones (London, 1995).
[93] *An Account*, 4.

titude, that the present calamities are purely owing to other members'.[94] Wagstaffe's list was thus produced for highly partisan purposes, aimed at vindicating the Tories and vilifying the Whigs. The tract was duly ordered by a Whig-dominated house to be burned by the common hangman. But in putting forward the concept that a minority of the House of Commons had to be distinguished from the majority (and hence collective) decision, the tract was pursuing the logic of publicly partisan politics.

Such partisan information conferred popular power. One of the chief promoters of the recoinage was Edward Clarke, MP for Taunton. Clarke's activity at Westminster was reported or misrepresented in Somerset by fellow MP John Sanford. The disruption that the recoinage caused to trade was undoubtedly severe in the short term, and Sanford exploited it, so that when Clarke attempted to return home in the summer of 1696 he was forced to flee to a local tavern for shelter from an angry mob and was then 'conveyed out the back way' to save his life. He had to spend the rest of the summer apart from his wife, a 'cruel separation forced upon us by the pride and malice of the most wicked and revengeful men living'. It was even suggested that a rabble would pull down Clarke's house and 'pull [him] in pieces'.[95] The incident is highly revealing. The activity of men at Westminster was not something unknown or abstract. In this instance a mob, politicized by economic hardship, could be manipulated by a rival politician by means of 'information' about his activity. The outcome of the affair is also illuminating. Believing that the rumours against her husband were spread as 'the forerunner of another Parliament', Clarke's wife, Mary, threw herself into politicking and electioneering. She met Taunton's aldermen to put them straight about her husband's actions and entertained their wives, showing that women could be invaluable in an electoral process from which they were ostensibly excluded by their sex. Moreover, rather than seek to punish the people who had momentarily flared against her and her husband, Mary set up poor relief schemes to alleviate the poverty in her area.[96] Disinformation needed to be countered by careful cultivation of the public so that they would be inclined to believe a different version of the 'truth'.

Blacklisting was a partisan business, in which both sides were culpable.

---

[94] Ibid., 5.
[95] *HOP II*, iii. 587. Wagstaffe was probably alluding to this when he noted that the people 'can hardly restrain their hands from offering violence to the persons and houses of the members'.
[96] I am grateful to Elizabeth Clarke for sharing her transcripts of the Clarke correspondence, now deposited at the HOP, with me.

In 1701 the Whigs published a 'black list' of MPs aimed at depicting the Tories as unpatriotic opponents of the war and more interested in attacking their rivals than protecting the national interest.[97] The Tories retaliated. *The Legionites Plot* (1702) objected to the attempt at 'libelling and stigmatising such members of the late house as stood most in the way of their [i.e. Whig] arbitrary designs'.[98] Tory crowds also sought to turn partisan truth inside out. Thus in November 1702 'a great bonfire was made at the Vine tavern door in Long Acre, where the mob obliged all persons that passed by to drink a health to the loyal gentlemen of the Black-list and to declare that they were the only persons that had preserved this nation from ruin'.[99] It was this affair that prompted James Drake, Tory physician and polemicist, into making the remarks quoted in the introduction about the lies propagated by the Whigs to subvert true elections.[100] Yet he agreed with the compilers of the blacklist that the best guide to men's principles was past actions, in and out of parliament:

If a candidate for parliament had ever sate in that house before, the electors ought to be satisfied how he attended, and how he voted, especially in all critical and important questions . . . if the candidate has never been a member before, the next certain indication is, his conduct in his own county on all publick occasions. The electors shou'd examine what sort of men he constantly favour'd? what party he has always joyn'd? and for want of surer and closer information, they may weigh him in their standard without danger of committing any error in consequence.

Drake (emulating in print what the Tory mob had done in practice) therefore reprinted the 'blacklist' at the end of his tract but gave it a new reading by suggesting that, far from being villains, the MPs listed were 'strenuous asserters of the liberties and rights of the people'.[101] Drake accepted an intrinsic link between representations in print or sermons and representations at the polls; but sought to counter the 'lying' slant put on an apparently impartial list by reframing its context and meaning. Party meant that the same text and information could be read in two fundamentally different ways. And to trump the Whigs, he now added a new list of MPs, this time intended to undermine them.

[97] *A List of One Unanimous Club of Members of the Late Parliament* (1701).

[98] *Legionites Plot*, 21. The blacklist, it was alleged, had been 'very carefully by the party dispers'd throughout the whole nation'. cf. *An Answer to the Black List* [1701]; *The Source of Our Present Fears*, 27.

[99] Strathmore MSS at Glamis Castle, box 70, folder 2, bundle 14, newsletter 19 Nov. 1702.

[100] *Some Necessary Considerations*, 3.

[101] Ibid., 14, 16, 23–8. He claimed they had promoted the Triennial Bill, a scrutiny of accounts, asserted the rights of the House of Commons, opposed a standing army, and backed the 1701 Act of Settlement.

The ability of lists to misrepresent and be read in more than one way was also evident in a dispute in 1705 over MPs who had supported the high-church attempt to tack a bill against occasional conformity onto a supply bill.[102] Few went so far as Bishop Burnet, who in 1705 organized 'a publick entertainment' at Salisbury in order to disseminate the blacklist of those who had voted for the Tack and hence prevent their re-election.[103] But as one Tory response indicated, the list of Tackers had 'been dispers'd abroad since the rising of both Houses of Parliament, to misrepresent such members as have shewn themselves worthy patriots in defence of the Church establish't, in order to render 'em suspected to the people of England at the ensuing elections'.[104] The Tory author claimed that it had

always been the practice of this pretended moderate party, to anticipate the Dissolution of Parliament, by scattering abroad lists of such worthy members as have been impediments to their designs, on purpose to prepossess their electors against 'em.

But, by reglossing the lists to show those blacklisted as patriots one could warn the 'poor, unwary, credulous people', and uncover the attempt 'by fraud and apparent falshoods' to win over their votes.[105] The lists of MPs' activity became part of a struggle over rival definitions of what it was to be a 'patriot', a term that was becoming increasingly powerful and necessary to appropriate as a validating label.

In a partisan age lists appeared to offer certain information but raised problems about interpretation. Even the basic accuracy of lists became a partisan matter. *A List of the Honourable House of Commons that Voted For and Against the Clause for the Hanover Succession in the Year 1702* (1710) and *A Test Offer'd to the Consideration of the Electors of Great Britain* (1710) provoked a controversy about the accuracy of their claims. A division of 13 February 1702/3 had been reproduced by them and appeared to show that there was just a single vote deciding the fate of the Hanoverian succession. The publication of the list was thus designed by the Whigs to show the anti-Hanoverian strain among the Tories and 'to hinder them being elected'.[106] But two Tories replied in print that the printed division was not,

[102] *A List of those Worthy Patriots* [1705].
[103] *Advice to the Gentlemen, Freeholders, Citizens and Burgesses* (1710), 4. See also *Seasonable Advice to Electors* (1705), 2, for hostility to Tackers.
[104] Subtitle of *The Tackers Vindicated* (1705). Cf. *The Countryman's Remembrancer* (1705); *A Word of Advice to the Citizens of London Concerning the Choice of Members of Parliament at the Ensuing Election* (1705), 7.
[105] *Tackers Vindicated*, 3–4, 5.
[106] *The False Test Set in a True Light* (1710), 1.

as it claimed to be, on the Hanoverian succession at all, but on a prior amendment barring anyone who had refused the abjuration oath from ever being readmitted to office.[107] The list was therefore portrayed by the Tories as a false and malicious reflection. To this the Whigs replied that the two divisions of the House stood or fell together and that therefore the lists were not misleading.[108] Although it was 'a logical truth' that the division was not over the Hanover amendment, 'it would be a mortal lye and a fallacy' to pretend that the first vote was not a cover for the second.[109] Thus there was truth and there was partisan, incomplete, truth. Voters were increasingly being asked to scrutinize the actions of MPs at Westminster in order to inform themselves 'rightly';[110] but the information provided by lists was partisan and potentially misleading. What was supposed to be a help to formulate right judgement could become a means to propagate prejudice and error.

The lists thus posed the same problems as other types of advice literature, apparently informative and accurate but often at the same time highly partisan and manipulative. This is neatly demonstrated in a tract of 1713, quoted at the head of the chapter, which warned voters about the print designed to advise voters. The pamphlet claimed to recommend men 'whether they were Whig or Tory', and yet could not refrain from being partisan. All the criteria offered by it for true judgement proved resolutely, if moderately, whiggish. Thus voters should choose men who were loyal to the church but who did not hypocritically make use of the cry 'the Church' and were in favour of toleration to dissenters; who were friends to the Dutch and to Hanover and enemies to France; lovers of the revolution and in favour of encouraging trade and credit.[111] To help voters make up their minds in the right (Whig) way, the author, despite all his earlier protestations, appended a list of those for and against the 1713 French commercial clauses.

---

[107] George Smalridge and Thomas Crosse, *A Detection of a Falshood* (1710), broadside. Crosse had a vested interest as a candidate for Westminster.

[108] *An Account of the Test Offer'd to the Consideration of the Electors* (1710), 1; *A Test Offered to the Consideration of Electors . . . to which is added . . . a reply to the Vindication* (1714), 18–20.

[109] *A Test Offered . . . to which is added . . . a reply*, 23.

[110] *A Tender and Hearty Address*, 17–18. In January 1715 Margaret Adams noted, in relation to the elections, that 'there is some pretty things in print which might help to open the eyes of the blind' (*Verney Letters of the Eighteenth Century*, ed. M. M. Verney, 2 vols. (1930), i. 326).

[111] [J. Oldmixon?], *Remarks on a Scandalous Libel Entitl'd a Letter from a Member of Parliament* (1713), 21–2.

REPRESENTATIVES OR DELEGATES?

One further dimension of the public 'advice' about elections demands comment. Advised and informed themselves, voters also sought to advise and inform their representatives, for the public was never merely an audience but also a participant. One form of representative participation was, as we saw in the last chapter, the address, and the right of the people to petition their MPs has already been discussed. The following discussion has a related but slightly different purpose. It argues that the problems of partisan interest, public judgement, and rationality, evident in the literature advising voters, also figured prominently in the debates about the 'instructions' to representatives.[112] In other words, the advice *from* the public raised questions about the nature of that public. If that public was itself a fiction hiding partisan groups, or popular sovereignty was dangerous because of the irrationality of the people, then it followed that mandates to MPs were also problematic. The issue of advice from voters to representatives once again centres on the issue of public judgement.

This section also seeks to make the point that the claim of MPs to represent the nation (rather than a particular set of constituents) was made, and contested, a century before Edmund Burke made his famous speech at Bristol in 1774 in which he enunciated the principle that MPs were representatives not delegates.[113] Argument about the extent to which MPs were responsible and independent of their constituents, representative of particular interests or a single national interest, had been rumbling since at least the 1640s, and especially in Leveller tracts.[114] When we examine the

---

[112] I. Kramnick, 'An Augustan Debate: Notes on the History of the Idea of Representation', in J. R. Pennock and J. W. Chapman (eds.), *Representation* (New York, 1968), discusses instructions during the administration of Walpole.

[113] Burke's speech of 3 Nov. 1774, together with his other views about representation are discussed by Pitkin, *Concept of Representation*, ch. 8.

[114] *England's Miserie* (1645), written about Lilburne's imprisonment by parliament and perhaps written by him, begins with a straightforward description of the House of Commons as the 'representative of the people' but develops the notion that MPs were merely the 'agents' of the sovereign people who had entrusted them with 'authority' (1–2, 6). Richard Overton's imprisonment in 1647 caused him to be even more assertive of individual authorization of representatives. He talked of the people as 'betrusters' who conveyed power 'by joynt and common consent' to 'elected deputies', 'members representative', 'representory deputies or trustees' (D. M. Wolfe (ed.), *Leveller Manifestoes of the Puritan Revolution* (New York, 1944), 162–9). See also Overton's 1646 Remonstrance (ibid., 113); G. Wither, *Letters of Advice* (1645), 13; J. North, *A True Looking-Glass* (1654), 3. For a discussion of restoration attitudes, see J. Miller, 'Representatives and Represented in England, 1660–89', *Parliaments, Estates and Representation*, 15 (1995), 125–32.

later Stuart debate we can see that it resumed discussions about the concept of representative over delegate, and that this became especially important because of the context of anxiety over the extent to which party promoted and legitimized the pursuit of self-interest and particular, minority, interests. Once again, then, the debate pushed in the direction of a collective national interest that could be represented through the political system. Let us take this last point first.

The doctrine of public interest suggested that the ideal representative, as well as the ideal voter, was to set aside private and partisan interest. An MP's duty was to the public. As one tract put it, his soul 'must soar up into the exalted height of an heroical virtue, and he is to believe that it is a pleasurable and noble enjoyment even to sacrifice himself and all private considerations for his country'.[115] But the sacrifice of private interest posed an interesting question when it came to representing the interest of the constituency over and against the interest of the nation. The same tract stated the dilemma:

> If the counties and corporations have anything particular in relation to their counties or corporations to be represented, they ought to chuse one that understands the nature of what they would have represented, or that is at least capable of being thorowly instructed in that matter. But at the same time that they chuse one for their particular purpose, they ought to consider that he votes for the whole commonwealth and therefore they must not chuse any man that is addicted only to their interest but should always deliberate whether he is of a publick and universal spirit as well as a proper advocate for them.

Constituency interests needed representation; but should those particular interests prevail over the national good? No: 'When the general good of England comes in competition' with that of the constituency, the ideal MP 'must consider himself as well and as more the representative of England than of that county or town for which he serves'. Only when he had 'consider'd the national interest' could he 'consider the interests of the body of the electors'.[116] The plurality and hierarchy of interests was thus a commonplace. As Defoe put it, MPs were 'representatives in a double capacity, separately consider'd, every member represents the people who chuse him, and all together represent the whole nation . . . every man represents the whole and acts for the whole, tho he is sent but from parts'.[117]

---

[115] *Some Reasons for an Annual Parliament as the Best Security for English Rights* [1702], in *State Tracts*, iii. 293.
[116] Ibid., 292–3.
[117] *The Freeholders Plea against Stock-jobbing Elections* (1701), 26.

The idea of national representation was, then, evident in the 1670s as well as the 1770s. Algernon Sidney made rather similar remarks to Burke, suggesting that MPs were representatives of 'the whole nation' rather than a particular county or borough.[118] Thus, he said, 'we always may and often do give instructions to our delegates; but the less we fetter them the more we manifest our own rights; for those who have only a limited power must limit that which they give; but he that can give an unlimited power must necessarily have it in himself.'[119] The context to this earlier debate therefore needs exploring.

At the heart of the later Stuart controversy lay a number of questions. If an MP was a 'trustee', could he break that trust and how? How far could the people claim a right to control the actions of their agent? How best might a representative legislature be made to reflect and respond to the people? And should the representative represent the majority view against that of a minority? These questions reflected a shift in thinking about representation, from considering a monarch who claimed to be the representative of the nation, to a parliament that claimed to be the representative of the people. That shift had begun in the 1640s and 1650s, but it was thought about again, and for a longer time, in the later Stuart period, because it was after 1689 that parliament became an enduring, reliable, point of contact between state and people through frequent elections and regular sittings. Such thinking also in part resulted from, and shaped, ideological positions about the role of the people. If the people were sovereign, then a number of things seemed to follow: they had a right to judge, needed information, and could hold their representatives to account. If the people were not sovereign, then their representatives were of limited relevance; or if parliament could establish claims to be the 'people', then limits were also unnecessary. Yet what is remarkable is how complex the positions of both Whigs and Tories became on these issues. Some Whigs championed the people's ability to limit their representatives, but others rejected this; some Tories sought to place strict limits and conditions on popular sovereignty whilst the high church wing developed a tendency to use popular allegiance to the church to their own advantage.

The ideological roots of regarding the people as superior to their representatives in parliament had both a religious and a secular tradition. During the Restoration, opposition to the penal laws on dissenters pushed

[118] *Discourses Concerning Government by Algernon Sidney*, ed. T. West (Indianapolis, 1990), 565. Cf. *Some Reasons for an Annual Parliament, State Tracts*, iii. 293.
[119] Ibid., 567–8.

some to claim that the people's natural freedom of conscience was superior to an act of parliament because it was made 'not by our representatives
but by the people themselves; and our representatives themselves limited
by them'.[120] A legalist tradition also saw the representative as limited by the
people. George Lawson attacked Hobbes for having equated representation with sovereignty: 'the word representative he either doth not understand or if he do, he intolerably abuseth his unwary and unlearned reader
by that term'.[121] For Lawson, a representative was simply a delegate having
a power to act, a 'trustee' and therefore limited.[122] This idea of limited trust
was often yoked to the idea of an ancient constitution. Thus one 1690 tract
claimed it was 'the ancient custom and undoubted right of all counties,
cities and buroughs, upon the sealing of their indentures of elections, to
deliver unto their respective representatives such instructions in writing as
they conceived most fit, either for their own particular good or the good of
the people in general'.[123] Such a view was endorsed by an interpretation of
the parliamentary writ as just such an instruction empowering a trustee.[124]
This contractural mentality, so analogous to everyday financial transactions, proved particularly important in encouraging instructions to MPs
over money: many of the addresses related to issues of taxation, trade, and
war.[125]

   Yet the ideology justifying the representative supremacy of parliament
over the people drew on the issues of interest, rationality, and partisanship
that we have already been discussing. As one pamphlet explicitly recognized, instructions were based on the idea that the electorate should trust

[120] [Sir J. Stewart], *Jus Populi Vindicatum; or, the People's Right to Defend Themselves* (1669), epistle to reader; *The Englishman* (1670), 9, 11; G. De Krey, 'Rethinking the Restoration: Dissenting Cases for Conscience, 1667–1672', *HJ*, 38 (1995), 70.
   [121] Lawson, *Examination of the Political Part of Mr Hobbs his Leviathan* (1657), 37–8.
   [122] C. Condren, *George Lawson's 'Politica' and the English Revolution* (Cambridge, 1989), 92, 159; Condren, 'Resistance and Sovereignty in Lawson's Politica', *HJ*, 24 (1981), 673–81; P. Miller, *Defining the Common Good: Empire, Religion and Philosophy in Eighteenth-century Britain* (Cambridge, 1994), 241–3. Lawson's work was republished in 1689.
   [123] *Proposals Humbly Offered to the Consideration of Those Who are to be Electors of Members* (1690), 1. Cf. Prynne, *Seasonable and Healing Instructions* [1660], broadside. The 'Funda-mental Constitutions' of Pennsylvania, probably drafted in the summer of 1681, required delegates to follow instructions from constituents because this did 'resemble the ancient con-stitution of England' (*William Penn and the Founding of Pennsylvania 1680–1684*, ed. J. R. Soderland (Philadelphia, 1983), document 26).
   [124] W. Prynne, *Seasonable and Healing Instructions* [1660], broadside; cf. Johnson, *A Letter from a Freeholder*, 21–2.
   [125] *The Best Choice*, 4; [Defoe], *The Original Power of the Collective Body of the People* (1702); *The Duke of Anjou's Succession Further Consider'd* (1701), preface; Wagstaffe, *An Ac-count of the Proceedings*, 3; *A Letter to a West Country Clothier and Freeholder* (1713), 17. For an earlier example see BL, 816.m.4, untitled and undated broadside, c.1654.

their own judgement.[126] To be sure, insulting the rationality of the people
was a dangerous game in an era of publicly contested politics; but it could
be avoided. One tactic was to suggest that the people simply did not have
the information on which to base valid judgements. As *An Account of Some
Late Designs* (1702) put it, electors were 'incapable of giving their advice' on
whether or not to go to war, for 'what could a freeholder know of the state
of Europe, so as to advise a parliament, when he had been following the
plough-tail ever since the peace?'[127] The growth of a national political culture, in which it was important to know the national interest, could thus
exclude popular involvement. Parliament was now taking over some of the
sanctity of the royal prerogative over war and peace. It needed passive but
not active popular consent. Secondly, as the title of the tract just quoted
suggests, it was easy enough to portray rival partisans as having a design to
subvert the true judgement of the people. Whig or Tory instructions
to MPs could thus be represented as emanating from self-interested minorities or, more sinisterly, those designing to subvert the liberties of the
nation.[128] The 1701–2 debate about the relationship between people and
representatives, one Tory tract claimed, was a sandstorm, deliberately
whipped up by the Whig Junto (at this time under impeachment charges)
to create trouble and division from which it could then profit. 'What can be
the design of throwing all this dirt and filth in the faces of our representatives in Parliament but to prejudice the people in future elections, in hopes
the electors will consent to sell their liberties?' The Whig aim was said to be
to obtain a subservient parliament that would allow the Junto to pursue its
own ends.[129] But it was not just a Tory critique of Whig populism. A moderate Whig tract condemned 'the new stratagem of electors of prescribing
to their representatives' as 'at best but a cover . . . to popularity, if not a
masque upon the face of rebellion, rendring all authority cheap and contemptible'. And it was an attempt by the 'little creatures' to dictate to 'better judgements'.[130]

Only in parliament, then, could the plurality of interests be arbitrated
properly. Thus a Tory tract made the point, later espoused by Jean-Jacques

---

[126] *A Letter to a West Country Clothier*, 18.
[127] *An Account*, 13.
[128] 'Advice to the Gentlemen and Freeholders of the County of Wiltshire to their Representatives in the Ensuing Parliament' (*c*.1701, copy in PRO 30/24/30/30 pt. III, f. 131), about the
need to contain France, was signed 'by a mighty body of gentry', but it had apparently
been drawn up under the third earl of Shaftesbury's influence (PRO 30/24/20/ff. 129–30,
Shaftesbury to Furley, 6 Jan. 1702).
[129] *England's Enemies Exposed*, 29, 33.
[130] *The States-Men of Abingdon* (1702), 7–8, 10–11.

Rousseau, that Englishmen were only free at election time. *England's Enemies Exposed* (1701) stated that once the people had made their choice 'the power and rights of the elector devolves intirely upon their representatives', creating a sort of parliamentary Leviathan.[131] The logic of the pamphleteer was, however, more based on the impossibility of reconciling different interests without a single umpire and on the ignorance of the mass of the people.

'How is it possible to know all the people's minds? . . . How is it possible to make all the people agree in their sentiments? . . . is not this the way to usher in disorder, confusion and every evil work? are yeomen, farmers and day labourers fit to be consulted with about abstruse affairs in government? are they fit to direct their representatives in parliament? Away with this silly stuff as the vulgar call it.'[132]

The appeal to rationality, and the need for a single, collective, and representative voice, could thus re-legitimate the exclusion of the people.

The position put forward here was similar to that outlined by Charles Davenant in 1704 when he warned about 'the danger of appealing to the people from their representatives in Parliament'.[133] Davenant attacked the doctrines that the people had not devolved all their power onto their representatives; that parliament was accountable to the people; and that it was always lawful to appeal to the people. He condemned those who censured the majority when it was not of their sentiment and believed the printed attacks on parliament to be 'appeals to the people' which were destructive to the constitution. The 1701 campaign of instructions, he believed, had called on the multitude 'to assume to themselves the whole administration of affairs; at least to wrest from their representatives that part of government they held'. This was wrong, he believed, because popularity was not an appeal to reason but to the wildness of the mob. 'The art of governing is to rule the many by a few; but when the many are suffer'd to sway, direct and lead the few, which way they please, tis quite returning into the wild state of nature and giving to force that empire and dominion, which reason and wisdom ought to have.' To set up a 'fourth estate'—a term coined here[134]—distorted the constitution. While the people could give advice to MPs, this was not binding, for MPs were 'representing the whole nation' as much as their individual constituencies. If the people had the last resort or

[131] Hobbes had allowed for his Leviathan to be an assembly as well as a prince.
[132] *England's Enemies Exposed*, 30, 42, 50.
[133] *Essays upon Peace at Home and War Abroad* (1704), section 1.
[134] Ibid., 31. *OED* gives first usage as 1752.

appeal, Davenant argued, 'then we are a democracy and not a kingly government'. 'When the commonalty have once made their choice, their whole power is devolv'd and delegated.'[135] *Leviathan's* transfer of representative power was reborn.

Defoe, as part of what should by now be apparent as a lively, contradictory and ongoing debate about representation, nevertheless attacked Davenant's reasoning and defended popular power. 'I wish the Commons of England in parliament . . . would let us know how far their power extends, with respect to the people they represent', he challenged. Defoe asserted that the people had a right 'to contradict and make void something their representatives may do, and consequently have some power which is not devolved upon the representatives'. He ridiculed Davenant's attempt to equate any complaint with tumult aimed against parliament: 'tis impossible the people of England, call them by the worst names you please, the rabble, the mob, the multitude, or any thing: I say, tis impossible the poor of England can ever, either by inclination or by contrivance, be brought to a dislike of parliaments as such'. Thus although the people were not a fourth estate 'yet they are the centre of the other three estates'. Even so, Defoe held a restricted view of the people, by whom he meant 'Negatively, not all the inhabitants, but positively all the freeholders . . . for all other inhabitants live upon sufferance.'[136] And, as we shall see, he did not always hold such an exalted view of the public. He reflected a more general dilemma about the extent of popular participation in representative government.

Davenant's parliamentary 'Leviathan' was not an uncontested one and challenges were made during the rage of party and beyond. Even so, the language of interest, reason, and a national voice served to extend the paradoxes of party: although contest and dispute made the later Stuart political culture an inclusive one, the forces created by that ferment could also be shaped to exclude its participants. Davenant believed that corruption was not just a matter of court bribery (though it was in his interest to say so, because his son had been given a government post!). Hostile to the 'giddy judgements' of the people in an age of partisanship, he argued that 'Liberty is equally unsafe where parliaments are to be frighted and influenced by popular clamours, as where they are to be corrupted by the ministers'. The English had found another via media to pursue: a path between the corruption of the court and the corruption of party zeal and

[135] *Essays,* 29–30.
[136] *Some Remarks on the First Chapter in Dr Davenant's Essays* (1704), 6–7, 12–14, 23–4.

popularity. And the irrationality of party zeal, he feared, was often the result of the manipulation of the press. Although Davenant defended press freedom, he attacked the 'strange licence of the press' in the summer of 1701, and thought that it 'rais'd so high a ferment, as brought the body politique into a raging and malignant fever'.[137] And he took up his pen on numerous occasions to write both for and against party.

THE DANGER OF APPEALS TO THE PEOPLE

> Popularity is a crime from the moment it is sought; it is . . . generally an appeal to the people from the sentence given by men of sense.[138]

Parliamentary authority thus in part derived some of its legitimacy from the people, but the public also represented a potential threat to it. To be sure, a fear of popularity, especially an appeal to the people through the press, was not new.[139] But it was explored with new urgency because the public now had, through frequent elections, print, and public credit, greater power. And the disposal of such power depended on public judgement. Printed electoral advice, like the poll itself, was necessarily an appeal to the judgement of the people. But print could be dangerous if the public did not know how to read it, or if they lacked the necessary skills of judgement in the first place. The danger of publicly contested politics was precisely that it exposed such incapacity. The author of the aptly named *Study to be Quiet* (1680) feared that although pamphlets were 'filled with lies and falsehood' men read them 'with delight and complacency'. Indeed, 'the sharper and more satyrical they are', the more such print found a 'ready and approved reception' so that the youth in particular 'were inscensibly tainted with dislike of the government'.[140] One cleric thus roundly dismissed the rational faculty of 'men, who were never blest with a liberal education, never taught to read; men so dull and stupid, that they cannot apprehend, much less remember the strength of an argument'. Surely, he moaned, 'persons under such ill circumstances are in no capacity to judge

---

[137] Davenant, *Essays*, 37–8, 46–8.
[138] *The Works of . . . Halifax*, 232; cf. Davenant, *Essays*, 23.
[139] R. Cust, ' "Patriots" and "Popular Spirits": Narratives of Conflict in Early Stuart Politics' (forthcoming).
[140] *Study*, 6.

The print, published in the election year of 1708, depicts the folly of the age. A 'Politician' full of Machiavellian schemes is given pride of place on the ass, though a jester laughs at him. At the back of the ass a puritan and a cavalier fight over who should ride, the one accusing the other of speaking nothing but lies. At the front a high churchman and a two-faced low churchman also dispute who should ride. The 'mob' flocks towards the scene of folly. The image may not be as ludicrous as it seems, for we know from his diary that William Coe fell off his horse in May 1721 because he had been at a 'slow trott reading' the *Northampton Mercury*. [Reproduced by courtesy of the trustees of the British Museum.]

for themselves, but may rely upon the judgment of their teachers'.[141] Another high-church cleric thought it a national sin that the people 'suffered themselves to be seduced by lies and greedily hearkened to the most improbable stories that were imposed upon them'.[142] A manuscript tract, 'The Misleading of the Common People', written at the accession of James II in 1685 and shortly before the general election of that year, argued that

[141] F. Gregory, *A Modest Plea for the Due Regulation of the Press* (1698), 12.
[142] T. Brett, *The Dangers of a Relapse. A Sermon* (1713), 9.

'great harm' had been done by their 'confiding and relying on others that misrepresented' their interests.[143]

This argument is easily associated with the high-church Tories of the 1680s; but in the late 1690s, as the tide turned against them, court Whigs also found it necessary to attack the apparent irrationality of the people. One author thus warned of the tyranny of the multitude:

> sure the world is turn'd topsy turvy and mens understandings grow downward or they could never think the multitude are invested with the highest piece of regality viz the judging of the publick good and controwling all; whose incapacity, levity and ignorance renders 'em unfit for any thing of this nature.[144]

Those in power who faced criticism or attack often feared that such assault was the result of the people's faulty judgement. But suspicion of popularity also extended to those disowning any party. As a moderate, ostensibly impartial, tract put it in 1705, 'these sorts of appeals from their representatives to the people, is making the rabble the judge and courting anarchy and confusion by a total dissolution of our constitution'.[145] At times, then, Tory, Whig, and the 'impartial' mistrusted the people's capacity for true judgement when presented with printed advice or misinformation.

CONCLUSION

This chapter has drawn attention to the ways in which print reflected the enlarged importance of the public and public judgement. The development of advice literature, specifically aimed at voters (but encompassing nearly all readers as though they were voters and addressing all voters as though they were part of a truly national political culture), suggests that the public was courted, cajoled, and manipulated through the press as it never had been before. Such print conceived of the public in ambiguous ways. On the one hand, the voter was idealized as rational, independent, and active; on the other, he was seen as the victim of partisan lies and misrepresentations. On the one hand, the electorate should be free of influence; on the other, it should discern reason and independence in established social élites. And the attack on partisans by rival partisans promoted the idealization of a discourse of public interest, independence, rationality, and impartiality. This discourse was shared by those who

---

[143]   BL, Sloane MSS 2753, ff. 1–17.
[144]   *Cursory Remarks Upon Some Late Disloyal Proceedings in Several Cabals* (1699), 10.
[145]   *The Ballance; or, A New Test of the High-Fliers of All Sides* (1705), 35.

believed neither party nor the court necessarily acted in the public interest. Such a discourse also helped to give political legitimation to those who owned property and wealth, since they could claim that these insulated them against the pursuit of private interest and corruption. The equation of representation with property-owners was nevertheless compatible with a neo-Harringtonian insistence that the public had widened over the course of the early modern period as a result of religious and economic change. From this point of view, participation and representation were absolutely compatible.

The chapter also examined the political dimension of early-enlightenment truth-claims. It showed that lists of MPs, that were apparently impartial pieces of information designed to aid public judgement, were, in fact, highly partisan and capable of being 'read' in contradictory ways. There was no such thing as a partisan 'fact'. Both the lists and the advice literature more generally thus reveal that contemporaries were highly suspicious of claims to impartiality and reason, since these could disguise partiality and cunning.

Finally, the chapter showed that public advice was a two-way process, from the public to MPs as well as vice versa. Yet the attempts to instruct or advise their representatives raised key problems about the nature of representation and public judgement. There were thus vigorous debates about the superiority of the public over MPs (with resolution mainly in favour of the latter), and over the dangers of an apparent appeal to popularity. Such anxieties were not new, but were sharpened by the increased power available to the public. A politically empowered people, misled and corrupted, now posed a significant threat—or one at least represented as such. We must now explore those anxieties more fully.

Part II

Public Discourse and Truth

Truth and falshood have chang'd places; and according to the mode of the times the very quality of it is inverted too . . . and what was this [popish] plot at last but a blasphemous slanderous imagination, made up of lies and contradictions? . . . the [people] were never cut out for the judging or the understanding of things; but plausible disguises and appearances, have with them the force and value of certain truths and foundations; and tis a hard matter to bring people out of the wrong that are not able to discern and to distinguish the right.[1]

[1] L'Estrange, *The Observator in Dialogue. The Third Volume* (1687), 34, 39.

INTRODUCTION

The men, who make no conscience of rebellion, will never stick at lying; because they can never hope to carry their point without it. They must defame and blacken, and dress up those in power like beasts of prey, before they can set on the People to worry them. And when you have deliver'd up your mind to the impressions of men, who have not known the way of truth; when the most beneficent designs are defil'd by filthy dreamers and the fairest actions deform'd by an evil tongue, and nothing comes before you in its native colour, you will find it almost impossible to see through these party-strains and misrepresentations and to form a right judgment against your affections.[2]

What matters is not what people were in themselves, but what they were doing to each other and saying about each other and against each other . . . What matters is not what was thought (and most thoughts are hidden from us) but what it was polemically advantageous to allege.[3]

The first part of this book explored the way in which the public was given enlarged roles in the later Stuart period. Widespread and frequent campaigns of addressing ensured large-scale participation in a national political culture. Similarly, frequent electioneering invoked the public as readers and voters on a scale hitherto unmatched. In both types of activity, the public was appealed to not just as a participant but also as a judge of public discourse. The addresses, though ostensibly aimed at the crown, were printed for public consumption and were intended to influence the way in which the people judged state affairs. Electioneering repeatedly appealed to the judgement of the public. The second half of this book examines contemporary anxieties about the nature of popular political judgement and the corrosive effect of public discourse. It focuses on fears generated by the apparently permanent and worrying division of the

---

[2] W. Reeves, *A Sermon Preach'd at the Assizes Holden at Abingdon, in the County of Berks, July 14 1713* (1713), 19–20.
[3] P. Collinson, *The Puritan Character. Polemics and Polarities in Early Seventeenth Century English Culture*, William Andrews Clark Memorial Library (Los Angeles, 1989), 16–17.

nation into two mutually hostile parties. It suggests that partisanship was regarded with suspicion, not just by those who disdained any party allegiances but also by the parties themselves. Both Whig and Tory, low church and high church, court and country, viewed each other as conspirators engaged in sinister designs against the public good.[4] Each saw the other as using public discourse to misrepresent the true state of affairs in order to manipulate the public into throwing its weight behind what were essentially private rather than national interests. The following chapters thus examine the nature of print and polemic, the misleading potential of party names, and the fictions that each side perceived to be perpetrated by the other. In short, the second part of the book examines the 'misrepresentations' referred to in the first of the quotations above and that contemporaries feared were being routinely practised in partisan struggle. The principle themes are therefore the nature of partisan polemic, perceptions about public discourse, contested truth-claims, and the consequences of contemporary anxieties.

Polemic: rhetoric or propaganda?

Concerns about meaning, truth, and misrepresentation commonly emerged in, and as a result of, printed polemic. There was a very widely held view, spanning the parties, that polemic, whether printed or delivered orally, was successful in misleading the people. Politicians needed to be able to explain why their views were being challenged, why elections were lost, and why popular opinion at times seemed to drift away from them. Polemic, it was alleged by one commentator hostile to both parties, was 'dispers'd, designedly to impose upon' the people; 'each contending party' put out 'gross and unwary representations' of the controversies at stake, with the result that the misled public had become 'factious and turbulent'.[5] Polemical misrepresentations were considered to be highly dangerous, especially in the light of their role in contributing to civil war a generation earlier. Indeed, the 'force of words' was stressed by Dr Robert South in a sermon delivered in May 1686. He observed

that the generality of mankind is wholly and absolutely governed by words and names, without, nay for the most part even against, the knowledge men have of

---

[4] M. Knights, 'Faults on Both Sides: The Conspiracies of Party Politics under the Later Stuarts', in J. Swann and B. Coward (eds.), *Conspiracies and Conspiracy Theory in Early Modern Europe* (Aldershot, 2004); M. Knights, 'Politics after the Glorious Revolution', in B. Coward (ed.), *A Companion to Stuart Britain* (Oxford, 2003).

[5] *The Moderator, or, Considerations Propos'd in Order to End the Unseasonable Debate Concerning the Legality of the Late Happy Revolution*, 2nd edn. (1710), preface.

things. The multitude or common rout, like a drove of sheep, or an herd of oxon, may be manag'd by any noise or cry, which the drivers shall accustom them to. And he who will set up for a skilful manager of the rabble, so long as they have but ears to hear, needs never to enquire, whether they have any understanding whereby to judge. But with two or three empty popular empty words . . . well turned and humoured; may whistle them backwards and forwards, upwards and downwards till he is weary; and get up upon their backs when he is so . . . for a plausible insignificant word in the mouth of an expert demagogue is a dangerous and a dreadful weapon.

The 'intoxication' of 'verbal magick' was so strong, he believed, that 'words are able to persuade men out of what they find and feel, to reverse the impressions of sense, and to amuse men with fancies and paradoxes'. South regretted 'that the greatest affairs, and most important interests of the world, are carried on by things, not as they *are* but as they are *called*'. Thus, he feared, good could be misrepresented as evil, and evil as good. Whether seen as magical or (in another common analogy) poison, words were seen as the means by which allegiance could be altered and reoriented, by which the body politic was sickened or made healthy.[6] John Locke, who devoted part of his *Essay Concerning Human Understanding* to the relationship between words and ideas, was thus far from being alone in warning about the abuse of language.[7]

Of course, we might simply say that this shows nothing more than that contemporaries had paid attention in their rhetoric classes and therefore that little had changed since the Renaissance. Rhetoric has become a subject of interest to historians of science and political thought as well as to literary critics.[8] But historians of politics and the state in the seventeenth

---

[6] South, *Twelve Sermons Preached Upon Several Occasions . . . The Second Volume* (1697), 314–57, Sermon ix, 'The Fatal Imposture and Force of Words'. The text of the sermon was Isaiah 5 : 20, 'Woe unto them that call evil good and good evil', a text used by South for three other sermons and often invoked in later seventeenth-century discussions about the way in which meaning could be inverted. South's sermon was quoted *in extenso* in the whiggish *A Letter from a Curate of Suffolk to a High-Church Member* (1712), which also discussed how words could mislead. For South, see G. Reedy, *Robert South (1634–1716): An Introduction to his Life and Sermons* (Cambridge, 1992), esp. ch. 4.

[7] South became Locke's correspondent (*The Correspondence of John Locke*, ed. E. S. de Beer, 9 vols. (Oxford, 1976–••), viii. 3591) when the two had a common enemy in Dr Sherlock.

[8] Shapin and Schaffer, *Leviathan*; P. Dear, ' "Totius in verba": Rhetoric and Authority in the Early Royal Society', *Isis*, 66 (1985), 145–61; B. Vickers, 'The Royal Society and English Prose Style: A Reassessment', in B. Vickers and N. Streuver (eds.), *Rhetoric and the Pursuit of Truth: Language Change in the Seventeenth and Eighteenth Centuries. Papers Read at a Clark Library Seminar by Brian Vickers and Nancy Struever* (Los Angeles, 1985); A. Gross, *The Rhetoric of Science* (1990); R. F. Jones, *Ancients and Moderns, A Study in the Rise of the Scientific Movement in Seventeenth Century England*, 2nd edn. (1961), esp. chs. 8 and 9; Skinner, *Reason and Rhetoric*; Condren, *Satire, Lies and Politics*; Raymond, *Invention of the Newspaper*, 128–30, 153–4, 177, and ch. 3; N. Smith, 'The English Revolution and the End of Rhetoric: John Toland's Clito

and eighteenth centuries have generally been relatively slow to follow these leads, even though it is clear that in 1700 rhetoric was far from dead. There was no simple transition to a scientific 'plain language' devoid of partiality and power.[9] Rhetoric is important as the language of politics, the means of persuasion, and hence of influencing judgement. For the partisan, aiming to convince the public of a certain viewpoint, this was important. Rhetoric sought to entrap the reader, making use of emotion as well as reason.[10] Moreover, rhetoric also instructed in the art of re-description—the skill of changing how something was interpreted by re-describing it.[11] The type of language games that characterized the later Stuart party conflict could thus be said to be grounded in rhetorical theory.

For these reasons, it is worth questioning the appropriateness of the term 'propaganda' to describe Stuart printed polemic. Why have so many early modern historians invoked an apparently anachronistic term rather than refer to rhetorical ploys?[12] In part the usage of 'propaganda' reflects a recognition—albeit often not articulated—that print changed rhetorical practices.[13] Charles Brent, rector of Christ Church in Bristol, was conscious of this when explaining how he had altered his sermon for the press and mused on 'the difference between speaking to the ear and the eye'. The former, he said, could be 'impos'd upon' by tricks of speech: 'he who has

(1700) and the Republican Demon', *Essays and Studies*, 49 (1996), 1–18; L. Mitchell, *Grammar Wars: Langauge as Cultural Battlefield in Seventeenth and Eighteenth Century England* (Aldershot, 2001); R. Ahrens, 'The Political Pamphlet: 1660–1714', in *Anglia*, 109 (1991), 21–43; Skerpan, *Rhetoric of Politics*; Montaño, *Courting the Moderates*; Downie, *Harley and the Press*; Urstad, *Walpole's Poets*.

[9] Vickers, *Rhetoric*, 24–5, 41–3. Sprat, *History of the Royal Society* (1667), ii. 20, urged that discourse should 'return back to the primitive purity and shortness when men delivered so many things, almost in an equal number of words'.

[10] Skinner, *Reason and Rhetoric*, 120–7.

[11] Ibid., ch. 4.

[12] B. Dooley, 'From Literary Criticism to Systems Theory in Early Modern Journalism History', *Journal of the History of Ideas*, 51 (1990), 465; B. Bailyn, *The Ideological Origins of the American Revolution* (Cambridge, Mass., 1967), p. ix, 95; K. Sharpe, *Criticism and Compliment* (Cambridge, 1987), 3–4; T. Cogswell, 'The Politics of Propaganda: Charles I and the People in the 1620s', *JBS*, 29 (1990), 187–215. For the concept of propaganda, see J. Ellul, *Propaganda, the Formation of Men's Attitudes, translated . . . by Konrad Kellen and Jean Lerner* (New York, 1973); D. Katz, D. Cartwright, S. Eldersveld, and A. Lee (eds.), *Public Opinion and Propaganda* (New York, 1954); R. Scribner, *For the Sake of Simple Folk: Popular Propaganda for the German Reformation* (Cambridge, 1981); Speck, 'Political Propaganda'; J. Downie and T. Corns (eds.), *Telling the People What to Think* (London, 1993); Harris, *London Crowds*; T. Harris, 'Propaganda and Public Opinion in Seventeenth Century England', in J. Popkin (ed.), *Media and Revolution: Comparative Perspectives* (Kentucky, 1995); Richards, *Party Propaganda*; J. Peacey, *Politicians and Pamphleteers* (Aldershot, 2004).

[13] Ramus and others sought to reconcile rhetoric to age of printed book (Skinner, *Reason and Rhetoric*, 110).

the knack of turning up his voice to the right pitch and key of his audience, does the business'. But print, he thought, acted differently, not least because he did not know his readers as he did his congregation. Aware that 'cool reasoning and calm sense' would 'not stir them' and that the eye 'looks closely, scans critically, pores thoughtfully, dwells capriciously upon every line', he reworked his argument in 'a livelier turn and spirit'.[14] Deprived of the advantages of speech, print had therefore to become bolder in order to retain the attention of readers of varied ability to weigh its message. Print could thus be subjected to leisured scrutiny and criticism in a way that rhetorical speech could not. Conventional rhetoric was often directed to influence a particular, limited, and known audience; yet the audience of print was often general, large, and anonymous. Renaissance rhetoric had been concerned primarily with persuading the monarch; but the later seventeenth-century audience was the public. Rhetorical concerns with gesture, memory, and pronunciation became irrelevant to printed discourse.

Rhetoric alone, then, fails to do justice to the changed context and demands of publicly competitive politics.[15] 'Propaganda' seems to fill some of the gap. Propaganda is co-ordinated; aware of the need for well-timed intervention; and adept at describing events and people in a way that plays on the psychological anxieties of its audience. And it often deals with simplified, binary stereotypes, lies, and inversions, playing on their fears and prejudices far more consistently than rhetoric. A significantly titled tract, *The Source of our Present Fears Discovered* (1703), alleged that a good deal of print was published to keep the people 'under continual alarms' of a French invasion, with fears of 'popery and wooden shoes'.[16] Whig writers were alleged routinely to invoke fear in their readers, and Tories were also, as we have seen, said to invoke the 'church in danger'.[17] Clearly early modern England was not a mass society in which the media of communication were all-pervasive or controlled by totalitarian regimes. Even so, the concept of propaganda confers agency to print, the pulpit, and other means of communication, particularly once the public was invoked as a political force.[18] Certainly contemporaries talked about the dangers of

---

[14] Charles Brent, 'An Essay Concerning the Nature and Guilt of Lying' (1702), dedication to Edward Colston.
[15] For a later period William Riker referred to the art of political manipulation, which he called 'heresthetics' (*The Art of Political Manipulation* (New Haven, 1986)).
[16] *Source*, 30–1, 37, 41. Cf. E. Settle's *The Character of a Popish Successor* (1681).
[17] *The Character of a Whig* (1700), 94–5.
[18] Achinstein discerns a mid-seventeenth-century 'transformation of the Renaissance humanist practice: rhetoric was turned to the common street' (*Milton*, 59).

rival groups *propagating* their ideologies.[19] There was a commonly held perception, from the 1670s onwards, that each 'interest' possessed organized and effective lie-machines. Propaganda is not an ideal concept, and we should treat it cautiously, aware of its overlap with the art of rhetoric; but several important elements of it, especially its binary world-view and stress on likely reader responses, are useful analytical tools when seeking to expose later Stuart prejudices and assumptions.

Party conflict as linguistic struggle

The party struggle was necessarily a struggle about the meaning of words. The bitterness of the rival interpretations of names, labels, phrases, and keywords struck contemporaries forcibly. As one pamphleteer explained, 'people of late are very hot and contentious, about things they seem to have no manner of notion of, except in name.' The author thought that they had 'been long led aside with sounds only, and set a madding about terms they have no meaning to'. The public needed 'clear and distinct significations', stripped of the 'cant and disguise, in which they have, a long time, been entangled, by the industry and artifice of such who find it in their interest to propagate error and mislead the common people.'[20] Fixed meaning was so elusive because partisan conflict created at least two interpretations. The same word, phrase, or even text was given more than one meaning. To appropriate a phrase coined by Howard Erskine-Hill to describe the language of jacobitism after 1714, we might talk of the double-vision of partisan discourse.[21] Whig cleric John Swynfen invoked such a concept when attacking the 'double entendres' that, he believed, had been deliberately planted in a high church declaration. 'It is shrewdly to be suspected', he thought, 'that it was drawn up with a direct view to this double meaning and worded as it is, purely that if one sense was liable to be struck at, another might be trumpeted up to ward off the blow.'[22]

Meaning was vigorously contested. Interconnected terms such as 'heir', 'hereditary', 'people', 'public good', 'commonwealth', 'church', 'religion',

[19] C. Leslie, *The New Association of Those Called Moderate Churchmen, With the Modern Whigs and Fanatics*, 3rd edn. (1702), 2; Leslie, *The Wolf Stript of his Shepherd's Cloathing* (1704), 3; W. Kennett, *The Wisdom of Looking Backwards, to Judge the Better of One Side* (1715), 330.
[20] *Reflections on the Management of Some Late Party-Disputes and the Notorious Abuse of the Words Church, Schismatick, Fanatick &c* (1715), 1–2.
[21] H. Erskine-Hill, 'Two-fold Vision in C18th Writing', *English Literary History*, 64 (1997), 909.
[22] Swynfen, *Objections*, 2–3.

'liberty', 'property', 'faction', and so on became the *subject* of debate. They became a lexicon of controversy. But the linguistic confusion of Babel was also created by private languages—what contemporaries were beginning in the later Stuart period to call 'cant'.[23] Secret, jargonized languages, were the preserve of particular groups rather than shared, common sense; and such language could be used to cover real meaning.[24] Indeed the words 'jargon', 'banter', and 'bamboozle' began to be used in the period, reflecting anxiety about words hiding and obscuring meaning. Words could, in another new verb, 'wheedle' men, flatter them with dissimulations.[25] Thus alongside, and part of, the contest over meaning there was an anxiety that language was being used to hide inner designs. Party itself appeared to encourage dissimulation, hypocrisy, and the pursuit of inner interests under an outer, legitimizing, veil of public good and validating slogans. Party not only conferred double-meanings, but also meant that partisans could themselves be taken in two ways, one constructed by outward actions and words, the other by inner, private, self-interest.

Redefinition, cant, dissimulation, or diversity of meaning and abuse of labels all led to epistemological uncertainty. Literary critics have, for some time now, been exploring a seventeenth-century language crisis. The following chapters suggest that the same epistemological crisis existed in the political sphere, which therefore needs to be related to a more general phenomenon. Indeed, anxiety about the effect of publicly competitive partisanship on language, truth, and the capacity for judgement was profound, not just an abstract concern but deeply embedded in the political culture. Yet it is also the case that these preoccupations had a creative side, for the very fictions that contemporaries discerned as being routinely generated by partisanship created new possibilities alongside the dangers they posed. Prose characterization, for example, became a literary plaything in polemical battles. Certainly this was not new; but it was carried to new heights. The characterization of the Englishman as John Bull in 1712 was only the most enduring of a series of representations: of dissenters, of party men, and of republicans. Moreover, a good deal of political debate took a pseudo-fictional form. The best polemicists were those able to

---

[23] The *OED* gives the 1680s as the earliest usage for cant in the sense of a peculiar jargon belonging to a sect, profession, social group and as a trick of words.
[24] The *OED* gives 1710 as the first usage of cant meaning phraseology that was not a genuine expression of sentiment, and 1709 for the affected use of religious language to convey an impression of piety. But see below for earlier usage.
[25] R. Head, *Proteus Redivivus; or, The Art of Wheedling* (1675), 2–3.

imagine themselves into the minds of their diverse audience and the prejudices of their opponents. Defoe's imaginative exploits are well known, but, as we shall see, there are many other examples of pamphleteers impersonating their rivals, or of writing dialogues in which they imagined sets of counter-arguments. This required skill when, as one writer put it, 'the difference between the Whigs and Tories is so great in everything, as if they were neither of one religion, country or nature.'[26] Partisan polemic also involved a process of claim and counter-claim, creating a narrative with a sense of history, a secular story with heroes and villains that could be followed in print and lived vicariously. In important ways, therefore, politics and literature were fused.

The fictions of partisanship

In the first half of his book we encountered several fictions: of the public; of the impartial, rational voter; of misrepresentations; and those deployed by petitioners and addressers. But the link between a representative society and fiction needs to be extended. Representation in either political or linguistic form creates a fiction. It seeks or claims to make present what is not present, it offers to make an image, copy, or idea of something which is absent and then make it act or perform in some way.[27] Hobbes recognized as much when he talked about a representer as an actor on a stage. Thus political actors and representatives were, he said, authorized fictions.[28] Indeed, he believed that 'there are very few things that are uncapable of being represented by fiction'. Hobbes's insight underlines the fusion of the political and the literary. The later Stuart period was not, of course, the first to make this connection (though we need more systematic mapping of it), but it was being made with a new intensity, urgency, and set of resolutions. Partisanship and a representational political culture had a fictional impulse.

The compiler of *The History of Associations* (1716), for example, believed that his age was a 'fabulous' one that had difficulty distinguishing between reality and 'fiction'. Partisan politics was a world of imagination and invention:

---

[26] *A Smith and Cutlers Plain Dialogue about Whig and Tory* (1690), 1.

[27] The type of representative fiction varies, from an exact likeness, to a depiction of an 'essence', an agent, or a symbolic depiction (Pitkin, *Concept of Representation*, 61, 86, 92, 113).

[28] Hobbes, *Leviathan*, ed. Tuck, 113.

most men now seem to be poetically inclin'd; they value not representing things as they are, but so disguise them in the relation, that they no longer appear to be the same. Our historians, ever affecting the stile of impartiality, are so far from it, that there is scarce a page to be read in their works, without perceiving that they are full of gall on the one side, and of flattery on the other. Our news-papers give us the same facts in such several dresses, that there is not more to be made of what was transacted the last week, than if it had happen'd before the flood. Our common discourse is never to be rely'd on; when we are told of any thing done in the next street, tis no more certain than if it had been in Japan, or Terra Australis Incognita. When men vouch a thing as eye-witnesses to it, good manners forbids us to contradict them, but at the same time good sense forbids us to believe them. What credit can be given to the common words of men, when so little regard is had to the most solemn oaths. In short, the poets first infected the world with their inventions instead of history, and now we have nothing but fictions instead of truth.[29]

Concern about the duality and inventions of the world of partisan politics was heightened by three factors. The first was the profusion of 'plots', which were revealed to and judged by the public. The Popish Plot (1678), the Rye House Plot (1683), and the Monmouth Plot (1685) all served to make this a particular feature of the late 1670s and early 1680s. But the rash of jacobite plotting after 1689 also required the public to believe 'evidence' presented to them (often by informers of uncertain credit) as truth, or reject it as fiction.[30] As the quotation by L'Estrange at the start of Part II emphasizes, contemporaries were highly aware of this dimension of partisan double-vision.[31] Importantly, such questions of judgement were not peripheral, but rather integral to partisan allegiance. Second, the frequent elections, addresses, petitions, addresses, and print controversies analysed in Part I all destabilized certain truths and generated two, or more, versions of it.[32] Third, new forms of public finance, such as the national debt, paper money, and stocks, depended on fiscal fictions dependent on public credit. As a result a preoccupation with duality, ambiguity, disguise, conspiracy, epistemological uncertainty, and fiction might be said to characterize later Stuart political culture. Such anxieties were not new; but they were intensified by the factors outlined at the beginning of this book and embedded in the practice of politics. They had become the norm, however

---

[29] *The History of Associations* (1716), 1–2.

[30] K. Loveman, 'Shamming Readers'.

[31] For an exploration of L'Estrange's preoccupation with deception see P. Hinds, 'Roger L'Estrange'.

[32] One tract attacked the 'surmises and empty nothings' with which readers were entertained (*Sober and Seasonable Queries*, 11).

aberrant or abhorrent that norm appeared to be. Partisan politics relied on the *routine* castigation of rivals as liars and frauds who pursued self-interest under the veneer of the public good and through the systematic deception of the public.

An outline of chapters 5–7

The remaining three chapters explore various aspects of the problem of how the public could make rational judgements amidst a public discourse that destabilized both the credibility of all political knowledge and the meanings of words and labels.[33] The following pages study how political knowledge was gained; how it could be abused; how 'true' knowledge could be discerned from 'false' knowledge and the consequences of error.[34] The public was being asked for, and offered, its opinion through petitions and addresses, through a series of elections and through the press. Yet partisanship was thought to render the grounds of public judgement (necessary for the formation of rational choice and informed opinion) extremely hazardous. The consequences of failure would be the subordination of free-born Englishmen to the tyranny of France and popery. At the heart of the later Stuart political culture there thus lay a series of fundamental ambiguities. The public was both a single-headed entity with a voice but also a multi-headed hydra. The public was a rational umpire whose decisions and opinions were fundamental to the structure of politics but also an irrational tool in the hands of manipulative politicians and frauds. The public was judge but its judgement was liable to be warped either by its own passions or by the manipulative language that surrounded it. The public had to make informed choices, but the information on which to base such choices was biased, filtered, and even distorted by partisanship.

[33] Viewing political culture in this way—as an intensification of longer term anxieties about uncertainty, truth-claims, and taxonomy—should enable the re-establishment of a dialogue between political and social history. An obvious overlap is with witchcraft, where similar issues of truth-claims and public judgement were at stake (see, for example, P. Rushton, 'Texts of Authority: Witchcraft Accusations and the Demonstration of Truth in Early Modern England', in S. Clark (ed.), *Languages of Witchcraft. Narrative, Ideology and Meaning in Early Modern Culture* (Basingstoke, 2001)). We have already noted the language of witchcraft to describe the power of political polemic. The issue of stereotypical labelling offers another point of overlap between strands of historical analysis.

[34] Dissimulation was the 'hallmark' of the seventeenth century, in Europe as well as England, but in the later seventeenth century 'a new notion of truth as the sum of probability rather than an absolute fact began to gain ground' (Dooley, 'News and Doubt', in B. Dodey and S. Baron (eds.), *The Politics of Information in Early Modern Europe* (London, 2001), 281, 287).

The public had to discern what was credible, but partisanship created a world in which the truth was relative and where credibility was fictional and unstable. Many of these ambiguities are still apparent in the way in which politics works today and may indeed be inherent to public politics *per se.*

Chapter 5 considers the way in which partisan public dialogue about politics was perceived, even by partisans, as dangerously corrosive and abusive. It highlights what many contemporaries regarded as an unusually libellous, slanderous, and querulous public discourse, both oral and written. Chapter 6 examines another aspect of the anxiety caused by the degradation of public discourse: the issue of political truth and its elusiveness in an age of partisanship. It suggests that a partisan political culture placed a great burden on the public to discern the 'truth' even though it simultaneously made truth a relative notion. Truth was particularly endangered by party, which strained language but in so doing also exploited fictional representations to full effect. The final chapter considers the consequences of such a political culture. It argues that by 1716 both Whig and Tory feared that the unwritten boundaries of public discourse were being transgressed. The Tories had long been convinced that the Whigs were a party of liars who used popularity for their own self-interested ends. By 1714, and especially as a result of the unrest in 1715, the Whigs were convinced not only that the Tories were master manipulators of public discourse but also that the people had lost their ability to judge and discern truth. The result was a decision to repeal the Triennial Act, that had guaranteed frequent elections. The chapter also argues that the evolution of politeness and an appeal to rationality was in some sense a response to this same set of problems, and that the consequences of adopting these informal rules governing public discourse were far-reaching for the political architecture and culture of Hanoverian England.

CHAPTER FIVE

The Evolution of Print Culture and the Libels of Public Discourse

> The bent and genius of the age is best known, in a free country, by the pamphlets and papers that come daily out, as the sense of parties and sometimes the voice of the nation.[1]

> Faction has a great advantage when it can dispers news so yt it shall be thought ye sence of ye people, for by yt means it will really become ye sence of ye people. By this means elections will be governed. For every idle burger will beleev a ly in print rather than an honest neighbour.[2]

Earlier chapters have explored sites where 'politics' and 'the public' met. Petitions, addresses, associations, and electioneering all necessitated some form of appeal to, and agency for, the public. Each of these points of contact between state and people relied in some sense on print. Print allowed petitions and addresses to evolve from their manuscript forerunners into something novel. Similarly, the publication of nationwide addresses and electioneering advice helped to expand a national political culture. And it will also have been evident that print seemed to fix misrepresentations and hence provoked counter-claims, sparking a contested public dialogue. This chapter therefore examines the role of print more closely. More specifically, it seeks to relate the expansion of vituperative printed polemic to perceptions about an increasingly abusive, libellous, public discourse.

In doing so there is always a danger of exaggerating the impact of the press. Indeed, recent work has stressed the continuing vitality of oral and

---

[1] W. Kennett, *A Register and Chronicle Ecclesiastical and Civil* (1728), preface.
[2] BL, Add. MSS 32,518, f. 36, notes by North.

manuscript cultures.[3] Poisonous words had long been a concern of those in positions of authority. Studies of prosecutions for seditious speech, dangerous sermons, and of manuscript libels in the sixteenth and early seventeenth centuries attest to the deep anxiety that publicly articulated words could induce.[4] Oral 'sedition', particularly at politically sensitive times, continued to be prosecuted. Tim Harris, Paul Monod, and Paula McDowell have shown how analysis of these can offer insights into popular allegiances and opinion in the later Stuart period.[5] Fear of printed poison has therefore to be seen against this wider culture of intermittently policed speech-acts, of which print was only a part. Libel was a term that applied to spoken sedition as well as a name commonly given to any controversial pamphlet.[6] We should also be wary about assuming that print alone tells us about popular opinion.[7] The impact of print is also questioned by the exhaustive work of the History of Parliament, suggesting that at the polls more traditional forms of influence, such as landowners, the church and the crown continued to hold enormous sway.[8] It is, moreover, important to place later Stuart developments in a broader context of a political culture that was in transition over the sixteenth and seventeenth centuries, with accelerated change after 1640.

Yet, despite all these caveats, contemporaries recognized the power of printed words and, as the remarks quoted at the head of this section make

[3] J. Barry, 'Literacy and Literature in Popular Culture: Reading and Writing in Historical Perspective', in T. Harris (ed.), *Popular Culture in England, c.1500–1850* (Basingstoke, 1995); M. Ezell, *Social Authorship and the Advent of Print* (Baltimore, 1999); Fox, *Oral*; H. Love, *Scribal Publication in Seventeenth-century England* (Oxford, 1993). Print continued to be copied into manuscript (*A Letter to Richard Steele Esq.* (1715), page opposite 1), pasted on walls (*Three Letters* (1689), 3) and read aloud (C. Leslie, *A View of the Times . . . in the First Volume of the Rehearsals* (1708), preface).

[4] Chapter 1, n. 52.

[5] Harris, *London Crowds*; P. Monod, *Jacobitism and the English People, 1688–1788* (Cambridge, 1989); McDowell, *Women of Grub Street*.

[6] William Denton's *An Apology for the Liberty of the Press* (1681), 6–7: if anyone who criticized the state 'represents falsly, it is then a libel and a crime'. For example, Narcissus Luttrell wrote on his copy of *An Address to our Sovereign Lady* [1704] that it was 'a scandalous libel on ye Commons in Parliamt' (Newberry Library, Chicago, Case 6A.159/45). See also his annotations in *The Luttrell File*, ed. S. Parks (New Haven, 1999). Between 1660 and 1720, nearly 300 tracts used the word 'libel', or variants such as 'libeller' or 'libellous' in their title, and a similar number were issued with 'scandal' or 'scandalous' in the title (ESTC).

[7] T. Harris, 'Understanding Popular Politics in Restoration Britain', in Houston and Pincus, *Nation Transformed*.

[8] *HOP I and HOP II*. Yet these do not systematically examine political print as a principal source, because it is less easy to use for surveys of individuals or even the constituencies they represented than other types of evidence. Relating MPs, constituencies, and parliament to a wider public and political culture would seem a methodologically beneficial step.

plain, saw in the press a form of national voice. Since the press interacted
with other forms of popular expression and organization, a focus on the
press should not be taken to mean that they are unimportant; rather that
print allows us one way of studying perceptions about public discourse.
Moreover, although the press had always been worrying to those in authority, there was something peculiarly interesting going on during the
later Stuart period: the press was seen as intrinsically linked to publicly
contested, partisan politics. The chapter therefore explores some of the
continuities and changes in print culture over the long seventeenth century. It begins by highlighting some of the innovations evident, particuarly
in the post-1695 free press, in order to stress that 1641 was not the only
significant watershed and that the longlasting fusion of politics and the
market could only flourish in the later period. I then examine some of the
ways in which print assisted in the transformation of early modern political culture, particularly from the mid-seventeenth century onwards. We
find that the conditions prevailing in the later Stuart period heightened
the transformative impact of print. Later Stuart news and polemic deepened, exacerbated, and extended earlier trends, features, and anxieties.
Moreover, print facilitated a national political culture, an ongoing public
debate that could hardly be closed down, the normalization of print as the
antidote to its own poison, and the fusion of the market and the political
system. Partisans also believed that loyalties and shared beliefs could, in
part, be forged and undermined through print and public discourse. The
Levellers and Quakers had already shown the potential that print offered
in the construction of identity and allegiance; and these insights were exploited to the full by the parties.[9] Whig and Tory were thus in part print
communities, defined not only by their own writers but also by those hostile to them. Print helped both to shape their identity, and to make them
recognizable to readers in the localities. The importance of this development will become clearer when the debate about the usefulness of party labels is examined in the next chapter. Partisanship thus realized some of the
potential of controversial print, and increased its transformative impact.
The result was that the interaction of print and party exacerbated long-
held anxieties about the abusive, seditious, and mendacious nature of
print. The press was perceived as facilitating and provoking the abusive

---

[9]   K. Peters, ' "The Quakers Quaking": Print and the Spread of a Movement', in S. Wabuda
and C. Litzenberger (eds.), *Belief and Practice in Sixteenth-century England* (Aldershot, 1998);
K. Peters, 'Quaker Pamphleteering and the Growth of the Quaker Movement in East Anglia,
1652–6', in D. Chadd (ed.), *Religious Dissent in East Anglia III* (Norwich, 1996); R. Foxley,
'Citizenship and the English Nation in Leveller Thought 1642–53', Ph. D., Cambridge (2001).

rage stoked up by publicly partisan politics because it allowed the wide-spread circulation of misrepresentations. But it was not just the controversial press that raised such fears, for an analysis of the coffee-houses, clubs, and electioneering reveals the articulation of very similar anxieties. Indeed, collectively the laments about the degradation of public discourse re-emphasize the degree of idealization apparent in the Habermasian notion of the public sphere dependent on reason and politeness.

The chapter therefore explores some of the inherent ambiguity of partisan print: it was a means to inform and persuade, but also to mislead and abuse; it aspired to rational, polite, communication but many feared it could easily become a tool for spreading slander and irrationality. Indeed, the degradation of the public sphere was apparent at its very inception. And these ambiguities became particularly important when public discourse had become part of the structure of politics in a more systematic way than ever before. The rage of party thus fostered a culture of libel, as each side sought to destroy the credit of the other; yet public refutation of a libel through print became the norm, so that print and party were in a sense made to do some of their own policing. The shift from pre-publication censorship to post-publication refutation, evident in the second half of the seventeenth century, was further proof of the rise of the public as a tribunal and umpire.

INNOVATIONS IN PRINT

Bestselling pamphlets and the rise of the periodical

Building on the remarks made in Chapter 1, it is first necessary to highlight some of the ways in which the later Stuart period witnessed innovation in terms of press output, organization, and structure. This helps us to understand how the public was created, sustained, informed, and manipulated.

As indicated earlier, change occurred in the scale and type of output. Although 1641 witnessed a remarkable opening of the floodgates, the output of the press declined in the 1650s and when it did regain its former level after the Revolution of 1689, it did so with a consistency that was new. Rather in the same way that parliament achieved regularity and permanency after 1689, so the press became a *reliable representative force*. Access to a press that was free from pre-publication licensing became the norm not the exception. And this normalization of the political press meant that it was a weapon with which everyone involved in the struggle for power had to come to terms.

The increase in titles is in part a reflection of the popularity of the pamphlet, one of the genres of print most suited to controversy. In his work on religious literature over the early modern period, Ian Green has questioned whether controversial literature sold as well as other genres.[10] Yet the bestsellers of the later Stuart period included many controversial pieces. *The Judgment of Whole Kingdoms* claimed to have sold 8,000 copies in seven months;[11] 10,000 copies of *The History of the Kentish Petition* were said to have been sold and prints were distributed to 'every freeholder in the county', dispersed by presbyterians and on market days, with 'men posted to read the libels' to the people.[12] Sacheverell's sermon, *The Perils of False Brethren*, which ran to eleven editions within a few months, famously sold about 100,000, a bestseller that had no equal in the eighteenth century.[13] Mark Goldie estimates that there were 300,000 copies of allegiance pamphlets in circulation in the years immediately after the revolution, over 20 per cent of which had more than one edition and a further 13 per cent received replies or defences, ensuring them a longevity beyond the merely ephemeral.[14] Nearly all such works appeared in pamphlet form, which reached its peak during the later Stuart period. We must return to the issue of pamphlet distribution and dissemination in a moment; but first we should look at the genre itself.

The pamphlet was a highly versatile format that had a long genesis that should not be under-estimated.[15] Capable of assuming different forms (letters, dialogues, essays, refutations, vindications, and so on), the pamphlet was ideally suited to making a public statement at a particular moment. It was thus highly suited to those who sought to make a bold, strategic, intervention in public discourse and partisan politics. Discussion of pamphlets thus became part of the political game, making timing of publication and authorship particularly important.[16] Moreover, the pamphlet was highly popular across the social scale. Thus, one contemporary historian of pamphlets remarked in 1715, 'there's scarce any degree of people but may think themselves interested enough to be concern'd with what is publish'd in pamphlets'. A pamphlet, being 'of a small portable

---

[10] I. Green, *Print and Protestantism in Early Modern England* (Oxford, 2000), 233.
[11] *The Art of Lying and Rebelling Taught by the Whigs* (1713), 3.
[12] C. Davenant, *Tom Double Return'd Out of the Country; or, the True Picture of a Modern Whig* (1702), 12–13.
[13] G. Holmes, *The Trial of Doctor Sacheverell* (London, 1973), 75.
[14] Goldie, 'Revolution of 1689', 479, 482.
[15] G. Orwell and R. Reynolds (eds.), *British Pamphleteers* (London, 1948), introduction; Raymond, *Pamphlets*.
[16] *The Luttrell File*, ed. S. Parks.

bulk, and of no great price, and of no great difficulty, seems adapted for every one's understanding, for every one's reading, for every one's buying and consequently becomes a fit object and subject of most people's choice, capacity and ability'.[17] In 1712 a tract advocating restraint on the press noted the time wasted by 'poorer tradesmen . . . in going about from one coffee house to another, poring upon seditious, heretical and treasonable papers'.[18] Their universality and their capacity to make political interventions meant that pamphlets could not be ignored.

But although pamphlets were bought in unprecedented number and were innovatively intertwined in the political strategies of the parties, perhaps greater *novelty* lay in the expansion of the periodical, and in particular the news periodical. The first great proliferation of printed newsbooks came in the 1640s. As Joad Raymond has shown, one might almost say printed news was 'invented' then.[19] Yet his claim that the lapse of the Licensing Act in 1695 was, therefore, 'not a watershed in the emergence of a public sphere of popular political opinion' seems to neglect later print density and new market forces.[20] The year 1695 was particularly significant for periodical publication because, more than pamphlet press, it was vulnerable to government censorship. For much of the later 1660s and 1670s there was only one, official, news periodical, *The London Gazette*. The lapse of licensing in 1679 and again in 1695 thus saw the proliferation of periodical titles.[21] More importantly, both lapses (coinciding with a form of politics that stimulated public appetite) encouraged expansion in the number of *issues* of each periodical (that is to say, the number of times it was published per week). 'Sixty four titles in 1642 produced 367 issues; in 1700 half as many titles produced four times as many issues.'[22] This can be clearly demonstrated with another graph, which shows the later Stuart period as achieving greater density of material. Based on data summarized in an appendix to this book my own count of periodical output in 1710 suggests that by Anne's reign there had been a step-change: 19 titles produced just

[17] M. Davies, *Eikon Mikro-biblike Sive Icon Libellorum; or, A Critical History of Pamphlets* (1715), 1–4.
[18] *Arguments Relating to a Restraint upon the Press*, 24.
[19] Raymond, *Invention*.
[20] 'The Newspaper, Public Opinion and the Public Sphere', in his *News, Newspapers and Society*, 128. Historians of the eighteenth century see 1695 as the turning-point (H. Barker, *Newspapers, Politics and English Society 1695–1855* (Oxford, 1998), 1).
[21] C. Nelson and M. Seccombe, *Periodical Publications 1641–1700. A Survey with Illustrations*, Occasional Papers of the Bibliographical Society, No.2 (1986), 11; Sutherland, *Restoration Newspaper*.
[22] Ibid., figs. 4, 5, pp. 14–15.

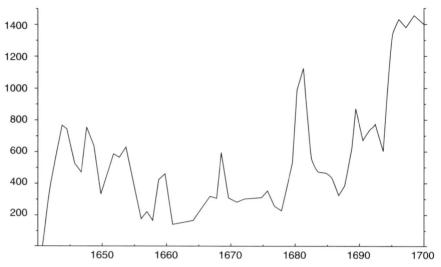

Issues of Periodicals per year, 1641–1700. (Source: C. Nelson and M. Seccombe *Periodical Publications 1641–1700* (1986)). [Reproduced by courtesy of the authors.]

over 2,300 issues, about three times the highest figure for the mid-seventeenth century.[23] Admittedly 1710 was a year of bitter controversy, but the figure brings home the massive expansion of the periodical press.

After 1695 news periodicals became a permanent and intrinsic feature of the political culture. Their proliferation was remarkable.[24] By 1709 there were 18 London periodicals, including the first daily, the first evening newspaper, 15 bi-weeklies, and 2 tri-weeklies. And the market was more secure—titles after 1695 were far less vulnerable to failure than their 1640s counterparts. This meant that readers could count on more regular and more frequent news; and on the longevity of their favoured paper. The number of *copies* of each issue was also impressive. In 1704 just nine news-

[23] See appendix. That figure omits some provincial periodicals for which evidence is sketchy as well as titles with runs of less than 50. It also omits Scottish and Irish output, for which the data are uneven, though inclusion would significantly increase the total, not least because Edinburgh and London each acquired their own prolific press, and because several important London titles were reprinted in both cities.
[24] For listings of titles 1660–1720, see *Cambridge Bibliography of English Literature* ed. G.Watson (1971), ii. 1255–1390; *Times Tercentenary Handlist of English & Welsh Newspapers, Magazines & Reviews, 1620–1920* (London, 1966); Nelson and Seccombe, *Periodical Publications*. For published extracts from periodicals, see W. B. Ewald, *The Newsmen of Queen Anne* (Oxford, 1946).

papers issued nearly 44,000 copies per week. In total about 2.3 million copies circulated that year, rising slightly to 2.4 million by 1712–13.[25] The variety of types of serial publication was, moreover, significantly wider in 1700 than in the 1640s, with an expanded sense of what news was and how to entertain as well as inform readers.[26] Periodicity was thus far more frequent, diverse, and deeper than it had ever been. The periodical press also became more national because the lapse of the law in 1695 removed the bar to provincial publication. The first newspaper to appear outside London was probably published in Norwich in 1701; certainly by the end of 1710 there were 13 provincial newspapers published in 9 towns. Although the number was temporarily dented by the 1712 Stamp Act, by 1723 there were 24 newspapers operating in the provinces.[27] These remarkable changes were the result of a mixture of market forces and the 'urban renaissance' but also demand created by political controversy and diversification of taste, as well as the abandonment of censorship. All these developments suggest a 'general thirst after news' and comment.[28]

To be sure, news-mania was far from being novel. Even before the civil war there was a sophisticated awareness about public affairs, stimulated not so much by print as by oral exchanges, at markets and fairs, inns and taverns, and by manuscript transmission through letters, libels, and ballads. News had always been a staple part of conversation and the impact of printed news can be exaggerated. Even so, news was evolving in interesting ways.

First, after 1695 print forced scribal news publication into a niche market. John Dyer's rabidly high-church scribal news still found buyers into Anne's reign; but his newsletter was an exception that proved the rule.[29]

---

[25] Barker, *Newspapers*, 30–1; J. R. Sutherland, 'The Circulation of Newspapers and Literary Periodicals 1700–30', *The Library*, 4th ser., 15 (1934), 110–24. Addison estimated there to be 'twenty readers to every paper' (*Spectator*, 10).

[26] Nelson and Seccombe, *Periodical Publications*, 17–18.

[27] G. A. Cranfield, *The Development of the Provincial Newspaper, 1700–1760* (Oxford, 1962), 16–17. Between 1701 and 1721 forty provincial newspapers were started (J. Raven, 'Book Distribution Networks in Early Modern Europe', in *Produzione e Commercio Della Carta e del Libro Secc. XIII–XVIII* (Florence, 1992), 583–630). But for government action leading to 'the virtual eradication of the non-Whig periodic press by mid-1716', see Hyland, 'Liberty and Libel', 868.

[28] *Spectator*, 452.

[29] Dyer had a number of brushes with authority, when his observations were perceived to have gone too far, but he continued to produce his newsletter. For action against him, see *CSPD 1691–2*, 475; *CSPD 1694–5*, 307; CLRO, SF 380, 7 Sept 1691; ibid., SF 394, 26 May 1693; ibid., SF 396, 6 Sept. 1693; PRO SP44/345, 86. If we are to believe Addison's caricatures, Dyer appealed particularly to bigoted Tory country parsons and fox-hunting squires who imbibed 'wrong notions and prejudices' (*Freeholder*, 22).

Thus although some of Dyer's election reports appeared in print and some newspapers aped the style of the newsletter—one by Ichabod Dawks even adopted a font emulating handwriting—print largely displaced scribal news.[30] The author (previously a scribal newsmonger) of the *London News-Letter* lamented in 1696 that he had been forced 'against my own inclination to appear in print, to recover if I can my former customers and preserve those few I have left, who as they often told me, will rather read a printed paper than a written letter'.[31] Second, printed periodicals were cheap and could cater for the specialist and politicized markets once cornered by scribal publication. Reader choice became particularly important in an age of partisan politics. Newspapers had always reported with a particular bias, but party shaped what was reported and how. In the reigns of William and Anne *The Post Boy, The Examiner, The Rehearsal* were all inclined to high church or Tory perspectives; *The Post Man, The Observator, The Medley* to a whiggish one. Other papers claimed self-consciously to report from a moderate, impartial stance, though many of these claims proved highly suspect, as we shall see. Thus not only were the 'facts' determined by ideological position but the reader could thus choose how his or her news would be filtered.

Third, this need to respond to reader demand in turn facilitated the diversification of periodicals, so that political news and affairs become a sort of interactive entertainment. This is particularly apparent in the development of a 'letters to the publisher' genre. This innovation owed much to John Dunton's *Athenian Mercury*, 1691–7.[32] Dunton assembled a team of writers whose sole purpose was to reply to queries sent in by readers, ranging across a broad swathe of 'current affairs'—moral, religious, social, scientific, and political issues. The reader was an active participant rather than a passive consumer, and the format was successful enough for others to copy it.[33] Whilst some of the letters published by periodicals might have

---

[30] *A Collection from Dyer's Letters Concerning the Elections* (1706); S. Morison, *Ichabod Dawks and his News-Letter: With an Account of the Dawks Family of Booksellers and Stationers 1635–1731* (Cambridge, 1931); *Newsletters to Newspapers: Eighteenth-century Journalism, Papers Presented at a Bicentennial Symposium*, ed. D. H. Bond and W. R. McLeod (Morgantown, 1977). Henry Crossgrove's *Norwich Gazette* derived some of its news from Dyer's newsletter (G. J. Guth, 'Croakers, Tackers, and other Citizens: Norwich Voters in the Eighteenth Century,' Ph. D., Stanford (1985), 216).

[31] *London News-Letter*, 1.

[32] H. Berry, 'An Early Coffee House Periodical and its Readers: The Athenian Mercury 1691–7', *London Journal*, 25 (2000), 15–33. Its 580 issues contained 5,000 questions and answers.

[33] *British Apollo* (1708–11), *Review* (1704–15), and *The Spectator*; B. Williams, 'Henry Crossgrove, Jacobite Journalist and Printer', *The Library*, 3rd ser., 5 (1914), 204–14; N. Glaisyer,

been fictitious, enough survive to make it impossible to dismiss them all as such.[34] There was thus a symbiotic relationship between periodical, reader, and correspondent that made it politically powerful. For example, one letter to the *Examiner* in 1710 claimed to be by a 'country member' whose habit was to 'constantly send a dozen of your papers down to my electors'.[35] Its author was thus involved in a triangular relationship with his constituents, via Westminster and the press. Moreover, the letter-based periodical often offered moral advice, alongside, and sometimes instead of, the news, making it a sort of secular homily 'heard' several times a week. Even if divines, such as Swift or Leslie, were periodical authors they derived authority from outside the pulpit; and there were many more such sermonizers who had no clerical training.

Market forces

Alongside these changes it must also be recognized that the structure of the press and the dissemination of material were increasingly sophisticated, reflecting the combination of commercial and ideological forces. In the last chapter we saw how election tracts were offered at a discount for bulk orders and this development was repeated for other pamphlets. Thus in 1711 *A Representation of the Present State of Religion . . . in Ireland*, sold at 4*d* but 'for encouragement of gentlemen to buy numbers, they shall have them at 30*s* per hundred'.[36] Similarly bookseller Thomas Harrison offered 'that useful and necessary book' *The Judgment of Whole Kingdoms and Nations* (which paraphrased Locke's *Second Treatise*) at wholesale as well as retail prices. Harrison even offered to lend the book for 'two days for nothing' provided it was not damaged.[37]

'Readers, Correspondents and Communities: John Houghton's A Collection for Improvement of Husbandry and Trade (1692–1703)', in *Communities in Early Modern England*, ed. Sephard and Withington (Manchester, 2000).

[34] R. P. Bond, *New Letters to the Tatler and Spectator* (Austin, 1959). In Feb. 1715, to correct what he thought was a false report of the Leicester election, Sir Thomas Cave sent a printed relation of the poll to the London coffee-houses, though he noted with regret that the *Post Man*, *Evening Post*, and *Post Bag* all refused to carry this rival version (*Verney Letters*, i. 329).

[35] Swift, *Prose Works*, iii. 89.

[36] BL, Harl. MSS 5,995 (68). Cf. [E.D.], *A Serious Representation to the People of Great-Britain Concerning the Pretender* (1715), price 4*d*; advertisement on reverse of title page: 'any gentlemen that have a mind to send any numbers into the country, may be furnished with what they please, with a very considerable allowance, by Mr Baker'. *A Letter from a Minister in Norfolk to his Parishioners* (1700) quoted a price of '8*s* per hundred'.

[37] *Proposals Made to the Booksellers of London and Westminster by T. Harrison* (BL, Harl. MSS 5996(134)). See also Ch. 2 n. 147.

PROPOSALS

Made to the Bookſellers of *London* and *Weſtminſter*,
by *T. Harriſon*, at the Weſt End of the *Royal-
Exchange*, in *Cornhill*.

THAT all Bookſellers may be encourag'd to Promote the Sale by Retail, as well
as by Wholeſale, to their Chapmen, that uſeful and neceſſary Book, call'd *The
Judgment of whole Kingdoms and Nations*, &c. I do henceforward Promiſe, That
they ſhall have the aforeſaid Book at the following Rates, *viz.* Three for 1 *s.* Thirteen for 4*s.* and Twenty ſeven for 8*s.* And whereas I have at the latter End of the
Contents given Notice, that any Perſon may read the aforeſaid Book two Days for
nothing, provided they do not damage it; I do promiſe to take all the aboveſaid Books
return'd, not damag'd, at any time. And whereas I have Printed the aforeſaid
Book in a large Character, on Nine Sheets and a Quarter of very fine Paper,
to be ſold to all Gentlemen at 1 *s.* per Book ; I do propoſe it to the Bookſellers
Three for 2 *s.* Thirteen for 8 *s.* Twenty ſeven for 16 *s.* *Note*, The Contents of
this Book are printed on two Leaves of Paper ; any Gentleman or Bookſeller may
have them Gratis to give and ſend to their Friends and Acquaintance.

Thomas Harrison sought to achieve maximum dissemination by offering discounts for bulk
purchases of *The Judgment of Whole Kingdoms*. The tract paraphrased John Locke's *Second
Treatise* and other statements of Whig ideology for a popular audience. It may have sold as
many as 8,000 copies in the space of seven months. It is clear from the quarto edition of 'very
fine paper', however, that Harrison also exploited a more genteel market. [Reproduced by
courtesy of the British Library.]

Discounts were clearly intended to appeal to the gentry who wanted to
distribute such material on a large scale. Entrepreneurs also sought to expand the market. Charles Povey, author of a bestselling electioneering
tract, opened 'a general office for publishing and selling books and pamphlets; as also for printing and dispersing all other papers or advertisements that upon any occasion are required by any person to be given away
gratis and which call for either a speedyer or general publication'. He
claimed to be able to increase sales tenfold.[38] Advertising for forthcoming
publications became ever more popular, with more and more notices
placed in the expanding periodical market and handbills announcing imminent or actual publication.[39] But innovation occurred at the higher end
of the market too, in the development of subscriptions and fine, folio editions of individual works or collections of controversial material suitable
for the gentleman's study.[40]

[38] BL, Harl. MS 5995 (170).   [39] BL, Harl. MS 5,995 (122).
[40] *Proposals Made*; *State Tracts*; *A Collection of State Tracts*; *A Collection of Poems on Affairs
of State*, 3 vols. (1689); *Poems on Affairs of State: From the Time of Oliver Cromwell*, 3 vols.
(1697–1707).

By all accounts dissemination was highly successful, particularly in towns and cities. Edmund Bohun, the last licenser of the press, thought that books 'have fallen so thick in all places that they have not escaped the soft hands of ladies, nor the hard fists of mechanicks and trades-men, and every man affects to seem well read in books'.[41] One 1690 tract was circulated and discussed so vigorously and variously that it was thought no one 'who for some weeks last past has lived anywhere but in a desert' could be ignorant of it.[42] A foreign visitor remarked that 'England is a country abounding in printed papers which they call pamphlets, wherein every author makes bold to talk very freely upon affairs of state, and to publish all manner of news'.[43] Defoe's pro-ministerial tracts were said to be 'brought up and sent away by the Carriers in Bundles, Carriage paid, to poyson or blind the poor Country'.[44]

The vulnerability of publishers to governmental action had fostered the development of 'trade publishers' who took on the risk of publishing controversial items and thus flourished in times of political crisis. Langley Curtis, Benjamin Harris, Richard Baldwin, John Morphew, and others thus became notorious names on the imprints of controversial literature.[45] It was also the case that publishing was becoming concentrated in the hands of 'congers' of publishers, who grouped together to spread risk but also to give them greater clout in the market. The spread of book piracy may also have been a factor, for it was claimed that booksellers had to charge more after 1695 because their books were pirated and sold cheaply.[46] Piracy certainly affected controversial material. 'There is no civiliz'd state, or city in the world', complained John How when he considered the state of the press, 'where such an extensive liberty is allow'd to any people as in this, where news, and all other sorts of papers, are suffer'd to be pirated, and cry'd about the streets by a parcel of vagabond hawkers, to the great prejudice and ruin of the just proprietors.'[47] This evidence suggests that the market for print was being exploited to the full. Indeed, piracy re-

[41] Bohun, *The Justice of the Peace* (1693), 23.
[42] *A Modest Attempt for Healing the Present Animosities in England Occasion'd by a Late Book Entituled A Modest Enquiry* (1690), 3 (referring to *A Modest Enquiry into the Causes of the Present Disasters in England* (1690)).
[43] *M. Misson's Memoirs and Observations in his Travels over England . . . Translated by Mr. Ozell* (1719), 203.
[44] *Remarks on a Scandalous Libel*, 4. For Defoe's distribution network, see *The Letters of Daniel Defoe*, ed. G. H.Healey (Oxford, 1955), 115–18.
[45] M. Treadwell, 'London Trade Publishers 1675–1750', *The Library*, 6th ser., 4 (1982), 99–134.
[46] J. How, *Some Thoughts on the Present State of Printing and Bookselling* (1709), 6–7.
[47] Ibid., 13. English print was frequently pirated at Dublin (R. Welch, 'The Book in Ireland', in Barnard and McKenzie, *The Cambridge History of the Book*, 716).

flected the emergence of the market, rather than the government, as the principal regulator of output for controversial print.

Those who distributed print, the hawkers, pedlars, and mercuries (many of whom were women) rose to record numbers in the capital. Just over 2,500 hawkers and pedlars were licensed 1696–7 when an act required it; only about a fifth of these were based in London.[48] Nehemiah Grew estimated that in Anne's reign there were about 4,000 in London who 'do nothing but sell trash under stalls, ballads, and papers of fals[e] news, tempting apprentices and children to spend money in useless and hurtfull things'.[49] More and more people appeared to eke a living out of print, leading to the emergence of London's 'Grub Street', a term first coined in the 1640s but which became far more commonplace in the later Stuart period.[50] The uncertain livelihood of those who lived off the expanded print marketplace was evident in a petition of 1704 from the journeymen printers who alleged that since the expiry of licensing they had 'become so numerous that there is scarce business enough for them all at present; and if they are confined to licensing, most of them, and their families, will be reduced to want'.[51]

London was still the capital of publishing but improved communications, rising provincial literacy, and, more importantly the lapse of the restriction on publishing outside London, opened up the potential of bookselling and publishing outside the capital and universities.[52] By 1700 there may have been about 200 booksellers operating in 50 different towns. Exeter, as 'the noted emporium of the west' had 'several printers' by 1715 and Plymouth had two printing houses 'both which subsist chiefly by publishing news-papers'.[53] It was not just newspapers and periodicals that

---

[48]   M. Spufford, *Small Books and Pleasant Histories* (London, 1981), 116, 120.

[49]   'The Meanes of a most Ample Encrease of the Wealth & Strength of England', *c.* 1707, Huntingdon Library MS 1264, f. 153. For female hawkers, see McDowell, *Women of Grub Street*, 55–62.

[50]   P. Rogers, *Grub Street: Studies in a Subculture* (1972); B. Hammond, *Professional Imaginative Writing in England, 1670–1740* (Oxford, 1997); McDowell, *Women of Grub Street*.

[51]   *CJ*, xiv. 338; Hammond, *Professional Imaginative Writing*, 5.

[52]   R. Burridge, *A New Review of London* (1721), 35–40 shows 149 places linked to London by coach and carrier. R. Houston, 'The Development of Literacy: Northern England 1640–1750', *EcHR* 35 (1982), 206–15, suggests that Newcastle literacy rates may have equalled London's by 1700. Two-thirds of adult males in Bristol were able to sign their names in later Stuart Bristol (Barry, 'Popular Culture in C17th Bristol', in Reay, *Popular Cultures*, 62–3). For provincial book trade, see Feather, *Provincial Book Trade*; and M. Harris, 'Print and Politics in the Age of Walpole', in J. Black (ed.), *Britain in the Age of Walpole* (Basingstoke, 1984).

[53]   B. Willis, *Notitia Parliamentaria or an History of the Counties, Cities and Boroughs in England and Wales* (1715), ii. 267, 292; BL, Harl. MS 5995 (152).

reached the provinces. Defoe built up a network of provincial contacts to whom he disseminated print and from whom, in return, he gathered news.[54] The clergy, too, acted both to disseminate (and restrict) what print was on offer. They allegedly took 'effectual care, that the country book-sellers, who get their livelihood by what they sell to them, to the schools and to the women, shall vend nothing but what they approve; by which means the people are kept in such ignorance, that they take a Whig and a Presbyterian to be the same thing'.[55] Even so, such power was increasingly difficult to enforce, especially in the towns. Provincial circulation was im-proved by the fact that circulating controversial material outside London first ensured it a longer life. Defoe himself noted in 1698 that anti-court titles were 'seen in the remotest countries of England before they were publish'd in London'.[56] Certainly there was a metropolitan perception that print circulated widely in the country and that it had considerable sway there.[57]

In terms of structure, then, the press became an available, reliable, and accepted part of political culture. It achieved record output, consistently high over an extended period, and innovated in terms of matching print to the demand of both market and politics. Paula McDowell has rightly ob-served that between 1640 and 1730 'political authority increasingly became a matter of competing public representations' and has termed this process the 'institutionalisation of a critical political press'.[58] This institutionaliza-tion was accelerated and confirmed in the later Stuart period by the in-creasing recognition that governments and partisans needed to propagate their own print and by the decision of government, in 1712, to tax rather than to censor print.[59]

[54] For example, Defoe established contact with a Norwich Whig, John Fransham, through whom he distributed the *Review* and his tracts, the former being read 'in the chief coffee houses' of the city where it was 'approved as the politest paper we have to entertain us with' (*Letters of Defoe*, 70–2).

[55] *A Letter to a Country Gentleman, Shewing the Inconveniencies which Attended the Last Part of the Act for Triennial Parliaments* (1716), 25.

[56] Defoe, *A Brief Reply to the History of Standing Armies in England* (1698), 25.

[57] *A Dialogue Between a Member of Parliament, a Divine, a Lawyer, a Freeholder, a Shop-keeper and a Country Farmer* (1703), 4–6, 32.

[58] McDowell, *Women of Grub Street*, 7.

[59] Downie, *Harley and the Press*, 117. As a result of the 1712 Stamp Act, weekly sales of news-papers fell from *c.*67,000 to *c.*44,000 and a number of titles went out of business (ibid., 159). For an outline of taxes on the book trade, see J. Feather, 'The English Book Trade and the Law 1695–1799', *Publishing History*, 12 (1982), 51–75.

THE IMPACT OF PRINT

These changes in practice nevertheless tell us relatively little about the impact of print. In order to assess that, or at least the perceived impact, we need to relate later Stuart print culture to that of the early modern period as a whole. This is not straightforward, since the notion of an early modern print 'revolution' has been challenged in favour of a model that allows for the continuing importance of oral, aural and, scribal, communication.[60] Even so, a number of the transforming features of print seem inescapable. This section seeks to outline some of the key ways in which such print (especially controversial print) helped to change political culture in the early modern period, especially in moments of crisis, such as the 1640s.[61] Only then can we assess the degree of change in the later Stuart period.

First, although in some ways an ephemeral medium, print was more permanent and enduring than the spoken word. This meant that print had an 'after-life', both at the time of publication and whenever it was re-read or re-issued. It was thus also a matter of public record that could be referred to and recycled. One of the consequences was that men's consistency (or lack of it) could be measured in part through their printed output or the printed record. Another was that republication was possible whenever a parallel situation appeared—sometimes over a long period of time. Alternatively the 'after-life' might be in a different location—Scotland or Ireland or the colonies, for example.

Second, for all the remarkable potency of early modern gossip and rumour, print could generally achieve a wider dissemination, in urban areas at least, particularly when the lapse of licensing controls in 1641 (and periodically thereafter) released a flood of printed material. The author of a printed libel could thus address not just one or two drinking companions,

[60] E. Eisenstein, *The Printing Press as an Agent of Change: Communications and Cultural Transformations in Early Modern Europe* (2 vols., New York, 1979). Her argument that print culture was subject to new notions of standardization, dissemination, and fixity, and that it subordinated oral culture to a public printed one, has been contested by Love, *Scribal Publication*; Fox, *Oral and Literate*; A. Fox and D. Woolf (eds.), *Oral Culture in Britain, 1500–1850* (Manchester, 2002); M. Hunter, 'The Impact of Print', *The Book Collector*, 28 (1979), 335–52; D. F. McKenzie, 'Speech–Manuscript–Print', *The Library Chronicle*, 20 (1990), 87–109; Johns, *Nature of the Book*.

[61] The following paragraphs draw on Zaret, *Origins of Democratic Culture*; Johns, *Nature of the Book*; Eisenstein, *Printing Press*; Achinstein, *Milton*; Freist, *Governed by Opinion*; Kemp, 'Idea of Liberty of the Press 1640–1700', Ph. D., Cambridge (2001); Raymond, *Pamphlets and Inventing the News*; Shevelow, *Women and Print Culture*; M. Warner, *The Letters of the Republic. Publication and the Public Sphere in Eighteenth Century America* (Harvard, 1990).

or even a room full of men, but a city and even the nation. As one pamphlet of 1681 put it, as a result of the lapse of pre-publication licensing, 'the mischievous conceptions of a single person, shall by the help of this dispatch, infect ten thousand in a few hours'.[62] And whereas rumour involved distorting Chinese whispers, fixed type ensured consistency of message.

Third, print was accorded agency. Print could be depicted as helping to subvert or challenge traditional public authorities, such as the monarchy or church, and replacing them with the power of the public. Print could be seen as a tool in the hands of those intent on undermining liberties, privileges, truth, and freedom. On the other hand, access to print was also seen as a means of preserving them. Print was thus a tool as well as a site of discourse. The public nature of that tool created a new political force. For public opinion could be invoked as a judge of printed appeals, even if contemporaries engaged in such activity simultaneously condemned others for acting in a similar fashion or disowned populist intentions. The power of print was thus simultaneously denounced and exploited; but it rested on, and in part created, the authority of the public. Print was thus a transformative but also an enabling medium.

Fourth, print 'magnified perceptions of chaos and disorder'.[63] It could spread fears about phenomena that were apparent or even imagined in one place to another. It thus made general what might be particular or even fictional. It could thus foster a conspiratorial outlook that was already ingrained in early modern mentalities. The link with a conspiratorial mindset was strengthened because what one printed oneself was always justifiable but what one's adversary printed could be viewed as conspiratorial; and print both facilitated conspiracy and acted conspiratorially by luring men into sedition.

Fifth, print was a dialogic medium: published claim provoked printed counter-claim, vindication, denial, or agreement. Such a dialogue was easiest to sustain during periods of press freedom—either when the laws regulating the press had lapsed (1641, 1679, 1695) or when the law was ineffectually enforced. The dialogue was necessary because the best way to counteract print, it came to be recognized, was through print. Print thus offered its own logic of self-justification. The more controversial print there was, the more need there was to enter into print to engage with it.

Sixth, polemical print favoured certain writing styles and the expression of polarities. It challenged conventional notions of how rhetoric worked

---

[62] T. Ashenden, *Some Reflections Upon a Late Pamphlet* (1681), 1.
[63] Zaret, *Origins of Democratic Culture*, 180.

and was a medium that facilitated slander, polemic, and satire. It delighted in mocking or even abusive criticism, in part because of conventions of anonymity. Printed polemic tended to polarize arguments, often favouring the irreverent or pugnacious expression of bold and uncompromising views, since fierce controversy sold better than quiet moderation. The anonymity offered by print heightened this trend. As one tract put it, 'a printed book never blushes, nor the author, if his name be not to it, but, like a boy that hath flung a cracker out of a garret window, pops in his head, and laughs only at the conceit of what mischief it may do'.[64]

Seventh, print appeared to confer credibility; but it could also lie, mislead, and undermine credibility through its inaccuracies, real or imagined. Paradoxically print not only fostered greater quantities of information but also offered conflicting accounts or explanations and hence appeared to make political or religious truth less obviously discernible and in some sense dependent on the viewpoint of the reader. This was particularly obvious in the medium of printed news. Periodicals competed to offer 'true' news and thus made truth something of a partisan affair.

Eighth, print stimulated and provoked readers. The periodicity of newspapers and periodicals, for example, created expectations in their readers of a narrative of politics. Readers were accorded an active role, either through techniques (such as printed queries that implied answers) or through implicit or explicit invitations to respond.

Ninth, print was part of a commercial as well as an ideologically divided world; indeed the two went hand in hand, for controversial print sold well. Print and partisanship both aimed at as wide an audience as possible and often adopted a number of strategies to ensure that they did so. Both could thus span popular and more élite readerships.

Tenth, print could create textual communities on a wider scale than was possible in a scribal culture. Some groups, such as the Levellers and Quakers, were so good at exploiting the potential of the medium that one might almost say they were in part created through print. Print could also enhance identities, including those relating to gender and nationality, and widen participation by marginal groups. Women could even begin to earn a living from their pens.

Eleventh, since print facilitated the advocacy of a particular programme to a wide number of people, able writers became politically important, and the timing of printed interventions and the 'tactical implications of political printing' became part of the process of political strife and negoti-

---

[64] *Arguments Relating to a Restraint Upon the Press* (1712), 13.

A female writer, flanked by portraits of Charles 1 and Queen Anne, gazes at her library stocked with books about the trial of 1648 and the church of England. The poem beneath the image attacked the 'treachery of the Whigs'. [Reproduced by courtesy of the Trustees of the British Museum.]

ation.[65] Print was thus a political tool and actor, capable of intervening quite dramatically in politics and having national impact. Indeed, contemporaries became preoccupied with examining, debating, and identifying such interventions. But, particularly after the lapse of pre-publication licensing, such interventions became a habitual way of doing things. Politics and print were thus entwined.

We do not have to prioritize print over other forms of discourse to recognize that collectively these factors had an impact on political culture. They made the public more important, both as judge and implied reader, and undermined notions of secrecy and consensus; they made print a political agent; and they created anxieties and opportunities for those in power or those who aspired to power. As features intrinsic, to a greater or lesser extent, in all controversial print, we should expect to find them evident in any moment of crisis that provoked print controversy from the 1640s onwards, and some of the features were evident as early as the 1580s or even earlier. But having mapped the culture of controversial print it

[65] Ibid., 205.

should now be easier both to emphasize how party print in some ways followed earlier patterns, but also to discern how it deepened, exacerbated, and extended earlier trends, features, and anxieties. Under the lens of party each factor outlined above became more obvious and powerful. Let us explore some examples of this.

PARTISAN PRINT AND ADVERSARIAL POLITICS

Print was often blamed by royalists for having alienated the affections of the people before the civil war. Roger L'Estrange was not alone when he repeatedly claimed that printed 'libells were not only the forerunners, but, in a high degree, the causes of our late troubles'.[66] The rhetorical ploy of the slogan '41 is come again' was powerful in part because of the association of 1641 with the collapse of print licensing.[67] Print was not an abstract, but a very real, danger to peace and unity. The metaphor of poisonous words thus took on new force, for the body politic really had sickened in the mid-century. Print poison became regarded as an *intrinsic and powerful part* of any partisan design to subvert church and state.

This was especially the case when, certainly from the 1670s, the press was seen as organized by the contending interests.[68] Certainly by 1714 (even if it was not, as John Downie suggests 'for the first time') 'both parties had fairly sophisticated means of producing and disseminating propaganda at their disposal'.[69] Party leaders took an interest in print as a political tool.

[66] *A Memento. Treating of the Rise, Progress, and Remedies of Seditions* (1682), 6. Cf. R. Atkyns, *The Original and Growth of Printing* (1664), epistle to the king.

[67] M. Nedham, *A Second Pacquet of Advices and Animadversions Sent to the Men of Shaftesbury* (1677), 8; *LJ*, xiii. 222.

[68] For Danby's appreciation of the advantages of 'directing some body to write both about the present state of things to give the world a better impression of them than they are now possessed with and to give constant weekly accounts of what is done at any time which may be for the satisfaction of men's minds', see BL, Add. MSS 28,043, f. 19v. Danby's policy towards the press is discussed more fully in Montaño, *Courting the Moderates*. Lord Chief Justice North was similarly canny (Sutherland, *The Restoration Newspaper and its Development* (Cambridge, 1986), 18; Knights, *Politics and Opinion*, 164–5). For writers and restoration government sponsorship, see L. Schwoerer, *The Ingenious Mr Henry Care, Restoration Publicist* (Baltimore, 2001); G. Kitchin, *Sir Roger L'Estrange. A Contribution to the History of the Press in the Seventeenth Century* (New York, 1971 rep.); J. G. Muddiman, *The King's Journalist 1659–89. Studies in the Reign of Charles II* (London, 1971 rep.). In the 1680s, governments attempted to cultivate a good press (Bodl. Tanner MSS 31, f. 22, Sprat to Sancroft, 11 Apr. 1685; All Souls Library, Oxford, Owen Wynne MSS, MSS 257 (56); BL, Add. MSS 34,515, p. 64, Johnston to——, 23 May 1688).

[69] Downie, *Harley and the Press*, 181.

John Somers and Charles Montagu, it was alleged, co-ordinated efforts during and after their impeachments in 1701.[70] Indeed, the degree to which the Whigs deliberately planned a press campaign was noted at the time. Tories claimed that the Whig 'trade in scurrilous lampoons, impudent libels, scandalous pamphlets, forg'd accusations and groundless calumnies has wonderfully improv'd since some of our late ministry put themselves openly at the head of 'em'.[71] Another Tory critic described how the Whig press operated in 1701 'to prepare the people for a new parliament'. Those who were 'solicitous for the nation' were smeared as church-papists, jacobites, and French-pensioners.

This was given out in a certain printed ballad, said to be written by a certain club of great men, which was then held not far from the King's head Tavern in Holbourn . . . The mob took the hint, for they had learn'd their cue to a tittle, and gave it out for gospel in an instant, nay, the story was improv'd, and gather'd like a snow-ball, as it was push'd forward.[72]

Thus, the Tory complained, 'the press had been us'd by 'em as an instrument of conveyance, thro which all their filth and ordure, their offals of scandal and indignity had hitherto pass'd, and they got ready rheams of malignity to make its way into the open light through that common-shoar, at the rising of the parliament'.[73]

It may well have been the case that partisan co-ordination of press campaigns was less coherent than many contemporaries thought. It often

---

[70] For Somers as patron, see Robert Adams, 'In search of Baron Somers', in P. Zagorin (ed.), *Culture and Politics from Puritanism to the Enlightenment* (Berkeley 1980), 165–202.

[71] *The Source of our Present Fears Discover'd*, 26–7; Downie, *Harley and the Press*, 42–3, 56; Swift, *A Discourse of the Contests and Dissentions* ed. F. H. Ellis (Oxford, 1967), 68–71. *England's Enemies Expos'd* (1701), preface, identified Charles Montagu as the shady figure behind the Legion Memorial, the Kentish petition and another tract, *The Present Disposition of England*, all of which could be 'joined together because they were contriv'd, publish'd, and encourag'd by persons in the same interest, and of the same kidney and complexion, that delight in sedition, calumny and detraction'. Montagu's authorship was denied in *The Present Disposition of England Considered. The Second Edition with the Addition of a Preface Occasioned by a Late Pamphlet Intituled England's Enemies Exposed* (1701), preface. This Junto Whig knot was, rather surprisingly, said to include John Darby, the printer of so much of the old Whig material. Darby's involvement suggests that the old and new Whigs had resumed an alliance against the resurgent Tories, an allegation that may account for a reference to 'Mongrel Whigs' (*England's Enemies Expos'd* (1701), 42). Page 28 refers to the fact that the publisher of the Legion Memorial was as well known 'as Darby ale to a Toper'. For a similarly coded reference to Darby, see W. Baron, *Regicides no Saints* (1700), 134; and E. Ludlow, *A Voyce from the Watchtower. Part 5, 1660–62*, ed. A. B. Worden, Camden Society 4th ser., 21 (1978), 20. *England's Enemies Expos'd*, 33, implied that the same authors and publishers responsible for the Legion Memorial were also behind *A Satyr upon Thirty Seven Articles* (1701).

[72] Tufton, *History of Faction*, 74–5.   [73] Ibid., 156.

A Tory satire against the Whigs, 1711. [Reproduced by courtesy of the Trustees of the British Museum.]

A Whig satire against the Tories, 1711. The identity of the parties was to some extent constructed through print and by means of stereotypical associations, as here in these collages of partisan prints. [Reproduced by courtesy of the Trustees of the British Museum.]

relied on the initiative shown by individual writers,[74] and publishers.[75] But the point is not just how organized the party machines were, but also how efficient they were perceived and said to be. What is striking is that both sides, and those who saw themselves as impartial, believed that party zealots were organized with intent to misrepresent public affairs. Indeed the concept of a centrally controlled press machine may rather be the product of (as well as contributing to) the conspiratorial mentality that was part of politics.

Party was thus seen as using print in dangerous ways. Indeed there was perceived to be a symbiotic relationship between party and print. Partisanship provoked print; and print helped to shape partisanship. Party and print were thus seen as working in very similar ways. In order to consider why, we must muse for a moment on the nature of partisanship. Partisans sought to represent a set of ideas in as convincing a manner to as many people as possible. We have already seen this in petitions, addresses, and electoral advice, all of which were printed. In other words, print enabled more successful partisanship. Partisans sought to foster allegiances to a set of principles and to leaders and hence build a community. Print fulfilled these ambitions, since it had the capacity to create identities or to link those who already shared similar outlooks and assumptions, even if those identities and groupings were fictional or less coherent and organized than the printed representation suggested.[76] As well as giving greater coherence to fellow supporters, however, partisans also sought, negatively, to divide their opponents. And here, too, the press could play an important role, since print could exploit tensions and doubts that existed within a rival

---

[74] In June 1711 Henry St John formed the Brother's Club by which 'a number of valuable people will be kept in the same mind, and others will be made converts to their opinions' (G. Parke (ed.), *Letters and Correspondence . . . of Henry St John*, 2 vols. (London, 1798), i. 246–7). By this St John meant to encourage writers to serve the Tory, or, more particularly, the St John brand, of Toryism. On the Whig side, Grey Neville, known ironically as 'Bishop' Neville because of his antipathy to the clerical hierarchy, stood bail for conroversial authors George Ridpath and Thomas Burnet, and there were hints that he financially supported other writers (*Post Boy*, 2706, 2765, 2783). Arthur Manwaring co-ordinated much of the Whig press effort in the second half of Anne's reign (*HOP II*, iv. 781–8). John Oldmixon and Richard Kingston are further examples of writers driven by ideological commitment, backed with varying degrees of governmental and party backing.

[75] 'it is not hard to guess the bookseller by his author and the author by his bookseller' (Pearse, *The Conformist's Plea for the Nonconformists*, 3rd edn. (1683), 'to the bookseller'); 'the dreadful names of Henry Hills and Henry Cruttenden in the title-page have been a fair warning to the reader not to venture any farther' (*A Vindication of a Sheet* (1688), 1).

[76] J. C. Davis, *Fear, Myth and History. The Ranters and the Historians* (Cambridge, 1986); M. Warner, 'The Mass Public and the Mass Subject', in B. Robbins (ed.), *The Phantom Public Sphere* (Minneapolis, 1993).

party. In terms of defining partisan identities and allegiances, therefore, the press helped to shape and even to create national party politics. Whigs and Tories were more recognizable to partisans in the localities because of the way in which they were described in the press; but reader responses to the press also created allegiance, or hostility, to the parties.

We can observe a parallel phenomenon in the later sixteenth and early seventeenth centuries over the identity of puritans and anti-puritans. Patrick Collinson has pointed to the importance of polemic in inventing puritanism.[77] Peter Lake has added that such polemic made puritanism more recognizable and allowed contemporaries to pigeon-hole each other, though he has also stressed the role of print in shaping a mentality that divided the world into binary opposites: papists and protestants; orthodox and heterodox.[78] As Stuart Clark has shown, print also facilitated perceptions of witches as inversions, in a binary world, of the proper order of things.[79] The creation of Whig and Tory identities owed a great deal to the invocation of such earlier polemical stereotypes. Indeed, many of the attributes of the puritan and roundhead were associated with the Whig (restless upstarts, hypocrites, rabble-rousers and so on), and the Tory was often depicted as the heir of the cavalier (passionate, pseudo-papists who hated the godly and favoured arbitrariness).[80] Yet the need to counteract these 'misrepresentations' took on a new imperative. For frequent electioneering meant that much of the political contest centred on the right

[77] P. Collinson, *The Puritan Character: Polemics and Polarities in Early Seventeenth-century English Culture* (Los Angeles, 1989); Collinson, 'Ecclesiastical Vitriol: Religious Satire in the 1590's and the Invention of Puritanism in J. Guy (ed)., *The Reign of Elizabeth, Court and Culture in the Last Decade* (Cambridge 1995).

[78] Lake, review of Collinson in *Journal of Ecclesiastical History*, 34 (1983), 627–9; Lake, 'Puritan Identities', *Journal of Ecclesiastical History*, 35 (1984), 112–23; P. Lake, 'Defining Puritanism—Again?' in F. Bremer (ed.), *Puritanism: Transatlantic Perspectives on a Seventeenth-Century Anglo-American Faith*, (Boston, 1993); P. Lake, *The Boxmaker's Revenge: 'Orthodoxy', 'Heterodoxy' and the Politics of the Parish in Early Stuart London* (Manchester, 2001); P. Lake, 'Anti-Popery: The Structure of a Prejudice', in R. Cust and A. Hughes (eds.), *Conflict in Early Stuart England* (1989).

[79] S. Clark, 'Inversion, Misrule and the Meaning of Witchcraft', *P&P*, 87 (1980), 98–127. For other binary divides, see also Scribner, *For the Sake of Simple Folk*; J. Walter, *Understanding Popular Violence in the English Revolution: The Colchester Plunderers* (Cambridge, 1999); A. Walsham, *Church Papists: Catholicism, Conformity and Confessional Polemic in Early Modern England* (Woodbridge, 1993); Vickers, *Rhetoric and the Pursuit of Truth*; E. Shagan, 'Constructing Discord: Ideology, Propaganda and English Responses to the Irish Rebellion of 1641', *JBS*, 36 (1997), 4–34.

[80] T. Corns, W. Speck, and J. Downie, 'Archetypal Mystification: Polemic and Reality in English Political Literature, 1640–1750', *Eighteenth-Century Life*, 7 (1982), 1–27; T. Canavan, 'Robert Burton, Jonathan Swift and the Tradition of Anti-Puritan Invective', *Journal of the History of Ideas*, 34 (1973), 227–42.

representation of the parties so that the public could judge properly; and the polemical representations of the parties could determine whether and how the war against France should be pursued. If, for example, the Tories could make their characterization of the Whigs (as moneyed men taking advantage of a long war for their own interest) stick, then peace on almost any terms seemed to become a possibility. The interaction between printed misrepresentation and representation at the polls, between print and the public, and between print and public credit therefore increased the importance of print wars.

Partisanship brought out the latent potential of print. It became a tool in the hands of partisans who sought to nurture, confirm, or undermine allegiance; and in this battle partisan organization of the press and access to the press were increasingly important. As Defoe put it: 'since this nation is unhappily divided into parties, every side ought to have an equal advantage in the use of the press'.[81] Perceptions, however, that one party had an unfair advantage over the other enhanced a conspiratorial mentality. Partisanship thus encouraged the production of more and more partisan print, in what amounted to a vicious circle. And as the dialogue between the parties enlarged, so the discourse became more enraged and vituperative. One tract of 1711 talked of the bitter language prevalent in coffeehouses, taverns, private houses, and the pulpits 'not manag'd (as formerly) with some sort of decency and good humour, but with meer scolding and the most scurrilous reflections; insomuch that (what I grieve to say) not only Christianity but civility and good manners seem to be laid aside and forgot'.[82]

This incivility, or impoliteness, in turn heightened the perception that partisan debate was increasingly libellous, deceitful, and dishonest. It encouraged the belief that the partisan press lied and invented to suit the political context. And this political culture was seen as pervasive, encompassing even the illiterate. 'Even those that can neither write nor read are become authors', complained one pamphleteer, 'by carrying some malicious tales to the next office of intelligence, whereby they may be undiscover'd and so unpunish'd, revenge themselves upon the reputation of an innocent neighbour'.[83] The perception arose that print was part of, and fostered, a culture of deception. As Marchamont Nedham, veteran newsmonger, put it, the newsmen presumed 'to misrepresent, argue and arbi-

---

[81] [Defoe], *An Essay on the Regulation of the Press* (1704), 12.
[82] *A Word to the Wise in a Letter to a City-Clergyman* (1711), 3.
[83] Ibid., 20.

trate the great affairs of state'.[84] Another observer thought partisan 'busie-
bodies' had 'little discretion' and that they received 'all they hear (especially
such things as will please their party) without examining the probability of
its being true or false' so that they spread malice like wildfire.[85] Some
thought such 'the way of guessing at political mysteries and then publishing as a matter of fact, a bare surmise, is the most dangerous piece of malice that can be exercised against government'.[86] This lying and fictional
dimension of political controversy is something to which we must return
in the next chapter.

For now, it is worth examining how party and controversial print shared
characteristics. Both were forms of representation that often claimed to
speak for the majority [o]f the nation rather than an individual or group.
Both thus fostered the notion of a public that could then be imagined and
invoked as umpire or judge.[87] Just as countless prefaces courted the reader
and asked him or her to judge the content, so partisans sought public
support. The success of both polemic and party relied on popularity and
knowing how to appeal pleasingly to the people. The high church writer
Charles Leslie said he had to draw the common people in through the
'pleasantry or fooling with which they were so much taken in other papers'.
He thus made 'no excuse for stile!' and wanted only that his 'meaning be
express'd easily'.[88] Publicly partisan politics was a representative struggle
that therefore exploited whatever medium made communication easy.

Yet the dialogue created by both polemic and party was an ongoing one
in which conclusion was elusive.[89] 'One book bears the bell away one
while and then presently comes out Reflections, Observations, Answers,
Replications and Exceptions upon it, till the press is so bepestered with
them', complained one observer.[90] Periodicals were often involved in a direct dialogue with each other—thus the *Examiner* and the *Medley* became
locked in an ongoing and vituperative commentary on each other as much

---

[84] *Christianissimus Christianandus; or, Reason for the Reduction of France* (1678), 73–4.
[85] *Study to be Quiet* (1680), 2.
[86] *Arguments Relating to a Restraint upon the Press*, 29–30.
[87] For the press conjuring the public, see *Shifting the Boundaries. Transformation of the
Languages of Public and Private in the Eighteenth Century*, ed. D. Castiglione and L. Sharpe
(Exeter, 1995), 4; Warner, *Letters of the Republic*, xiii–xiv.
[88] *A View of the Times*, preface.
[89] McKenzie, 'Speech–Manuscript–Print', 99–100. Dialogue is an ongoing construction of
knowledge and can extend across time and space (M. Macovski, *Dialogue and Literature*
(Oxford, 1994), 27–8).
[90] *Raillerie à la Mode* (1673), 22–3. Dialogue could also occur within a pamphlet when it
incorporated the body of a text that was to be refuted, allowing paragraph by paragraph
criticism.

as the 'news' they reported. Print also attempted to summarize and engage with other print in the form of reviews. Samuel Parker's monthly *Censura Temporum* (1708–10), for example, commented on 'the good or ill tendencies of books, sermons, pamphlets' from a high church perspective and this dialogue of print on print was itself couched in a dialogue form. Not all readers can have had access to such runs of material, but those with access to the coffee-houses or London probably did and many contemporary collections of controversial material bound tracts together in a way that suggests they recognized them as ongoing and linked dialogues. Such printed exchanges lacked any obvious conclusion; as one tract or periodical beat down another, so a new title sprung up to take the debate in a slightly different direction. As one tract remarked: 'we have answers and rejoynders multiplyed against each other daily . . . and this peevish progress of mutual dispute and contradiction, is likely to raign ad infinitum'.[91]

Partisanship acted in a similar fashion, pursuing an endless dialogue with an opponent. Partisanship was all about engaging with an opponent. We can glimpse this dialogic process through some reader responses to polemical print. For example, *Mr Hoadly's Measures of Submission to the Civil Magistrate Enquir'd Into and Disprov'd* (1711) provoked one reader to scribble furious notes at the front of his copy, alleging it to be the work of a jacobite. Such men were, the annotator wrote, 'in a close confederacy with Hell & France to undermine the revolution, unravell the succession & invade the union; this you may find through out the whole discourse'.[92] Once embarked on this line of thought the engaged reader found it difficult to stop, and his or her critical marginalia acted like an imagined conversation with the author, filling eleven pages at the end of the work with a handwritten vindication of Whig doctrine. Another anonymous (Tory) reader similarly sought to add a marginal voice to a printed dialogue. *Both Sides Pleas'd* (1710), in which a parson and gentleman argue over an alleged duty to resist tyranny, prompted the marginalia: 'so they pretended in the reign of Charles the 1st but they cut of[f] his head'.[93] And when the Whig gentleman of the printed dialogue claimed that resistance to tyranny extended only so far as the king's ministers and not the king, for that would be carrying things too far, the Tory reader wittily interjected in manuscript 'and so it will be'.[94] It was almost as though the reader was participating in

---

[91] Ashenden, *Some Reflections*, 1.   [92] Copy at BL, 4106.c.34.
[93] BL Sach.188/1(4).   [94] At p. 11.

the dialogue, using manuscript to add a private voice to the public debate. An active dialogue between reader and text, and between text and partisan, was also fostered by formats such as queries or questions, especially since these often employed cryptic shortening of names to elude prosecution.[95] Just as print was in dialogue with print, and the reader with print, so party was in dialogue with party, through the medium of print and through a constant process of electioneering.

Critics of party politics and print pointed to the restrictions both placed on individual opinion and judgement. Print, like party, introduced a form of

tyranny . . . in as much as the opinions and judgment, intentions and meaning, fortunes and reputation of men may by this means be and are daily traduced, over-awed, ridiculed, insulted, ensnared and trampled upon; in the most unavoidable and irremediable manner that can be express'd.[96]

The press was an 'envious monster which spares no age, sex, quality or condition; but gnaws and pollutes sacred and secular things and persons alike; observes no law, rule nor decorum but insults and overbears with uncontroul'd rage whatever it lights upon'.[97] The liberty of the press, it was alleged, thus removed freedom of conversation and reputation, exposing men 'to the reproaches and indignities of a rude Mob, without coercion, redress or amends'.[98] This, the author claimed, was no less than a form of 'slavery'. Very similar things were said about partisans.[99] Party and press were thus perceived as both misrepresentative and dangerously inflammatory, for 'a civil war began with ink may end in blood'.[100] In short, party and polemic could subvert rational discourse with dangerous consequences. Partisan print was thus seen as passionate and abusive, what contemporaries called 'Billingsgate language', when argument was reduced to the heated exchanges allegedly perfected by fishwives. A tract of 1673, for example, referred to the 'scolding of a ragged-canting crew of Billingsgate Rhetoricians'.[101] Similarly in 1701 the Legion Memorial was said to have

---

[95] One Edward Rud annotated his copy of electioneering tracts, *Queries for Queries* and *Queries. Numb. II* (both 1710), to show who was meant by the allusions in them (copies at Trinity College, Cambridge, N.8.59 (1 and 12)).

[96] *Arguments Relating to a Restraint upon the Press*, 18.

[97] Ibid., 19.   [98] Ibid., 20.

[99] *Works of Halifax*, 225–7; S. Clement, *Faults on Both Sides* (1710); *Faults on No Side* (1710), 2, 4; J. Locke, *Of the Conduct of the Understanding*, ed. F. Garforth (Columbia, 1966), 35, 104–5.

[100] *Arguments Relating to a Restraint upon the Press*, 45.

[101] *Raillerie à la Mode*, 34, 53.

broken 'the common rules of civility' by giving 'opprobrious language' to the House of Commons in what amounted to 'Billingsgate' abuse.[102] To be sure, 'Billingsgate' was not invented in the later Stuart period.[103] But the rage of party was echoed in the rage of language and both caused concern. What seemed to matter was mastery of the negative aspects of rhetoric: scorn for an opponent; the depiction of enemies as laughable, evil, and corrupt; irony, sarcasm, and mocking deference; ambiguous words to describe people or things; rhetorical questions that intended to mislead; the pretence of yielding to an argument in order only to disparage it; repudiation of an imagined objection; humourous understatement; deliberately inappropriate and undignified terminology to belittle and deface high matters with low words; and speculation about disaster as the outcome of an alternative proposal. Emotion, too, had to be exploited to the full, even if it meant using it to override the rationality of the audience.

This section has highlighted ways in which the impact of controversial print, evident before the Restoration, was deepened by the partisan political culture of the later Stuart period. It has suggested that print and partisanship shared similar characteristics and worked closely to promote each other. Print was a tool in the hands of the partisan; but the partisan was also in some ways the product of the print debates. The press is important, then, because it was often intrinsic to partisan politics.

COFFEE-HOUSE AND CLUB DISCOURSE

The railing, abusive nature of partisan print, outlined in the previous section and explored further later in the chapter, raises questions about the applicability of Habermasian notions of reasoned and polite debate. For Habermas, greater public discourse reflected the public use of private reason. Yet for many observers of the first age of party the greater ventilation

---

[102] *England's Enemies Expos'd* (1701), 38. Mary Astell compared 'disputes in print and disputes at Billingsgate' (R. Perry, *The Celebrated Mary Astell* (Chicago, 1986), 206). For just a few other uses of 'Billingsgate', see *Jack out of an Office* (1705), 3; Defoe, *History*, preface; Huntington Library, Stowe MSS 57, James Brydges to Drummond, 15 July 1710; J. Oldmixon, *Essay on Criticism* (1728), 58; BL, Add. MSS 70421, f. 264, newsletter, 9 Nov. 1710; *The Kentish Men* (1701), 3; Defoe, *The Political Sow-Gelder; or, The Castration of Whig and Tory* (1715), 9; *Source of our Present Fears Discover'd*, 25; *Character of a Whig* (1700), 22; C. Lawton, *Civil Comprehension* (1705), 6; *Reasons for a War against France* (1715), 3; *A Second Letter to the Right Honourable Robert Walpole* (1716), 21.

[103] Lake and Quester, *Antichrist's Lewd Hat*, 521–3; J. Black, 'The Rhetoric of Reaction: The Marprelate Tracts (1588–9): Anti-Martinism and the Uses of Print in Early Modern England', *The Sixteenth Century Journal*, 28 (1997), 707–25.

of public opinion exposed the irrationality and abusive nature of a good deal of public discourse. Whereas Habermas sees a structural shift from a vibrant emergent public sphere to a modern stagnant one, from the exercise of private reason in public matters to the passive consumption of artificial and manipulated debate, I shall argue that the emergence of the 'first public sphere' was marked by contemporary fears of a highly *irrational*, abusive, and manipulative form of public discourse. In other words, irrationality or the perceived degradation of critical-rational public debate was apparent at the very inception of the public sphere. Or rather, reason and irrationality were seen to be in a struggle with one another. Let us turn to those sites privileged by Habermas, the coffee-house and the club, to explore this tension further.

Coffee-houses have been claimed as prime sites of the emerging public sphere. Habermas saw in them a public space dedicated to commercial and literary, and then political, discourse, where conventions dictated a rational equality between participants.[104] They have also been seen as arenas of urban, polite, sociability, and commerce. They were certainly a new forum. After their introduction to England in the early 1650s, they proliferated, so that by 1700 there were at least 500 in London and they were common in most market towns.[105] They appear to epitomize what was new about later Stuart political culture and to symbolize a new representative space. As Swift remarked, some mistook 'the echo of a London coffee-house for the voice of the kingdom'.[106] It was the coffee-house that contemporaries identified as a scene of a national political voice and public debate that was outside governmental control. Yet it is easy to exaggerate their novelty. Public discourse had long flourished in alehouses, taverns, and inns, which existed in large numbers throughout the nation,[107] or in market places, highways, and fairs. In what ways, then, did they innovate and contribute to a different, more rational and accessible, type of public discourse?

---

[104] Habermas, *Structural Transformation*, 32–3; S. Pincus, ' "Coffee Politicians Does Create" ', 811.

[105] Borsay, *English Urban Renaissance*, 145; Pincus, ' "Coffee" ', 811–14; C. J. Sommerville, *The News Revolution in England* (Oxford, 1996), 77; J. Harris, 'The Grecian Coffee House and Political Debate in London 1688–1714', *London Journal*, 25 (2000), 1–13; Spurr, *England in the 1670s*, 165–78.

[106] Swift, *Prose Works*, vi. 53–4.

[107] Grew estimated that in Anne's reign 'at least an 8th part of the houses' in London were drinking dens, with possibly 154,000 throughout England (Huntingdon Library MS 1264, ff. 149). A similar proportion prevailed in York (Withington, 'Urban Political Culture', table 2.13). One estimate put the number of taverns in 1689, outside of London, Essex, and Surrey, at 47,455 (Bodl. MS Carte 81, ff. 790–2). See also, P. Clark, *The English Alehouse: A Social History, 1200–1830* (London, 1983).

Unlike the alehouse, the coffee-house was idealized as 'an academy of civility', open to all.[108] The coffee-drinker was not impassioned like an alehouse sot, but represented as sober and calculating. He (and depictions were often gendered) had his wits about him in order to conduct private transactions or to hear and read about public business. The news and the prints were thus not *incidental* to coffee-house culture, but rather *essential* to it. Print, politics, and news were intrinsic to the coffee-house. This was an age 'when talking politics at a coffee-house is no longer an amusement, but the main business that's pursued'.[109] Some of this talk was, in the 1680s at least, stimulated by scribal news;[110] but increasingly it was the availability of print on the coffee-table that was commented on. 'You have all manner of news there',[111] commented one foreign observer. The coffee-house was 'a mint of intelligence . . . the rendezvous of idle pamphlets and persons more idly employed to read them'.[112] Prints were spread out over tables and occasionally available to buy or borrow.[113] Some news-junkies went to coffee-houses specifically to read the variety of papers and manuscript libels that would be on display.[114] But the coffee-house was not just a venue for private reading; consuming the print culture was far more commonly a shared and hence sociable experience. Prints were read aloud or discussed. Indeed, the licence of speech to be found there was compared to, and provided a justification of, printed debate. 'What I write is with as much liberty, and little care, as people discourse in coffee houses, where we hear the state-affairs of nations adjusted, and from thence guess at the humor of the people and at the times', wrote Thomas Sheridan.[115] Sir

---

[108] *Coffee Houses Vindicated* (1673) (in *Harl. Misc.* vi. 473); *Misson's Memoirs*, 39; B. L. de Muralt, *Letters Describing the Character and Customs of the English and French Nations* (1726), 82–3 [written in the early 1690s]. See also Ch. 1, n. 152.

[109] *Enquiry into the Inconveniences*, 5.

[110] John Croker wrote to secretary of state Middleton from near Dartmouth on 25 June 1685: 'I presume to acquaint yr Ldship that if ye publick news-letters be such elsewhere as they are at Dartmouth coffee-house, they may help to make ye people, already crazy, to run starke mad' (BL, Add. MSS 41803, f. 322). In 1686 lord chancellor Jeffreys denied Bishop Compton a copy of the articles against him, but quipped that if he had 'been so desirous of a copy of the commission, for a penny it might have been had at a coffee house' (BL, Verney MSS, M/636(41) Dr Panton to Sir Ralph Verney, 11 Aug. 1686).

[111] *Misson's Memoirs*, 39.

[112] *The Character of a Coffee-House* (1673) in *Harl. Misc.*, vi. 465.

[113] Houghton's *Collection for the Improvement of Husbandry and Trade*, Vol. 6 No. 129, 18 Jan. 1694/5: 'Walsal the coffee man against Cree Church in Leadenhall Street keeps a library in his coffee room for his customers to read. He also buys and sells books.'

[114] HMC Hastings, ii. 268–9, 271.

[115] Sheridan, *Discourse*, 10. The claim to free speech was invoked to justify the freedom of the press: 'there is no authorized licenser for talk, preaching, writing, but men may speak, preach and write at their peril; and why they should not print and publish at their peril too,

Thomas Player resented how 'the common people talke anything, for every carman and porter is now a statesman; and indeed the coffee houses are good for nothing else'.[116] They were spaces 'where every little fellow in a camlet cloke takes upon him to transpose affairs both in Church and state'.[117] Such 'free' speech was notable and even compared to the dissenters' conventicle.[118]

Perhaps because of that, the Restoration government contemplated how to control the coffee-houses.[119] The boldest attempt was a proclamation of 29 December 1675, declaring them to be 'common assemblys to discours of matters of state news & great persons' and therefore to be suppressed as 'a comon nuisance'.[120] That attempt failed, though a proclamation was issued to forbid the circulation of false or scandalous news in them, and individual coffee-houses and their owners were prosecuted.[121] Early in October 1688 lord chancellor Jeffreys again ordered Middlesex JPs to suppress all coffee-houses and other public houses that either dealt in newsletters or exposed newspapers.[122] There were, however, no further systematic attempts to do so after the Revolution. Whereas before 1688 coffee-houses were discussed in terms of their challenge to legitimate authority, by Anne's reign they were being thought of 'as a tool for the construction of a "polite public"'. Indeed, in the pages of the *Tatler, Spectator*, and *Guardian* they were represented as 'a site for conversable sociability conducive to the improvement of society as a whole'. From then on, coffee-houses provided a means by which 'those excluded from the

the reason seems to be the same' (*Supplement (to the Paper called, Reasons Humbly offered to be Considered before the Act for Printing be continued &)*, n.d., *c.*1692/3, broadside); *Locke Corresp.*, v. 294–5; Locke, *Political Essays*, ed. M. Goldie (Cambridge, 1997), 331, 337.

[116] *Letters Addressed from London to Sir Joseph Williamson*, ed. W. D. Christie, Camden Society, NS, 9, 2 vols. (1874), ii. 63.

[117] *Character of a Coffee-House* (*Harl. Misc.*, vi. 465).

[118] R. North, *Examen; or, An Enquiry into the Credit and Veracity of a Pretended Complete History* (1740), 138–9; *Heraclitus Ridens*, 12; E. Ward, *The School of Politicks; or, The Humours of a Coffee-house* (1690), 2 ('state conventicle').

[119] *The Bulstrode Papers*, ed. A. Morrison (London, private, 1897), 221–2; Sommerville, *News Revolution*, 79. B. Cowan, 'The Rise of the Coffeehouse Reconsidered', *HJ*, 47 (2004), 21–46.

[120] BL, Add. MSS 32518, f. 227v; Spurr, *England in the 1670s*, 176–7.

[121] *CSPD 1675–6*, 497; W. Rye, *Depositions Taken before the Mayor and Aldermen of Norwich* (Norwich, 1903), 157; *Presentment of the Grand Jury for the County of Kent . . . 12 Mar. 1682* (1683); B. Lillywhite, *London Coffee Houses* (1963), 20.

[122] *The Ellis Correspondence: Letters Written during the Years 1686, 1687 and 1688*, ed. G. A. Ellis, (2 vols. London, 1829), ii. 243. Ironically, however, James had also sought to use the coffee-houses to his advantage: *Seven Papers* (1689), 26, alleged that James's electoral agents had ensured that papers were 'exposed in coffee houses and houses of publick entertainments for the information of the country'.

"political nation" presumed to sit in judgement of politics'.[123] They were another example of the growing importance of public judgement.

As venues for sociability and discussion the rise of the coffee-house was matched by that of the club. Indeed, Peter Clark suggests that 'between the Glorious Revolution and the death of George II clubs and societies matured as a national social institution'.[124] Like the coffee-house, the club acquired a certain legitimacy after 1689. The word club itself gained a positive meaning alongside its pejorative sense as a suspicious band of men or cabal.[125] The clubs also provided semi-private venues where free discussion of state affairs and printed news could be had. Roderick Mansell, a member of the infamous Green Ribbon Club, described how

some persons, it seems, according to the custom of the town converse, do divert themselves in clubs at coffee houses, taverns &c where with a certain frankness of conversation, agreeable to a people that abhor starcht pedantry, they toss the Gazets and intelligences up and down; and . . . now in the career of discourse, some one perhaps applauds what is discommendable, another censures that of which he is no competent judge.[126]

As this suggests, individual clubs acquired particular reputations and clienteles, which could be highly partisan.[127] Such political clubs became quite common, not just on the Whig but also on the Tory side, and not just in London. The Tory Lord Fermanagh was advised, for example, that at the Crown inn the Chesham postmaster held a weekly club of supporters who requested Fermanagh to send free copies of the newspapers.[128] York's coffee-house, Parker's, was said to be the 'common rendezvous of the political tribe'.[129] And the clubs could become means of mobilizing and advising voters. A Whig club in London thus drew up lists of candidates for common council elections, allocated funds, and organized canvassers, even appointing 'a proper person . . . in each ward to solicit the poor sort of people' for their votes.[130] The toasts that were customarily offered in clubs

---

[123]   Klein, 'Coffee-house Civility', 32–3, 43.   [124]   Clark, *British Clubs*, 60.
[125]   For its pejorative connotation, see Dr Williams Library, 'Entring Book' of Roger Morrice, R 57; *A Seasonable Caution to all Loyal Subjects* (1690), 2.
[126]   Mansell, *An Exact and True Narrative of the Late Popish Intrigue* (1680), introductory 'solemn address'.
[127]   E. Ward, *The London Spy*, ed. A. L. Hayward (London, 1927); Kirk, 'London in 1689–90', 658.
[128]   *Verney Letters*, i. 308. Interestingly Fermanagh sent both the Tory-inclined *Post Boy* and its rival, the whiggish *Post Man*.
[129]   Capt. Bland, *The Northern Atalantis* (1713), 33.
[130]   *London Politics 1713–17: Minutes of a Whig Club 1714–17*, London Record Society, 17 (1981), ed. H. Horwitz, 1–2, 9.

could also serve to bind a party together. It is true that many clubs were non-partisan and that their sociability could represent a 'retreat from the party conflicts'.[131] Even so, like the coffee-house the club was another new representative body, a small, self-describing and self-governing community operating within the larger civil society.

Yet both coffee-house and club could pose challenges to sociability, civility, and rational conversation. These tensions are apparent in the *Remarques on the Humours and Conversations of the Town* (1673), a dialogue divided between 'Pensive', who seeks to flee town because the 'clamours of a country-mob at the choice of a knight of the shire', and 'Sociable', who attempts to lure Pensive and his cousin 'Sir Jovial' into staying to enjoy the pleasures of the town. Sociable argues that the town offers conversation with men of sense and fine ladies, as well as books; but Jovial counters that the books were only 'some scurrilous pamphlet, or a novel . . . forgot as fast as read and not worth the remembering'. He went on to complain that

> politicks are so plenty here in town, that there's not a trader, even from the topping merchant to the humble translator, but has his share in modelling the government; and for fear they shou'd shoot wide of their mark, the weekly Observator holds forth in a wretched manner upon occurrences for their better instruction . . . coffee house politicks are but fewel to factions, and fosterers of ripening rebellion.[132]

Town conversation, he thought, did not edify or please, but gratified hate and lust.[133] He condemned town tatlers who knew 'so little that they cannot distinguish between apparent dissimulation and reality . . . chance and inclination, not reason, guiding them in the choice'. Although everyone, 'from the groom to the lord, from the prentice to the alderman, from the chambermaid to the countess', could read, the coffee-houses where they met were 'a perpetual hurry of news, business, polliticks, plots and conspiracies and battles, medlies and confusion of sounds and discourses'. Not surprisingly, the public lacked judgement.[134]

Indeed, the coffee-house was often depicted, like partisan polemic, as promoting abusive railing and irrationality. As the author of *Raillerie à la Mode* complained, 'it is a vicious sort of buffoonery that this mistaken age is ready to cry up for a high acquir'd ornament and piece of refin'd

---

[131]   Clark, *British Clubs*, 461.
[132]   *Remarques*, 16, 41–2.
[133]   A conclusion shared by Sarah Cowper—see Ch. 2.
[134]   *Ibid.*, 49, 55–6, 62, 107.

education, while a sober judgment or modest innocence is as much mistook and exploded for mere Dullness and Ignorance. He that can abuse another handsomely is presently applauded for a shrewd wit'.[135] These charges were often repeated. 'I believe tis these coffee houses that furnish the inhabitant of this great city [London] with slander, for there one hears exact accounts of every thing done in town, as if it were but a village', observed one visitor.[136] Critics believed the coffee-houses taught the 'art of scandal and detraction'; it was there that the people divided 'into sides and factions', where feuds and animosities began, and where they fell 'from arguing and disputing to thwarting and quarreling', stoked by 'paper fuel'.[137] 'What is conversation now-a-days', moaned one cleric, 'but a match at fencing, where we falsifie a blow to make that part unguarded which we design to strike?' It would, he said, 'introduce a greater curse than that of Babel, were not good words by long abuse grown to be but words of course, and well known to signify nothing'.[138]

There was thus perceived to be a vituperative, licentious, discourse associated with the partisan political culture found in coffee-house and club. A *True Protestant Bridle* (1694) suggested that this would 'shrivel their present majesties by degrees into a meer fairy queen and an emperour of the moon'. Nothing was more lamentable than 'speaking evil of persons illustrious' which any half-wit could do.

Hence it comes to pass that every notion-struck tradesman and purse-proud mechanick (whose learning and education never carried him higher than the Gazette or compting-book) can run down the whole ecclesiastick order with an infallible wink or nod . . . and represent the mild, the peaceable, the salutary doctrine of non-resistance . . . as an antichristian Mormo and bugbear to a kingdom.[139]

The combination of partisan politics, print, and new sites facilitating public discourse was thus thought by some—until Anne's reign mostly Tories—to foster seditious or abusive speech. The Tory Ned Ward thus observed that

though the promotion of trade and the benefits that arise from humane conversation are the specious pretences that every tippling club or society are apt to assign as a reasonable plea for their unprofitable meetings; yet most considerate men,

---

[135] *Raillerie à la Mode*, 3.
[136] Muralt, *Letters*, 82–3.
[137] *Arguments relating to a Restraint upon the Press*, 25, 39. The tract depicted the Grecian tavern, which was noted for its free discourse.
[138] W. Reeves, *The Nature of Truth and Falshood* (1712), 21–2.
[139] [T. Rogers], *True Protestant Bridle*, 3–5.

who have ever engag'd in such sort of comportations [*sic*] have found by experience that the general end thereof is a promiscuous encouragement of vice, faction and folly.[140]

In any club, Ward argued, there were always leaders, 'men of ill design', who, 'when once they find they have reputation, argument or cunning enough' imposed 'their own interested suggestions or partial sentiments or reports upon the rest of their associates' and 'loaded' the virtuous 'with undeserv'd calumny'.[141] The healths drunk in them created reputations but also distorted or destroyed them. 'By these sort of stratagems', Ward feared, 'first publick societies and next whole nations are often misled into dangerous errors; and tavern clubs have been frequently made the proper vehicle in which our politick emperics have convey'd their poison into the heart of the kingdom. Nor, indeed, have there been any plots, or conspiracies in any reign, but what have been first hatch'd and then nourish'd in these sort of societies.'[142] Rather than a Habermasian public sphere of reasoned discourse, these Tory critics saw sites of irrationality, incivility, and conspiracy—or at least titillated shocked readers with such representations. Licentious public discourse was nothing new; but the political power of the public, exercised in part through new forms of sociability, posed new dilemmas.

But it was not just Tories who hated the licentiousness of public discourse. In 1698–9, for example, the 'new Whigs' faced criticism over the maintenance of a standing army.[143] In language reminiscent of defenders of the court a decade or so before, one court Whig tract suggested that no vice was more common than that of speaking ill against illustrious persons: 'he is accounted the wittiest man and staunchest member of his party that dares calumniate the loudest'. Indeed, 'the leudness of the tongue' had become 'so epidemical in the nation' that the common people were 'grown to such excesses in their pragmatical censuring the actions of their superiors, as is unsufferable to the loyal and sober part of mankind'. This created a licentious age 'when every private person, that thinks he has half a dram of brains about him, shall arraign the actions of his superiors'. Thus, it was asserted, 'kinging the multitude is only a trick to weaken the monarchy'

[140] Ward, *The Secret History of Clubs* (1709), 1. See also his *School of Politicks* and *The Humours of a Coffee House: A comedy* (1707). For Ward, see H. W. Troyer, *Ned Ward of Grub Street: A Study of Sub-literary London in the Eighteenth Century* (London, 1968).
[141] Ward, *Secret History*, 6–7.
[142] Ibid., 7–8.
[143] L. Schwoerer, *No Standing Armies! The Anti-army Ideology in the Seventeenth Century* (Baltimore, 1974).

and introduce arbitrary power.[144] Court whiggery could thus see dangers in popularity, believing that there was 'a blind side and weak part in the populace, that easily yields to any assault', for most 'naturally love to hear great men spoken ill of'. The author did not blame the people so much as those who sought to mislead them. Wicked men, it was claimed, frequented 'publick places . . . to exaggerate the faults and misfortunes of the government'. Thus 'the spring and progress of all our causeless fears and jealousies' was due to the 'industry of seditious men's trafficking for news; and employing a sort of idle pedling people, to range up and down in quest for fresh intelligence' which was then taken to the 'seditious clubs'.[145] In such depictions, therefore, public discourse was represented as lively but abusive, libellous, scurrilous, and dangerous. The rage of party, many contemporaries felt, pushed the boundaries of speech and print to new limits. And when both sides were the butt of that discourse, both found it highly uncomfortable and even reprehensible.

A CULTURE OF PUBLIC LIBEL AT ELECTIONS

> fame, reputation and honour, as they are the greatest
> incentives to all good and vertuous actions, so they as
> much terrify men from committing base and unwor-
> thy ones. . . . this law of reputation (if I may so call it)
> influences men more than all other laws whatever.[146]

A culture of libelling was, of course, nothing new. When it was rumoured that one of the impeachment charges against Lord Somers would include adultery, Sarah Cowper noted in her diary that

Some crie out, that when men are accused upon the publick score, it is base to rake into their private lives; But it is nothing new, yᵉ same was done by the D[uke] of Buck[ingham] in the reign of Char[les] 2ᵈ. Whatever party accuses, they throw all the dirt they can find at those they wou'd beat down, tho' themselves do the very same thing.[147]

---

[144] *Cursory Remarks*, 2, 10, 20.   [145] Ibid., 42, 65–6.
[146] *A Letter to a Member of Parliament Shewing that a Restraint on the Press is Inconsistent with the Protestant Religion and Dangerous to the Liberties of the Nation* (1698), *State Tracts*, ii. 623. The author is unknown, but was an admirer of Locke, whose work on human understanding is singled out for particular praise (625). Toland has been suggested as a likely candidate.
[147] Herts. RO, Panshanger (Cowper) MSS D/EP F 29, 90.

She might have gone back further, at least to the early Stuart period.[148] Nevertheless, a preoccupation with libelling in the later Stuart period was the result of the conjunction of a number of factors. First, the 'rage' of party produced passions that were bent on publicly denigrating persons. Second, party and an enlarged print culture increased the amount of information available to the public about figures of authority. Third, frequent elections placed a premium on the credit of candidates— 'reputation is power', remarked South.[149] The destruction of personal credit was therefore also a political, party act. Fourth, the lapse of the Licensing Act meant that after 1695 the statutory limits of public discourse were drawn by the laws of treason, libel, slander, defamation, and sedition. It also fostered a shift from manuscript to printed libel.

We can examine the culture of libel by examining electioneering. Having examined print and public discourse in coffee-houses and clubs, and found a consistent strain of contemporary lament, it will come as no surprise that electioneering offered another occasion when the partisan political culture appeared to corrupt manners and knowledge.

During any publicly contested electioneering, the characters of individual candidates were scrutinized for exploitable chinks. As one tract put it, 'no man stands a candidate . . . but has all his faults from his cradle written on his forehead, or thrown into his dish, at such a time, tho they were conceal'd from all the world before . . . [all is] expos'd to publick censure'.[150] Another pamphlet suggested that during election time 'license is given to all manner of scandal; if a candidate has been guilty of a crime committed with the utmost secrecy, and never heard of before, he is sure to have it published, with additions, before the election is over. All the faults of a man's life, and of his family and dependents, he must expect to hear of, and to hear it often repeated.'[151] A Tory, lamented that 'divers otherwise well meaning men amongst the credulous commons, were 'so very silly as to believe their lies & slanders'.[152] Defamation, as a result, seemed part of the political process. As another tract explained, 'No man can form such a just judgment of things and persons as is necessary to the making a right choice, without some true previous knowledge of both; for want of which

---

[148] See works listed, Ch. 1, n. 54.
[149] R. South, *Twelve Sermons Preached upon Several Occasions* (1692), 248.
[150] *The Subjects Case*, 5. Cf. CUL, Sel. 3.237, item 34, W. Glover to Edmund Bohun, 7 March 1689/90: 'they have spread abroad a great many black and slanderous lies both before & since the election, for the blasting the reputation of honest & good men'.
[151] *Art of Parliamenteering*, 17.
[152] CUL, Sel. 3.237, item 34, Glover to Bohun.

some mens good names have been scandalously defamed and the nation imposed upon by false representations and popular colours.'[153]

A Norfolk parson agreed. In a sermon published under the title *Truth and Sincerity*, Thomas Rawlins lambasted, as the general election of 1713 loomed large, the 'ludicrous and senseless reflections generally made upon candidates of the brightest characters'. Men's reputations, he said, were battered with lies and every public action misrepresented 'with the most bitter and degrading invectives' that sought to give 'a sinister turn to every thing that is transacted for the publick good'.[154] The marquis of Halifax similarly complained that some electioneering was like 'raising a kind of petty war in the country or corporation . . . omitting to spread no report, whether true or false, which may give an advantage by laying a blemish upon a competitor'.[155]

The culture of credit might thus be extended beyond the scientific, social, or economic into the political. Just as credit conferred truth and wealth, so it also conferred political legitimacy and helped voters to decide between candidates and parties. The credit of individuals was essential for successful election; and the credit of a party could reinforce that of an individual and offer a network of supportive contacts that would raise it yet further. Parties thus competed to construct representations of their creditworthiness. Just as financial credit was not static but a process of maintaining a reputation, so party politics was a process of competition to detract from the credit of a rival and to bolster the credit of a friend. Frequent elections necessarily meant that the preservation of credit and reputation, at both personal and party level, was vital. Thus in 1699 the merchant MP Sir Henry Furnese, who had gained 'great credit and esteem' among the voters of Bramber, prosecuted John Sturt of Steyning for 'saying, proclaiming and publishing . . . false and scandalous words'. Sturt had circulated rumours that Furnese was bankrupt, and in September 1698, during public discussions in London about the election, declared that Furnese was 'as great a rogue as any highway-rogue that ever was on the road', that he lived 'by nothing but cozening and cheating', and that 'they are all rogues that chose Sir Henry Furness'. Such smears, Furnese alleged, brought him 'into distrust and discredit'. He not only brought a law suit but also published a copy of the indictment. Its publication was evi-

---

[153] *English Advice to English Freeholders* [1705], 1.
[154] Rawlins, *Truth and Sincerity Recommended in a Sermon against Lying* (1713), 18–19.
[155] *Works of Halifax*, 143.

dently intended to vindicate his reputation, though it must also have had the effect of giving greater currency to Sturt's words, which were printed in full.[156] The case suggests that public credit—of particular importance, of course, to a merchant—was at stake, particularly for electioneering purposes, and that there was a symbiotic relationship between reputation in political life and reputation in other dimensions.

More frequently, however, the libels and slanders made against candidates were not prosecuted and we learn of them through reports in the press or election petitions to parliament, as the following examples illustrate. Frederick Tilney was alleged to have been attacked as a pensioner of France because he had used French coins, though the newsletter that carried this news was itself condemned as containing 'scandalous observations'.[157] Sir William Franklyn allegedly 'dispersed scandalous reportes of Mr Christie before the election, on purpose to alienate Mr Christie's friends'.[158] John Cholmley and Charles Cox procured their election at Southwark, it was said, by threats and 'dispersing scandalous papers'.[159] In Herefordshire in 1710 'further to influence votes for Mr Price, scandalous libels were printed and dispersed reflecting upon the privilege of the House of Commons'.[160] At Chester, alderman Street 'was active to bring aspersions on Sir Thomas Grosvenor on purpose to keep him off from being a parliament man'.[161] In 1702 Sir Robert Davers, the electoral rival of John Hervey, spread news of a quarrel between Hervey and a neighbour over timber 'to make a noise in ye court & country, to blast [his] reputation' and frustrate his election at Bury.[162] James Grahme wrote to a freeholder of Westmorland in September 1700 to clear himself and his son 'from aspersions malitiously spread about the country'.[163]

Printed satires also picked on certain MPs for personal vilification. Charles Davenant was alleged to have been 'found in a tavern treating for a miss with Jenny Cromwell to refresh himself after his political labours' with a French agent.[164] At Amersham in 1679 Sir William Drake had been called 'a papist and a pensioner'; but although his opponent, Algernon Sidney, regretted such 'licence' of speech he thought 'that Sir William

---

[156] Sir H. Furnese, *Sir Henry Furness's Case against Mr John Sturt* (1699). Ironically Furnese himself had a reputation for spreading false news (*Remarks by Way of Answer, Paragraph by Paragraph to the Character of a Modern Whig &c* (1701), 9).
[157] *Collection of Dyer's Letters*, 5, 16.   [158] *CJ*, x. 376.
[159] *CJ*, xvi. 421.   [160] *CJ*, xvi. 422.   [161] *CJ*, x. 492.
[162] *The Letterbooks of John Hervey*, (3 vols. Wells, 1894), i. 172.
[163] HMC 10th report, appendix. iv, 335.
[164] *The Whigs Thirty Two Queries and as Many of the Tories in Answer to Them* (1701), 15.

must suffer as well as others'. In any case, he remarked, 'such language was then and still is used of himself every day by Sir William and his friends'.[165] In February 1690 John Verney wrote to his father that 'as for the false storyes raised on you to lessen your interest with the burgesses, I doe not wonder at it, because tis usuall where there is contests for parliamt men; I onely wish the Burgesses may have witt enough to judge them'.[166] So prevalent were such arts that in one Tory tract a Whig allegedly confesses that his party employed 'a number of lying spirits . . . in all corners of the kigdom, especially in the intervals of parliament, to fill the nation with clamours against the patriots of the Ch[urch]. This licentious abuse of criminating candidates in elections, hath been carried to such a height by us, that were a man reputed never so honest before, yet, no sooner is he chose a M[embe]r of the H[ous]e of C[om]m[on]s, and sticks close the interest of the Ch[urch], but he presently becomes a publick enemy and as such we brand him, and teize him and seek to tire him out.'[167]

It is clear from these and many other examples that might be produced that electoral slander against, and misrepresentations of, individuals were routine. Misrepresenting candidates orally or in print was thus part of the political game of adversarial politics. But even when the *ad hominem* attack was avoided, there was a good deal of mud-slinging against the characters of the *parties*. For example, a 1705 high-church election tract warned that a low churchman was 'a false-hearted, popular timerous, time-serving man, who at any conjuncture, can be so kind and complaisant, so civil and good natur'd, to lay aside his religion, to violate his most solemn oaths, his duty and conscience'. The high churchmen were, for their part, of course, sincere and honest but had been 'misrepresented; ill stories designedly spread to blemish the reputation of our late sitting members and to make way for the advancement of some invidious, revengeful or ambitious person'.[168] Libel and slander thus applied to parties as well as to their candidates.

Indeed, contemporaries became particularly anxious about the amount of print that sought to damage each party's reputation and identity. 'The pamphlets do now pelt and blacken the whigs in virulent manner to hinder their election for the next parliament', remarked Sarah Cowper in 1713.[169]

[165] *The Case of Algernon Sidney Esq.* [1680].
[166] BL, Verney papers, microfilm 44, John to Sir Ralph Verney, 18 Feb. 1689/90.
[167] *The True Picture of a Modern Whig Reviv'd. Set forth in a Third Dialogue between Whiglove and Double at Tom's Coffee-house* (1707), 25–6.
[168] A *Dialogue* (1705), 11, 13–14.
[169] Herts. RO, Panshanger MSS D/EP F 34, 266.

A Tory election tract of 1714 complained that 'swarms of pamphlets and libels have issued from' the Whig press, and 'great drifts of them . . . were
daily dispersed through the country, to influence elections'.[170] Each side
believed this flood of print was packed with slander, libel, and malicious
lies. *England's Enemies Expos'd* (1701) accused the Whig leader Charles
Montagu of writing a pamphlet that made such vague allegations against
the Tories that they could not be rebutted. The Whigs, it was said, gave 'men
a liberty to scandalise the innocent . . . and to slander the' Tories for 'the
misdemeanours of a few of their members'. Montagu was therefore in turn
attacked for his 'base and sordid arts, in mis-representing men and things',
and for having 'but a mean opinion of his readers understandings, that he
thinks to banter them into a belief, that his suggestions are matters of fact,
only by calling whore first and asking trifling questions, practis'd only by
common jilts and scolds, but abhorr'd by men of sense and ingenuity'. He
'musters up all his powers of malice and Billings-gate rhetorick, to bespat-
ter those that he thinks have detected and supplanted him'.[171] Here, then,
the public and political credit was discussed in language familiar to social
historians investigating the defence of personal reputation.

The law of libel

The key question, as Verney observed in the quotation cited above, was
whether or not the public could see through the libel and slander against
individuals and parties. One way to try to ensure that they did was to use
the law of libel to use the power of the state to delegitimize a misrepresentation. Yet when we examine attitudes to the law of libel we find that it offered little in the way of security of reputation, for individual or party. The
result, ironically, was an appeal to the equally uncertain, but increasingly
powerful, court of public opinion. It was recognized that one of the best
defences against libel was through print, even though, ironically, this
risked provoking yet more abuse.

   A libel could be directed against a private individual or against the magistrate or public persons. The private was taken to be a public matter when
the public injury of private reputation led to breach of the public peace.[172]

[170] *The Management of the Four Last Years Vindicated*, 4, 6.
[171] *England's Enemies Exposed*, 3, 11, 18–19.
[172] *English Reports*, 77, King's Bench Division (1907), vi. 250–1; F. Holt, *The Law of Libel*
(New York, 1978, rep. of 1812 edn.); R. H. Helmholz (ed.), *Select Cases on Defamation to 1600*,
Selden Society, 101 (1985); M. L. Kaplan, *The Culture of Slander in Early Modern England*
(Cambridge, 1997), ch. 1.

Defining a libel, however, was not easy. Seditious libel was introduced by statute in 1275, and originally primarily aimed at protecting the monarch from false rumours; but its extent was always vague and decided principally by common law. This placed power of definition in the judge. Chief justice Scroggs declared in 1680 that the jury had only to decide whether or not the accused had actually written an offending piece, not whether the offence amounted to libel against the state (only after 1792 did the *content* also come within the remit of the jury).[173] On the other hand, in cases where private persons were concerned, individuals had the power to bring cases and therefore test the boundaries of precedent decisions. This situation made for a very vague and broad definition, and testing the law meant defining the limits of acceptable political expression. The definition of libel was thus a barometer of legitimate and illegitimate discourse.

Although there was a widening of the offence of libel after the Revolution to include the government and ministers,[174] the limits were still very unclear, as the trial of the Whig newswriter John Tutchin in November 1704 showed. Tutchin was alleged to be 'a daily inventor and publisher of false novelties, and of horrible and false lies' in his paper *The Observator*. Tutchin's defence rested in part on the claim that he could not be condemned as scandalous or malicious since he had not mentioned any particular person by name but merely alleged that there were mismanagements in the ministry. The prosecution countered that since he and others had asserted that the ministry had taken French money, he had been scandalous and instilled 'wicked principles into the minds of men, sheltering themselves under the plausible pretences of defending the rights and liberties of the people. And that if mercenary scribblers were allowed such uncontrolled freedom, no government could be safe'. The attorney-general thus alleged that 'every one knows a libel is a libel, though particular persons are not named'. Yet a packed courtroom—so full that the crowd spilled out into the street—heard Tutchin escape on a technicality, because although the jury found him guilty of composing and publishing the pieces, they did not find him guilty of writing them in London, as the indictment claimed.[175] Tutchin's writing prompted a parliamentary

---

[173] Feather, 'English Book Trade', 67; D. Thomas, *A Long Time Burning: The History of Literary Censorship in England* (London, 1969).

[174] *Mercurius Politicus* was prosecuted for representing the revolution as the 'destruction of the laws of England' and libelling the Queen and government (Trin. Term. 5 Anne (1706), *Queen* v. *Dr Brown*).

[175] *The Tryal and Examination of Mr John Tutchin* (1704), broadside; *State Trials*, xiv. 1095–199, quotations at 1124, 1127. Cf. G. Wither, *The Prisoner's Plea* (1661), 17–18.

bill to restrain the 'licence' of the press but the measure came to nothing.[176]

The case left the extent of libel against the government unclear. But it had also illustrated the danger that, particularly in an age of party, such prosecutions could backfire, for failure to convict seemed to confirm the truth of the allegations and prosecution might itself arouse public sympathy. This was particularly evident in the reaction to the impeachment of Henry Sacheverell, whose sermons were alleged to have shown 'a wicked, malicious and seditious intention to undermine and subvert Her Majesty's government' and 'defame the administration'.[177] Although Sacheverell was convicted, the public displays of support for him served only to confirm his suggestion that the church was in danger.

There were, in any case, many ways of evading accusations of libel, as Swift explained in relation to attacks on Richard Steele. 'First we are careful never to print a man's name out at length; but as I do that of Mr St—le: so that although everybody alive knows who I mean, the plaintiff would have no redress to any court of justice. Secondly by putting cases; thirdly, by insinuations; fourthly, by celebrating the actions of others who acted directly contrary to the persons we would reflect on; fifthly, by nicknames either commonly or stamped for the purpose which everybody can tell how to apply.'[178] Another trick was to adopt modes of writing which dissimulated meaning—irony, satire, and allegory proved very difficult to prosecute—or to impersonate a rival.[179] There were, of course, some successful prosecutions that showed that even these evasive techniques were dangerous. Defoe was imprisoned for his ironic impersonation of a rabid high churchman in *The Shortest Way with Dissenters* and Steele was expelled from the House of Commons for libel, even though he had argued that the ostensible (and innocent) meaning of his words ought to prevail over an inner one which readers chose to interpret as defamatory.[180] But this matter of inner and outer meanings proved particularly problematic

---

[176] *CJ*, xiv. 278.   [177] Preamble to articles of impeachment.

[178] Swift, *Political Tracts 1713–19* ed. H. Davis (1953), 54. In a government case brought in 1711 it was, however, decided that defamatory writing using only one or two letters of a name was libellous if the contraction could only refer to one person (Holt, *Law of Libel*, 213, 243; (Trinity Term, 12 Anne (1711), Queen vs Hurt)). For the prevalence of such techniques see Zwicker, 'Reading the Margins', 109; ibid., *Lines of Authority*, 4–8.

[179] *State Law or the Doctrine of Libels Discussed and Examined* (1729), 58.

[180] Steele, *Mr Steele's Apology for Himself and his Writings; Occasioned by his Expulsion from the House of Commons* (1714), 54. Readers were not always taken in. [N.N.] *Old Popery as Good as New* (1688) claimed to be by a friend to the church, but the reader of the BL copy marked it as being 'by the worst of mortals, a virulent fanatick or hypocritical papist' (BL, T.763(36)). See also, *Post Boy*, 2778, 2843.

for libel prosecutions. Defoe's *And What if the Pretender should come?; or, Some Considerations of the Advantages and Real Consequences of the Pretender's Possessing the Crown of Great Britain* (1713) was a libel only if read at face value, and he pleaded 'ironical writing'.[181] Ambiguous and fictional writing proved a headache for the government. The removal of pre-publication licensing thus did not remove the need for imaginative and fictionalized forms of political writing, and may actually have encouraged them as a means of avoiding prosecution.

Ironically, libel could also be denied under the cover of plain speaking or telling the truth.[182] One Tory tract of 1703 thus argued that 'What is true can't be scandalous. Because the word scandal, in the sense of our law, implies a wrongful and generally a malicious aspersion.' Readers, it said, must distinguish between 'falsities' and 'unseasonable truths'.[183] Yet in a partisan political culture it was precisely this distinction that proved so elusive, for party was a lens in which a rival truth could be read as a lie. For example, if a jacobite claimed that William was oppressing the people because his war burdened them with taxes, was this a lie, a half truth, or the whole truth? The answer, of course, lay with the allegedly impartial judgement of the people. It was this area of conflicting truths that made satire such an effective weapon. Satire thus played with the uncertain boundaries between 'falsities' and 'unseasonable truths'. For these reasons formal prosecution, though still an option, needed to be accompanied by public refutation and hence by another appeal to the public as umpire. Although prosecutions continued to occur, public refutation and counter-accusation were prized because they, in turn, influenced public opinion. This strengthened a move towards informal methods of constraining public discourse.

We can see this in two responses to libel in William's reign. The first of these concerned the City of London's mayoral elections of 1692. Two Tory candidates, Sir Jonathan Raymond and Sir Peter Daniel, had their reputations attacked in print.[184] Edmund Bohun drafted a response:

---

[181]   But in the case of Dr Joseph Browne, prosecuted in 1706 for *The Country Parson's Honest Advice*, a satire of William Cowper, it was ruled that irony was libellous if the jury so interpreted it (Holt, *Law of Libel*, 107, 233).

[182]   For the longer history of this figure of speech, see D. Colclough, 'Parrhesia: The Rhetoric of Free Speech in Early Modern England', *Rhetorica—A Journal of the History of Rhetoric*, 17 (1997), 177–212.

[183]   *The Source of Our Present Fears Discover'd*, 4–5. It praised the plain-speaking of J. Drake, *The History of the Last Parliament* (1702).

[184]   *Advice to the Livery-men of London in their Choice of a Lord Mayor, on Michaelmas Day, 1692* (1692); and *A Letter from a Country Gentleman to an Eminent but Easy Citizen who was Unhappily Misguided in the Fatal Election of Sir John Moore for Lord Mayor of London at Michaelmas 1681* (1692).

There is a very unjust and wicked custome taken up by some who pretend a mighty zeale for their Majesties interest by printed papers as well as by private whispers to blacken and defame all those that stand candidates for any imployment in the city or countrey and ripping up the whole series of mens lives, misrepresenting what is good or harmless, aggravating what is amiss and too often inventing what never was. They indeavour to have all those they dislike thought the worst of men.[185]

Bohun thought all this tended 'directly to the rendering the government cheap and unsteady'. But ironically for a man shortly to be made one of the last licensers of the press, Bohun appreciated that print could work against print. He felt that the Whig attacks were 'so black and passionate that they are their own antidote', and he printed his work with an explicit appeal to 'the judgment of all the citizens' (as well as God) to find in his favour.[186] Instead of formal prosecution, then, a frequent response to a controversial 'libel' was refutation in print.

   Such a solution is also evident in the second example, which concerns the fascinating physician and speculator Hugh Chamberlen. He thought that a tract, *A Dialogue between Dr H.C. and a Country Gentleman* (1696), which discussed his proposed land bank, was a libel because of the 'manner of its coming abroad, having been plentifully dispersed in town and country, without either the authors or printers name'. It had been 'scatter'd up and down in coffee houses' where people might be misled by its 'nonsense'.[187] Chamberlen's response was to take up his pen and publish a vindicating reply, refuting the 'libel' that 'maliciously' sought to undermine his credit—the very thing necessary for an aspiring founder of a bank. Print was thus both the means to damage reputation but also a way to secure public vindication and hence restore credit. This worked by invoking public opinion as a 'tribunal' that was as, if not more, powerful than any court.[188] Libel was thus not something just treated by courts; it was a concept that was part of the printed duel between partisans. And in this sense the public acted as a form of censor. Yet in an age of party the censor, though claiming impartiality, was as partisan as the audience of print. Indeed, party acted as its own kind of censor, through its constant censure of rival opinions. And, as the next chapter explores in more detail,

---

[185]   CUL, Sel.3.238, item 214.
[186]   Bohun's manuscript defence, shorn of its prefatory fulminations, duly appeared in print, as *The Vindication of Sir Jonathan Raymond Alderman of London, from the Aspersions Cast upon him by Two Injurious Libells*. Bohun collected two copies at Sel.3.238, items 220 and 221.
[187]   *An Answer to a Libel Entituled A Dialogue between Dr H.C. and a Country Gentleman* (1696), 1–2.
[188]   *Mercurius Politicus; or, An Antidote to Popular Mis-representation*, 1.

the nature of party meant that there was always a part of the public that might judge something true which the other half judged to be false and libellous.

> A free press is the pulse of the body-politic, from which it would be impossible for the wisest state-physician to discern, or prevent the public distempers, unless it is suffer'd to beat free without a ligature.[189]

If the law of libel was an uncertain ally, and refutation of libel a time-consuming and uncertain affair, might there still be a case for safeguarding against abusive, irrational, misrepresentative public discourse by regulating the press? The solution adopted at the Restoration had been to try to insist that words had to be licensed by the state before publication. As we have already seen, this system (only ever partially effective) lapsed in 1679 and although the law requiring pre-publication licensing was reimposed in 1685 (for seven years), and renewed in 1693, it disappeared for good in 1695.[190] Even so, there were some, well beyond that date, who continued to advocate some form of suppression. A tract of 1701, invoking the authority of Bacon, noted that 'a Wise and Great States Man has long since observed that the currency and superabundancy of libels is a sign of a sickly state and is such a dangerous attempt against the tranquillity and safety of the kingdom, that the first promoters, divulgers and encouragers of them, ought to be taken up and by the severity of their punishment, be made publick examples'.[191] The call for restrictions on the press was one often made by those who feared the corrosive effect of the press on religious as well as political belief. The high church Tory Simon Harcourt, for example, urged prosecution of seditious print and warned a grand jury about the 'unthinking men who believe everything they see in print, be it never so false, whereby [thei]r principles are debauched & poisoned'.[192] The

---

[189] W. Lawrence, *Marriage by the Moral Law of God Vindicated* (1680), 166, cited by Kemp, 'Ideas of Liberty of the Press', 164.
[190] Astbury, 'Renewal of the Licensing Act'.
[191] *England's Enemies Expos'd*, 25.
[192] BL, Harl. MS 5137, f. 253, Jan. 1704/5.

national church, it was asserted, was a guide to truth and hence its license was itself a guide of rectitude. *A Letter to a Member of Parliament Shewing the Necessity of Regulating the Press* (1699), argued that 'the generality of mankind are scarce able or at leisure to detect the false colours of an artificial harangue', much less make a judgement on the merits of the religious controversies, so that 'every thing that appears in publick must pass for orthodox, unless it has some publick note of distinction fixed upon it'.[193] A licence could thus be seen as a piece of advice about the truth of the print.

Clerics therefore used convocation both to condemn unorthodox print and to call for new curbs on the press.[194] High churchmen believed that *vox populi* was not necessarily the voice of god but could be that of the devil.[195] Francis Atterbury, for example, attacking what he saw as a tribe of impertinent scribblers, remarked that 'when every individual member of the society pretends to give rules of government, the consequence can be no other than confusion'. His whole design was to show that 'according to the vulgar proverb, the cobbler ought not to go beyond his last, which they all now do, superciliously playing the statesman and taking on them to regulate all affairs, as well civil as ecclesiastical'. Atterbury provocatively alleged that in fact 'the Voice of the People is the cry of Hell, leading to idolatry, rebellion, murder and all the wickedness the Devil can suggest'.[196] The removal of clerical censorship, together with the flood of hostile (and, to them, irreligious) print, convinced many clerics that the press posed a considerable threat to the church and to belief. This sentiment was put in the mouth of Queen Anne when she opened parliament on 9 April 1713, expressing her displeasure 'at the unparalleled licentiousness in publishing seditious and scandalous libels. The impunity such practices have met with has encouraged the blaspheming everything sacred, and the propagating opinions tending to the overthrow of all religion and government'; she urged a new law 'to put a stop to this growing evil'.[197] There were indeed

---

[193] *Letter*, 23, 39, 41–2. cf. Gregory, *A Modest Plea.*

[194] G. V. Bennett, *The Tory Crisis in Church and State, 1688–1730* (Oxford, 1976), 137. For a satire of high church views, see BL, Add. MS 70267, which contains a printed tract *c.*1704 attributed in letter 41 to Defoe (*To the Honourable, the C-s of England Assembled in P-t. The Humble Petition and Representation of the True Loyal and Always Obedient Church of England, Relating to the Bill for Restraining the Press*).

[195] Atterbury, *The Voice of the People no Voice of God* (1710), 4. Cf. *A Letter to a Modern Dissenting Whig*, 14.

[196] *Voice of the People*, 4–6.

[197] *CJ*, xvii. 278.

a number of attempts to reimpose censorship; and prosecutions against the press persisted, using the laws of treason, sedition, and (from 1698 onwards) blasphemy.[198]

Nevertheless there was a growing ambiguity in such attitudes from the 1640s onwards. For many advocates of licensing or suppression also used the press not only to advocate those views but also to engage in the public discourse that they sought to restrict.[199] One pamphleteer observed that he did not have 'the vanity to believe myself able to make converts, for our affections and prejudices are too strong to be alter'd by better writing than I can pretend to' but he did hope 'to confirm those who are dispos'd to believe right' and this necessitated replying to a critic, otherwise the public 'may suspect I acquiesce in his contradiction'.[200] Refutation was thus as important as prosecution. Indeed, over the later Stuart period there was a shift, from regulation of controversial print through pre-publication censorship to refutation via a press restrained by the market and taxation. We do not need to exaggerate the efficiency of the licensing system to discern this important change.[201] Nor do we need to play down the religious motivation of those urging that print be free to mirror and promote liberty of conscience[202] to appreciate that the press was increasingly seen as a guarantor of all civil freedoms. As one Whig tract justifying the liberty of the press argued, restriction of it had led to slavery of all types under James II and therefore 'Secure but the liberty of the press and that will, in all probability, secure all other liberty.'[203] Some commentators suggest that it was

---

[198]   Feather, 'The Book Trade in Politics: The Making of the Copyright Act of 1710', *Publishing History*, 8 (1980), 19–44; L. Hanson, *The Government and the Press 1695–1763* (Oxford, 1936), 8–11; P. Monod, 'The Jacobite Press and English Censorship 1689–95', in E. Cruickshanks and E. Corp (eds.), *The Stuart Court in Exile and the Jacobites* (London, 1995); F. Siebert, *Freedom of the Press in England 1476–1776* (Urbana, 1952); T. Crist, 'Government Control of the Press after the Expiration of the Printing Act of 1679', *Publishing History*, 5 (1979), 49–77.

[199]   Kemp, 'Ideas of Liberty of the Press'.

[200]   *A Supplement to Faults in the Fault-Finder* (1710/1), 26.

[201]   Some commentators discern a powerful system of pre-publication censorship (Siebert, *Freedom*; A. Patterson, *Censorship and Interpretation: The Conditions of Writing and Reading in Early Modern England* (Madison, Wisc., 1984); J. Clare, *Art Made Tongue-Tied by Authority* (Manchester, 1990)). Others, however, question its efficiency and consistency (B. Worden, 'Literature and Political Censorship in Early Modern England', in A. C. Duke and C. A. Tamse (eds.), *Too Mighty to be Free: Censorship and the Press in Britain and the Netherlands* (Zutphen, 1987); S. Lambert, 'The Printers and the Government, 1604–37', in R. Myers and M. Harris (eds.), *Aspects of Printing From 1600* (Oxford, 1987); Kaplan, *Culture of Slander*; Barnard, *Cambridge History of the Book*, 3).

[202]   Stressed by Worden, 'Literature and political censorship', and Kemp, 'Ideas of Liberty of the Press'.

[203]   *A Letter to a Member of Parliament* (*State Tracts*, ii. 624).

only in the 1720s that the concept of freedom of press as a bulwark of liberties became formulated, but this would be to post-date an important development.[204] For it was not just the crown that was perceived as a threat to liberties: in an age of partisan rivalries Whig and Tory or high church and dissenter were regarded as equally destructive.

The need to offer an antidote to the poisonous words of a rival justified the entry into print even of those who disliked an appeal to the people. Mary Astell argued, in 1704, that apart from 'making a figure in the world' the only reasons for publishing pamphlets were 'either to strengthen a party, that is, in other words, to embroil the state by working on the fears and jealousies of the weak and injudicious and by soothing the humours and designs of the vicious and turbulent; or else by way of antidote, to fortifie the honest and well-meaning, against the poison of the common sort of pamphleteers'.[205] Clearly she saw herself in the latter category, for all her own attempt to 'strengthen a party'. Indeed, partisan print could thus claim a measure of loyalty to the queen, state, or church. In a passage which prefigures Swift's Gulliver pissing out a fire at the Lilliputian palace, *A Dialogue betwixt Whig and Tory* (1710) argued that

tho the sacred majesty of kings (I am sensible) ought not in common cases to be approach'd by every little busy-body, or frivolous remonstrance-maker; yet when our prince's palace is on fire, and his sacred person in the midst of the flames, the meanest of his subjects hath the privilege then to give him warning of his danger, and to assist to quench the fire.[206]

From asserting the necessity of publishing antidotes it was a short step to claiming a duty or even right to publish, in the *public interest*.[207] William Denton thus justified his entry into print on the grounds that it was 'every mans duty to contribute what he can towards the support of that government under which he lives'.[208] This sense of duty and conscience was clearly evident in the publications of Robert Crosfeild, a self-appointed thorn in the government's side who sought to expose corruption in the

[204] Downie, *Harley and the Press*, 118–19.
[205] M. Astell, *Moderation Truly Stated; or, A Review of a Late Pamphlet Entituled Moderation a Vertue* (1704), 1–2.
[206] *Dialogue*, prefatory 'To the King'.
[207] R. Kingston, *True History of the Several Designs and Conspiracies . . . from 1688 till 1697* (1698), preface.
[208] W. Denton, *Jus Regiminis; Being a Justification of Defensive Arms* (1689), Advertisement to the Reader, 7. Denton had earlier written *An Apology for the Liberty of the Press* (1681). Cf. L'Estrange, *A Short Answer to a Whole Litter of Libels* (1680), 15; Toland, *The Militia Reform'd* (1698), 4, 6.

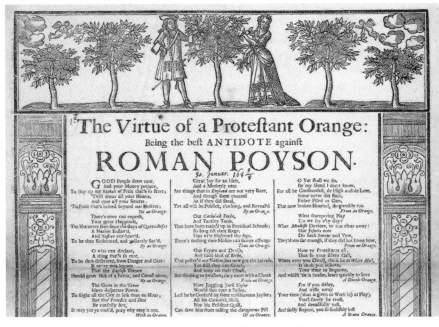

Both William himself and the print that represents him are antidotes against popish poison.
[Reproduced by courtesy of the Houghton Library, Harvard University.]

1690s. Although arrested six times during William's reign, and interrogated by the House of Lords, he continued to use print to articulate his claims, 'the press being kept open to the intent corruption should be detected', even though it was the publication of some of his accusations that got him into trouble.[209] In one of those pieces Crosfeild asserted that to put a restraint on the press 'is the way, infallibly, to ruin the nation'.[210] Crosfeild attempted to use the press to castigate the pursuit of private interests under the pretence of public good, and he seems to have regarded both parties as having their noses in the trough of corruption. But he also clearly saw print as an antidote to corruption of the national interest. An

[209] *A Vindication of the Constitution of the English Monarchy and the Just Rights of the People* (1703), 7–9 (I ascribe this to Crosfeild on grounds of style and content). He wrote nine other tracts listed in ESTC. Samuel Baston's *A Dialogue Between a Modern Courtier and an Honest English Gentleman* [1697] was also written with his 'knowledge and approbation'.
[210] Crosfeild, *England's Warning-Piece* (1704), 3.

appeal then, of loyalty to state, government, nation, or 'truth'—any collective that overrode particular interest—could thus justify print.[211]

Even if we admit, then, that pre-publication censorship was far less efficient in the pre-1640 period than was once thought, that the drive for freedom of expression was rooted in claims for religious liberty, and that the changes of the later Stuart period were therefore perhaps more the culmination of a transformation rather than a revolution in their own right, we can still discern important shifts. First, being able systematically to counter print with print became essential as well as desirable for anyone, or any party, aspiring to power. The licensing system was 'superseded by a different attitude towards literature, which attempted not to suppress it but to exploit its popularity' for the government.[212] Walpole's administration learned this lesson well.[213] It was another essential consequence of the rise of the public and the importance of public judgement. Second, partisan use of the press could justify and legitimize a printed counter-response, particularly if the riposte appealed not just to the rival party interest but also to the national interest. Third, public discourse had to be regulated by means other than pre-publication censorship. Fourth, the later Stuart period carried the logic of print self-justification to its natural conclusion. The consequences of this were that, in the absence of pre-publication licensing, informal rules governing public discourse became ever more necessary, and, as we shall now see, the definition of what constituted poison and its antidote was necessarily relative to partisan allegiances.

---

[211] Section 13 of *Letter to a Member of Parliament Shewing that a Restraint on the Press is Inconsistent* linked freethinking to the liberty of the press. This notion was attacked by Gregory, *Modest Plea*, 21.

[212] Downie, *Harley and the Press*, 149. Downie nevertheless under-estimates the extent of earlier ministerial sponsorship.

[213] S. Targett, 'Government and Ideology During the Age of Whig Supremacy: The Political Argument of Sir Robert Walpole's Newspaper Propagandists', *HJ*, 37 (1994), 289–317; Targett, ' "The Premier Scribbler Himself": Sir Robert Walpole and the Management of Political Opinion', M. Harris and T. O' Malley (eds.), *Studies in Newspaper and Periodical History. 1994 Annual* (Westport, 1996), 19–33; Urstad, *Walpole's Poets*; M. Harris, 'Print and Politics'; M. Harris, *London Newspapers in the Age of Walpole: A Study of the Origins of the Modern English Press* (Rutherford, 1987); J. Black, *Walpole in Power* (2001), ch. 6; D. Stevens, *Party Politics and English Journalism 1702–42* (1916).

CHAPTER SIX

Truth and Fiction in the Age of Party

THE PROBLEM OF TRUTH

The previous chapter examined contemporary fears that public discourse was threatened by irrationality, abusiveness, and libel, all of which made judgement about politicians and their policies difficult. As we saw, contemporaries feared that polemic might be deliberately misleading. This chapter explores the question of truth and political lying in more detail, suggesting that it was a central concern to all participants and their a udience, and that the political culture of the later Stuart period was one preoccupied with the language of politics, fiction, and truth-claims. Fierce conflict between parties placed enormous pressure on language and manners. Through the everyday practice of partisan politics, therefore, issues that are far more associated with an eighteenth-century enlightenment agenda, such as rationality, truth, and fact, were routinely discussed.

Party politics, as we have seen, offered divergent views about what was true. The bi-polar mentality of Whig and Tory meant that what was right and true for one side was wrong and erroneous for the other. As Henry St John, later viscount Bolingbroke, put it in 1709, 'no man looks on things as they really are, but sees them through that glass which party holds up to him'.[1] Seven years earlier he had referred to party as one of the 'false optics' through which men viewed things.[2] Yet each of the parties believed that it had truth on its side, as the titles of numerous pamphlets and periodicals made clear.[3] Each item of partisan print vied to represent a certain viewpoint as true by condemning its rival or opposite as erroneous.

---

[1] *Camden Miscellany* 26 ('Letters of Henry St. John' ed. H. T. Dickinson), Camden Society, 4th ser., 14 (1975), 147.

[2] BL, Add. MSS 72489 ff. 98–99v, Henry St. John to Sir William Trumbull, 21 Aug. 1702. For an exploration of the metaphor of sight, see Achinstein, 'Uses of Deception'.

[3] ESTC lists almost 6,500 items, published 1675–1720 with 'true', 'truth' or 'false' in the title.

Such profuse competition exacerbated anxieties about truth-claims. Truth lay in the eye of the partisan and adherence to party could either distort truth or so prejudice the partisan that truth could, or would, not be recognized. Dryden had said as much in 1681: 'Wit and Fool are consequents of Whig and Tory: and every man is knave or an ass to the contrary side'.[4] Addison noted that any public figure to the partisans was 'like an object seen in two different mediums' and thus had 'two contrary characters, as opposite to one another as light and darkness'.[5] The political struggle was thus a competition between and over rival representations and truth-claims.

Yet, whilst raising questions about where truth lay, partisan politics also undermined the status of the traditional means of validating truth-claims: the monarch and church. Instead (or more accurately, as well), there was a new, but to many observers, an uncertain or even vacillating umpire, the public. As we have seen, petitions, addresses, public oaths, frequent elections, and a free press all placed the public as judge of state affairs, not just as a non-instrumental spectator but as an active participant in the political process. Publicly adversarial politics thus not only institutionalized rival truth-claims but also championed as arbiter a public that, it was feared, either lacked the capacity to discern truth or could be manipulated into mistaking truth for error. This was even more dangerous because the public had considerable power to affect public affairs, through the polls, through the public credit necessary to fight war, and through informal pressures, such as petitions and addresses. Truth, then, was a party political issue. Indeed, just as historians of science have investigated the problem of how contemporaries distinguished error from truth, and just as social or religious historians and literary critics have stressed the importance of means of establishing credibility and certainty, so a political history of truth also needs to be mapped.

Once the public was constituted as an umpire of politics, what was important was not so much what was true but what the public *thought* was true or could be *made to believe* was true. The marquis of Halifax, for example, concluded that the popish plot 'must be handled as though it were true, whether it were so or not, in those points which were so generally believed by the city or country, as well as both houses'.[6] The prevalence of revelations about plotting in the later Stuart period made public perceptions

---

[4] *Absalom and Achitophel* (1681), 'To the reader'.
[5] *The Spectator*, 125.
[6] H. C. Foxcroft, *A Character of the Trimmer. Being a Short Life of the First Marquis of Halifax* (Cambridge, 1946), 76.

all-important, for frequently the 'evidence' was laid out before a fascinated nation. The public decided what to believe as true; and hence it could create truth and error. Yet the consequences of error being mistaken for truth were far-reaching. Hobbes had already seen how a shift towards a representational world was dangerous unless meaning, even of good and evil, could be fixed by the sovereign. Thus for him one of the chief causes of the dissolution of a state was the 'false' doctrine 'that every private man is judge of good and evil actions' because from this 'men are disposed to debate with themselves and dispute the commands of the common-wealth; and afterwards to obey or disobey them, as in their private judgements they shall think fit'.[7] And all this, he suggested, stemmed from a false concept of representation.

Whig and Tory seemed to make judgement a private, partisan, self-interested affair. A Tory tract lamented that, 'the people being duly appriz'd that the governors and magistrates had no sort of power or authority but what they deriv'd from them, they assum'd to themselves this privilege of creating right and wrong'.[8] The Whigs were alleged 'to confound the people in their notions of good and evil', and 'left every man to be his own judge in all cases whatsoever, and no obligation by way of conscience left to any government'.[9] Good and evil had become private or party judgements. As the rage of party increased, all sides began to fear that there was a paradox at the heart of publicly competitive politics: an appeal to the people was an integral part of such politics but it was also the root of the problem. For it was in the very appeal to the public's judgement about what was true that truth could itself become subverted.[10] Truth was both conveyed by public discourse; but also undermined by it. This was no abstract problem. For the public was being asked repeatedly, through frequent elections, to judge and make choices, at a time of war against the most powerful military force in Europe. Failure to discern the true choice in these circumstances threatened to be catastrophic.

One of the obstacles to discerning right and wrong was language itself. Without agreement over the meaning of words, the values they represented could hardly be clear. Yet partisans routinely disputed the true definition of words. For example, John Somers defined 'abdication' as

[7] *Leviathan*, 223.
[8] *The Danger of Moderation* (1708), 3.
[9] *True Picture of a Modern Whig Reviv'd*, 14–15.
[10] We can glimpse something similar in the mid-century (Achinstein, 'Uses of Deception', 178–82).

resigning governance, whereas (he said) the word 'desertion', which might have been used to describe James's flight, meant only a temporary 'bare withdrawing'.[11] When the House of Lords sought to remove the word 'abdicated' from the key motion about the crown and replace it with 'deserted' their action led to a trial of political strength between the two Houses and between the parties. It was the ensuing division in the Commons on 5 February 1689 on the amendment that in turn provided the basis for a printed list of Tories that was used to persuade the electorate to reject them, as we saw in Chapter 4.[12] A controversy over the meaning and significance of words that embodied rival ideologies thus became not just a Westminster business but the concern of voters up and down the land. Publicly contested politics was thus fought out over the interpretation, meaning, and applicability of key words and slogans. This process occurred routinely, though we encountered a particularly dramatic example of it in Chapter 3 in the conflict in Norwich in 1696 over the word 'revenge'. Such linguistic disputes were not limited to the high-profile clash over the succession. Instead they became endemic to the new political culture. Plurality of opinion, it was suspected, caused or was caused by, the false applications of meanings to key words and concepts.

Contemporaries thus worried about the nature of public discourse. This chapter focuses on these concerns about how truth was obscured, distorted, and misrepresented, especially through the abuse of words. Party appeared to distort language in a number of ways. The meaning of words and phrases was contested and destabilized.[13] Political labels misrepresented the true nature of political ideologies and positions. Polemic used or misused rhetorical practices to manipulate and deceive readers, to appeal to their passions rather than their reason. Political languages seemed like secret codes, part of the means by which a conspiratorial group furthered their designs by gulling the public with jargon or meaningless words. And as language became fractured, invested with contested and partisan meanings, it seemed to unravel, for language relied on a shared, common, sense. Moreover, political lying appeared to be a commonplace of the culture of party—indeed, an inherent part of the means by which parties operated. Political lying in turn created unease about the prevalence of self- or particular interests and the absence of sincerity. This

---

[11] J. Oldmixon, *Memoirs of the Life of John Lord Somers* (1716), 19–21.

[12] *A Letter to a Friend* (1690).

[13] Contestation creates 'imaginary categories' (M. de Certeau, *Capture of Speech and other Political Writings . . . translated by Tom Conley* (Minneapolis, 1997), 64).

chapter therefore examines the ways in which contemporaries feared that public discourse might lead to error as much as truth. And it also explores the ways in which such 'errors' could be seen as fictions. Building on the suggestion of John Downie that the rise of the political press 'prepared the way for the tremendous growth of the popularity of fiction', the chapter concludes by examining some of the ways in which fiction and politics fused.[14]

Uncertainty about the nature of truth, the stability of meaning, the sincerity of public words and how to discern lies was certainly not new to the later Stuart period. These were issues that had long affected religious debate, 'science', rhetoric, and the impact of print.[15] Once civil war had broken out, rival truth-claims in the political sphere had, moreover, focused on the duality of meaning, insincerity, lies, and misrepresentation.[16] The uncertainties of the post-1660 period were thus not unknown in early modern England. Nor was uncertainty merely the creation of party politics. John Spurr's suggestive analysis of the 1670s highlights the importance of disguise and dissimulation in the restoration political and literary culture. Spurr sees these as a reflection of the uncertainties engendered not only by politicians but also by shifts in communicative practices.[17] So my argument is not that such anxieties were new; nor that epistemological uncertainty was novel. Rather, I suggest that party conflict led to an important *intensification* of longer term phenomena, to quite unprecedented proportions, so that a preoccupation with the abuse of language for political ends became a commonplace, *embedded* in the political culture and part of the representational politics that was gaining hold. Each of the five factors identified at the beginning of the book as prompting change—frequent elections, a free press, challenges to the church, a financial revolution, and ideological conflict over the root of authority—constituted threats to fixed and secure notions of truth, knowledge, certainty, meaning, and understanding. These factors created a new context in which the instabilities and ambiguities of meanings *were part of* everyday political struggle. It could hardly be otherwise when Whig and Tory were them-

---

[14] Downie, *Harley and the Press*, 14–15.

[15] See ch. 1 and E. Leites (ed.), *Conscience and Casuistry in Early Modern Europe* (Cambridge, 1988); E. Rose, *Cases of Conscience: Alternatives Open to Recusants and Puritans under Elizabeth and James I* (Cambridge, 1975); A. Jonsen and S. Toulmin, *The Abuse of Casuistry: A History of Moral Reasoning* (Berkelely, 1988); P. Zagorin, *Ways of Lying: Dissimulation, Persecution and Conformity in Early Modern Europe* (Cambridge, Mass., 1990).

[16] Raymond, *Invention of the Newspaper*, 128, 211–12, 221–5, 276–7; Achinstein, 'Politics of Babel' and 'Uses of Deception'.

[17] Spurr, *England in the 1670s*.

To preach up Truth, some say tis not a time | But since ỹ Truth offends, I'll vex you more
False Brethren allwaies think ỹ Truths Crime | And shew ỹ face of Truth you've wrongd befor

The image, and the verse beneath it, represent Dr Sacheverell as the face of Truth; but his Truth was regarded by others as highly partisan and even erroneous. He holds the portrait of Charles I; but the 'truth' about Stuart failures as a cause of 'civil war' or 'rebellion' was also bitterly contested. The word 'Truth' appears in each line of the verse caption. [Reproduced by courtesy of the Trustees of the British Museum.]

selves representational constructs that appeared to shift their meaning over time and space.

The appeal to the public in this context exacerbated a state of epistemological uncertainty, in which readers, voters, writers, and representatives were disorientated by their inability to take things at face value. This has, in part, been recognized by literary scholars as a causal factor in the emergence of the novel. McKeon argues that the news-books of the mid-seventeenth century made claims to authentic truth that were denied by opponents as fiction. He identifies a dialectic in which the claim to historicity provoked the accusation of romance. This, he suggests, destabilized genres. The loosening of historicity shook other genres which relied on conceptions of 'true history', such as biography, autobiography, and travel narratives. McKeon nevertheless saw this process as driven primarily by the destabilization of social categories resulting from the emergence of a 'capitalist' market. Money and credit—outward appearances—now marked the value of men. This process, he suggests, raised questions about virtue; and when questions about virtue and truth coincided, the conflation produced the novel.[18] So although McKeon identified epistemological crisis, he did not explore the political partisanship that helped to create it. Paul Hunter has also stressed the importance of journalistic fictions for the novel, though he too emphasizes social factors, particularly urbanization, as the key motors of change.[19] The historian can build on these insights but also relate them to the political culture set out in previous chapters. In turn it may be that such analysis helps to place Defoe, Swift, and their readers in a wider context.[20] If it is the case that the practice of partisan politics helped to deepen a culture of fiction and epistemological uncertainty, then Defoe and Swift become more readily understandable (though unusually talented) practitioners of arts that surrounded them, and their readers emerge as well versed to expect and consume such material.

[18] McKeon, *Origins of the English Novel,* 48, 87–9, 91, 205–11, 266.
[19] Hunter, *Before Novels.*
[20] For a recognition of the importance of 'didactic material' see ibid., 226–7. Leonard Davis sees parliamentary statutes, newspapers, advertisements, and handbills as novelistic and suggests that fact and fiction are not distinct categories (*Factual Fictions,* 7–8). Achinstein has stressed the 'ways in which political thinkers resemble creative writers in their fiction-making' (*Milton,* 7). See also, Eilon, *Faction's Fictions* and R. Zimbardo, 'The Late Seventeenth Century Dilemma in Discourse', in J. D. Canfield and J. P. Hunter, *Rhetorics of Order/Ordering Rhetorics in English Neoclassical Literature* (Newark, NJ, 1989). Most recently, Kate Loveman has placed the literary and political culture of deception at the heart of an explanation for the rise of the novel (Loveman, 'Shamming Readers').

THE DANGEROUS ARTS AND ARTIFICES OF
POLITICAL LANGUAGE

In 1711 the Tory periodical the *Examiner* noted that 'it is Machiavel's Observation that the people when left to their own judgment, do seldom mistake their true interests' but that 'they are to be deceiv'd by several means' and could be 'deluded' into slavery. The issue's author, Swift, thought that Britain now faced a similar danger from 'the lowest Plebeans' who sought to obtain and preserve their power 'by representing the nobles and other friends to the old government, as enemies to the publick'. The effect of their false discourse, 'in conjunction with a great depravity of manners, and a weak or corrupt administration', was to produce a state fever. The 'madness of the people hath risen to such a height as to break in pieces the whole frame of the best instituted governments', he claimed. The arts and artifices of public discourse were thus seen as highly dangerous. Yet Swift also believed that, with his paper's help, 'such great Frenzies being artificially rais'd . . . will certainly decline of themselves, settling like the sea after a storm and then the true Bent and Genius of the People will appear'.[21] Partisan writers (though, of course, Swift eschewed the label) thus believed that the people could both be led astray and corrected through public discourse, even though the correction of misrepresentation involved, in the eyes of their rivals, employing the same misrepresenting arts to do so. Thus the *Examiner* and its rival Whig periodical, the *Medley*, were involved in an increasingly vituperative attempt to neutralize the poison of each other's words. Words had temporarily sent the nation mad, but equally they could help restore sanity.[22]

Words of whatever type were accorded a high degree of agency by contemporaries, especially when they mused on the origins of riot or rebellion. High churchman Charles Leslie, for example, believed that the abuse of words had caused the revolution of 1641 and threatened to do so again. 'Four Ps carry'd on the whole revolution of forty-one', he claimed; 'these were, people, parliament, property and popery. By vertue of the word people and their ORIGINAL POWER they overturn'd the government . . . the inchantment of these words is not yet over with us'.[23] An essential part of such anxiety was rooted in the recognition that words could misrepresent as well as represent. A perceived disparity between 'words and things' was

---

[21] *Examiner*, 25.
[22] Cf. *The Observator*, 1.
[23] *The Rehearsal*, 7–14 April 1705.

an ongoing concern throughout the seventeenth century, for their divorce was thought to result in disunity, conflict, and even chaos. But, as this section suggests, the arts of partisan politics centred on a deliberate and misleading misuse of discourse, so anxiety about the disparity between words and things was bound to increase. The practice of politics thus embedded heightened sensibilities about this danger into the later Stuart political culture. And because this was a national political culture, it involved the smallest boroughs in the land.

The problem of 'words' was dealt with philosophically by John Locke. He wondered 'whether the greatest part of the disputes in the world are not merely verbal, and about the signification of words'.[24] He saw 'the abuse of words' as responsible for bringing 'confusion, disorder, and uncertainty into the affairs of mankind'.[25] Words, he insisted, were signs that must be properly defined, for that was the only way to achieve truth and harmony.[26] Indeed, the proper use of words defined truth: 'Truth is the marking down in words, the agreement or disagreement of ideas as it is. Falsehood is the marking down in words, the agreement or disagreement of ideas otherwise than it is.'[27] Words and ideas therefore had to correspond; words had accurately to represent ideas and concepts. But all too often 'if the idea be not agreed on, betwixt the speaker and hearer, for which the words stand, the argument is not about things, but names.'[28] Thus the 'sure and only way to get true knowledge is to form in our minds clear settled notions of things, with names annexed to those determined ideas'. Unfixed meanings, he warned, could be used 'in several senses to serve a turn'.[29] The lover of truth was thus to avoid rhetoric and sophistry, even though such arts served 'so well to propagate' opinions and 'procure . . . credit in the world'. He recommended an alternative 'more jejune and dry way of writing', that appealed to simple reason and demonstration.[30] Locke saw party—by which he meant in particular religious factions and sects but also political parties—as one of the main threats to truth, when combined with the other prejudices of education and custom.[31] 'Interest or party', he remarked, 'commonly content themselves with words which have no dis-

[24] Locke, *Essay Concerning Human Understanding*, Bk III, ix. 6.
[25] Ibid., Bk III, x. 12.
[26] For Locke and semiotics, see H. Aarsleff, *From Locke to Saussure: Essays on the Study of Language and Intellectual History* (London, 1982), 27.
[27] Locke, *Essay*, Bk IV, v. 9.
[28] Ibid., Bk III, xi. 6–7.
[29] Locke, *Of the Conduct*, 68.
[30] Ibid., 118–19. He called a club in the early 1690s the Dry Club.
[31] N. Wood, *The Politics of Locke's Philosophy* (Berkeley, 1983), 101–9.

tinct ideas to them'.[32] The 'constant din' of a party could falsely connect ideas that should remain independent and 'this gives sense to jargon, demonstration to absurdities, and consistency to nonsense, and is the foundation of the greatest, I had almost said of all the errors in the world'.[33] Everyone's 'natural reason' could be 'spoiled and lost only by assumed prejudices, overweening presumption and narrowing our minds'.[34]

Locke—and Richard Burthogge before him or George Berkeley after him—gave philosophical coherence to ideas about the abuse of words.[35] But observations about the disparity between words and things, about the way in which blind adherence to a party abused the understanding, and about the danger of misrepresentative words and labels could be found routinely expressed in partisan polemic. Thus Danby's apologist Marchmont Nedham in 1677 warned against those who were 'wont to be carried away with the mere sounds of words; are too apt to be carried away by phansie and mistake it to be understanding'. He noted that the critics of the court 'tickled' the people 'with frequent mentions of *ancient laws, the good old laws and ancient customs of England*, and like phrases; which make a noise, and great noises usually take the weaker sort of people; yea and engage them too'.[36] The idea that 'words' misled the public into false allegiance helped contemporaries to explain why their rivals gained the upper hand. Nedham was thus quite explicit that an appeal to the ancient constitution was a way of talking, a rhetoric, that could deceive readers unless they were taught how to understand or 'read' it. Nedham identified other misleading phrases (such as 'property, right and liberty') which the 'faction' used to ensnare 'the injudicious part of the world, which are always much the major part of mankinde, who . . . are not able to judge whether discourses be made rationally or not, till the sophisms or cheats of such crafty writers be discovered'.[37] The faction, he said, sprinkled 'flowers of rhetoric in all their writings and discourses: they work upon the people with them as witches do with charms, characters and spells, to bewitch the multitude with an opinion against the court' and make them 'run headlong into civil wars'.[38] In the previous chapter we saw discourse likened to

---

[32] Locke, *Of the Conduct*, 35.
[33] Locke, *Essay*, Bk II, xxxiii. 18.
[34] Locke, *Of the Conduct*, 38–9.
[35] *The Philosophical Writing of Richard Burthogge*, ed. M. W. Landes (Chicago, 1921), 13, 15, 26; G. Berkeley, *A Treatise Concerning the Principles of Human Knowledge*, ed. C. M. Turbayne (New York, 1970), 240, 242–3.
[36] *A Second Pacquet of Advices and Animadversions Sent to the Men of Shaftesbury* (1677), 11.
[37] Ibid., 18–19.
[38] Ibid., 62.

poison; here, the image is one of witchcraft.[39] Party was a malevolent moving spirit.

Nedham's critique lay at the core of the high church and Tory response to the print of their opponents. The Tories were convinced that the Whigs had a set of misleading words. Liberty was prime among these, as one tract made clear. The word

> has been a protection of all sorts and degrees of criminals and debauchees; it can swear and fight, plunder and kill through all the points of the compass: backbiting, perjury and libelling of princes; sodomy, incest and all the unnatural lusts have defended themselves with the pompous name of liberty.[40]

Another Tory tract agreed: 'Liberty but perverted into Contention for superiority is but trepanning and deluding men into slavery; catching them with words and decoying them with nets and snares.'[41] Charles Leslie observed that 'This Publick Liberty is the word and cry of the party. But when you ask them what they mean by it, or where they would fix it? they cannot tell.'[42] Another Tory writer identified the Whigs' idols as the words 'liberty, property and life', and that whilst liberty rightly defined was good the Whigs meant by it only 'a licence to resist and depose their sovereign'. Such word-play was 'no new thing' for

> in the days of their ancestors in 41 and 48, the usurpers were call'd keepers of the liberties of their country! Perjury was call'd obeying of providence! A transformation of the Church into a Babel was call'd glorious reformation! The kingdom in a blaze, was call'd Gospel light! Extinguishing all remorse, compasion and good nature was call'd subduing of the passions! And then, as well as now, by the same Whiggism, to be independent of law and free form subjection to princes, when they fancy themselves griev'd, was, and is call'd Liberty![43]

The point here is that words were used in a deliberately dishonest way to mobilize and mislead an unthinking multitude. Thus a 1707 Tory tract suggested that 'liberty and property' was a phrase that 'deluded' the 'weaker sort of people' 'into a misunderstanding of their representatives' and into 'a disposition to tumults'. The 'design, by raising of dust, is to throw it in the peoples eyes, that they may not discern right from wrong' and hence allow

---

[39] Cf. South's 'magic' of words [p. 211].

[40] T. R., *A True Protestant Bridle* (1694), 13–14.

[41] *An Answer to Mr Stephens Sermon . . . Printed for the Use of the Cal Head Club, in Order to their Conversion* (1700), 8.

[42] Leslie, *The New Association, Part II* (1703), 27.

[43] W. Robertson, *The Liberty, Property and Religion of the Whigs* (1713), 4–6. Cf. T. Sprat, *A True Account and Declaration of the Horrid Conspiracy Against the Late King* (1685), 2–4.

The buzzwords of Liberty and Slavery were frequently deployed in polemic, though their meaning was disputed and to some extent contingent upon party allegiance. This image formed the frontispiece to *A Dialogue Betwixt Whig and Tory* (1710), which had already had three earlier editions. [Reproduced by courtesy of the Trustees of the British Museum.]

the Whigs to become 'by the help of a popular uproar, establish'd in a governing posture'.[44] The Whigs, it was alleged, sought to 'to stun the people's heads and confound their understandings, and by downright dint of impudence to make 'em believe contrary to their experience and their senses'.[45]

Yet anxiety about the abuse of words was shared by the Whigs, especially when trying to explain the rise of toryism in Anne's reign. One tract, for example, argued that the Tories had played with language even at her accession: 'the first thing we heard off [*sic*] was *retrieving* England's *honour*: a word meant for a reproach to the management under the late King'.[46] In the same speech Anne had promised support for 'those who were most zealous' for the church, a phrase which the high Tories construed as meaning 'the utter suppressing and extirpation of the Dissenters'. It was this 'zeal

[44] *True Picture of a Modern Whig Reviv'd*, 38–9, 43.
[45] J. Trapp, *Character and Principles*, 9–10.
[46] *A Supplement to the Faults on Both Sides: Containing the Compleat History of the Proceedings of a Party Ever Since the Revolution* (1710), 35.

for the church' that allowed Sacheverell to claim that 'he could not be a true son of the Church of England who did not lift up a banner or flag of defiance against the dissenters'. The high churchmen, the Whigs complained, had thus put 'the most wicked construction . . . upon Her Majesty's words MOST ZEALOUS'.[47] Yet in turn, when prosecuted, Sacheverell himself claimed that his words had been misconstrued by the low churchmen and Whigs. He told the House of Lords that 'it hath been my hard fortune to be misunderstood, at a time when I endeavour'd to express my self with the utmost plainness; even the defence I made at your Lordships bar, in hopes of clearing the innocence of my heart, hath been grievously misrepresented'.[48] He further complained that 'when my words were capable of two senses, the worst and most invidious, tho at the same time the most strain'd and unnatural construction, has been always made of them'. He had 'been accus'd of meaning the direct contrary to what' he said.[49] His lawyers exploited the doubts about authorial intention by suggesting that the meaning of his words was not as clear as the Whigs claimed.[50] The trial became an extended exercise in textual criticism, an investigation into whether the words actually printed or said constituted the slander and sedition that was claimed or whether there were not ways in which they could be understood far more innocently.

Tracts published during the jacobite unrest of 1714–16 sought to show how much of the dispute between the parties centred on words and their meanings. One Whig tract, for example, noted 'how far some terms of religious import have been perverted, to the breaking in upon the very boundaries of good and evil'. The weak people had, it alleged, been 'impos'd upon' and 'been made instruments of a great deal of mischief by being hurryed into false cries and misrepresentations of things'. The press and the pulpit thus bore the responsibility for misleading the people, because they misused words and slogans. Contention focused on abused words: 'People of late are very hot and contentious about things they seem to have no notion of, except in name . . . [they have been] set a madding about terms they have no meaning to'.[51] The 'silly multitude' had thus fallen prey to

---

[47] *A Supplement to the Faults on Both Sides*, 37–8. For the 1705 election Sir John Pakington had a banner made with the design of a church falling and the inscription 'For Queen and Church Pakington' (HMC Portland, iv. 189).

[48] *The Speech of Henry Sacheverell DD Upon his Impeachment . . . March 7, 1710* (1710), dedication to House of Lords.

[49] Ibid., 2.

[50] Holmes, *Trial*, ch. 8.

[51] *Reflections on the Management*, 1–2.

the notorious sophistry, and tricking way of writing, which some defenders of the High-Church notions make use of. They first get the reader as far from any settled meaning to the word *schism* as they can, and then come round upon him with some horrid crime they would have him think of the like nature; and awaken his apprehensions and even fears of damnation, at the thoughts of such guilt.[52]

As a result the people were 'strangely of late warped in their understandings'.[53]

The author thus discerned a struggle to capture the meanings of words. He condemned Tory polemicists for their 'misapplication of several hard words, with which they expect to amuse the weak and ignorant, and work them into such wicked purposes as they find it in their interest to prosecute'.[54] In language reminiscent of Locke, the author claimed that in counfounding terms men 'overturn, as far as in them lies, the very principles of knowledge'. And all this was part of a political design, 'a cover to some ill designs upon the publick good'.[55] Francis Atterbury's technique in this respect came in for criticism. He had referred to the execution of jacobites as 'violences and slaughter' and called those who disagreed with him 'the blood-thirsty, the political butchers, state chirurgeons and the like'. This was dismissed as an attempt to 'divert his readers' from the real meaning of words and hence from his sedition.[56]

The 'blind multitude', claimed another Whig writer, had been deluded by misleading phrases.[57] Another complained that whenever an 'honest, well-meaning people' were infatuated and misled it always

proceeded from some popular word, misunderstood by those who make the most use of it, and are most noisy in its defence. Anyone who has observed the rise and progress of certain words, put into the mouths of a deluded populace for these last ten years, will agree with me that this is that case at present.

The tract suggested that the current buzzword was 'mercy'. It had been

whined and canted in the pulpit, and been poured into half the tea and coffee that has been drunk for these two months throughout the whole nation. The word

[52] Ibid., 22–3. For the dispute over 'fanatic', see 29–30.
[53] Ibid., 24.
[54] Ibid., 33. The impact was deepened by the printer, who used 'frightful black characters' (43).
[55] Ibid., 47, 53.
[56] *Freeholder*, 31 commenting on Atterbury, *An Argument to Prove the Affections of the People of England to be the Best Security to the Government* (1716).
[57] Povey, *Inquiry into the Miscarriages*, 7.

itself conveys a very good idea but as it is used by the partizans, it seems the patron of all the vice, folly and nonsense that can be committed.[58]

By the time of the Hanoverian succession, therefore, the Whigs ascribed popular disaffection to the power of words to mislead the public. Both sides, ironically, recognized that a good deal of the partisan struggle involved disputing the meaning of key words and phrases.[59]

Contemporaries even listed them for us.[60] 'Monarchy, Prerogative, Liberty, Property, the Church, Popery and Fanaticism are words that in this kingdom enchant and enflame and almost bereave us of our senses', observed Charlwood Lawton.[61] John Toland agreed and capitalized the relevant words: 'MONARCHY therefore and a COMMONWEALTH, WHIGS and TORIES, HIGH and LOW-CHURCHMEN, FORSWEARERS and NON-SWEARERS, TOLERATION, NATURALIZATION, the BALANCE OF EUROPE, the DANGER OF THE CHURCH but (above all things) the word CHURCH it self.'[62] As the marquis of Halifax observed, 'the world hath of late years never been without some extraordinary word to furnish the coffee-houses and fill the pamphlets. Sometimes it is a new one invented and sometimes an old one revived.'[63] Indeed, pamphleteering was often a case of associating a jumble of these pejorative or contested terms. Thus, as one writer put it,

Let but any one take a few rattling words for his materials, such as schismatic, atheist, rebels, traitors, miscreants, monsters, enthusiasts, hypocrites; Lord's anointed, sacred majesty, God's vicegerent; impious, blasphemers, damnation; stir these together in a warm head and after a little shaking, bring them out, scum and all, distribute them into several periods and your work is half done.[64]

Another word (and concept) redefined under the pressure of party politics was 'English', which became particularly charged in 1702, after Queen Anne described her heart as 'entirely English'. Deemed to be a reflection on the Dutch William, and hence on the Revolution, the word was taken up by high church Tories. One election tract listed all the types of dissembling Whig imaginable, but ended with the claim that a Tory was 'the reverse, or the character of a true Englishman', who could be trusted for 'the integrity

---

[58] [Defoe?], *The Mercy of the Government Vindicated* (1716), 4–5.
[59] The *Spectator* often did this (M. Ketcham, *Transparent Designs: Reading, Performance and Form in the Spectator Papers* (Athens, Ga., 1985), 133–4).
[60] Some are explored in Ashcraft, 'Language of Political Conflict'.
[61] Lawton, *A Second Letter Concerning Civil Comprehension* (1706), 3.
[62] Toland, *State-Anatomy*, preface.
[63] *Works of Halifax*, 104.
[64] T. Bradbury, *The Lawfulness of Resisting Tyrants*, 2nd edn., (1714), preface.

and truth of his words'.[65] Partisans thus competed to claim Englishness
and appropriate the label 'patriot'. John Dennis thus praised the electorate
for knowing that 'he is most an Englishman who does most for England's
happiness; and who prefers a foreigner that endeavours to support it,
before an Englishman that attempts to enslave it; and esteems one who was
born a Dutchman, or perhaps a German, but is become an Englishman,
before one who was born indeed an Englishman, but is become an errant
Frenchman'.[66] For him, an Englishman was obviously a Whig and Englishness something politically defined.

Such keywords and slogans were, as this suggests, particularly useful in
electioneering. 'Papist' and 'courtier' were frequently invoked in order to
besmirch a candidate. As one tract observed, 'there hath scarce been an
election of the new Parliament, where any ancient royalist was a competitor, but that some rascall would brand him with the title of masked papist
or courtier; which is now a character almost as obnoxious to the rebellious
commonalty as the former, a resemblance too much of the late rebellion'.[67]
Although this 'cant' was becoming a little 'threadbare' from overuse by the
end of Anne's reign—by 1701, it was claimed, the spread of atheism and toleration had weakened the impact of religious slogans, which had been
replaced by commercial 'cant', such as 'trade' and 'public credit'[68]—the
language of popery and arbitrary government was still an effective tool
against the Tories.[69] Popery, in particular, was a word that put a 'blind' on
the people and hampered their ability to judge.[70] Swift similarly observed
in 1710 that 'the word Pretender is a term of art' used by the Whigs to castigate anything they disliked.[71] The high churchmen also felt that 'Tacker'
was another label deliberately coined to destroy their credit.[72] On the other

[65] *Character of a Whig*, 122–3.
[66] *The Danger of Priestcraft* (1702), 3–4. Roger Morrice referred to the Whigs as the 'English party' or those of the 'English interest' in the Commons throughout 1689 (Dr Williams Library, Entring Book, MS Q 495, 547, 552, 579; see also 535, 590 for 'the anti-English party' as the Tories).
[67] W. L., *A Letter from an Impartial Hater of the Papists* [1680], 1. Cf. J. Nalson, *The Complaint of Liberty and Property against Arbitrary Government* (1681), 1.
[68] A. Hammond, *Considerations Upon Corrupt Elections of Members of Parliament* (1701), 7. Cf. 'Trade is as Good a Cry as Church the latter being, as it is secur'd, beyond all possibility of danger' (*Remarks on a Scandalous Libel*, 20).
[69] *Post Boy*, 1802; S. Tufton, *The History of Faction, alias Hypocrisy, alias Moderation* (1705), 171–2.
[70] L'Estrange, *Remarks on the Growth and Progress of Non-Conformity* (1682), 19.
[71] *Examiner*, 15. In 1705 the Commons had tried to forbid such sloganizing as prejudicial to free elections (*CJ*, xiv. 557).
[72] John Dyer maintained, however, that Tacker was a word which 'the phanaticks thought to have made a bugbear amongst the freeholders and other electors, [but] proves in most

The Modern Champions (1710) shows Sacheverell, fictionalized as 'Jehu Hotspur', and Hoadly, as 'Balthazar Turn-Coat', fighting each other with slogans. Hotspur had a cloak of hypocrisy and fought, as the accompanying text made clear, with accusations of 'tolleration', 'rebellion', 'moderation', 'regicide', and 'anarchy'. Balthazar fought back with 'non-resistance', 'passive obedience', 'superstition', 'jacobitism', 'tyranny', and 'persecution'. At about this time the third earl of Shaftesbury wrote: 'Every one takes party and encourages his own side "this shall be my champion!"' The image, like others reproduced in this book, carries Luttrell's annotations. [Reproduced by courtesy of the Houghton Library, Harvard University.]

side, 'dissent' was a bugbear word, used to smear the Whigs. Henry Care said that the penal laws had given 'every ill-natur'd man an opportunity to stigmatise any of his neighbours with some nick-name of religion, as a phanatick, a papist, a presbyterian, an anabaptist, a Whigg or the like; and by that means presently ruine his reputation, trade, employment, estate or person'. He urged men to restore amity to a nation 'that had almost banisht all civil conversation'.[73]

Religious labels as party tools

Contemporaries sensed that religious labels were being invoked in a struggle for power. Just as the high churchmen believed 'popery' was being used

places a badge of honour, that recommends those gentlemen to them' (*A Collection from Dyer's Letters*, 9–10).

[73] Care, *Draconica; or, An Abstract of all the Penal Laws*, 2nd edn., (1688), 33.

to undermine them, so the Whigs resented the politicized slogan of 'the Church in danger'. 'This danger of the church seems to be a mere bug-bear; that is trumped up only to justle some out and thrust others into the great posts and offices both of church and state', remarked one tract.[74] *The Church Not in Danger* (1707) agreed that the slogan was used by the 'self-designing sophister' who 'prostituted the venerable name of the church to the service of a party' and used an 'equivocating sort of cant . . . to obscure his sordid design of calumniating the Queen and the estates of the realm'.[75] These disputes were significant, because it was intrinsic to the Whig argument that the high church Tories invoked religious labels in order to maintain secular power. John Dennis claimed that 'priestcraft' was 'an art by which designing men, in order to their own advantage, make that pass for religion upon the unthinking part of the world, that is neither dictated by the law of the nature nor included in the written religion of the country'.[76] High church Tories, it was claimed, thus defined religion incorrectly in order to advance their power. Dennis therefore sought to redefine religion in terms of private faith.[77] Another Whig pamphleteer similarly believed the Whigs had been 'too long and too artfully represented and mis-represented' as enemies to the church.[78] The accusations of 'priestcraft' thus reflected a growing sense that religious discourse was being used as a political tool. Richard Steele, addressing the clergy in 1714 in a tract called *The Crisis*, observed that 'all the dissatisfactions which have been raised in the minds of the people owe their rise to the cunning of artful men' who used the church 'to cover and sanctify their own practices upon the affections of the people, for ends very different from the promotion of religion and virtue'. Such misrepresentation threatened the 'crisis' of the pam-

---

[74] Swynfen, *Objections*, 23. cf. *The Church Not in Danger* (1707); [Defoe?], *An Humble Address to our Sovereign Lords the People* (1715), 7; *The Danger of the Church Enquir'd Into* (1710), 7.

[75] *Church not in Danger*, 4–5. Cf. *A Smith and Cutlers Plain Dialogue about Whig and Tory* (1690), 1–2.

[76] *Danger of Priestcraft*, 6.

[77] Cf. *A Letter to a Conscientious Man* (1720), 6.

[78] *The Whigs Warning-Piece, as Drawn from the Late Picture of a Modern Whig* [1701?], 4. For the deployment of the 'church in danger' as an electioneering slogan, see *Naked Truth; or, Phanaticism Detected. Recommended to the Serious Consideration of all True Protestants, Particularly to the Electors of Members to Serve in the Ensuing Parliament* (1705); *A Word of Advice*. One Whig observed 'It is impossible to imagine what an influence the crying the church in danger has among the vulgar in this county' even though the high churchmen 'never go to church, but for the most part atheists and libertines' (Lincs. RO, Monson MSS 7/13/124, Gervase Scrope to Sir John Newton, 1 July 1710). When Sarah Cowper saw voters coming from the 1713 Hertfordshire election 'Bawling forth High: Church huzza', she noted 'Oh monsters! Why shou'd any be concern'd for what may became of such profane miscreants who triffle thus with religious matters?' (Herts. RO, MSS D/EP F34, 282).

phlet's title. Under the veil of such hypocrisy, 'the laws of our country, the powers of the legislature, the faith of nations, and the honour of God may be too weak considerations to bear up against the popular though groundless cry of the Church'.[79] The language of religion was thus being used for political ends.

The Tory, claimed the Whigs, deliberately used words to pervert right judgement, 'making use of the Church as if it were a word only and the laws as if they knew not the right use of a word in them'.[80] Indeed, the Tory had 'got a new English Dictionary' by which he had

the assurance to address and make speeches, clamour and dispute, in the most contradicting, impertinent and treasonable terms, without being either understood or censur'd. His argument is maintain'd by his bullying noise, unparallel'd impudence and in an abominable jargon of hard words, with which he amazes and deludes the ignorant, and confounds the understandings of the wise. Talk soberly of religion and he slaps you over the face with heresy, schism, fanaticism, and faction and calls you confounded Whigg, and so you are confuted. Urge never so modestly legal fundamental rights and mention irregularities, and the privileges and authority of British Parliaments, and he cries out faction, disloyalty, you ruin the kingdom, arraign the government, distrust the Q[ueen] &c.[81]

A low church cleric, Robert Lumley Lloyd, preached a sermon in which he warned that the 'poor unthinking vulgar have been spirited up into a dangerous rebellion, with these monstrous unintelligible watch-words put into their mouths, namely, high church, or low church.[82]

'Moderation' was another keyword linked to religious disputes which appeared to be invoked for particular, political ends.[83] The high churchmen thought moderation meant 'nothing but lukewarmness in religion' and indifference to the church, and that it was used to undermine their grip on power in the early and late years of Anne.[84] Again, then, contemporaries recognized the artifice of words. *The Moderation, Justice and*

---

[79] *The Crisis, or, A Discourse Representing, from the Most Authentick Records, the Just Causes of the Late Happy Revolution* (1714), preface.

[80] *The Character of a Modern Tory* (1713), 14.

[81] Ibid., 19–20.

[82] For defining high church as 'a rebellious, discontented factious party, utter enemies to our Queen and the present constitution', Lloyd was 'pelted and libell'd, paper without end' (Kennett, *Wisdom of Looking Backwards*, 153–4). But for a discussion of the low church label, and a rejection of it as a short hand for Whig, see R. Warner, 'Early C18th Low Churchmanship: The Glorious Revolution to the Bangorian Controversy', Ph.D., Reading (1999).

[83] For an extended discussion of this point, see M. Knights, 'Occasional Conformity and the Representation of Dissent: Hypocrisy, Sincerity, Moderation and Zeal', in D. Wykes (ed.), *Parliament and Dissent* (forthcoming).

[84] *The Memorial of the Church of England* (1705), 27.

Manners of the Review censured Defoe's 'sophistical way of writing' which had 'seduced' some and accused him of abusing the nation 'with pretensions of peace and moderation whilst nothing less was at his heart'.[85] One could not take religious labels at face value, it was being suggested, because they were being used to hide private and group interests. They were a pretence under which to hide rather sinister political ambition. As Edmund Hickeringill, rector of Colchester, put it, 'if dismal and bloody villainies be commonly varnish'd with religion, then this may inform us, that the most plausible pretexts of religion are always suspicious, since so seldom sincere'. Thus 'Politicians that plot rebellion, and mutiny, do but give out a religious watch-word, and the people straight give the word about and are up in arms for God and his cause'.[86] Taking religious discourse at face value, it is suggested, misled contemporaries; and it may also mislead historians into under-estimating the politics behind 'a religious watch-word'.

The problem of party identities and their labels

Party labels were thus dangerous representations and fictions. A good deal of partisan polemic was aimed at constructing such representations or challenging the 'fictions' created by rivals. The identities of the parties were thus the product both of the protagonists and of their antagonists, who were locked in a battle of redefining each other. Thus, while much of the historiographical debate over parties has centred on the question of whether or not they existed, it might be more helpful to examine the ways in which allegiance to them involved identification with a rhetorical construct. Just as with national identity, so political, religious, and social identities were also 'imagined' and constructed by their antipathy to an 'other'. As Swift observed, a 'Whig forms an image of a Tory, just after the thing he most abhors, and that image serves to represent the whole body'.[87] Difference gave meaning; and stereotypes helped to create political fictions.[88]

This process was not new; but the labels used to describe the parties, and the ways in which those labels represented stereotypes, nevertheless acquired a novel importance because, certainly by Anne's reign, the labels were themselves a guide to voters and readers. As one tract put it, 'the general method of enquiry about members for parliament is whether they are

---

[85]   *The Moderation, Justice and Manners of the Review* (1706), 3.

[86]   *A Sermon Preach'd on the 30th of January* (1700), 14, 18.

[87]   *Examiner*, 34. Cf. The Tory was 'in many ways the reverse of' the Whig (*A Letter to the Gentlemen and Freeholders of the County of Dorset* (1713), 29).

[88]   See also Ch. 5, nn. 78–81.

Whigs or Tories'.[89] Indeed, 'in every county or borough, where there is an opposition, the competitors will be generally distinguish'd and known to you all by the two names beforementioned'.[90] Thus, if the representation of the parties was misleading and fictional, this had potentially devastating consequences for the nature of political choice. The very names of the parties were thus important in helping men to decide how to vote. As one pamphleteer complained, men had found an easier way of 'judging the worth and character of men' than by evaluating their principles and actions. This was 'by marks or names, which immediately by one stroke upon the eye or the ear, convey the whole knowledge of a man to you as perfectly as if you had been acquainted with him from his cradle'. The labels Whig and Tory were thus set up 'as the Tower-mark to warrant the value and weight of all the current men in the kingdom; so that every man now passes or is cry'd down in the country, is receiv'd or rejected above; according as he is tender'd under one of these names'.[91] Yet such labels could lead to error in the voters' choice, if the word did not match the 'thing'. The marquis of Halifax saw this danger:

Amongst all the engines of dissention, there hath been none more powerful in all times, than the fixing names upon one another of contumely and reproach, and the reason is plain, in respect of the people, who tho generally they are uncapable of making a syllogism or forming an argument, yet they can pronounce a word; and that serveth their turn to throw it with all their dull malice at the head of those they do not like; such things ever begin in jest, and end in blood.[92]

In very similar words secretary of state William Trumbull observed that 'distinctions by names' were dangerous, 'used only to please the ill-judging mob who love words of reproach beginning often in jest but too often ending in violence and confusion'.[93] Taxonomy was intrinsic to the political contest.

The problems inherent in the names of Whig and Tory struck that acute observer of British politics, du Rapin Thoyras, who sought to explain the terms to both a foreign and an English audience at the end of our period. Rapin thought that 'many are Whigs or Tories, without having a clear no-

---

[89] *A Letter to the Gentlemen and Freeholders of the County of Dorset*, 28; cf. *A View of the Present Divisions in Great Britain, by the Leaders of the Parties, which May Encourage a French Invasion* (1708), 3.
[90] *Advice to the Electors of Members for the Ensuing Parliament of Great Britain* (1708), 2.
[91] *Danger of Moderation*, 4, 6.
[92] *Works of Halifax*, 47–8.
[93] BL, Add. MSS 72,510 f. 82–83v, Trumbull to Anne Delaune, on verso of letter from Delaune, 13 May 1711.

tion of the party they have embrac'd'.[94] The labels were, he thought, 'very obscure, and equivocal terms, because they do, or at least ought to carry along with them many different ideas, according to the occasion upon which it is used'. Thus 'the names Whig and Tory inspire certain confused ideas, which few people are able rightly to disentangle'.[95] And this confusion gave opportunities for a partisan 'to blacken his adversary with the most odious faults any of the same party are guilty of'.[96] The uncertainty and changeability of the meaning of party labels was, however, noted by many others before him. The high churchman Joseph Trapp observed that 'the word Whig, indeed, like all other words that have been long in use, has run thro various significations'.[97] So too 'Tory' according to a Whig critic. That party had, allegedly, 'renounced their former Tory principles, even so far as to run into the other extreme, and that instead of submitting all things to royal will and pleasure they are now for depressing the prerogative and exalting the power of the Commons'. 'A Tory's acting like a commonwealthsman' was to be suspected as insincere. Indeed, they would repeal the triennial act 'tomorrow' if they had power.[98]

The shift in the idea of Whig and Tory, discerned by this pamphleteer, has been echoed in modern accounts of party realignments. The Whigs, historians agree, divided into 'old Whigs', who maintained a suspicion of the executive powers of the crown, and 'new' or 'modern Whigs', who sought to reconcile revolution principles to their support for royal powers. Similarly, a new Tory party emerged after the Revolution, the fusion of churchmen with those whose country mentality meant that Whig corruption in office was too much to swallow. Yet these shifts caused problems for contemporaries, for the same words, Whig and Tory, continued to be used to describe groups that had shifted meaning. Unless carefully defined, there was a strong danger that word and idea could become divorced and lead to error.

The idea that the party labels had indeed become an unsound guide to public judgement was probed extensively in a controversy in 1710. *Faults on Both Sides* claimed that the parties had shifted their identities, so that their original labels were no longer an accurate reflection of the men they described. Thus the court Whigs, by their sacrifice of the public for private advantage, had 'in their actions really turn'd Tories, though they still

---

[94] R. de Thoyras, *The History of Whig and Tory from the Conquest to the Present Time* (1723), v. The work was written in Feb. 1716.
[95] Ibid., 57–8.   [96] Ibid., 59.
[97] Trapp, *Character and Principles*, 3.
[98] *Candidates Try'd*, 2–3.

affected to be counted as good Whigs as ever'. And, it was alleged, many 'Tories themselves became Whigs in practice', joining with 'old staunch Whigs' who had never abandoned their principles.[99] In a similar vein, Hoadly argued that the Tories had abandoned their principles of passive obedience and thus were no longer really Tories.[100] In other words, the public should not rely on party names as accurate guides of what the parties stood for.[101] But of course they *were* relied on and the role of much of the electoral advice literature was to define what each party label meant. Since 'the whole kingdom is divided into Whig and Tory and ever was and will be distinguished by that which these names do signifie, it concerns us to understand them, that we undo not ourselves by following the wrong side in our votes or otherwise'.[102]

Distinguishing what the parties really stood for from the fictional depictions of them was difficult, for even those who claimed to offer impartial assessments proved disingenuous. In January 1713, for example, a new periodical, the *Britain*, seemed to want to reconcile the parties, believing that 'the differences between the honest men of either party are not founded on essentials but merely on opinion'.[103] Thus, it was claimed, 'the difference is in the main more in words than things'.[104] Yet this pose of impartiality and reconciliation was in fact a veneer to woo the reader. As early as the fourth issue Narcissus Luttrell detected its partisan bent, dismissing it as 'a silly Whig paper'.[105] Indeed, its author may have been John Oldmixon, who had assisted Arthur Maynwaring in writing down the Tory *Examiner*.[106] The guise of impartiality could thus itself be a partisan fiction.

The meaning, or even existence, of Whig and Tory is evidently crucial to understanding the politics of the period; yet the names used by historians for historical analysis were also used by contemporaries as part of the political game. Sir John Plumb claimed that the contours of the two parties were always apparent to contemporaries. Unlike historians, he suggested,

[99] *Somers Tracts*, 4th collection, iii. 304–5.   [100] Ibid., 285.
[101] Alternatively, it might be polemically important to contend that the meaning of the labels had *not* changed. See *Advice to the Electors*, 1.
[102] *Smith and Cutler's Plain Dialogue*, 1. Luttrell noted it to be 'a Whigg thing exposing ye Tories & applauding ye Whiggs as ye only good persons' (BL, Cup 407.ee.15, film of copy in the Newberry Library, Chicago).
[103] *The Britain*, 1.
[104] Ibid., 19. Cf. *The Necessity of Peace and Union Among Members of the Church of England, Proving that the Names of Whig and Tory are Mischievous and Unreasonable* (1715), 4–6, 17–18.
[105] Endorsement on *The Britain*, 4 [Burney].
[106] *The Britain*, 12, defended Maynwaring.

who are often bewildered by the complexities of party politics, 'contemporaries were less distracted and they rarely had difficulty, at least after the middle 1690s, in distinguishing Whig from Tory'.[107] This is true in the sense that for most of the period contemporaries did discern a bipartisan struggle. But it obscures a contest that permeated the printed polemic of the period about what precisely Whig and Tory meant. In other words, the identity of Whig and Tory can be confusing to students of the period precisely *because* the labels Whig and Tory were themselves contested terms with fluid meanings. Political identities were thus representations that needed to be created through contests over names and labels; and they were shifting. Indeed, many contemporaries worried that they were fighting about Whig and Tory when they had lost sight of what those terms meant.

Cant and the secret meanings of words

One of the effects, then, of the polemic and adversarial contest was to create partisan languages whose meanings were only partially shared; and to create disputes over labels and keywords. The result was that partisan meanings and language created an obscurity intended to promote a party rather than the national interest. One Tory complained that all his rival's 'discourses are obscure and enigmatical, like the Devils in the Delphic Oracle; you may understand his words but never reach his meaning. The corruption of reason was the generation of his wits, and the spirit of lying and slandering is the height of his improvement'. The Whig, it was said, had a passion for 'confounded jargon, Billingsgate rhetorick' and his 'words are Hebrew characters; if he says he will do anything for you, tis as much as if he had sworn he would not, and you must always spell him backwards before you can read him'. [108] The Whigs supposed that 'the nation, by fine words, may be led about, as the bears are by the fiddle'.[109] They were double-dealers 'who paint their faces like Jezebel, and peep into the world with the outside varnish of *liberty, toleration, moderation, self-preservation* and such like insinuating and deluding cant'.[110] Publicly competitive politics threatened to overwhelm society with a flood of hypocritical cant.

---

[107] Plumb, *Growth*, 130.
[108] *Character of a Whig*, 3–4, 22, 30.
[109] *True Picture of a Modern Whig Reviv'd*, 36.
[110] H. Pugh, *The True Nature of Religious Zeal* (1710), 22. Pugh was deeply concerned about hypocrisy (9, 18).

Party produced a pressure, akin to that of casuistry, by which the meaning of words and terms became subject to specialized and even private meanings. Just as economic plurality and diversity were reflected in the proliferation of terms to describe the specialization of the economy,[111] so religious and political plurality led, it was believed, to the development of specialized languages. The fear of the dissolution of a shared language was already apparent by the restoration.[112] But the number of politically and religiously inspired plots during the Restoration period increased anxiety about the prevalence of 'cant'—language that dissimulated its real meaning and was only readable by those who knew its code. Cant allowed designing politicians to disguise their sedition.[113]

Thomas Sprat, who had urged the use of plain language in his *History of the Royal Society*, wrote an account of the 1683 Rye House Plot in which he stressed the cant used to disguise the activities of the plotters, in both their verbal and written exchanges.[114] As one of the plotters confessed, 'things were expressed under new words', thereby creating 'a new language'; extra words, without 'sense', were inserted between 'real' words, so that the 'method of reading became the more mysterious and intricate'.[115] Seditious cant adapted the jargon of the merchant, the lawyer or the medic. After 1689 the plotters were jacobite rather than Whig, but the cant was the same. In 1696 Thomas Percival even satirized Sprat by producing a parallel history of the plot to assassinate William and a parallel focus on jacobites' cant: 'the king was sometimes call'd the Spark . . . the little gentleman &c . . . the insurrection was stil'd *the general point*, the assassination *the taking off the spark* and *striking at the head*.'[116] The jacobites were thus alleged to work under a 'passive cant of non-resistance' to levy war, just as Sprat had claimed the radical Whigs had done.[117]

---

[111]   T. Blount, *Glossographia* (1670), To the Reader.

[112]   For secret languages, see L. Potter, *Secret Rites and Secret Writing: Royalist Literature 1641–60* (Cambridge, 1989); Achinstein, 'Politics of Babel'; Smith, *Literature and Revolution*, 26. See also Hobbes, *Leviathan*, chs. 4, 24, and 31.

[113]   L'Estrange even claimed that publishers used cant to describe the print they produced (*Considerations and Proposals* (1663), 6).

[114]   Sprat, *True Account*, 40 and appendix, 7. For a discussion of plotting cant see Ashcraft, *Revolutionary Politics*, 383–9.

[115]   Sir G. McKenzie, *A True and Plain Account of the Discoveries Made in Scotland, of the Late Conspiracies against His Majesty and the Government* (1685), 18. See also, Sprat, *Copies of the Informations and Original Papers Relating to the Proof of the Horrid Conspiracy* (1685), 23, 77, 93.

[116]   T. Percival, *The Rye House Travestie* (1696), 28, paralleling Sprat, *History*, 53. For jacobite use of the same terminology, see Dr Williams Library, Morrice Entring Book, Q276.

[117]   *The True Patriot's Speech to the People of Rome Answer'd Paragraph by Paragraph* (1708), 2.

Swift's fears about private, partisan, languages are well known.[118] But his anxiety was widely shared. The world seemed upside down, claimed one tract sympathetic to dissent, because people misapplied meanings: 'behold on the one hand vertue termed vice, sobriety debauchery, religion faction, pious and peaceable assemblies riots and routs and punished as such'.[119] In other words, the partisan definitions of words and phrases could create private languages. Dissenting ministers were thought to specialize in such double-speak, preaching 'in words metaphorical and ambiguous and . . . obscurely in phrases and odd schemes of speech, not understood and scarce intelligible'. They 'preached not Christ but their own dreams'.[120] *A New Dictionary . . . of the Canting Crew* (1699) thus sought, in part, to explain the dialect of dissenters 'who affect a disguised speech and disguised modes of speaking . . . as gypsies and beggars have their peculiar jargon'.[121] Party, too, created such cant. Defoe thus wrote *An Essay at a Plain Exposition of that Difficult Phrase a Good Peace* (1711), in which he noted that the 'various constructions' put on the phrase 'a good peace' varied 'as interest, party and opinion leads them'.[122] In turn, such cant helped to *create* party allegiance. As one critic of a clerical address put it, talking to the people in 'a language in which the sense of words is perverted' and words understood in one sense nevertheless 'made to speak another sense and to signifie the direct contrary . . . serv'd not only to *distinguish* but even to *form* and *make* parties'.[123]

Party conferred different meanings on the same words and thus created not just sectional but also competing languages. Swift admitted that when discussing hereditary right, for example, 'both parties are apt to be a little dubious in some of their terms, and (as modern philosophers) express it, fix different ideas to the same words'.[124] If readers and hence the public authorized meaning, as they did in publicly contested adversarial politics, then fixing the meaning of words became extremely difficult. Defoe nevertheless insisted that words should be intelligible to readers, with common and shared senses, otherwise 'a man may speak

---

[118] Eilon, *Faction's Fictions*; *Examiner*, 16.
[119] *The Second Part of the People's Antient and Just Liberties Asserted* (1670), 4. The difference over the word 'riot' was particularly important, since it was the basis for legal prosecution of religious conventicles in the 1680s—see T. Ellwood, *A Discourse Concerning Riots* (1683).
[120] J. Glanvill, *A Seasonable Defence of Preaching* (1703), 41, 78.
[121] Entry for 'Canting-Crew'.   [122] *Essay*, 12.
[123] Swynfen, *Objections*, 3–4, 10.
[124] Eilon, *Faction's Fictions*, 69, citing *Discourse on Hereditary Right* (written 1712, published 1775), 1–2.

in words, but [be] perfectly unintelligible as to meaning; he may talk a great deal but say nothing.'[125] It was in part to avoid this abuse of words that he and others made proposals for a formal academy to stabilize language.[126]

The art of political lying

> Almost every age hath been remarkably infamous for
> some prevailing iniquity more than other; and how
> justly this we live in may be call'd by way of eminence,
> the Lying age, you all, I presume, very well know.[127]

Cant imperilled a common language; but political lying was an even more sinister threat, threatening to destroy 'the use of talking'.[128] Lying was thought to be intrinsic to partisan politics. In the *Art of Political Lying* (1712) John Arbuthnot referred to the common practice of 'spreading and propagating' lies.[129] He drew up a mock prospectus for a book, in which he depicted politics as 'an elaborate and endless glass-bead game of lies'.[130] He defined political lying to be 'the art of convincing the people of salutary falsehoods for some good end . . . [but] by good he does not mean that which is absolutely so, but what appears so to the artist'.[131] The people, his text satirically asserted, had no right to political truth but possessed a right to invent and spread lies, which was often the only way to pull down governments that they were weary of.[132] Arbuthnot found both political parties guilty of lying and employing others to lie for them. Conal Condren speculates that the overflow of printed information, together with the apparent dishonesty of international diplomacy, may have led not to certainty but to an impression that lying was endemic.[133] But this impression was also the inevitable consequence of party politics.

Of course, political lying was not new and Nigel Smith has shown that

---

[125] *Essays Upon Several Projects* (1702), 37.

[126] Sprat, *History of the Royal Society*, 42–4; Swift, *A Proposal for Correcting, Improving and Ascertaining the English Tongue* (1712); Oldmixon, *The British Academy: Being a New-Erected Society for the Advancement of Wit and Learning: With Some Few Observations Upon it* (1712).

[127] R. L. Lloyd, *A Sermon Preach'd at St. Paul's Covent-Garden, on the 30th of January, 1711* (1712), 6. For other remarks by Lloyd about lying, see Kennett, *Wisdom*, 258–9.

[128] *Works of Halifax*, 253.

[129] Condren, *Satire, Lies and Politics*, 179.

[130] Ibid., 123.   [131] Ibid., 178–81.

[132] Ibid., 178–9.   [133] Ibid., 125–6.

the association of lying and print was made in the 1640s when the freedom of the press 'radically destabilised conceptions of truth, trustworthiness and authority'.[134] Indeed, the art of lying needs to be set against the much longer preoccupation with casuistry and dissimulation outlined earlier. What, then, was different about the later Stuart period to justify the quotation at the head of this section which asserted the age to be characterized by lying? Lying, dissimulation, and disguise had generally been applied to matters arising out of religious controversy or where religious oaths had been invoked to support civil measures; but in the later Stuart period, they came to be considered inseparable from publicly competitive politics. We have already seen how words could be made to mislead and how meanings became unstable under the pressure of a partisan political culture. More than that, however, each side believed the other to be guilty of systematic and intentional lying, dissimulation, and disguise. Misrepresentation, it was feared, had become central to the way that the political system worked and exacerbated longer term fears of conspiracy, hypocrisy, and insincerity.

In the previous chapter we encountered Thomas Rawlins lamenting the abusive nature of public discourse, especially at election time. At the heart of his critique lay a concern with lying. Rawlins complained that 'never in any place or time did the spirit of lying become so daring and impudent, as it has of late among us; it appears openly, without veil or masque, and flies in the face of our superiors at noon-day, without fear or shame, at least without fear of punishment'.[135] Another cleric, John Edwards (significantly the son of Thomas 'Gangraena' Edwards, who had seen dissimulation as a characteristic of mid-century sectarianism), agreed. 'I know of no vice in the whole list of immorality that is less excus'd or spar'd throughout the sacred pages than this of lying' but none the less, he lamented, it was a common practice and lying touched 'the tongue and head and heart of a politician'.[136] Edwards highlighted the perception that lying and dissimulation were embedded in partisan public discourse. At first addressing his remarks about religious controversy, he observed that 'we live in a dark world and are misled into wrong conceptions of things because the ignorant and insane have here the majority of votes'.[137] This was important because he felt that men were incapable of discerning error:

---

[134] *Literature and Revolution*, 28, 358.
[135] *Truth and Sincerity*, 18–19.
[136] Edwards, *Some New Discoveries of the Uncertainty, Deficiency and Corruptions of Human Knowledge and Learning* (1714), 66, cf. 150–2.
[137] Ibid., 1.

'the right conception of things are very scarce and opinion and conjecture are in their place and consequently error is entailed on mankind'.[138] Error was prevalent because lying, and hence uncertainty, was everywhere, not just in the religious sphere. Thus 'we might make the like reflections of un-certainty on Politicks, which are admired by some as a more exalted degree of knowledge. But if we could look into the springs and engines that set the heads of the greatest politico's on work, we should find that imagi-nation, conjectures and suppositions have the greatest ascendant over these men.'[139]

Edwards admitted that 'it is a hard task to be a politician, because so vast a stock of knowledge, judgment and experience is required to it' and the modern world was full of 'unexpected revolutions, new and uncommon springs of war and peace'. The modern politician, he felt, lacked a guide from history, for the classics were

not sufficient to direct us at this day when there are such projects and attempts as no history relates, no former annals ever acquainted us with. There are no certain rules in policy now; for from what hath been, we cannot tell what shall be; because there are new scenes and variety of changes continually starting up in all parts of the world.[140]

The result was

a great deal of legerdemain, trick and artifice; between which and true wisdom there is as wide a difference as between stock-jobbing and fair-trading. The chiefest art of state hath been generally to dissemble. The great mystery of it is to keep the ignorant and vulgar (who are always the most) in false apprehensions of what is to be done and never to let them know the true measure of things. This in plain Eng-lish is politic lying . . . the study hath been to appease the people, not to make them happy. I appeal to impartial minds, whether in such politicks there be any thing solid and certain, any thing to be depended upon.[141]

Dissimulation, tricks, lying were thus deliberate means to delude the people. The result was a political culture in which nothing was certain.[142]

Lying, then, was perceived to be all-pervasive, and responsible for much of the division and rage of party. Each party accused the other of lying, for neither side saw the other as putting forward honest differences of opin-ion—or at least *represented* the other party as acting dishonestly. Party

---

[138] Edwards, *Some New Discoveries*, 4.   [139] Ibid., 62.
[140] Ibid., 63.   [141] Ibid., 64.
[142] For the resulting riddles of policy, see Trapp, *The Age of Riddles; or, A True List of Cer-tain Extraordinary Positions, Formerly Call'd Contradictions, but now Distinguish'd by No Name at All* (1710).

thus spread distrust of politicians. And those who claimed to be aloof from party saw a conspiracy of lies from both bodies. We might apply this set of anxieties to the problems of 1701 to show how far they penetrated political debate. The Tory charge against the Whig junto in that year was that they deliberately manufactured a dispute between the 'people' and their representatives in parliament by falsely suggesting that the people had a right to compel their MPs. So Tory critics of the infamous 'Legion Memorial' saw it as a 'meer piece of forgery', the natural outcome of a party dedicated not to 'honesty and truth', as Legion claimed, but to lying (Legion, after all, was the biblical devil who tried to 'misrepresent actions and be a false accuser').[143] 'To hear a modern Whig talk of truth is as ridiculous as to hear your physician say he is glad to see you in health', quipped another tract.[144] And the Whig rumour-monger John Freke was made to say (in a *fake* printed letter!) that 'a malicious lye is more heeded and propagated than any true vindication'.[145] In 1702 Charles Davenant, who had helped to pen Freke's bogus letter and was therefore well-placed to know, complained that 'a lye shall reach to forty thousand persons, of which not the twentieth part come in a long time to be put right'.[146]

Whig lying again headed Tory concerns in 1710. One pamphlet, for example, attacked Whig scribblers for 'breaking down the fences of truth, government and religion and treating their illiterate, impatient and undistinguishing readers with malicious suggestions and fictitious accusations'.[147] Swift, too, alleged that the art of political lying had been 'cultivated these twenty years past' and was now applied 'to the gaining of power and preserving it, as well as revenging themselves after they have lost it'. A political lie was, he said, 'sometimes born out of a discarded statesman's head, and thence delivered to be nursed and dandled by the Rabble. Sometimes it is produced a monster and licked into shape; at other times it comes into the world completely formed and is spoiled by the licking'. But whatever its form, the political lie had, he said, been 'the Guardian

---

[143] *England's Enemies Expos'd*, 26, 28–30.
[144] *History of the Kentish Petition, Answer'd*, 7.
[145] Davenant (with Harley), *A Letter from the Grecian Coffee House* (1701), 6.
[146] *Tom Double*, 13. Cf. *Examiner*, 15. 'There is not a place in the world so fruitful in lying stories as London, and, though the falseness of these stories is usually within two or three days laid open to the world, yet the people are ready to receive new ones, and to believe them till they also are detected' (*Letters Addressed to . . . Williamson*, i. 133). Sir Thomas Burnet thought ' 'tis very easie in a sheet to contain more plausible falsehoods than shall be answer'd in twenty, and whilst the sheet comes to every one's hands, the answer can neither be bought nor read by half the people whom those lies deceiv'd' (*The True Character of an Honest Man Particularly with Relation to the Publick Affairs* (1712), 19).
[147] Ward, *The Galloper; or, Needs Must When the Devil Drives* (1710), preface.

spirit of a prevailing party for almost twenty years. It can conquer a kingdom without fighting, and sometimes with the loss of a battle'. Indeed
Swift alleged that the political power of junto Whig Lord Wharton rested
on his art of lying:[148]

the superiority of his genius consists in nothing else but an inexhaustible fund of
political lyes, which he plentifully distributes every minute he speaks . . . he never
yet considered whether any proposition were true or false, but whether it were con-
venient for the present minute or company to affirm or deny it . . . the only
remedy is to suppose that you have heard some inarticulate sounds without any
meaning at all.[149]

Since the Revolution, Swift claimed, a set of men had brought the nation to
the brink of ruin yet 'by the means of perpetual misrepresentation, [we]
have never been able to distinguish between our enemies and friends'. The
Whigs thus used lies 'for deciding elections and influencing distant boroughs' because otherwise the honest landed interest was too strong for
them. Only now were the people being 'undeceived by true representations
of persons and facts'.[150] The high-church Joseph Trapp agreed. 'Nothing is
more remarkable in the Whigs', he protested, 'than their unparallel'd impudence in lying. They will positively affirm the most unheard of absurdities in reason, and the most notorious falsehoods in fact; especially in
matters of calumny and slander'.[151]

   Lying was thus claimed to be central to Whig methods but also to Whig
ideology. *The Art of Lying and Rebelling* (1713) attacked an oft-reprinted
Whig tract *The Judgment of whole Kingdoms*, which summarized Locke's
Second Treatise and justified popular sovereignty. The Tory author accused
the pamphlet of deliberately misleading its readers: 'the ignorant, who
read this rhapsody of lyes, conclude the author of it a mighty read man in
all history and take all he says for infallible', whereas really he was a bad historian and liar:

scarce a paragraph is clear from perverting the truth or making some malicious insinuation. Would mankind but give themselves the trouble of enquiring into the
truth of facts, as represented to them by factious writers, they would not be so
easily seduc'd and infested with pernicious notions. Every man has not leisure nor
opportunity to turn to so many books as a designing writer can quote; but most
men might be inform'd, in some measure, by others, who are able to satisfy their

---

[148] Lord Wharton boasted that 'a lie well received is as good as if it were true' (*DNB*).
[149] *Examiner*, 15.
[150] Ibid.; F. H. Ellis (ed.), *The Examiner and The Medley* (Oxford, 1985), xlii–xliii.
[151] Trapp, *Character and Principles*, 24.

reasonable curiosity. The mischievous pamphlet here spoken of is certainly calculated for the meaner sort, who never read above a sixpenny paper and conclude
that all they see in print is infallibly true. That such ignorant persons should be deluded is no wonder; but to see others of a higher sphere, who might easily undeceive themselves, wilfully deluded by such wretched works is really amazing.[152]

The Tories believed that the Whig concept of contract (of which no one
could produce the 'original') was only a mere 'phantom' and the Whig
good old cause was supported by 'shams and falshood'.[153] Whig ideology
was thus alleged to be *based* on a fiction as well as faction, and advanced by
frauds.[154] Similarly, *Cameronian Whigs no Patriots* (1713) attacked republican agents who spread false reports 'on purpose to amuse and affright the
credulous and unwary; and tis impossible to describe with what indefat-
iguable industry these retailers of lyes and stock-jobbers in forgery spread
volumes of scandal throughout the kingdom against our worthy patriots
the TACKERS'.[155] The Whig writer, another tract claimed, filled people's
heads with stories, replacing proof with 'imposture and invention. There's
not a whimsical story passes in the town that is capable of being improv'd
into a scandal or illusion but it's presently furnish'd up, for the service of
the malcontented; and when there wants matter of fact for a ground to
work upon, tis his care to supply it with fancy or suggestion.'[156] Occasionally Tories were sanguine about the ability to counter Whig lies. Lord chief
justice North, for example, thought that Whig lying during 1679–81 had
been 'bafled and destroyed by printing'.[157] But such optimism was usually
short lived.

Yet the Whigs were equally convinced that the Tories intentionally lied
to the people. The allegation that James II's son, smuggled in a warming-
pan to replace the 'real' but dead infant, was a 'fictitious prince', was only
the best-known example.[158] Whig allegations of Tory lying became partic-

---

[152] *Art*, 19, 29–30.
[153] *The Thoughts of an Honest Whig, Upon the Present Proceedings of that Party* (1710), 13.
The idea that an original contract contained a caveat allowing resistance 'ought to be slighted
as a most extravagant fiction' (*Antiquity Reviv'd* (1693), 72).
[154] Ashcraft, 'Language of Political Conflict', examines how plotters were forced 'to create
a world of fictional discourse in order to meet the practical demands of communication' (5).
See also, Erskine-Hill, 'Two-fold Vision'.
[155] *Cameronian Whigs*, 18.
[156] *Character of a Whig*, 99.
[157] BL, Add. MSS 32,518, ff. 34, 220.
[158] *LG*, 3755 (Saltash address, Nov. 1701). *A Full Answer to the Deposition and to All Other
Pretences and Arguments Whatsoever Concerning the Birth of the Prince of Wales* (1688) included an engraved plan of Whitehall so that readers could follow the precise route taken by
the 'warming pan' baby.

ularly acute in Anne's reign. In 1711 it was alleged that in one work Swift disdained 'undeniable truths' and 'invented the sense of words'. And it was noted that, as Swift's tract had been published just before the parliamentary session opened, one could conclude that 'the great skill in dealers of political lies consists in knowing how to time them nicely'.[159] John Toland's *State-Anatomy* argued that the 1710–14 Tory ministry 'carry'd all their projects with palpable lying, and that indeed their whole administration was but one continu'd series of falshoods and impostures'. He was insistent that the Tories had 'been doing nothing else but spreading of lies (except when they were busy'd in pillageing, demolishing and murdering) ever since the late Queen's death'.[160] Another Whig tract of 1716 suggested that when the people expressed their joy at George I's accession, the Tories 'sent their emissaries and incendiaries into the several counties of the kingdom (into some, on my own knowledge) to spread false reports, and to cast villainous reflections on the government, and to mislead and poyson the minds of the people'. The key lie was that the Pretender was 'a person of wonderful accomplishments, of heroick courage and deep understanding; when all the world knows, and some of his adherents confess and lament, that he is the very reverse, a poor, mean-spirited, despicable thing and little better than a coward and an ideot'.[161] Political lying, then, could even re-present the personalities of would-be monarchs.

The claim that the Tories/jacobites were adept liars was pursued by Addison in the periodical, the *Freeholder*, early in 1716. He noted that lies now abounded, particularly about the danger to the church. 'The emissaries of the party are so diligent in spreading ridiculous fictions of this kind, that at present, if we may credit common report, there are several remote parts of the nation in which it is firmly believed, that all the churches in London are shut up; and that if any clergyman walks the street in his habit, 'tis ten to one but he is knock'd down by some sturdy schismatick.'[162] He mockingly suggested that, as in Turkey, the houses of men who authored 'notorious falshoods' should be painted black. If this were done, 'this metropolis would be strangely chequer'd; some entire parishes wou'd be in mourning, and several streets darken'd from one end to the other'.[163] And all this, he said, was the inevitable consequence of partisan politics: 'every Man in a publick station ought to consider, that when there are two different parties in a nation, they will see things in different lights'. The Tories were thus

---

[159] *A Defence of the Allies and the Late Ministry* (1711), 1, 3–4.
[160] *State-Anatomy*, 87–8.
[161] *A Second Letter*, 15–16.
[162] *Freeholder*, 7.   [163] Ibid., 17.

fictionalizing politics through their lying and Addison saw it as his duty to 'undeceive my countrymen' from the 'mutual intercourse of credulity and falshood'. And, he insisted, misrepresentations would in the end backfire, for 'the reasonable and unprejudic'd part of mankind' would see through them. Others were not so sanguine.[164] The author of *Treason Detected* (1715) argued that the jacobites exercised extravagant practices on the people 'who wanting proper means of information, are oblig'd to take things at second hand and are liable to gross mistakes'. Indeed, 'slanders are directed to the rabble, and are forg'd in the furnace of hell, purely for the delusion of the mobb'.[165]

The divided political culture thus dealt in what everyone agreed to be delusions and fictions even if they could not agree on what was real. The Whig periodical the *Observator* called the high church as conjured up by Henry Sacheverell 'a fiction, a church of the brain, supported by a little, in-significant, trifling number of brainless people; and the people of England are no more concern'd about that Church, than about the institutions of government laid down in Moor's Utopia, Harrington's Oceana, or Bacon's New Atlantis'.[166] Imagined fictions pervaded the political culture, imagined both in the sense of fancied and as something 'uncertain, imperfect . . . opposite in some measure to real'.[167] We must now explore this fictional world more fully.

THE FICTIONS OF PARTISAN POLITICS

That truth was something contested and hence constructed, as a representation, is a point that has attracted the attention of literary scholars, particularly those seeking an explanation and context for Defoe's works.[168] Defoe's fiction was often presented as fact, and his political work often played with fiction. Even the circumstances surrounding his publications appeared to involve deception. Thus in 1715 he wrote a *Secret History of the White Staff* to defend Harley's reputation. When this was attacked by Old-mixon, Defoe wrote a second part, to which Oldmixon again, but also Francis Atterbury and Abel Boyer, responded. Someone with a knowledge

---

[164] Ibid.   [165] *Treason Detected*, 7, 13.
[166] *Observator* 4: 89. Its editor, Tutchin, was, of course, reacting against the charge that dissent was, as an earlier work put it, the product of 'corrupt imaginations and phantasies' (*The Character of a Phanatique* (1660), broadside).
[167] *True Picture of a Modern Whig Reviv'd*, 59.
[168] See above.

of the press published a secret history of the *Secret History*, claiming that
the whole spat had been a Grub Street ruse to sell copy and that 'the same
people employing other hands, have been the editors not only of the books
themselves, but also of several of the answers to these books, causing the
deceiv'd people to dance in the circle of their drawing'.[169] As the mere product of a market in which political literature was in demand, the controversy became a 'continu'd fiction'. The 'facts' presented were either false or
had 'romance' mixed with them. Thus much of the print controversy, it
was claimed, was merely manufactured by booksellers for a 'credulous'
people who believed 'everything which pleases them, and call everything
which they do not approve of, false'.[170] Readers were imposed on to 'believe
lies and things which have no foundation but in the crazy preposses'd
imaginations of a party' or which were the result of booksellers' simple desire that their print 'may sell'.[171] And the problem was a 'national' one, for
'it is not just a single person that is deceiv'd here, but the whole body of the
people are banter'd and made fools of'.[172] Politics was thus consumerist
entertainment, its arguments existing only to sell texts.[173] But, although
literary scholars have rightly observed this phenomenon and seen its
importance for the emergence of the novel, the processes of fictionaliza-
tion in the new political culture need to be explored more systematically.
Partisan politics contained a fictional impulse. In recognizing this, Defoe
and Swift emerge only as the most brilliant exemplars of a wider trend of
polemical writers preoccupied with the problem, and using the arts, of
fiction.

      One of those fictional arts, the personalization of truth, virtue, and in-
terest—a process seen as part of the rise of individualism and a concept of
the 'self'—can also be related to the process of partisan politics.[174] Michael
Mascuch has suggested that around 1700 'innovations in journalistic
publishing and in social control . . . helped to establish in the popular
imagination a new form of self-consciousness: the concept of an active,

---

[169] *The Secret History of the Secret History of the White Staff* (1715), 8. Sherman, *Finance and
Fictionality*, 60, 66, attributes it to Defoe but this is rejected by Furbank and Owens and explicitly denied by the tract at p. 28. It may have been the work of William Pittis whose career
is explored in T. F. Newton, 'William Pittis and Queen Anne Journalism', *Modern Philology*,
33 (1935), 169–86, 279–302.
[170] *Secret History of the Secret History*, 12, 15, 22, 24.
[171] Ibid., 30, 32.   [172] Ibid., 3.
[173] Sherman, *Finance and Fictionality*, 57–66.
[174] Greenblatt has argued that the Renaissance witnessed a period of 'increased self-
consciousness about the fashioning of human identity as a manipulable artful process' (*Renaissance Self-fashioning*, 2); see also Charles Taylor, *Sources of the Self* (Cambridge, 1989); and
Eisenstein, *Printing Press*, 225–46 for the importance of print and identity.

Polemical writers (here Daniel Defoe and John Tutchin) were depicted as 'two-fac'd subjects' with more than one persona and sex. But the problem of two-facedness was also a more general problem in a partisan political culture. A character called 'Turn-around' was, for example, used to satirize the Tories in a tract of 1707. [Reproduced by courtesy of the Houghton Library, Harvard University.]

independent, and secular personality'.[175] But if a new consciousness was emerging, it was in part because the self, self-identity, and private interest were becoming playthings of polemical, partisan, exchanges. For example, the Whig Richard Steele wrote to the Stockbridge electors in the form of a fictional letter, signed as though from an 'English Tory', to a fictional Nestor Ironside. This letter was then published in the *Guardian*. Swift had great fun with the resulting identity crises: 'to render this matter clear to the very meanest capacitie, Mr English Tory, the very same person with Mr Steele, writes a letter to Nestor Ironside Esq; who is the same person with English Tory, who is the same person with Mr Steele; and Mr Ironside, who is the same person with English Tory, publishes the letter written by English Tory, who is the same person with Mr Steele, who is the same person with Mr Ironside'.[176] Steele (and others, as we shall see) were playing with the ambiguity of identity, and he did so because political personas were at least ambivalent if not deceptive. The way in which politicians and polemicists could be seen in two different ways by the public is a point

---

[175] *Origins of the Individualist Self: Autobiography and Self-Identity in England, 1591–1791* (Stanford, 1996), 136.
[176] Swift, *Prose Works*, viii. 8.

driven home visually in *A Character of a Turn-Coat* [1707]. This depicted the double, turn-around nature of politics at the time, the reader having literally to turn the page to continue with an inverted piece of text that was all about dissembling. As the page is rotated, the engravings of heads change their identity. The accompanying poem also ridiculed the people for their 'janus' attitude to kings: vilifying them as soon as they were dead. Even gender is destabilized, 'as by these pictures you may plainly see | he that was a man, a woman seems to be | and she that did a woman represent | by change into another form is sent'. The sheet might be read as a satire against Tutchin and Defoe, whose names are asterisked, and hence against polemical writers who created fictions, but equally against the double-faced people as a whole: 'thus two-fac'd subjects, stock'd with impudence/with any oaths for interest will dispense'.

The ambiguity and double-ness of partisans also foregrounded the issue of hypocrisy. Sophistry—intentionally deceptive argument—was seen as the preserve of both the partisan and the hypocrite (and it is significant that the image reproduced on p. 288 depicting Sacheverell shows him with the cloak of hypocrisy).[177] An anxiety about hypocrisy was not new, of course, and had a long association with 'puritans';[178] but in the later Stuart period it permeated the political culture, not least because it threatened the ability of the public to make informed choices at the polls.[179] Anxieties that had once dominated in the religious sphere thus came to preoccupy the political too, as inherent in partisanship. The problem of sincerity became acute because insincerity frustrated the ability to discern what was politically true.

The fictional impulse of later Stuart political culture

There are a number of ways in which the fictional potential of party can be explored. One, considered in more detail elsewhere, is party history.[180] *A*

---

[177] A satire of the Whigs made them declare: 'Interest is our aim, rebellion is our doctrine, Hipocrisy is our cloak, Murders our intention, religion we have none, and the devil is our master' (*Mr Ferguson's Lamentation for the Destruction of the Association and the Good Old Cause* (1683), 3).

[178] Collinson, *Puritan Character*, 6, 11, 21; W. P. Holden, *Anti-Puritan Satire 1572–1642* (Hamden, Conn., 1954).

[179] For discussions of hypocrisy, see J. Sklar, 'Let us not be Hypocritical', *Daedalus*, 108 (1979), 1–25; P. M. Spacks, *Privacy. Concealing the Eighteenth-Century Self* (Chicago, 2003); and M. Knights, 'Occasional Conformity' (forthcoming). I intend to write more fully on this theme, across the early modern period.

[180] See my 'Whig and Tory History', *Huntington Library Quarterly* (forthcoming).

New Dictionary of the Terms Ancient and Modern of the Canting Crew (1699), defined Whigs as 'the republicans or commonwealthsmen, under the name of patriots and lovers of property'. This was a stock representation, creating the image of dissemblers who sought the good old cause under the veneer of the public good.[181] Such partisan uses of the mid-century crisis were common. The promoters of an address from Pembroke in 1682 reflected 'deliberately upon that bloody history of the late rebellion, carried on by ambition and enthusiasm, in which many well-meaning, unwary men, infatuated by the canting declarations and gilded promises of those times, were unfortunately involved to the ruine of the best of kings, the purest of churches and the most equal of governments'.[182] The Whigs, it was alleged, were dissimulating republicans. To the Whigs, however, such a representation of their past was a fictional misrepresentation. To achieve it the Tories were said to 'have inverted the very sense of words and things . . . for with some of these men, at present, loyalty to our king is republicanism, and rebellion passive obedience'.[183] 'What strange magick spell lies hid in the word commonwealth! It frights men like a goblin', observed some advice to electors.[184] The Tories, it was said, thus made use of a 'mere fantastical imaginary fear of a commonwealth'.[185] This was perhaps best illustrated by the Calves Head Club, depicted in numerous prints as the headquarters of 'republican monsters'. Yet much of the literature about the club was just fiction: the product of Ned Ward's imagination, built up in pamphlets that swelled from year to year with poetical anthems allegedly sung by the radical Whigs. John Kenyon and others have doubted if the Calves Head Clubs ever existed.[186] Even Ward claims to have thought at first that the club was 'a story . . . contrived on purpose to render the republicans more odious than they deserved' and that it was a 'fiction', until, he said, he heard a Whig confirm it. There is some evidence that the clubs did exist.[187] But what is important here is that the fiction that the clubs were widespread became a core element in high church polemic from the press and pulpit. And that fiction was more important than the truth about the clubs. The representation of a satire became credible.

[181] In 1689 a Pontefract voter publicly told Sir William Lowther that he would not support 'any such Commonwealth's man as you are'. Lowther was elected in 1695 only 'after that he had clear'd himself from being a Puritan' (*Diary of Abraham de la Pryme*, 69, 73).
[182] *LG*, 1728.   [183] *Freeholder*, 29.
[184] *Claims of the People*, 33.
[185] W. Stephens, *A Letter to His Most Excellent Majesty King William III* (1699), 11.
[186] Kenyon, *Revolution Principles*, 77; J. Timbs, *Club Life of London* 2 vols. (London, 1866), i. 27.
[187] I will make this case elsewhere.

There is a methodological point that needs stating here, though it has been implicit in much that has gone before. The reception of a political message might be shaped as much by the polemical and semi-fictional allegations of its opponents as by those who sought to explain and justify it. Stereotypes are a semi-fictional genre: part rooted in what is credible or feared, but also exaggerated, elaborated, and imagined representations beyond what is real.[188] But stereotypes are part of public discourse. Thus the history of political discourse needs, in part, to be constructed from the representations put forward by the rabid critics of any set of ideas. Indeed, the way in which an ideology was mythologized and depicted by opponents could help shape how proponents of the ideology articulated it and how they acted. One might almost say that the triumph of oligarchical whiggery was testimony to the enduring impact of high church polemic. Fictions need to be taken seriously.

Rather than exploring the fictional representations of the past, however, this section will mainly be concerned with another construct: credit. Previous chapters have already stressed the importance of credit to electioneering. But it is worth thinking more about it. Once the public was a political umpire, the credit it conferred and constructed became important, not just to the political structure but also to the economy. Moreover, a key problem facing the public in that process was how far to take outward appearance as representative of inner worth. The public, which could not be expected to know politicians or polemicists personally, had nevertheless to decide on their credit-worthiness. They had to 'know' them, and yet often lacked the relevant information.[189] The danger, then, was that they would rely on the outward show and hence misjudge.

The stereotype of the grasping and unscrupulous Whig financier might serve as a case study of these issues. At the heart of the representation lay the allegation that such a man (and party) was a fraud, a hypocrite who spoke about public interest but who 'really' sought only his self-interest. *The True Picture of a Modern Whig Reviv'd* (1707) defined such a modern Whig as 'one, who has no concern at all for the publick good, when oppos'd to private gain; he will sacrifice his duty to his prince, his country and his God, to persons from whom he has any prospect of advantage, or of power, though never so distant, and never so mean or destructive of the publick

---

[188] Stereotypical representations of the past involve a double fiction, since partisan history is itself open to the accusation of being fabricated to serve a turn.

[189] This may explain the public appetite for intimate 'knowledge' about public figures. The lives of Sarah and John Churchill, for example, were minutely examined and DelaRiviere Manley's 'secret lives' seem also to have fed such cravings.

Double vision: the coffee-house mob (see the image reproduced on p. 19) has been transformed into the Calves Head Club, which allegedly celebrated the execution of Charles I. The image remains almost the same (though the print on the table, has been replaced by the dishes of calves' heads) but the title requires it to be read differently, with an explicit stress on sedition and the enduring divisions of the 1640s. [Reproduced by courtesy of the Trustees of the British Museum.]

good. He is, in short, a patriot without honesty, a politician without common understanding; and wit without common sense'.[190] Another Tory polemicist agreed that there was 'a race of men who thrive and grow rich by war . . . Their constant cry is *Liberty Oh! the danger of English Liberty and property; no tyranny, no slavery, no tyranny*: yet who but themselves ever preferr'd the interest of an exotick state to that of their native kingdom; or were so profusely lavish of the blood, lives, liberties and estates of their brother Britains?'[191] This stereotype was echoed across the country. The rash of Tory addresses in 1712 and 1713 harped on the theme that the Whigs were political vampires who had sucked the nation dry. Ilchester's address thus referred to the 'close designs of those who so long triumph'd in the misery of their fellow subjects, sacrificing their blood and treasure to insatiable avarice and ambition'. Radnor's referred to disloyal men who, 'to gratifie their own resentments, ambition and sordid avarice, labour to obstruct your royal intentions'.[192] Nottinghamshire's attacked 'self-interested and ambitious persons whose private advantage was term'd the public good; and whose delight was in war because their impunity and their gain depended upon it'.[193] Tenby's address suggested that the war had been 'begun upon publick views but conducted to private purposes and sinister designs, to gratify the insatiable ambition of others, to enrich the factious and impoverish your faithful subjects'.[194] The Whigs had, it was suggested, used the war to sink 'the landed interest of England till it was unable to oppose their pernicious designs'.[195] The Whigs were thus proscribed as self-interested, ambitious, dissemblers who purported to be 'publick patriots' but were really 'private oppressors'.[196]

The Whig had 'more shapes than proteus', and used the resulting confusion as a cover for self-interest; thus the Whig was nothing more than a hypocrite, who protested one thing but sought another in a form of 'politick masquerading'.[197] It is significant that Davenant's representation of the new Whig, the significantly named Tom Double, rose through the Whig ranks based on his ability to invent credit through the lottery, bank, exchequer bills. Nor was it a coincidence that the archetypal new Whig, Charles Montagu, was the chancellor of the exchequer who presided over such fiscal innovations. Montagu was depicted as a 'rapacious filcher' who

---

[190] *True Picture*, 44–5.   [191] *Cameronian Whigs*, 10.
[192] *LG*, 5043.   [193] *LG*, 5046.   [194] Ibid.
[195] *LG*, 5033 (Cheshire).   [196] *Freeholder*, 29.
[197] *Character of a Whig*, 1. The tract listed the types of whiggery, but they were bound together by a common hypocrisy, a word used numerous times in the text (39, 63, 66, 98, 106, 108).

stole other people's ideas (including their literary and economic projects) and lined his own pockets with public money. 'Magpie' Montagu thus epitomized the dissimulation, greed, and self-interest associated with the new Whigs. While the nation groaned under the fiscal burden he imposed on it, the money raised was 'whor'd away or piss'd against the walls'.[198] Montagu's failings were thus said to be representative of the rest of his party's. Just as we saw words and the things they represented appeared to have become divorced under the pressure of partisanship, so too the politicians themselves appeared in a double-light, with an outer public mask divorced from, but hiding, sinister private designs. The modern Whig was a fraud. And that fraud was financial and literary as well as political.

We can see these interconnections clearly in the debates over recoinage, masterminded by Montagu and the Whigs. As a result of 'clipping' silver in order to melt it down and literally forge new money, the coin was, by 1695, about 48 per cent deficient in weight and, as a result, British money bought less and less when used abroad to pay for England's large standing army.[199] Its representational value thus outstripped its intrinsic value, with the result that the export of bullion in order to pay and supply the armed forces was bleeding the country dry. The Whigs therefore sought to recoin, recalling the old and reissuing it in a form that could not be so easily debased. The debates about recoinage did not always run along party lines but they centred on issues to do with representational values, which we have already seen as central to public discourse. The public thus gave credit to the value of words, the value of money, and the value of a politician or polemicist.

We have just seen the linkage between the public credit of a politician and new systems of fiscal credit. But how were words and money linked and given value by the public? To answer that we need to examine the process of recoinage. The shortage of silver raised the market value of gold. This meant that the relational values of silver and gold were distorted. Not only did this allow silver to be bought 'cheaply' (with inflated gold) and hence exported by money dealers, with the result that the new silver coin would be lost as fast as it could be minted, but the instability of relationships between the metals also hampered trade. This problem posed the question of whether money had a *representational* or *intrinsic* value. Was

---

[198] *England's Enemies Expos'd*, 9, 12–13, 18.
[199] W. Lowndes, *A Report Containing an Essay for the Amendment of the Silver Coins* (1695), 106–7, 159.

money like words: constantly circulated and exchanged, given sense and value by the public, but also potentially debased?[200] One tract made this connection explicit: 'how can truth subsist with falshood, or what agreement can there be between the real intrinsick value of the silver and the false denominative price of gold[?]' The author continued that monetary value was determined by 'opinion and consent' which could 'not be imposed upon by the fraudulent artifices of particular men, nor even be controlled by the power of absolute princes, nor by any other sovereign power whatsoever'.[201] The solution was for public opinion—formed by 'the mob (as we call them), and the ordinary and middling traders (who are the bulk of the nation . . .) . . . in conjunction with the public receipts (the Exchequer, Excise, Custom-House) and the Bank of England'—to refuse to accept golden guineas as being worth more than 22s.[202] In other words, the value of money, like that of words and civil society, lay in the credit accorded by the public. 'Tis mere opinion that sets a value upon money', asserted Newton.[203] Public credit was thus a matter of finance but also of words and Defoe wanted to make it 'as criminal to coin words as money'.[204] A mass of print was produced in order to influence public discourse on the topic, creating an explicit link between verbal representation and the value of money.[205] John Freke, for example, complained in December 1695 that 'the monyers are . . . busie buzzing hard words and unintelligible cant' into MPs' heads.[206] For him, fraud was thus linguistic and economic. The secular world of the financial revolution thus had an important impact on political culture.

The interaction between outward appearance and inner reality, and between credit, credibility, print, and politics, can be seen again in the case of one such 'monyer', William Chaloner. He was the author in 1695 of *Reasons Humbly Offered against Passing an Act for Raising £1,000,000 for Making Good the Deficiency of the Clipt-Money*, which argued (against Whig policy) for a devaluation of the currency. Chaloner also alleged that the

[200] C. Caffentizis, *Clipped Coins, Abused Words, and Civil Government* (New York, 1989).
[201] *A Letter to a Gentleman in the Country Concerning the Price of Guineas* [1695/6], 2.
[202] *A Word in Season about Guineas* (1695), 3. See ch. 4 for a discussion of the controversial list of MPs who had tried to argue down the value of guineas.
[203] J. Craig, *Newton at the Mint* (Cambridge, 1946), 42.
[204] Defoe, 'Of Academies', *An Essay upon Projects* (1697), 237; Nicholson, *Writing and the Rise of Finance*, 235, 244–5.
[205] J. K. Horsefield, *British Monetary Experiments, 1650–1710* (London, 1960), bibliography, lists 501 titles relevant to debates on money and banking published between 1690 and 1700.
[206] *Locke Correspondence*, v. 475.

Mint—headed by Whig MP Isaac Newton—was incompetent at producing the new coin and offered parliament his own inventions to stop counterfeiting. Despite Newton's opposition, parliament accepted his machines. Newton's response was to have Chaloner imprisoned in Newgate for seven weeks and to gather as much information about him as he could in order to prove him a fraud. He uncovered that Chaloner had started life as 'a japanner in clothes threadbare, ragged and daubed with colours' who 'turned coiner and in a short time put on the habit of a gentleman'.[207] Thus, rather than resolving fraudulent coinage, as he claimed to want to do, Chaloner was himself the most accomplished counterfeiter and trickster, who had almost literally coined himself. Moreover, his dissimulation was linked to politics. He had been paid money by the government for the discovery of jacobite print, but Newton alleged that Chaloner had obtained a copy of a tract and then had forty more copies printed in order to be able to inform on the printer—he was as adept at pirating words as money.[208] Chaloner, now depicted as a jacobite sympathizer, was convicted of false coining and executed on 4 March 1699.

Literary historians have recently made good use of the notion of public credit and its role in the development of the novel. They have noted that the innovations of the financial revolution relied on fictions, such as paper money, a standing debt, a bank, stocks, and the stock market.[209] This interpretation owes much to John Pocock, who argued that land gave way to movable forms of property and credit based on the value of opinion. In this process credit became a discourse; the market placed a value not on real, solid, things but on how real things were represented and discussed. In the tension between words and things, words had won out; they had themselves become things, objects of desire because they conferred value. Pocock argued, moreover, that once established, a system of public credit necessitated dependence on the public's confidence in the government's ability to repay the debt at some imagined future date. 'Government is therefore maintained by the investor's imagination concerning a moment which will never exist in reality'.[210] Literary scholars have run with these

[207] Craig, *Newton*, 124; PRO, Mint 19/1, f. 501.
[208] Ibid., 18–19. For clippers and jacobitism, see M. Gaskill, *Crime and Mentalities in Early Modern England* (Cambridge, 2000).
[209] National debt stood at about £1 million at the time of the revolution; by 1697 it stood at £16.7 million and though it fell briefly during the peacetime years of 1697–1702, it reached £21.4 million by 1710 and £54 million by 1720 (B. Mitchell, *British Historical Statistics* (Cambridge, 1988), ch. 11, table 7).
[210] Pocock, *Virtue, Commerce and History*, 112.

insights. Sandra Sherman, for example, argues that the commercial market of Defoe's world generated a notion of 'fiction'.[211] Colin Nicholson traces the ways in which literary, political, and economic projects coincided in the writings of the Tory opposition to Whig power.[212] And James Thompson suggests that changes in political economy were instrumental in the rise of the novel.[213] This link between the financial revolution, the rise of new literary forms, and the emergence of the 'public' is also present in Habermas's work.

But the link between opinion, credit, and *partisan politics* remains under-explored and is worth emphasizing here. Public credit relied on political representations of the parties and their leaders. Public discourse of political affairs was thus an integral part of the evolving financial system, and frequent elections had a place in establishing the state of creditworthiness. Credit and public opinion were thus entwined. As Charles Davenant and Benjamin Hoadly put it, credit 'hangs upon opinion' and 'publick credit is . . . like private reputation; obtained by a series of good conduct made up of a multitude of good actions'.[214] For Defoe credit was 'the essential shadow of something that is not' and depended on 'the honour of the public administration in general and the justice of parliaments in particular'.[215]

This reliance of public credit on public opinion and political representations was unnerving. For Davenant there was a dangerous link between a new system of politics and a new system of finance, both of which depended on the public.[216] Anxieties about party and credit were thus linked. Critics of both saw a propensity among their fellows to give value to the fictional or misleading, to what was not real or true.[217] They saw a mismatch between words and things—indeed, even the severing of the link between the representation and the represented. For example, Defoe accused stockjobbers (those who manipulated the stock market to make profit out of financial speculation) of working by 'trick, cheat, wheedle, forgeries,

---

[211] *Finance and Fictionality*, 2.
[212] *Writing and the Rise of Finance*.
[213] *Models of Value*.
[214] *The Political and Commercial Works of that Celebrated Writer Charles D'Avenant*, ed. by Sir C. Whitworth, 5 vols. (1771, repr. Farnborough, 1968), i. 151; Hoadly, *The Fears and Sentiments of all True Britains* in *A Collection of Several Papers Printed in the Year 1710* (1718), 95.
[215] *An Essay Upon Public Credit* (1710), 6; *Review*, iii. 3, 126 and vii. 166.
[216] I. Hont, 'Free Trade and the Economic Limits to National Politics: Neo-Machiavellian Political Economy Reconsidered', in J. Dunn (ed.), *The Economic Limits to Modern Politics* (Cambridge, 1990).
[217] Baston, *Thoughts on Trade*, 7–12.

falsehoods and all sorts of delusions; coining false news, this way good, that way bad; whispering imaginary terrors, frights, hopes, expectations, and then preying on the weakness of those whose imaginations they have wrought upon'.[218] Yet his allegation could be reproduced almost word for word, as we have seen, in a political context. And hence it is no surprise that Defoe, and others, made the connection between politics and stock-jobbing (particularly at election time, when votes could appear to be bought and sold) quite explicit.[219] Politicians became 'stock-jobbers'. Fraudulent politics and fraudulent money-making went hand in hand. The new credit system was only possible because of the regularity of parliamentary sessions and parliamentary taxation.[220] Credit was linked with representation; but the new credit systems also, it was claimed, in turn corrupted the representational system by allowing government to bribe MPs and electors. As Swift put it, the new men of money raised themselves by taxing landowners, so that many of them 'were able in time to force the election of burroughs out of the hands of those who had been the old proprietors and inhabitants'.[221]

But the relationship between representational politics and the fiction of the market-place went deeper. Stocks had 'an imaginary value'. On the one hand, this was dangerous. The stock-jobber could delude people, as in the 1720 financial bubble, 'into a much higher opinion of the value of those stocks than they were really worth, so that they bought them at extravagent prices'.[222] Stock-jobbers, 'by forging false news, raise and fall the stocks'.[223] Indeed, stock-jobbers were thought to thrive in times of war and public calamity, when their seditious lies were more likely to be believed and further undermine stability.[224] Like words, the stock market could parallel the tower of Babel in producing confusion.[225] But, on the other hand, stocks might be useful as representations of public credit and opinion. The link between public discourse, public opinion, and public credit could thus now in some measure be charted, for by 1715 it could be asserted that credit

---

[218] *The Anatomy of Exchange Alley* (1719), 3–4.
[219] Ibid., 42; Defoe, *Freeholders Plea Against Stock-Jobbing Elections*. Cf. *Examiner*, 13.
[220] For a whiggish argument suggesting that capital markets could not develop without constitutional and institutional limits to governmental arbitrary power after 1689, see D. C. North and B. R. Weingast, 'Constitutions and Commitment: The Evolution of Institutions Governing Public Choice in Seventeenth-Century England', *Journal of Economic History*, 49 (1989), 803–32.
[221] Swift, *Prose Works*, ii. 70.
[222] *Letter to a Conscientious Man*, 13–14.
[223] Baston, *Thoughts on Trade*, 7.
[224] Ibid., 8–9.
[225] *The South Sea Scheme Detected* (1720), 8.

was 'the best indication of the people's satisfaction'.[226] Stocks, then, were another voice of the public. The value of stock was thus affected not only by economic conditions but also by news of foreign crises and the state of the conflict between the two parties.[227] Moreover, the value of the market was now routinely reported in periodical form for public consumption, so the capacity of the stock-owning public to influence value was enhanced.[228] The market, like elections, was thus a means of gauging the 'public' and fluctuations in the market might reflect shifts of public mood.[229] This link between public politics and public credit was made explicit by Addison. He painted an allegorical vision of public credit as a beautiful virgin who swoons when frightened by phantoms representing tyranny, anarchy, atheism, bigotry, republicanism, and the Pretender; but she recovers in the presence of liberty, moderation, religion, and Hanover.[230] Addison's vision therefore reflected political circumstances. The stock market rendered the discursive public sphere instrumental in the affairs of government. Stocks and other forms of investment linked public credit and public opinion; and fiscal probity became an essential component of political credibility.[231] This in part explains the longevity of Walpole's administration after the South Sea Bubble of 1720. But it also helps further to explain the rise of the language of interest, in which economic, national and personal interest coincided.[232] And the incorporation of matters of public finance into the political system added an economic break to the rage of party. As Hont puts it, 'commercial society, in other words, set clear limits to ideological politics'.[233]

---

[226] *LG*, 5293.

[227] *Locke Correspondence*, vii. 198–9, 231, 248, 288, 384, 388.

[228] L. Neal, *The Rise of Financial Capitalism. International Capital Markets in the Age of Reason* (Cambridge, 1990), ch. 2.

[229] On the day of the motion for the Schism Bill in 1714 the stocks fell by 2 per cent (BL, Add. MSS 72,496 ff. 141–2, 14 May 1714). Carruthers, *City of Capital*, argues that politics influenced economics and that Whig and Tory penetrated the stock market.

[230] *Spectator*, 3.

[231] In 1707–9 there were about 10,000 public creditors in England, rising to about 40,000 by 1720 (Dickson, *Financial Revolution*, 262, 273).

[232] Steve Pincus has suggested that, after 1689, with the economy the 'central object of governance', the language of national interest prevailed over that of the godly ('The Making of a Great Power? Universal Monarchy, Political Economy and the Transformation of English Political Cultures', in *The European Legacy*, 5 (2000), 531–45; Pincus, 'From Holy Cause to Economic Interest: the Study of Population and the Invention of the State', in Houston and Pincus, *A Nation Transformed*, 287).

[233] 'Free Trade', 68.

Value of Bank of England Stock, Showing the Interaction of Politics and Public Credit.[234]

September 1694	57 (Uncertainty overpublic finance)
November	70
December	76
January 1695	90
March	99
December	100
January 1696	108
February	83 (Assassination attempt; rival land bank scheme)
March	82
August	70 (Recoinage crisis)
October	60
December	73 (Bank asked to loan government £2.5 million)
January 1697	55
February	51
September	98 (Conclusion of peace)

These shifts did not pass unnoticed. Swift observed that the 'wealth of the nation, that used to be reckoned by the value of the land, is now computed by the rise and fall of stocks'.[235] He feared that the representative indicator of English worth had thus changed from land to commerce. Thomas Baston similarly reckoned that 'most weak people take stocks to be the weather glass of the state; and as they ebb or flow, rise or fall, so they judge of the health or sickness of the publick'.[236] The politicization of economic forces was also apparent. The opponents of Sir John Moore, who had complied with the court during 1682 shrieval election, took their revenge by engineering a run on one of his associates, who was a banker, resulting in several insolvencies.[237] In 1710 the Whigs also sought to use public credit as a political issue, arguing that a change of ministry would be financially destabilizing.[238] One pamphleteer sympathetic to

---

[234] For graphs of the London stock price index 1698–1734, see Neal, *Rise of Financial Capitalism*, figs. 3.1–3.3.

[235] Swift, *Prose Works*, iii. 6.

[236] Baston, *Thoughts on Trade*, 7.

[237] Houghton, *Collection of Letters for the Improvement of Husbandry and Trade*, 13.

[238] BL, MS Add. 70,421, ff. 139–40, Dyer's newsletter, 15 June 1710; [Sir T. Burnet], *Truth if you can Find it* (1712), 4–5. In July bank stock had fallen to 113.5, and to 107 by the end of August, but Dyer thought this not representative of public confidence but a 'contrivance of the Whigs' (ibid., 163, 165, 169, 172, 197–8).

Harley and the incoming Tories was outraged at this blatant piece of
political stock-jobbing. He argued that 'though we daily see that these
stocks are run up and down by the new science of stock-jobbing, yet this
can never be truly said to operate any thing upon the real intrinsick value,
which can never be moved otherwise than by the known profit or loss upon
it'. The political manœuvres were thus represented as being divorced from
the intrinsic value of bank stock and hence deceitful to the public.[239]

Public discourse about the danger of a change of ministry was, the
Tories claimed, thus no more than a form of stock-jobbing, creating a
misrepresentative price and a problem for public credit. This, of course,
did not stop a Whig pamphleteer from observing how the public credit
had fallen as the credit of a Tory ministry rose: bringing in 'hot, mad, raging Tories . . . will, in my weak judgment, quite finish the tragedy and destroy that [fiscal] credit which was wounded before. No man will venture
his money in Tory hands; they have no honour, no regard to the publick
good, or to private right, otherwise than as it suits with their party'. In
other words, public credit relied on the Whigs. Public credit did rally in
1710 despite the change of ministry; but issues of public credit and public
opinion were again entwined at the 1713 general election, when peace with
France was hotly contested by rival economists and partisans.[240] All this
mattered; it had electoral consequences. Public credit was also now something important to state formation. The public's judgement could have
far-reaching implications for the economy and the war. Party politics,
then, had become intermeshed with the inherently fictional forms of public credit. Representative politics thus acquired a new dimension, unimag-
inable before the creation of a public debt. Defoe even worried that debt
heightened the instability of opinion: 'our debts are the main article that
darken our circumstances, and makes every rumour alarm us; every conspiracy, tho supported by beggars and mad men, seem formidable to us'.[241]
Truly this was a different world from the 1640s or even the Restoration. The
representative fiction of public credit had a real impact.

Imagined dialogues and personifications

Besides the fictional impulse of partisan history and a linkage between
representational politics and the fictions created by new forms of finance,

---

[239] *Faults on Both Sides* (1710), *Somers Tracts*, 4th collection, iii. 315.
[240] Defoe told Oxford during the election of 1713 that the 'disputes upon the subject of the
commerce with France are carried on not merely as a dispute about trade . . . but as an arrow
shot at the present administration' (*Letters of Defoe*, 418–19).
[241] *Fair Payment No Spunge* (1717), 17.

we might also look to the fictional potential of polemic. In particular, we might examine one common format, the dialogue between two or more fictionalized characters.[242] Relatively little has been written about the genre, but it is important to our understanding of public discourse.[243] Such dialogues played with distinctions between private and public, for they were public versions of allegedly private conversations and also seemed to reveal to the public the private motives of individuals and their parties.[244] Thus, like the recoinage and public credit, they turned on notions of inner and outward designs. Perhaps more importantly, the characters in some of the dialogues also began to reflect the fictional creativity that has been so far indicated in other areas. Again, this was not unique to the later Stuart period; the use of imagined protagonists verbally exchanging ideas in order to explain and explore concepts and arguments was as old as classical antiquity.[245] But the exploitation of print dialogue in the age of party was remarkably creative.

Polemical print dialogues sometimes claimed to represent actual conversation. One, for example, claimed to be 'an account of what is said at Child's and Tom's Coffee Houses for and against Sacheverell'.[246] The tract was very successful, running to four editions, presumably becoming the subject of the coffee-house discourse that it sought to reproduce.[247] Yet the representation of speech in print inevitably involved a degree of fiction and some authors revelled in the deception involved. One pamphlet thus purported to be *A Certain Information of a Certain Discourse. That Happen'd at a Certain Gentleman's House in a Certain County. Written by a Certain Person then Present, to a Certain Friend Now at London. From Whence You May Collect the Great Certainty of the Account* (1713). This tract played with the 'certain' truth-claims made in its title, for as its dialogue is about to begin the 'author' dramatically stops one of the characters from speaking:

[242] McKenzie, 'Speech-Manuscript-Print', 102–3.

[243] E. Merrill, *The Dialogue in English Literature*, Yale Studies in English, 42 (1911); M. Macorski, *Dialogue and Literature* (Oxford, 1994); Raymond, *Pamphlets*, 218–20; Green, *Print and Protestantism*, 373–8; P. Burke, 'The Renaissance Dialogue', *Renaissance Studies*, 3 (1989), 1–12; Sawyer, *Printed Poison*, ch. 5.

[244] Another genre that worked in a similar fashion was the published letter (J. Brewer, 'This, That and the Other: Public, Social and Private in the Seventeenth and Eighteenth Centuries', in Castiglione and Sharpe (eds.), *Shifting the Boundaries*, 12–16.

[245] For a discussion of 'ventriloquy' during the mid-century crisis, see Peacey, *Politicians and Pamphleteers*, 225, though he claims the deceptions were always apparent.

[246] Sir John Saint Leger, *The Manager's Pro and Con or an Account of What is Said* (1710), subtitle.

[247] A tract by Marchmont Nedham even used the reconstruction of a coffee-house conversation to argue for the need to 'lay aside disputings', an attempt to use public discourse to restrict itself (*Christianissimus Christianandus*, 78).

hold, he shan't begin, till I have answered an objection which may be made by the reader how I came to be present and not say a word all the time. Why perhaps I am the spectator, who never talks in any company; no, that, says my reader, I'm sure you are not. Well then perhaps I am Philologus [the Whig country gentleman of the dialogue] or perhaps I am one that listened at the door, or perhaps, I spoke and wont tell you what I said, or perhaps I held my tongue.[248]

Here the 'certain discourse' was filtered by the reporter—or 'spectator'—who intrudes himself into the print only to offer no explanation of his part and remain unidentifiable—even though it is on his credibility that the 'certain' account rests.[249]

Dialogues proved a popular, accessible, and adaptable form. The word 'dialogue' was used in the titles of 113 printed items between 1660 and 1680, but 267 times in the period 1680–1700 and 486 times in the next twenty years, 1700–20.[250] Many periodicals adopted a dialogic format. L'Estrange claimed it was 'more familiar and entertaining' than others.[251] Yet the dialogue was also viewed with suspicion by some who feared it too prone to drollery. One author asked readers to excuse the levity of his dialogue by looking on it 'as a common discourse, wherein a greater liberty and freedom of speech is taken than in compos'd orations'.[252] A Whig cleric complained that the way of dialogue was 'fitter for a droll than a defence', not least because the author could manipulate his characters like puppets.[253] The dialogue was thus both popular but also manipulative, and hence ideally suited to partisan politics in which rival opinions and binary divides were represented to the public and in which a politics of entertainment was essential.

Dialogues allowed the author to construct either a didactic exchange, in which one of the participants occupied a dominant, tutoring role, or a less-controlled discussion, in which free-ranging debate took place. The pres-

---

[248] Sir T. Burnet, *Certain Information*, 5–6.

[249] The spectator as an outward mask for the inner self is explored in Ketcham, *Transparent Designs*.

[250] Calculated from ESTC. *Plain Dealing Concerning the Penal Laws and Tests. Delivered in a Dialogue* (1688), 1, suggested that toleration undid the 'pad-lock' that had shut the mouths of dissenters.

[251] *Observator*, 9 Jan. 1683/4.

[252] *A Dialogue Between the Author of Whigs no Christians and a Country Gentleman* [1715?], Preface to the Reader.

[253] W. Bisset, *The Modern Fanatick. Part II* (1710), 2. Cf. 3rd Earl of Shaftesbury, *Characteristics of Men, Manners, Opinion, Times*, ed. J. M. Robertson, 2 vols. (Gloucester, Mass., 1963–4 edn.), ii. 338.

sure of partisan politics, which placed a premium on the victory of one set of ideas over another, ensured that the didactic model was the more common. Imagined dialogues were thus often used as a vehicle for rebutting the arguments that a rival might put up,[254] and such polemical debates weighted the conversation clearly in favour of one of the participants. Rival opinions, rather than being portrayed at their most persuasive or strongest, were often put forward in a caricatured, easily defeated fashion. Rather than being designed to explore the truth through the collision of rival opinions, such dialogues became mere polemic. It was for this reason that the third earl of Shaftesbury bemoaned the state of the philosophical dialogue, which he saw as having fallen victim to the demands of 'our party pamphlets'.[255] Bernard de Mandeville similarly lamented that 'partial men' wrote dialogues 'in which the [victims were] . . . visibly set up on purpose to be knock'd down'.[256] Rather than pursue free debate, partisan dialogues suggested that truth lay only on one side. They aimed at conviction rather than conversation. Ciceronian didacticism thus prevailed over Platonic speculation. Henry Neville had floated solutions to what he saw as England's structural problems in his dialogic *Plato Redivivus*; but in a partisan age his independent speculation was condemned.[257] Partisan polemic thus sought to control and narrow what was true. It could hardly be otherwise, for the danger inherent in every dialogue was that the articulation of a rival opinion might put ideas into the reader's mind. The dialogue, unless tightly controlled, threatened to give a voice to opinions that the author sought to counter.

Even so, polemical dialogues were persuasive because they gave the appearance of a free debate—and hence increased the appearance of impartiality—despite their fixed outcome. A good example, whose title gives all away, is *A Dialogue betwixt Whig and Tory alias Williamite and Jacobite Wherein the Principles and Practices of Each Party are Fairly and Impartially Stated; that thereby Mistakes and Prejudices may be Remov'd from amongst us, and All those who Prefer English Liberty and Protestant Religion to French*

---

[254] The process of deciding between rival versions is, as Hannah Arendt put it, not just 'a dialogue between me and myself, but finds itself always and primarily, even if I am quite alone in making up my mind, in an anticipated communication with others with whom I know I must finally come to some agreement' ('Crisis in Culture', in *Between Past and Future* (New York, reissued with additional text, 1968), 220).

[255] Shaftesbury, *Characteristics*, ii. 337. For Shaftesbury the dialogue form was the 'politest and best way of managing even the graver subjects' and for treating philosophy. (Klein, 'Shaftesbury and the Progress of Politeness', 206–211)

[256] *The Fable of the Bees. Part II* (1729), preface, vi–vii.

[257] Robbins, *Two English Republican Tracts*, 17.

Slavery and Popery may be Inform'd how to Chuse Fit and Proper Instruments for our Preservation in these Times of Danger (1693).[258] The title identified Tory with jacobite but then went on to claim impartiality, which in this context meant not a free and fair discussion but an explicit and polemically charged attempt to persuade the public to avoid French 'slavery'. The author claimed he had 'impartially made a collection' of arguments used by parties against each other so that the king could decide 'to become intirely an Englishman' by choosing the Whigs. The king was thus the nominal audience; but printing the dialogue meant that the reading public was the judge, temporarily occupying the place of the king in arbitrating between the parties.[259] For all his protestations of impartiality, truth, and public service, the author's partisan intentions were—intentionally—clear.[260]

Yet these partisan dialogues often played on the disparity between public and private motives and it was here that most fictional potential existed. The exposé of an individual's inner (and real) character necessarily meant the exploration of the 'self' and also some attempt at 'realistic' characterization. Dialogue could thus be used as public exposure of confessions made in the 'privacy' of intimate conversations. Indeed, the confessional form gave additional validity to the admissions that one of the speakers— and hence one of the parties—had base and sinister motives. 'Private' speech thus conferred authenticity on a fabricated, public confession of evil motives. The dialogue lent itself to the suggestion that parties operated conspiratorially. The reader was temporarily placed as an eavesdropper on the seditious confessions of plotters. Thus *The True Picture of a Modern Tory: in a Dialogue between Jack and Ned; Two Agents from the Jacobite Party* (1702) purported to be a conversation between two plotting Tories/jacobites, allowing its Whig author to explain the tactics that the Tories/jacobites used to seduce the people to support them. Thus, in a subversion of catechistic dialogues, one speaker tutors the other in the arts of sedition. The most important example of this type of confessional dialogue, however, was a series written by Charles Davenant, who dramatized politics in prose just as his father William Davenant had in plays for the

---

[258] Two editions in 1693; reprinted in *State Tracts*, with a date of Nov. 1692; reprinted again in 1710. Once ascribed to Defoe, it was probably by Ben Overton. The frontispiece is as Illustration 24.

[259] *State Tracts*, ii. 372.

[260] Ibid., 376. Cf. *The True Picture of an Ancient Tory in a Dialogue between Vassal a Tory and Freeman a Whig* (1702); *England's Corruptions and Mismanagements Discover'd. In a Dialogue between Trueman and Legion* (1702).

Caroline stage.[261] The brilliance of the dialogues lay in their creation of a fictional Whig character, Tom Double, whose name epitomized his ability to pursue private designs under the cover of party and the public interest.[262] The reader is allowed to hear Tom's 'private', spoken explanation of his double-dealing. Tom's designs are thus exposed in public, to the reader, though the conversation remains 'private' between the two characters who meet away from public gaze. The reader, armed with this knowledge, can then act accordingly when confronted by a Whig, for the private dialogue will echo in his mind.

Davenant fully explored the fictional potential of the dialogue. But the conjunction of the fictional and the real, of the public and private, and hence the uncovering or unmasking of the corrupt, was also apparent in the representation of the dialogue at the Cowper family table, discussed in Chapter 2. It can also be discerned in another important series of dialogues, by Dr John Arbuthnot, who created the enduring character of John Bull.[263] The point of the dialogues is that Bull was a simple, credulous man, who understood little and could easily have the wool (he is a clothier, after all) pulled over his eyes. Bull was honest but careless and thus constantly being cheated—and cheated on by his wife.[264] The dialogue form made it easy for Arbuthnot to allegorize politics as a familial story, in which domestic but also foreign news becomes literally a domestic discussion and in which the English were duped by the politics around them. In the dialogues public affairs—the relations between states—become privatized and then revealed for what they really are. In the final tract in the series, *Lewis Baboon Turn'd Honest*, John Bull (now styled 'politician') finally sees through the deceptions put on him. Bull and Lewis Baboon (France) settle their dispute by means of each discerning their 'interest'.[265]

---

[261] Davenant, *The True Picture of a Modern Whig, Set Forth in a Dialogue between Mr. Whiglove & Mr. Double, Two Under-Spur-Leathers to the Late Ministry* (1701, 7 edns. by 1705); *Tom Double Return'd* (2 edns.); *Sir Thomas Double at Court, and in High Preferments. In Two Dialogues, between Sir Thomas Double and Sir Richard Comover, alias Mr. Whiglove* (1710). Another tract which appropriated Tom Double, *The True Picture of a Modern Whig Reviv'd*, was probably not his work. For attributions, see D. Waddell, 'The Career and Writings of Charles Davenant 1656–1714', Ph.D., Oxford (1954), appendices.

[262] Davenant was himself attacked for doubleness when he and his son accepted minor office: 'The advocate for Hypocrisie could not act more becomingly, than by doing himself the very thing which he defends, and justifying one odious sort of dissimulation with another' (*The True Tom Double; or, An Account of Dr Davenant's Late Conduct and Writings* (1704), 21).

[263] Arbuthnot, *The History of John Bull*, ed. A. Bower and R. Erickson (Oxford, 1976); M. Taylor, 'John Bull and the Iconography of Public Opinion in England, c.1712–1929', *P&P*, 134 (1992), 93–128.

[264] *History of John Bull*, 9.

[265] Ibid., 93, 111.

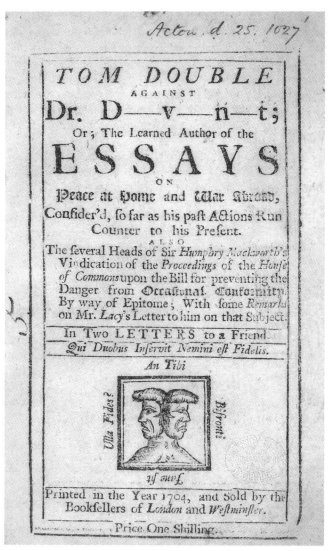

Acton. d. 25. 1027

TOM DOUBLE

AGAINST

Dr. D——v——n——t;

Or; The Learned Author of the

ESSAYS

ON

Peace at Home and War Abroad,

Confider'd, fo far as his paft Actions Run
Counter to his Prefent.

ALSO

The feveral Heads of Sir *Humphry Mackworth's*
Vindication of the *Proceedings* of the *Houfe*
of *Commons* upon the Bill for preventing the
Danger from Occafional Conformity.
By way of Epitome; With fome *Remarks*
on Mr. *Lacy's* Letter to him on that Subject.

In Two LETTERS to a Friend.
Qui Duobus Infervit Nemini eft Fidelis.

An Tibi

Ulla Fides? *Bifronti*

uf auuf

Printed in the Year 1704, and Sold by the
Bookfellers of *London* and *Weftminfter*.

Price One Shilling.

Tom Double, the representation of a two-faced politician, was a brilliantly imagined characterization of the 'modern Whig'. However, when its author, Charles Davenant, appeared to backtrack on his earlier support for the Occasional Conformity Bill, he was himself vilified as the two-faced Janus shown here. Print heightened such perceptions of double-dealing, for it fixed statements of belief and allegiance and made deviations from them seem hypocritical. [Reproduced by permission of the Syndics of Cambridge University Library.]

It is also worth noting that the Bull dialogues show how such works could be situated in the world of artisans, yeomen farmers, and freeholders who populate them and who constituted a considerable section of the urban voting class.[266] Conviction of the readers of partisan dialogues could be enhanced through the creation of characters (or caricatures) with whom the reader could identify, either because they were representative of a type or because they were humorous, or both. The representation of the public as artisan was thus possible. One electoral advice tract depicted *A Smith and Cutler's Plain Dialogue* (1690). Another dialogue, *Both Sides Pleas'd* (1710), took the form of a debate between high church Tory and a low church Whig, between 'a Sacheverellite parson and an Hoadlean gentleman', but it took place among the 'tradesmen (of each party)', who were a tailor, butcher, apothecary, smith, and a waterman. Indeed, the Whig gentleman makes his point by explicit reference to the artisanal world:

you that are bakers, should not be so much griev'd for the loss of a penny loaf as for the over or under-baking a whole batch of bread. And so also in relation to all other trades. That is, every man should moderate his desires, his hopes, his fears, his sorrow, and all his passions in such a due proportion as the particular thing, which at any time occasion'd any of these passions, might reasonably require. And now, to apply it to the government, people should not be immoderately solicitous who did act in such or such particular great offices, as long as the duty of each office was RIGHTLY discharged . . . if all proper METHODS are taken to preserve both CHURCH and STATE, it matters not which, to the people in general, whom her Majesty employs as the principal instrument in such our preservation.[267]

Representing politics in some measure meant creating character actors to speak the relevant parts.[268] Here it is worth recalling Hobbes's concept of the sovereign as a representative 'person' who 'is the same that an Actor is, both on the stage and in common conversation' and that the people were 'authors' of their sovereign.[269] Hobbes made the theoretical point that the polemical dialogues make: that representation was a fictional process of authorship and acted conversation. The Hobbesian representer as actor was a fiction; but the fiction was real in printed partisan dialogue.

---

[266] Cf. *A Dialogue between a Member of Parliament, a Divine, a Lawyer, a Freeholder, a Shopkeeper and a Country Farmer* (1703); Swift's 'Drapier's Letters' series of the 1720s.

[267] *Both Sides Pleas'd*, 6–7.

[268] Dialogues could also create personifications of abstract concepts (for example, *A Dialogue Betwixt Moderation and Constitution* (1714)).

[269] *Leviathan*, 112.

Fictions and the representation of the self

I want to end this chapter speculatively by wondering whether, given all
this, the political culture of the later Stuart period may have opened
significant possibilities for self-fictionalization and fictional biography.
There may be an important link between party, a concern with the 'self',
and the emergence of novelistic prose fiction. These are very large and
complex topics that I wish to tackle elsewhere at more length, so my intention here is merely to be suggestive. We have seen that party made great use
of the press, invoking and wooing readers, embroiling them in a restless
dialogue that could almost be seen as a form of public entertainment. The
fate of the parties seemed to offer a narrative of changing fortunes and
imagined futures. We have also seen party playing with the notion of truth
and identity—including the very identity of the parties themselves—and
with the idea of politicians as dissimulating, hypocritical, deceitful, du-
plicitous, and insincere, men (often gendered in this way) who hid their
core 'self' under a cloak of religion or political party. To be sure, the puritan had for long been depicted along rather similar lines; but his or her self
had in some sense remained constrained by the strictures of the puritan
way of life. Puritanism constructed boundaries of conduct. What was particularly worrying in the age of party was that the potential for deception
was now almost without bound (conscience having been devalued by
the pursuit of interest), and the deceivers now had not just the wealth of
the church but also the power and riches of the state at their disposal. The
scope for self-interest was enormously expanded. As one writer lamented,
people put 'self before the publick'.[270] Worse still, one's own identity was
now rendered uncertain by the partisanship of others. One 'honest' clerical author put this rather well when, in the wake of the Sacheverell trial, he
realized that he and his type were seen differently by his enemies. 'The trial
of the doctor last winter has brought every man upon his trial; and I must
no longer take my self for granted, while the world is discussing me; for
tho, when I turn my eyes inward, I look like the same man, and feel no
sensible alteration in my self; yet in the eyes of others, I perceive, I begin
to look dubious. With the violent Whigs, I am a Tory; and with the violent
Tories, a Whig.'[271] The double-vision of party thus rendered perceptions of
the self unstable.

[270] Baston, *Thoughts on Trade*, 180. Cf. CUL, Sel.3.238 item 416, William Cooke to Edmund
Bohun, 18 Jan. 1693, 'we are over growne with selfishness'.
[271] *The Declaration of an Honest Churchman Upon Occasion of the Present Times* (1710),
3–4.

Party polemic may also have accustomed prose writers to assume fictional personas. Both Defoe and Swift did so, but they reflected a wider culture, inherent in prose polemic from the Elizabethan Martin Marprelate onwards but certainly polished in the later Stuart period. One technique, besides creating the type of dialogue characters already discussed, was for partisans to impersonate one another. Under disguise of belonging to the opposite party, an author could expose his rivals' 'true' motives.[272] An example may be found in 1710, in an extended pamphlet controversy initiated by *Some Thoughts of an Honest Tory upon the Present Proceedings of That Party* (1710). The title was highly misleading, for the 'honest Tory' was no other than Benjamin Hoadly, the Whig cleric who preached Lockean doctrine and epitomized everything an 'honest Tory' abhorred.[273] Hoadly's tract was thus a deliberate—and dishonest?—fabrication of opinion, a fictionalizing of views which he imagined or hoped might be held by moderate Tories.[274] This did not fool contemporaries. The author of *Faults on Both Sides*, which responded to the tract, suspected the author had 'only assumed the name of a Tory, but [was] indeed a crafty Whig at the bottom', and a later tract directly accused Hoadly of the cheat.[275] Hoadly was not the only one, however, to have assumed a fictional identity. A reply, *The Thoughts of an Honest Whig*, was thought to have been written by an anonymous Tory or jacobite—one reader noted on his copy that 'the bent of this mans discourse shows him to be disaffected to the government'.[276] *Faults on Both Sides*, which ostensibly was of no party, was also the product of a fictional character. It claimed on the title page to have been written by 'Richard Harley'. No other tract by a Richard Harley is known to exist. The real author was probably Simon Clement, who had previously published on the Whig side in the exchanges about the recoinage and the Bank of England. But other hands were also thought to have been involved and it is quite possible that the mention of Harley in the title was deliberate, since the appeal to moderate opinion on both sides of the party divide was entirely in line with the policy of Robert

---

[272] Though for this to work the deception was almost always designedly transparent to careful readers.

[273] An effigy of Hoadly and his books were burned in March 1710 (Strathmore MSS at Glamis Castle, box 75, bundle 6, newsletter 30 Mar. 1710).

[274] A similar fictional pretence was present in *A Supplement to the Faults on Both Sides*, which was presented in the form of a dialogue between 'Steddy' (an old Whig) and 'turn-around', who had been seduced by the Tories for a short while before abandoning them.

[275] *Somers Tracts*, 4th collection, iii. 291; *Thoughts of an Honest Whig*, 6, 10.

[276] Manuscript note on CUL, Syn.7.70.28/1. There *were*, however, Whigs who blamed leaders of their own party (*Letterbooks of John Hervey*, i. 266, 271).

Harley.[277] 'Harlequin' and 'trickster' Harley was himself a politician accused of adopting a number of different personas, as contemporaries charted his apparent shift from whiggery to toryism.[278] In this pamphlet exchange, then, Whig, Tory, and critic of both were all fictions. The apogee of partisan polemic was thus bound to accentuate the inherently creative playfulness of the genre.

The conspiratorial nature of party also meant that plotting and politics encouraged fictionalizing possibilities, or at the very least a destabilization of truth-claims that bordered on the imaginary.[279] Not only was the testimony of key witnesses uncertain, but their lives seemed also to have been the ultimate in self-fashioning. We have already met William Chaloner, a consummate fraud hounded to death by Newton, but the best example of a semi-fictional, semi-autobiographical character is William Fuller, who first wormed himself into the court of James II and subsequently became a double-agent for the Williamite regime.[280] Fuller maximized his revelations through a very skilful use of the press, issuing a number of sensationalist tracts that sought to prove that the 'Pretender' (the future 'James III') was, as the Whigs claimed, a 'sham'. Yet Fuller was himself a sham, spending a lifetime extorting money by pretending to be a gentleman of quality. Many of his pamphlets were autobiographical—his 'evidence' could not be told without some account of his personal activity (not least to explain how he could both be loyal and also able to reveal conspiracy), but the versions of his life were fluid, dramatic, and sometimes contradictory.[281] And without access to secret information about state affairs, the public could only come to a view about the credibility of what he said by evaluating his life and assessing the probability of his printed evidence.

---

[277] *The Faults on Both Sides* was 'supposed to be written by Ld Pet[erboroug]h and the accurate Mr Fletcher' (BL, Add. MSS 72,495 ff. 26–7, Bridges to Trumbull, 25 Oct. 1710). But for Clement as the author, see Downie, *Harley and the Press*, 121. For Clement's career, see also Gauci, *Politics of Trade*, 189.

[278] *HOP II*, iv. 244–80.

[279] For a connection between plotting and the plots of contemporary drama, see Braverman, *Plots and Counterplots*.

[280] G. Campbell, *Impostor at the Bar: William Fuller 1670–1733* (London, 1961). Fuller used 'cant' in his letters to ministers (Nottingham University Library, Portland papers, PwA447–50).

[281] *The Life of William Fuller, Gent.* (1701); *Mr William Fuller's Trip to Bridewell* (1703); *The Whole Life of Mr William Fuller* (1703); *The Sincere and Hearty Confession of Mr William Fuller* (1704); *Truth at Last or Mr William Fuller's Free Account of his Books (or Narratives) and Public Transactions* (1708). He also wrote an unpublished account, about which I hope to write elsewhere.

This was important enough for MPs to spend a good deal of time sifting his claims, especially when he made assertions about the complicity of politicians. At times he admitted that his allegations were fabricated. During the rise of the high church Tories at the beginning of Anne's reign, for example, he claimed that he had 'been deceived and deluded by some men that call themselves Whigs' and that the Whig journalist John Tutchin had helped him to concoct his story.[282] But at other times he retracted his confessions.[283] Parliament condemned him as 'a notorious impostor, a cheat and a false accuser', King's Bench found him guilty in 1703 of being a 'common liar', and a series of pamphlets, written both by jacobites and Williamites, sought to expose him as such, delighting in uncovering the cheats he had performed on the public.[284] Yet the possibility that he might just be telling the truth meant that it was always impossible to dismiss what he said as a pack of lies. Fuller knew this and exploited that anxiety and uncertainty to the full. Indeed, he seems to have relished the fictions he wove and his autobiography became a rogue romance.[285] When hostile biographers sought to expose him, Fuller in turn called them 'snarling, impudent liars'.[286] He alleged, for example, that Richard Kingston, self-appointed defender of the regime and compiler of several versions of Fuller's life, was himself a cheat: not a cleric, as Kingston claimed, but a tailor who had copied a certificate found in a parson's old breeches and then passed himself off as being in orders 'to which he was never justly intituled'.[287] Fuller was a convicted fraud who nevertheless offered his testimony of jacobite plotting and the warming-pan baby as though his word was truth and claimed all his detractors were liars. He then disowned his claims, reclaimed them, and then claimed their falsity again, as the political wind

---

[282] *Mr William Fuller's Trip to Bridewell* (1703), 32; Campbell, *Impostor*, 215, 225.

[283] *The Tories Looking Glass* (1716), for retraction. In the preface to his *Twenty Six Depositions* (1702), Fuller wrote that 'if what I write be not Truth, I am, I own it, of all men the most wretched and a villain'.

[284] *The Life of William Fuller, the Late Pretended Evidence* (1692); *The Truest Account of Mr Fuller's Discovery of the True Mother of the Pretended Prince of Wales* (1696); R. Kingston, *The Life of William Fuller, alias Fullee, alias Fowler, alias Ellison . . . The First and Second Part* (1701); *The Cheater's Speculum; or, The New English Rogue* (1700); *The English Rogue Revived; or, The Life of William Fuller, Cheat-Master-General of Great Britain* (1718).

[285] For earlier rogue lives and fiction, see A. F. Kinney (ed.), *Rogues, Vagabonds and Sturdy Beggars: a New Gallery of Tudor and Early Stuart Rogue Literature* (Amherst, 1990), introduction. During the Popish Plot, Thomas Dangerfield (like Fuller, a 'double agent') was depicted by Elizabeth Cellier as *The Matchless Rogue* (1680), and Fuller claimed that, as a youth, he had been fascinated by a printed life of Dangerfield (*The Whole Life of Mr William Fuller* (1703)).

[286] Campbell, *Impostor*, 154.

[287] Fuller, *Twenty Six Depositions* (1702), preface.

dictated. When we reread either the pamphlet storm about him or his claims, we appear to have entered a world in which truth has become a mere plaything.

I am not suggesting that a partisan political culture was *responsible for* the rise of the novel or of autobiography. Clearly the emergence and development of genres is far more complicated. But a number of the features associated with such a political culture may well have provided a perfect breeding ground: an appeal to the people as participatory readers; a blurring of fact and fiction; the development techniques of personification and characterization through explorations of dissimulation and deception; the unshackling of the self; and the epistemological uncertainty of partisan language. Readers of partisan polemic did not have to seek out imaginary worlds; rather, claimed both partisans and their critics, they had these daily thrust upon them.

SUMMARY

The second part of this book has examined the impact of partisan politics on public discourse and found that the public judge, identified in the first section, was perceived to face a crisis of judgement. For although public choice was repeatedly offered at the polls, in the petitioning and addressing campaigns, and through the press, the ability of the people to make informed, rational, impartial decisions was questioned by nearly all participants. We have identified a number of ways in which contemporaries feared that public judgement was being misled:

1   The parties were engaged in a systematic, organized attempt to deceive the nation. It was not just the government that sponsored such campaigns, but the parties themselves.
2   Party discourse was railing, abusive, scandalous, and impolite. The passion and rage of party obscured cool reason and blighted proper judgement.
3   Each party made use of misleading and emotive slogans.
4   The same words and phrases were given different meanings by the parties, and meaning became destabilized by the capacity of party to see and define the same thing in two different ways. The authority of the monarch and/or church to define contested terms was challenged by the new, but vacillating and manipulable, authority of the public. In what amounted to a Hobbesian nightmare, party's appeal to the public could thus offer private definitions of truth and moral values.

5   The parties specialized in cant and jargon, creating privatized rather
     than shared languages.

6   Parties delighted in and polished the art of political lying, which be-
     came seen as intrinsic to the way in which they propagated themselves.
     There was a perception that lying and misrepresentation were used as
     a means of gaining power.

7   In such a culture, fictions and uncertainties became part of the politi-
     cal contest.

8   As representations themselves, the identity of Whig and Tory was the
     result of a contest over rival sets of representations, so that although
     voters and readers routinely used the labels as an aid to judgement, the
     labels were, it was feared, misleading.

9   Contemporaries were thus convinced that party was conspiratorial
     because it allowed inner, private, designs to be hidden under a veneer
     of public interest, and hence that it fostered hypocrisy and dissimula-
     tion of the real self. The partisan political culture offered a space in
     which to explore fictionalized selves and in which each side routinely
     accused the other of creating sets of fictions. The polemic routinely
     provoked by party conflict, and bought in massive quantity during
     the period, similarly accustomed readers to fictionalized worlds and
     hence this partisanship had wider cultural impact.

These features are observable not just in the canonical works of the period,
but were embedded in everyday partisan discourse, a discourse that, as we
have seen, was part of a national culture. And the set of anxieties about
public judgement was shared both by partisans and by those who attacked
parties. The result was a form of politics that was seen as inherently deceitful, self-serving, hypocritical, conspiratorial, and fictional. This was a self-
consciously 'modern' form of public politics—the word being applied
pejoratively to emphasize the prevalence of Machiavellian, secularized,
and interest-driven politics.[288]

   Although Whigs and Tories simultaneously accused each other of such
faults, there were periods in which such anxieties were heightened. The
polarities were most stark at moments of crisis, such as 1679–83, after
the Revolution and particularly in the reign of Queen Anne. Thus,
although the factors mapped out in this book are in many ways intrinsic to
polemical competition, and hence to be found earlier, especially in the
1580s and 1640s, there was a later Stuart intensification of features that

---

[288] 'Modern' was used in 274 titles or issues of titles 1640–60, 352 times 1660–80, 654 times
1680–1700 and 536 times 1700–20 (ESTC).

thrived wherever conflict occurred and an appeal to the public was made. And the expanded capacity of the public, together with new roles for it in terms of electioneering, addressing, and maintaining public credit, served to institutionalize practices that can be discerned (less consistently) earlier on. The epistemological uncertainties, rival truth-claims, and fictions of the later Stuart period were not unprecedented in early modern England. Nor was uncertainty merely the creation of party politics. Indeed, I hope that this work has relevance to students of politics in other periods and places, for there are important continuities in the nature of public political conflict—and many of these persist into the twenty-first century. But the implications are also partly time-specific. For intensified fears and a perception that the abuse of representative practices had become embedded in political culture provoked reaction, as the final chapter will show. What was regarded as the debased nature of public discourse gave rise to both formal and informal rules that strove after an idealized form of political dialogue. In 1716 the Whigs, now convinced that the public had been temporarily seduced by high church and jacobite lies and misrepresentations, repealed the Triennial Act in favour of one requiring general elections only once every seven years. This was an attempt to restrict public judgement. But there were also informal strategies to contain an abusive and irrational public discourse. The most important of these was an ever-stronger stress on reasoned and polite argument as a counter to the emotive passion aroused by party allegiance. Thus, although the anxieties about public discourse mapped out here can be found earlier as well as later, the rage of party in the later Stuart period did have an important transformative effect on political culture that helped to shape the eighteenth century.

CHAPTER SEVEN

Consequences

> nature will not allow any thing to continue long that
> is violent.[1]
>
> no book or story full of scandal is publish'd but it ob-
> tains immediate credit, even though told of a person
> whose good character we are well acquainted with
> and altho' no manner of evidence be brought to it.
> . . . Strange! Have the common people no judgment?
> Are they a meer mobile?[2]
>
> What wild opinions have possesst mankind,
> And made their judgment lame and reason blind?[3]

Preceding chapters have suggested the prevalence of a national political culture that was perceived to be full of passionate rage, irrationality, intemperate language, sophistry, debased rhetoric, lies, name-calling, dissimulation, conspiracy, and hypocrisy. It was a political culture in which forms of representation and misrepresentation seemed entwined. All this meant that the first age of party politics raised fundamental and perhaps worryingly unanswerable questions about the relationship between the public, information, and the nature of representation. On the one hand, the period saw the maturing of a large, increasingly well-informed, public that was frequently asked to make judgements about state affairs, to choose between contradictory representations of affairs, and then to represent its own views. On the other hand, the press, petitions and addresses, the polls, coffee-houses, clubs, and political language—the very means by which the public was expanded, informed, and represented—could be misused to spread misrepresentations. This dilemma was not entirely new—the public as a target for persuasion had, of course, been key to the Reformation—but it took place in new circumstances, such as a free press,

---

[1] *Works of Halifax*, 198.
[2] *Supplement to Faults in the Fault-Finder*, 25.
[3] E. Ward, *A True History of the Honest Whigs. A Poem* (1710), 3.

frequent elections, new types of public credit, and polarized political ideologies. If the questions about sincerity, truth-claims, and the nature of the public were not new, they were nevertheless being asked with a new urgency, in a new context. Contemporaries duly worked out a set of ideals by which to conduct politics and much else besides, and this chapter explores those ideals and their consequences.

The partisan nature of later Stuart politics acted dialectically. Out of the struggle between two competing parties emerged ideals and practices that acted in part to defuse the bitterness of the conflict. Alongside, and in a large measure in reaction to, the abusive irrationality of partisan politics contemporaries set out how politics might be conducted. Hostility to the excess or even existence of party was in part based on much older notions of civility, unity through uniformity, and the common good. Yet the repeated castigation of the behaviour of partisans redirected these older concepts and languages along lines far more familiar to students of the eighteenth century. These included the culture and language of politeness, rationality, public interest and happiness, sociability, a mature print market, and lessons in reading texts critically and how to see through manipulative discourse. The characteristics prized in this *ideal* political culture were the inversion of the partisan and we have already seen them implicitly invoked throughout this book.[4] The appeal to such ideals did not, however, eradicate party. Indeed, the longevity of party conflict merely served to reinforce them. But they could help contain it, and perhaps even, by so doing, ensure that it survived as an acceptable, permanent, feature of political life.

An idealized form of public discourse and practice was worked out, developed and disseminated through day-to-day engagement in publicly competitive politics, through the press and in the boroughs, rather than being imposed from above. The practice of politics thus helped to establish the languages of politeness, reason, interest, and sociability. This helped to constitute a political enlightenment. What this study stresses is that the routine process of publicly competitive politics provoked each side to castigate irrationality, sophistry, and slanderous abuse. The irony is that even the most passionate of zealots could contribute to this process. For we can find Whigs, Tories, as well as those who hated both parties, articulating common ideals. Since all sides were, at some stage between 1675 and 1720, the victim of each other's partisan passions they each had a

---

[4] Ironically, however, politeness exacerbated anxiety about hypocrisy and dissimulation, so it was not a simple panacea.

common experience that helped to spread a common sense of redress, even though they continued to revile each other. This is why there is no clear-cut party identity for the new political culture, though very clearly after 1714 it did benefit one party, the Whigs.

The first half of this chapter will examine the informal means by which contemporaries sought to remedy the problems associated with public discourse. But besides the appeal to reason, politeness, moderation, majority, critical reading, and fine writing, a decision was also made to terminate, or at least drastically redesign, the grand experiment in frequent elections. In 1716 the Triennial Act that guaranteed elections at least every three years was repealed. The second half of the chapter will then consider some of the implications of these developments.

THE IDEAL POLITICAL CULTURE

The ideal language of politics was the inverse of the irrational, abusive, misleading, lying, uncivil, hypocritical, and conspiratorial discourse that characterized the rage of publicly competitive politics. The following sections explore some of the facets of this process of idealization, which focused on the need for a rational, polite, moderate, clearly defined form of discourse.

Rational discourse

At one extreme of the stress on reason that sought to counter impassioned partisanship we find the emergence of political science and political arithmetic, 'the art of reasoning by figures, upon things relating to government'.[5] Numbers rather than words, or words used like numbers, it was thought, might produce a more certain and impartial form of public discourse. As Sir William Petty put it, 'instead of using only comparative and superlative words, and intellectual arguments, I have taken the course (as a specimen of the political arithmetick I have long aimed at) to express my self in terms of number, weight, or measure . . . leaving those [arguments] that depend upon the mutable minds, opinions, appetites and passions of

---

[5] Davenant, *Discourses on the Public Revenues* (1698), in *Political and Commercial Works of . . . Davenant*, i. 128. Sir William Petty's *Two Essays in Political Arithmetick* (1687) gave name to it. The genre is discussed by J. Hoppit, 'Political Arithmetic in Eighteenth Century England', *EcHR*, 49 (1996), 516–40; P. Buck, 'Seventeenth Century Political Arithmetic: Civil Strife and Vital Statistics', *Isis*, 68 (1977), 67–84.

particular men, to the consideration of others'.[6] Since in mathematics there could be no disparity between symbol and the thing it represented, the mind was freed from prejudice, taught to reason rightly and was offered a higher degree of certainty.[7] This was why John Arbuthnot called political arithmetic 'the true political knowledge'.[8] A mathematical language was a way of appearing to exclude personal judgement and achieving objectivity and certainty in the public sphere.

Yet, for all its apparent certainty, a mathematical language for politics was often ruled inappropriate or dismissed as a cover for bias. The trick of using figures to convey a spurious rationality was well known. The anonymous author of *The Danger of Moderation* (1708) likened the fashionable logic to that of Hobbes 'which is very properly styl'd the art of computation or counting; where to add is to affirm, to subtract is to deny, and the conclusion of the syllogism is the summ . . . but you must know this new political arithmetick is of a different kind from that which is purely mathematical; for there the same proportions always hold . . . but according to the new way of counting it's quite otherwise. For sometimes it may so happen that 5 shall prove more than 10.'[9] Five often proved ten when it came to computing election results. A count of votes seemed to offer numerical certainty; yet a majority could be changed and challenged, at the poll, during the scrutiny or, in parliament, at the elections committee or on the floor of the House. And a huge number of election petitions and cases offered rival arithmetic to 'prove' their point.[10] Numerical argument was, then, often only another way of being partisan. Thus a tract of 1716, by cleric Matthias Earbery, significantly entitled *Elements of Policy Civil and Ecclesiastical, in a Mathematical Method*, concluded that its anti-Hanoverian argument could only be disproved if the author's definitions or axioms were refuted. Even so, there *was* a reply, that sought to beat Earbery at his own 'rational way'.[11]

    [6] *The Economic Writings of Sir William Petty*, ed. C. H. Hull, 2 vols. (New York, 1963–4), i. 244.
    [7] Davenant, *Political and Commercial Works*, i. 128. Locke, Hobbes, and Arbuthnot all advocated the certainty of mathematical meaning.
    [8] *The Life and Works of John Arbuthnot*, ed. G. A. Aitken (Oxford, 1892), 412 quoted by Hoppit, 'Political Arithmetic'.
    [9] *Danger*, 3.
    [10] To give just one example, *The Case of Sir Thomas Lee* [1699] sought to counter an election petition by setting out the rather complex mathematics of voting to show how individual voters had to be discounted. Lee claimed the sums showed he had a majority of 7 'and were there no greater majority these do as much give the right as 700 could have done'. The printed case frequently discussed the 'credit' of the evidence about the majority.
    [11] *An Answer to a Late Pamphlet Entitled Elements of Policy Civil and Ecclesiastical, in a Mathematical Method. By a Member of the Hanoverain Society in Oxford* (1716), 23. There was

Political arithmetic restricted discourse to a narrow group of competent specialists.[12] But its claim to rational objectivity, impartiality, moderation, public good, and degree of certainty were valuable antidotes to partisanship. These ideals, on which we must now focus, were often invoked by material that was explicitly hostile to the extremes of party and that appealed to moderation and reason. *The Second Part of the Character of a Good Man, Neither Whig nor Tory* (1682) described someone 'that avoids all modern exasperating names of distinction . . . and makes a very charitable construction of other men's words and actions, and never quarrels with them because they use different vestures, gestures and modes of expression'.[13] The idealized good man was one who was 'very cautious of running into extreams and in things of a controversial nature inclines to believe the moderators to be the wisest men'. He 'entertains his private opinions with great modesty and reservation, and is never positive in doubtful matters, nor tenacious of his own sentiments, as if he had monopolized the infallible chair; nor doth he think anything true meerly because he once thought it so, but is ready to change his opinion, when better information leads him to it, and thinks he does not undervalue his judgment by so doing'.[14] Moderation meant allegiance to principles and judgement based on independent reason, rather than blind obedience to the name of a party or its leaders. 'I mind not whose opinion it is, but how far it is agreeable to TRUTH and REASON', one author announced (in capitalized Gothic font, to drive the point home).[15] The author then set out the fiction of rational politeness as violated by partisan rage:

When a man of any temper or judgment reads the pamphlets that are daily publish'd of both sides, and in conversation hears the noise and violent disputes the zealous of each party maintain, with the little reason couch'd in a multiplicity of words, where abundance of heat passes for sense and reason, he wou'd wonder that any lover of truth or justice shou'd be against *Moderation*. One side calls the other Jacobite, High-Flier, Tory, Perkinnite &c the other returns the compliment, and clamours mightily with the exprobations of Whig, Phanatick, Republican, Forty One Man and the like. Thus they endeavour to stigmatise each other's arguments with names instead of confuting them by reasons . . . whereas in right reason the argument ought to be look'd on, not the person or his principle who urges it, or what side he is of. A just friend to truth wou'd take this method, and all who do not are truly *high-fliers* on one side or the other and therefore equally criminal.[16]

another reply in 1718, *The Old Constitution and Present Establishment in Church and State Honestly Asserted*, suggesting that Earbery's remarks had some longevity.

[12] T. Porter, *Trust in Numbers: The Pursuit of Objectivity in Science and Public Life* (Princeton, 1995), viii, 217.
[13] *Second Part*, side 1.   [14] Ibid., side 2.
[15] *Ballance*, 37.   [16] Ibid., 43, cf. *Spectator*, 117.

By 'moderation' the author meant 'that we admit no heat against our neighbour for differing with us in opinion, or principles of religion, for there can be no heat against our neighbour without passion, and all that is passionate is irrational, as well as unchristian . . . we ought not to be violent against our neighbours for not believing as we do because it is no means of conviction of a free rational creature; it is impossible to force the mind by violence'.[17] Another tract also castigated the 'factious rage' of the parties, occasioned when men contended 'with madness and fury about mere names'.[18] Beneath the misleading labels the author was sure that 'we should find (cou'd we judge with moderation and impartiality) a great many on both sides, nay I believe the far greater number, zealous lovers of their country; tho very different in their notions of government. And how plain a truth this is, will appear to any person [who] will make an inquiry into the principles of each party, with that unbias'd temper [that] becomes a man that searches after truth.'[19] Reason thus involved moderation and toleration. As one cleric put it (when preaching about party strife), 'Moderation in general will amount to the due observation of a mean betwixt all unjustifiable excesses in matters of difference and contest among men, proceding from a just amplitude and ingenuity of spirit, and aiming alwaies at the advancement of the most publick and extensive good'.[20] The principles of religious toleration were thus to be extended to all forms of rational disagreement; and such moderation, even though it despised party, could push towards political pluralism.[21]

Ideally, it was thought, the reader should be presented impartially with evidence and facts, as in the courtroom. Thus the author of the Royal Society's polemic in favour of plain language, Bishop Sprat, promised in one printed vindication to tell the truth 'as carefully as if I were upon my oath' and to tell 'all the truth I can remember and nothing but the truth'.[22] This mimicry of court procedures and protocol bolstered claims to credibility, impartiality, and certainty.[23] Addison's *The Late Tryal and Convic-*

---

[17] *Ballance*, 44.
[18] R. Burton, *A Modest Enquiry into the Rise and Growth of Party Distinction Among Us* (Dublin, 1714), 5.
[19] Ibid., 6.
[20] G. Tullie, *Moderation Recommended in a Sermon* (1689), 4. Tullie had just cited Grotius.
[21] Ihalainen, *Discourse on Political Pluralism*, 11, 119.
[22] Sprat, *A Relation of the Wicked Contrivance*, 3rd edn. (1692/3), 7.
[23] Evidence and fact were thus routinely discussed. For example, Trapp's *Most Faults on One Side* (1710), 36–8, claimed that dissenters had, after the Sacheverell trial, participated in destroying their own meeting houses. [S. Clement], *A Vindication of the Faults on Both Sides* (1710), refuted this as an attempt to 'bid defiance to truth' and offered very detailed account of what had really happened so as to put it 'out of doubt'. True judgement, *Faults on Both Sides*

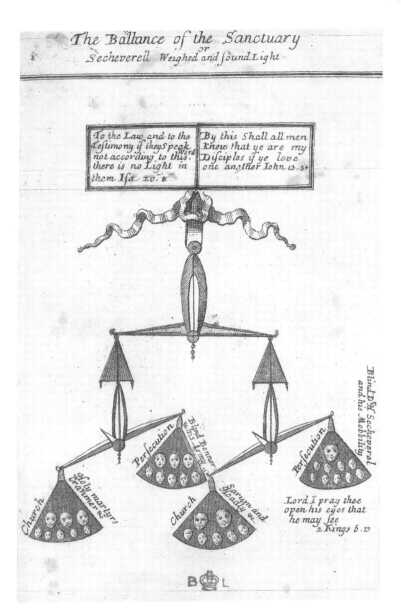

The Ballance of the Sanctuary
or
Sacheverell Weighed and found Light

To the Law and to the Testimony if they speak not according to this Word there is no Light in them Isa. 10. 8

By this shall all men know that ye are my Disciples if ye love one another Iohn 13. 34

Persecution

Blind Bonner & his Army &c

Persecution

Blindd of Sacheverell and his Mobility

Church Holy martyrs Cranmer &c

Church Ferrum and Blondly &c

Lord I pray thee open his eyes that he may see 2 Kings 6. 17

B L

The image shows a legalistic, commercial, but also mathematical, attempt to measure truth—and the high church zealot Sacheverell is 'found light'. [Reproduced by courtesy of the British Library.]

tı.... _ount Tariff (1713) literally placed 'Goodman Fact' on trial. Fact was 'a plain-spoken person and a man of very few words. Tropes and figures are his aversion. He affirms everything roundly without any art, rhetorick or circumlocution.'[24] He 'never applies to the passions or prejudices of his audience' and accused Count Tariff of 'having misrepresented him in many cunningly-devised speeches'. Count Tariff only challenged Fact by 'railing and calling names'.[25] But rational discourse avoided slander and abuse; and their employment was thought to prove irrationality.[26] Thus, argued another pamphleteer, 'in matters of dispute tis unbecoming any man to reflect upon those that happen to differ in their opinions from him; and when men come to that, it gives a shrewd suspicion that the cause is weak . . . where we build our notions upon reason and fairly offer our reasons to examination, tis not raillery but reason ought to decide it'.[27] In 1715 a tract complained that 'railing accusations' were made 'instead of sound arguments, and Billingsgate expressions are made to supply the place of demonstration'. Reacting against this, the author promised to avoid using

odious appellations, such as the writers of this age are conversant in, nor give vent to the spirit of detraction so much in practice with exasperated and injudicious tempers; but so demean myself as to shew no ill will to the persons of evil counsellors, while I am pointing out the fatal consequences of their pernicious consultations.[28]

Slander and name-calling, it was said, were not only irrational but impeded the rational process of judging. A Perswasive Oration to the People of Great Britain (1716) attacked jacobite rebels but its author recognized that he had 'to keep within the bounds of decent language' and did not believe that 'a violent tongue strengthens' any cause.[29] Adherence to reason, with its associated attributes of moderation, and civil, forensic language became an important informal idiom of restraint, particularly once formal means—pre-publication licensing, religious uniformity, infrequent par-

---

argued, could only be achieved 'by avoiding the extremes of all parties and comparing matters of fact' (Somers Tracts, 4th collection, iii. 327–8, 367, 372–3). But Faults in the Fault-Finder attacked Faults on Both Sides for being 'erroneous' and offered 'a small collection of proofs from undeniable evidence' (3).

[24] The Miscellaneous Works of Joseph Addison, ed. A. C. Guthkelch, 2 vols. (London, 1914), ii. 267.

[25] Ibid., 268–70.

[26] A Letter from J.B alias Oldcutt, to his Friend Mr Jenks (1679), 2.

[27] A Letter to Mr B—a North Wiltshire Clergyman, Relating to an Address from that Archdeaconry to the Queen (1710), 4.

[28] [W. Pittis], Reasons for a War with France (1715), 3–4.

[29] G. Waldron, Perswasive Oration, dedication.

liamentary sessions—disappeared. Linguistic and social conventions could thus help to fill a gap left when government ceased to be so active in regulating religious worship and print.

But it was not just those who claimed to be of no party, or who sought to reconcile the parties, that articulated the ideal of a rational public discourse, for partisans invoked it in order to delegitimize their opponents.[30] Reason was particularly useful for Whigs seeking to challenge an existing dominant discourse, because it invalidated, delegitimized, and even proscribed other languages.[31] Tory argument based on custom and history could thus be undercut at a stroke. Algernon Sidney, for example, declared that all the records in the world were 'nothing to the question, which is concerning reason and justice; and if they are wanting, the defect can never be supplied by any matter of fact, tho never so clearly proved'.[32] The language of reason could thus supply the legitimacy otherwise conferred by historical precedent, an essential strategy when the Whigs' historical interpretation of the ancient constitution was attacked as shaky.[33] Reason could even override the law.[34] Reason was 'the test and touch-stone of laws, and . . . all law or power that is contradictory to reason, is ipso facto void in it self, and ought not to be obeyed'.[35] One tract thus depicted Tories as vassals because they possessed a blind loyalty instead of a rational one based on law. Thus, whereas in the dialogue the Tory 'Vassal' defines 'Loyalty to be an entire subjection to the will of the king', the Whig 'Freeman' answered that obligation was founded on individual consent to the law, and that law, 'being enacted by the representatives of the people in parliament', was 'the act and deed of the whole people'. Freeman further alleges 'you Tories never judge according to reason'. The Tories were told they were 'so bigotted to an opinion, and so misled by an implicit faith, that you deny your selves the use of your reason'. In this discourse, reason, consent, representation, and true loyalty became associated concepts. Irrationality was thus more than a failure to think clearly; it led to a programme that infringed civil liberty.[36]

---

[30] Sacheverell attacked the prejudice and impartiality of his Whig and dissenting opponents (*The Nature and Mischief of Prejudice and Partiality* (1704)).

[31] The language of reason aimed to exclude appeals to emotional keywords, such as 'the Church'.

[32] Sidney, *Discourses*, 493–4.

[33] J. G. A. Pocock, *The Ancient Constitution and the Feudal Law* (Cambridge, 1957).

[34] *The Reasonableness of Toleration* (1687) argued that reason could abolish a law if it contravened it (30).

[35] Defoe, *Original Power*, 2.

[36] *True Picture of an Ancient Tory*, 5, 19, 24.

The partisanship possible in the invocation of reason is clearly evident in a tract by defender of the revolution, Richard Kingston. He promised in *Apothegmata Curiosa* (1709) to comply with 'the rules of decency, as not to insert anything in the whole, that might offend a chaste eye, a sober ear, or a religious heart, or disoblige any contending sect, faction or party'.[37] The tract duly set out maxims to guide public discourse. 'Conversation should be the most agreeable pleasure of life; but then it must be regulated'; 'opinion is but the dawning and twilight of knowledge . . . let opinions be held; but let them be held with moderation, only as opinions.'[38] 'Extreams are to be carefully avoided in politicks.'[39] But among the maxims was the explicitly whiggish claim that 'the great end of government is the happiness of the govern'd society and the happiness of a govern'd society consists in the enjoyment of liberty, property and the free exercise of religion, all which we owe, under God, entirely to the late Revolution and those principles upon which it is founded'.[40] The acceptance of Kingston's Whig ideology was packaged along with a way of talking, with the implication that to reject reasonable and moderate discourse was to reject reasonable and moderate whiggery. This was precisely the tactic pursued by Addison and Steele in their far more famous attempts to inculcate moderation and reason in the *Spectator* at a time when high-church Toryism was rampant and violent.

The same linkage of a type of public discourse and a partisan political programme can be seen in a tract of 1702. Ostensibly it sought to 'allay this publick phrensy' by reconciling the parties; but it also aimed to vindicate the impeached Whig peers.[41] And this dual feat was accomplished through a stress on an idealized form of discourse. Thus the author had

observed both in the conversation and writings of those zealous men that signalize themselves for parties, that justness and reason are things they seldom consult; and that a man is a fool, or a knave, an honest man and a wise man, as he is of this or the other faction, not according to the reasons he urges, the candour or honesty of his life. This passion, that prevails thus in these gentlemen, it is, that splits us into these unhappy divisions, when union is the only thing that can preserve us from a speedy ruin. Peruse we the pamphlets of either party and we find them equally guilty of heat and scandal, and accusations of the highest nature, while both pretend, at the same time, to be thus eager and violent, out of zeal for the publick good; in this one

---

[37] *Apothegmata*, epistle to reader.
[38] Ibid., 23, 75–6. Cf. maxim 373: 'We should use moderation in our discourses'.
[39] Ibid., 70.   [40] Ibid., 46.
[41] *The Moderator; or, A View of the State of Controversie betwixt Whigg and Tory. By a true English Man of no party* (1702), 4.

point, both Whigg and Tory agree; that is, they both allow in their pretences to it, that the publick good is the aim both ought to regard in all their disputes.[42]

But the real or true public good was not difficult to discern, the tract claimed; and in doing so, the author revealed Whig stripes. The Whig peers were 'worthy patriots' and the Tories' pretext of acting for the public good was 'specious'. In fact, the tract claimed, the Tories aimed at nothing but 'private malice'.[43] The claim to moderate between the parties, and the castigation of passion, heat, and private interest were all invoked in order to lend credibility to a defence of the Whig leaders.[44]

Yet although it worked in the Whigs' favour, it would be wrong to call the language of reason and politeness *merely* whiggish. Thus the ideal of moderating honesty was invoked by *The Introduction to the Reconcilers* (1713), but this time on the High Church side. At first the author appeared impartial. He thought his undertaking would appeal to 'every honest man' but not to the party wranglers, for whom 'the heat of the dispute has rais'd a smoke and a mist before their understandings, which has made them miss truth; nay, few on both sides do rightly understand the grounds their principles turn upon'.[45] Yet the tract ended with comments attacking dissent and in favour of Dr Sacheverell, who was praised for having 'screw'd somewhat too high than too low'.[46]

Sometimes the language of rational evidence was appropriated by the most rabid of partisans. Thus the high-church *Most Faults on One Side* (1710) refuted the Whig 'slander' that jacobites were Tories but then protested that when Tories accused the Whigs of being men of 'Republican and Rebellious principles' they produced 'evidence and prove what we assert'.[47] Of course, this did not stop the hostile *A Supplement to the Faults on Both Sides* from asking, from the Whig side, 'where is the matter of fact'?[48] Reason, and the language of fact, was thus a cunning rhetorical ploy invoked by both sides, and seen as such. Appeal to reason invalidated other arguments and undercut the languages on which those arguments were based. 'Rationality' was intolerant of anything that could be represented as 'irrational' and was therefore a powerful polemical tool. The Tory author

---

[42] Ibid., 4–5.   [43] Ibid., 19, 33.
[44] 'One may venture to affirm that all honest and disinterested Britons of what party soever, if they understood one another, are of the same opinion in points of government: and that the gross of the people, who are imposed upon by terms which they do not comprehend, are Whigs in their hearts' (*Freeholder*, 10).
[45] *Introduction*, 5.
[46] Ibid., 25. The partiality of the periodical was attacked by the Whigs (ibid., 14).
[47] *Faults on One Side*, 31.
[48] *Supplement to the Faults on Both Sides*, 57.

of *England's Enemies Expos'd* (1701) appreciated this, and not only invoked reason to claim the superiority of parliament over the people but also warned that the Whigs tried the 'trick' of passing off their rival theory 'upon the world under the title of the law of reason' even though, it alleged, reason was 'a profess'd enemy to their principles'.[49]

Locke had attempted to show readers how to discern truth from falsehood[50] but implicitly, of course, this truth was politicized, for he wanted to show readers how to discern a Whig, low church truth, which he thought was reasonable. Locke was an advocate, even architect, of Whig ideology and was closely associated with leading Whig politicians. He, of course, may have been sincere in believing that he was the impartial, rational, man depicted in his own work. But we are faced with the possibility that the discourse of reason had its own form of cunning. The impartiality of reason could be invoked to support a partisan argument. To those hostile to that partisan argument, the 'reason' employed could appear far from impartial and polite. Locke was himself taken to task for vindicating his *Essay concerning Human Understanding* in 'an angry style' and of having 'misrepresented and perverted the sense' of a reply to it.[51] The discourse of impartiality, rationality, and plain speaking could thus be invoked by party polemicists as a justifying, legitimizing, strategy. Even so, there is a further irony, in that such a discourse also militated against the excesses of party by condemning party rage and the abusive language that it provoked. Thus the invocation of impartiality, rationality, and purity of language was both a tactic to legitimize partisan discourse and, once invoked, a restraint upon it. The discourse of impartiality, rationality, and plain speaking was thus facilitated, spread, and increasingly invoked by the very phenomenon, partisan and polemical politics, that it would help to contain. Rather than Plumb's 'growth of political stability', sharply accelerated after 1714 and under Walpole, we might thus discern a dialectical, cultural process at work far earlier.[52] Walpole was its representative rather than its architect.

---

[49] *England's Enemies Expos'd*, 35.
[50] *Essay Concerning Human Understanding*, Bk iv, chs. xv–xvi.
[51] T. Burnet, *Second Remarks upon an Essay* (1697), 1–3. For a discussion of Locke's own misuse of words see 21, 28–30.
[52] Plumb, *Growth of Political Stability*, 158, suggests that in 1714 political instability looked set to continue but 'within a decade all was changed: aided both by events, and by the tidal sweep of history, a politician of genius, Robert Walpole, was able to create what had eluded kings and ministers since the days of Elizabeth I'. For interesting critiques of Plumb, see Halliday, *Dismembering the Body Politic*, 21–4 (questioning Plumb's equation of division with instability); C. Roberts, 'The Growth of Political Stability Reconsidered', *Albion*, 25 (1993), 237–55.

Defoe called reason 'the Almighty's representative' in the souls of men, a divine mechanism that exposed truth.[53] Reason was, agreed Toland, 'that faculty of the soul which discovers the certainty of any thing dubious or obscure, by comparing it with something evidently known'.[54] Reason was thus akin to conscience but usurped it as a surer guide, untainted by enthusiasm. The political and literary critic offered a form of casuistic, rational advice, allowing the individual to judge wisely and ensure against being misled. Reason was universal and, it was thought, could determine nearly all secular affairs.[55] Reason offered a tool to discern public truths and was put forward as the antidote to partisan passion, as the umpire of contest. Rationality thus became an ideal, though, as we have seen, the language of rationality proved no solution to the problem of sincerity and may even have exacerbated anxieties about the way in which outward behaviour and discourse could dissemble.[56]

Possession of reason conferred the ability to make public judgements. If the public was to be a judge it had to act through reason. Yet the Whigs were ambiguous about the degree to which all men possessed sufficient rationality; or rather they were not at all confident that all men had either the training or leisure to develop their reason and resist being misled.[57] The paradox of whiggery was that, on the one hand, as a set of ideas and a language, it encouraged men to think for themselves and, on the other, as a party, it marshalled them to follow a concerted line and cast doubts on the rationality of the people. Whiggery both upheld the power of the people and restricted it, especially when irrationality was equated with the uneducated, the unleisured, the uninformed, and those who lacked financial independence.[58] Conventions of rational politeness thus narrowed the public voice. The reaction against the rage of party, and the resulting embrace of polite reason, help to explain the shift towards, and justification for, Whig oligarchical rule.

The restrictive and exclusive nature of the language of polite reason can best be seen in the way in which it limited the role of women and those without leisure. In some ways, of course, conventions of politeness

---

[53] Defoe, *Jure Divino* (1706), dedication.
[54] Toland, *Christianity not Mysterious* (1696), 12–13.
[55] For limits to reason, see Boyle, *A Discourse of Things above Reason* (1681).
[56] The development of the 'sincere' ideal had a long gestation from the 16th century onwards. See J. Martin, 'Inventing Sincerity, Refashioning Prudence', in *American Historical Review*, 102 (1997), 1309–25.
[57] See, for example, Locke, *The Reasonableness of Christianity*, 2nd edn. (1696), 282.
[58] For remarks on the narrowing function of politeness and rationality, see T. Woodman, *Politeness in the Age of Pope* (Toronto, 1989), 22, 27; Wood, *Politics of Locke's Philosophy*, 117.

enhanced the role of women as moderators of conversation, and certainly women helped to construct the language of politeness. Women, for example, had sought to preserve a notion of conversation against the masculine rage of party. Sarah Cowper thought that 'the party rage which of these late years is very much crept into conversation is in its nature a male vice, and made up of angry passions, repugnant to the softness and modesty which is natural to the female sex.'[59] Yet the female public role was not revolutionized by the attack on patriarchal political theory, because female rationality was questioned and because attitudes to gender themselves became subject to the vagaries of partisanship.[60] Similarly the mob (the term coined in the 1680s) was also depicted as irrational and although there were periodic claims that *vox populi* was *vox dei*, the idea (essential to modern democracy) that popular opinion was right by definition was not yet accepted. Indeed, a rational choice might well not be the choice of the mob. And it is significant that Steele's *The Plebeian*—itself a rather unlikely title for a periodical by an architect of bourgeois politeness—was said to appeal 'to men's passions and not their reasons'.[61]

Reason was thus a powerful language but also an intolerant and exclusive one. The representation of any argument as irrational was a key polemical and rhetorical ploy. The ideal of reason, to which men of all (or no) sides aspired or at least professed to, thus often hid a partisan dimension. The language of reason, politeness, moderation, and public good possessed its own cunning, its own rhetorical force that delegitimized opponents whilst justifying impartiality. Yet the more frequently it was invoked by partisans and by those who attacked partisanship, the more embedded an ideal it became and hence, ironically, a cultural restraint on party zeal.

Hoadly: a Whig perspective

To illustrate further some of the complexity and even partisanship of the invocation of reason, politeness, and the public good, a brief examination of the work of Benjamin Hoadly is instructive. Hoadly was used by high-church Tories as a representative, or stereotype, of the low church Whigs.[62]

---

[59]   Herts. RO, Panshanger MSS D/EP F 33, 328.
[60]   Weil, *Political Passions*, 231–5.
[61]   *The Plebeian*, 11.
[62]   There is a vituperative biographical sketch of him in H. Vaughan, *From Anne to Victoria* (London, 1931); and see N. Sykes's essay in *The Social and Political Ideas of some English Thinkers in the Augustan Age*, ed. F. J. C. Hearnshaw (London, 1967 repr., first published 1928), ch. 6; but we need a good intellectual biography.

Hoadly was a deeply controversial figure, even on his own side, and the degree to which he was representative of low church opinion is debatable. Nevertheless, his notoriety ensured that his ideas were disseminated and at the centre of public discussion.[63] And they neatly show how far later Stuart discourse had become concerned with enlightenment ideals.

In a sermon of 29 September 1705, Hoadly claimed that 'the end of all humane authority is the good of the public' and 'the public happiness of mankind'.[64] It was therefore 'highly requisite that all in authority should be happy in a public spirit, and a true regard to the public interest', avoiding being 'led by private interests' or 'ambition'.[65] The sermon was attacked for its excessive stress on the plea of public good, and the argument was rebuffed by one tract that rehearsed the old patriarchalism.[66] Hoadly's reply was that 'prejudices' must be set aside in order to discern the truth, which had been 'borne down by words and passions'.[67] He himself, he claimed, endeavoured to make his own work 'as inoffensive' as he could to his enemies, leaving 'nothing in it that might disturb them, besides argument and the best reasoning I was capable of; assuring them that I do not esteem myself infallible, or above the instruction of better argument and better reasoning, whenever they shall please to offer it'. Hoadly spoke the language of public good, happiness, and moderate rationality in order to advance Whig and low-church claims. If governors acted against the end of their institution and attempted the ruin of the society, he said, 'it is lawful and glorious for these subjects to consult the happiness of the public, and of their posterity after them, by opposing and resisting such governours'.[68]

Hoadly also warned about the problem of language. In *The Nature of the Kingdom, or Church, of Christ* (1717), which sparked a massive print war, he asserted that

one of those great effects, which length of time is seen to bring with it, is the alteration of the meaning annexed to certain sounds. The signification of a word, well known and understood by those who first made use of it, is very insensibly varied, by passing through many mouths . . . in common discourse; till it often comes to

---

[63] The 'Bangorian controversy', over his views, involved a large paper war 1717–18. *The Works of Benjamin Hoadly*, 3 vols. (London, 1773), ii. 383–401 lists many of them.

[64] *Works of Hoadly*, ii. 20–1. Hoadly's writings were burned at Exeter in 1710 (BL, Add. MSS 70,421, f. 78, newsletter, 1 April 1710).

[65] *Works of Hoadly*, ii. 25.

[66] *The Plea of Publick Good not Sufficient to Justify the Taking up Arms against our Rightful and Lawful Sovereigns* (1706); *An Enquiry into the Nature of the Liberty of the Subject* (1706).

[67] He later made a distinction between authority and power so that his own argument could be better understood (*Works of Hoadly*, ii. 25).

[68] Ibid, ii. 37, cf. 109.

stand for a complication of notions, as distant from the original intention of it, nay as contradictory to it, as darkness is to light.[69]

This was important because

> words and sounds have had such an effect (not upon the nature of things, which is unmoveable but) upon the minds of men in thinking of them; that the very same word remaining (which at first truly represented one certain thing) by having multitudes of new inconsistent ideas, in every age and every year, added to it, becomes itself the greatest hindrance to the true understanding of the nature of the thing first intended by it.[70]

Hoadly applied this Lockean analysis to 'religion', a word that, he said, had come to mean man-made forms rather than Christ's law.[71] He therefore built a plea for the proper definition of words into his larger argument for a rational and moderate discourse.

Arguing for the supremacy of Christ's rule over the interpretation of the church, the sermon caused uproar. 'The distraction of men's minds, of different sentiments and parties was so great on this occasion . . . that for a day or two the common business of the City was at a stand, little or nothing done on the Exchange, and even many shops shut up', Hoadly admitted (or boasted).[72] He nevertheless claimed to take criticism in his stride, stating that 'calmness' was 'the happiest circumstance of a reasonable mind' and a sign of sincerity.[73] Yet when a committee of convocation took his doctrine to be destructive of church authority and the position of the monarch as head of the church, Hoadly attacked their *Representation* as a misrepresentation.[74] Claiming that he merely wished to be heard with 'impartiality', Hoadly made his appeal to the 'judgment of all', claiming that he rejoiced in sincere, rational public debate. 'I can truly say that I rejoyce as sincerely in the liberty we enjoy in this nation when it is made use of in a Christian way against my own doctrines as when it is used for them; because it tends, both to discover what is true and at length to fix it in the minds of men'. But he resented the 'personal affronts and indignities' unleashed on him from pulpits. Hoadly's language thus mirrored his ideology. He supported sincere, polite, rational, tolerant, and diverse argument, attention to the power of words to mislead, and to a justification of popu-

---

[69] *Works of Hoadly*, 402.   [70] Ibid.

[71] Hoadly's attempts at redefinition were attacked (C. Place, *The Thoughts of an Honest Whig; or, The Scheme of the Bishop of Bangor's Sermon before the King Examin'd in its particulars* (1717)).

[72] *Works of Hoadly*, ii. 429.   [73] Ibid., 411.

[74] Hoadly, *An Answer to the Representation Drawn up by the Committee of the Lower-House of Convocation* (1717).

lar resistance, public good, and private faith. And, though he claimed impartiality, he applied all this to the subordination of the church to a concept of public good, so that he was accounted a partisan who legitimized pluralism.

The language of interest and majority

The idealization of the rhetoric of reason and the disdain for partisan misrepresentations had other implications. Reason put value on consistency of outward performance and speech, so that inconsistency was a yardstick of irrationality or of hypocrisy and dissimulation. Thus the Whigs were condemned for piling 'contradiction upon contradiction, and falsity upon falsity'.[75] Narcissus Luttrell noted on his copy of Henry Care's *Draconica* (1688) that the author's inconsistency 'made manifest that what he wrote was not for religion or conscience, which he before did pretend, but meerly for interest'.[76] Conscience, then, appeared to have given way to interest. Reason could help to penetrate private 'interest' and peel away the dissimulating rhetorics and masks that were of such concern. Marchmont Nedham declared in the 1650s, when the language of interest first really gained ground, that 'interest is the true zenith of every state and person, according to which they may certainly be understood, though clothed never so much with the specious disguise of religion, justice and necessity'.[77] Defining interests offered certainty and a way of seeing through disguise, making it possible 'to surely know . . . how to judge' anyone's design.[78] If a man did but 'state his own interest aright, and keep close to it, it will not lie to him or deceive him' but prevent him from being 'drawn aside by specious pretences'. Nedham saw interest as a way of cutting 'through the slie insinuations and perswasions of cunning men', exposing the pursuit of private

[75] *Thoughts of an Honest Whig*, 15. For allegations of inconsistency, see J. Northleigh, *Parliamentum Pacificum* (1688), 56; *Vox Cleri Pro Rege* (1688), 'To the reader'.
[76] Annotated copy at BL, T.2330(33).
[77] *The Case Stated Between England and the United Provinces* (1652), 23. For discussions of the language of interest, and the associated language of reason of state, see N. Von Maltzahn, 'From Pillar to Post: Milton and the Attack on Republican Humanism at the Restoration', in *Soldiers, Writers and Statesmen of the English Revolution*, ed. I. by Gentles, J. Morrill, and B. Worden (Cambridge, 1998); S. Pincus, 'Neither Machiavellian Moment nor Possessive Individualism: Commercial Society and the Defenders of the English Commonwealth', *American Historical Review*, 103 (1998), 705–36; A. Houston, 'Republicanism, the Politics of Necessity and the Rule of Law', in Houston and Pincus, *Nation Transformed*; J. A. W. Gunn, *Politics and the Public Interest in the Seventeenth Century* (London, 1969); M. Viroli, 'The Revolution in the Concept of Politics', *Political Theory*, 20 (1992), 473–96.
[78] Nedham, *Interest will not Lie* (1659), preamble.

interest under the cover of the public good.[79] A later, long discourse about 'almighty interest' claimed it was 'the undoubted cause of all the transactions of the politick world' and that men acted 'as if they were all downright Hypocrites'; interest showed what men 'will not own'.[80] Discerning interest thus offered a means of gaining certainty and right judgement, the two qualities most at risk in publicly competitive politics. We have already encountered appeals to interest, made during electioneering but in the polemic exploring hypocrisy and dissimulation. 'Interest' seemed to offer a way to cut through such deceptions and to get at the 'truth'.

Nevertheless, interest was, like reason, highly ambiguous. On the one hand, neo-Machiavellians recognized that men would follow their own interests and that the art of government involved fitting authority to interest; on the other, the pursuit of private interest was often condemned as hostile to the public good.[81] Defining the public interest, therefore, was contentious. Who judged it? How was it discerned? How could the competing claims of rival interests, articulated through the variety of legitimate platforms offered by the state, be arbitrated? The vitality of publicly contested politics reflected an ongoing struggle between parties using different representative platforms to appropriate the arbitration of the public interest and the public good. Grand juries, petitions and addresses, the press, and parliament were legitimate, but rival, voices that claimed to speak for the public interest. Partisans frequently sought to redefine their opponents as pursuing private interests and private benefits. The contest to represent the public interest thus necessarily constructed a model in which parties and their leaders were seen as conspiring against the good of the nation.[82] And the general pursuit of interest, noted one pamphleteer, made it vain 'to pretend to unanimity'.[83]

Interest, like reason, might also be said to have had whiggish overtones. Two of the cunning words of politics were 'consent' and 'majority'. Both, of

---

[79] Nedham, *Interest will not Lie*, 3.

[80] D. Abercromby, *A Moral Discourse of the Power of Interest* (1690), Author to the Reader.

[81] Trenchard, *A Short History of Standing Armies in England* (1698), preface, argued that 'a government is a mere piece of clockwork . . . it is certain that every man will act for his own interest; and all wise governments are founded upon that principle: so that this whole mystery is only to make the interest of the governors and governed the same'. Yet the work is regarded as a classic statement of 'old' Whig principles, which valued the public good over, and often against, private interest. Cf. 'All government is interest, and the predominant interest gives the matter or foundation of the government' (*Political Works of . . . Harrington*, 836).

[82] Knights, 'Faults on Both Sides'. Gunn suggests 'public interest' was a claim associated with non-participant governments (Ball and Hanson (eds.), *Political Innovation*, 196).

[83] *Party No Dependance: Containing an Historical Account of the Rise and Fall of Parties* (1713), 2.

course, had a long history. But the language of interest and reason gave them a new importance, for a majority might show where the public interest lay and the public would only consent to what was in their interest. A majority principle was the way to arbitrate a divided society and preserve a decision-making capacity; and it was also the means by which disagreement could still confer consent.[84] So long as there was a willingness to recognize the binding power of a majority decision, even vehement hostility to governmental action could be contained within an expectation of allegiance and peaceable unity. Once again, frequent elections are important here, for electoral disputes were resolved on the majority principle. They hence served to embed for practical reasons the doctrine articulated most clearly in the contract theory of Hobbes and Locke.[85] But an appeal to the 'major part' was also common in the preamble of many a petition or address that could not command unanimous consent.[86] And polemic frequently sought to represent its viewpoint as that of the majority. The factors highlighted as shaping political culture thus helped to embed the majority principle. That was crucial to the development of a representational society, but it could only really flourish under certain conditions prevalent in the later Stuart period: when uniformity was no longer the goal; when physical force as a means of resolving conflict was abandoned; when there was a concept of a public opinion or interest; when there were communicative and representative practices that allowed the character and voice of the majority to be expressed; and when the majority agreed not to persecute the minority merely for its opinion.

The problem, however, lay in how the majority was to be discerned, for the majority was itself often a representational construct.[87] A minority could be represented as a majority; or a majority might be said to have been achieved as the result of misrepresentation. The whole of the political system was geared towards representing the majority or claiming to represent it, slighting opponents as representing a minority or sectional interest, and trying to persuade the majority to back a certain set of principles or men. Moreover, many were uncertain that the majority of the

---

[84] W. Kendall, *John Locke and the Doctrine of Majority Rule* (Urbana, 1965).

[85] A high church author argued that the majority principle was used 'not because the greatest number are the wisest and best; for it is commonly otherwise; but because there would be endless disputes who are wisest and best, whereas there can be no doubt about the majority' (*An Enquiry into the Nature of the Liberty of the Subject* (1706), 19).

[86] For example, Penzance's address in 1712 came from the 'gentlemen, merchants, tradesmen and others, being the majority of the principal inhabitants' ((*LG*, 5051). Cf. ibid., 5270 (Portsmouth), 5302 (Saltash)).

[87] Defoe, *A Fifth Essay at Removing National Prejudices* [1707], 5–6.

people were always wise, rational, and capable of judging when they were being misled. The acceptance of the majority principle was thus tempered by the recognition that the majority itself was no proof of rectitude and might need extraordinary guidance.

Consent was, of course, necessary for any majority choice to emerge. But it went much further than that, for the notion of consent conveyed all the idealization of individual and public judgement that we have been exploring. Even so there was little agreement about whether or not consent had to be active, rather than passive. Direct consent was predicated on the idea of a close and active relationship between the individual and his representative institutions, and hence reconciled participation and representation. Indirect consent, on the other hand, involved a much more passive relationship, in which the representative was given a great deal of autonomy; expectations of participation were weak. The debate over the degree to which MPs were representatives or delegates, explored earlier, was one aspect of this ongoing tension. And it was, at least in the short term, resolved in favour of passive consent. Addison's *Freeholder* announced that the British 'happy constitution' ensured that 'the bulk of the people virtually give their approbation to every thing they are bound to obey and prescribe to themselves those rules by which they are to walk'.[88] Addison thus replaced the active citizen embroiled in partisan rivalries with the spectator and virtually represented freeholder.[89]

The critical public and public criticism

> the public realm is constituted by the critics and the
> spectators and not by the actors or the makers.[90]

Polite reason, the language of interest, majorities, and consent were all part of the preoccupation with public judgement in a representative society. Another dimension of this, linked also to the diversity of printed opinion, was textual criticism. Partisan conflict encouraged authors to see each other's arguments as literary as well as political pieces. In other words, style was another aid to public judgement. Thus Joseph Trapp accused the author of the *Supplement to the Faults on Both Sides* of 'false English'. In

---

[88] *Freeholder*, 1.
[89] For virtual representation, see P. Langford, 'Property and Virtual Representation in Eighteenth-Century England', *HJ*, 31 (1988), 83–115.
[90] 'Judging', appendix to Arendt, *The Life of the Mind* (1981), 262.

turn *A Vindication of the Faults on Both Sides* attacked Trapp's work for its poor style, by which 'he discovers the meanness of his own talent, and shews that he is but (what some call) a Haberdasher of small-wares'.[91] Trapp was thus termed 'Mr Critic', because he was both politico-religious and literary critic (as a high church polemicist and professor of poetry his two functions were entwined).[92] Argument, wit, and style were fused, so that an attack on style was an attack on ideology, and vice versa. In this vein, argument and true wit had, it could be claimed, been replaced by scurrilous railing or dullness.[93] Hoadly's fictional 'Honest Tory' complained that he could 'hardly meet with any one thing writ on our side but what is either inhumanly dull or inhumanly abusive; what is enough to make either the man very sick or the Christian very melancholly'.[94] Thus, the mock-lament ran, Tory 'wit is dwindled with our honesty and our sense hath forsaken us together with our plain-dealing'. This simple dullness was because everything seemed fitted for 'the capacity of watermen, porters, carmen and plowmen, leaving gentlemen and men of common sense to shift for themselves'.[95] And a (fictional) Whig neighbour said he found 'the party-writings of the Tories as void of wit as I ever thought their cause to be of reason'. Instead of wit, then, there was just abuse. Tory tracts were alleged to be 'void of sense and good manners, sparing neither dead nor living, insulting the one beyond example, and abusing the other beyond patience'.[96] According to this tract, then, the Tory case relied on lies and abusive language rather than argument, and rested on an attempt to trick the unthinking lower orders into supporting them. The Tories were represented as lacking manners and sincerity; and lack of wit was evident to anyone who read their work. One tract attacking Charles Davenant's hypocrisy thus made 'many reflections on his style'.[97] A refined style of writing was important because it was instrumental in the process of influencing the public; and its absence could indicate a lack of rational argument.

[91] Trapp, *Most Faults on One Side*, postscript, 5; *Somers Tracts* 4th collection, iii. 367.

[92] Ibid., 369. Trapp's lectures on poetry were praised in 1713 by Henry Felton as examples of polite criticism (P. Wilson, 'Classical Poetry and the Eighteenth century Reader', in Rivers, *Books and their Readers*, 88).

[93] Pope most famously used dullness against the Whigs, but it is clear dullness was associated with partisanship more generally. See also, A. Williams, 'Whig Literary Culture: Poetry, Politics and Patronage, 1678–1714', Ph.D., Oxford (2000).

[94] *Somers Tracts*, 4th collection, iii. 288.

[95] Ibid., 288. [96] Ibid., 289.

[97] *The True Tom Double*, 27.

Criticisms of style became intrinsic to partisan polemic. Response and counter-response necessitated careful attention to text, form, and style as well as content. Partisan authors thus engaged in extended exercises in textual appreciation. For example, a tract of 1710 reproduced a letter concerning an Essex election and then offered comments on it. Its *first* remark was about the bad English employed in the letter ['several gentlemen of the county of Essex HAS done. . . .]: 'this is not true grammar and not fit for a candidate of so great and loyal a county as Essex is', it complained. It then went on to correct the letter's English. The claim that one candidate would be 'violently' opposed was ridiculed; 'vigorously', it was said, was more appropriate.[98] Bad grammar and poor style, it was being suggested, implied bad or impolite politics. Such textual deconstruction, blending literary and political criticism, applied to anything presented to the public and no author was immune. In 1705 an attack on the Whig journalist John Tutchin observed that in his writings 'even her Majesty's speeches were taken to pieces.'[99]

Political censure, then, often involved a process of extensive literary criticism, in which style and language were carefully scrutinized.[100] This process was necessary because, as Defoe observed, men habitually wore masks that needed deconstructing.

This, Sir, is an age of plot and deceit, of contradiction and paradox; and the nation can hardly know her friends from her enemies; men swearing to the government and whishing it overturn'd; abjuring the pretender, yet earnestly endeavouring to bring him in; eating the Queen's bread and cursing the donor; owning the succession and wishing the successor at the devil; making the marriage (UNION) yet endeavouring the divorce; fawning upon the toleration yet railing at the liberty—it is very hard under all these masks, to see the true countenance of any man—there are more kinds of hypocrisie than that of occasional conformity—and the whole town seems to look one way and row another.[101]

Since men habitually hid their motives, textual analysis was another way of trying to uncover their true designs. Defoe's comments had been prompted by an exchange between Henry Sacheverell and his low church critic, William Bisset. Bisset's literary style had played an important part in

---

[98] [I. Sharpe], *This is the Time; or, Serious Advice to a Country Friend Concerning the Election of Members of Parliament* (1710), 1.

[99] Tufton, *History of Faction*, 117.

[100] *Some Critical and Politick Remarks on a Late Virulent Lampoon Call'd Faction Display'd* (1704).

[101] Defoe, *A Letter to Mr Bisset Eldest Brother of the Collegiate Church* (1710), 9–10.

the contest, for whilst he claimed to write 'plain English', his adversaries claimed his style was 'pulpit buffonry . . . fitter for the playhouses' and accused him of 'the deformation of scripture as well as English'.[102] Literary style was thus scrutinized as a means of uncovering authenticity, veracity, and intent. To be sure, textual analysis was not new but it was becoming routine. 'There have been always criticks', remarked the earl of Mulgrave, 'but I believe there was never such an age and nation for that humour as ours is at present'.[103]

Richard Steele, whose prose is now taken as the epitome of the polite style, offers an excellent example of literary criticism used for political effect. In 1714 he was expelled the House of Commons for writing libels. But, in a tract addressing 'all the rest of mankind' against the judgement of the House of Commons, Steele complained that his enemies had 'misrepresented me in every part of my character', and misread his work. 'It would be very unfair to separate my words, and to pronounce a meaning in them, which I have not expressed, when that which I have expressed, is a positive denial of having entertained any such meaning . . . by this way of arguing, it is not in the power of words to be free from unwarrantable hints and innunendos'. Partisans, he was suggesting, read their own prejudices into a text and threatened to make any common understanding impossible. Steele thus ironically (and self-consciously) appealed to the argument made in Sacheverell's defence that 'if there be a double sense, in either of which these words are equally capable of being understood', the law erred 'on the side of mercy' and thus 'a subject of England is not to be made criminal by a labour'd construction of doubtful words'.[104] The reader was appealed to as an impartial judge (over and above the parliamentary judge), and urged to find Steele not guilty. Right-reading was essential for public judgement.

The search for veracity amid competing public discourse inevitably pushed men into analysing language as well as content. Habermas saw the literary and political public spheres as developing separately, with the literary coming first.[105] But the one helped to formulate the other, and

[102] *B-ss-t B-sh-t; or, The Foulness of More Plain English* (1704), 5–6.
[103] *Works of John Sheffield*, ii. 259.
[104] *Mr. Steele's Apology for Himself and his Writings* (1714), in *Tracts and Pamphlets by Richard Steele*, ed. R. Blanchard (London, 1967), 292, 299, 307, 317, 335–6.
[105] Habermas, *Structural Transformation*, 29. T. Eagleton, *The Function of Criticism* (1984), argues that 'seen historically, the modern concept of literary criticism is closely tied to the rise of the liberal, bourgeois public sphere in the early 18th century' (10). Nancy Streuver discerns an early eighteenth-century 'transformation of rhetoric into criticism' (Vickers and Streuver (eds.), *Rhetoric and the Pursuit of Truth*, 83).

criticism was both a literary and a political activity. Indeed, it could hardly be otherwise when conventions of anonymity encouraged literary criticism as a means to identifying the author.[106] Commentators on political polemic *were* critics. They scrutinized work in order to discover inconsistencies, mistakes, and unreasonableness. Such a fine attention to the detail of another's argument led to an appreciation of the way in which it was written or in which words were misused. Marchmont Nedham thus claimed he had 'to play the Grammaticaster', when dissecting the usage of a tract critical of the court, because the misuse of prepositions had perverted the author's definition of the law.[107] Sacheverell was criticized for his style as well as his inflammatory content. His sermon was dismissed as 'a rhapsody of incoherent and ill-digested thoughts, dress'd in the worst language that could be found'.[108]

Tory and Whig could define good and bad writing. This is why the Whig John Dennis could remark, looking back on the temporary triumph of toryism, that since the accession of Anne 'taste' had disappeared:

For the greatest part of that time a fatal delirium seems to have seiz'd upon Great Britain; an epidemical stupidity, which has done more mischief than the most raging plague. For during the greater part of that time, have not two thirds of the nation believ'd and declar'd that white is black, that black is white; that virtue is detestable, that vice is amiable; that wisdom is contemptible, that folly is estimable; that we are to hate, slander, to curse our deliverers; to love, to extol, to bless our destroyers; that tis better to fall down and adore the devil than to worship God in spirit and in truth; that true religion can have no support but from atheism and idolatry; that liberty can only be upheld by tyranny, property by beggary, trade by bankruptcy.[109]

As David Womersley has argued, between 1660 and 1750 criticism was for many 'openly and deliberately co-ordinated with other areas of their lives,

---

[106] For example, *The Mercy of the Government* claimed that the author of the anonymous *An Argument to Prove the Affections of the People the Best Security of the Government* (1716), could 'be discovered only by the likeness of stile and manner to some other pieces, so that the critical world are divided in their opinions to whom to attribute this celebrated performance' but suspected a bishop (23). It was, indeed, by Bishop Francis Atterbury.

[107] Nedham, *Second Pacquet*, 21.

[108] [W. Fleetwood], *The Thirteenth Chapter to the Romans Vindicated from the Abusive Sense Put upon it. Written by a Curate of Salop* (1710), 1. For another attack on Sacheverell's bad style, see Kennett, *A True Answer to Dr Sacheverell's Sermon before the Lord Mayor, Nov. 5 1709* (1709), 4–6, 10–12.

[109] *Remarks upon Mr Pope's Translation of Homer* (1717), 2 (*The Critical Works of John Dennis*, ed. E. N. Hooker, 2 vols. (Baltimore, 1943), ii. 116).

in particular with their political lives'.[110] Party and criticism were intimately connected, for, it was feared, what was 'formerly the art of judging well, is now become the pure effect of spleen, passion and self-conceit'.[111] Alexander Pope agreed and his *Essay on Criticism* (1711) was thus in part an attack on the type of partisan and debased criticism that was so common to his world. The attack by Pope and others on the Whig authors John Dennis, Richard Blackmore, and John Oldmixon, whose writings were depicted as dull and workmanlike, was thus a politicized and familiar response.[112]

As both Whigs and Tories recognized, criticism was necessary as advice to unwitting readers. Mary Astell warned that 'most readers are superficial, men of short views, of great prejudices and passions, and therefore no wonder that they are best pleas'd with writers of their own depth'. She advised her imaginary (and ironically male) reader to be more critical. 'I would intreat him neither to believe me or any other writer on our bare word, to take nothing upon trust, but to see with his own eyes, and to judge according to his own understanding; to be of no party, no opinion, because this relation or that great man are of it; because it is plausible, because it will serve a present turn, or make a fortune, or even because one has been of this opinion formerly'. Yet she knew that 'a pert jest or a sly reflection, a probable slander or even a down right calumny' that had the right 'gingle of sounds' would 'pass with very many readers for arguments and demonstrations'.[113] And Astell, of course, was far from being an impartial writer, for her high church allegiance was made utterly clear.

The Whigs also turned to criticism to help the reader discern the truth. White Kennett's remarkable book *The Wisdom of Looking Backwards* (1715) was published 'to judge the better of one side and t'other by the speeches, writings, actions and other matters of fact on both sides, for the four years last past'. The volume collected details about pamphlets and other print, arranged in two columns: one of material in favour of the high churchmen and the other of material against them. To these Kennett added his own

---

[110] *Augustan Critical Writing*, ed. D. Womersley (London, 1997), xii.

[111] S. Cobb, *Discourse on Criticism* (1707), reproduced in *Augustan Critical Writing*, 201.

[112] Oldmixon, in revenge, blamed English critics for not distinguishing between different kinds of wit and hence praising 'Sir William Temple, and Sir Roger L'Estrange, the Tatler and the Spectator . . . though their manner is as different as their faces' (*Essay on Criticism*, 44).

[113] Astell, *Moderation Truly Stated*, 2–3.

observations on the prints. Since he was also the author of several tracts in the period, the volume represents an extended commentary on the press, from the perspective of both reader and author, aimed at offering criticism so that the public judged aright.[114] Both sides, then, tried to use criticism to neutralize their political opponents. The deconstruction of texts occurred over form as well as content.

Finally, the guidance of the critic became increasingly attractive and necessary as the volume of print increased. Ironically, once a state censor had been abandoned, an informal censor was needed to filter and comment on the profusion of public discourse. Isaac Bickerstaffe, the fictional persona of the *Tatler*, set himself up as a self-conscious censor, and the term 'censor' was then taken up by others.[115] Thus *The Principles and Practices of the Present Sett of Whigs Defended* (1713) claimed to be written 'by the censor of Great Britain'.[116] An essential part of the censor's role—and indeed how he or she exercised his authority—was criticism of style as well as content. In other words, the censor of print and politics was also and inevitably a literary critic. Whereas the state censor had the power to alter text, the critic censor suggested the ways in which any text fell foul of standards of content and style. The licenser had invoked the authority of the state; the critic invoked the authority of the public and a concept of taste. The licenser had done things to texts; the censor or critic used text to do things to other texts. The censor or critic used language to act on and to shape reader response, recognizing that words were the best tools against words.

THE REPEAL OF THE TRIENNIAL ACT

Whosoever wou'd our follies know
And how much lewder ev'ry day we grow,
Let him but once to an election go . . .
You'd think elections made and members stood
Both in defiance of the publick good . . .

---

[114] It was based on BL, Lansd. MSS 1024, a journal noting the appearance of tracts and his comments on them, from 1681 to 1714, that becomes a diary and commonplace book.

[115] Cf. A. Goldgar, 'The Absolutism of Taste: Journalists as Censors in C18th Paris', in *Censorship and the Control of Print*, ed. by R. Myers and M. Harris (Winchester, 1992).

[116] Subtitle. Cf. *The British Censor* (1712); *The Censor* (1717); [S. Parker], *Censura Temporum: The Good or Ill Tendencies of Books, Sermons, Pamphlets &c Impartially Consider'd* (1708).

> All stunn'd and senseless in the drunken fray
> They shit and spew their liberties away.[117]

As we have seen, one of the key factors shaping later Stuart political culture was the frequency of elections. Proponents of the Triennial Bill had argued that frequent parliaments were 'the right of the people', 'the only thing that will settle this government on a lasting foundation' and ensure MPs were 'the true representatives of the people'.[118] But in 1716 the Triennial Act, enacted in 1694 by the Whigs to ensure that elections were held at least every three years, was repealed by the same party.[119] How can this apparent shift away from revolution principles, by both people and the Whigs, be accounted for?

This book has argued that the political culture fostered by frequent electioneering was characterized by anxieties about the prevalence of a manipulative, lying, slanderous, conspiratorial, and misrepresenting public discourse. It has also been suggested that it was during electioneering that words and phrases became most abused, that lies became most prevalent, that incivilities became most apparent, and that reason appeared most threatened. The key moment of public judgement thus became the very occasion by which public judgement was corrupted and rendered irrational. This seemed to be apparent from the standpoint of 1716. In 1688 the 'people' had helped to put William on the throne; but in 1715 they threatened to ease George I out of it. The paradox was noted at the time by one cleric, who thought 'a more gross delusion has scarce ever been seen, than for men to be almost distracted for fear of popery and arbitrary power at one time and to appear by their conversations and writings so little apprehensive of them at another, and all within the space of three and twenty years'.[120] The repeal of the 1694 Triennial Act appeared to be the means by which public misjudgement could be neutralized and misrepresentation

---

[117] *Suffragium; or, The Humours of the Electors* (1702), 4, 6–7.
[118] Grey, *Debates*, ix. 393, 413. Cf. Nottingham University Library, Mellish papers, Me 150–89/2 Saunderson to E. Mellish, 14 Feb. [1693]; Me 150–89/11, same to same, 11 Dec. 1694.
[119] In 1708 there had been talk of suspending the Triennial Act 'for a year or two' when a jacobite invasion seemed imminent (Cheshire RO, Arderne MSS, DAR/H/14, Sir Edward Lawrence to Sir John Crew, 2 Mar. [1708]). Similar rumours had circulated the previous November but John Hervey dismissed them as 'only bruited about by ye malice of ye Tories to blacken our friends ye Whiggs by an insinuation of their becoming unnatural enough to destroy their own issue for ye serving a present purpose' (*Letterbooks of John Hervey*, i. 229–30).
[120] J. Woodward, *The Divine Right of Civil Government* (1712), dedication, iv. He noted that contemporaries played with dangerous words as 'children play with edged tools til they cut themselves'.

could be defeated. Frequent elections and the excesses of party politics generated a revulsion against incivility, irrationality, and social inversion, sentiments that fostered the cultivation of civility, politeness, and social segregation. In turn, these linguistic and social conventions, once embedded in the political culture, undermined the rationale for frequent elections. An examination of the polemical arguments for the repeal allows us to explore these issues.[121]

Before turning to contemporary perceptions of electioneering, however, it is important to recognize social and economic pressures that also appeared to be reorienting the nature of the public and questioned the participatory role of the people in the representative system.[122] One of these was the politics of poor relief.[123] During the rage of party, the cost of poor relief spiralled. In Norwich, for example, the burden became 'very uneasy' to the rate-paying inhabitants. John Fransham, with whom Defoe had corresponded, kept figures showing that in 1690 poor relief in the city had cost £1,920, but had risen inexorably, to £2,559 in 1700, £4,908 in 1710, and peaked at £7,464 in 1720.[124]

There were less dramatic, but still very significant, rises elsewhere.[125] The amount raised in poor relief rocketed after the Restoration, but particularly after 1689. An inquiry in 1696 concluded that poor rates in England and Wales amounted to £400,000, three times the amount raised by charitable donations and, hence, as Paul Slack claims, tantamount to a

---

[121] The pamphlets may have been co-ordinated: two use the same phrase (*A Second Letter to a Friend in Suffolk Occasion'd by a Report of Repealing the Triennial Act* (1716), 34, and A. Sykes, *The Suspension of the Triennial Bill the Properest Means* (1716), 32).

[122] Steve Hindle has suggested that even in the seventeenth century the parish 'became oligarchic', with the chief inhabitants representing themselves not just as the most honest, most able men, but also *as* the parish (Hindle, 'A Sense of place? Becoming and Belonging in the Rural Parish, 1550–1650', in Shepard and Withington (eds.), *Communities in Early Modern England*, 109). Hindle's work suggests social pressures working towards a more representative society.

[123] I intend to write about this more fully elsewhere.

[124] Norfolk RO, Frere MS NNAS safe II 1a–b, MS History of Norwich by Benjamin Mackerell *c*.1737. The city erected a workhouse in 1712 and Fransham was appointed clerk to the Board of Trustees. In 1720 he published *An Exact Account of the Charge for Supporting the Poor of the City of Norwich*, which contains figures for each parish. For the relationship between poor relief and electioneering, see also D. G. Stuart, 'The Parliamentary History of the Borough of Tamworth, Staffordshire, 1661–1837', M.A., London, (1958), 26.

[125] Hindle, 'Power, Poor Relief, and Social Relations in Holland Fen, *c*.1600–1800', *HJ*, 41 (1998), 67–96; P. Clark and P. Slack (eds.), *Crisis and Order in English Towns, 1500–1700* (London, 1972), 20, 34; H. French, 'Chief Inhabitants and their Areas of Influence: Local Ruling Groups in Essex and Suffolk Parishes 1630–1720', Ph.D., Cambridge (1993), 79.

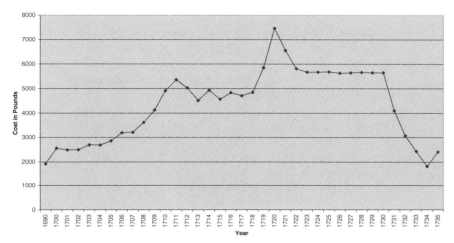

Poor Relief in Norwich, 1690–1735.

rudimentary 'but organised system of public welfare'.[126] The rise in poor relief was in part due to the impact of war against France, which dislocated parts of the economy. The continuation, and type, of war, became controversial and a good deal of the political heat in 1710–13 centred on the inability of the country to sustain further conflict. Severe economic disruption and social polarization had also been the result of the financial measures taken by the Whigs to finance the war. The recoinage in the mid-1690s had proved particularly painful, since the circulation of coin virtually ground to a halt in some parts and this led to unrest which continued in the later 1690s under the pressure of bad harvests. For example, *The Complaint of English Subjects* (1700), by Richard Newnam of Tiverton, deplored the decay of trade, which he attributed to 'the revolution of the late coin'. Newnam complained that the rich used the recoinage to get richer—though he reckoned that the wealthy and the devil would 'drive my truth to the wall with disdain . . . and then it shall pass for truth as if they were innocent and myself guilty of accusing them maliciously and wrong-

---

[126] P. Slack, *The English Poor Law 1531–1782* (Cambridge, 1995), 21–2; P. Slack, *Poverty and Policy in Tudor and Stuart England* (London, 1988), 170–3 and ch. 9.

fully'.[127] The poor, not the landed, were the real victims of the new financial
system and massive hike in taxation. They were certainly unable to take
advantage of the new stock market and system of public credit, except for
the lotteries.[128]

Yet partisan electioneering, it was complained, turned men away from
pursuing trades that could alleviate their poverty. Thus a tract of 1701
argued that feuds produced by elections 'make people factiously pursue
the interest of a party to the neglect of the public and the ruin of trade'.
People's time was now spent 'caballing at a tavern'; talking politics at a coffee-house was no longer amusement 'but the main business that's pursued'. Trade flourished best, by contrast, when 'private men seldom
concern themselves with public management'. In short, 'parties endanger
the peace and ruin the trade of the city'.[129] Frequent elections and party
politicking thus clashed with an increasingly aggressive commercial culture perceived to be threatened by partisanship. 'The great decay of our
woollen manufacture is by our most eminent traders very much ascribed
to the late frequent riots and commotions among the ordinary people,
whose minds have been taken off from their respective callings and occu-
pations, interrupted in a course of industry, and turned to other matters by
frequent elections', moaned one writer.[130] Electors supported themselves
not through industry, it was suggested, but through the market of their
votes.[131] Elections had taught men 'the value of their votes. The Question
is not now, who is best qualified to serve his country, but who is the best
bidder.'[132] As another pamphleteer put it, 'abundance of drunkenness,
swearing, cursing, quarrelling and debauchery of all sorts are not only the
necessary attendants upon elections; but the preludes to them for some
months before; during that time, the voters are indispos'd for labour,
neglect the business of their particular callings, contract habits of idleness
which tend to the impoverishing of their families and the decay of trade.'[133]
In 1716 the Whig defender of the Revolution of 1689, James Tyrell, urged
the gentry to resist bribing and treating the people, since they had made

[127] *Complaint*, 13.
[128] *Reasons to Support the Proposal for Granting Divers Sorts of Annuities Such as the
Common People May be Able to Compass* (1705).
[129] *Enquiry into the Inconveniencies of Public . . . Elections*, 4–6.
[130] *The Alteration of the Triennial Act Considered* (1716), 14.
[131] Ibid., 15.
[132] *A Letter to a Friend upon Occasion of the House of Commons Passing a Bill, Intituled an
Act for Enlarging the Time of Continuance of Parliaments* (1716), 26.
[133] Ibid., 17–18 (mispaginated, *recte* 25–6).

themselves 'wholly to depend upon the interest and favour of a beggarly and corrupt mobb, which makes not further difference of persons but as they will fill their bellies with beef and ale or their pockets with ready cash'.[134] The issue of electoral corruption thus became linked to perceptions of the poor and of the people more generally.

The polarized social consequences of war, unprecedented levels of poor relief, and new forms of capitalism tended to accentuate long-held views about the unsteadiness, irrationality, dependence, corruptibility, and dangerousness of the mob, at a time when public judgement and the language of rationality, independence, and virtue were central to public discourse. The resulting unease about the 'public' was particularly evident when contemporaries mused on electioneering. Sarah Cowper, reflecting on how 'very busie' the people were in December 1707 preparing for a general election (which occurred in May the following year), at first displayed a whiggish sympathy for the virtue of the people and then, in a throw-away line, dismissed it as no longer relevant to her corrupt age:

one may sometimes perceive that the body of a people has juster views for the pub-lick good and pursues 'em with greater uprightness than the nobility and gentry, who have so many private expectations and perticuler interests that hang like a false balance upon their judgments, and may possibly dispose 'em to sacrifice ye good of their country to the advancment of their own fortun^{es} wheras the gross of ye people can have no other prospect in changes and revolutions than of publick blessings that are to diffuse themselves thro' ye whole state in general. To mee it seems this observation holds not good in this age wherein riot and drunkeness carrys the choice.[135]

Electioneering thus tended to militate against the idea of a rational multi-tude interested in the public good, instead helping to portraying the pub-lic as irrational and self-interested. Shortly after the 1708 election, Sarah Cowper called the mob 'that enemy of reason, vertue and religion' and in 1712 she observed the English to be 'mad' and changeable.[136]

Electoral feuding was seen as provoking impolite behaviour. Codes of civility and politeness were thus both being violated by the process of par-tisan politics and then reinforced as contemporaries sought to idealize a better way of doing things—and even to construct politeness as the

---

[134] Tyrrell, *His Majesty's Government and Ministry Vindicated* (1716), 49.
[135] Herts. RO, Panshanger MSS D/EP F 32, 141.
[136] Ibid., F 34, 152, 204. Interestingly, she specifically included irrational gentry among the 'mob'.

To the Electors of an Alderman for the Ward of QUEEN-HITHE.

WHEREAS an Evil and Pernicious Custom has of late very much prevail'd, at the Election of Aldermen for this City, by Treating at Taverns and Ale-houses, thereby engaging Many unwarily to give their Votes: Which Practice, appearing to Sir *Ambrose Crowley* to be of dangerous Consequence to the Freedom of Elections, he hath avoided the Excess thereof. Nevertheless, to make an Acknowledgment to this Ward for their intended Favour, he hath deposited in the Hands of Mr. *John Midgley*, one of the present Common-Council, Four hundred and fifty Pounds, to be dispos'd of as follows, provided the said Sir *Ambrose Crowley* be the Alderman, *viz.*

All such that shall Poll for Sir Ambrose Crowley, *shall have one Chaldron of good Coals* Gratis.
And half a Chaldron to every one that shall not Poll against him.
And the Remainder to be laid out in a Clock, Dial, or otherwise, as the Common-Council Men of the said Ward shall think fit.

And if any Person shall refuse to take the said Coals to himself, he may assign the same to any Poor Electors in the Ward.

I do acknowledge to have received the said Four Hundred and Fifty Pounds, for the Purposes above-mention'd, for which I have given a Receipt

Witness, James Hallet,   John Midgley.
Jeremy Gough,
Edward Davis.

N. B. Whereas several Persons have already engaged to Poll for Sir *Benjamin Green*. It is hereby farther declared, That every such Person as doth Poll for Sir *Benjamin Green*, and doth also Poll for Sir *Ambrose Crowley*, shall each of them receive a Chaldron of Coals *Gratis*, on the Proviso above-mention'd.

A handbill of 1709 shows how sophisticated the purchase of votes had become, even for aldermanic elections, in London by Anne's reign. Although he condemned the 'evil and pernicious custom' of bribery, Sir Ambrose Crowley went on to offer free coal in return for votes. He lost the election, but was elected for Andover in 1713; a petition against his election had alleged bribery. [Reproduced by courtesy of the British Library.]

opposite of what they saw around them. *A Dialogue; or, New Friendly Debate* (1705), for example, argued that the aggressive tactics of the low churchmen were 'a piece of incivility'. Such men were 'acting contrary to the character and practice of a gentleman; tis like the raising of a civil war amongst us at every election'.[137] Frequent elections prevented voters from being polite:

It is well, if in the first year, they can be brought to pay one another the civility of the hat; and if in the second, they can bear being in the same room together and seem dispos'd, if the cessation were to continue for some time, to come to a better understanding; the third year comes a new election, the hostilities are renewed and thus our divisions are perpetuated.[138]

Elections were also condemned for promoting foul language, disrespect for social superiors, and uncivil feuds. In 1710 the Whig grandee Sunderland was forced out of Coventry by a crowd of 'near 800' who treated him with 'vile language'.[139] Elections, it was said, had debauched the people: 'the country is on such occasions filled with drunkenness, opprobrious language, impious oaths and execrations, with violence and party rage, and often with bloodshed'.[140] Public discourse became abusive. 'Riots, tumults, mutual abuses, odious nick-names, personal affronts are kept alive and warm from three year to three year by men of design and dexterity in the management of other men's passions', cried one author, who believed they led to scenes 'of bestial intemperance'.[141] Elections had become 'a true representation of the ancient bachanals', 'a corruption of morals', and, Richard Hampden observed, had led to 'dissolution of manners'.[142] And the press reported incidents of unruly conflict as though they were representative of all elections, and hence (rather as it could spread panic about crime) fostered fears of a society in crisis.

One important element of the perceived incivility was disrespect to social superiors. So long as MPs were elected 'by popular election', one author lamented, the 'mob pretends to extraordinary liberties whilst the

---

[137] *Dialogue*, 5.
[138] *A Letter to a Friend upon Occasion of the House of Commons Passing a Bill*, 19 (mispaginated, *recte* 27).
[139] BL, Add. MS 70,421, f. 235–6, newsletter 7 Oct. 1710.
[140] *Alteration of the Triennial Act Considered*, 13.
[141] [Defoe], *Arguments about the Alteration of Triennial Elections* (1716), 2.
[142] Sykes, *Suspension of the Triennial Bill*, 7–8; *A Letter to a Friend upon Occasion of the House of Commons Passing a Bill*, 24; Hampden, *A Speech Made in the House of Commons, by Richard Hampden Esq.* (1716), 6.

bustle holds'.[143] This inversion of social norms was apparent in a printed dialogue of 1716 between two innkeepers, who sought to retain frequent elections out of self-interest to preserve their trade. During their conversation it became apparent that such 'little men' held sway over gentlemen. If the act was repealed, the Tory innkeeper was made to complain,

we shall not have our masters in that subjection and dependence that we used to have. You know that for a year before, and for some months after an election, there was no riding through the town, without calling upon some of us, and being very civil and familiar with us; knowing us all by our Christian names, saluting our wives and daughters, and enquiring after our sons, and a world of other complaisant things, besides the never examining or disputing our reckonings; and now and then, some of our corporation got a small office, by their interest.

There were hardly 'ten gentlemen in England' who were not 'weary of securing their elections, so frequently, by such poor and unworthy meanness as they are put to'.[144] Another tract complained that a gentleman's house became little more than an inn at which electors 'riot and carouse and drink and smoak day and night'.[145] Some 'have their houses fill'd with company they care not for, and are not only forc'd to endure the rudeness and noise of a drunken crew, but to drink and be drunk with them'. Candidates dared not return home, it was alleged, 'for fear of being devour'd by whole troops of hungry voters'.[146]

Such inversion, it was suggested, was not only impolite but also criminal. At election times the electors became 'petty princes' who 'destroy the game, pilfer, steal and do anything but work', while the candidates courted them 'with low submission'.[147] Another author pointed out that frequent elections undermined effective enforcement of the game laws: 'the game keeper is generally a person that has a vote, for which reason he may regale himself with hare and partridge, or if he please sell them, whilst the poor lord of the manor must content himself with plain beef and mutton. If you offer to put the law in execution against him, an election will soon be at hand and you must expect he will vote against you.'[148] Gentlemen were

---

[143]   *Considerations Relating to our Choice*, 45.
[144]   *The Innkeepers Opinion of the Triennial Act* (1716), 9–11. According to one account, there were two-thirds more alehouses by 1716 than in 1694 (*A Letter to a Country Gentleman Shewing the Inconveniences*, 10).
[145]   *An Epistle to a Whig Member of Parliament, Concerning the Triennial Bill* (1716), 3.
[146]   *A Letter to a Country Gentleman Shewing the Inconveniences*, 9–10.
[147]   Ibid., 8.
[148]   *An Epistle*, 6–7. For a discussion of the political implications of the game laws, see E. P. Thompson, *Whigs and Hunters: The Origin of the Black Act* (London, 1975).

subjected to 'the insolent humours of every pitiful wretch that has a vote'.[149]

The incivility of the polls was also dangerous because it ousted reason. Frequent elections, it was argued, had accelerated the drift towards bribery, corruption, debauchery, and even idleness, creating a dependent rather than independent, thinking people. Few electors were 'sensible of or consider the consequences one way or other attending their country by the choice their votes may help to make'.[150] The Tory ministry of 1710–14, the Whigs complained, had used 'mobbs, riots and tumults' to keep up the spirit of the crowd against truth and right: 'they thought it their interest to govern by the passions of the crowd'. Such passions pushed out reason: 'all reasons founded upon party only, separate from the good of the publick, are such as ought not to weigh with any one; whenever things are carried to such a height as to be looked upon as good or bad, only because done by such a party a man is engag'd in, tis plain the publick must be neglected'.[151] And along with reason, the Tories had abandoned civility and politeness. Their 'good breeding' was turned inward, 'all within themselves', so that the 'pretious commodity . . . call'd courtesy' was withdrawn from all but their own club.[152] The language of polite reason thus justified the repeal of the Triennial Act. The Tories were irrational and enraged and a critical public had become a credulous, censorious, public, incapable of rational judgement. The Whigs had been 'scandalously represented amongst the ignorant people, who implicitly swallow down the artificial reports'.[153]

Popular irrationality was pervasive because electioneering was the occasion *par excellence* for political lying and the abuse of language. The people not only sold their rationality to the highest bidder, but were also misled by those who used frequent elections to perpetrate the grossest lies

---

[149] *An Epistle*, 10. Edward Nicholas visited every householder of Shaftesbury who had voted for him to thank them. While some voters were embarrassed to see a gentleman so 'demean himself', the steward observed that 'this and more must be done in such a borough as ours' (John Rylands Library 76/27, Greene to Nicholas, 15 Jan 1701, cited in D. R. Hainsworth, *Stewards, Lords and People: The Estate Steward and his World in Later Stuart England* (Cambridge 1992), 154).

[150] *A Letter to a Friend in Suffolk Occasion'd by a Report of Repealing the Triennial Act* (1716), 15.

[151] *A Second Letter to a Friend in Suffolk*, 29. The turning-point of 1710 was explicitly recognized (Burton, *Modest Enquiry*, 5).

[152] *An Impartial Account of the Behaviour of the Tories*, 30.

[153] *Whiggism Vindicated* (1715), 8. Cf. 'Sure the world is turn'd topsy turvy and mens understandings grow downward or they could never think the multitude are invested with the highest price of regality viz the judging of the public good' (*Cursory Remarks Upon Some Late Disloyal Proceedings*, 10).

and misrepresentations of individuals and parties. The Triennial Act had produced 'vollies of lies and taunts', 'ten thousand lies are rais'd to defame each antagonist'.[154] The fear that the people could be misled by misrepresentations, sophistry, and sinister 'arts' has been highlighted throughout this book. Such fears gripped the Whigs in 1715–16 when they saw four years of high church toryism as having corrupted the people through a deliberate and sinister campaign of misrepresentation waged via pulpit and press.[155] One Whig writer alleged that immediately after the accession of the new king the Tories

> sent their emissaries and incendiaries into the several counties of the kingdom (into some, on my own knowledge) to spread false reports, and to cast villainous reflections on the government, and to mislead and poyson the minds of the people.

He was shocked how the press 'swarmed' with scurrilous print.[156] And 'artifices and lies', the Whigs argued, were a prelude to rebellion.

In early 1716 Addison devoted several issues of *The Freeholder* to highlight 'the most wicked artifices' used to promote the jacobite cause. He lamented 'the mints of calumny' that were spread and the people's failure to read rightly.[157] The 'self-interested and designing leaders cannot desire a more ductile and easy people to work upon', he sighed. Addison saw political lying as the inevitable consequence of partisan politics, and only the rational and the unprejudiced would see the truth through the smears of misrepresentation: 'when there are two different parties in a nation, they will see things in different lights. An action however conducive to the good of their country, will be represented by the artful and appear to the ignorant as prejudicial to it'. Given such double-vision, then, right judgement was essential.

One explanation for the unrest was that the people had been misled by the arts and sophistry of the jacobites and Tories, and thus lost their skills of judgement. The mob had become the playthings of conspiratorial politicians who used them 'as workmen use their tools'.[158] The decay of popular virtue and judgement was seen as the product of Tory lies and misrepresentations. The people had become corrupted by priestcraft and tricked by high churchmen into irrationality and passion. The apparent

[154] Sykes, *Suspension of the Triennial Bill*, 7–8.
[155] *The Tories Unmask'd* (1715), 27–8, 35, 37; *An Impartial Account of the Behaviour of the Tories*, 1–11, 16–17; *The Zeal of the Tories for the Church and State* (1715), 8.
[156] *A Letter to the Right Honourable Robert Walpole* (1716), 15.
[157] *Freeholder*, 7, 14, 17.
[158] [Defoe], *A Hymn to the Mob* (1715), 30.

power of Tory 'misrepresentations' between 1709 and 1716 removed Whig confidence in the ability of the 'people' to discern 'truth'.[159] The 'favour of the multitude' was mere 'quicksand'.[160] 'I think the disposition of the people's minds far from being suitable to the business of an election', Richard Hampden said.[161]

Before the Triennial Act, the Whigs suggested, it had been safe to trust the people and it had been right to call *vox populi vox dei*. But 'since then vox dei would have been turn'd into vox diaboli'. The people had changed their principles 'and become the reverse to what they were before'.[162] A majority of the common people were now, it was admitted, 'bare-fac'd and open against the government' and 'if the pleasure of the people, violent and obstinate as they are at present, must be complied with, such measures must be taken as no patriot could bear'.[163] Treason ran 'into common discourse . . . riots and assaults pass for frolicks'.[164] It was clear that the people had been seduced. 'The minds of the people are not yet recover'd from those groundless prejudices, which have been instill'd into them by the king's enemies.'[165] The clergy's cry of 'the church' had corrupted the people, even though it was a 'snare' which filled 'the minds of weak men . . . with groundless fears and apprehensions, unspeakable rage towards their fellow-subjects, wrong ideas of persons whom they are not acquainted with, and uncharitable interpretations of those actions of which they are not competent judges'.[166] The people, 'oblig'd to take things at second hand', were 'liable to gross mistakes'. Indeed, 'slanders' were 'forg'd in the furnace of hell, purely for the delusion of the mobb'.[167] Freeholders, who before the 1694 act had been 'plain, honest and well-meaning people', had

[159] *Reflections on the Management of Some Late Party-Disputes*, dedication; H. Morley (ed.), *Famous Pamphlets* (London, 1886), 176–8 (Steele, 'The Crisis').
[160] Ibid., 246.
[161] Hampden, *Speech*, 8. As recently as 1714 he had refused an agreement between Whigs and Tories in Buckinghamshire to share the county seats—designed to heal 'the divisions and uneasiness the county has long lay'd under upon account of elections'—because he feared that it would 'take from the freeholders both now and for ever their right of voting'. He declared that he would stand 'by my self, that the freeholders may have an opportunity to assert their right of election and to dispose of their own votes as they shall most judge for their service and advantage' (*Verney Letters*, i. 317, 319).
[162] *A Letter to a Country Gentleman Shewing the Inconveniences*, 18.
[163] Sykes, *Suspension of the Triennial Bill*, 13, 26.
[164] *Alteration of the Triennial Act Considered*, 13.
[165] Ibid., 21.
[166] *Freeholder*, 37. cf. *Alteration of the Triennial Act Considered*, 14.
[167] *Treason Detected in an Answer to that Traiterous and Malicious Libel, Entitled, English Advice* (1715), 7, 13.

become corrupted.[168] The people therefore had to be governed by their rational representatives. As Defoe put it, 'it is true, we have a notion that in England the people govern . . . but suppose it to be true, this is properly the people represented, not the people gather'd together; in short, it is in the parliament in a House, not the rabble in a street'.[169]

Deeper poverty and a heavier financial burden, when coupled with frequent elections and misleading public discourse, appeared to have created a corrupt people who saw elections not as rational choices but as occasions to extort money and treats from their superiors. The conviction that the press and pulpit misled men, that the mob was increasingly open to electoral manipulation, that such behaviour violated codes of rationality and civility all pushed towards a repeal of one of the root causes of these symptoms: frequent elections. These were no longer the instrument to preserve liberty but 'the bulwark of licentiousness'.[170] Long parliaments were no longer depicted as posing a threat; indeed 'the longer a parliament continues, the less danger there is of their giving up their own or their elector's rights'.[171] The Septennial Act would instil real virtue again.

To be sure, the act was a Whig measure. But by 1716 the ill effects of electioneering had been felt under both parties, so that Tory criticism of the Septennial Act was rather ambiguous.[172] Vicious electioneering, it was stressed, damaged Whig and Tory gentlemen alike. Indeed, one brilliantly imagined reconstruction of the evils of corrupt elections argued that both sides had been guilty in promoting 'sordid mean steps' to promote 'the common people to be their legislators'. MPs of all sorts, it was said, thus 'ungentleman themselves in descending to the sordid methods of courting the rabble in the town'. The author was horrified

to see a gentleman of birth and fortune, going through a country village from alehouse to alehouse, drinking belch with every butcher, be hail-fellow-well-met with every tanner and tinker; stand cap in hand to a room full of drunken boors, cringing and whining, Gentlemen, I beg the favour of your votes, then slavver and kiss their wives, and with their tongues put guineas into their mouths, as they kiss the beastly creatures; call them Madam and ladies when they are hardly able to bear the stench of the brandy, tobacco and what's worse that fumes from them: to see this

---

[168] *A Letter to a Country Gentleman Shewing the Inconveniences*, 9.
[169] Defoe, *Hymn*, preface, ii–iii.
[170] Sykes, *Suspension of the Triennial Bill*, 12. Yet *British Advice* (1715) had refuted Atterbury's allegation that the Whigs would repeal the Triennial Act, on the grounds that this was 'the bulwark of their liberty' (18, cf. *Treason Detected*, 25).
[171] *A Letter to a Country Gentleman Shewing the Inconveniences*, 11–16.
[172] *An Epistle*, 11.

done in the open town, with hundreds of unconcern'd people looking on and laughing at them, and which is worse, most justly abhorring the baseness of spirit that can act in this manner . . . Is this the spirit and blood of a gentleman?[173]

It is clear that the author had the smallest and most venal boroughs most in mind, but he specifically alleged that similar things were acted the nation over, 'as well in county elections as in those of cities and borough towns'.[174]

Of course, there was some Tory opposition to the proposed Septennial Act, and ten hostile petitions against the measure were presented to the House, declaring frequent elections to be both a guarantee of liberty and a part of the constitution.[175] The independently minded Archibald Hutcheson vigorously defended the electorate. 'How low and mean soever they may be, they are still the people of England', he protested. Although they had been depicted as idle and debauched they were still 'a brave and gallant people'. If, he went on, MPs deprecated them it was as though the Commons was setting itself up as a third estate 'entirely independent of them', an innovation that would necessarily lead to more coercive forms of government.[176] A protest by peers was even publicized in the *Evening General Post*, proclaiming that frequent parliaments were 'required by the fundamental constitution of the kingdom' and that 'the House of Commons must be chosen by the People; and when so chosen they are truly representatives of the people; which they cannot be so properly said to be when continued for a longer time than that for which they were chosen; for after that time they are chosen by the parliament and not the people'. The protest claimed that the argument in favour of seven years could be used 'for continuing it still longer and even to perpetuate it, which would be an express and absolute subversion of the Third Estate of the Realm'. Yet the newspaper's writer and publisher were forced by the Lords to kneel to hear a formal reprimand.[177]

Although Tory arguments against the bill were dismissed as another example of their capacity for linguistic deception, many Whigs also had qualms about reversing such a revolution principle, not least because it

[173] *The Candidate: Being a Detection of Bribery and Corruption* (1715), 9, 12, 14. The tract was once thought to be Defoe but this is now disputed. Cf. *A Letter to a Country Gentleman Shewing the Inconveniences*, 9–10.
[174] *The Candidate*, 18.
[175] *CJ*, xviii. 429–32.
[176] *Parl. Hist.*, vii. 358–9 (see 292–379 for other speeches).
[177] *LJ*, xx. 331–2, 341, 344–5. Wilkins, the publisher, was later prosecuted for his part in an anti-trinitarian tract (*LJ*, xxi. 231–2, 235).

smacked of undermining another, namely liberty of opinion.[178] One critic of the measure mocked the Whig argument that 'if you take away that liberty, and compel all men to be of the opinion of some one, you then destroy the seeds of schism and contention'.[179] After the repeal of the Triennial Act electors would not have 'so much as Hobson's choice'. According to the Whigs, the satire continued, 'as you are to have no opinions of your own, so you cannot fall into those divisions which have miserably distracted both Church and State'.[180] The repeal would erode the freedom of Englishmen by curtailing their 'share or consent' in the government. The new Whigs, it was alleged, now blamed the people for beginning any 'publick dissention' and wanted all to 'go on in a quiet, regular, peaceable train of hardships'.[181] The repeal of the Triennial Act united men only by placing them 'in bonds'; it removed party names, but merely substituted 'the common appellation of slaves'.[182]

Another critical tract argued that the repeal of the Triennial Act was itself founded on a lie, a party 'trick' designed to misrepresent the Tories by raising groundless fears about them and the people. A 'set of men' it argued, had made use of 'some incidents' in order 'to misrepresent the affections of the people in general, the better to carry on their own schemes'. And the lie that the Tory ministry had designed to 'bring in the pretender' actually encouraged the jacobites, so that they 'did imagine and vainly perswade themselves of the reality of these assertions'.[183] Rhetoric, it was claimed, deliberately exaggerated the jacobite threat in what then became a self-fulfilling prophecy. But the author also found that the Septennial Act was intolerant of different opinions. 'In all places where there is liberty, there are different opinions, and different parties, and some have reasoned it necessary for the preservation of the whole it should be so, and when they recommend themselves to the people by the emulation of their services to the publick, the contest is far from being hurtful.'[184] Besides

---

[178] *A Second Letter to the Right Honourable Robert Walpole*, 21–4, 27–33. It was also alleged that Locke's *Two Treatises* had been misapplied by Tories seeking to unsettle the Whigs (17–18). Many Whigs were 'squeamish and difficult about this bill' (*An Epistle*, 20).

[179] *The Suspension of the Triennial Act the Certain Way to Unite the Nation* (1716), sig. A. The tract mocked Sykes, *Suspension of the Triennial Act the Properest Way to Unite the Nation.*

[180] *Suspension . . . the Certain Way*, sig. A1ᵛ.

[181] Ibid., sig. A2ʳ.   [182] Ibid., sig. A4ʳ⁻ᵛ.

[183] *The Triennial Act Impartially Stated, Shewing 1. That the Law was made for Securing the Liberties of the People . . . and is Now Become a Fundamental Part of our Constitution . . . II That the Many Plausible Arguments Insinuated for Repealing this Act are Fallacious and Inconclusive and the Consequences thereof may be Fatal to the Publick* (1716), 19–20.

[184] Ibid., 27–8.

indicating the power of political lies, the tract was a testament to how far publicly competitive politics had inculcated values of plurality and a representative society, and how far public discourse would remain the key battlefield even after the repeal of the Triennial Act. For all the qualms, and precisely because public discourse had assumed such prominence, the Septennial Act became law; yet ironically its passage was a testament to how much had changed. It was necessitated by the moves towards a representative society.

A REPRESENTATIVE PUBLIC: A TORY PERSPECTIVE

The shift towards a representational culture, and its consequences, can be seen in two pamphlets published in 1710 by Conyers Place, a Tory cleric who mainly involved himself in theological dispute but who also attempted to arbitrate between the two parties.[185] The works allow us to summarize contemporary perception about partisanship and to show its impact on attitudes about politics and public discourse. The first of the tracts, *The Arbitration; or, The Tory and Whig Reconcil'd* (1710) rehearsed themes that have run throughout this book. Place thus expressed shock that the vituperativeness of party politics had inverted vice and virtue:

> Rage and fury are the vertuous qualities that make darlings on both sides. He that has said most bitter things, and done most despite to the adverse party, is the man of merit . . . speaking virulent things, without shame or decency, out of all character makes you presently a confessor . . . to abuse or to have been abused make you equally famous . . . and when you are a party-man, an honourable word escaping you, a favourable thought discover'd of the opposite, is as much as your Whig or Torydom is worth.[186]

Place had a 'hypothesis' that 'neither party are so bad as the other make them' and that 'honest men would agree, did they understand one anothers meaning but right'.[187] The epistemological problem was that

---

[185] Place (1665–1738) was educated at Cambridge and then, after ordination, served as Master of Dorchester Grammar School 1689–1736. He was also rector of Woodford, Dorset. In 1709 he wrote against Matthew Tindal and both in 1710 and later locked horns with Hoadly.

[186] *Arbitration*, 3–4. Cf. Place, *A Sermon Preach'd at Dorchester During the Time of the Assizes March the 18th 1705* (1705), 22: 'Mens Interests are their Zeal and their Humours their Consciences'.

[187] *Arbitration*, 5, 32.

some 'politick muster-masters' made tools of honest men, partly by invoking 'two nick-names to distinguish folks by', so that there was 'such an
over-heat of thought and disorderly fermentation as obstructs all fair discretion and manly judgment'.[188] In this 'excess of partiality' men considered 'nothing but that outside denomination truly or falsely affix'd'. 'Party
judgment' was thus irrational; there was 'nothing so monstrously improbable' that it would not believe.[189] And it was a 'dotage on party names and
character that confounds all' for the public reduced issues to personalities
and judged the merits of any one person 'by his party nick-name'. Public
judgement had thus become corrupt when sacrificed to party, for it hin-
dered 'all the tedious trouble of examination and deliberation'.[190] The tract
ended with a plea that the two parties declare peace, not by reconciliation
of principles 'which are too incurably wide to be closed', but by tolerating
each other. Each should have 'such a tolerable opinion of each other as
will secure the nations peace'.[191] Place thus implicitly accepted the existence of the parties, but sought to moderate the conflict between them,
convinced that much of their misunderstanding resulted from a failure of
communication.

Certainly Place wanted concessions from the Whigs more than from the
Tories; but he saw toleration of difference as the way to achieve unity. This
was also the thrust of his second tract, which recognized that both Whig
and Tory were 'too great to be violently crusht' and hence that diversity had
to be accommodated.[192] Every man, he said, understood things differently
and this produced a 'variety of judgment'.[193] This diversity of taste necessitated a tolerant attitude. Governments, he said, should not 'cramp' men's
conscience but leave open 'all the ways that are innocent' by which men
might comply.[194] To be sure, Place was criticizing what he believed was a
form of Whig intolerance and political exclusivity; but, in doing so, he was
enunciating principles inconceivable to most church of England men a
few decades earlier.

But even more importantly Place saw representation as the means to
achieve stability. He suggested that representation was the means by which
the 'natural inseparable right of every subject' could be maintained peace-

---

[188] *Arbitration*, 9–10.
[189] Ibid., 11–12.   [190] Ibid., 13–14.   [191] Ibid., 36.
[192] *The True English Revolutionist* (1710), preface, iv.
[193] Ibid., 6. Cf. *Spectator*, 197, written by Budgell, advised readers to 'avoid disputes as much
as possible . . . Nothing can be more unjust or ridiculous than to be angry with another, because he is not of your opinion. The interests, education and means by which men attain their
knowledge are so very different, that it is impossible they should all think alike.'
[194] *True English Revolutionist*, 26.

fully. Thus the 'true revolutionist' 'looks upon this right of the subjects determining their Soveraign to be the very first article of representative trust, which makes good all the rest of the conveyance . . . He takes representation to be the only method by which the members of his country's constitution can do any political act.'[195] The solution to diversity of opinion was to abide by the principles of representation, for men were bound by their representatives' decision. The decision of the representatives was the people's 'own political act, tis the form of it that is every man's judgment, and that which conscience is therefore to follow and obliged by'. Men should not, he insisted, posit their private judgement against their 'politick', representative, judgement.[196] The diversity of private judgement could thus be made peaceful and practicable when it found an overriding representative judgement, centred on parliamentary representation.

Though he does not use the term, the representative general will becomes that which all men are obliged to follow. Place was certainly no Hobbes or Rousseau but he argued that representation was the only means by which many private wills could be reduced to a single will which was then binding on individuals. Place thus reflected the increasing reliance placed on accommodating forms of representation, both in terms of the conduct of public discourse and of the power of the representative assembly, as a means of re-establishing unity. In a sense, Place had replaced the leviathan of the prince with that of the people and monarch represented in a sovereign assembly and hence acting as a unified public.[197] Equally important is Place's readiness to use the press to articulate his views. Besides advocating parliamentary representation he implicitly regarded print as another key representative institution. Like parliament, public discourse, when rightly self-regulated, could be a positive as well as a negative force. Contemporaries referred to elections, petitions and addresses, the stock market, and the press (Davenant's 'fourth estate') as though each were some form of representation of the national will. Each measured the pulse of the nation or the bent of the people. And each of these sites was not just representational but was also capable of exerting a political power that could not be ignored.

The cleric's arguments are also interesting because they reflect a belief that religion as it had been traditionally practised was being challenged by forces that were now unchecked. Forces of ambition, greed, selfishness, irreligion, debauchery, even atheism in a man-made, materialistic world

---

[195] Ibid., 30–1.   [196] Ibid., 31, 37–8.
[197] Importantly, however, he argued this was England's old constitution (Ibid., 12–13).

seemed to him, unrestrained. Men talked less about providence than the luck of lotteries.[198] In other words, many perceived the two revolutions of the seventeenth century to have produced a *moral* crisis once the restraint of traditional religious practices and structures was weakened (for good or ill, depending on party viewpoint). Modernity thus smacked of corruption and the pursuit of self-interest, with potentially devastating consequences. An unbridled public was a frightening prospect. As one critic put it in 1716, whereas once it had been in the power of the prince to oppress, it was now 'in every one of his subjects power to tyranize over one another, so that we have only taken this power from him, to lodge it in ours selves'.[199] Conventional religion found such power difficult to confront. Politicking clerics seemed only to attract 'contempt and hatred' so that, one writer claimed, 'the whole clergy is torn, defam'd and vilify'd between the two parties'.[200] Partisan debate about the succession, for example, eroded key Christian values: 'the being of Christianity must be lost in the fog, and smoke and stink and noise and rage and cruelty, of our quarrel about a king.'[201] Party destroyed Christian neighbourliness. As one tract remarked, 'making parties to be elected hath raised such feuds and differences between neighbours and near relations, that hospitality and indeed brotherly love and charity is at a low ebb'.[202] The decay of true religion was blamed on the vituperativeness of party politics. Jonathan Swift, who had been no stranger to party polemic, sermonized about the loss of Christian brotherly love, remarking that 'men's very natures are soured and their passions inflamed when they meet in party clubs, and spend their time in nothing else but railing at the opposite side'.[203] To be sure, this was not the first or last perceived moral crisis but its causes were rather unlike those of

---

[198] Providence was invoked in letters by both Edward Clarke and Robert Harley, (particularly to their fathers), but largely disappears from their correspondence after the mid-1690s. A history of late seventeenth- and eighteenth-century attitudes to providence (no doubt linked to a history of Calvinism) is needed. For some discussion, however, see Claydon, *William III*; Rose, *England in the 1690s*, 19–21, 196–201; J. Spurr, ' "Virtue, Religion and Government": The Anglican Uses of Providence', in Harris, Seaward, and Goldie (eds.) *Politics of Religion*, 29–47; J. C. D. Clark, 'Providence, Predestination and Progress', *Albion* 35 (2003), 559–89.

[199] Baston, *Thoughts on Trade*, 106.

[200] *Introduction to the Reconcilers*, 13.

[201] Defoe, *Reasons against the Succession of the House of Hanover* (1713), 2. The bulk of the tract's argument is ironic, but the opening passages, from which the quotation is taken, serve to sketch the rage of party.

[202] *A Friendly Letter to Such as Have Voices in Election of Members to Serve in Parliament* (1695), broadside.

[203] Swift, *Prose Works*, ix. 176.

its predecessors. And alongside all this the era of pragmatism and the professional politician had, it seemed, arrived as part of a 'modern' politics.[204] By 'modern' many meant something pejorative, a set of politicians who habitually dissimulated their private designs.[205] It is perhaps no coincidence that the term 'prime minister' appears to have been coined at this time by Jonathan Swift.[206]

Although frequent elections, at least at a national scale, were removed from the equation, the shift towards a representative polity, given such a mighty push under the later Stuarts, continued after 1716.[207] Debates about private and public interests; about the manipulation of the public through a debased form of public discourse; about the nature of party and political diversity; about the fictional nature of politics; about reason, moderation, politeness; and about representation, participation, and delegation all continued to ignite passions throughout the century.

But more work needs to be done on the creativity and nature of party, on the impact of partisan discourse, and the role of party in the development of the state in order to show the ongoing importance of a culture of partisanship. The potential can also be seen in the promotion of an enlarged sense of the state as a national and international entity. Party politics strengthened the state in a number of ways. The power of parliament's representative voice was enhanced *vis à vis* other legitimate voices of the

---

[204] Ihalainen, *Discourse on Political Pluralism*, 91–6, argues that in the early eighteenth century the words 'politic' and the increasingly used 'political' were becoming synonymous and losing their pejorative status. But he also notes that the idea of wicked politicians drew on earlier stereotypes.

[205] South, *Twelve Sermons* (1692), 434, 440, 460–6. For contemporary attitudes to 'modern', see Ihalainen, *Discourse on Political Pluralism*, 74–80; and bibliography for its pejorative use in titles.

[206] Swift, *Prose Works*, iv. 17. Oldmixon discussed the novelty of the term in *Reflections on Dr Swift's Letter to the Earl of Oxford* (1712), 30. The term was also used in 1712 in *Arguments Relating to a Restraint upon the Press*, 31, and in 1715: Kennett, *Wisdom*, 253, 266. For usage in the 1690s, see *OED*. Roger Morrice commented in his 'Entring Book' for 1677 that 'Danby is prime minister of state' (Dr Williams Library, Morrice Entring Book P, f. 58), but the word 'prime' is interlineated over another word and might have been the product of a later revision.

[207] The vitality of politics is explored in a growing volume of literature, but see especially Rogers, *Whigs and Cities*; Rogers, *Crowds, Culture and Politics in Georgian Britain* (Oxford, 1998); Wilson, *Sense of the People*; Halliday, *Dismembering the Body Politic*, pt 3; B. Harris, *Politics and the Nation: Britain in the Mid-Eighteenth Century* (Oxford, 2002); H. T. Dickinson, *The Politics of the People in Eighteenth-Century Britain* (Basingstoke, 1995); Monod, *Jacobitism*; J. Brewer, *Party Ideology and Popular Politics at the Accession of George III* (Cambridge, 1976); L. Colley, *In Defiance of Oligarchy: The Tory Party 1714–1760* (Cambridge, 1982); F. O'Gorman, 'Campaign Rituals and Ceremonies: The Social Meaning of Elections in England, 1780–1860', *P&P*, 135 (1992), 79–115.

people, and openly partisan debates at Westminster scrutinized, critiqued, and hence improved the efficiency of state activities—particularly by exposing corruption.[208] Parties with a national applicability bound as well as divided the nation, for party ideology operated vertically and helped to paper over the social and economic gulf that widened during the period under the pressure of invigorated capitalism.[209] Parties also spoke a language of patriotism to legitimize their different voices, offering another vertical bond. And the vibrancy of local politics energized the state, as competitors sought to wrest the levers of power from each other. The state, as we have been reminded, was a social construct, with power negotiated by a series of key players. By the late seventeenth century those players were partisans whose negotiations were coloured by party. At a personal level this could change the perameters of negotiation and distort perceptions of equitable governance. But the appropriation of the legitimate institutions of the state as platforms for political parties could also strengthen those institutions as each side competed to control them. So a system that rested on a struggle over representation helped to foster a sense of national identity and an empowered state. Party was intrinsically divisive; yet this process of division could be hugely creative and actually foster strong links within a community. The struggle for uniformity might have been abandoned but that only redoubled efforts to find a whole within which the parts could fit, to find communities of interest where a single community proved impossible.

Historians have tended to focus less on the nature of partisan culture than on the ins and outs of party manoeuvrings at local and national level. This book has tried to redress this neglect by examining the implications of the first sustained attempt to explore public representational politics. Previous chapters have attempted to map the way in which publicly adversarial politics and public discourse combined to create real anxieties. As we have seen, contemporaries across the political spectrum were convinced

---

[208] *View of the Present Divisions*, 16. The whole issue of party and corruption needs analysis. The work of Caroline Robbins and J. G. A. Pocock on the eighteenth-century commonwealthsmen suggests that the court was the most feared agent of corruption; but previous chapters have suggested that party needs to be added back into the equation, as both a positive and a negative force, and that corruption needs to be seen in political, religious, moral, economic, cultural, and linguistic terms.

[209] Morgan suggests the temporary fraternization of candidates and electorates during the first age of party had a 'make-believe quality to it, a temporary pretending that people were equal when everybody knew they were not' and acted as 'a legitimising ritual in which the populace renewed their consent to an oligarchical power structure' (*Inventing the People*, 199, 206).

that each party, far from offering impartial advice to rational readers and voters, was engaged in attempts to foster lies, misuse words, and destabilize meanings as part of a design to mislead the public. The invocation of the public as arbiter was thus seen as problematic. Yet it was also—as the analysis of petitions, addresses, electoral advice, and print revealed—integrated into the formal and informal mechanisms of the state. As England entered the eighteenth century, its political culture appeared to be shifting towards a more representative form, not in the sense of a democracy but a society in which public representation, and representation of the public, had become central to the political process.

Appendix
The Principal Periodicals in the Reign of Queen Anne

Information about serials prior to 1702 can be found in C. Nelson and M. Seccombe, *British Newspapers and Periodicals, 1641–1700. A Short-title Catalogue of Serials Printed in England, Scotland, Ireland, and British America . . . With a Checklist of Serials Printed 1701–March 1702* (New York, 1987). There is, however, no comparable bibliographical study for the post-1695 period. The list below therefore represents a rough attempt to map out the number of titles, the number of issues, and (where possible) the number of copies produced for periodicals with runs of 50 issues or more. More information, and listing of minor serial publications, can be found in *The New Cambridge Bibliography of English Literature Vol. 2 1660–1800*, ed. G. Watson (Cambridge, 1971); and W. R. and V. B. McLeod, *A Graphical Directory of English Newspapers and Periodicals, 1702–1714* (Morgantown, 1982). The ESTC is adding data to its definitive listing and, when complete, the project's findings will supersede the data offered here.

The Bristol Post-Boy: 340 issues between 1702 and 1710; weekly.

The British Apollo: 411 issues between 1708 and 1711 (at first bi-weekly, but from no. 80, tri-weekly); circulation approx. 1,500 copies.

The British Merchant: 103 issues between 1713 and 1714, bi-weekly; circulation of about 1,200 copies at start.

British Mercury: 474 issues between 1710 and 1714, tri-weekly.

Daily Courant: 3,984 issues between 1702 and 1714, daily; founded 1702 (until 1735); circulation of about 850 copies in 1712, but 600 in 1713.

Dawks's News Letter: 596 issues between 1710 and 1714, first appeared 1696 (until 1716), tri-weekly; circulation of about 200 copies.

The Dublin Gazette: founded c.1705 (until 1726); Dublin publication; 129 issues by 1706, 2,659 by 1726.

The Dublin Intelligence: founded 1708 (continued as *Edward Waters' Protestant Dublin Intelligence* and then as *The Dublin Weekly Intelligence*, until 1710); 64 issues by 1710.

The Dublin Mercury: founded 1705 (until at least 1706); 85 issues by 1706.

Dublin's Post-Man: founded 1714 (continued under similar title until 1727).

The Edinburgh Courant: founded 1705 (continued as *Scots Courant* in 1710, until 1720); 2,251 issues by 1720.

The Edinburgh Gazette: founded 1699 (until 1707, then continued as Scots Postman until 1709 and then in various permutations of those titles until 1715).

The English Post: 1700–?19 May 1708, three times a week so over 1,300 issues by close; tri-weekly; circulation of *c*.400 in 1704.

The Evening Post: begun 1700, 1,191 issues by 1708; daily at first, but soon tri-weekly; circulation of 2,280 copies in 1712, 1,900 in 1713.

The Examiner: 268 issues between 1710 and 1714, mainly bi-weekly; circulation of *c*.1,370 in 1712 and 1920 in 1713 (repr. Edinburgh and Dublin).

Female Tatler: 111 issues between 1709 and 1710, tri-weekly.

Flying Post: 3,523 issues by 1714. Founded 1695 (until 1733); tri-weekly; circulation of *c*.400 in 1704 and 1,350 in 1712 (repr. Dublin).

General Remark on Trade: founded 1705 (until 1708); 440 issues; tri-weekly.

The Guardian: 175 issues in 1713; daily; circulation of *c*.1,200; sequel was *The Englishman* that had 95 issues 1713–15; tri-weekly.

Heraclitus Ridens: 63 issues 1703-4, bi-weekly.

Impartial Occurrences: published in Dublin, uncertain date of foundation, 61 issues by 1704.

Lloyd's News-Letter: founded *c*.1710, published in Dublin, possibly 221 issues by 1714.

The London Gazette: 5,247 issues by 1714; founded 1665; bi- and tri-weekly; circulation of *c*.6,000 in 1704, 6,500 in 1714, and 5,100 in 1712 (repr. Dublin 1700–3).

London Post: 1,079 issues between 1702 and 1705; founded 1699 (until 1705); tri-weekly; circulation of *c*.400 in 1704.

The Medley: 90 issues between 1711 and 1712; mostly bi-weekly (repr. Dublin).

The Mercator: 181 issues between 1713 and 1714; tri-weekly.

Mercurius Politicus: 51 issues in 1705, bi-weekly.

The Moderator: 50 issues in 1710, bi-weekly.

The Newcastle Courant: 67 issues in 1711; tri-weekly, continuing after 1714.

The Newcastle Gazette: 308 issues by 1712; founded 1710.

The Night Post: at least 68 issues, ?1711–?1713.

The Norwich Gazette: 406 issues by 1714; founded 1706 (until 1749); mostly weekly.

The Norwich Post: 594 issues by 1712; founded 1701.

The Norwich Post Man: 135 issues 1706–9.

The Observator: 1,060 issues 1702–12; bi-weekly; circulation of *c*.1,000 in 1704.

The Post Boy: 3,001 issues by 1714; founded 1695; circulation of *c*.3,000 in 1704 and 3,650 in 1712; tri-weekly.

The Post Man: 11,050 issues by 1714; founded 1695 (until 1730); tri-weekly; circulation of *c*.3,870 in 1704, 3,800 in 1712, and 2,000 in 1713 (repr. Dublin from 1707).

The Protestant Postboy: 123 issues; 1711–12, tri-weekly (repr. Dublin).

The Rehearsal: 298 issues 1704–9; weekly and bi-weekly.

The Review: 1,354 issues 1704–13; weekly, bi-weekly, and tri-weekly; circulation of *c*.400 in 1704 and 280 in 1712.

Sam Farley's Exeter Post-Man: 556 issues by 1711; date of foundation uncertain.

The Spectator: 635 issues 1711–14 (with hiatus 1712–14); mostly daily; circulation of *c*.11,400 in 1712.

The Stamford Mercury: weekly, ran 1713–32.

The Supplement: 753 issues between 1708 and 1712 (307 for 1710–12); tri-weekly.

The Tatler: 330 issues between 1709 and 1711; tri-weekly (repr. Edinburgh and Dublin).

The Weekly Pacquet: 473 issues 1712–21; weekly; circulation of *c*.250 in 1712 and 470 in 1713.

The Worcester Post Man: 267 issues by 1714; founded 1709; continued after 1714.

Select Bibliography

MANUSCRIPT SOURCES

All Souls Library, Oxford
  Owen Wynne MSS.

Bodleian Library
  Carte MS 81
  Eng. Hist. b.209–10 diary, notes and speeches of Sir Richard Cocks.
  Eng. Hist. c.487, Ludlow's Memoirs.
  Eng. Hist. c.711, Roger Whitley's diary 1684–97.
  Eng. Hist. c.712, Whitley's commonplace book.
  Tanner 31 and 459.

British Library
  Add. MSS 32,518–20, papers of Lord Chief Justice North.
  Add. MSS 34,515 transcripts of Johnston correspondence.
  Add. MSS 41,803, Middleton papers.
  Add. MS 70,420–1, Dyer's newsletters 1709–10.
  Add. Charter MSS 76,108–23, 1,710 addresses.
  Eg. MSS 3,348, Danby papers.
  Harl. MS 5,137 Sir Simon Harcourt's common-place book, 1705.
  Harl. MS 5,995–6 (on microfilm in Rare Books), printed ephemera.
  Hargrave MSS 149, parliamentary journal of Henry Booth 1677–81.
  Lansd. MSS 1,024, Kennett's journal.
  Sloane MSS 2,753, ff. 1–17, 'The misleading of the Common People'.
  Verney MSS on Microfilm.

Cambridge University Library
  Bohun collection (rare books, interleaved with correspondence).

Corporation of London Record Office
  Sessions Files.

Dr Williams Library, London
  MS 31.P, Q, R Morrice Entring Book.

Essex Record Office
  Essex RO, T/A 98, common-place book of William Holgate.

Hertfordshire RO
  Hertford Borough Records.

Panshanger (Cowper) MSS D/EP F29-35, Sarah Cowper's diary. (F 29, vol. 1, 1700-2; F 30, vol. 2, 1703-4; F 31, vol. 3, 1705-6; F 32, vol. 4, 1706-9; F 33, vol. 5, 1709-11; F 34, vol. 6, 1711-13; F 35, vol. 7, 1713-16).
Verulam MSS

Huntington Library, San Marino
MS 1264, tract by Nehemiah Grew.

Liverpool RO
920/MD/172 diary of Sir Willoughby Aston.

Norfolk RO
Norwich City Records
Frere collection.

Public Record Office
C213/182 and C213/184, Norwich association rolls, 1696.
Mint 19/1, Newton papers re William Chaloner.
Shaftesbury papers
State papers, SP29, SP35.

Transcripts of manuscript sources at the History of Parliament Trust
Canterbury Corp. Archives, CC/A/C 8, burghmote minute book 1695-1744.
Cheshire RO, Arderne MSS.
Chester RO, Earwacker MSS.
Chester RO, Assembly Books.
Cornwall RO, Carew papers.
John Rylands Library, Manchester, Mainwaring of Peover MSS.
Lincs. RO, Monson MSS.
Nottingham University Library, Portland papers.
PRO Ireland, Wyche MSS 1/222.
Strathmore MSS, Glamis Castle.

THESES AND UNPUBLISHED WORKS

Adams, B., 'The Body in the Water: Religious Conflict in Hertford, 1660-1702', Ph.D., London (2000).
Challinor, P. J., 'The Structure of Politics in Cheshire, 1660-1715', Ph.D., Wolverhampton Polytechnic (1984).
Cunnington, E., 'The General Election of 1705', M.A., London (1939).
French, H., 'Chief Inhabitants and their Areas of Influence: Local Ruling Groups in Essex and Suffolk Parishes 1630-1720', Ph.D., Cambridge (1993).
Glaisyer, N., 'The Culture of Commerce in England 1660-1720', Ph.D., Cambridge (1999).

Guth, G. J., 'Croakers, Tackers, and other Citizens: Norwich Voters in the Eighteenth Century', Ph.D., Stanford (1985).

Hopkins, P., 'Aspects of Jacobite Conspiracy in England in the Reign of William III', Ph.D., Cambridge (1981).

Kemp, G. H., 'Ideas of Liberty of the Press, 1640–1700', Ph.D., Cambridge (2001).

Loveman, K., 'Shamming Readers: Deception in English Literary and Political Culture *c.* 1640–1740', Ph.D., Cambridge (2003).

Marshall, D. N., 'Protestant Dissent in England in the Reign of James II', Ph.D., Hull (1976).

Stuart D. G., 'The Parliamentary History of the Borough of Tamworth, Staffordshire, 1661–1837', M.A., London (1958).

Triffitt, J. M., 'Politics and the Urban Community. Parliamentary Boroughs in the South West of England 1710–1730', Ph.D., Oxford (1985).

Waddell, D., 'The Career and Writings of Charles Davenant 1656–1714', Ph.D., Oxford (1954).

Walker, R., '"Ordinary and Common Discourse": The Impact of the Glorious Revolution on Political Discussion in London 1688–1694', Ph.D., Sheffield (1998).

Warner, R., 'Early C18th Low Churchmanship: The Glorious Revolution to the Bangorian Controversy', Ph.D., Reading (1999).

Williams, A., 'Whig Literary Culture: Poetry, Politics and Patronage, 1678–1714', Ph.D., Oxford (2000).

Withington, P., 'Urban Political Culture in Later-Seventeenth-Century England: York 1649–1688', Ph.D., Cambridge (1998).

PRINTED WORKS

Post-1750 editions of primary material

Addison, J., *The Miscellaneous Works of Joseph Addison*, ed. A. C. Guthkelch, 2 vols. (London, 1914).

An Address from the Gentry of Norfolk and Norwich to General Monck in 1660, ed. H. Le Strange and W. Rye (Norwich, 1913).

Arbuthnot, J., *The History of John Bull*, ed. A. Bower and R. Erickson (Oxford, 1976).

Bond, R. P. (ed.), *New Letters to the Tatler and Spectator* (Austin, 1959).

The Bulstrode Papers, ed. A. Morrison (London, private, 1897).

Cocks, Sir R., *The Parliamentary Diary of Sir Richard Cocks*, ed. D. W. Hayton (Oxford, 1996).

A Collection of Scarce and Valuable Tracts . . . selected from . . . private libraries; particularly that of the late Lord Sommers (first collection 1748; second 1750; third 1751; fourth, 1752).

Davenant, C., *The Political and Commercial Works of that Celebrated Writer Charles D'Avenant*, ed. Sir C. Whitworth, 5 vols. (London, 1771, rep. Farnborough, 1968).

Defoe, D., *The Letters of Daniel Defoe*, ed. G. H. Healey (Oxford, 1955).

Dennis, J., *The Critical Works of John Dennis*, ed. E. N. Hooker, 2 vols. (Baltimore, 1943).

Dunton, J., *The Life and Errors of John Dunton*, 2 vols. (London, 1818).

The Ellis Correspondence: Letters Written during the Years 1686, 1687 and 1688, ed. G. A. Ellis, 2 vols. (London, 1829).

Ellis, F. H. (ed.), *Swift vs Mainwaring: The Examiner and The Medley* (Oxford, 1985).

Filmer, Sir R., *Patriarcha and other Writings*, ed. J. P. Sommerville (Cambridge, 1991).

Grey, A. (ed.), *Debates of the House of Commons, from the Year 1667 to the Year 1694*, 10 vols. (London, 1763).

Gunn, J. A. W., *Factions No More: Attitudes to Party in Government and Opposition in Eighteenth Century England, Extracts from Contemporary Sources* (London, 1972).

The Harleian Miscellany: A Collection of Scarce, Curious, and Entertaining Pamphlets and Tracts, as well in Manuscript as in Print, Found in the Late Earl of Oxford's Library, 12 vols. (London, 1808-11).

Harrington, J., *The Political Works of James Harrington*, ed. J. G. A. Pocock (Cambridge, 1977).

Hervey, J., *The Letterbooks of John Hervey*, ed. S. H. A. H., 3 vols. (Wells, 1894).

Hoadly, B., *The Works of Benjamin Hoadly*, 3 vols. (London, 1773).

Hobbes, T., *Leviathan*, ed. R. Tuck (Cambridge, 1996).

—— *De Cive: The English Version*, ed. H. Warrender (Oxford, 1983).

Kenyon, J. P. (ed.), *The Stuart Constitution 1603-88* (Cambridge, 1969).

Kirk, Rev. R., 'London in 1689-90', transcribed by D. Maclean, *Transactions of the London and Middlesex Archaeological Society*, NS 6 (1929-32), 487-97, 652-61; NS, 7 (1936 for 1935), 133-57, 304-18.

Letters Addressed from London to Sir Joseph Williamson, ed. W. D. Christie, Camden Soc. NS, 9, 2 vols. (1874).

Locke, J., *Works*, 10 vols. (London, 1823).

—— *The Correspondence of John Locke*, ed. E. S. de Beer, 9 vols. (Oxford, 1976-).

—— *Political Essays*, ed. M. Goldie (Cambridge, 1997).

—— *Of the Conduct of the Understanding*, ed. F. Garforth (New York, 1966).

Two Treatises of Government, ed. P. Laslett (Cambridge, 1960).

London Politics 1713–1717: Minutes of a Whig Club 1714–17, ed. H. Horwitz, London Record Society, 17 (1981).

Ludlow, E., *A Voyce from the Watchtower. Part 5, 1660-62*, ed. A. B. Worden, Camden 4th Series, 21 (1978).

Luttrell, N., *A Brief Historical Relation of State Affairs, from September 1678 to April 1714*, 6 vols. (Farnborough, 1969).

—— *The Luttrell File*, ed. S. Parks (New Haven, 1999).

Manley, D., *The New Atalantis*, ed. R. Ballaster (London, 1991).

Marvell, A., *The Complete Works in Verse and Prose of Andrew Marvell*, ed. A. B. Grosart, 4 vols. (London, 1872–5).

Montesquieu, C-L, Baron de, *De L'Esprit des Lois* (1748), trans. as *The Spirit of the Laws* by A. M. Cohler, B. C. Miller, and H. S. Stone (Cambridge, 1989).

Morley, H. (ed.), *Famous Pamphlets* (London, 1886).

Petty, Sir W., *The Economic Writings of Sir William Petty*, ed. C. H. Hull, 2 vols. (New York, 1963–4).

Pryme, A. de la, *The Diary of Abraham de la Pryme*, ed. C. Jackson, Surtees Soc., 54 (Durham, 1870).

Reresby, Sir J., *Memoirs of Sir John Reresby*, ed. A. Browning (Glasgow, 1936).

Rugg, T., *The Diurnal of Thomas Rugg 1659-1661*, ed. W. L. Sachse, Camden Society, 3rd series, 91 (1961).

Robbins, C. (ed.), *Two English Republican Tracts* (Cambridge, 1969).

Rye, W. (ed.), *Depositions Taken before the Mayor and Aldermen of Norwich* (Norwich, 1903).

3rd earl of Shaftesbury, *Characteristics of Men, Manners, Opinion, Times*, ed. J. M. Robertson, 2 vols. (Gloucester, Mass., 1963–4 edn.).

St. John, H., *Camden Miscellany*, 26 ['Letters of Henry St. John', ed. H. T. Dickinson], Camden Society, 4th ser., 14 (1975).

——— *Letters and Correspondence . . . of Henry St John*, ed. G. Parke, 2 vols. (London, 1798).

Sidney, A., *Discourses Concerning Government by Algernon Sidney*, ed. T. West (Indianapolis, 1990).

Steele, Sir R., *Tracts and Pamphlets by Richard Steele*, ed. R. Blanchard (London, 1967).

Swift, J., *A Discourse of the Contests and Dissentions*, ed. F. H. Ellis (Oxford, 1967).

——— *The Prose Works of Jonathan Swift*, ed. H. Davis, 13 vols. (Oxford, 1939–68).

——— *Political Tracts 1713-19*, ed. H. Davis (1953).

Verney Letters of the Eighteenth Century, ed. M. M. Verney, 2 vols. (1930).

Ward, E. [Ned], *The London Spy*, ed. A. L. Hayward (London, 1927).

Wootton, D. (ed.), *Divine Right and Democracy: An Anthology of Political Writing in Stuart England* (Harmondsworth, 1986).

Womersley, D. (ed.), *Augustan Critical Writing* (London, 1997).

Pre-1750 books, pamphlets, and poems
Only titles cited in the text are listed here

Abercromby, D., *A Moral Discourse of the Power of Interest* (1690).

An Account of Some Late Designs to Create a Misunderstanding betwixt the King and his People (1702).

An Account of the Full Tryal and Examination of Spencer Cooper Esq. (1699).

An Account of the Test Offer'd to the Consideration of the Electors (1710).

An Address to our Sovereign Lady [1704] [sometimes attributed to Maynwaring].

The Addresses Importing an Abhorrence of an Association (1682).

Advice to the Electors of Members for the Ensuing Parliament of Great Britain (1708).

Advice to the Gentlemen, Freeholders, Citizens and Burgesses (1710).

Advice to the Livery-men of London in their Choice of a Lord Mayor, on Michaelmas Day, 1692 (1692).

The Alteration of the Triennial Act Considered (1716) [sometimes attributed to Defoe].

An Answer to a Letter from a Gentleman in the Country, Relating to the Present Ministry (1699).

An Answer to a Paper Entituled A Letter to a Friend (1690).

An Answer to Mr Stephens Sermon . . . Printed for the Use of the Calves Head Club, in Order to their Conversion (1700).

An Answer to the Black List [1701].

Antiquity Reviv'd, or the Government of a Certain Island (1693).

Arguments Relating to a Restraint Upon the Press Fully and Fairly Handled in a Letter to a Bencher from a Young Gentleman of the Temple (1712).

The Art of Lying and Rebelling Taught by the Whigs (1713).

The Art of Parliamenteering (1722).

Ashenden, T., *Some Reflections Upon a Late Pamphlet* (1681).

Astell, M., *Moderation Truly Stated; or, A Review of a Late Pamphlet Entituled Moderation a Vertue* (1704).

Atkyns, R. R., *The Original and Growth of Printing* (1664).

Atterbury, F., *An Argument to Prove the Affections of the People of England to be the Best Security to the Government* (1716).

—— *English Advice to the Freeholders of England* (1714).

—— *The Voice of the People no Voice of God* (1710).

B-ss-t B-sh-t or the Foulness of More Plain English (1704).

The Ballad; or, Some Scurrilous Reflections in Verse . . . Answered (1701).

The Balance; or, A New Test of the High-Fliers of All Sides (1705).

Baron, W., *Regicides no Saints* (1700).

Barrington, J. S., *A Dissuasive from Jacobitism: Shewing in General what the Nation is to Expect from a Popish King and in Particular from the Pretender* (1713).

Baston, S., *A Dialogue Between a Modern Courtier and an Honest English Gentleman* [1697].

Baston, T., *Thoughts on Trade and a Publick Spirit* (1716).

The Best Choice for Religion and Government in a Conference between Sir Anthony, a Latitudinarian; John Ponteus, a Religion-Broker; Mr. Maggot, an Independent; Mr. Mouth, a Gifted-speaker; and Friend Henry, an Undeceiv'd Quaker (1697).

The Best Choice of Parliament-Men Considered (1701).

The Best Means to Defeat the Expectations of the Enemies to the Government (1690).

Bisset, W., *The Modern Fanatick. Part II* (1710).

Bland, Capt., *The Northern Atalantis; or, York Spy* (1713).

Blount, T., *Glossographia* (1670 edn., first published 1656).

Bohun, E., *The Justice of the Peace* (1693).

—— *The Vindication of Sir Jonathan Raymond Alderman of London, from the Aspersions Cast upon him by Two Injurious Libells* (1692), authorship concluded from CUL, Sel.3.238 item 214.

Booth, H., *The Speech of the Honourable Henry Booth Esq.* (1681).

—— *Lord Del-r's Speech* (1688).

—— *The Speech of the Right Honourable, Henry Earl of Warrington, upon his being Sworn Mayor of Chester, in Novenber [sic] 1691* (1691).

—— *The Speech of the Right Honourable Henry Earl of Warrington, Lord Delamere, to the Grand Jury at Chester. April 13. 1692* (1692).

—— *A Collection of Speeches of the Right Honourable Henry late Earl of Warrington* (1694).

—— *The Works of the Right Honourable Henry Late L[ord] Delamer* (1694).

Both Sides Pleas'd; or, A Dialogue Between a Sacheverelite Parson, and an Hoadlean Gentleman (1710).

Boyle, R., *A Discourse of Things above Reason* (1681).

Bradbury, T., *The Lawfulness of Resisting Tyrants*, 2nd edn. (1714).

Brett, T. *The Dangers of a Relapse. A Sermon* (1713).

Brent. C., *An Essay concerning the Nature and Guilt of Lying* (1702).

British Advice to the Freeholders of Great Britain (1715).

The British Censor (1712).

Browne, J., *The Country Parson's Honest Advice to my Lord Keeper* (1706).

Burnet, G., *An Enquiry into the Measures of Submission to the Supream Authority* (1688).

Burnet, T., *Second Remarks upon an Essay* (1697).

Burnet, Sir T., *A Certain Information of a Certain Discourse. That Happen'd at a Certain Gentleman's House in a Certain County* (1713).

—— *The True Character of an Honest Man Particularly with Relation to the Publick Affairs* (1712).

—— *Truth if you can Find it* (1712).

Burridge, R., *A New Review of London* (1721).

Burton, R., *A Modest Enquiry into the Rise and Growth of Party Distinction Among Us* (Dublin, 1714).

Cameronian Whigs No Patriots (1713).

The Candidate: Being a Detection of Bribery and Corruption (1715) [sometimes attributed to Defoe].

The Candidates Try'd; or, A Certain Way how to Avoid Mistakes in Choosing Members (1701).

Care, H., *Draconica; or, An Abstract of all the Penal Laws*, 2nd edn. (1688).

Cary, J., *A Vindication of the Parliament of England* (1698).

The Case of Algernon Sidney Esq. [1680].

The Case of Sir Thomas Lee [1699].

The Case of Spencer Cowper Esq. (1701).

A Catalogue of the Names of the Members (1654).

A Caution to the Good People of England, about the Choice of Members for the Ensuing Parliament (1690).

A Caveat for my Countreymen in General (1660).

Chamberlen, H., *An Answer to a Libel Entituled A Dialogue between Dr H. C. and a Country Gentleman* (1696).

The Character of a Modern Addresser (1710).

The Character of a Modern Tory (1713).

The Character of a Phanatique (1660).

The Character of a Whig (1700).

The Cheater's Speculum; Or, The New English Rogue (1700).

The Church Not in Danger (1707).

The Claims of the People Essayed (1701).

[Clement, S.], *Faults on Both Sides* (1710).

——— *A Vindication of the Faults on Both Sides* (1710).

Coffee Houses Vindicated (1673).

A Collection from Dyer's Letters Concerning the Elections (1706).

A Collection of Addresses (1710).

A Collection of Poems on Affairs of State, 3 vols. (1689).

A Collection of Several Papers Printed in the Year 1710 (1718).

A Collection of State Tracts: Publish'd on Occasion of the Late Revolution in 1688. And During the Reign of King William III (London, vol. 1, 1705; vol. 2, 1706; vol. 3, 1707).

Collins, A., *Priestcraft in Perfection* (1710).

[Comber, T.], *Three Considerations proposed to Mr William Penn . . . which may be Worthy the Consideration of all the Quakers and of all my Dissenting Brethren also that have Voyces in the Choice of Parliament-men* [1688].

Considerations on the Nature of Parliaments and our Present Elections [1698].

Considerations Relating to our Choice and the Qualifications of Our Members of Parliament (1711).

[Cooper, A. earl of Shaftesbury?], *Some Observations Concerning the Regulating of Elections* (1689).

The Countryman's Remembrancer . . . who were Most for Promoting the Bill against Hypocrisie, Heresie, and Schism, alias, Occasional Conformity (1705).

[Cowper, W.], *The Case of the Ancient Burrough of Hertford in Relation to their Electing Burgesses* [1688/9]—not in ESTC, copy at Herts. RO, bor. recs. 23/331.

Crosfeild, R., *England's Warning-Piece* (1704).

——— *A Vindication of the Constitution of the English Monarchy and the Just Rights of the People* (1703) [ascribed to him on grounds of style and content].

Cursory Remarks Upon Some Late Disloyal Proceedings in Several Cabals (1699).

The Danger of Moderation (1708).

The Danger of the Church Enquir'd Into (1710).

Davenant, C., *Discourses of the Public Revenues* (1698).

——— *Essays upon Peace at Home and War Abroad* (1704).

——— *Sir Thomas Double at Court, and in High Preferments. In Two Dialogues, between Sir Thomas Double and Sir Richard Comover, alias Mr. Whiglove* (1710).

——— *Tom Double Return'd Out of the Country; or, The True Picture of a Modern Whig* (1702).

——— *The True Picture of a Modern Whig, Set Forth in a Dialogue between Mr. Whiglove & Mr. Double, Two Under-Spur-Leathers to the Late Ministry* (1701).

——— (with Harley, R.) *A Letter from the Grecian Coffee House* (1701).

Davies, M., *Eikon Mikro-biblike Sive Icon Libellorum; or, A Critical History of Pamphlets* (1715).

A Declaration and Vindication of the Loyal-hearted Nobility, Gentry and others of the County of Kent and City of Canterbury that they had no Hand in the Murder of our King (1660).

The Declaration of an Honest Churchman Upon Occasion of the Present Times (1710).

A Defence of the Allies and the Late Ministry (1711).

Defoe, D. *The Anatomy of Exchange Alley* (1719).

——— *And What if the Pretender should come? or, Some Considerations of the Advantages and Real Consequences of the Pretender's Possessing the Crown of Great Britain.*

——— *Arguments about the Alteration of Triennial Elections* (1716).

——— *A Brief Reply to the History of Standing Armies in England* (1698).

——— *An Essay at a Plain Exposition of that Difficult Phrase a Good Peace* (1711).

——— *An Essay on the Regulation of the Press* (1704).

——— *An Essay upon Projects* (1697).

——— *An Essay Upon Public Credit* (1710).

——— *Essays Upon Several Projects* (1702).

——— *Fair Payment No Spunge* (1717).

——— *The Freeholders Plea against Stock-jobbing Elections* (1701).

——— *A Fifth Essay at Removing National Prejudices* [1707].

——— *The History of the Kentish Petition* (1701).

——— *A Hymn to the Mob* (1715).

——— *Jure Divino* (1706).

——— *A Letter to a New Member of the Ensuing Parliament* [23 Dec. 1701 as printed date] (1702) [possible ascription of authorship].

——— *A Letter to Mr Bisset Eldest Brother of the Collegiate Church* (1710).

——— *Mr. S-r. The enclosed memorial you are charg'd with, in the behalf of many thousands of the good people of England* (1701), cited as the *Legion Memorial.*

——— *A New Test of the Sence [sic] of the Nation Being a Modest Comparison Between the Addresses to the Late King James and those to her Present Majesty* (1710).

——— *The Original Power of the Collective Body of the People* (1702).

——— *The Political Sow-Gelder; or, The Castration of Whig and Tory* (1715).

——— *Reasons against the Succession of the House of Hanover* (1713).

——— *The Secret History of the White Staff* (1715).

——— *The Shortest Way with Dissenters* (1702).

——— *Some Remarks on the First Chapter in Dr Davenant's Essays* (1704).

Defoe, D., *Two Great Questions Considered. I. What is the Obligation of Parliaments to the Addresses or Petitions of the People* (1707).

———— *A Word Against a New Election* (1710).

Dennis, J., *The Danger of Priestcraft to Religion and Government* (1702).

Denton, W., *An Apology for the Liberty of the Press* (1681).

———— *Jus Regiminis; Being a Justification of Defensive Arms* (1689).

A Dialogue Between a Member of Parliament, a Divine, a Lawyer, a Freeholder, a Shopkeeper and a Country Farmer (1703) [sometimes attributed to Davenant].

A Dialogue between a Quaker and his Neighbour in Hertford, about the Murder of Mrs. Sarah Stout (1699).

A Dialogue between Dr H. C. and a Country Gentleman (1696).

A Dialogue Between the Author of Whigs no Christians and a Country Gentleman [1715?].

A Dialogue Betwixt Moderation and Constitution (1714).

A Dialogue betwixt Whig and Tory (1710)—a reprint of a 1693 tract with the same title but a different subtitle.

A Dialogue; or, New Friendly Debate (1705).

[Drake, J.], *Some Necessary Considerations Relating to All Future Elections* (1702).

———— *The History of the Last Parliament* (1702).

Dryden, J., *Absalom and Achitophel* (1681).

The Duke of Anjou's Succession Further Consider'd (1701).

Earbery, M., *Elements of Policy Civil and Ecclesiastical in a Mathematical Method* (1716).

Edwards, J., *Some New Discoveries of the Uncertainty, Deficiency and Corruptions of Human Knowledge and Learning* (1714).

The Electors Right Assented (1701).

Ellwood, T., *A Discourse Concerning Riots* (1683).

The Engagement and Remonstrance of the City of London, Subscribed by 23,500 Hands (1659).

England's Corruptions and Mismanagements Discover'd. In a Dialogue between Trueman and Legion (1702).

England's Directions for Members Elections (1660).

England's Enemies Expos'd, and its True Friends and Patriots Defended (1701).

English Advice to English Freeholders [1705].

The Englishman (1670).

An Englishman's Thoughts of the Present State of Affairs (1701).

The English Rogue Revived; or, The Life of William Fuller, Cheat-Master-General of Great Britain (1718).

An Enquiry into the Inconveniences of Public and the Advantages of Private Elections. With the Method of a Ballott (1701).

An Enquiry into the Nature of the Liberty of the Subject (1706).

An Enquiry; or, A Discourse between a Yeoman of Kent, and a Knight of a Shire, upon the Prorogation of the Parliament to the Second of May, 1693 [1693], possibly by John Hampden and John Wildman.

An Epistle to a Whig Member of Parliament, Concerning the Triennial Bill (1716).

The False Test Set in a True Light (1710).

Ferguson, R., *A Representation of the Threatning Dangers* (1688).

Fleetwood, W., *The Thirteenth Chapter to the Romans Vindicated from the Abusive Sense Put upon it. Written by a Curate of Salop.* (1710).

Fransham, J., *An Exact Account of the Charge for Supporting the Poor of the City of Norwich* (1720).

The Free State of Noland (1696, rev. and expanded 1701).

A Friendly Letter to Such as Have Voices in Election of Members to Serve in Parliament (1695).

A Full Answer to the Deposition and to All Other the Pretences and Arguments Whatsoever Concerning the Birth of the Prince of Wales (1688).

Fuller, W., *The Life of William Fuller, Gent.* (1701).

———— *Mr William Fuller's Trip to Bridewell* (1703).

———— *The Whole Life of Mr William Fuller* (1703).

———— *The Sincere and Hearty Confession of Mr William Fuller* (1704).

———— *The Tories Looking Glass* (1716).

———— *Truth at Last or Mr William Fuller's Free Account of his Books (or Narratives) and Public Transactions* (1708).

———— *Twenty Six Depositions* (1702).

Furnese, Sir H., *Sir Henry Furness's Case against Mr John Sturt* (1699).

Glanvill, J., *A Seasonable Defence of Preaching* (1703 edn.).

———— *The Grand Memorandum* (1660).

Gregory, F., *A Modest Plea for the Due Regulation of the Press* (1698).

Gumble, T., *The Life of General Monck* (1671).

[Halifax, Marquis of], *Some Cautions Offered to the Consideration of those who are to Chuse Members to Serve in the Ensuing Parliament* (1695).

Hammond, A., *Considerations Upon Corrupt Elections of Members of Parliament* (1701).

Hampden, R., *A Speech Made in the House of Commons, by Richard Hampden Esq.* (1716).

Harrington, J., *Roger L'Estrange's Queries Considered; and Some Queries Put* [1690].

———— *Some Queries Concerning the Election . . . Together with a Reply* (1690).

Harrison, T., *Proposals Made to the Booksellers of London and Westminster by T. Harrison* [not in ESTC, copy at BL. Harl. MSS 5996 (134)].

Head, R., *Proteus Redivivus; or, The Art of Wheedling* (1675).

The Hertford Letter Containing several Brief Observations on a Late Printed Tryal, Concerning the Murder of Mrs. Sarah Stout (1699).

The History of Associations (1716).

The History of the Kentish Petition, Answer'd Paragraph by Paragraph (1701).

Hickeringill, E., *A Sermon Preach'd on the 30th of January* (1700).

Hoadly, B., *The Election Dialogue between a Gentleman and his Neighbour in the Country* (1710).

Hoadly, B., *An Answer to the Representation Drawn up by the Committee of the Lower-House or Convocation* (1717).

——— *The Jacobite Hopes Reviv'd by our late Tumults and Addresses* (1710).

——— *The Nature of the Kingdom; or, Chuch of Christ* (1717).

——— *The True Genuine Tory-Address* (1710).

How, J., *Some Thoughts on the Present State of Printing and Bookselling* (1709).

An Humble Address to our Sovereign Lords the People (1715) [sometimes attributed to Defoe].

The Humble Desires of the Knights, Gentlemen, Ministers, Freeholders and Inhabitants of the County and Burrough of Leicester (1659).

An Impartial Account of the Behaviour of the Tories (1716).

The Innkeepers Opinion of the Triennial Act (1716) [sometimes attributed to Defoe].

The Introduction to the Reconcilers (1713).

Jack out of an Office (1705).

Johnson, S., *A Letter from a Freeholder to the Rest of the Freeholders of England* [1689].

The Judgment of Whole Kingdoms and Nations (1710).

Jura Populi Anglicani . . . Answer'd, Paragraph by Paragraph (1701).

Kem, S., *King Solomon's Infallible Expedient* (1660).

Kennett, W., *A Register and Chronicle Ecclesiastical and Civil* (1728).

——— *A True Answer to Dr Sacheverell's Sermon before the Lord Mayor, Nov. 5 1709* (1709).

——— *The Wisdom of Looking Backwards, to Judge the Better of One Side* (1715).

The Kentish Men (1701).

King, W., *The State of the Protestants of Ireland* (1691).

Kingston, R., *Apothegmata Curiosa* (1709).

——— *The Life of William Fuller, alias Fullee, alias Fowler, alias Ellison . . . The First and Second Part* (1701).

——— *True History of the Several Designs and Conspiracies . . . from 1688 till 1697* (1698).

Lawton, C., *Civil Comprehension* (1705).

——— *A Second Letter Concerning Civil Comprehension* (1706).

The Legionites Plot (1702).

Leslie, C., *The New Association of Those Called Moderate Churchmen, With the Modern Whigs and Fanatics*, 3rd edn. (1702).

——— *The New Association, Part II* (1703).

——— *The Wolf Stript of his Shepherd's Cloathing* (1704).

——— *A View of the Times . . . in the First Volume of the Rehearsals* (1708).

——— *The Good Old Cause; or, Lying in Truth* (1710).

L'Estrange, R., *L'Estrange his Apology* (1660).

——— *Citt and Bumpkin* (1680).

——— *Considerations and Proposals in Order to the Regulation of the Press* (1663).

——— *A Memento. Treating of the Rise, Progress, and Remedies of Seditions* (1682).

——— *Remarks on the Growth and Progress of Non-Conformity* (1682).

———— *A Short Answer to a Whole Litter of Libels* (1680).

———— *Some Queries Concerning the Election of Members for the Ensuing Parliament* (1690).

A Letter from a Citizen of Worcester (1710).

A Letter from a Clergy-Man in the Country to a Minister in the City (1689).

A Letter from a Country Gentleman to an Eminent but Easy Citizen who was Unhappily Misguided in the Fatal Election of Sir John Moore for Lord Mayor of London at Michaelmas 1681 (1692).

A Letter from a Curate of Suffolk to a High-Church Member (1712).

A Letter from a Minister in Norfolk to his Parishioners (1700).

A Letter from a Person of Quality to his Friend, about Abhorrers and Addressors (1682).

A Letter from an Impartial Hater of the Papists [1680], by W. L.

A Letter from J.B alias Oldcutt, to his Friend Mr Jenks (1679).

A Letter to a Conscientious Man (1720).

A Letter to a Country Gentleman, Shewing the Inconveniences which Attended the Last Part of the Act for Triennial Parliaments (1716) [sometimes attributed to Defoe].

A Letter to a Friend in Suffolk Occasion'd by a Report of Repealing the Triennial Act (1716).

A Letter to a Friend upon Occasion of the House of Commons Passing a Bill, Intituled an Act for Enlarging the Time of Continuance of Parliaments (1716).

A Letter to a Friend, Upon the Dissolving of the Late Parliament (1690).

A Letter to a Gentleman about the Election of Members for the County of Cambridge (1690).

A Letter to a Gentleman in the Country Concerning the Price of Guineas [1695/6].

A Letter to a Member of Parliament Shewing that a Restraint on the Press is Inconsistent with the Protestant Religion and Dangerous to the Liberties of the Nation (1698).

A Letter to a Member of Parliament Shewing the Necessity of Regulating the Press (1699).

A Letter to a Modern Dissenting Whig (1701).

A Letter to a New Member of the Honourable House of Commons; touching the Rise of all the Imbezzlements and Mismanagements of the Kingdom's Treasure from the Beginning of the Revolution until this Present Time (Amsterdam [London?], 1710).

A Letter to an Elector Containing Powerful Persuasives to Vote for our Most Worthy Patriots the Whigs Next Election (1713).

A Letter to a West Country Clothier and Freeholder (1713).

A Letter to Mr B—a North Wiltshire Clergyman, Relating to an Address from that Archdeaconry to the Queen (1710).

A Letter to Richard Steele Esq. (1715).

A Letter to the Gentlemen and Freeholders of the County of Dorset (1713).

A Letter to the Right Honourable Robert Walpole (1716) [sometimes attributed to Defoe].

The Life of William Fuller, the Late Pretended Evidence (1692).

A List of One Unanimous Club of Members of the Late Parliament (1701).

A List of One Unanimous Club of Voters (1679).

A List of the Honourable House of Commons that Voted For and Against the Clause for the Hanover Succession in the Year 1702 (1710).

A List of those Worthy Patriots [who voted for the Tack] [1705].

Lloyd, R. L., *A Sermon Preach'd at St. Paul's Covent-Garden, on the 30th of January, 1711* (1712).

Locke, J., *The Reasonableness of Christianity*, 2nd edn. (1696).

The Lord Delamere's Letter to his Tenants at Warrington, in Lancashire, Answered; by One of his Lordship's Tenants (1688).

Lowndes, W., *A Report Containing an Essay for the Amendment of the Silver Coins* (1695).

McKenzie, Sir G., *A True and Plain Account of the Discoveries Made in Scotland, of the Late Conspiracies against His Majesty and the Government* (1685).

Mackworth, Sir H., *Free Parliaments; or, A Vindication of the Fundamental Right of the Commons of England* (1704).

The Management of the Four Last Years Vindicated . . . Recommended to all True Englishmen, against the Election of a New Parliament (1714).

Mandeville, B., *The Fable of the Bees. Part II* (1729).

Manley, D., *The Secret Memoirs and Manners of Several Persons of Quality* (1709).

Mansell, R., *An Exact and True Narrative of the Late Popish Intrigue* (1680).

Maynwaring, A., *The King of Hearts* [1690].

—— *Advice to the Electors of Great Britain; Occasioned by the Intended Invasion from France* (1708).

A Memento for the People about their Elections of Members for the Approaching Parliament (1654).

The Memorial of the Church of England (1705) [sometimes attributed to William Pittis, James Drake, and Henry Pooley].

The Mercy of the Government Vindicated (1716) [sometimes attributed to Defoe].

Meriton, H., *A Sermon Preacht at the Cathedral Church in Norwich* (1696).

Misson, H., *M. Misson's Memoirs and Observations in his Travels over England . . . Translated by Mr. Ozell* (1719).

The Moderation, Justice and Manners of the Review (1706).

The Moderator; or, A View of the State of Controversie betwixt Whigg and Tory. By a true English Man of no party (1702).

The Moderator; or, Considerations Propos'd in Order to End the Unseasonable Debate Concerning the Legality of the Late Happy Revolution, 2nd edn. (1710).

A Modest Attempt for Healing the Present Animosities in England Occasion'd by a Late Book Entituled A Modest Enquiry (1690).

A Modest Enquiry into the Causes of the Present Disasters in England (1690).

Molyneux, W., *The Case of Ireland's Being Bound by Act of Parliament in England* (1698).

Mr Ferguson's Lamentation for the Destruction of the Association and the Good Old Cause (1683).

Mr Hoadly's Measures of Submission to the Civil Magistrate Enquir'd Into and Disprov'd (1711).

Muralt, B. L. de, *Letters Describing the Character and Customs of the English and French Nations* (1726).

Naked Truth; or, Phanaticism Detected. Recommended to the Serious Consideration of all True Protestants, Particularly to the Electors of Members to Serve in the Ensuing Parliament (1705).

Nalson, J., *The Complaint of Liberty and Property against Arbitrary Government* (1681).

The Necessity of Peace and Union Among Members of the Church of England, Proving that the Names of Whig and Tory are Mischievous and Unreasonable (1715).

Nedham, M., *Christianissimus Christianandus; or, Reason for the Reduction of France* (1678).

———— *Interest will not Lie* (1659).

———— *A Second Pacquet of Advices and Animadversions Sent to the Men of Shaftesbury* (1677).

A New Dictionary of the Terms Ancient and Modern of the Canting Crew (1699) [by B. E.].

Newnam, R., *The Complaint of English Subjects* (1700).

North, R., *Examen; or, An Enquiry into the Credit and Veracity of a Pretended Complete History* (1740).

Northleigh, J., *Parliamentum Pacificum* (1688).

The Old and Modern Whig Truly Represented (1702) (sometimes attributed to C. Davenent).

The Old Constitution and Present Establishment in Church and State (1718).

Old Popery as Good as New (1688) [by N. N.].

Oldmixon, J., *The British Academy: Being a New-Erected Society for the Advancement of Wit and Learning: With Some Few Observations Upon it* (1712).

———— *Essay on Criticism* (1728).

———— *The History of Addresses* (part 1, 1709; part 2, 1710).

———— *Memoirs of the Life of John Lord Somers* (1716).

———— *The British Empire in America*, 2 vols. (1708).

———— *Reflections on Dr Swift's Letter to the Earl of Oxford* (1712).

———— *Remarks on a Late Libel Privately Dispers'd by the Tories* (1715).

Party No Dependance: Containing an Historical Account of the Rise and Fall of Parties (1713).

The Patriot's Proposal of the People of England Concerning the Ballot, the Best Way of Choosing New Representatives in Parliament (1705).

Percival, T., *The Rye House Travestie* (1696).

Pearse, E., *The Conformist's Plea for the Nonconformists*, 3rd edn. (1683).

Petty, Sir W., *The Political Anatomy of Ireland* (1691).

———— *Two Essays in Political Arithmetick* (1687).

Petyt, G., *Lex Parliamentaria* (1690).

Pittis, W., *Reasons for a War with France* (1715).

Place, C., *The Arbitration; or, The Tory and Whig Reconcil'd* (1710).

—— *A Sermon Preach'd at Dorchester During the Time of the Assizes March the 18th 1705* (1705).

—— *The Thoughts of an Honest Whig; or, The Scheme of the Bishop of Bangor's Sermon before the King Examin'd in its particulars* (1717).

—— *The True English Revolutionist* (1710).

Plain Dealing Concerning the Penal Laws and Tests. Delivered in a Dialogue (1688).

The Plea of Publick Good not Sufficient to Justify the Taking up Arms against our Rightful and Lawful Sovereigns (1706).

Political Aphorisms; or, The True Maxims of Government Displayed (1690).

Poems on Affairs of State: From the Time of Oliver Cromwell, 3 vols. (1697–1707).

Pope, A., *An Essay on Criticism* (1711).

The Popish Damnable Plot against our Religion and Liberties Fairly Laid Open (1680).

[Povey, C.], *An Inquiry into the Miscarriages of the Last Four Years Reign, . . . Presented to the Freeholders of Great Britain against the Next Election of a New Parliament* (1714).

The Present Disposition of England (1701) [perhaps by C. Montagu].

The Present Disposition of England Considered (1701).

Presentment of the Grand Jury for the County of Kent . . . 12 Mar. 1682 (1683).

The Principles and Practices of the Present Sett of Whigs Defended (1713).

A Proclamation against Tumultuous Petitions (1679).

Proposals Humbly Offered to the Consideration of Those Who are to be Electors of Members (1690).

Prynne, W., *A Remonstrance and Declaration of Severall Counties, Cities and Burroughs* (1648).

—— *Brevia Parliamentaria Rediviva* (1662).

—— *Seasonable and Healing Instructions . . . to be Seriously Recommended . . . to . . . Knights and Burgesses* (1660).

Push, H., *The True Nature of Religious Zeal* (1710).

Raillerie à la Mode (1673).

Rawlins, T., *Truth and Sincerity Recommended in a Sermon against Lying* (1713).

A Ready Way to Prevent Bribery [1689].

The Reasonableness of Toleration (1687) [sometimes attributed to William Penn].

Reasons for a War against France (1715).

Reasons to Support the Proposal for Granting Divers Sorts of Annuities Such as the Common People May be Able to Compass (1705).

Reflections on the Management of Some Late Party-Disputes and the Notorious Abuse of the Words Church, Schismatick, Fanatick &c (1715).

Reeves, W., *A Sermon Preach'd at the Assizes Holden at Abingdon, in the County of Berks, July 14 1713* (1713).

—— *The Nature of Truth and Falshood* (1712).

Remarks by Way of Answer, Paragraph by Paragraph, to the Character of a Modern Whig &c (1701).

Remarks on a Scandalous Libel Entitl'd a Letter from a Member of Parliament (1713) [sometimes ascribed to John Oldmixon].

Remarks Upon the Most Eminent of our Anti-Monarchical Authors (1699).

Remarques on the Humours and Conversations of the Town (1673).

A Reply to the Hertford Letter (1699).

A Reply to the Second Return (1682).

A Representation of the Present State of Religion . . . in Ireland (1711).

Robertson, W., *The Liberty, Property and Religion of the Whigs* (1713).

Rogers, T., *A True Protestant Bridle* (1694).

Roscommon, earl of, *A Letter from Scotland* (1681).

Sacheverell, H., *The Nature and Mischief of Prejudice and Partiality* (1704).

——— *The Perils of False Brethren, Both in Church and State* (1709).

——— *The Speech of Henry Sacheverell DD Upon his Impeachment . . . March 7, 1710* (1710).

Saint Leger, Sir J., *The Manager's Pro and Con or an Account of What is Said* (1710).

Sarah, the Quaker, to Lothario, lately Deceased, on Meeting him in the Shades (1728).

A Satyr upon Thirty-Seven Articles (1701).

The Scottish Echo to the English Legion (1707).

Seasonable Advice to Electors (1705).

A Seasonable Argument to Perswade all the Grand Juries to Petition for a New Parliament (1677).

A Seasonable Caution to all Loyal Subjects (1690).

A Seasonable Memento to all the Electors (1689).

A Second Letter to a Friend in Suffolk Occasion'd by a Report of Repealing the Triennial Act (1716).

A Second Letter to the Right Honourable Robert Walpole (1716).

The Second Part of the Character of a Good Man, Neither Whig nor Tory (1682).

The Second Part of the People's Antient and Just Liberties Asserted (1670).

The Secret History of the Secret History of the White Staff (1715) [sometimes attributed to Defoe but possibly by William Pittis].

A Serious Address to the Commoners of England Concerning the Approaching Elections (1705).

A Serious Representation to the People of Great-Britain Concerning the Pretender (1715) [by E. D.].

Settle, E., *The Character of a Popish Successor* (1681).

Seven Papers (1689).

The Several Proceedings and Resolutions of the House of Commons (1701).

Sharpe, I., *This is the Time; or, Serious Advice to a Country Friend Concerning the Election of Members of Parliament* (1710).

Sheffield, J., [Duke of Buckingham], *The Works of John Sheffield . . . Duke of Buckingham* ed. A. Pope, 2 vols. (1723).

Sheridan, T., *Discourse of the Rise and Power of Parliaments* (1677).

Shippen, W., *Faction Display'd* (1704).
——— *Moderation Display'd* (1704).
Smalridge, G., and Crosse, T., *A Detection of a Falshood* (1710).
A Smith and Cutlers Plain Dialogue about Whig and Tory (1690).
Sober and Seasonable Queries Humbly Offered to All Good Protestants . . . The Second Edition with Considerable Additions by Another Author (1679).
Some Advice Humbly Offered to the Consideration of the Several Electors of Parliament-Men for this Great City [1689].
Some Critical and Politick Remarks on a Late Virulent Lampoon Call'd Faction Display'd (1704).
Some Observations on the Tryal of Spencer Cowper (1701).
Some Reasons for an Annual Parliament as the Best Security for English Rights [1702].
Some Remarks upon Government (1689).
[Somers, J.], *The Security of English-men's Lives* (1681).
——— *Jura Populi Anglicani; Or, The Subjects Right of Petitioning* (1701).
The Source of our Present Fears Discover'd (1703).
The South Sea Scheme Detected (1720).
South, R., *Twelve Sermons Preached upon Several Occasions* (1692).
——— *Twelve Sermons Preached Upon Several Occasions . . . The Second Volume* (1697).
Sprat, T., *Copies of the Informations and Original Papers Relating to the Proof of the Horrid Conspiracy* (1685).
——— *The History of the Royal Society* (1667).
——— *A Relation of the Wicked Contrivance*, 3rd edn. (1692/3).
——— *A True Account and Declaration of the Horrid Conspiracy Against the Late King* (1685).
State Law; or, The Doctrine of Libels Discussed and Examined (1729).
State Tracts: Being a Collection of Several Treatises Relating to the Government, Privately Printed in the Reign of K. Charles II (London, part 1, 1689; part 2, 1692/3).
The States-men of Abingdon (1702).
Steele, R., *The Crisis; or, A Discourse Representing, from the Most Authentick Records, the Just Causes of the Late Happy Revolution* (1714).
——— *Mr Steele's Apology for Himself and his Writings; Occasioned by his Expulsion from the House of Commons* (1714).
[Stephens, E.], *Authority Abused by the Vindication of the Last Years Transaction and the Abuses Detected* (1690).
[Stephens, W.] *Dick and Tom: A Dialogue about Addresses* (1710).
——— *A Letter to His Most Excellent Majesty King William III* (1699).
Stewart, Sir J., *Jus Populi Vindicatum; or, The People's Right to Defend Themselves* (1669).
Study to be Quiet (1680).
The Subjects Case (1701).
Suffragium; or, The Humours of the Electors (1702).
A Supplement to Faults in the Fault-Finder (1710/1).

A Supplement to the Faults on Both Sides: Containing the Compleat History of the Proceedings of a Party Ever Since the Revolution (1710) [sometimes attributed to Defoe].

A Supplement (to the Paper called, Reasons Humbly offered . . .) [1693].

The Suspension of the Triennial Act the Certain Way to Unite the Nation (1716).

Swynfen, J., *The Objections of the Non-Subscribing London Clergy against the Address* (1710).

Sykes, A., *The Suspension of the Triennial Bill the Properest Means* (1716).

The Tackers Vindicated (1705).

A Tender and Hearty Address to all the Freeholders and other Electors (1714).

A Test Offer'd to the Consideration of the Electors of Great Britain (1710).

A Test Offered to the Consideration of Electors . . . to which is added . . . a reply to the Vindication (1714).

The Thoughts of an Honest Whig, Upon the Present Proceedings of that Party (1710).

Thoyras, R. de, *The History of Whig and Tory from the Conquest to the Present Time* (1723).

Three Letters (1689).

Toland, J., *Christianity not Mysterious* (1696).

——— *The Danger of Mercenary Parliaments* (1698).

——— *The Militia Reform'd* (1698).

——— *The State-Anatomy of Great Britain* (1717).

The Tories Unmask'd (1715).

[Trapp, J.], *The Age of Riddles; or, A True List of Certain Extraordinary Positions, Formerly Call'd Contradictions, but now Distinguish'd by No Name at All* (1710).

——— *The Character and Principles of the Present Set of Whigs* (1711).

——— *Most Faults on One Side* (1710).

——— *The True Genuine Modern Whigg-Address* (1710).

Treason Detected in an Answer to that Traiterous and Malicious Libel, Entitled, English Advice (1715) [sometimes attributed to Defoe].

Trenchard, J., *A Short History of Standing Armies in England* (1698).

The Trial and Determination of Truth in Answer to the Best Choice for Religion and Government (1697).

The Triennial Act Impartially Stated, Shewing 1. That the Law was made for Securing the Liberties of the People . . . II That the Many Plausible Arguments Insinuated for Repealing this Act are Fallacious and Inconclusive and the Consequences thereof may be Fatal to the Publick (1716).

A True Account of the Lord Delamere his Reception and Wellcome in Cheshire [1689].

A True Catalogue; or, An Account of the Several Places . . . where . . . Richard Cromwell was Proclaimed Lord Protector [1659].

True English Advice to the Kentish Freeholders [1702].

The True Englishman's Choice of Parliament-Men (1698).

The True Genuine Tory-Address and the True Genuine Whig-Address, Set One Against the Other (1710).

The True Patriot's Speech to the People of Rome Answer'd Paragraph by Paragraph (1708).

The True Picture of a Modern Whig Reviv'd. Set forth in a Third Dialogue between Whiglove and Double at Tom's Coffee-house (1707).

The True Picture of an Ancient Tory in a Dialogue between Vassal a Tory and Freeman a Whig (1702).

A True Protestant Bridle (1694) [by T. R.].

The True Tom Double; or, An Account of Dr Davenant's Late Conduct and Writings (1704).

The Truest Account of Mr Fuller's Discovery of the True Mother of the Pretended Prince of Wales (1696).

The Tryal and Examination of Mr John Tutchin (1704).

The Tryal of Spencer Cowper (1699).

Tufton, S., *The History of Faction, alias Hypocrisy, alias Moderation* (1705).

Tullie, G., *Moderation Recommended in a Sermon* (1689).

Tutchin, J., *The Mouse Grown a Rat* (1702).

Tyrrell, J., *His Majesty's Government and Ministry Vindicated* (1716).

—— *Patriarcha Non Monarcha* (1681).

A View of the Present Divisions in Great Britain, by the Leaders of the Parties, which May Encourage a French Invasion (1708).

A Vindication of a Sheet (1688).

A Vindication of the Constitution of the English Monarchy (1703).

Vox Angliae; or, The Voice of the Kingdom (1682).

Vox Cleri Pro Rege (1688).

Vox Patriae; or, The Resentments & Indignation of the Free-born Subjects of England (1681).

Vox Populi, Vox Dei: Being True Maxims of Government (1709), reprinted as *The Judgment of Whole Kingdoms* (1710).

Wagstaffe, T., *An Account of the Proceedings in the House of Commons* (1696).

Wagstaffe, W., *The State and Condition of our Taxes Considered . . . with Some Directions to the Freeholders of Great Britain, Concerning the Choice of the Next Parliament* (1714).

Waldron, G., *A Perswasive Oration to the People of Great Britain* (1716).

Walpole, R., *A Short History of the Parliament* (1713).

Ward, E. [Ned], *The Galloper; or, Needs Must When the Devil Drives* (1710).

—— *The School of Politicks; or, The Humours of a Coffee-house* (1690).

—— *The Secret History of Clubs* (1709).

—— *A True History of the Honest Whigs. A Poem* (1710).

What has been, May be; or, A View of a Popish and an Arbitrary Government in a Recapitulation of the Barbarities of the Late Times (1713).

Whiggism Vindicated. In a Letter to a Tory (1715).

The Whigs Warning-Piece, as Drawn from the Late Picture of a Modern Whig [1701?].

The Whigs Thirty Two Queries and as Many of the Tories in Answer to Them (1701).

Willis, B., *Notitia Parliamentaria or an History of the Counties, Cities and Boroughs in England and Wales*, 2 vols. (1715).

Wither, G., *The Prisoner's Plea* (1661).

—— *Letters of Advice* (1644).

Woodward, J., *The Divine Right of Civil Government* (1712).

The Worcester Triumph (1710).

A Word in Season [1690].

A Word in Season about Guineas (1695).

A Word of Advice to the Citizens of London Concerning the Choice of Members of Parliament at the Ensuing Election (1705).

A Word of Advice unto all those that have a Right to Choose Parliament Men (1690).

A Word to the Wise in a Letter to a City-Clergyman (1711) [sometimes attributed to Joseph Rawson].

Wroe, R., *A Sermon at the Funeral of the Right Honourable Henry Earl of Warrington* (1694).

The Zeal of the Tories for the Church and State (1715).

PERIODICALS

(Date begun and editors in brackets)

The Britain (1713, ?J. Oldmixon).

British Apollo (1708, A. Hill and M. Smith).

The Censor (1717, L. Theobold).

Censura Temporum (1708, S. Parker).

Collection of Letters for the Improvement of Husbandry and Trade (1681, J. Houghton).

The Examiner (1710, W. King and J. Swift).

The Freeholder (1715, J. Addison).

Heraclitus Ridens (1681, E. Rawlins or T. Flatman).

London Gazette (1666).

London Journal (1720, J. Pitt).

London News-Letter (1696, ?F. Leach).

The Loyal Protestant and True Domestick Intelligence (1681, N. Thompson).

The Medley (1710, A. Maynwaring and J. Oldmixon).

Mercurius Politicus (1705, J. Drake).

The Observator in Dialogue (1681, R. L'Estrange).

The Observator (1702, J. Tutchin).

The Plebeian (1719, Sir R. Steele).

The Post Boy (1695, A. Roper).

The Post Man (1695, J. de Fonvive).

The Rehearsal (1704, C. Leslie).

The Review (1704, D. Defoe).

The Spectator (1711, J. Addison and R. Steele).

SECONDARY WORKS

Achinstein, S., *Milton and the Revolutionary Reader* (Princeton, 1994).
—— 'The Uses of Deception: From Cromwell to Milton,' in K. Z. Keller, and G. J. Schiffhorst (eds.), *The Witness of Time. Manifestations of Ideology in Seventeenth Century England* (Pittsburgh, 1993).
—— 'The Politics of Babel in the English Revolution', in J. Holstun (ed.), *Pamphlet Wars: Prose in the English Revolution* (1992).
Ahrens, R., 'The Political Pamphlet: 1660–1714', in *Anglia*, 109 (1991), 21–43.
Amussen, S., and Kishlansky, M., *Political Culture and Cultural Politics in Early Modern England: Essays Presented to David Underdown* (Manchester, 1995).
Ashcraft, R., *Revolutionary Politics & Locke's Two Treatises of Government* (Princeton, 1986).
—— 'The Language of Political Conflict in Restoration Literature', in *Politics as Reflected in Literature, Papers presented at a Clark Library Seminar 1987* (1989).
—— and Goldsmith, M., 'Locke, Revolution Principles, and the Formation of Whig Ideology', *HJ*, 26 (1983), 773–800.
Astbury, R., 'The Renewal of the Licensing Act in 1693 and its Lapse in 1695', *The Library*, 5th ser., 33 (1978), 296–322.
Atherton, I., 'The Press and Popular Political Opinion', in B. Coward (ed.), *A Companion to Stuart Britain* (Oxford, 2003).
Aylmer, G., *The Crown's Servants: Government and Civil Service under Charles II, 1660–1685* (Oxford, 2002).
Baldwin, G., 'The "Public" as a Rhetorical Community in Early Modern England', in Shepard and Withington, *Communities in Early Modern England*, ch. 11.
Ball, T., Farr, J., and Hanson, R. L. (eds.), *Political Innovation and Conceptual Change* (Cambridge, 1989).
Barker, H., *Newspapers, Politics and English Society 1695–1855* (Oxford, 1998).
Barnard, J., and McKenzie, D. F., *The Cambridge History of the Book in Britain. Vol. 4: 1557–1695* (Cambridge, 2003).
Baskerville, S., Adman, P., and Beedham, K. 'The Dynamics of Landlord Influence in English County Elections 1701–1734: The Evidence from Cheshire', *Parliamentary History*, 12 (1993), 126–42.
Behrens, B., 'The Whig Theory of the Constitution in the Reign of Charles II', *Cambridge Historical Journal*, 7 (1941), 42–71.
Beiser, F., *The Sovereignty of Reason: The Defense of Rationality in the Early English Enlightenment* (Princeton, 1996).
Bennett, G. V., *The Tory Crisis in Church and State, 1688–1730: The Career of Francis Atterbury, Bishop of Rochester* (Oxford, 1976).
Berry, H., *Gender, Society and Print Culture in Late Stuart England: The Cultural World of the Athenian Mercury* (London, 2003).

——'An Early Coffee House Periodical and its Readers: The Athenian Mercury 1691–1697', *London Journal*, 25 (2000), 15–33.

Blanning, T. W., *The Culture of Power and the Power of Culture. Old Regime Europe 1660–1789* (Oxford, 2002).

Bond, D. H., and McLeod, W. R. (eds.), *Newsletters to Newspapers: Eighteenth-century Journalism, Papers Presented at a Bicentennial Symposium* (Morgantown, 1977).

Borsay, P., *The English Urban Renaissance: Culture and Society in the Provincial Town 1660–1770* (Oxford, 1989).

Braddick, M., *The Nerves of State. Taxation and the Financing of the English State 1558–1714* (Manchester, 1996).

—— *State Formation in Early Modern England c. 1550–1700* (Cambridge, 2000).

——and Walter, J. (eds.), *Negotiating Power in Early Modern Society: Order, Hierarchy and Subordination in Britain and Ireland* (Cambridge, 2001).

Braverman, R., *Plots and Counterplots: Sexual Politics and the Body Politic in English Literature, 1660–1730* (Cambridge, 1993).

Brewer, J., *The Sinews of Power: War, Money, and the English State, 1688–1783* (New York, 1989).

British Parliamentary Lists 1600–1800, ed. G. Ditchfield, D. Hayton, and C. Jones (London, 1995).

Brooks, C., 'The Country Persuasion and Political Responsibility in England in the 1690s', *Parliament, Estates and Representation*, 4 (1984), 135–46.

Bryson, A., *From Courtesy to Civility. Changing Codes of Conduct in Early Modern England* (Oxford, 1998).

Burns, J. H. with Goldie, M. (eds.), *The Cambridge History of Political Thought 1400–1800* (Cambridge, 1991).

Burke, P., Harrison, B., and Slack, P. (eds.), *Civil Histories. Essays Presented to Sir Keith Thomas* (Oxford, 2000).

Burtt, S. G., *Virtue Transformed: Political Argument in England, 1688–1740* (Cambridge, 1992).

Caffentizis, C., *Clipped Coins, Abused Words, and Civil Government* (New York, 1989).

Campbell, G., *Impostor at the Bar: William Fuller 1670–1733* (London, 1961).

Canavan, T., 'Robert Burton, Jonathan Swift and the Tradition of Anti-Puritan Invective', *Journal of the History of Ideas*, 34 (1973), 227–42.

Carruthers, B., *City of Capital: Politics and Markets in the English Financial Revolution* (Princeton, 1996).

Castiglione, D., and Sharpe, L. (eds.), *Shifting the Boundaries. Transformation of the Languages of Public and Private in the Eighteenth Century* (Exeter, 1995).

Champion, J., *Republican Learning: John Toland and the Crisis of Christian Culture, 1696–1722* (Manchester, 2003).

—— *The Pillars of Priestcraft Shaken: The Church of England and its Enemies, 1660–1730* (Cambridge, 1992).

Clark, J. C. D., *English Society, 1688–1832: Ideology, Social Structure and Political Practice During the Ancien Regime* (Cambridge, 1985).

—— *English Society, 1660–1832: Religion, Ideology and Politics during the Ancien Regime*, 2nd edn. (Cambridge, 2000).

Clark, P., *British Clubs and Societies, 1580–1800: The Origins of an Associational World* (Oxford, 2000).

Claydon, T., *William III and the Godly Revolution* (Cambridge, 1996).

—— 'The Sermon, the "Public Sphere" and the Political Culture of Late Seventeenth-Century England', in L. A. Ferrell, and P. McCullough (eds.), *The English Sermon Revised: Religion, Literature and History 1600–1750* (Manchester, 2001).

Cogswell, T., 'The Politics of Propaganda: Charles I and the People in the 1620s', *JBS*, 29 (1990), 187–215.

—— Cust, R., and Lake, P. (eds.), *Politics, Religion and Popularity. Essays in Honour of Conrad Russell* (Cambridge, 2002).

Coleman, D., 'Politics and Economics in the Age of Anne: The Case of the Anglo-French Trade Treaty of 1713', in D. Coleman and A. H. John (eds.), *Trade, Government and Economy in Pre-Industrial England* (1976).

Colley, L., *In Defiance of Oligarchy: The Tory Party 1714–1760* (Cambridge, 1982).

Collinson, P., *The Puritan Character. Polemics and Polarities in Early Seventeenth-century English Culture* (Los Angeles, 1989).

—— 'Ecclesiastical Vitriol: Religious Satire in the 1590's and the Invention of Puritanism', in J. Guy (ed.), *The Reign of Elizabeth I: Court and Culture in the Last Decade* (Cambridge, 1995).

Condren, C., *Satire, Lies and Politics: The Case of Dr. Arbuthnot* (Basingstoke, 1997).

—— *The Language of Politics in Seventeenth-Century England* (Basingstoke, 1994).

Corns, T., Speck, W., and Downie, J., 'Archetypal Mystification: Polemic and Reality in English Political Literature, 1640–1750', *Eighteenth-Century Life*, 7 (1982), 1–27.

Cowan, B., 'Reasonable Ecstasies: Shaftesbury and the Languages of Libertinism', *JBS*, 37 (1998), 111–38.

—— 'The Rise of the Coffeehouse Reconsidered' *HJ*, 47 (2004), 21–46.

Craig, Sir J., *Newton at the Mint* (Cambridge, 1946).

Cranfield, G. A., *The Development of the Provincial Newspaper, 1700–1760* (Oxford, 1962).

Cressy, D., *Literacy and the Social Order: Reading and Writing in Tudor and Stuart England* (Cambridge, 1980).

—— 'Binding the Nation: The Bonds of Association 1584 and 1696', in D. J. Guth and J. W. McKenna (eds.), *Tudor Rule and Revolution* (Cambridge, 1982).

Crist, T., 'Government Control of the Press after the Expiration of the Printing Act of 1679', *Publishing History*, 5 (1979), 49–77.

Cruickshanks, E., Handley, S., and Hayton, D. W., *The History of Parliament. The House of Commons 1690–1715*, 5 vols. (Cambridge, 2002).

Davis, L., *Factual Fictions: The Origins of the English Novel* (New York, 1983).

De Beer, E. S., 'The English Newspapers from 1695 to 1702', in R. Hatton and J. S. Bromley (eds.), *William III and Louis XIV. Essays 1680–1720* (Liverpool, 1968).

De Krey, G., *A Fractured Society: The Politics of London in the First Age of Party, 1688–1715* (Oxford, 1985).

—— 'Rethinking the Restoration: Dissenting Cases for Conscience, 1667–1672', *HJ*, 38 (1995), 53–83.

Diamond, L., and Gunther, R. (eds.), *Political Parties and Democracy* (Baltimore, 2001).

Dickinson, H., 'How Revolutionary was the "Glorious Revolution" of 1688?' *British Journal for Eighteenth-Century Studies*, 11 (1988), 125–42.

—— *Liberty and Property: Political Ideology in Eighteenth-Century Britain* (London, 1979).

—— *The Politics of the People in Eighteenth-century Britain* (Basingstoke, 1995).

—— 'The Eighteenth Century Debate on the Sovereignty of Parliament', *TRHS*, 5th ser., 26 (1976), 189–210.

Dickson, P. G. M., *The Financial Revolution in England: A Study in the Development of Public Credit, 1688–1756* (London, 1967).

Dooley, B., 'From Literary Criticism to Systems Theory in Early Modern Journalism History', *Journal of the History of Ideas*, 51 (1990), 461–86.

—— and Baron, S. (eds.), *The Politics of Information in Early Modern Europe* (London, 2001).

Downie, J. A., *Robert Harley and the Press: Propaganda and Public Opinion in the Age of Swift and Defoe* (Cambridge, 1979).

—— and T. Corns (eds.), *Telling the People What to Think* (London, 1993).

Duffy, M., *The Military Revolution and the State 1500–1800* (Exeter, 1980).

Eagleton, T., *The Function of Criticism: From the Spectator to Post-structuralism* (1984).

Eastwood, D., *Government and Community in the English Provinces 1700–1870* (Basingstoke, 1997).

Eilon, D., *Faction's Fictions: Ideological Closure in Swift's Satire* (Newark, NJ, 1991).

Eisenstein, E., *The Printing Press as an Agent of Change: Communications and Cultural Transformations in Early Modern Europe*, 2 vols. (New York, 1979).

Erskine-Hill, H., 'Two-fold Vision in C18th Writing', *English Literary History*, 64 (1997), 903–24.

Feather, J., *The Provincial Book Trade in Eighteenth-century England* (Cambridge, 1985).

—— 'The English Book Trade and the Law 1695–1799', *Publishing History*, 12 (1982), 51–75.

—— 'The Book Trade in Politics: The Making of the Copyright Act of 1710', *Publishing History*, 8 (1980), 19–44.

Fletcher, A., *The Outbreak of the English Civil War* (1981).

Fox, A., *Oral and Literate Culture in England 1500–1700* (Oxford, 2000).

Foxcroft, H. C., *A Character of the Trimmer. Being a Short Life of the First Marquis of Halifax* (Cambridge, 1946).

Freist, D., *Governed by Opinion: Politics, Religion and the Dynamics of Communication in Stuart London, 1637–1645* (London, 1997).

French, H. R., 'Social Status, Localism and the "Middle Sort of People" in England 1620–1750', *P&P*, 166 (2000), 66–99.

Furbank, P. N., and Owens, W. R., *Defoe De-attributions: A Critique of J. R. Moore's Checklist* (London, 1994).

Garrett, J., *The Triumphs of Providence: The Assassination Plot of 1696* (Cambridge, 1980).

Gauci, P., *The Politics of Trade. The Overseas Merchant in State and Society, 1660–1720* (Oxford, 2001).

Glaisyer, N., 'Readers, Correspondents and Communities: John Houghton's A Collection for Improvement of Husbandry and Trade (1692–1703)', in Shepard and Withington (eds.), *Communities in Early Modern England* (Manchester, 2000).

Goldie, M., 'The Unacknowledged Republic: Officeholding in Early Modern England' in T. Harris (ed.), *The Politics of the Excluded c. 1500–1850* (Basingstoke, 2001).

—— 'The Roots of True Whiggism, 1688–1694', *History of Political Thought*, 1 (1980), 195–236.

—— 'The Political Thought of the Anglican Revolution', in R. Beddard (ed.), *The Revolutions of 1688* (Oxford, 1989).

—— 'The Revolution of 1689 and the Structure of Political Argument', *Bulletin of Research in the Humanities*, 83 (1980), 473–564.

Goldsmith, M. M., *Private Vices, Public Benefits: Bernard Mandeville's Social and Political Thought* (Cambridge, 1985).

Green, I., *Print and Protestantism in Early Modern England* (Oxford, 2000).

Greenblatt, S., *Renaissance Self-fashioning: From More to Shakespeare* (Chicago, 1980).

Griffiths, P., Fox, A., and Hindle, S. (eds.), *The Experience of Authority in Early Modern England* (Basingstoke, 1996).

Gunn, J. A. W., *Beyond Liberty and Property: The Process of Self-Recognition in Eighteenth-Century Political Thought* (Kingston, 1983).

—— *Politics and the Public Interest in the Seventeenth Century* (London, 1969).

Habermas, J., *The Structural Transformation of the Public Sphere*, trans. T. Burger (Cambridge, 1989).

Hacking, I., *The Emergence of Probability* (Cambridge, 1975).

Hainsworth, D. R., *Stewards, Lords and People: The Estate Steward and his World in Later Stuart England* (Cambridge, 1992).

Haley, K. H. D., *The First Earl of Shaftesbury* (Oxford, 1968).

Halliday, P., *Dismembering the Body Politic: Partisan Politics in England's Towns, 1650–1730* (Cambridge, 1998).

Hammond, B., *Professional Imaginative Writing in England, 1670–1740* (Oxford, 1997).

Handley, S., 'Provincial Influence on General Legislation: The Case of Lancashire, 1689–1731', *Parliamentary History*, 16 (1997), 171–84.

—— 'Local Legislative Initiatives for Economic and Social Development in Lancashire, 1689–1731', *Parliamentary History*, 9 (1990), 14–37.

Hanson, L., *The Government and the Press 1695–1763* (Oxford, 1936).

Harkness, D. A., 'The Opposition to the Eighth and Ninth Articles of the Commercial Treaty of Utrecht', *Scottish Historical Review*, 21 (1924), 219–26.

Harris, B., *Politics and the Rise of the Press: Britain and France 1620–1800* (London, 1996).

Harris, J., 'The Grecian Coffee House and Political Debate in London 1688–1714', *London Journal*, 25 (2000), 1–13.

Harris, M., *London Newspapers in the Age of Walpole: A Study of the Origins of the Modern English Press* (Rutherford, 1987).

—— 'Print and Politics in the Age of Walpole', in J. Black (ed.), *Britain in the Age of Walpole* (Basingstoke, 1984).

Harris, T., *London Crowds in the Reign of Charles II: Propaganda and Politics from the Restoration until the Exclusion Crisis* (Cambridge, 1987).

—— *Politics under the Later Stuarts: Party Conflict in a Divided Society 1660–1715* (London, 1993).

—— 'Propaganda and Public Opinion in Seventeenth Century England', in J. Popkin (ed.), *Media and Revolution: Comparative Perspectives* (Kentucky, 1995).

—— (ed.), *The Politics of the Excluded* (Basingstoke, 2001).

Harris, T., Seaward, P., and Goldie, M., *The Politics of Religion in Restoration England* (Oxford, 1990).

Hayton, D. W., *The History of Parliament. The House of Commons 1690–1715. Introductory Survey* (Cambridge, 2002).

—— 'The "Country" Interest and the Party System, *c.* 1689–1720', in C. Jones (ed.), *Party and Party Management in Parliament 1660–1784* (Leicester, 1984).

Hearnshaw, F. J. C. (ed.), *The Social and Political Ideas of Some English Thinkers in the Augustan Age* (London, 1967 repr.; first published 1928).

Henning, B. D. (ed.), *The History of Parliament. The House of Commons 1660–1690*, 3 vols. (London, 1983).

Herrup, C., 'The Counties and the Country: Some Thoughts on C17th Historiography', *Social History*, 8 (1983), 169–81.

Heyd, M., *'Be Sober and Reasonable': The Critique of Enthusiasm in the Seventeenth and Early Eighteenth Centuries* (1995).

—— 'The Reaction to Enthusiasm in the Seventeenth Century: Towards an Integrative Approach', *JMH*, 53 (1981), 258–80.

Hill, C., 'James Harrington and the People', in C. Hill, *Puritanism and Revolution* (London, 1968).

Hindle, S., *The State and Social Change in Early Modern England c. 1550–1640* (Basingstoke, 2000).

Hinds, P., 'Roger L'estrange, the Rye House Plot and the Regulation of Political Discourse in Late Seventeenth-Century London', *The Library*, 7th Ser. 3 (2002), 1–31.

Hirst, D., *The Representative of the People? Voters and Voting in England under the Early Stuarts* (Cambridge, 1975).

Holmes, G., *The Electorate and the National Will in the First Age of Party* (Lancaster, 1976).

—— *British Politics in the Age of Anne* (London, 1967; rev. 2nd edn., 1987).

—— (ed.), *Britain after the Glorious Revolution 1689–1714* (London, 1969).

—— *The Trial of Doctor Sacheverell* (London, 1973).

—— *The Making of a Great Power. Late Stuart and Early Georgian Britain 1660–1722* (Harlow, 1993).

—— and Jones, C., 'Trade, the Scots and the Parliamentary Crisis of 1713', *Parliamentary History*, 1 (1982), 47–77.

Holstun, J. (ed.), *Pamphlet Wars: Prose in the English Revolution* (1992).

Holt, F. L., *The Law of Libel* (London, 1812).

Hont, I., 'Free Trade and the Economic Limits to National Politics: Neo-Machiavellian Political Economy Reconsidered', in J. Dunn (ed.), *The Economic Limits to Modern Politics* (Cambridge, 1990).

Hoppit, J., 'Political Arithmetic in Eighteenth Century England', *EcHR*, 49 (1996), 516–40.

—— *A Land of Liberty? England 1689–1727* (Oxford, 2000).

Horsefield, J. K., *British Monetary Experiments, 1650–1710* (London, 1960).

Horwitz, H., *Parliament, Policy and Politics in the Reign of William III* (Manchester, 1977).

Houston, A., *Algernon Sidney and the Republican Heritage in England and America* (Princeton, 1991).

Houston, A., and Pincus, S. (eds.), *A Nation Transformed: England after the Restoration* (Cambridge, 2001).

Hunter, J. P., *Before Novels: The Contexts of Eighteenth Century Fiction* (New York, 1990).

Hyland, P. B., 'Liberty and Libel: Government and the Press During the Succession Crisis in Britain, 1712–1716', *EHR*, 101 (1986), 863–88.

Ihalainen, P., *The Discourse on Political Pluralism in Early-Eighteenth Century England. A Conceptual Study with Special Reference to Terminology of Religious Origin* (Helsinki, 1999).

Johns, A., *The Nature of the Book: Print and Knowledge in the Making* (Chicago, 1998).

Jones, C. (ed.), *Britain in the First Age of Party, 1680–1750: Essays Presented to Geoffrey Holmes* (London, 1987).

——— (ed.), *Party and Management in Parliament, 1660–1784* (Leicester, 1984).

Jones, D. M., *Conscience and Allegiance in Seventeenth-century England: The Political Significance of Oaths and Engagements* (Rochester, 1999).

Jones, D. W., *War and Economy in the Age of William III and Marlborough* (Oxford, 1988).

Kaplan, M. L., *The Culture of Slander in Early Modern England* (Cambridge, 1997).

Kendall, W., *John Locke and the Doctrine of Majority Rule* (Urbana, Ill., 1965).

Kent, J., 'The Centre and the Localities: State Formation and Parish Government in England *c.* 1640–1740', *HJ*, 38 (1995), 363–404.

Kenyon, J. P., *Revolution Principles: The Politics of Party, 1689–1720* (Cambridge, 1977).

Ketcham, M., *Transparent Designs: Reading, Performance and Form in the Spectator Papers* (Athens, Ga., 1985).

Kishlansky, M., *Parliamentary Selection: Social and Political Choice in Early Modern England* (Cambridge, 1986).

Kitchin, G., *Sir Roger L'Estrange. A Contribution to the History of the Press in the Seventeenth Century* (New York, 1971 repr.).

Klein, L., *Shaftesbury and the Culture of Politeness* (Cambridge, 1994).

——— 'The Third Earl of Shaftesbury and the Progress of Politeness', *Eighteenth Century Studies* 18 (1984–5), 186–214.

——— 'Coffee-house Civility, 1660–1714: An Aspect of Post-Courtly Culture in England', *Huntington Library Quarterly*, 59 (1997), 30–51.

——— 'Politeness and the Interpretation of the British Eighteenth Century', *HJ*, 45 (2002), 869–98.

——— 'The Political Significance of "Politeness" in Early Eighteenth Century Britain', in G. Schochet (ed.), *Politics, Politeness and Patriotism*, Folger Institute Center for the History of British Political Thought Proceedings, Vol. 5 (Washington, 1993).

——— 'Liberty, Manners and Politeness in Early Eighteenth Century England', *HJ*, 32 (1989), 583–604.

Knights, M., *Politics and Opinion in Crisis, 1678–1681* (Cambridge, 1994).

——— 'London's "Monster" Petition of 1680', *HJ*, 36 (1993), 39–67.

——— 'London Petitions and Parliamentary Politics in 1679', *Parliamentary History*, 12 (1993), 29–46.

——— 'Petitioning and the Political Theorists: John Locke, Algernon Sidney and London's "Monster" Petition of 1680', *P&P*, 138 (1993), 94–111.

——— 'Politics after the Glorious Revolution', in B. Coward (ed.), *A Companion to Stuart Britain* (Oxford, 2003).

——— 'Faults on Both Sides: The Conspiracies of Party Politics Under the Later Stuarts', in J. Swann and B. Coward (eds.), *Conspiracies and Conspiracy Theory in Early Modern Europe* (Aldershot, 2004).

——— 'Occasional Conformity and the Representation of Dissent: Hypocrisy, Sincerity, Moderation and Zeal', in D. Wykes (ed.), *Parliament and Dissent* (forthcoming).

Kramnick, I., 'An Augustan Debate: Notes on the History of the Idea of Representation', in J. R. Pennock and J. W. Chapman (eds.), *Representation* (New York, 1968).

Kroll, R., *The Material World. Literate Culture in the Restoration and Early Eighteenth Century* (1991).

Kugler, A., *Errant Plagiary. The Life and Writings of Lady Sarah Cowper 1644–1720* (Stanford, 2002).

Lake, P., with Questier, M., *The Antichrist's Lewd Hat. Protestants, Papists and Players in Post-reformation England* (New Haven, 2002).

—— 'Puritans, Papists, and the "Public Sphere" in Early Modern England: The Edmund Campion Affair in Context', *JMH*, 72 (2000), 587–627.

Landau, N., 'Independence, Deference and Voter Participation: The Behaviour of the Electorate in early C18th Kent', *HJ*, 22 (1979), 561–83.

Langford, P., 'Property and Virtual Representation in Eighteenth-century England', *HJ*, 31 (1988), 83–115.

—— *Public Life and the Propertied Englishman, 1689–1798* (Oxford, 1991).

Love, H., *Scribal Publication in Seventeenth-Century England* (Oxford, 1993).

Manin, B., *The Principles of Representative Government* (Cambridge, 1997).

Mah, H., 'Phantasies of the Public Sphere: Rethinking the Habermas of Historians', *JMH*, 72 (2000), 153–82.

Mascuch, M., *Origins of the Individualist Self: Autobiography and Self-Identity in England, 1591–1791* (Stanford, 1996).

McDowell, P., *The Women of Grub Street. Press, Politics and Gender in the London Literary Marketplace 1678–1730* (Oxford, 1998).

McKenzie, D. F., 'Speech–Manuscript–Print', *The Library Chronicle*, 20 (1990), 87–109.

McKeon, M., *The Origins of the English Novel 1600–1740* (Baltimore, 1987).

McLeod, W. R., and McLeod, V. B., *A Graphical Directory of English Newspapers and Periodicals, 1702–1714* (Morgantown, 1982).

Markley, R., *Fallen Languages. Crises of Representation in Newtonian England 1660–1740* (New York, 1993).

Miller, J., 'Public Opinion in Charles II's England', *History*, 80 (1995), 359–81.

—— 'Representatives and Represented in England, 1660–89', *Parliaments, Estates and Representation*, 15 (1995), 125–32.

Miller, P., *Defining the Common Good: Empire, Religion and Philosophy in Eighteenth-Century Britain* (Cambridge, 1994).

Monod, P. K., *Jacobitism and the English People, 1688–1788* (Cambridge, 1989).

—— 'The Jacobite Press and English Censorship 1689–95', in E. Cruickshanks and E. Corp (eds.), *The Stuart Court in Exile and the Jacobites* (London, 1995).

Montano, J., *Courting the Moderates. Ideology, Propaganda and the Emergence of Party, 1660–1678* (Newark, NJ, 2002).

Morgan, E., *Inventing the People. The Rise of Popular Sovereignty in England and America* (New York and London, 1988).

Morison, S., *Ichabod Dawks and his News-Letter: With an Account of the Dawks Family of Booksellers and Stationers 1635–1731* (Cambridge, 1931).

Muddiman, J. G., *The King's Journalist 1659–89. Studies in the Reign of Charles II* (London, 1971 repr.).

Muldrew, C., *The Economy of Obligation: The Culture of Credit and Social Relations in Early Modern England* (Basingstoke, 1998).

Myers, R., and Harris, M. (eds.), *Aspects of Printing from 1600* (Oxford, 1987).

Neal, L., *The Rise of Financial Capitalism. International Capital Markets in the Age of Reason* (Cambridge, 1990).

Nelson, C., and Seccombe, M., *Periodical Publications 1641–1700. A Survey with Illustrations*, Occasional Papers of the Bibliographical Society, No.2 (1986).

Newton, T. F., 'William Pittis and Queen Anne Journalism', *Modern Philology*, 33 (1935), 169–86, 279–302.

Nicholson, C., *Writing and the Rise of Finance: Capital Satires of the Early Eighteenth Century* (Cambridge, 1994).

North, D. C., and Weingast, B. R., 'Constitutions and Commitment: The Evolution of Institutions Governing Public Choice in Seventeenth-Century England', *Journal of Economic History*, 49 (1989), 803–32.

O'Brien, P. K., 'The Political Economy of British Taxation, 1660–1815', *Economic History Review*, 2nd ser., 41 (1988), 1–32.

—— and Hunt, P., 'The Rise of a Fiscal State in England 1485–1815', *Historical Research*, 66 (1993), 129–76.

O'Gorman, F., *Voters, Patrons and Parties: The Unreformed Electoral System of Hanoverian England 1734–1832* (Oxford, 1989).

Ogg, D., *England in the Reigns of James II and William III* (Oxford, 1984 edn.).

Pagden, A. (ed.), *The Languages of Political Theory in Early-Modern Europe* (Cambridge, 1987).

Patey, D., *Probability and Literary Form: Philosophic Theory and Literary Practice in the Augustan Age* (Cambridge, 1984).

Peacey, J., *Politicians and Pamphleteers* (Aldershot, 2004).

Pettit, P., *Republicanism: A Theory of Freedom and Government* (Oxford, 1997).

Phillipson, N., 'Politics and Politeness in the Reigns of Anne and the Early Hanoverians', in J. G. A. Pocock (ed.), *The Varieties of British Political Thought 1500–1800* (Cambridge, 1993).

Pincus, S., ' "Coffee Politician Does Create": Coffeehouses and Restoration political culture', *Journal of Modern History*, 67 (1995), 807–34.

—— 'Neither Machiavellian Moment nor Possessive Individualism: Commercial Society and the Defenders of the English Commonwealth', *American Historical Review*, 103 (1998), 705–36.

Pitkin, H., *The Concept of Representation* (London, 1967).

Plumb, J., 'The Growth of the Electorate in England from 1600 to 1715', *P&P*, 45 (1969), 90–116.

Plumb, J., *The Growth of Political Stability in England, 1675–1725* (London, 1967).

Pocock, J. G. A., *The Machiavellian Moment: Florentine Political Thought and the Atlantic Republican Tradition* (Princeton, 1975).

—— 'The Ideal of Citizenship since Classical Time', *Queens Quarterly*, 99 (1992), 33–55.

—— *Virtue, Commerce and History. Essays on Political Thought and History, Chiefly in the Eighteenth Century* (Cambridge, 1985).

—— 'The Myth of John Locke and the Obsession with Liberalism', in J. G. A. Pocock and R. Ashcraft (eds.), *John Locke* (Los Angeles, 1980).

—— 'Post-Puritan England and the Problem of the Enlightenment', in P. Zagorin (ed.), *Culture and Politics from Puritanism to the Enlightenment* (Berkeley, Calif., 1980).

Poovey, M., *The History of the Modern Fact: Problems of Knowledge in the Sciences of Wealth and Society* (Chicago, 1998).

Porritt, E., *The Unreformed House of Commons: Parliamentary Representation before 1832*, 2 vols. (New York, 1963).

Porter, R., *Enlightenment. Britain and the Creation of the Modern World* (London, 2000).

Price, J. M., 'A Note on the Circulation of the London Press 1704–14', *BIHR*, 31 (1958), 215–24.

Ransome, M. E., 'The Press and the General Election of 1710', *CHJ*, 6 (1939), 209–21.

Raven, J., 'Book Distribution Networks in Early Modern Europe', in *Produzione e Commercio Della Carta e del Libro Secc. XIII–XVIII* (Florence, 1992), 583–630.

Raymond, J., *The Invention of the Newspaper: English Newsbooks, 1641–1649* (Oxford, 1996).

—— *The Pamphlets and Pamphleteering in Early Modern Britain* (Cambridge, 2002).

—— 'The Newspaper, Public Opinion and the Public Sphere', in J. Raymond (ed.), *News, Newspapers and Society in Early Modern Britain* (London, 1999).

Reay, B. (ed), *Popular Cultures in England 1550–1750* (1998).

Redner, H., *A New Science of Representation: Towards an Integrated Theory of Representation in Science, Politics and Art* (Westview, Conn., 1994).

Richards, J., *Party Propaganda Under Queen Anne: The General Elections of 1702–13* (Athens, Ga., 1972).

Richter, M., *The History of Political and Social Concepts* (New York, 1995).

Rivers, I. (ed.), *Books and their Readers in Eighteenth-century England* (Leicester, 1982).

—— *Reason, Grace, and Sentiment: A Study of the Language of Religion and Ethics in England, 1660–1780*, 2 vols. (Cambridge, 1991 and 2000).

Roberts, C., 'The Growth of Political Stability Reconsidered', *Albion*, 25 (1993), 237–55.

Robbins, B. (ed.), *The Phantom Public Sphere* (Minneapolis, 1993).

Robbins, C., *The Eighteenth-Century Commonwealthman* (Harvard, 1961).

Rock, P., 'Law, Order and Power in late C17th and early C18th England', in S. Cohen and A. Scull (eds.), *Social Control and the State* (Oxford, 1983).

Rogers, P., *Grub Street: Studies in a Subculture* (1972).

Rogers, N., *Whigs and Cities: Popular Politics in the Age of Walpole and Pitt* (Oxford, 1989).

—— *Crowds, Culture and Politics in Georgian Britain* (Oxford, 1998).

Rose, C., *England in the 1690's: Revolution, Religion and War* (Oxford, 1999).

Rubini, D., *Court and Country 1688–1702* (London, 1967).

Rudolph, R., *Revolution by Degrees. James Tyrrell and Whig Political Thought in the Late Seventeenth Century* (2002).

Sawyer, J., *Printed Poison: Pamphlet Propaganda, Faction Politics and the Public Sphere in Early Seventeenth-century France* (Berkeley, 1990).

Schaffer, S., 'Defoe's Natural Philosophy and the Worlds of Credit', in J. Christie and S. Shuttleworth (eds.), *Nature Transfigured. Science and Literature, 1700–1900* (Manchester, 1989).

Schochet, G., 'Vices, Benefits and Civil Society: Mandeville, Habermas and the Distinction between Public and Private', in P. Backscheider and T. Dystal (eds.), *The Intersections of the Public and Private Spheres in Early Modern England* (1996).

Schwoerer, L., *The Ingenious Mr Henry Care, Restoration Publicist* (Baltimore, 2001).

—— *No Standing Armies! The Anti-army Ideology in the Seventeenth Century* (Baltimore, 1974).

Scott, J., *England's Troubles: Seventeenth-century English Political Instability in European Context* (Cambridge, 2000).

—— *Algernon Sidney and the Restoration Crisis, 1677–1683* (Cambridge, 1991).

Scribner, R. W., *For the Sake of Simple Folk: Popular Propaganda for the German Reformation* (Cambridge, 1981).

Seaward, P., *The Cavalier Parliament and the Reconstruction of the Old Regime, 1661–1667* (Cambridge, 1989).

Shapin, S., *A Social History of Truth: Civility and Science in Seventeenth-century England* (Chicago, 1994).

—— and Schaffer, S., *Leviathan and the Air-pump: Hobbes, Boyle, and the Experimental Life* (Princeton, 1985).

Shapiro, B., *Probability and Certainty in Seventeenth-century England: A Study of the Relationships between Natural Science, Religion, History, Law, and Literature* (Princeton, 1983).

—— *A Culture of Fact: England, 1550–1720* (London, 2000).

Sharp, B., 'Popular Political Opinion in England 1660–1685', *History of European Ideas*, 10 (1989), 13–29.

Sharpe, K., *Reading Revolutions: The Politics of Reading in Early Modern England* (New Haven, 2000).

Sharpe, K., and Zwicker, S. (eds.), *The Politics of Discourse: The Literature and History of Seventeenth-century England* (Berkeley, 1987).

—— (eds.), *Refiguring Revolutions: Aesthetics and Politics from the English Revolution to the Romantic Revolution* (Berkeley, 1998).

—— (eds.), *Reading, Society and Politics in Early Modern England* (Cambridge, 2003).

Shepard, A., and Withington, P. (eds.), *Communities in Early Modern England: Networks, Place and Rhetoric* (Manchester, 2000).

Sherman, S., *Finance and Fictionality in the Early Eighteenth Century: Accounting for Defoe* (Cambridge, 1996).

Shevelow, K., *Women and Print Culture: the Construction of Femininity in the Early Periodical* (1989).

Siebert, F., *Freedom of the Press in England 1476–1776* (Urbana, Ill., 1952).

Skerpan, E., *The Rhetoric of Politics in the English Revolution, 1642–1660* (1992).

Skinner, Q., *Liberty before Liberalism* (Cambridge, 1998).

—— *Visions of Politics*, 3 vols. (Cambridge, 2002).

—— *Reason and Rhetoric in the Philosophy of Hobbes* (Cambridge, 1996).

Sklar, J., 'Let us not be Hypocritical', *Daedalus*, 108 (1979), 1–25.

Smith, H. L. (ed.), *Women Writers and the Early Modern British Political Tradition* (Cambridge, 1998).

Smith, N., *Literature and Revolution in England, 1640–1660* (New Haven, Conn., 1994).

—— 'The English Revolution and the End of Rhetoric: John Toland's Clito (1700) and the Republican Demon', *Essays and Studies*, 49 (1996), 1–18.

Sommerville, C. J., *The News Revolution in England: Cultural Dynamics of Daily Information* (Oxford, 1996).

Speck, W. A., *Tory & Whig: The Struggle in the Constituencies, 1701–1715* (London, 1970).

—— 'Political Propaganda in Augustan England', *TRHS*, 5th ser., 22 (1972), 17–32.

Spurr, J., *England in the 1670s: 'This Masquerading Age'* (Oxford, 2000).

Stevens, D., *Party Politics and English Journalism 1702–42* (1916).

Stewart, L., *The Rise of Public Science: Rhetoric, Technology and Natural Philosophy in Newtonian Britain 1660–1750* (Cambridge, 1992).

Sutherland, J. R., 'The Circulation of Newspapers and Periodicals 1700–1730', *The Library*, 4th ser., 15 (1934), 110–24.

—— *The Restoration Newspaper and its Development* (Cambridge, 1986).

Sweet, R., 'Local Identities and a National Parliament, *c.* 1688–1835', in J. Hoppit (ed.), *Parliaments, Nations and Identities in Britain and Ireland 1660–1850* (Manchester, 2003).

Targett, S., '"The Premier Scribbler Himself": Sir Robert Walpole and the Management of Political Opinion', *Studies in Newspaper and Periodical History*, (1994), 19–33.

Thompson, E. P., *Whigs and Hunters: The Origin of the Black Act* (London, 1975).

Thompson, J., *Models of Value: Eighteenth-century Political Economy and the Novel* (Durham, NC, 1996).

Thompson, M., 'The Reception of Locke's Two Treatises of Government 1690–1705', *Political Studies*, 24 (1976), 184–91.

Treadwell, M., 'London Trade Publishers 1675–1750', *The Library*, 6th ser., 4 (1982), 99–134.

Tully, J. (ed.), *Meaning and Context: Quentin Skinner and his Critics* (Cambridge, 1988).

Urstad, T. S., *Sir Robert Walpole's Poets. The Use of Literature as Pro-Government Propaganda 1721–42* (Newark, NJ, 1999).

Vallance, E., 'Loyal or Rebellious? Protestant Associations in England 1584–1696', *The Seventeenth Century*, 17 (2002), 1–23.

—— 'The Decline of Conscience as a Political Guide: William Higden's *View of the English Constitution* (1709)', in H. Braun and E. Vallance (eds.), *Contexts of Conscience in Early Modern Europe 1500–1700* (Basingstoke, 2004).

Van Horn Melton, J., *The Rise of the Public in Enlightenment Europe* (Cambridge, 2001).

Van Leeuwen, H. G., *The Problem of Uncertainty in English Thought 1630–1690* (The Hague, 1963).

Vickers, B., 'The Royal Society and English Prose Style: A Reassessment', in B. Vickers and N. Streuver (eds.), *Rhetoric and the Pursuit of Truth: Language Change in the Seventeenth and Eighteenth Centuries. Papers Read at a Clark Library Seminar by Brian Vickers and Nancy Struever* (Los Angeles, 1985).

Viroli, M., 'The Revolution in the Concept of Politics', *Political Theory*, 20 (1992), 473–96.

Walcott, R., *English Politics in the Early Eighteenth Century* (Oxford, 1956).

Warner, M., *The Letters of the Republic. Publication and the Public Sphere in Eighteenth-century America* (Harvard, 1990).

—— 'The Mass Public and the Mass Subject', in B. Robbins (ed.), *The Phantom Public Sphere* (Minneapolis, 1993).

Webb, S., and Webb, B., *English Local Government from the Revolution to the Municipal Corporations Act* (1906).

Weil, R., *Political Passions. Gender, the Family and Political Argument in England 1680–1714* (Manchester, 1999).

Williams, A., *Poetry and the Creation of a Whig Literary Culture 1680–1715* (Oxford, 2004).

Willman, R. 'The Origins of "Whig" and "Tory" in the English Political Language', *HJ*, 17 (1974), 247–64.

Wilson, K., *The Sense of the People: Politics, Culture and Imperialism in England, 1715–85* (Cambridge, 1995).

Withington, P., 'Two Renaissances: Urban Political Culture in Post-Reformation England Reconsidered', *HJ*, 44 (2001), 239–68.

—— 'Views from the Bridge: Revolution and Restoration in Seventeenth-century York', *P&P*, 170 (2001), 121–51.

Withington, P., 'Citizens, Community and Political Culture in Restoration England', in A. Shepherd and P. Withington (eds.), *Communities in Early Modern England* (Manchester, 2000), 134–55.

Wood, N., *The Politics of Locke's Philosophy: A Social Study of 'An Essay Concerning Human Understanding'* (Berkeley, 1983).

Woodman, T., *Politeness in the Age of Pope* (Toronto, 1989).

Worden, A. B., 'The Question of Secularization', in A. Houston and S. Pincus (eds.), *The Nation Transformed* (2001).

Young, J., 'The Scottish Parliament and National Identity from the Union of the Crowns to the Union of Parliaments 1603–1707', in D. Brown, R. Finlay, and M. Lynch (eds.), *Image and Identity: The Making and Re-making of Scotland through the Ages* (Edinburgh, 1998).

Zaret, D., *The Origins of Democratic Culture: Printing, Petitions, and the Public Sphere in Early-Modern England* (Princeton, 2000).

—— 'Religion and the Rise of Liberal-Democratic Ideology in 17-Century England', *American Sociological Review*, 54 (1989), 163–79.

—— 'Petitions and the "Invention" of Public Opinion in the English Revolution', *American Journal of Sociology*, 101 (1996), 1497–555.

Zimbardo, R., 'The Late Seventeenth Century Dilemma in Discourse', in J. D. Canfield and J. P. Hunter (eds.), *Rhetorics of Order/Ordering Rhetorics in English Neoclassical Literature* (Newark, NJ, 1989).

Zook, M., *Radical Whigs and Conspiratorial Politics in Late Stuart England* (Pennsylvania, 1999).

Zwicker, S., *Lines of Authority: Politics and English Literary Culture, 1649–89* (New York, 1993).

—— 'Politics and Literary Practice in the Restoration', in B. K. Lewalski (ed.), *Renaissance Genres: Essays on Theory, History and Interpretation* (Harvard, 1986).

—— 'Language as Disguise: Politics and Poetry in the Later Seventeenth Century', *Annals of Scholarship*, 1 (1980), 47–67.

—— 'Lines of Authority: Political and Literary Culture in the Restoration', in K. Sharpe and S. Zwicker, *The Politics of Discourse* (Los Angeles, 1987).

—— 'Reading the Margins', in K. Sharpe and S. Zwicker (eds.), *Refiguring Revolutions: Aesthetics and Politics from the English Revolution to the Romantic Revolution* (Berkeley, 1998).

Index